End

oing through this book for the fifth time, all ten chapters, I got the conviction that this book is unique in a very special way.

The narrator's journey through thorny and cruel paths of life was one that no person could pass through without having deep roots in faith and trust in the Almighty God.

This is a truly inspiring message, and more so, a roadmap that guides the reader to a better life, better judgment and a better approach to issues.

For me, this was well documented, and vividly designed to shape anyone who's willing to accept the precepts herein.

I confess that I have read many spiritual books, but none have had the amazing revelations that this book contains, not to forget the many Biblical references that are quite relevant to each chapter.

In brief, every chapter is well expounded in relation to our day-to-day life. How our Lord Jesus wants us to live, contrary to what human beings have stage managed and the contrary life as far as Christianity is concerned.

S/Sgt. Andrew Rekeny

This message is super well written and incredibly interesting. I wish you all the luck in moving this book forward.

Ben

We've all read many books over the years but this book you hold in your hands now is by far the most significant of your life aside from the Bible.

This book is going to take you on an incredible journey that can't help but change the way that you view faith, marriage and family- forever.

You shall see that there is no limit to what God can do. His power, and the power of love that comes from God. That through obedience to God's word no matter what, is the only key to a truly successful life...and after life. God's amazing love is so powerful that it can melt away all pain, hurt, bitterness and hatred, allowing you to live a life in the love of God.

-M.B.-

This is by far the most exhaustive book on marriage and family. No issue is left unturned, and the way he takes us to our relationship with God is truly amazing. This book should be given to EVERY child from around twelve years of age to cling to alongside of their Bible for the rest of their lives.

Jaime Blanco

We've all read many books over the years but this book you hold in your hands now is by far the most significant of your life aside from the Bible itself. This message is a real eye opener.

This book is going to take you on an incredible journey that can't help but change the way that you view your faith, marriage and family forever.

You shall see that there is no limit to what God can do. His power, and the power of love that comes from God. That through obedience to God's word no matter what, is the only key to a truly successful life...and after life. God's amazing love is so powerful that it can melt away all pain, hurt, bitterness and hatred, allowing you to live a life in the love of God.

Judith Wong

We would encourage you to watch for other books by Pastor and Evangelist Dr. John Bishop D.D., some of which are in progress:

-**Only Believe** *A book of repentance, revival, and the Christian walk*

-**What About the Biblical Perspective of Christmas?**

- **Yokana's Brief Bible Synoptic Notes, A Pastoral Study guide**

- **The Message of Daniel** – *A Literal, Historical, and Prophetical look*

-*Also my messages from Revelations given unto me by the Holy Spirit;*

The Pentecostal Movement.

Message From the Cross.

Xenophobia and the Christian

The End Times

This message published

in loving memories of

my dear wife and children

BECOMING ONE

*An Expository on Marriage,
Family, and the Family of God*

PASTOR & EVANGELIST
DR. YOKANA MUKISA

XULON PRESS

Xulon Press
2301 Lucien Way #415
Maitland, FL 32751
407.339.4217
www.xulonpress.com

Unless otherwise indicated, Scripture quotations taken from the King James Version (KJV)–*public domain.*

Paperback ISBN-13: 978-1-66282-507-1

Hard Cover ISBN-13: 978-1-66282-508-8

Ebook ISBN-13: 978-1-66282-509-5

ABOUT THE AUTHOR

Pastor and Evangelist Dr. John Bishop D.D. AKA Mobiliza Yokana Mukisa, is the founder and director of Lighthouse of Blessed Hope Ministry. He was called in a vision in 2005 to East Africa where he set Spiritual fires. He suffered many trials, tribulations, and persecutions. This book was written while in prison in Kenya, where he was held hostage for over nine years. He was sentenced to thirteen years by the court, but condemned to death by the prison system, for bringing Christ to their Country. He was told "we don't need or want White man's God in this country". He has been tortured, poisoned, drowned, and strangled; denied medical care and left for dead, with no help from his Embassy, Kenya has done all it could to destroy God's messenger, ministry, and message, by trying to kill this Pastor...but God has other plans...Phil. 2:27, John 16:20 and Job 41:22. And then cast out by his family after being released from prison. God will turn our sorrows into joy. Matt 4:10-12, Read this for this Pastor is living by God's promise and in the hope of His fulfillment of promises of restoration, deliverance and joy that he might live to testify and bring glory to His mighty name, Psalm 118:17. Read also 1ˢᵗ Peter 4:12-14. The Pastor was called (invited) to Kenya to be introduced into villages there, when through the prejudice, and extreme corruption of Kenya, CID, the courts, the prison, Kenyatta Hospital, He endured persecution and conditions beyond human comprehension, but God has remained faithful and by his side, constantly revealing to him of His presence- and while several MD's have said 'I can't believe that you are still alive', or 'It is a miracle that you are alive', while being denied any treatment, He has been diagnosed as terminally ill, and is struggling with a few life threatening conditions, but he still managed to compile his notes together and through God's grace and mercy for you, allowed the impossible there in Kenya prisons- to get this powerful message out to the world. Many others told the Pastor that your God must really love you to survive all of this.

TO GOD BE ALL THE GLORY

DEDICATION

Becoming One is dedicated to the world, for all who are genuinely seeking a closer walk with our Father, The Creator of All; and a better marriage.

This message was divinely inspired and I dedicate this message to my wonderful and beautiful wife who I pray for without ceasing. This message I also dedicate to all the pastors; As well as for all of you who are single, engaged, married, separated, divorced, and widowed.

With special thanks to my friends; as well as those who claimed to be, as they helped teach me God's truths through the pain and suffering that they inflicted upon me. Many thanks also to those who encouraged me to write and share the ministry in written form to reach more people. Most of all, I thank you Heavenly Father for being my best friend and for giving me these words to share.

A special thank you to a few people of Uganda, who heard the messages that God sent through me, and encouraged me to write these messages for all to hear. Also, very special thanks to my dear wife who shared twenty wonderful years of my life and for too many things to list here, as well as our wonderful blessings from God– our children, the innocent victims. My wife's name has been withheld throughout this message to protect her from the shame of her actions. She was a victim of her "friends". Regardless of the outcome, those years were such a blessing, but I never cease praying for her and my precious children.

Thank you to all the folks who assisted me in publishing this message.

I also wish to sincerely thank the new Officer-in-charge, Henry Kisingu who trusted in me enough to allow me to use my laptop (the only inmate out of three thousand three hundred to have a computer, and in my room yet! He gave me a private room) so as to put together these messages and even was so kind as to assist me in the printing of them when they were about one fifth done so others could begin reading the messages, and who has brought about some very positive changes in that prison.

And a very special thank you to S/Sgt. Andrew Rekeney, one of a kind, an angel sent from above, who encouraged me through some of my darkest hours, and who provided me with paper, pens, and encouragement. in order to transform thousands of notes from the Holy Spirit written on backs of biscuit boxes into these messages. May God always bless you and your family.

And an extremely special thank you to my Lord and Savior Jesus Christ, for entrusting me and sharing these messages with his servant, and being faithful to His promises, who preserved me, the strength and protection to survive in order to share these messages with the world and testify of how wonderful He is.

Table of Contents

ABOUT THE AUTHOR VII

DEDICATION IX

INTRODUCTION XVII

WHAT IS A FRIEND? XXVII

WARNING XXXIV

PERSONAL NOTES XXXV

CHAPTER 1 1

THE BLESSED CHILDREN 1

CHILDREN ARE A BLESSING 1

PARENTAL RESPONSIBILITY..................... 3

UNPLANNED CHILDREN.......................... 4

PERSONAL NOTES 24

PERSONAL NOTES 25

CHAPTER 2... 27

THE RIGHTEOUS MAN, HUSBAND, AND FATHER.................. 27

MEN 27

HUSBANDS 31

DADS 42

MEN IN THE CHURCH AND COMMUNITY 44

PERSONAL NOTES 55

CHAPTER 3...57

THE PRECIOUS WOMAN, WIFE, MOTHER...........................57

WIVES...75

MOTHERS 93

WOMEN IN THE CHURCH AND COMMUNITY.............. 101

PERSONAL NOTES 109

PERSONAL NOTES 110

CHAPTER 4... 112

AN INTRODUCTION TO BETROTHAL 112

DATING 116

BETROTHAL.. 128

PERSONAL NOTES 147

PERSONAL NOTES 148
CHAPTER 5...150
    THE SACRED MARRIAGE 150
        THE CEREMONY....................................162
        AFTER THE CEREMONY 178
        THE WEDDING (FIRST) NIGHT 181
        PERSONAL NOTES 191
CHAPTER 6...193
    BEHIND THE VEIL 193
        PREGNANCY....................................... 254
        PERSONAL NOTES 270
        PERSONAL NOTES 271
CHAPTER 7... 273
    MARRIAGE AND FAMILY 273
        BE COURAGEOUS—DON'T COMPROMISE..................... 299
        REVERENT BEHAVIOR.............................304
        CONTROLS HER TONGUE 305
        PERSONAL NOTES 318
CHAPTER 8 320
    FORGIVENESS IS A FORM OF LOVE 320
        PERSONAL NOTES 338
        PERSONAL NOTES 339
CHAPTER 9...342
    DIVORCE...342
        DIVORCE AND THE CHURCH 358
        REMARRIAGE AFTER DIVORCE 397
        RETURNING TO THE PATH OF RIGHTEOUSNESS 402
        PERSONAL NOTES 437
CHAPTER 10...439
    BUILDING BLOCKS FOR BUILDING BRIDGES 439
        PERSONAL NOTES 455
CHAPTER 11 457
    THE FINAL CHAPTER 457
        PERSONAL NOTES 468
EPILOGUE 469
    MY PERSONAL NOTE TO YOU................................. 505
        REPENT FOR THE KINGDOM OF HEAVEN IS AT HAND! 527

May God bless you as you meditate and reread
this message and apply it to thy marriage and/
or family. 527
PERSONAL NOTES 528
Appendix A 529
    Index to Scriptural References 529
Appendix B 547
    Topical Index 547
Appendix C 552
    Footprints In The Sand 552
Appendix E 553

The Lord hath given me a burden for repentance

The Lord hath given me a burden for marriage and family

He hath given me this message to share

I am blowing the trumpet,

I am delivering His message, and warnings

Behold, heed His words

Repent, return ye to the path of righteousness

And be blessed

For the time is come, and the end is near.

Genesis 1:1, 31 In the beginning God created...

God saw that everything He created

was very good

INTRODUCTION

Greetings in the name of our precious Lord and Savior Jesus Christ! It is such a blessing for me to be here with you today to testify what the Spirit of God has inspired me to share with you regarding marriage and the spiritual walk. This book is like two books in one, intimately linked together.

I was encouraged to write books while serving as a missionary in Uganda being told Your messages are so unique and what we need today, but with the ministry I had no time. I ended up being taken hostage and placed in prison where I wrote several books and messages. I was held in a Kenyan prison, where I had no access to anything but my precious Bible, so with the Spirit's help, I started to write. This message is entirely divinely inspired. While in prison, I came to realize that most people today are in a prison; spiritually, emotionally, and/or physically, whether in a prison, disabled, or whatever. While I can't free you from your prison while I am in mine, I can introduce you to the One who can free you just as He did me. You'll always have at least two friends if you shall allow and accept them, God and myself. While I am anxious to be free from my physical bondage, I always desire to be bound to my Lord and Savior. I am honored and blessed to be able to share with you His message, and consider myself blessed and honored that He chose me to pen these precious revelations, to be shared with you. It is truly my prayer that these words shall bring you to repentance, to restore and/or strengthen your family, marriage to your spouse and as well as to the Living God.

Many of us have read books and/or heard messages on marriage and family, and thus I hesitated writing another book on this same issue, however, God said write, so here it is. This message is divinely inspired, not from Pastor John, but from God Himself as Galatians 1:2 says, For I neither received it of man, neither was I taught it, but by the revelation of Jesus Christ It was an amazing revelation to me, and I pray that it will be for you as well. Every time that I read this message, the Holy Spirit reveals to me new insights.

I will open this message with the warning that this message is going to get very personal. We shall very discretely touch on the anatomy and physiology of sex, and what it all represents spiritually. It is also going to pierce many of you like a two-edged sword and convict you. This in fact is my prayer and I believe it is God's desire and purpose for allowing me to share these precious words. Please, don't get up and walk away, for the pain is temporary that can bring everlasting joy to you. This message may be the turning point in your life, a strengthening or rekindling of your marriage, a restoration of your marriage, and effect changes that may enhance thy family, each member of your family, as well as thy spiritual walk. Stay with me and hear—listen to what God has to say to you, please. Proverbs 22:20-21. Hosea 4:6 tells us that *My people are destroyed due to a lack of knowledge.* So, with that having been said, I bring you to Romans 12:2 *And be not conformed to this world: but be ye transformed by the renewing of your mind, that ye may prove what is that good, and acceptable, and perfect, will of God.*

I believe that God wants His word taught not only as a history book, which it is, but making it come alive and practical in our lives today. Also, I believe that through Christ's teachings, and speaking to me, that His word is triphasic. That is, it has three parts or aspects to it. First, it is literal, what it says, it means, what it says happened, happened. Secondly, it is prophetic. It is God's way of showing us what will occur in the future. We don't need fortune tellers, we have God, Hallelujah! And thirdly, God's word is a parable, just as Christ spoke when on this earth. All of His word really occurred, but also is symbolic of our lives today in relation to Him. In this message, I will be freely floating between the three.

In dealing with the issues of marriage and family as well as the roles of men, husbands, fathers, women, wives, mothers, children, men's and women's roles in the church and community, as well as many issues facing us today, It is my sincere prayer that each of us shall walk away from this message a convicted and changed person, whether you are single, engaged, married, widowed, separated, or divorced.

When God started me on this quest I went to my knees, searched the Scriptures, and hardly ate or slept while God spoke with me.

I believe that God never gives us an experience without being able to use it to help us grow spiritually, and allow us to be able to assist others, so I shall be sharing some personal information with you as well, as it relates to the subject matter being presented today. All the while however, I wish the focus to be on God not Pastor John, Amen!

To begin with, as I always like to do, I wish to begin by asking a few questions to get you focused and thinking. Don't think too much however or you shall miss out on some important lessons here.

1. Why is the Bible devoted so much to marriage or is it?

2. Why is God so opposed to polygamy, adultery, homosexuality, etc.? Or is He?

3. What is the big deal about adultery? Everybody does it.

4. Why is God so opposed to divorce or is He?

5. Why does God use he or she; him or her, masculine or feminine, to describe Israel and others? Why did Jesus have to ride into Jerusalem on the back of a **male** colt?

6. What is the condition of your marriage, and do you desire better?

7. What is the condition of your spiritual life?

8. Why did God create marriage in the first place? And is it really so important to Him?

I pray that these few questions not only trigger your thinking, but also pique your interest and curiosity, so here we go on. I shall give you a bit more for you to ponder. What history book have you seen that has romance and love stories such as those of the Bible? One only has to look at Ruth and Song of Songs to name but a couple. Why? God is a romantic. He is so full of love, and He created us and desires for us to be also a romantic and as full of love as He is. The commandment to love the Lord thy God with ALL your heart, soul, and mind, with absolute and total devotion, and to thy neighbor as thyself, Matthew 22:37.

This my dear brothers and sisters, is the most unusual message I have ever heard on marriage, and it shall be followed by the most unusual request or petition for most of you, so don't go away mentally or physically, and **don't skip ahead. The information presented is in an order as to prepare you for the next part.**

Many years ago, God gave me a message on marriage and family. As a result, I did some marriage and family classes and counseling, all Bible based. A part of me always worried what people would think, but in reality, it really doesn't matter what people think, what matters is what God thinks. If He gives me a message to share, so be it. Years later, He called me into the ministry and called me into various places of the world, and finally into East Africa, where He gave me a heart and message on repentance, revival, and strengthening the Christian walk. I obeyed and here I am today. After the few years, the message no less important actually increases in importance daily. But why is repentance important? It leads to revival; revival of the Spirit of God in our lives, as well as those of our families, churches, communities, and our nations. Yes... our families, hence the importance of revival in ourselves and in our families, bringing the importance of repentance, and reviving the families through the word of God, so here I am today, still preaching repentance and the Christian walk, but marriage and family as well.

Many decades ago, I thought myself very low, and still do. 'You're ugly, good for nothing...' even though I was often praised by others and all my life thrown into leadership and teaching roles... I never dated, but always since I can first remember, I talked with my best friend, God. I never believed I would ever get married nor have children. In 1986 God brought an absolutely beautiful young lady into my life who claimed to be a virgin and a Christian. I prayed and asked God, really??? Then in my human frailty I wrestled with God. We are from different religious, cultural, language backgrounds, but love is a universal language, and...God! She was so beautiful, why would she want me? He told me that she was the one, so I flew the eight thousand± miles to Malaysia to meet her, and marry her, after spending only a couple of weeks trying to speak with her and her family, got their blessings and asked them to please stop arranging proposals, as I wanted her, and that God had ordained her for me.

A true story about one man and his family, a few years into their marriage, they conceived their first child. During initial visits with the MD, he did a test that is only accurate in about one in twelve cases, and based on the results; they were hounded the next seven months to abort the pregnancy! That they believed was murder folks and God opened her womb, blessed us with a child, and my God doesn't make mistakes! He explained to the MD that they would accept their child regardless what God chose to bless them with. Delivery time came; the MD pushed them to allow him to do a cesarean section on her, for no reason! He fought for his wife and child and said no, they would trust God and allow a normal healthy delivery, as God designed. His wonderful wife listened to him and they delivered a beautiful and totally healthy son.

The following year, they conceived again. The pregnancy was healthy and happy for eight- and one-half months, until... sudden death. The MD wouldn't believe him that their precious gift was dead. I must interject here that he had twenty-four years in medicine so he knew what he was talking about.

So, after about two weeks of fighting with the MD, they delivered Joshua-dead and already decaying. He was perfect but dead. It was a problem inside the placenta not with their child. God knew that they could handle this with His strength, so He allowed this tragedy to happen. Because of this experience God placed a couple of other families in their path in subsequent years who experienced similar experiences and they were able to help the others through and be there for them in the love of God.

The following year they conceived again and a happy and healthy pregnancy, but!!! His wife had made some new 'friends' who claimed to be Christian. He warned her against them as he had an uneasy feeling about them. They convinced his wife that her husband didn't know what he was talking about, and there was nothing wrong with having a C-section. He knew that the MD had ill intentions for his wife. The MD told his wife and him that she needed a C-section without reason again, but told his wife that she would lose this child also without a C-section, which wasn't true, all was fine. He said no. His wife said yes. He told her the consequences, and she told him you don't know what you are talking about, oh friends how that hurt him. It wasn't his pride he explained to me, but concern for his wife, so why? First, like Eve, she took the authority away from her husband, and his ability to protect her, as well as bowing to other gods, and secondly, he knew what the MD was planning to do with her. You don't know what you are doing...stupid... but!!! Isn't that exactly what we are doing to God through our direct and indirect disobedience to Him?

He fought for her; they had security come and restrain him while she stripped herself in front of several people on their command-medical staff and public, the whole time with her beautiful smile, and allowed herself to be penetrated in various orifices. She then went with them into surgery. Later when he was finally allowed into the operating room, she had been raped by the MD, and had suffered a stroke. She was badly torn apart from one side to the other, and was lying in a large pool of blood, which was running off onto the floor. She was left open, in pieces, bleeding... and their precious gift from God, their son was dead, while just minutes before the mutilation he was fine (by sonogram). This man had to resuscitate their son. He survived but with residual damages, such as mentally slow and weak in the right hand and arm, as the MD had yanked it out of its socket. The LNorthern California hospital and MD left his wife for dead, and he had to put her back together, close her up, get IV's and medications into her to save her life. She sustained permanent damage as well as disfigurement. The court, State Board of quality medical assurance, and AMA refused to do anything to stop this, man or the hospital from hurting others, and this MD had a reputation he found out later of this type of activity and worse. After all of this was said and done, he left medicine because though he was very highly respected by patients and staff, he didn't wish to be a part of a system that would allow MD's and hospitals to participate in such heinous crimes and no protection from the government, or medical oversight boards on the state or national levels. He believes also the God used this to take him to greater levels. Why do I call this action a rape when she undressed herself and went with him? Because it was not consensual, and his pants were down when this man entered the room! I give you this brief outline of what happened as an example that there are consequences for sin and disobedience-physically, mentally, and most of all spiritually.

It was shortly after this time that his wife and him were talking, and he attempted to explain how wrong what she did was from a biblical perspective, and the consequences which she refused to accept, and she confessed to me that before we were married, having been active before marriage like so many other girls are now days. He told me that he was even more devastated. God, why? You said... I trusted you God; I forgave my wife. But this was the beginning of the end.

She grew closer to her worldly friends, got her U.S. citizenship fraudulently, filed false reports, lied to her husband and grew progressively withdrawn from their marriage and more materialistic.

He explained that he had always prayed for a daughter, a sister for his sons. His wife entered into menopause early from all of the trauma, and he was so hurt, but kept laying up his petition before God. Dear friends, after two- and one-half years of menopause, his wife's womb was reopened and they were with child. They were so excited and scared because a perinatologist had said after reviewing her records, that because of the trauma, she would never be able to conceive and that if she did by some miracle (we fell into this category for it truly was a miracle) conceive, that it would cost her and their child their lives. In spite of it all, he loved God and his wife. He prayed daily for his wife and child. This time she was in her forties as well, but God is in control! Not taking any chances, he cared for them at home the entire pregnancy. No MD saw her at any time. Then one fine evening, the time came and he delivered his little miracle. His wife lived; His...baby girl was perfect. As soon as he saw that she was a girl, he cried. They just delivered a precious daughter. His sons were so excited, that night that they stayed awake in the living room waiting to see and hold their new baby sister; such a wonderful experience for them all. God was with them, He blessed them, but his wife so drawn by the world couldn't see this and allowed herself to be pulled further away by her friends and the enemy. He had long forgiven her, but then she began beating His sons until SHE was too tired to even stand up, the boys were hiding in their room when he returned home from work. He tried to work with her, to love her, but her friendship with the world grew stronger and stronger, and allowed her friends to come between us, and between God Almighty and herself.

His wife was from a very poor family and so she had little education. She had dreams when they got married of being a stay-at-home mother, continue her art work which her family discouraged, she had a natural talent for art. She also dreamed of learning to play the violin. All three of these he was able and happy to fulfill during their marriage.

More and more she withdrew from their marriage, and grew in friendship with the world. She lied to the U.S. Government to obtain her citizenship (he wasn't aware at the time). She removed her head covering, threw it on the floor and cursed their marriage. She lied to the police, social service, and court, broke her vows before God and her husband and walked out of the marriage taking his children with her. No notice was given prior, but when he returned home from work, there was a note saying that she loved him and hoped that he would forgive her. This behavior and the lies were not his wife, but...her friends. His wife was a simple, beautiful, loving, caring, kind, compassionate, sympathetic young lady who apparently loved the world more than God. He warned her but the first time she was hooked, she was taken into the hands of men and women of the world who sought to destroy and did, hurt her and nearly cost her and their precious blessing of a son their lives. The second time took her away from her vows to God and her husband, into the hands of evil people of the world and deep into the darkness of Satan's domain.

His eldest son also left him a note saying that he loved him but knew that he could care for himself but that his mama would need help. She refused to speak with any pastors or friends of theirs, but went instead to known adulterers, alcoholics, drug and porn addicts, and the world. Just before she left, she destroyed all of his works- nearly complete for his Doctoral dissertation, which was called Idolatry, Adultery, and Pornography in the pulpit. His sons also made a choice (?) to go the way of the world (mother) rather than holding onto righteousness (papa), this concept you will understand more as we proceed further in this message.

He prayed about fighting for his wife and especially his wonderful children. The attorneys said that the courts there in Wyoming are so corrupt that no matter how abusive she was, she would get the children, and that knowing some of her friends, that if he went to court, his life may be jeopardized. One of her male friends already had made an attempt on his life, tried to kill him, and the local police would do nothing. He lost his house just to get away from him, so that he couldn't find him. This cost him his job. God told him that just as He lets His bride, His children who who desire to run from Him, to go, so should he. He reminded him of Paul's teaching that if an unbeliever leaves, let them leave. God also had given him a peace about not going to court, for it is a sin. In 1st Corinthians

6:6 we see *but brother goeth to law with brother and that before unbelievers. Now therefore there is utterly a fault among you, because you go to law one with another. Why do ye not rather take wrong? Why do ye not rather suffer yourselves to be defrauded? Nay, ye do wrong, and defraud.* Also, in 1ˢᵗ Corinthians 7:15-16 we are told, *But if the unbelieving depart, let him (or her) depart... but God hath called us to peace; for what knowest thou, o man, whether thou shalt save thy wife.* A few pastors reminded him that she couldn't be a true believer in God or His Word and walk out on her vows, and her marriage. Isaiah 29:13; 30:1-9.

He suffered a heart attack, his heart actually stopped and he had to be resuscitated, and praise God, no damage to his heart. The MD's who treated him said that it was a miracle that he survived for the loss of a spouse after so many years of marriage generally yields death within six months. God is powerful, and he will never leave Him.

After twenty mostly wonderful years of his life with this wonderful wife and children, it was over. His wife didn't know to do any of this; it was all the work of Satan, her friends, the world. He wasn't mad at her, in fact he hurt for her, and to this day, he prays for each of them. She and most people fail to realize or recognize what the Bible, what God Almighty says about marriage, about friendship with the world, divorce, lies, deceit. Why marriage is so important to God. All of this said I want to say that while what she did was wrong, literally, we all make mistakes, and spiritually, and in this message I'll explain why. I also wish to tell you that a few years later, God revealed to him why this happened, not justifying her actions but understanding God's works. But I also want to tell you that God is still in control. He turns a crisis into a blessing. Job lost all, but in the end, he had twice as much as he started with. God didn't cause Job's tragedy, or this mans, but He allowed Job's trials and this mans. He took him into an amazing mission that wouldn't have been possible with a wife and children, economically and safety wise, although with God all things are possible. The above story is real.

What Is A Friend?

The Bible says in John 15:13, *Greater love hath no man than this, that a man lay down his life for his friends.* Jesus Christ set the example for us to follow. This is not to say that everyone is going to be killed for someone else, but that we should have the heart to do so, if called upon to do so. Christ died for all, even those who crucified Him! What does this tell us? That we are to love all men, no matter what color, what sex, what age. No matter what they do or don't do for you. No matter what they say or don't say. We are to love all, no exceptions. And that includes within marriage.

Jesus said in Matt 26:24, *...but woe unto the man by whom the Son of man is betrayed!* Christ before He gave up His Spirit, asked our Father to forgive them (those who betrayed and crucified Him). Yes, I believe that His forgiveness included Judas, but this is another lengthy subject. I believe that the sin that came after the betrayal is the sin for which Jesus said Woe... Suicide is nothing more nothing less than murder of oneself. When you commit murder against yourself, there is no time to ask forgiveness or to repent for the sin, and this unforgiven sin is carried with you before the judgment seat. Also, you cannot intentionally kill someone you love, and hatred is a sin. So, Jesus forgave his worst enemies, those who killed Him. Therefore, we are to forgive those who trespass against us just as Christ has forgiven us. Forgiveness is an act of love!

To have a friend in word only is not a friend. Jesus said that He loves us so much that He wishes that none should perish. He also loves enough that He has given us a free choice to accept His friendship or not. He encourages our walk, and is ALWAYS there for us. Jesus NEVER leaves us nor forsakes us!

A person who says that they love you, but constantly lie and deceive to avoid you, to extort money, get a baby, or to obtain material things, etc.; but who desires to spend no time with you, and offers you no encouragement in your godly walk, is not a friend, no matter how much they claim to love you.

The Bible also says to love neither the world nor the things of the world. Friendship with the world is enmity with Christ! What is a friend? Among other things, a friend is;

> Someone who doubles our joys and divides our sorrows,

> Someone who understands our silence and comes in when the world goes out.

> Someone who accepts you for who you are rather than what you have.

> Someone who you can trust, who will always be totally honest with you, and who you can always count on.

> Someone who helps us keep up the pace,

> Someone who whispers words of encouragement, and shouts praise.

> Someone who puts others first

> and someone who will challenge you to become the person God desires you to be.

Brothers and Sisters in Christ, before you begin this message, I want you to know that I have not yet attained the high calling to which God has called me, to be in perfect obedience and faithfulness to Him. I struggle daily against the temptations of selfishness, pride, anger, self-pity and all the other sins of the flesh. When I speak of the evils of the age, I am often speaking to that which I have known personally. When I refer to the great need of repentance and personal holiness before God, I include my own continuing need each and every day to do the same. When I speak about the church, I do not mean any individual denomination. We are admonished in 2nd Corinthians 13:5 to *Examine yourselves, whether ye be in the faith; prove your own selves. Know ye not your own selves, how that Jesus Christ is in you, except ye be reprobates?*

It is essential that we take this command seriously and subject ourselves to God's plumb line as seen in Amos 7:7-8, His revealed word, the Holy Bible. Knowledgeable reformation minded Christians are concerned about many aspects of the lowered standards and conduct displayed in much of the present-day Church; many are doing nothing about it however, while many more are needed. The Holy Spirit recently gave me another revelation and told me to write it, so I have a message available entitled The Pentecostal Movement.

Today I am going to approach marriage in a way that I've never heard before. This message is totally inspired by God and is truly enlightening both for marriage as well as for your spiritual walk.

James 4:4 tells us that *friendship with the world is enmity with God*. I cannot emphasize this enough, nor could the Holy Spirit, for He repeated this idea many times, in fact I have found this in over fifty different scriptures! God used this and other miracles to take me into remote villages of Africa to share His word and His love. You will hear me repeat a few concepts over and over, because of how important they are.

Enough for an introduction; we shall now speak about the literal and spiritual aspects of children. May God bless each of you richly as you hear what the Spirit of the Living God has to say, Amen.

Clear your hearts and minds and listen closely to what the Holy Spirit has to say to you personally. Don't stop if the message pierces you, pray and read till the end...

Though I have been credited with writing this message, I take no credit other than the penmanship. This beautiful, wonderful and powerful message was given to me by the Holy Spirit to share with you, and to Him give I all the credit, the glory and thanks.

Most importantly, this message is divinely inspired, that is, what He told me to write, I wrote. It is subsequently the result of me asking questions to God, then listening to the voice of God as He responded. He entrusted this divine revelation to me to share with the world. He heard my petition and soon the springs of living water swept over my heart and mind. I spent many hours in the night (Psalm 16:7), Matt 10:27 tells us that *What I tell you in darkness, that speak ye in light, and what ye hear in the ear, that preach ye upon the housetops* Job 33:15-16 says *In a dream, in a vision of the night, when deep sleep falleth upon men, in slumberings upon the bed; Then he openeth the ears of men, and sealeth their instruction,* and day, listening and writing what He revealed unto me. Other revelations will be covered in other books I am writing. Often His answers brought about more questions, but God provided the wisdom contained herein. I am no writer, but I praise God for hearing me, for His precious answers, and for helping me through this writing. God loves you and me so much and He desires this message to be shared around the world. He hath called me to open your eyes and to turn you from the darkness of the evil one of this world to the Light, from the power of Satan unto God, that you may receive forgiveness of sins and inheritance among them which are sanctified by faith in Jesus Christ, and for this cause, the Christians went about slandering me, persecuting me and sought my life, but the God that I serve and preach unto you this day is far stronger than all of the demons of this world. He allowed them their fun but never my life, that I may continue to praise Him and testify of His mercy and grace. He resurrected me from these nearly ten years in the pit of hell called Kenya, and placed me upon the mountain so that I may shout praises unto Him and testify to the world that Jesus Christ is the Lord of Lords and the King of Kings! They wanted me dead so badly! One attorney even told me These people want you dead so badly they can taste your blood. They are already dividing up your property knowing that you won't get out of there alive. One pastor came and saw my condition and asked if they could pray for me. Several senior Christian officers (they were all SDA) laughed at them and said Why waste your time and ours? Can't you see that he is dying? We are just waiting to bury him. Imagine! Since the Christ whom I serve was willing to suffer and to die for my sins, should not I likewise be willing to suffer even unto death for Him? I call this the pit of hell, not only because of my experience but what I observed while in Kenya those few times I was there.

As the Holy Spirit spoke this message to me, it raised many questions in my mind, which I freely and humbly asked Him. Some He hath elected to answer and the information is thus contained herein these pages; the rest are not yet answered, if He so chooses to answer, then the material shall be made available in any subsequent editions, if not I'll assume that the answers are not for us to understand yet.

I know the worldly view of dating, male and female roles, sex, divorce, adultery, homosexuality, etc. but...God was the Creator of marriage and family, so let us look at what is His intent and why He created these along with His feelings and directives for this. In this critical message we shall attempt to guide each of us back to the path of righteousness, and see how God feels about us **BECOMING ONE** in marriage as well as in the family of God, therefore, this message may not be politically, socially, traditionally or even legally correct, but it is biblically correct. While reading it you must make choices, just as Daniel when he continued with God rather than the law.

I'm not going to get much into cultural ramifications as that is an entirely different issue; I am strictly teaching God's word, and this is what He wants, not what man or cultures have dictated.

He desires for you to be His bride. **Please... read this message carefully and prayerfully**, while listening to hear His call to you. Live for Him. Follow the precepts herein for your spiritual walk as well as for your marriage relationship. Get back on the straight and narrow path and hold on to Him. Understanding marriage helps us to understand our place in the family of God and vice-versa as you will see throughout this message.

May God richly bless you as you read on; there are many more scriptures relating to the topics in this message, but I believe that I am giving unto you enough to get the points across. As you read God's word, you will see that the precepts you learn in this book will make the Bible a lot more understandable. This message from God is very powerful and piercing. Please, again don't stop. Read and reread time and again cover to cover. I believe if you do, you like those who read the manuscript read it several times and asked for more. Read, pray, repent, revive, and be blessed. I also wish to encourage you to actually **look up** each verse and read them **in context** to get even more of the significance of each verse and topic. God bless you. Read this message carefully and prayerfully. Read the scriptures in context in God's word, preferably the Standard KING JAMES VERSION or better yet, the 1611 translation of the King James Bible, as it is the most accurate translation available. Don't get mad and close the message, but be glad, and pray, allow the Holy Spirit of the Living Almighty God to work in your life. Many shall be hurt by this message for we are all sinners, but allow God to turn this hurt this spirit of conviction to transform your life as well as that of your family. God wants to work in your life or He wouldn't have given you this message. The question is will you allow Him to? Revelation 3:20 tells us *Behold, I stand at the door and knock: If any man hear my voice and open the door, I will come into Him.* Let us all be filled today with the Spirit of the Living God.

We see in Matthew 5:6 *Blessed are they which do hunger and thirst after righteousness: for they shall be filled.* It is my prayer that you are or you wouldn't be hearing this message today.

One additional comment that I wish for each of you to understand! I speak in this message a few very truthful facts about my wife, but I need for you to understand that **I do not** condemn her for these things which she did...We are all sinners and make mistakes. I love her very much and pray for her return! All that she did **are common** mistakes that so many women make that are considered to be 'socially correct' today, but not biblically correct! Also, if you hear something that convicts you, don't beat yourself up over it, as we all do what we think is best by cultural upbringing and standards, that is why this message is so critical, to restructure our thinking and ways according to Christ's standards rather than cultural and tradition.

Again, **please don't skip ahead.** The information presented is in an order as to prepare you for the next part. And please make use of the page at the end of each chapter designated **PERSONAL NOTES**, to write your own personal notes to reinforce the material that you are reading, questions, and what comes to your mind for you personally to improve yourself, your Christian Walk and your marriage and family. May God bless you as you pass through this critical message, AMEN.

WARNING

Open and read this message with great care, with an open heart, mind, and soul; be prepared to be pierced through with His sword of conviction to your very core! This may be the greatest message you will ever read aside from God's word itself; and be brought to thy knees in repentance for restoration and revival according to the word of God, it will cut you through, turn you inside out so that thou mayest be cleansed.

PERSONAL NOTES

Psalms 127:3 lo, children are an heritage of the Lord

CHAPTER 1

The Blessed Children

Before we get into marriage, I want to discuss the roles and responsibilities of each member, the children, the men, and the women. Then we will be better prepared to discuss marriage, and further explain the reason that God gave this outline in a spiritual sense.

In Genesis 1:1 we read *In the beginning God created*! Then we skip to verse 26 and see *Let Us make man in Our image.* The animals were already created, so man is man, not apes or fish, man is man, in the image of God was man created. In Genesis Chapter two and three, we see all of creation was created from...nothing. Then God created man in His own image from the dust of the earth. Then He made woman from man, Gen 2:22, for man verse 20. Then God created through Adam and Eve, children.

CHILDREN ARE A BLESSING

Children, we read in Psalms 127:3 and 5, *Lo, children are a heritage of the Lord; and the fruit of the work is his reward.* **Happy** *is the man that has his quiver full of them. They shall not be ashamed...* Why are children created? In

Jeremiah 1:5 we read *before I formed thee in the belly I knew thee, and before thou camest forth out of the womb I sanctified thee...* In Psalm 139:13-15 we read *thou hast covered me in my mother's womb. I will praise you for I am fearfully and wonderfully made...my substance was not hid from thee, when I was made in secret.* We are made by God, for God.

I know a family of nineteen, and only one pregnancy bore twins. I asked them one day about it. The husband wanted no children, she did. She obeyed her husband and used birth control. One day however, God opened her womb in spite of the birth control, and her husband was beside himself. The day came for her to deliver their first child. He was by her side. He cried after seeing his firstborn and said to his wife, Let's have another. Now after seventeen, he told me that if God should bless them with another, they shall once again rejoice, even though everyone around puts us down. They said hurtful comments such as population control ... Haven't you ever heard of birth control? (Which we shall discuss in a later chapter), Don't you know how to say no? More on this also in a later chapter. How can you afford so many? God provides my dear friends. I told him not to listen to the world, listen to God. He had quit working full time and went to working half of the year and the other half was spent serving God. He cares for his family, and God cares for him.

Psalm 128:3 tells us, *Thy wife shall be as a fruitful vine by the side of thine house, thy children like olive plants round about thy table.* Look at the beauty, the unity of the family here. I had some other friends who had ten plus children, but God always provides, Jehovah Jireh, when we surrender ourselves and trust Him fully.

I need to begin here also by telling you that our precious little ones are children, not kids, as kids are baby goats!

In Genesis 31:35, we see the children were to stand before their parents, as a show of respect. Then again in 1st Kings 2:19, we see that Solomon bowed before his mother. I believe that we need to bring respect back. The Bible teaches us to train up a child in the way that they should go. If we don't teach respect to our children, how will they know to respect others

2

especially their life partners and their bosses, when they get older? And this is a big problem today, many young people don't respect one another, and unfortunately, don't respect themselves. Children should be taught to respect their elders, to stand before them, to offer up their chairs, to address them in a proper manner, not by first name... Even in 1ˢᵗ Kings 2:3 we see that Solomon the king, around 20 years of age, bowed before his mother out of respect.

In scripture, I see only a couple of specific commands for children. The first is in Exodus 20:12, the fifth commandment, also repeated in Ephesians 6:1-3, *Children, obey your parents in the Lord: for this is right. Honor thy father and mother, that it may be well with thee, and thou mayest live long on the earth.* This command is reiterated in Colossians 3:20.

I read this over many times for many years. I was always impressed that this was seemingly the only scripture dealing with the roles and responsibilities of children. Why? And if this is all God tells us, then why do our parents have so many rules? To Abraham, Moses, Israel, and to us, God said obey me, listen to me, and follow me.

Well, to explore this, we need to examine the other aspect of children in God's word. Parents are taught in Proverbs 22:6 to *train up a child in the way he (righteousness) should go and when he is old, he will not depart from it.* And how is a parent to do this? God tells us also in Proverbs 13:24 *He that spareth his rod hateth his son, but he that loveth him chasteneth him.* Again, in Proverbs *He that spareth his rod, spoils his child* depending on translation.

PARENTAL RESPONSIBILITY

𝕿 *rain up a child in the way he should go.* Deuteronomy 11:19 tells us to teach our children from the time we wake up until we go to sleep. Teach what? Teach the precepts of God, His word and His law. We need to teach His word by mouth and by example. Do as I say and not as I do, doesn't work and has no place in the Christian family. In the Christian walk we are to be Christ-like. Jesus taught by word and by example. He lived His word. This being said, in marriage there should be no secrets. We can't hide from God, ask Jonah. And we shouldn't hide anything from the partner that God hath ordained for us. We also must ALWAYS be honest with our children. How can we teach God's precepts to be honest and upright, and then lie to our children about family issues, questions that they ask, Santa Claus, Easter bunnies... when they find out the truth (and they will), they shall look at you and wonder, Hmmm they said we must not lie, yet they've lied to me all of these years... so... I guess it's Okay to lie, and if Santa is a lie... maybe God is also a lie??? Please read more about x-mas in my book **WHAT ABOUT THE BIBLICAL PERSPECTIVE OF CHRISTMAS**. Teach your children the word of God and His precepts. If this were done, we wouldn't be in the sorry condition that we are in presently. You are now being fed the true word, begin today reading God's word, apply it to your life, and teach God's word and precepts to thy children, and have them teach their children.

UNPLANNED CHILDREN

eing honest includes and brings into mind the subject of adoption. If you've adopted a child, be honest with them. Always be honest, with one another and with thy children.

Giving up a child to adoption is not a godly option. If God blesses you with a child, **you** are who He wishes to rear up the child, leave the rest to God.

I need to tell you parents and children right here and now; there are no such things as unwanted or unplanned children, accidents! These are terrible things for the child to hear! They may be by your parent's feelings in which case they should be ashamed! Each and EVERY pregnancy, child is a product of God. He designed and created each of us and had a purpose and a plan as we are told in Jeremiah 29:11, for each of us and He created you just the way that He wanted and needed you to be. There is a place that you alone are to fill, something you are to do which nobody else can. The place God calls you to is where your innermost peace and joy meets the world's deepest hunger and needs. Your parents, shame on them, may not have wanted or planned you; But God Almighty did want and plan you. You may have been an accident for your parents, shame on them, but you were no accident to God. We are told these precious words in Psalms 139:14 *I will praise thee; for I am fearfully and wonderfully made: marvellous are thy works; and that my soul knoweth right well.* Isaiah 49:5, *And now, saith the Lord that formed me from the womb to be his servant, to bring Jacob again to him, Though Israel be not gathered, yet shall I be glorious in the eyes of the Lord, and my God shall be my strength.*, and Jeremiah 1:5 *Before I formed thee in the belly I knew thee; and before thou camest forth out of the womb I sanctified thee, and I ordained thee a prophet unto the nations.*

I know of a couple that was unable to bear children but they had a genuine heart for them. They ended up adopting thirty children from all over. They adopted abandoned babies, orphans, Latin, oriental, Indian, African, as well as Caucasians. They were such a beautiful family.

If you are an adopted child and confused, don't be. Listen, we are all adopted children into the wonderful family of God IF we choose to accept Him as our Father. Why did your birth parents give you up? Only they know, and it's not important, their loss. What is important is that they didn't hate you enough to abort you, and that you have parents who chose you above all other children, to love, teach, protect, and provide for you, and for all of this you should be praising God. Don't look back, look forward, knowing that regardless of what happened- looking back to the past, the living Almighty God has a purpose and a plan for you or He wouldn't have brought you into this world. We aren't the choice of our parents; we are God's choice. So, don't live for people, live for God. Look to Him...Serve Him. Don't spend precious time searching for thy birth parents for life is too short. Live for God looking forward, fulfill His purpose for your life and look forward with joy unto the finish line of your life, eternity with God. My precious friends, never be ashamed of having been adopted, rejoice that there was a couple who love you enough to sacrifice their time, money, mercy... for you were bought with a price, just as those of us who accept Christ, who loves us enough to sacrifice himself and paid the price for us, for our sins, that we may have life eternal with a Father who loves us so very much. Your parents love you enough that they purchased you for a price, and have sacrificed for you.

Also, very important, love thy parents, forgive thy birth parents, they will never know what a blessing, what a special person they gave away! Think about this. If you parents are considering a divorce (May God touch your hearts and you reconcile before hurting yourselves and thy children), I need to explain a very important biblical principal regarding your children. Contrary to the courts of today, IF... You children should ALWAYS stay with thy father and Father-just as we as His children should ALWAYS stay with our Father, this is His plan.

My boys were beyond the age of accountability and they chose to leave the father and follow sin, for which there is a judgment day. I shall explain this in a little while. Dear children, pray always for your parents, your family, but establish a relationship with your father and never let him go. (You need to have a special relationship with your mother in the worldly sense, don't get me wrong). But don't allow yourself to fall into sin. My eldest wrote me a note saying that he knew that I could take care of myself but mom needs help. This is a sweet reason (poor boy needing to be torn into making such a decision). God is able to take care of Himself, but He still deserves us to follow and serve Him rather than the sinful ways of the world. My second son left no note so I don't know his heart.

I wish to encourage parents to use cloth diapers and avoid plastic bottles. We are called to be good stewards of God's creation, and plastic is not at all healthy for the environment. Plastic is also not good for the body, and children who use cloth diapers are much less prone to developing diaper rash, infections, and other problems. Reusable (cloth) is also much less expensive, so that your (God's) money can be used for better purposes. It is better for the environment, God's creation. God created cotton, man invented plastic.

Another important issue and I know that there will be great controversy about this, but...the issue of vaccinations. The body is the temple of God and we should not violate His temple. By injecting bacteria and viruses into His temple, doesn't that sound like a grievous violation of His temple? Vaccinations have been well documented to cause an increase in immune-mediated diseases such as diabetes, asthma, MS, ADD/ADHD, autism, and cancers; as well as autoimmune diseases, strokes, seizures, brain damage, sudden death, learning disabilities, and the list goes on, and includes death! Yet, many who are immunized get sick anyway, and in fact, the epidemics of old were ended BEFORE the vaccines were widely dispersed. One must weigh the advantages with the disadvantages of them. I chose none for my children. At birth many hospitals routinely place eye drops in the infant's eyes in case of gonorrhea. If you and your partner are true Christians, you aren't out playing around and don't need to worry about the in case, also, these same eye drops blinding the child for around three days, which are a critical period for infant bonding. We refused those as well, and our children are fine. For more information on immunizations, you may contact Immunization Action Coalition at www.immunize.org; National Network for immunization information at www.immunizationinfo.org; or the National Vaccine information center at www.909shot.com or call 1800-909-SHOT. You may also go to National Institute of health at www.nih.gov, National vaccine injury comp. program at www.hrsa.gov/csp/vicp, or vaccine adverse events reporting system at www.fda.gov/cher/vaers. Immunizations, now days they are pushing for more and more vaccinations for our precious children including but not limited to flu, shingles, HPV, meningitis, hepatitis. Dear friends, I believe that our Lord God, our Creator, the Creator of this universe and all that it contains, created us as we need to be. By injecting all of these organism's dead or alive, is not how God, our Creator, the Master Designer, planned. By all of these vaccinations, you are not only increasing immediate risk factors but long term as the immune system is being revamped from how God designed it to be, predisposing one to immune deficiency conditions, cancers, etc. Again, I am not here telling you what to do, merely stating an opinion to consider, you make your choice after careful thought and prayer for your children. Another vaccine that is in the works is for the covid. This vaccine I would encourage nobody to take, but it is your choice. It actually works on the RNA of your body which is a critical part of the DNA which controls your entire body-growth and development as well as functions within. This is essentially producing Genetically modified people, what next? Control your reproduction, longevity...? I need again to say that I am not telling you to use or not to use vaccinations, I am merely providing you with some information to consider and pray about. The final decision is between you and God. I am not advising to do go one way or the other. Do what God leads you to do. I am merely documenting an issue for you to pray about for your own family. It is between God and you. Every year they are adding more and more vaccines. Have they been thoroughly tested? How healthy are they? What are the risks versus benefits?

Listen to Solomon's words in Proverbs 1:2-10, 15. *The fear of the Lord is the beginning of knowledge: but fools despise wisdom and instruction. My sons hear the instructions of thy father and forsake not the law of thy mother; for they shall be an ornament of grace unto thy head and chains about thy neck. My son, if sinners entice thee, consent thou not. My son, walk not thou in the way with them; refrain thy feet from their path.* We should, as children of God, hear the instruction of our heavenly Father or be chastised by Him. We should obey the law of the Lord for it directs our path. We must look to Rachel in Genesis 31:35. It was customary for a child of any age to stand in the presence of their parents, a show of respect as we just discussed. We need to teach our children respect, the way that they should go, Proverbs 22:6.

Children tend to be followers, thus the need for the proper instruction by the parents both by word and by example, and discipline as is necessary. We are shown in 1ˢᵗ Samuel 3:13, the consequences of not disciplining our children, *For I have told him that I will judge his house for ever for the iniquity which he knoweth; because his sons made themselves vile, and he restrained them not,* and we see the results in today's society. In 1ˢᵗ Samuel 8:5-8, we see the children of God failed to realize that they already had a King, the King of Kings, but they desired to be like everyone else (vs. 5), worldly, rather than seeking God. There are of course, consequences for your choices, and as James 4:4 tells us that *friendship with the world is enmity with God.* We as His children, must choose to listen to and obey our Father, this begins by example in early childhood by assuring that children honor, listen to, and obey their earthly father, who should teach their children not to conform to the world, but rather to the precepts of God, to listen to and be obedient unto Him. Since the man is the head of the house, the wife should honor her husband's wishes regarding child-rearing. This is something that should be discussed before it becomes an issue and then the child begins to play one parent against the other, a very bad and dangerous situation for all involved.

God never commanded parents to teach the A B C's or 1 2 3's and science, but God did... God did...God did say in Deuteronomy 6:7 *and thou shalt teach them* (the Ten Commandments, statutes, God's Word*) diligently unto thy children, and shalt talk of them when thou sittest in thine house, and when thou walkest by the way, and when thou liest down, and when thou riseth up.* Speak of God, not idle chatter, the statutes, the ordinances, the love, mercy, and grace of God. Even less reason for the big push today for more women in college, and increased benefits to women unavailable for men... In Deuteronomy 4:9 we are told to teach the statutes and law to thy sons and thy son's sons. Now, I ask you, why only the sons? Well, physically because the woman is subject to their fathers or husbands, so the men need to know the law so that they may oversee their wives, daughters, as well as their sons;

Spiritually, because sons (righteousness) need the law to keep them on the right path.

One may ask, why did God make rules for Adam in the first place? to test him and then to guide him after he fell. As a parent, I know that I provided a shelter, love, and protection for my children, as does God. I know that I had to make rules to guide and protect them, to keep them safe and on the correct path. Disobedience could lead to disaster and/or death, look both ways before crossing the street... just as our disobedience to the law of our heavenly Father or...rejecting our Father... leaving us as orphans, lost, and alone, and...cast into eternal death and damnation. He provides love and protection if we will choose to listen, accept and obey Him. We choose to disobey... and look at the results! God's ways are always the best way; God's time is always the best time. God doesn't lie, so we can always trust Him in all things, Amen. We are told in Amos 3:2 *You only have I known of all the families of the earth: therefore I will punish you for all your iniquities.* We see the special privileges that God gave Israel by choosing them increased their moral and ethical standards and responsibilities, and did not exempt them from judgment. Those of us who are the chosen, those of us who choose to receive Jesus Christ as our Lord and Savior have greater responsibilities to listen to, be obedient to and serve Him and are not exempt from judgment and chastisement as some think. Whom the Father loveth, He chastises.

In Proverbs 19:18 we read, *chasten thy son while there is hope and let not thy soul spare for his crying.* Psalm 23:4 *Thy rod and thy staff they comfort me.* They what? They comfort me. 2 Samuel 7:14 tells us, *I will be his father and he shall be my son. If he commits iniquity, I will chasten him with the rod of men, and with the stripes of the children of men.* In Proverbs 22:15 *foolishness is bound in the heart of a child, but the rod of correction shall drive it far from him.* Proverbs 23:13-14 *withhold not correction from the child, for if thou beatest him with the rod, he shall not die. Thou shalt beat him with the rod, and shalt deliver his soul from hell.* Proverbs 29:15, 17 *The rod and reproof give wisdom, but a child left to himself bringeth his mother to shame. Correct thy son and he shall give thee rest, yea, he shall give delight unto thy soul.* I shall explain why I covered these verses shortly as I put this picture together for you. Satan is wreaking havoc now as many areas are making laws against child discipline.

The second command for children is found in Matthew 23:9. We are not to call any *man your father upon the earth: for one is your Father, which is in heaven.* So, dad, papa... but not happy Father's Day. Catholics shouldn't call their leader's father. No God-fearing person should call anyone but God, Father. God alone is our Father. Throughout scripture you see he, she, him, and her. He or him always refers to righteousness, and to God. She or her always refers to sin and the sinner, which is all of us, all men and women, all of mankind. The Spirit reminded me, all the covenants were made between God and men, not women; and only men were called to be circumcised, not women. Why? because of God's relationship with man. 1st Corinthians 11:7 tells us that *man was made in the image and glory of God, but the woman is the glory of man.* She was made from man for man. The fall of the family is a reflection of Spiritual decline. Father disciplines his son, not mother her daughter (in scripture) because God (He) disciplines those He loves. Does He only love men? No! He loves the righteous, men or women, but men are symbolic of righteousness. God desires to bring the righteous sinner to repentance, back on or onto the path of righteousness that leads to salvation and eternal life with Him in heaven. Sin doesn't desire righteousness, so in the spiritual sense, all men begin life as she, and some men and women are he in the spiritual sense. In Proverbs 1:8 we see that instruction and wisdom come from God (Father). The law is for sinners (she) to lead us back onto the correct path. Please keep the spiritual and earthly definitions of men and women separate, as you will see this throughout this message and the significance of it. I had discussed this issue with a priest (a Catholic father) and he attempted to justify this title but the scriptures that he used simply didn't justify disobedience to God's Word.

A child always tries to be like his father, imitate and be like him. Likewise, the truly spiritual should strive to be like our Heavenly Father, to be Christ-like Matthew 18:1-5

Adam did not fall because he ate of the fruit, but because he listened to the voice of his wife rather than the voice of God, Gen 3:17 and we shall explain this in more detail later. We see this also in Genesis 16:2 between Abram and Sarai.

Eve, the first woman, brought also sin into the world. This is a clue in our reading and interpreting scripture. Israel, when wandering those forty years, when they were walking with God, God called them he. When they went astray, they were called she. Children represent the true believer, the truly spiritual, the chosen, and the justified.

In a literal perspective, God chooses whose womb He shall open and when, the choice isn't ours. Oh, you say, but the cycle, the rhythm... I studied and worked in medicine for over thirty years, do you know how long a sperm cell can live in the vagina? And remember that Jesus Christ was born of a virgin, no sperm. Variables in the vagina affect fertility, but who is in control of all this? Not man or woman, but God. Will you have one child or twenty? It is all in God's plan, not mans. NO birth control can one hundred percent prevent pregnancy, except for a complete hysterectomy (removal of ALL of the woman's reproductive organs). Without going into more detail yet, I wish this point to be clear to all. We shall discuss this more later. Now for the scriptures I just reviewed, allow me to reveal to you the spiritual aspects.

God the Father chastens those who He loves, His children, so that we may walk in His path, to be Christ-like, and not to turn to the left or to the right onto the paths of sin. He disciplines us because He loves us and because He desires the best for us. The best is eternal life with Him. We are all sinners, men and women, and the believer should find comfort in His discipline, knowing even though it may hurt for a time, that He loves you or He wouldn't care enough to discipline you. He loves and disciplines us so that we may walk the path by His side. If He was not to discipline us, we would be lost, spoiled, eternally in hell, therefore we who love and trust God our Father, we as His children must be obedient to Him. In Proverbs 13:18 we are told, *Poverty and shame shall be to him that refuseth instruction: but he that regardeth reproof (discipline) shall be honored.* Part of this obedience involves being obedient to God's laws, which were given in order to draw us closer to Him. Amen. Now, parents, we are not talking about abuse. God never abuses us, and neither should we abuse our children. Discipline is a means to correct a child's evil, sinful ways, and guide them to the path of righteousness, and it is always done with love, not anger. Abuse is an action of anger against a certain behavior. Also, this discipline should not be by the judgment of our personal likes or dislikes, but judgment of the child's behavior in relation to what God's word teaches, the way that they should go. This is God's way, not mans. God's chosen people, His children, He trains up, then He allows us to be tried and tested. If you prove disobedient and fail the tests, He will discipline to make you stronger. He does all of this with love for us. Whom He loves He chastises, so children, obey thy parents in the Lord, or you should be disciplined with love to help you to grow stronger, wiser, and upright.

We are to train up our children in the ways of the Lord not the ways of the world (James 4:4). That means as Deuteronomy 6:6-7 tells us, in the precepts of God's word, and we are to discipline our dear children according to God's will, not our own likes and dislikes, teaching them to use their God given brains rather than computers and artificial intelligence.

Parenting- When you are yelling at your children, your marriage partner or to God, do you think that they can hear you any better? No. It only serves to make you feel better. Yelling is from anger, not love. Discipline must always be done with love just as when God disciplines us. I think of Sheriff Andy Taylor who had a son, and he never raised his voice at home or at work. He always corrects with a soft, caring voice. When you are yelling and then beating...this is abuse, not discipline. We must be careful how we talk to our children, our marriage partner, and to God and be sure that it is ALWAYS with love. We read in Jeremiah 31:9 They shall come with weeping, and with supplications will I lead them: I will cause them to walk by the rivers of waters in a straight way, wherein they shall not stumble: for I am a father to Israel, and Ephraim is my first-born. Further we read in verses 18 and 19 I *have surely heard Ephraim bemoaning himself thus; Thou hast chastised me, and I was chastised, as a bullock unaccustomed to the yoke: turn though me, and I shall be turned; for thou art the LORD my God. Surely after that I was turned, I repented; and after that I was instructed, I smote upon my thigh: I was ashamed, yea, even confounded, because I did bear the reproach of my youth.* Please note here, the discipline leading to repentance and turning away from the wicked ways. We further read in Hebrews 12:5-11 *And ye have forgotten the exhortation which speaketh unto you as unto children, My son, despise not thou the chastening of the Lord, nor faint when thou art rebuked of him: For whom the Lord loveth he chasteneth, and scourgeth every son whom he receiveth. If ye endure chastening, God dealeth with you as with sons; for what son is he whom the father chasteneth not? But if ye be without chastisement, whereof all are partakers, then are ye bastards, and not sons. Furthermore, we have had fathers of our flesh which corrected us, and we gave them reverence: shall we not much rather be in subjection unto the father of spirits, and live? For they verily for a few days chastened us after their own pleasure; but he for our profit, that we might be partakers of his holiness. Now no chastening for the present seemeth to be joyous, but grievous: nevertheless afterward it yieldeth the peaceable fruit of righteousness unto them which are exercised thereby.*

Parents, you must practice a daily routine (every evening Bible reading/study, prayer, and song). This should be inclusive of EVERY member of the family, Deuteronomy 6:6-7.

Children, even if you don't think that your parents love you remember that God is your Father, and He will always love you. You parents should always love your dear children as they are Gods precious gifts to you.

Childbirth is such an amazing event, experience. As I read the scriptures, I think of what Adam must have been wondering as he watched Eve's abdomen get bigger and bigger. I wonder how Eve felt with this first experience of its kind. I wonder about the rupturing of the membranes and the amniotic fluid gushing out, how they both felt, what was going through their minds. Then the birth of little Cain. What an experience! Today we know about this wonderfully amazing event, and what a blessing it is. But along with the joy of this spectacular event, there are tremendous responsibilities and challenges that lie ahead. It is a life changing event and one that both parents must accept and be prepared for. But the biggest responsibility that a parent has is to rear the child in the ways of the Lord.

The Bible teaches parents to:

- Be a good example for them to follow, Genesis 18:19, Titus 2:2, and others

- Instruct children in righteousness, Psalms 78:5, Proverbs 22:6 and others

- Provide for our children, 2 Corinthians 12:14

- Govern with kindness, Ephesians 6:4, Colossians 3:21

- Discipline our children, Proverbs 29:15 and 17

The Bible also shows us examples of parenting mistakes so that we may learn from them, such as;

- Rebekah playing favorites with her children, Genesis 25:28, and Joseph did the same with his children in Genesis 37:3.

- Eli was unable to rear his own children but was entrusted with rearing Samuel. 1 Samuel 3:10-14.

- 1st Samuel 8:1-6 shows that Samuel was a deficient father as well as David committed adultery, murder, and set a bad example for his son to follow, Manasseh sacrificed his sons to demons, 2 Kings 21:1-9. And many other examples of parenting in scripture. But while there were bad examples, there were also some good examples as well;

○ Mordecai, who adopted Esther, 2:7 and Esther saved the Jews.

○ We see Job who prayed and interceded for his children, Job 1:4-5, etc.

But having shown these examples, I need to say that it is a choice you make to be a good parent or not, but how a child turns out is ultimately their choice, based upon your influence. If you choose to be an alcoholic and your child turns out to be an alcoholic, is it your fault? Yes, but also the child chose to follow your ways, rather than choosing to abstain from alcohol.

We also are not called to send our children off to boarding schools, baby sitters, day care, etc. for others to train up. I and many others today home schooled our children. As God has blessed you with children, He has likewise ordained **you** to train up that child, just as God our Father trains us up. God chose this child at this time in this place, and He chose you to be the parent, to bring this gift into the world, and to bring up this child for Him. He chose you to nourish, to breastfeed, spiritually nourish this precious child. Is that child your child? No, the child belongs to God, He just loaned this child to you to rear for Him, temporarily to care for His child. Our Father never gives us up to other gods to train or to discipline us. Never! If He did, what would happen? We would not have the training that God ordained for us. Neither can others train up the child God ordained for us, for your children, God's children.

Something else that I feel compelled to share. I had three wonderful children. All three were different, were unique. My eldest son had a heart of gold, very loving and caring, always could be found helping people. Time out was a severe punishment for him. My second son also had a good heart, was a comedian. He could always make people laugh, and cheer them up. Time out never worked for him. My daughter was still young, but she loved to help cook. The point is this. My second son always tried to be like his big brother, and he wanted to be treated the same. But he wasn't his brother He was he. They had different personalities, interests... I treated each differently but loved each the same. Christ created each of us unique and He wants us to be us, not to be like anyone else. We are to be ourselves and to separate ourselves from the world, not to be like everyone else. He gives each of us special gifts and talents to be used for His purpose and plan that He has for each of us, for His glory, and He loves us all the same, while treating each of us differently.

My wife was tested by her 'friends' as was the woman spoken of in the intro and just as we all are. I have been tested by the loss of a family I loved very much. I lost everything that I had ever worked for, including gifts collected from countries, as well as those that my wife and children made for or gave me. I've been stoned, torched twice, thrown into prison and tortured in Africa for the cause of Christ. Even though God may treat you differently, God loves you the same. Being a dad is difficult; imagine being God, the Father of all! But remember, the better the child, the easier it is for the father, and for our Father.

One more point, I'm inspired to write regarding this. If we aren't/weren't married to Christ, we cannot be His children. Those who aren't married to Him are illegitimate children, children of the devil. Think about this my dear friends.

Children, you must be careful in choosing your friends, and remember that we are all children of God so this equally applies to all of us. Unfortunately, many young people make the choice to associate with other young people who are involved in alcohol, drugs, smoking, gangs, criminals, etc. in order to fit in or belong. Many young ladies associate with prostitutes or sexually promiscuous girls and all these young people wind up walking down the same deadly path. This path is dangerous physically, leading to death, prison, HIV and other diseases, unplanned and unwanted pregnancy, etc. as well as spiritually as this leads you away from the path of righteousness leading to the gates of heaven, and rather leading them straight to hell, all because of the choice that they make. Choose your friends wisely. Choose those who lift you up, keep you on the right path. And listen, good friends are hard to find, but no friend is better than a bad friend. And you will never be without a friend if you stay on the path of righteousness because God will always be by your side.1ˢᵗ Corinthians 15:33 tells us *Be not deceived: evil communications corrupt good manners*. Attend a bad church, read bad books, watch bad movies, listen to sermons by heretics...your spiritual life will rot away and before you know it, you'll be lost, broken, behind bars, or lying in a hospital bed. Remember, this applies to our children, but also to all of us as we are all children of God.

God rejoices over each of the children that are saved. He desires that all are saved, that His family be large, yet while many today desire small families, our Father desires a full house. God however gives each of us a free choice; each of us is free to choose the right path, adoption into His family, or the path of destruction, sin, leading to death and eternal damnation. The latter is not God's will but your choice. It is not God's fault, only yours. You make the choice. Think about what the Spirit is saying here my dear friends. We have but one Father, God in heaven. We are His children, and we need to listen to and obey Him. We need to trust and obey Him that it may be well for us, unto salvation and eternal life. He loves us but allows us to leave Him and join unto other gods, Satan, but while Satan may give you a piece of cake, he will never love you.

There is an old adage that a child should be seen and not heard, but I tell you that a child should be heard, for they have much to share. Jesus loves the little children and so should we. If a child is not taught how to speak and when to speak, or when not to speak, and then allow them to practice, how will they ever learn, just look at Isaiah 53:5. And, one must recall that Josiah, king of Judah for thirty-one years began at the age of eight years old! And he did right in the sight of the Lord!

Remember, the children of God murmured forty years in the wilderness because of disobedience and no love of the Father who delivered them. Children when they begin to venture out on their own in independence need first to forgive their parents, so that they may venture out without carrying the baggage of hatred, resentment, and unforgiveness into the world. Your parents, most of them did the best that they knew how, but we are all human and make mistakes. Jesus forgave His family so that He could minister unto others. He later disowned them, saying where is my mother, my brothers or sisters? Matt 12:48. We must also forgive our dads just as we must forgive God, why all the trials and tribulations, persecutions? Why me?

Isaiah 30:9 says *This is a rebellious people, lying children, children that will not hear the law of the Lord.* Why? because of a lack of godly parenting and discipline. Look at the children today. Look at their parents.

As Christians, we first need to pull the log from our own eye... we need to set priorities in our homes for child rearing; we need to be selfless, have objectives, godly vision to love others and serve Him; We need to be role models- admitting mistakes, and living a godly lifestyle, we need to be involved with our family, and have godly expectations for a godly lifestyle for your children.

Children are a gift from God. You must understand that God is in control of a woman's womb, not her or the man, or birth control. Whenever He chooses to open thy womb, rejoice and be glad, you are the chosen! Praise Him. You see in the spiritual realm, the true believer is chosen by God, to receive the free gift of salvation, because He already knows your heart that you will make the choice to follow Him. Many are called but few choose to truly accept God and the free gift of salvation that He offers. They refuse to confess, repent and become a new member of the family of the Living God.

Oh children, you are so special to God. The Bible teaches us in Matthew 19:14 *Suffer not a little child to come unto me.* We are to be as little children Jesus taught. We are not to lose a child for any reason, to abortion, adoption, prostitution, nothing, for God chose this child, each of us at this time for you the parent to train up and prepare for God to use. Rearing up a child is an awesome responsibility, and it takes commitment. It takes quality time spent with your child each and every day. Rejecting a child is rejecting God, and refusing the precious gift and blessing that He wishes to bestow unto you. I've been to crusades and churches where certain church leaders refused to allow children to respond to the altar call. Oh, the shame. Jesus called the little children to come unto Him. One should never turn away a child or anyone who desires to sanctify themselves to God and accept His free gift of salvation, any more than would God ever reject you. He loves us all so very much.

In Deuteronomy 21:18 we see the instruction for a stubborn and rebellious son who will not obey the instruction of the father. In verse 21 we are told that he is to be removed from the city and stoned to death. Those who are stubborn and refuse to accept Christ and obey Him shall reap eternal death outside of the city of heaven.

Psalm 127:13 *...the fruit of the womb is his reward,* just as we are His children, the fruits that we harvest by being His servants, His helpmates, sewing seeds, watering and harvesting is God's reward. But...we must remember Matthew 18:3-6 ... *except ye be converted and become as little children, ye shall not enter into the kingdom of heaven. Whosoever therefore shall humble himself (righteous) as this little child, the same is greatest in the kingdom of heaven, and who shall receive one such little child in my name receiveth me. But whoso shall offend one of these little ones which believe in me, it would be better for him that a millstone was hanged about his neck, and that he were drowned in the depth of the sea.* The humble mentioned includes trusting and openness with God; A willingness to learn with a heart to obey.

And then Jesus continues in Matthew 19:14 saying *Suffer little children to come unto me and forbid them not: for of such is the kingdom of heaven.* simple as a child folks.

The opening words of Isaiah 1:2,10 tells us *I have nourished and brought up children, and they have rebelled against me.* Why? because of a lack of childlike faith, because of a lack of godly parenting and discipline.

Parents, you must practice a daily routine (every evening Bible reading/study, prayer, and song). This should be inclusive of EVERY member of the family regardless of how young or old. Read Deuteronomy 6:6-7 teach precepts to children

Proverbs 17:25 tells us *A foolish son is a grief to his father, and bitterness to her that bare him.* Then we continue in Proverbs 19:26-27 *He that wasteth his father, and chaseth away his mother, is a son that causeth shame, and bringeth reproach. Cease, my son, to hear the instruction that causeth to err from the words of knowledge.*

1ˢᵗ Samuel 15:23

What about the children who for one reason or another left home and their families? We are all children of the Most-High God; we all have strayed away from Him just as in the parable of the Prodigal son. He returned, repented, and was restored. And so must we return to our heavenly Father in repentance, and be restored into His family; and so should the children who have wandered or strayed away from their parents. This includes running away. If you are truly abused-physically, sexually, mentally, then seek assistance from a godly pastor and/or the local police and receive the counseling and assistance that you need, but you must find forgiveness in your heart for thy parents whom God hath given unto you.

What is the role of the church in all of this? As God's servants, we are to call the children unto God. Matthew 19:14, as such if a child presents him or herself unto the church building or member, they should be heard. If the situation is not one of abuse, then they should be returned to their parents and you may act as a mediator between parents and child if needed. If the child is abused physically, emotionally, or spiritually, then take that child in and care for them until the proper help can be arranged.

Philosophers say that grownups take the world for granted. That they allow themselves be lulled into the enchanted sleep of their boring routine of life. Jesus said the same thing-unless you become as a little child... Such is the truth in religion. We become complacent. This message is meant to awaken, revive and restore you back to God and what is most important in life, marriage, and family. We must stop taking God (and Satan) for granted. Satan has craftily used this world and the things of it to pull people off of the path of righteousness and God hath sent me to try to pull the lost sheep back to His flock.

Even if you don't think that your parents love you remember that God is your Father, and He will always love you. You parents should always love your dear children as they are Gods precious gifts to you.

Children, and we are all the children of God as well as of our parents, you have heard what I have said here. Now I must challenge you, Cain the first born, lost his blessings as did Reuben and Simeon the first and second born, because they proved themselves unworthy. But Shem the first born proved himself worthy. Are you proving yourself worthy or are you losing your blessings?

We are all children of the Most-High, the Almighty God, our Father, and we must make the choice of whether or not to love Him with a pure, clean heart; to fully submit to His authority, and obey Him at all times and at any cost, just as the adopted children that we are must. Galatians 4:5 *To redeem them that were under law; that we might receive the adoption of sons.* This tells us that the righteous, the justified shall be adopted into the family of God. *I have nourished and reared my children, and they rebelled against me. Hear the word; give ear unto the law of our God.* Dear friends, I read this and just hear and feel the pain in His sweet voice as He agonizes over this. He created you and me, He has loved, He hath provided...and yet...most of us have rebelled against Him. I nourished and reared my children; I delivered three of my children. They rebelled, as did my wife, my bride, I know some of the pain that God must feel when we are disobedient and/or turn from Him and walk away, after all He hath done for us. In 1ˢᵗ Timothy 5:1-2 we are told *Rebuke not an elder, but intreat him as a father: and the younger men as brethren; the elder woman as mothers; and the younger as sisters, with all purity.* I do believe that this practice should be reenacted as a sign of respect rather than a child calling an elder by first name, or as 'the old man/lady... Growing up is not a matter of how big or tall or how old you become, but rather how wise you become. I pray that this message will awaken you and get you on the path of righteousness with God, and your marriage and family. Amen.

To further assist you in understanding this message, ask yourself and perhaps discuss in a group the following two questions.

1. What would have happened if Adam and Eve had of conceived a child BEFORE the fall?

2. Could God cause a woman to conceive a perfect child today? And if so, what would be the consequences?

PERSONAL NOTES

_____

_____

_____

_____

_____

_____

_____

_____

_____

_____

_____

_____

_____

_____

_____

_____

PERSONAL NOTES

Job 1:1 That man was perfect and upright, and one that revered God and eschewed evil

CHAPTER 2

The Righteous Man, Husband, and Father

In Eccliastes 7:28 we read *...one man among a thousand have I found; but a woman among all those have I not found.* Let us look at God's word here.

As I stated earlier in the previous chapter, in scripture whenever God says he, him, his, He is referring to God and righteousness, the justified people, men and women, so my dear brothers and sisters please keep this in mind and as we hear this message, consider both the physical and spiritual context. You will better understand this concept as we proceed through this message.

MEN

In Titus 2:6-8 we see *Young men likewise exhort to be sober minded in all things showing thyself a pattern of good works in doctrine showing uncorruptness, gravity, sincerity. Sound speech that cannot be condemned...* In Leviticus 10:9 *do not drink wine or strong drink...* I believe that these are very important and are self-explanatory. Alcohol inhibits sexual performance, but more importantly it deadens your senses to be able to appreciate and enjoy this beautiful and wonderful time and your wife who God created and blessed you with. Just look at what happened when Noah drank in Genesis 9:21-25, and Lot in Gen 19:32. There is a reason that they are called spirits.

1st Thessalonians 4:3-5 also tells us *that we should abstain from fornication; That every one of you should know how to possess his vessel in sanctification and honor; not the passion of lust, even as the gentiles* (non-believers) *which know not God.* What vessel is he talking about here? our bodies, those of the men and women who are saved, who are the vessels of the Holy Spirit. We need to care for and bring honor unto His temple, not give into lusts and enticements of the world of Satan, as the unbelievers do.

We see the example of Job who was upright, and didn't fall when tried, even when his wife told him to curse God and die. She tried to entice her husband to sin and die, just as Eve did Adam, only Adam caved in and did die. Job's 'friends' all condemned him, the people who were closest to him and knew him best. Look at how crafty Satan is. You must be strong. You must always be on your guard. You must be strong in the word of God. In Matthew 4:1-11, we see Christ in the wilderness forty days, then tempted by Satan, tried and tested by the enemy. What I wish for you to see here is how did Christ respond and defeat the enemy 1n each of the three temptations? By quoting scripture; God's word is so powerful and it is final. *It is written.* It is so important for us men to be diligently studying the precious word of God and pray for understanding.

Men, we must love our God, ourselves, our wives, our children, our neighbors. We must totally surrender ourselves to God and if married, to our wives as God hath done for us.

We must care for orphans and widows. Why does God refer specifically to these two groups? Orphans have no papa, and they need love and guidance, just as we need from our Father in heaven. Widows have no husband to love, guide and protect them. Widows represent the lost souls that are in need of someone to love them, to guide, lead them to a saving knowledge of the Bridegroom, Jesus Christ.

We are to visit the sick as well as those in prison. When people are down, it's a great time to reach out to them, showing them the love of God, His mercy, and grace, and leading them to or encouraging them in the Lord.

In Genesis 3:9 we read *And the Lord called unto Adam, and said unto him, where art thou?* This is a scripture that many of us have heard or read many times over, but... what does it really say? Dear brothers and sisters, I wish for you to see a few important points here. First, God called Adam, not Eve. Man is accountable before God for his wife and children, just as Jesus justifies us before God. Secondly, a man is not to see another woman other than his wife. God walked this earth in the form of a man, so symbolically shouldn't see Eve (after the fall). God created man in Their own image, that is in the image of God, for service unto God, then He created woman from man for man. God created man to serve Him, He created woman to serve man, to be a helpmate for her husband. So, in a spiritual sense, God is calling the righteous (man) unto Himself. Thirdly, I wish for you to see here that God called Adam...Adam didn't call God. God, even in our sinful nature, still loves us and calls us to come unto Him. Adam didn't turn from Eve; He still loved her in spite of her sins. Now let us read on in verse 12. *And the man said, the woman whom thou gavest to be with me, she gave me of the tree and I did eat.* Again, I wish to bring to light a few points. First, who did Adam blame? He blames God and Eve. He accepts no responsibility. Did he know it was the forbidden fruit before he ate of it? No, but that is an issue for another time. The point is that he didn't accept responsibility for his actions because mankind is weak and that is why it is time for us all to repent and pray for the strength which can only come from God, to be more Christlike and overcome the enemy. Eve sinned, but **you** God, gave her to me. Did Adam ever blame Satan or himself? No. Men, I want you to know that we are accountable before God; we need to take the authority that God intends for us, and with that authority comes accountability. Gen. 3:12 Adam spoke the truth but blamed Eve rather than accept the responsibility, so God made man to be the responsible part and holds him accountable for his wife and children. What does God want from us? Tend my sheep, teach my laws and ordinances. Tend to the orphans and the widows; visit the sick and those in the prisons. I need to remind you that the sick isn't just those in the hospitals, not just the physical, but the emotional and spiritual as well. Those in prison aren't just those behind iron bars, but also those with physical handicaps, terminal illness, etc. Care for the poor, give of yourself and of your (God's) possessions. Did you ever hear someone say, or say to yourself, how can I give, I've a family to care for; or when I get enough, then I'll give to... Oh friends, so many excuses come from the devil. If you want blessings, you must bless. You must humble yourself and sacrifice. God doesn't give so that you can hoard, He gives you to use for His glory and purpose. If you want more money, you must use what He hath provided for His glory. If you want forgiveness, you must forgive, if you want to be loved, you must love. In the Old Testament when Moses was collecting offerings to build the tabernacle, the people gave willingly, with a pure heart, and Moses had more than he could use. The people didn't suffer, rather they were blessed. Let us jump now to the New Testament book of the Acts of the Apostles. Here we see that the people sold ALL that they had, and created a community pool so that nobody lacked anything and nobody had excess. Why? God provides, Amen. And if you ever get to hear or read my abbreviated testimony in my book **'ONLY BELIEVE'**, you'll see that He still provides for those He loves today, I am living proof of this, and I praise you Jesus.

Beauty is more than skin deep; it is your very heart, soul, and mind, not your appearance. Look over at Isaiah 53:2 ... *he hath neither form nor comeliness: and when we shall see Him, there will be no beauty that we should desire Him.* Who is Isaiah speaking of? Jesus Christ and God! Men and women, are you listening?

Men need to rise up and pray for the families today and every day, intercede for each of them. And remember Proverbs

11:4 *Riches profit not in the day of wrath: but righteousness delivereth from death*

We read in 1ˢᵗ Corinthians 13:11 *When I was a child, I spake as a child, I understood as a child, I thought as a child: but when I became a man, I put away childish things.* I ask you today, after hearing this message, evaluate yourself, are you a really a man? What must I do to improve myself, to be more of a man, more Christ-like?

Men, a good prayer for us to pray today is to please give us the strength of Samson, the wisdom of Solomon, the courage of Paul, and the faith of Daniel, Amen.

HUSBANDS

𝕱 irst of all, I encourage young men rather than having bachelor parties with alcohol and women, to have instead a nice meal with a few Christian friends, and should include your dad, your dad in law, and your pastor. Instead of dirty jokes, sex, etc., allow these men to share with you that they have learned along the way, sharing godly knowledge and wisdom from their Christian marriages, and provide godly advice and answers to any questions that you might have. They should offer up prayers for you and your new family. We read in Proverbs 1:8-9, *My son, hear the instruction of thy father (righteousness and God) ... For they shall be an ornament of grace unto thy head, and chains about thy neck.* With these, who needs jewelry?

The second commandment given by God was 'to leave father and mother (they had none) and become one. Why this command? Because out God already knew that Eve would fall resulting in death and thus mankind would have to reproduce -Genesis 2:24.

The third commandment given by God our Creator was for women to bare children – Genesis 3:16.

The fourth commandment given was That the husband is to rule over his wife, calling the men into leadership positions and women into submission, Genesis 3:16.

And the fifth commandment is for the MAN to work, if he is able 2nd Thessalonians 3:10.

There was a time I was in the hospital and the people around a neighboring bed were talking, laughing, and praying. Part of the prayer was for one of the men's wives who was getting ready to give birth. After the prayer, I called for the man to come over, and told him, you were just praying for your wife, but who did you pray to? He replied God of course. I continued; do you believe in the Bible as God's inspired word to us? Yes. I continued, then you should be down there with your wife. Did you make love to her or merely have sex with her on that beautiful night nine months ago? What's the difference? he asked. I continued, IF you love your wife as God ordains and commands, you should be down there with her, comforting and loving her. He responded No way would I want to see...and do you hear that screaming. You think I want to be by her side listening to that? I replied, yes my friend, I hear that screaming, but God ordained you to be the lord and savior of your family, that God set the example for us to follow. Your wife was given to you by God to be a helpmate for you, not to serve you or as a slave, or sex toy. God our Bridegroom, Husband, serves us by providing, protecting and comforting us, and we are as husbands to serve Him by serving and loving one another, especially our wives. You need to humble thyself, go down there and save her from the bad spirits and those women who are yelling at her. Experience the greatest miracle of humankind-the birth of God's blessing to you. This blessing is God's gift to you, and your wife is an instrument that He uses, you should be there to receive this precious gift. By being there also, you will relieve about ninety percent of her pain and suffering. Also, I would never allow anyone to speak to my wife the way they are to your wife. You my friend need to be there for her and be her lord and savior as God hath ordained you to be. Serve her, let her know that she is not alone, that you will be by her side no matter what, be there for her. Are you being, are you showing her the example of the God we serve? He is with us even during the worst of trials, and He humbled Himself to the point of death for you and for me. Think about it. The room was dead silent. He left. What happened after that I know not. About fifteen minutes later, the screaming stopped. Whether he went or not, she had the baby. I pray that he accepted God's word through me, and that his wife received a true husband from then on, and that the lives of the others in the room were changed as well.

The husband's role includes a responsibility to pray daily for his wife and children, the willingness to read and instruct them in the scriptures (but they must be willing to accept the teachings), protect them from all evil (but they must be willing to accept the protection), to be the man of God they need us to be and to practice the spiritual discipline of fasting.

Men need to start being servant/leaders Ephesians 5:23-25, selfless, give up their desires in order to serve their wives and meet the needs of the family, practicing self-denial for the good of the family, sacrifice for the family, with a servant's heart, set aside your desires in order to serve others, i.e. your wives for starters.

Men, we need to humble ourselves serve, and, care for our wives. We need to be Christ-like, the lord and savior, the high priest of our families, and we see in Hebrews 5:1-10 the qualifications of the high priest. Are you qualifying?

Numbers 30:2 tells us *If a man vows a vow unto the Lord... he shall not break his word. He shall do all that proceedeth out of his mouth.* Men, the marriage vow that you take is binding-until death do us part, just as God has and always will keep His word to us for all eternity.

Jump down now to verses 6-8. *If she had at all an husband, when she vowed...wherewith she bound her soul, and her husband heard it and held his peace at her in the day that he heard it then her vow shall stand...But if her husband disallowed her on that day that he heard it, then he shall make her vow which she vowed...of none effect, and the Lord shall for-give her.* You are responsible for your wife and family before God, just as Jesus Christ takes responsibility for each of us, His bride, and His children. Her husband, as we see in verse 13, *Every vow...her husband may establish it, or her husband may make it void,* is in authority, given by God, to be responsible for his family, just as Jesus Christ is responsible for each of us. He either justifies before the Father, or He doesn't. We need to love, trust, obey and submit unto our Father in heaven, just as the wife needs to love, trust, obey and submit to her husband's God given authority, but men, you must be worthy just as Jesus is worthy of our love.

I must include here on husbands Proverbs 18:22 which tells us that *whoso findeth a wife findeth a good thing, and obtaineth favor of the Lord.*

Men, all of this being said, yes, you have the God given authority and status, but... with all of this; comes an awesome responsibility. You are to love your wives as Christ loves the church-the true believers, the truly spiritual. This vow, this covenant is not one-sided. You must do your part. In Ephesians 5:24 we read *therefore as the church is subject unto Christ, so let the wives be subject to **their own** husbands **in every-thing***. Be worthy of the high calling as husband. James 4:4 tells us that *Friendship with the world is enmity with God.* I cannot emphasize this enough, nor could the Holy Spirit; for He hath had this written in various forms at least fifty-four times that He has shown me. You must be a friend to your wife (and children) rather than of the world. God used this and other miracles to take me into the remote villages of East and Central Africa as a missionary. This command to love your wife is reiterated in Colossians 3:19.

Men, you are to provide for thy family. In Exodus 16:16, the Lord commanded what? Every **man** gathers according to the number of your household...no more and no less (no hoarding). From the time of Adam, man was to work and provide for his family, the woman is to stay at home as a helpmate. Proverbs 23:4 tells us *Labor not to be rich...* There was no storing; the Israelites were to take what they needed, no more, no less.

Hoarding money in the bank and food in the closet show a lack of faith and trust in the same God who promised that He would supply your needs.

Once betrothed (married), men you need to remove the pants literally and spiritually from your wives, and put them back on yourselves. Replace the pants with long skirts, dresses, kimonos, saris, gomas, whatever, for your wives, we'll discuss clothing in a while. The pants should also be replaced on your daughters as well.

Men, you must take the role of leadership, lordship of thy family, and take responsibility for them. For Adam it wasn't Eve's fault (only indirectly) that Adam ate. It wasn't God's fault. Come on men, it was Adam. Where was he when Eve was being tempted by the enemy? Why wasn't she by his side so that he could protect and guide her? God gave us men the responsibility and leadership roles in the family, church, and community. In Jeremiah 44:15 we see that the men who knew their wife's idolatrous practices would be judged for it. Man is to be responsible for his wife and children; therefore, he must lovingly be in control. This is an active role, not a passive role as in lazy or slack men. Do you really believe that our God is somewhere up there relaxing in a recliner, feet up, sipping on a beer and watching television? Dear friends, not the God that I serve!!! My God is a very active God, who is always awake and working in my life every minute of each and every day. You must be strong, bold, and active in the life of your family. Look over at 2 Thessalonians 3:10 which tells us *...if any **would not** work, neither let him eat.* The men also need to intercede for their families as Job did and as Isaac did in Genesis 25:21 where we read, *And Isaac intreated the Lord for his wife, because she was barren: and the Lord was intreated of him, and Rebekah his wife conceived.*

We need as husbands need to earn a living to support our families so long as we are able, but not to chase after wealth or riches. Many families suffer because of the husbands' obsession with making money, that the family suffers neglect. Many a family would gladly have traded the richer lifestyle for a husband/dad who spent time with them. Work should never be the central focus of our lives, God first, family second, work last as God will provide. We are told in Proverbs 23:4 *labor not to be rich.* We are also instructed in Luke 12:15-21 telling us ... *Take heed, and beware of covetousness: for a man's life consisteth not in the abundance of the things which he posesseth,* and then proceeds to tell a parable. Take a few moments please to read and reflect upon this parable...men and women.

Ephesians 5:25 says very clearly for husbands, *love your wives, even as Christ loves the church and gave His life for it.* How strong these words are my dear brothers. How much Christ loves the church-loves you and I; this is how much we should love our wives.

Remember men, back in the garden of Genesis, God gave man a wife as a helpmate, not a playmate, but a blessing. Though she is a helpmate, you are to be in charge, and responsible, accountable for your family. You are the lord, the high priest of your home. You should always listen to your wife, for God can speak to you through her, as can Satan. Ultimately, therefore, decisions are to be made by God and you. In Genesis 3:17 we read, *unto Adam he* (God) *said,* to who? To Adam, God said *because thou hast harkened unto the voice of thy wife...* You must understand, Adam's sin wasn't that of eating of the forbidden fruit, which was the curse of Eve. Adam's curse was relinquishing his leadership role in the family, as well as for being obedient and subject to his wife rather than to God. What would have happened had Job harkened unto the voice of his wife when she told him to curse God and die?

In 1st Peter 3:7 we are told, *likewise, ye husbands, dwell with them (your wife) according to knowledge, giving honor unto thy wife, as unto the **weaker** vessel, and being heirs **together*** (you are now one*) of the grace of life, that,* listen friends, *that your prayers be not hindered!* Did you hear that? Look at how serious marriage is to God. We'll discuss marriage later, because first it is important to understand God's design first of children, men, and women.

Following one of the few disagreements in our marriage, my wife decided to call the number for a popular radio Christian psychologist whose counseling center told her that the man has no authority over his wife (thus saying that God has no authority over us, His bride). They went on to inform her that women can do whatever they wish with their bodies and may submit to whoever she wishes, (thus adultery and idolatry). They went on to tell her that there is nothing wrong with abortions (not that this was even an issue with us), my dear friends, this is the peril of psychology. It teaches self rather than God, and is the basis of Eastern religion where 'I am god', and humanism as well. Christianity and psychology are conflicting, contradictory terms. God's word says in 1st Corinthians 7:4 that *the wife hath not power over her own body but the husband does. And likewise the husband hath not power over his own body, but the wife.* Memucan law in Esther 1:22 says that every man should bear rule in his own house. In continuing with 1st Peter 3:7, the entire Bible explains what God is like and how He deals with us as a fallen people, a weaker vessel. God is love. God is forgiving, patient, caring. Men...are you listening?

Husbands, throughout Scripture God tells us how much He loves us, and cares for us, and so should we love and care for our wives. He honors us as a weaker vessel, He cares and provides for our needs, just as we should for our wives that He hath blessed us with. God is the head of the church just as we are to be in our homes. As men, you cannot serve two masters, Luke 16:13. You must always put God first, then your wife, then yourself in that order. If you place your wife before God, for sure your marriage, and you, shall fall. We saw on the previous pages in Exodus 16:16 that the man is to provide for his family. We are to be Christ-like. Take time to ponder this in relation to your life, your career, as a husband, as a dad, are you being Christ-like or are there areas that you need to work on? Meditate upon this, pray and become the man, husband that God desires you to be.

Men, your clothing, your priestly garments, must be respectable at all times, and bring honor to God, to your family, and to yourself. It should be modest, long sleeve, long slacks. The temple must be covered, and NO hats. We'll discuss this more later.

Ecclesiastes 9:9 tells us men to *Live joyfully with the wife whom thou lovest **all** the days of the life of thy vanity, which he (God) hath given thee under the sun... for that is thy portion in this life.*

Proverbs 5:15-19 finally, tells us men *Drink waters out of thine own cistern, and running waters out of thine own well. Let thy fountains be dispersed abroad, and rivers of waters in the streets. Let them be only thine own, and not strangers with thee. Let thy fountain be blessed: and rejoice with the wife of thy youth. Let her be as the loving hind and pleasant roe; let her breasts satisfy thee at all times, and be thou ravished always with her love.* I'm sure that most of you have heard or read these passages many times, but what do they mean? This figurative language literally refers to intercourse within a marriage, and that ye should find mutual content with thy wife. Then He asks, should thy fountains beget children by an adulteress, a prostitute? Verse 20 says *And why wilt thou, my son, be ravished with a strange woman, and embrace the bosom of a stranger?* Fountains here actually refer to children, water represents people or nations throughout scripture. He presents here a healthy, godly view of sex, which is to be engaged in and enjoyed **only** within a marriage, and having many children, (rivers of waters), Amen.

Husbands and dads, you must be very careful what you say. Being quick with the tongue rather than prayer, landed Daniel in the lion's den and John the Baptist without a head, Mark 6:26. Also what you say will be absorbed by your wife and children, and may well be repeated. Be quicker to listen and slower to speak, this is why God gave us two ears and only one mouth.

It is important to note that throughout the scriptures and still today, it is the men who are broken, not the women. Why? Because God breaks the righteous to bring them higher on the mountain and closer to Him.

A man's goodness has nothing with to do his salvation, for we know from Ephesians 2:8-9 that salvation is by faith, not by works.

A good man is God-fearing, Acts 10:1-2. We see Cornelius who sought God, he commanded one hundred people in the Roman army, and he was a man of position.

A good man is diligent to study the scriptures, 2ⁿᵈ Timothy 2:15. *Study to shew thyself approved unto God.*

A good man loves God's words, Psalms 119:165. *Great peace have they which love thy law, and nothing shall offend them.* He uses God's words when trials and temptations come along.

A good man always obeys God's words, Psalms 37:31. *The law of his God is in his heart. None of his steps shall slide.*

A good man is a man of prayer, Psalms 77:2. *In the day of my trouble, I sought the Lord. My sore ran in the night, and ceased not: my soul refused to be comforted.* A good man has a prayer life. He prays for his family, his wife/wife to be, his children, and his children's children.

A good man is a soul winner, Daniel 12:3. *And they that be wise shall shine as the brightness of the firmament; and they that turn many to righteousness as the stars forever and ever.*

A good man worships God, Genesis 24:26. *And the man bowed down his head and worshipped the Lord.* He attends church and engages his family in Christian fellowship.

A good man provides for himself and his family, 2ⁿᵈ Thessalonians 3:10. *Forever when we were with you, this we commanded you, that if any would not work, neither should he eat.*

A good man does not beat up or abuse his wife or children physically, emotionally, mentally, or spiritually.

A good man will lead his family, Genesis 18:19. *For I knew him that he will command his children and his household after him, and they shall keep the way of the Lord, to do justice and judgment, that the Lord may bring upon Abraham that which He hath spoken of him.*

A good man serves the Lord, Joshua 24:15. *And if it seem evil unto you to serve the Lord, choose you this day whom ye will serve; whether the gods which your fathers served that were on the other side of the flood, or the gods of the Amorites, in whose land ye dwell; but as for me and my house, we will serve the Lord.*

A good man is a wise man, Ecclesiastes 7:25. *I applied my heart to know and to search and to seek out wisdom and the reason of things and to know the wickedness of folly even of foolishness and madness.*

A good man is humble, John 3:30. *He must increase but I must decrease.*

A good man waits on God, 1st Thessalonians 5:21. *Prove all things, hold fast that which is good.*

Psalms 37:23, *The steps of a good man are ordered by the Lord, and he delighteth in his way.*

You know, Nehemiah, an often-forgotten biblical character, was a man of God and should serve as a great example for men to follow. Let us look at some of his attributes. I have actually written an entire message on this man. Take some time and read this powerful book and you will see that Nehemiah;

- Was responsible and disciplined

- Commanded respect

- Leader-he led Israel

- He was a successful Governor

- He had a vision and plan

- He was sensitive to the needs of others

- He had intimacy with God

- He was honest and had integrity

- He was unselfish

- He was in the scriptures

- He was faithful to exercise his duties

- He was straight forward he wasn't a yes man or big-mouthed

- He listened to concerns and came up with solutions
- He did his homework properly
- He added value
- He remained silent until he was ready
- He offered God's plan rather than his own
- He stood for justice
- He practiced what he preached
- He refused to be bought off
- His work led to the restoration of the scripture

Are you a Nehemiah? Are you being Christ-like, or are you of the world? You cannot serve two masters! Take a few minutes and ponder this.

Husbands must fulfill his duties unto his wife-1st Corinthians 7:3. This includes spiritually, mentally and emotionally, this includes meeting her physical needs as well. There is a growing doctrine (of man) that a pastor is not to show affection or have relations with his wife. God says otherwise. If you get married, you have responsibilities to your wife, and her needs, for intimacy, time, a listening ear... It is interesting that while this doctrine is growing, so is the number of extramarital affairs among church leaders.

Men must respect their wives who are imperfect just as you are. We see in Matthew 1:18-19 *Now the birth of Jesus Christ was on this wise: When as his mother Mary was espoused to Joseph, before they came together, she was found with child of the Holy Ghost. Then Joseph her husband, being a just man, and not willing to make her a publick example, was minded to put her away privily.* Note that even though he thought that his betrothed had sinned against him, he still respected her enough to want to protect her!

We are told in Genesis 18:19 regarding Abraham but should be equally applicable to all men, *For I know him, that he will*

command his children and hos household after him, and they
will keep the way of the LORD, to do justice and judgment...*
My dearest brothers, can God truthfully say this of you?

DADS

Jn Deuteronomy 11:19 we read, *and ye shall teach them*
(God's law, God's word) *to your children, speaking of
them when thou sittest in thine house, and when thou walkest in the way, when thou liest down and when thou risest
up.* This doesn't say in front of the television. Quality time with
thy family is the time together without any distraction. Shut
off the television, the radio, the telephones, the computer...and
dedicate thyself to thy family.

The Bible says to pray without ceasing, and in relation to
family, what do we see? In the first chapter of Job, we see that
Job was blessed with seven sons and three daughters. In verse
5, Job prayed for his family. He sanctified them before God.
Job was lord of his home, and we should follow his beautiful
example, praying for our families, praying with our families,
and being there for our families.

In Genesis 18:19 *For I know him (Abraham) that he will
command his children and his household after him, and they
shall keep the way of the Lord...* Can God say this about you?

Men, you can't be a coward, lazy, or anything, God gave
you a powerful position-the king, lord, the pastor, the leader
of your family, so wear the pants, and this must start from the
day that you become betrothed, if not before.

You must earn a living to support your family, but not be in
pursuit of wealth. Many families and marriages have suffered
because of a father who was obsessed with making money, and
neglected the family in order to seek riches. Most wives and
children would much prefer a humbler life in order to have
time with their husband/dad. Work should never be the central focus in your life, God and family should be the central core.

Husbands, each time that thy wife conceives, thou shouldst lay thy hands upon the head of thy wife and pray for her, bless her, sanctify her, praise God for her and pray for her safety, God's protection over her throughout the pregnancy and delivery. Then layest thy hands upon her womb and pray for this thy child, thy precious gift/ reward from God. Bless thy child, sanctify him or her, praise God for this precious gift and pray for God's protection throughout the pregnancy, and for God's provision, protection, and blessings for their lives, that they may serve God.

Fathers must

1-Pray daily with thy wife, also with your wife and children

2-Lead the family and read the scriptures to them daily

3- Set a Christian example- no adultery, observe the Sabbath day and keep it holy, set boundaries, dress appropriately and modestly, limit TV viewing, etc.

In Genesis God honored Abraham in 18:19 saying, *For I know him, that he will command his children and his household after him, and they shall keep the way of the Lord.* Can he say that about you? If you turn over into the Book of the Proverbs, 17:6 you are told, *Children's children are the crown of old men; and the glory of children are their fathers.*

Finally, in the book of Malachi 1:6 the LORD told this prophet and us *A son honoureth his father, and a servant his master: if then I be a father, where is mine honour? And if I be a master, where is my fear? sweareth the LORD of hosts unto you, O priests, that despise my name.* You are the priest of your home, are you honoring the LORD, are you fearing Him? You are the role model for your wife and children to draw them unto our heavenly Father, an awesome responsibility for all of us men.

The church has God; your wife only has you. You need to be there for her. As a husband, you must be the front-line fighter in the battle against the enemy. Unfortunately, today the women become the fighter to save the marriage, but men, it must be you! We see many species in the animal kingdom the male protects and defends his mate, aren't we created to be smarter than they? Also, I must add here that in Judges 4:4 Barak trusted a woman rather than God, think about it. How often do men listen to women (their wives) to please them rather than listening to God?

Note in scripture and in general practice today (though less so) that it is always the man (dad) that is to give away his daughter in marriage, not the mother. If she has no dad, then who can give her away properly?

MEN IN THE CHURCH AND COMMUNITY

This takes us to 1st Timothy 3. The leaders of the church must be a male, blameless, the husband of one wife. Please dear friends...male, the husbands of one wife, men, not women are to be church and community leaders. He must be vigilant, sober, good behavior, hospitable, apt to teach, not given to wine or strong drink, not a bully, not greedy (hear this pastors), patient, not a brawler or covetous; One that ruleth well in his house, having his children in subjection. Not a novice, new believer, babe in Christ, but well grown in the Spirit and the blood of Christ, and must be of good report.

God and this world need men, real men, who cannot be bought or sold, men who are honest and true, men who are not afraid to be straight forward and stand for the right regardless of the consequences. We need faithful and true men.

The great need in this world is men, servants of the Most-High, men who cannot and will not be bought or sold, men who deep down are truly honest and sincere, men who fear not to call sin by its right name, men who are sure footed who can stand for the right no matter the consequences, no matter what others say or do to or about you. A man who is willing to stand for God and serve God, to take the leap of faith and pick up the cross and follow Him. Jesus says in Luke 10:2 *The harvest is great, but the labourers are few.* Will you take that leap and join me and the small labor force? Will you men dare to pick up the cross and follow Him? In Matthew 27:32 we see that Simon had to be compelled to pick up the cross. Coerce him coerce means to force, induce, pressurize, compel, intimidate, persuade. God doesn't compel anyone, He just asks you, but gives you freedom of choice. He will never twist your arm, but... just remember all that He did and is doing for you.

If a man is unable to manage his family, how can he manage to be a leader in the community, politicians and other leaders, are you listening? If you are corrupt or abusive in the family, are you truly going to behave any differently outside? I believe not and God's Word confirms this.

Pastors and all men, sexual relations within marriage is important and commanded by God. Do not neglect thy wife and her various needs.

In the church and community, he must be a leader, a good example of Christ at all times, anywhere and everywhere that he goes, pure and upright, and without sacrificing his family.

An old cliché says 'like father...like son, but I pose the question to you today, are you truly like our Father? Are you being Christ-like in your speech and in your actions?

Unfortunately, most men today fall way short of God's expectations. We are called to be Christ-like, but most are following the world, the customs and traditions of man, the ways of our fathers. Ask yourself, are you morally upright and prayerful? Are you filled with lust? Are you prone to drinking or smoking, using prostitutes, or committing adultery or fornication of any kind? Are you keeping any bad company? Are you following the vain customs and traditions of man rather than looking to God in ALL things? Are you involved in ungodly behavior, activities, or speech? Are you being lazy for God or for your family? Need I go on or has this list already included you? My point is not to judge or condemn us as I shall allow the word of God to do so, but in love so that we may be convicted and alter our ways to walk the path of righteousness. Pray this through. Allow the conviction from the Holy Spirit to amend thy ways and allow Him to be your guide back onto the path of righteousness and keep you on this path once you have arrived. This is so important because by His word shall we be judged by Him. By our works shall our faith be used to share the love of God or hatred of Satan. By our works shall our heart of faith be witnessed by others and by God. Though we are saved by faith alone, our works are a manifestation of our faith; therefore, faith without works is dead.

Dear friends, if you are following and I hope that you are, the family is a type of the family of God, the church. The husband is a 'type' or representation of God, of righteousness. The wife represents the law for sinners. In Hebrew, the terms male and female literally mean the piercer and the pierced. We are all God's children, called to honor and to obey Him. Children, obey your parents, God is our Father. Now dear brothers and sisters, I haven't said many words about men, but the words are powerful and represent a tremendous responsibility to carry. We need the help of our wives and our children. We can't do it without God who is faithful and willing to give us and be our strength and courage, if we seek Him, and humble ourselves. Humility is not a weakness as the world sees it, but strength in God's eyes. The fact that many men today are not turning to and submitting unto God is one of the main reasons the family is so broken today. Look at Ezekiel 23, where the two mountains with female names represents the trouble in Jerusalem.

Proverbs 27:23 says to *be diligent to know the state of thy flocks and look well to thy herds*. Husbands, dads, leaders, care for and look after thy families with the love of God.

Another issue I was led to speak about, another way of defiling the body, the temple of God. Turn with me to Leviticus 21:4-5. *He shall not defile himself, being a chief man among his people, to profane himself. They shall not make baldness upon their heads, neither shall they shave off the corner of their beard, nor make any cuttings in their flesh.* Turn back a few pages to Leviticus 19:28, ...*nor print any marks upon you.* Your body is the temple of the living God, not to be pierced, tattooed, head shaved, or beards shaved. Head shaving throughout scripture is a sign of shame and humiliation. In 1ˢᵗ Chronicles 19:4 you'll note that the shaving was more humiliating than having their garments cut off. There are several references to this in scripture. Ezekiel 44:20 goes on to say *Neither shall they shave their heads, nor suffer their locks (hair) to grow long; they shall only poll their heads.* Poll means to cut short. As a Christian, should we be ashamed or humiliated when we serve such a mighty God? I think not! In 2ⁿᵈ Samuel 10:4-5, we see David's men went to bring good tidings to these other men. These other men judged wrongly and shaved half of the heads and beards of David's men. David's men were humiliated and were told by David not to return to their land until the hair on their heads and beards grew out. In grief and sorrow people shaved their heads. The only exception I have been shown in scripture is at the end of the seven years of a Nazarite vow.

I heard of a Hispanic man who had tattoos on his left side for his dad and brothers and tattoos on his right side were for his life. While I go along with scripture against tattoos, I see an allegory here that we must learn from the past but we who are truly born again, must separate from this world as well as our past and begin to live for God.

In Colossians 3:22-24 we are told, *Servants, obey in all things your masters according to the flesh: not with eye service, as men pleasers: but in singleness of heart fearing God: and whatsoever ye do, do it heartily as to the Lord, and not unto men; knowing that of the Lord ye shall receive the reward of the inheritance for ye serve the Lord Christ.*

Now in this space as we end this chapter on men and prepare to discuss women, other sins that men and women do to defile themselves and the temple of God would include makeup and jewelry. Let us look here at what God's word says about this and why.

Let us begin by turning back in time to the book of Exodus. Before Israel departed from Egypt, they were told to gather as much gold and silver jewelry as they could from the Egyptians. Then at Mount Sinai, what happened? The jewelry that was to be used for building the tabernacle of God was instead used to make an idol, the golden calf. After this the people were told by God to remove all of their jewelry. In Exodus 33:5-6 *Ye are a stiffnecked* (stubborn and disobedient) *people. I will come into the midst of thee in a moment* (Jesus is going to return in a moment without any notice, and as the brides in Matthew 25:1-13, many shall be caught unprepared*): and consume thee: therefore put off thy ornaments* (Jewelry) *from thee, that I may know what to do unto thee* (submission, obedience, humility). *And the children of Israel stripped themselves of their ornaments* ... for good. Why? Because gold became more precious than God and for many today, it still is.

Next, let us jump to the book of 2ⁿᵈ Kings 9:30 which tells us *And Jehu was come to Jezreel, Jezebel* (a cursed woman and a whore) *heard of it, and she painted her face and tired her hair* (adorned with jewels).

Now, let us look at Esther 2:12 and 17. In verse 12, Esther went through all of the preparations required to come before the king, but in verse 15 when her turn came to come before the king, she could have anything she wanted to 'beautify' herself like all the others did, but she took nothing but what was required and then in verse 17, we see that the king loved her above all others.

Go over now to Ezekiel 23:40 *for whom thou didst wash thyself, paintedst thy eyes and deckedst thyself with ornaments.* This was done for strange men, men that she didn't know, prostituting herself!

Now to the New Testament book of 1 Timothy 2:9 ...*that women adorn themselves in modest apparel, with shamefacedness* (modest*) and sobriety; not with braided hair (hair with gold and pearls), or costly array.* 1ˢᵗ Peter 3:3-4 goes on to tell us *whose adorning let it be not that outward adorning of plaiting of the hair,* (again braiding with gold and pearls*), and of wearing of gold, or of putting on apparel* (costly). See also Colossians 3:18-20, 2nd Samuel 6:20-21, Jeremiah 7:29, Ezekiel 44:20, Isaiah 35:2-4, Deuteronomy 22:5, and there are many more. Here we see that we are to care for the temple of God. Makeup, lotions, etc., block the pores and prevent the skin from doing what God ordained it to do, and may cause serious problems within God's temple later in life.

I took three average looking prostitutes to an area where they were unknown, and paid them to be out there for four nights and NOT to accept any proposal, but to record every contact. The first night I had them in a nice long dress high collar, long sleeve and a bonnet, they wore no makeup. They had not one proposal. The next night they were in a nice skirt and blouse, with their hair loose, they had one to two proposals in one hour. The third night, I had them in hot pants and a tank top, where they averaged fifteen proposals in one hour. The last night, I had them in a halter top and a tight very mini skirt and a lot of makeup, which gave them an average of twenty-three proposals in one hour, the last two nights were clothes that they normally wore). You may ask yourselves why I did this. These women were paid to keep them out of strange men's beds, and to prove that how one dresses does in fact influence how people look at you and how they respond and treat you. After this I spoke with the three women who said that they felt much better about themselves when they dressed nicely the first two nights. They also stated that the manner of speech during the propositions deteriorated with the deterioration of dress, and that the dress of the men proposing also deteriorated as their dress deteriorated. And yet, so many today justify poor and immodest dress saying that it doesn't matter. In fact, it is an indicator of how you feel about yourself, and how others will think and act towards you. A truly spiritual individual will desire to dress in a modest manner as it reflects who we are to others, as well as the fact that we must remember why God clothed us in the first place. Do you desire for your sins to be covered? It is interesting to note that while Peter taught this to the Jews, Paul was off teaching the gentiles, they agreed on this issue even though they were miles apart physically because the

Holy Spirit spoke this to both of them, and they both wrote the same about how women ought to dress and behave.

I covered several verses to make a point. The verses speak for themselves, and you'll find more as you read through scripture. We are clearly not to wear jewelry. But what about wearing wedding rings you may ask? Since this is a message on marriage. A wedding band is jewelry, isn't it? Yes, it most certainly is, so a Christian, a protestant should not wear them. A ring does nothing for a marriage, other than waste a lot of money that would be much better used for God and your family. Furthermore, what is the origin of the wedding bands? Do you see anywhere in scripture where anyone was given or wore wedding bands? No. The origin of the wedding bands again takes us back to the Roman Catholic Church. Not only are rings not scriptural, but as protestants (protest against Catholicism), we are to do just that, protest against, not join with her ways. Whenever you wear rings, you violate the Scriptures, God's word. You violate scripture and validate Catholicism over God. You cannot serve two masters, Luke 16:13, so...who will you serve? *As for me and my house, we shall serve the Lord,* Josh 24:15. Oh dear friends the shame how far off the path of righteousness we have fallen, and God is calling each of us to repentance today. When a woman becomes engaged, what is the first thing she wants and gets? The same thing that everyone looks at when she announces her engagement, a ring. Why?

You may then ask how people know that you are married if you don't wear a ring. Does it really matter what people think? What God thinks is what is important. Also, I always spoke lovingly of my wife and children, so there was never any doubt that we were married. The rings don't make or sustain a marriage, only God and the two of you can. Jewelry is a form of idolatry and greed, both of which are opposed to God's will.

Makeup. Why not makeup, painting your face, lips, eyes, nails? I take you back to Genesis chapter 2. God created man in His own image. He created woman from man. After creation, God looked and saw that **all** was good (perfect). God does not make mistakes. My dear sisters, are you getting this? When you wear makeup firstly, you are telling God that He didn't do a good enough job and that secondly, you know better than He does how you should look. He is the potter and we are the clay. Do we have any right or the knowledge to correct God or tell Him that He isn't good enough and we know better how we should look? How to do it correctly? I think not! Be proud, be honored, be content, be happy with who and how our Master Creator designed you and never be ashamed or embarrassed to show your face to the world, show the world the wonderful miracle of God's creation, Amen. Thirdly, this includes messing with your hair, coloring, tinting, straightening...God knows best. Are you graying? Praise God, you are crowned with silver, Prov 20:29. Not to put marks or cuttings on your skin, certainly would include piercing, tattoos, etc. Plain and simple, your bodies are the temple of God and we must honor our temples. How would you feel going into a church (temple) full of holes (piercing), graffiti (tattoos), and different colors of paint all over (makeup, hair color...) Chances are you would be appalled and probably turn away. What about God when you do this to His temple? In Jeremiah 4:30 we read ...*Though thou clothest thyself with crimson, though thou deckest thee with ornaments of gold, though thou rentest thy face with painting, in vain shalt thou make thyself fair; thy lovers will despise thee...* In Esther the king didn't choose the other women, he chose Esther who was plain and simple.

Blasphemy is a very serious thing and is punishable by death, see Leviticus 24:16-hell!!! When you put on all that make up to make yourself beautiful you are in essence blaspheming God telling Him that He didn't do a good enough job and that you know better than He does how you should look. Appreciate what God created, and allow those around you to appreciate God's creation as well. After all, who are you trying to impress, God or man?

When you put on a bathing suit, you must still remain modest, but unfortunately most women and men cover much more with their undergarments than they do with their bathing suits. Getting into the water is no excuse for immodesty. In fact, wearing nothing would be far less provocative than the skimpy things people wear today to the pool or beach!

Men, I take you to Numbers 18:1 ... *thou shalt bear the iniquity of the sanctuary, and the iniquity of your priesthood* Remember you are the high priest of the temples of thy family. If your wife, sons or daughters start defiling their temples, you as high priest bear the iniquity before God.

Back to the clothing! In Deuteronomy 22:5 *the woman shall not wear that which pertaineth unto a man, neither shall a man put on a woman's garment: for all that do so are abominations unto the Lord thy God.* In the garden God covered Adam and Eve, not because being naked was a sin, for they were created naked and without sin. He covered not their physical selves but their sinful being, their sinful nature, just as those who confess Jesus Christ as Lord and Savior, God's Son, have their sins covered by the blood of Jesus Christ. God covered Adam and Eves sins and our sins are covered if we'll **ONLY BELIEVE**; Imagine nude beaches where nobody cares because there is nothing left to the imagination. Even in pornography, the person covers her or himself just enough to be provocative. Imagine living in a village where nobody wore clothes, or one in which they wore very little...I have worked there, people don't care, they don't think about being naked as it is a fact of life, nothing provocative. This chapter is brief as we shall be discussing this throughout this message. We see in 2nd Samuel 13:18 that Tamar had *a garment of divers colors upon her, for with such robes were the king's daughters that were virgins appareled.* This as in the coat of Joseph in Genesis 37:3 indicated special love and status. We are as daughters in that we are sinners, of the Almighty King of Kings and as such we need to dress accordingly and modestly. I lived for a few years in a country where all of the virgin girls wore nice simple long dresses, whereas the non-virgins wore pants. I also am shown here that virgin women (and men) should stand out- perhaps even wear white (as sign of purity) dresses until or if she loses her virginity, as virginity, contrary to modern thought, is in fact something to be proud of and encouraged.

Even the international symbol for a woman is a figure in a skirt; a man is a figure in pants. What? Must we change to a single symbol of the figure in pants...you already have unisex clothing...do you want unisex public restrooms as well? Perhaps I shouldn't mention this because there unfortunately are many men and women who would enjoy this. In Africa they have some of these because of poverty. Just how far off the path do you wish to travel before stopping and considering your ways?

I also wish to say here that if your parent or if married, your partner encourages you to dress in a more conservative manner, a godly manner, don't resent them, but be honored that they love you enough to want to assist you in being godlier in thy appearance. In Zephaniah 1:8 we are told *And it shall come to pass in the day of the Lord's sacrifice, that I will punish the princes, and the king's children, and all such as are clothed with strange apparel.*

Men take care of thy temples, but remember the words of Paul's first letter to Timothy 4:8 *For bodily exercise profiteth little: but godliness is profitable unto all things*

When I was in the hospital the dozen times while being held hostage, I requested a pastor, but all that I could get was a priest, no protestant clergy! While in prison, most of the people from churches that came to see us were females, and don't get me wrong, they were a blessing, but...where are the men??? Most were from the Catholic church. Where are the pastors? Nobody likes hospitals, nobody including myself wants to be inside a prison, but God calls us men to the great commission found in Matthew 28:19-20 and Isaiah 61:1-2, Isaiah 58:6-8 and Matthew 10:6-16. Today the great commission of our Lord and Savior has become the great omission! The villages I was in had never seen a white man before and a couple villages had never heard of Jesus Christ, where are the men? I pray for revival, and let us stop the delaying of the return of our Lord! Each of us were placed here for a specific purpose in God's overall plan, there is no room or time for laziness. I am calling all of us men to wake up and get busy...for the Lord our God.

Men, God created you and then woman to help you. He gave the responsibility of leadership to the man and with this responsibility comes accountability, both to God as well as to thy wife and children. After the fall God addressed Adam the man. Adam failed to be responsible, protect and care for his wife and so she fell. Men continue to fail in this today. It is time for each of us to man up and resume the leadership role that God ordained for us, to protect and to provide for our wives and our children. The women are counting on us not to fail them again, and so is God. Men, even if your wife steps in your way or tries to usurp authority, stand firm for God and for her. Sometimes she does this because you are failing, other times because of her sinful nature. Don't be like Adam, be responsible.

Men, when you die to self, become selfless rather than selfish is when you begin to live and be blessed. When you die to self and live for God and family, you begin to be fulfilled and more blessings will come your way. When you die to self, you begin to live eternal life. In Ezekiel 22:30, we see, *And I sought for a man among them, that should make up the hedge, and stand in the gap before Me in the land, that I should not destroy it, but I found none.* Today men, I am calling for you to be the one to stand up for God, and be one of the few good men for God's kingdom. Amen.

For further reading, please read Psalm 128.

PERSONAL NOTES

Proverbs 31:10 *Who can find a virtuous woman? For her price is far above rubies*

CHAPTER 3

The Precious Woman, Wife, Mother

Men, please pay special attention as well as women to this chapter, for in the spiritual context; we are all women- sinners by nature and thus in need of salvation.

We read in Jeremiah 9:20 *Yet hear the word of the Lord, O ye women, and let your ears receive the word of His wrath, and teach your daughters wailing...* Who was Jeremiah talking to here, the women? No, he was speaking to the people of Judah, the sinner's, men and women. God desired the people, the sinners to hear His word, repent, and then teach it to their children.

Women, just as many men have failed in their God given roles and responsibilities, so have the women of today. You see it in the families, you see it in the work place, you see it in politics, you see it in... the churches. I, like God's word, will spend more time discussing women, but if you listen and pay attention, and don't get offended, you shall certainly understand why and I pray that it will change your perspective; you will grow stronger men and women, and begin to fight against woman's lib, equal opportunity, etc. Those of you who read God's word, have you noticed that so much more is focused on women than on men? Is God sexist? Absolutely not! A reminder here to open your minds, as the Bible talks of him, he or his, He is referring to God and the righteous. Whenever the Bible discusses she or her, it is referring to us the sinners. Who is the sinner? all of us, men, women, and children. Do you find this 'oppressive' as so many of the world claim today? If so, then it is no wonder that so many have walked away from the Lord and the path of righteousness today as well, for this is symbolic of our relationship with Christ...the true believer is the bride of Christ! We see this again in 1st Corinthians 7:1 because she represents the sinful nature of man. Titus 3:4 speaks of women (sinfulness), hidden man of the heart, (righteousness and perfection). Again in 1st John 2:12-14, why only children (innocence) and men? Are women to be excluded? Absolutely not! Again, men represent righteousness and the perfection of God, so, he only addresses the righteous for sinners will be judged and cast out. Yet again we see in 1st John 3:1 sons of God, not daughters, because the masculine represents the righteousness and perfection of God and He has no part with sin. These are just a few examples, as you will find this throughout Scripture.

We see in 2nd Chronicles 8:11 *And Solomon brought up the daughter of Pharaoh out of the city of David unto the house that he had built for her: for he said, my wife shall not dwell in the house of David... Because the places are Holy.* The sinners (wife, woman) would not be accepted into the Holy place (heaven) but shall be judged, for salvation is only for the righteous. Who are the righteous? those who believe and accept Him, those who are justified by Him. In practical terms, men and women who are saved shall enter heaven. Sinners, unbelievers, men and women shall be judged. Turn with me to Mark 15:40-41. Why the specific mention of all the women? Equally important is the question where are the men? The answer is simple if you are following with me here. The women are representing the sinner and the sinners need Jesus. Where are the men, the righteous? They are also there and of course God was there. But important is that we as sinners need Christ. He is our only hope. He alone is our salvation.

I saw an acronym one time for a virtuous woman- RISKS

R= takes risks and is righteous

I= integrity and takes initiative

S= sacrifice

K=Knowledge

S= Simplicity and service

I see this as a vital part of our lives. There is a risk when one becomes a husband or a wife. It is risky to walk with the Lord, but if you don't, you shall be judged and condemned. Let the world hate you, but let God love you.

Who were the first at the tomb of Jesus? the women. We as sinners need to come before the cross in confession and repentance. We need to die to sin and resurrect as a new creature in Christ Jesus. If we do this, our lives will never be the same.

Very simply, and women don't like to hear this today, but a woman's place is in the home. Proverbs 7:11 says, *she is loud and stubborn: her feet abide not in her house.* Genesis 31:1-3, look at what happened. Now I am not justifying his actions which were clearly wrong, but... if she was at home where she belonged, nothing could have happened. Home or by her dads, or husbands' side is where she can be safe and protected; Ruth and Proverbs 31, a keeper of the home. Literally, we'll see over the next several pages, time and again why women should be in the home, but I need to add here that when not at work or church, the man should also be with his wife, to love, care, nurture, and protect her as God does for us. Note frequently that I will be saying 'your husband' but if you are single or widowed, then replace husband with dad.

Let us look at Isaiah 3:12. *If we suffer, we shall also reign with Him; if we deny Him, He will also deny us. As for my people, children are their oppressors, and **women rule over them.** Oh my people, they which lead thee cause thee to err, and destroy the way of thy paths.* Dear brothers and sisters, these verses are so loaded, but what I wish you to see at this time is first, the child oppressors. Why are the children oppressed? Because the women are stubborn and refuse to stay at home and care for the home and for the children that God blessed thee with. This causes all to suffer. Then we see the women rule over them. Look at equal opportunity, quotas, woman's rights, etc. creating and pushing women more and more into the workplace, into management, politics, etc., placing men into subjection under them. Women not working will decrease the workplace affairs, adultery, etc. Single women by staying at home under the protection of their dads, are not exposed to the workplace environment and the risks of being out there in the world. In 1st Timothy 2:12 we see, *But suffer not a woman to teach, not to usurp authority over the man, but to be in silence.* This is so clear, just as clear to me is the reason why; and please listen closely, because this is not from Pastor John, but inspired by the Holy Spirit. Man is an allegory of God and woman is an allegory of the sinners. We the sinners are not to take authority away from God our Father, our Bridegroom though many today try. No, we are called to humble ourselves and submit to His authority, and to be obedient unto Him; Likewise, the woman to her husband. Men, you should not submit or surrender to a woman's authority, for in God's eyes, she has none. Women should leave their jobs. Men should leave their jobs, transfer to another department; leave your church...whatever it takes, but never submit to a woman. Adam did and look at what happened. Set an example, lead others onto the correct path, and see the blessings from God for your obedience unto His word rather than the ways of this world. Whenever my wife was disobedient unto me, something happened. She went home to visit her family, and called to ask me about going to a Catholic church with her family for a function. I explained to her that as a Christian, she shouldn't subject herself to such spirits so not to go. She went and caught her hair on fire, other such events occurred with disobedience. Colossians 3:18 reiterates this command to submit yourself unto thy husband.

In Genesis 2:23, Adam named his wife. He named her Havah, related to the word hayah- a Hebrew word meaning to live. Jews to this day have an expression lehayim-meaning to life! Thus, Havah can be interpreted as life giver, as Eve was the ancestor of the human race, thus we are all family. Eve however as well as being a life giver, also became the death giver as well, as her sin brought death upon all of mankind. Thus, women throughout scripture represent sin, whereas man, made by God, for God, represents God and righteousness. Woman was made from man, for man. I ask you, why in Leviticus 12 do women need to be cleansed and purified and not man?

My dear sisters, you may say whoa, today we are liberated! God's response to this is two-fold. First, the Bible, God's word, was written for yesterday, today, and forever more, not just for a particular time or place. Women are to assume their God given roles just as men are. For a woman to have authority over a man is to say that we the sinner can have authority over God, that we may take the place of God. Some women got together some years back, got together for a women's retreat. They were from two protestant denominations. When they returned to their homes, they were worshipping the goddess, Diana! What would have happened if they were at home with their husbands, and caring for their families? One only has to look into the book of Ezekiel 8:10 and we are shown the same thing, the women weeping over the gods, including Tammuz. Take a look over at Acts 19:27, 35, and 37. We are not equal to nor have we authority over God. Job's wife told Job to curse God and die. Now, you say, "but Pastor, the Bible teaches that we are equals, husbands and wives, joint heirs with Jesus." But only if we have fellowship, trust and obey, and look to Him in all that we say and do. We are not equal to God, so women are not equal to men. Women were created from man for man, to be a helpmate for her husband. I ask you, why in Leviticus 12 do women need to be cleansed and purified and not men?

Secondly, what are you liberated from?... from biblical teaching? From God's word? God forbid. God's plan is perfect; He knows what He is doing. In Titus 2:3-5, we see that ...*Women likewise, that they be in behavior as becometh holiness, not false accusers, not given to much wine, teachers* (of women) *of good things, that they may teach the young **women** to be sober, to love their husbands, to love their children, to be discreet, chaste, **keepers at home**, good, obedient to their **own** husbands, that the word of God be not blasphemed.* Are you listening? Isn't this what I just spoke about in our relationship with God? Thus, it is with women's role to her husband. Marriage is an allegory of our relationship with God.

1st Timothy 5:13 goes on further to tell us *they* (women*) learn to be idle, wandering about from house to house, tattlers also, and busybodies, speaking things they ought not.* In other scriptures, it also talks about gossip. This ought not to be. Stay at home, be a keeper of the home, love thy husband and thy children. Remain under the shelter and protection of thy husband. Imagine you or your daughter calls your husband crying for help. Help me!!! Then nothing, the line goes dead. He jumps up, leaves work and runs home to care for you. He arrives home quickly, only to find his house empty. You aren't there. He goes in a panic all over looking for you. All this time, he is risking his life, while you are mad at him because...he didn't come to your defense. Where is he anyway? As he is asking himself where could she be? Why isn't she at home or by my side so that I could protect her, where she belongs...? How can I protect her if she isn't under my covering? God feels the same way. He calls us to rest under the shadow of His wings, Israel wandered off and suffered... When they repented, turned from their wicked ways, then He healed them. They returned to the shadow of His wings. However, many never made it back to His protection, and they perished. You can't swim in the evil, worldly ways and expect God's protection, nor can your husband protect you or guide you when you wander off from under his shelter. And I need to remind you that just as we saw with Eve, when the woman, the weaker vessel, is out from under the covering of her husband, she is vulnerable to Satan's attacks of all sorts, including sexual, because she is sinning. She is in violation of God's will and plan. Remember the story of Dinah who was out wandering about and was raped, Genesis 34:1-2. This fact is why Paul goes on to admonish young ladies in 1ˢᵗ Timothy 5:14 *I will therefore that the younger women marry, bear children, guide the house, give none occasion to the adversary to speak reproachfully.* This way instead of wandering and being tempted (or the tempter deliberately or not), the woman can be at home, under the covering and protection of their own husbands and avoid any trouble (sin). He is not however commanding all women to marry, simply suggesting in order to protect them. Until marriage, the young lady should remain in the house of under dad and be under his covering and protection.

Following the Westgate incident in Kenya as I wrote this, I was reminded of how important it is to let parents, spouse know everywhere that you are going not to spy, but for your own protection, as well as just out of a respect for one another in the family. This bit of information may save your life one day, and/or alleviate a lot of unnecessary stress upon your loved ones, knowing that 'no, none of my family is there.'

I need also to put a sideline here while we are discussing women. In scripture we see talk of the evil woman; see Revelation 17:1, 19:2. These refer to the false church, also called a whore. Dear friends are you hearing this? 1ˢᵗ Samuel 28:7 Saul sought someone to call the king from the dead to help him, but...he didn't seek just anyone did he? He called for a woman. There are many false churches today. We need to get away from denominationalism, divisions amongst us, and return to the pure, unadulterated, word of God. Just as Satan used Eve because she was the weaker vessel, so Saul sought out a woman to commit the evil deeds. In Genesis 34:1-3, she, the Israelites in sin, was out in the world rather than separating from the world, and being at home with God. Once in the world, Satan will use lusts and enticements to lure you further and further from your home. My wife was an example of this. If you are not at home with your husband, you are not at home with God, you are out in Satan's domain and you are in extreme danger. Let us look over into the book of Zechariah 5:7-11. *And behold, there was lifted up a talent of lead: and this is a woman that sitteth in the midst of the ephah, and he said, this is wickedness. And he cast it into the midst of the ephah; and he cast the weight of lead upon the mouth thereof. Then I lifted up mine eyes, and looked, and, behold there came two women...and he said unto me, to build it an house in the land of Shinar* (Babylon. Evil was removed from Israel and tossed to Babylon, the land of idolatry, the biblical name for modern Rome-Catholic) *and it shall be established, and set there upon her own base.* This is God's word, not mine but remember, we are all sinners, women, who only by accepting Jesus Christ as our Lord and Savior, can we become men (righteous).

Is the woman always evil? No! We see here the scriptures tell of the good woman, Revelation 14:4, 2nd Corinthians 11:2 which refers to the true church, the handful of truly spiritual believers, also called a virgin, unadulterated. Men and women were created to makeup man (righteousness). Man needs the woman and woman needs the man.

Let's go back to Genesis 3:9 as we discussed in the last chapter, where God called Adam, rather than Eve. We must look at the fact that God calls the righteous, the justified home, but the sinners shall be judged. Acts 13:50 tells us that *the Jews stirred up the devout and honorable women... and raised persecution against Paul.* Why the women? These were good women. The woman is a weaker vessel and easier for Satan to stir up.

I also need to share with you Ecclesiastes 7:28 again, saying *Which yet my soul seeketh, but I find not: one man among a thousand have I found; but a woman among all those have I not found.* This verse challenges me my dear friends. Today will you be one in the thousand? That one in a thousand was Jesus Christ, but aren't we called to be Christ-like? Oh, to be Christ-like, to walk by His side and to hear Him call me friend. Then turn with me over to the Song of Songs 8:9 which is very interesting but people often overlook its significance. It tells us; figure this out in a history book! *If she be a wall, we will build upon her a palace of silver, and if she be a door, we will enclose her with boards of cedar.* Sounds strange, doesn't it? So, what is He trying to tell us here? The Shulamite woman was recalling her brothers' thoughts of when she was young. But...

what does this all mean to us today? The wall signifies resisting temptation, she would be rewarded. Dear friends; God calls us to resist the temptations of this world, of Satan, so that He may reward us with eternal life in heaven by His side, Hallelujah. But...the door represents a loose person, who needs discipline.

I went quickly through the Bible in 2011, and made a list of all of the women and why they were mentioned, as I was curious. I wrote forty-eight names, out of which ten had nothing really good or bad to say about them at first glance. Twenty-six were evil and murderous, prostitutes, disobedient to husband and to God, idolatrous, false prophetesses, etc. Only twelve were cited for godliness. Many are called but few are chosen, Matthew 22:14.

In 1ˢᵗ Corinthians 14:34-35 we read *Let your women keep silence in the churches for it is not permitted unto them to speak; but they are commanded to be under obedience as sayeth the law. And if they will learn anything, let them ask their husbands at home: for it is a shame for women to speak in the church.* So, you see, just as we are to come before God to seek His teaching, His guidance for our lives, so should a woman to her husband. As we are to be obedient to God and His law, so must a woman to her husband. Women (the sinners) are to be subject to and under obedience (to God) as sayeth the law (we are to be obedient to God's law). If as the Bible teaches, a woman is not to speak in the church, and she is not to usurp authority over a man or to teach a man, then how can she be a church leader? Timothy also is told this in his first letter from Paul 2:11-12., in which Paul says *let a woman learn in silence with all subjection* (just as we are to be before God) *but I suffer not a woman to teach, nor usurp authority over the man, but to be in silence,* This is humility and we have already discussed the spiritual parallel for this.

My dear sisters, I told the men earlier that they need to remove your pants and that they are once again to wear the pants in thy family, for this is God's plan. So, what are you wearing now? Are you willing to give up the pants, surrender all in obedience to God and to thy husband?

In 1ˢᵗ Timothy 2:9 we are told that *Women adorn themselves in modest apparel, with shamefacedness and sobriety: not with braided hair, or gold or pearls, or costly array.* Your clothing should be high neck, long sleeve, full length skirt or dress, not tight fitting or transparent. Take a look at Revelation 17:4. *And the woman was arrayed in purple and scarlet color, and decked with gold and precious stones and pearls, having a golden cup in her hand full of abominations and filthiness of her fornication.* In 1ˢᵗ Peter 3:3-4 again we read, *When adorning, let it not be that outward adorning of plaiting the hair, and wearing of gold or putting on* (costly) *apparel, but let it be the hidden man* (righteousness) *of the heart, in that which is not corruptible, even the ornament of a meek and quiet spirit, which is in the sight of God of great price.* You see, in these verses that we, men and women, are to dress modestly, and we aren't to waste money on fancy or stylish clothing and jewelry, but let our hearts be our beauty. Furthermore, this should be our attitude and manner before our Lord and Savior. In Ezekiel 23:40 He tells us, *and furthermore, that ye have sent for men-* (be they righteous or false gods, idols) *to come from far, unto whom a messenger was sent, and lo, they came: for whom thou didst wash thyself, paintedst thy eyes,* (makeup), *and deckedst thyself with ornaments,* (jewelry). Read Genesis 35:4 and Exodus 32:1-2. Respectable and honorable apparel reflects a godly woman and man's inner self. It shows respect of God, others around you, as well as thyself. You have seen the word shamefacedness a few times in scripture. This term means modesty. We see in this passage of Ezekiel that a godly woman should not wear makeup or jewelry, nor should a man.

Secondly, using make-up and painting yourself is a way of telling God that He didn't do a good enough job when He created you and that you know better than He does. Are you better than God? He created you to look the way that He wants you to look. He chose your dad and husband to help you to be what He wants you to be, same thing with painting of nails, shaving legs and pelvic area. God designed your body the way that He wants you to be. You cannot improve on God's creation. And most men, especially Christians, prefer simplicity in a woman; they, like the King and Esther, like and appreciate God's creation as it is. Cutting your hair likewise; for a woman is to have long hair. In some cultures, a woman's husband brushes her long hair as a show of his love for her. Be who and what God created you to be.

Now, let us turn to 1st Corinthians 11:9-15, ...*that the head of every man is Christ, and the head of the woman is the man, and the head of Christ is God. Everyman praying or prophesying, having his head covered, dishonoreth his head. But every woman that prayeth or prophesieth with her head uncovered dishonoreth her head, for that is even as if her head were shaven.* Need I remind you that the Bible teaches us to pray without ceasing, therefore men should never have their heads covered, and a woman should keep her head covered. Are you hearing this? In 1st Corinthians 11:3-15, *Judge for yourselves: is it comely that a woman pray unto God uncovered? Doth not nature itself teach you, that, if a man has long hair, it is a shame unto him? But if a woman has long hair, it is a glory to her: for her hair is given unto her for a covering.* Women's head should always be covered and a man's head should never be covered. Women did in fact cover their heads up until the 1960's, when the liberation movement began. We shall continue *for if it is a shame for a woman to be shorn or shaven, let her be covered.* Remember the Bible teaches that it is a shame and humiliation to have the head shaved. *For a man indeed ought not to cover his head, forasmuch as he is the image and glory of God: but the woman is the glory of man. For the man is not of the woman, but the woman for the man.* Man was not created for sin. *For this cause ought the woman to have power on her head because of the angels.* The covering is a sign of man's authority (God's) over the woman (sinner). The unwillingness to cover her head signifies her unwillingness to recognize and accept the authority of God and her husband, just as sinners do not accept the authority of God, and this would offend the angels. It is also important to note that the covering in verse 15 is a different word (peribolaion)from the covering in verse 5-6 (Katakalupto-a veil). The point here is that the hair is given as a covering in the natural or physical realm, whereas the veil or head covering is the spiritual realm. Also, the hair, along with the veil, represents the outer curtain into the temple, the veil, the inner-the holy of holies. So, we can see here first for men to wear hats, caps, hoods, etc., is a sin, whereas a woman with her head uncovered is in sin. The head covering that I am discussing here is of the hair not necessarily the face as is seen in Genesis 38:15.

Turn over now to 1ˢᵗ Corinthians 3:16-17 and let us summarize this discussion. *Know ye not that ye are the temple of God, and that the Spirit of God dwelleth in you? If any man defile the temple of God* (the righteous), *him shall God destroy: for the temple of God is holy, which temple ye are.*

Who did the Jews stir up in Acts 13:50? The devout and honorable women. Also please note that There were no female angels in scripture, because God can have no part with sin and the feminine is symbolic of sin. Only masculine can be justified (declared righteous) so the angels by nature must be masculine.

Ye women as these verses demonstrate, you are not equal to man, just as we as sinners are not equal to God. God did not create woman equal to man in the physical sense, but equal in the spiritual. In spite of what the world teaches, independent mind set of today, we are to separate ourselves from the ways of the world. Men are physical, women are emotional beings; men and women have different needs and desires, different abilities, strengths and weaknesses because God created us this way and if done properly, the two complement each other. This is a good, not a bad thing, God didn't make any mistakes.

When Moses divided the blood of the sacrifice and sprinkled it equally on the altar and on the people, he beautifully depicted the equality that exists in marriage. In the covenant relationship between Yahweh and Israel there was no question of their being equal partners, nor was there in marriage any question of man and woman being equal partners. This marriage was consummated when the Glory of God entered the Holy of Holies, and the marriage was made legal with the public vows and signing of the covenant in blood. Marriage is a legal agreement before God, and a physical agreement. The church can never be Israel and Israel can never be the church.

This woman's lib, independence, equality, etc., is not God's plan or will. You women from the beginning were created to be helpmates for the men who were created to be helpmates in serving God. Men didn't choose to be men with their awesome responsibilities any more than women chose to be women with their awesome responsibilities. Just think, on top of your other blessings, you alone are blessed to be able to incubate a precious life, feel God's creation, and give birth, then nourish this precious gift with thy breasts. No man can do this or experience the wonders of these blessings. If you are obedient and submissive, loving and honoring your husband, you do so to God and His Son Jesus Christ our Lord. Then are we justified, declared righteous and brought up to be heirs with Christ. Galatians 4:7 tells us *wherefore thou art no more a servant, but a son* (righteous, justified before God), *and if a son, then an heir of God through Christ.* Oh, praise you Father, how blessed we are! Though we are never truly equal to God, likewise women, if you will love, honor, obey, submit thyself unto thy husband and to his God given authority, you too shall be a joint heir, but never equal to him. Now husbands, having said all of this, this message places you in a tremendous position, and awesome responsibility, as lord of thy home; Responsibility beyond compare. You must love thy wife as Christ loves the church, and was willing to suffer and die for her, Ephesians 5:25. You must be willing to sacrifice everything for her, and do anything within the confines of scripture to earn her love, respect, and honor, just as Jesus did and does for us. Just as God, you are to always be there for your wives and families, to help and protect them, whatever they need physically, emotionally, and spiritually. Just as Jesus is our mediator, our intercessor before God our Father; just as men must intercede for their families, just as we saw Job doing.

We see in Mark 6:24 the daughter never seeks God, but her mother, which sin resulted in the death of John the Baptist. We go back and reenter that fateful day in the garden. Why wasn't Eve by Adam's side where he could have guided her along the path of righteousness and protected her from the enemy? By that one act of plucking that fruit from the tree of knowledge of good and evil, everything changed forever. Aside from breaking the very first commandment of God that one act was actually three sins. Allow me to explain this in brief, because many women are still eating of the forbidden fruits of the world today-money, sex, jobs, fashion, school... first, in disobedience to God and His law. Women are to be caretakers at home. They are to be obedient to God and His laws, as well as her husband. Secondly, she took the authority away from her husband. Adam told her not to eat of the fruit. Women are frequently doing their own thing because they are independent, they are liberated, they can do whatever they wish, or so the world leads them to believe. They are disobedient, disrespecting, dishonoring her husband, again a violation of God's law, then she cries when she gets violated. My wife told me thanks to her friends, you don't know what you are talking about. How disobedient, disrespectful and dishonoring can you be, but she suffered the consequences, as did our son and ultimately our marriage. I honestly don't believe that I have ever heard eight words that ever caused me as much pain as those did. There are always consequences for your actions. And thirdly, Eve exercised authority over the man, in telling him to eat of the fruit of which he had no way of knowing was from the forbidden tree, but that is another story. So, one simple but deliberate act; caused Eve to commit three sins, which destroyed all of mankind forever, as well as plants and animals. When women today do the same, families and others are destroyed. Dear sisters and brothers, this is so serious, please take some time to reflect upon this and ask thyself, ask God, what am I doing and how can I get back on the correct path of righteousness, to bring honor unto God and thy family, as well as unto thyself.

I was excited meeting new people, pastors here in this foreign land. It wasn't long before they were leading me down the wrong paths. Once I was going west with a Pastor friend, but he got called somewhere else, so he was sending me with another Pastor. This pastor though did not take me to where

I was supposed to go, to villages who were anxiously awaiting my arrival! Instead, he took me to his home and left me until it was time to return, while he was out visiting with family and friends, Pastors, before I knew what was happening, instilled a spirit of aloneness and depression.

One must be careful when choosing 'friends' and keep checking to see if they are leading you on the correct path and offering words of encouragement to strengthen your walk, or are they hindering you?

Let us go a step further. Turn with me and look at Proverbs 1:4-10; 8:4, etc. Note repeatedly the man, my son... always masculine, for God gives to man, and women are to receive from their husbands, or dads if single. 1st Corinthians 14:35, just as we are to receive instruction from God not from the world.

After all of this, you my sisters may feel picked on, and may be asking yourselves, are women really bad? Absolutely not! Remember that women represent all of us, for we are all sinners and fall short of the glory of God. We are all sinners saved only by the grace of our Lord and Savior Jesus Christ. She is simply representing sinners perhaps because Eve first sinned, and the fact that God did create man for Himself, and women for men. However, God doesn't make mistakes and women are a wonderful, beautiful, and precious gift from God. In Genesis 19:14 also, I wish for you to see here that the son-in-law (men represents righteousness) were sucked up by the sins of the world (Jews), whereas the daughters of Lot (women represent the sinners), held onto their father (gentiles), prophetic of the end times, but also pertinent for us today, as we all need to forsake the ways of the world and hold on to our heavenly Father, Amen! Note that in 1st Peter 3:4 why hidden man of the heart when he was talking to women here? Again, because man represents righteousness and perfection which he is looking for here, while women are an allegory of the sinful nature of mankind. I think also of Hannah in 1st Samuel 1, who came before the Lord in total self-surrender, setting a wonderful example for us, for if as sinners we will surrender ourselves unto God and sacrifice ourselves for Him, He will bless us as He did Hannah.

Before we close this segment, I must bring you to Deuteronomy 28:56 in which Moses warns us to be careful, *The tender and delicate woman among you, which would not adventure to set the sole of her foot upon the ground for delicateness and tenderness, her eye shall be evil toward the husband of her bosom, and toward her son, and toward her daughter,* It all began with Eve. If you'll turn to Psalms 148:12, you will see in context that he is listing everything to praise the Lord, but in this verse, *Both the young men, and maidens; old men, and children:* Now, I ask you, why were not women listed herein? It again is because women represent evil, sinfulness, and sinfulness does not worship God. This is in striking contrast to what Solomon tells us in Proverbs 31:26-29, *She openeth her mouth with wisdom; and in her tongue is the law of kindness. She looketh well to the ways of her household, and eateth not of the bread of idleness. Her children arise up, and call her blessed; her husband also, and he praiseth her. Many daughters have done virtuously, but thou excellest them all.* But remember how he begins in verse 10 *Who can find a virtuous woman? For her price is far above rubies.*

I saw the following, author unknown but thought to share it with you:

- A godly woman doesn't just sit there.
- She knows that we cannot eat air,
- She works hard around the house to keep it clean, safe, and attractive.
- A woman is wise
- A godly woman dresses modestly,
- She does not leave her chest bare,
- As she knows that her body is for her husband's eyes only,
- She maintains her nails clean,

- And her hair neat.

- She soaks herself in a hot water bath

- Lathered with perfumed soap.

- She comes to bed with her husband.

- She calls to check on her husband's parents

- They laugh on the phone.

- She jokes with her in-laws,

- And plays with their last-born child,

- She advises her brother in laws,

- And shops with her sister in laws,

- She loves her in laws.

- A godly woman cooks delicious meals,

- As she knows the way to a man's heart,

- She packs some food

- And gives to a neighbor,

- Or perhaps even to the local police officer or anyone for no reason.

- She donates some of her belongings to the needy,

- She finds favor from those who admire her generous deeds,

- And her gracious hospitality,

- But most of all from her husband.

  ○ Women are to submit to the man-but not to submit to abuse-physical, emotional, mental, and/or immorality at any time, there a woman must draw the line just as we as believers are to be obedient to the law up to the point where they tell you to do or not do something contrary to God's law. Anyway...

Are you aware that there are women in some cultures who call their husbands daddy, because her husbands are given the responsibility and authority from her dad, so this is another way in which she honors and demonstrates her respect and honor for her husband?

I need to make mention here also that with all of the discussion today of empowering women, when you empower a woman, you empower a whole family and nation in sin, against God's plan and will. You also disempower the men whom God ordained to be in power and authority. God ordained man to care for the family, so empowering the women actually because of the sinful nature, tears down and destroys the family, church, and the nation. Did God give us power and authority over Him? I believe not.

Finally, my sisters, I wish to refer you to 1st Corinthians 7:28 which tells us that *If a virgin marry, she hath not sinned.* Please note that God is very specific, a virgin, so please save thyself for marriage. Offering of yourself as a chaste virgin to your marriage partner (if God chooses you one) is the best gift that you can offer him and to God. IF you do so, then I believe that you shall spiritually remain a virgin until you commit adultery, fornication, or divorce.

In the spiritual sense, all men and women are born as women, for all are born into sin and woman is symbolic of sinners, however, we must praise God, we all, men and women have the opportunity to become men- symbolic of righteousness, simply by accepting our Lord and Savior Jesus Christ. In the physical sense however, we are who and what our Lord God created us to be, man or woman, and we need to accept and rejoice over His choice for us. Being a woman doesn't make us bad, men and women are judged by how they live in submission and obedience to God and in relation to their sex.

We see in 1st Corinthians 12:18-25 that women are so important, but must be in the role where God placed them just as men must. Women are to be in the submissive role to assist men, just as we, the truly spiritual are to be submissive to assist God.

WIVES

Many women begin and end their marriage with lies and paying men for sexual favors. In Ezekiel 16:32-34 we read *but as a wife that committeth adultery, which taketh strangers (those outside of marriage), instead of her husband! They give gifts to all whores: but thou giveth thy gifts to all thy lovers and hirest them that they may come unto thee on every side for thy whoredom. And the contrary is in thee from other in thy whoredom, whereas none followeth thee to commit whoredoms, for that thou givest a reward, and no reward is given unto thee.* Dear friends, this includes anyone except thy husband. We shall discuss this in greater detail later, but for now we shall jump down to verse 38 which tells us *and I will judge thee, as a woman that breaks wedlock and shed blood are judged, and I will give thee blood (death) in fury and jealousy.* Our sins put Christ on the cross and shed His precious blood. Oh, dear sisters, to drive God to fury and jealousy! Fear God, women and love thy husbands only! Forsake the world and love God and God alone. My wife came from darkness to the Light, and then chose to return to darkness worse than before. Don't make the same mistakes. Be honest, the truth always surfaces, but even more importantly, when you lie to thy betrothed or husband, or anyone for that matter, God knows!

Wives, there are four main behaviors that women make that tend to destroy marriages. Allow me to discuss these briefly for thy benefit. First, her behavior chases away her husband, Secondly, in her gossip to others. What happens in thy home stays in thy home, unless a pastor is needed to help resolve problems; Third in her listening to friends or family. When you marry, you leave your family; your dad turns all authority over to thy husband. You become one with thy husband. Satan seeks to destroy godly marriages and loves to use family and friends, those closest to you. And fourth, her lack of willingness to trust, obey, love and care for her husband and children, to surrender all unto him, just as we are to surrender all unto God.

Wives need to be helpers for their husbands, needs to know she is needed Genesis 2:20-22, submissive to their own husbands, voluntary subordination to the authority (their own husband) Ephesians 5:22-24. Mothering is a priority over other interests, and time and devotion is critical. Let us also look at Titus 2:4-5. Are we as sinners not called to be servants of our bridegroom?

The Bible throughout teaches that a woman is to love and to serve (help) her husband, as we are to love and serve God. Sarah called her husband lord, a term for strong respect and honor, see Judges 19:27 and Gen 18:12, and 1ˢᵗ Peter 3:6. She is to have only one husband just as we are to serve only one God, the Lord God Almighty. Anything more is idolatry and adultery, more on this shortly. Our God is a jealous God, and He has good reason to be after all that He has done for us. Men, women are to serve, to help you, not be your slave and do your work for you. We serve God, but He serves us. Jesus humbled Himself and knelt down before each of His disciples to wash their feet. You likewise must serve thy wife; it is a two-way street. Remember that the Bible teaches do unto others as you would have them do unto you.

A husband and wife should only listen to God and each other, if necessary, some godly mediator or advise from a truly spiritual Pastor. Anyone else, use extreme caution, just as Job's wife and friends. You need to sanctify thyself to each other and unto God. You need to sanctify thy marriage and family from the world and its ways, for *friendship with the world is enmity with God*, James 4:4.

Revelation 12:4 tells us that *a virtuous woman is a crown unto her husband, but she that maketh ashamed is as rottenness in his bones.* A virtuous woman turns a man's house into a home, in Proverbs 14:1 *Every woman buildeth her house but the foolish plucketh it down with her hands.*

Ephesians 5:22-24 tells us *Wives, submit yourselves unto* **your own** *husband as unto the Lord. For the husband is the head of the wife (as God is head over us) even as Christ is the head of the church, and He is the Savior of the body.* If this woman spoken of earlier had of submitted unto her husband, she and his son would not have suffered, nor would theirr marriage, because one's sin affects many. There are consequences for your choices in life, blessings for obedience, and curses for disobedience to God's law. One needs only to look at Israel's wanderings in the wilderness those forty years! Therefore, in verse 24 *as the church* (the believers) *is subject unto Christ, so the wives be to their own husbands in everything.* Any disobedience to thy husband is disobedience to God and His law. Following the analogy of Eph 5:21-33, where the husband is the head of the wife and the wife represents the body: then divorce depicts cutting a head off the body or severing a body from the head, and is seen as murder in the sight of God, and of course murder is a sin against God and man, a breaking of one of His commandments!

2nd Timothy 3:6 *For this sort are they which creep into houses, and lead captive silly women laden with sins, led away captive with divers lusts.* We must all be on guard against the world and the enemy who tries in any and every way possible to throw us off the path. The woman being the weaker vessel, Satan attacks more, the husband must protect her, but he can only protect her if she is obedient and submissive unto his authority, just as we must be unto God. In Genesis 3:16 we are told *and he shall rule over thee!!!* This occurred only after her sin. Look at Eve. The wife's obedience is required just as God requires our obedience unto Him. She must submit to her husband, just as we must unto God. She must surrender all, leave the world behind and truly become one with him physically, emotionally, and spiritually, as the true believer must before God, no other gods, Exodus 20:3, no other men. We go back to Genesis 3:8, back to the garden, there are so many lessons in the garden. What are we seeing now? We see Adam and his wife, not Adam and Eve, but Adam and his wife, indicating ownership, possessiveness, a unity, the God of all creation sees man and wife as one with the husband as the head.

In Esther 4:8 God calls us to think only upon Him and His word. Fear not, only believe, trust Him, and give ourselves fully unto Him, and have none other, just as the woman should to her husband. Jump down now to verse 12 which depicts purity, and virginity. We need to separate ourselves from the world and to sanctify ourselves unto God and unto each other. We need to serve Him and Him alone, just as a woman is instructed to do unto her own husband. Then in verse 16, Jesus is invited into your heart and life, you surrender all. In Revelation 3:20 we see *Behold, I stand at the door and knock. If any man* (righteous) *hears my voice, and opens the door, I will come into him, and I will sup with him, and he with me.*

1st Peter 3:1 tells us *Likewise, ye wives, be in subjection to **your own husbands**...* just as sinners need to be unto God. Furthermore, in 1st Corinthians 7:10 you are commanded *Let not the wife depart from her husband.* No if's, ands or buts, or unlesses, no exceptions! You are not to leave and we shall discuss this also in more detail later, the reasons why, but you are not to leave thy husband just as we are not to leave God our Father. Pray for thy husbands, but don't ever leave them. What did Jesus say? Forgive seventy times seven, infinity.

In Ezekiel 16:38, God says, *I will judge thee as a woman who breaks wedlock, and shed blood are judged.* Women that break wedlock we'll discuss later, but again if we leave Him, we shall be judged, what a fearful thought! But note here also, that He equates breaking wedlock with murder. See Revelation 21:8. This is shown again in Jeremiah 3:20, where He tells us *Surely as a wife treacherously departeth from her husband, so have ye dealt treacherously with me, o house of Israel, sayeth the Lord.*

Wives do you truly love thy husbands? Men and women, my dear friends, do you truly love God? If so, have complete faith in God and in your husband, Faith requires trust and obedience to him. Wives, you should never resist or refuse thy husband, unless he asks you to do something in opposition to God's word. You should always be there for him. You should always welcome him and encourage him, physically, emotionally, spiritually, and sexually. We should always trust and obey God; we should never refuse Him. We should always be there for Him and always welcome Him into our lives, Deuteronomy 6:5 tells us in our heart, soul and mind.

In Esther 1:12, we see Vashti refused to come before her husband, the king when he called for her, as when we refuse to submit unto God. Vashti disobedient to her husband caused her fall. Esther obedient to the king, prospered. Esther said no initially (the sinner) then repented and came before the king (God) and saved the chosen people. The woman's disobedience has consequences, earthly and spiritually. When God calls us, we must obey lovingly, or there are consequences. Jump down now to verse 16-18, and we shall see that when we turn from God, it affects all those around us, just as does a woman's disobedience to her husband. Others may follow in thy footsteps of sin and fall into the same pits. My wife and my relationship were so close and wonderful, I always gave God the glory and praise. Others though saw and their marriages and spiritual walks were strengthened. But...when she left, several people said that if that is what your God is all about and allows, we don't need Him. I tried to undo the damage done Him, but actions speak louder than words. So, neighbors and friends are affected as are our children, which we shall also discuss later, as well as my wife and I; I ended up having a heart attack, a broken heart.

In Esther 1:12, 17 we see that the wife's disobedience to her husband was and is not to be tolerated. Wives must submit (Sarah called Abraham, lord and bowed down to him) just as we, the brides of Christ should submit and bow down before our Lord and Savior. The sin if not punished (accountability) will spread like wildfire amongst the people, Women equals the sinful people, the false church. You cannot serve two masters, God and self, we must be selfless and commit unto God, women unto thy husbands. And what happened? Vashti's refusal to come before the king is a parable of a sinner refusing to come to Christ at His call. The consequences are being cast out into the lake of fire, and replaced by gentiles who will accept by faith-Esther. We see that Esther was transferred from the adoption of man (Mordecai), to the adoption by the King (God)

Let us jump to verse 22, where we again see that the man is to be the ruler, the high priest, the lord of the home, just as God is to be the ruler over us, His children.

Thou shalt love the Lord thy God with all of your heart, soul and mind, Deut 6:5, we just looked at this but you must realize that this is also how you sisters must love thy husbands.

In Genesis 3:6 we are told, *And when the woman saw that the tree was good for food, and that it was pleasant to the eyes, and a tree to be desired to make one wise, she took of the fruit thereof, and did eat, and gave also to her husband with her, and he did eat.* Now, let us dissect this verse. First, I wish you to see that God through Adam, her husband, told her not to eat of this tree, so she was disobedient to God and to her husband, which brings consequences. She was obedient to only one and that was Satan, the enemy. She fell for a few reasons. First, the lusts and enticements of the world, but as believers we are to be separate from the world, 1st John 2:15. Secondly, she listened to the world, Satan, rather than to God and her husband. She ate, she fell, but look...that wasn't enough. She knew that she did wrong, so she decided to entice her husband to eat so that he would also fall, to bring him down with her. My dear sisters, please, for God's sake, your husband's sake, and your sake, obey thy husband in the Lord. Submit and surrender all unto him. My wife through her lack of submission and obedience to God and I, and to her parents; unto the lusts and enticements of this world, and listening to the world through her friends, *friendship with the world is enmity with God*, James 4:4. The consequences though fell upon her, God, friends, neighbors, our children, and I, just as Eve's sin fell upon all of mankind.

In 1st Chronicles 15:29 we are shown Michal, David's wife, and whom David loved so much, but here she was mocking him when instead of watching him from the window, she should have been by her husband's side. Her heart was not right before her husband or God. As a consequence, she was barren unto her death, God closed up her womb. I pray that you are hearing this message. Let us continue.

Back to Eve; Above all of this Eve deceiving of herself in three ways is the same as found in 1st John 2:16. She disobeyed the word of God and her husband. She believed the lies of Satan, listening to the lies of Satan, listening to the world, rather than to the truth of God's word. Then she placed her own will above that of God and her husband. Dear brothers and sisters, are you hearing this? Are you listening? This is so serious in marriage and our relationship with Christ. You are a helpmate, you must submit to thy husband fully and cheerfully, just as we sinners are to submit to God rather than our own wills. There is only one exception to this, if your husband asks you to do something contrary to God's word, or to deny Christ. These are two things that God would never do or ask you to do. While I do not agree with what the king requested of Vashti, it wasn't contrary to God's word per se, so therefore she should have humbled herself and been obedient.

Also, what Eve did as we see in 1st Timothy 2:14, is that she took the authority away from her husband. Dear friends, we cannot take the authority away from God and expect things to work out well. In Isaiah 3:12 we see this point again, *as for my people, talking of their wickedness, children are their oppressors, and women shall rule over them; O my people, they which lead thee (the women) cause thee to err, and destroy the way of thy paths.* There is one path of righteousness, and women are not to lead, have authority, nor are men to submit to the authority of a woman.

Please turn with me now to Hosea 3:2-3, *So I bought her to me for fifteen pieces of silver, and for a homer of barley, and an half homer of barley; (dowry which we shall discuss in chapter 4, but buying a woman equals prostitution) and I said unto her, thou shalt abide for me many days (until death); thou shalt not play the harlot, and thou shalt not be for another man, so I will also be for thee.* Are you listening my dear sisters?

Don't try to look wealthy and don't be too conventional- use discretion. You may use seduction in the home, and elegance together to keep your husband awake. You don't need a lot of clothes, just the right clothes.

One final note before we move on. Bath-Sheba bowed before her husband David, as we see in 1st Kings 1:31. Sarah called Abraham, her husband, lord. This is the complete surrender and submission, which God desires from women to their husbands, as well as from us, the sinners unto Him.

My dear sisters, I want you to know that being a stay-at-home wife and mother is **not** an oppressive role, but rather God's design, His will. It is a blessing as He uses that to protect you from the perverseness of the world. It is an honorable role that yields many blessings. It is not oppressive for us to be subject unto our Lord and God.

Women did stay at home until again the early 1960's, then... women's lib, burn the bra...why? What purpose did that serve? Then came the pants, they began to take over the jobs and seats in the schools that once belonged to the men, leaving the men with no place to go. Then came 'equal opportunity', which isn't equal, it's qualified or not, if you are a woman or a foreigner, you get the position. You didn't need to meet the same standards as the white male, because the law requires a certain percentage now to be women or minorities, if you are a foreign woman so much the better. This subsequently lowered the standards and quality of services provided in medicine, law, education...and then came the Iraq war. The women who joined the military for pay and benefits now said 'we can't go, we have families, and other excuses. They wanted the salary but didn't wish to do the job. In the U.S. how many women, let's be honest here, do you see laboring on street repairs, climbing utility poles... no, they are standing on the street holding the stop/slow sign to move traffic, but demand equal pay, and get it.

My dearest sisters, if you wish to read more on what God's word has to say about you wearing pants, read Genesis 1:27 and 3:21, Exodus 28:40-42, Leviticus 6:10 and 16:4, Deuteronomy 22:1-30, 2nd Kings 9:30, Proverbs 7:10, 14:12 and 31:25, Nahum 3:5, Acts 10:34, Rom. 14:2-3, 1st Corinthians 11:1-34, Galatians 3:28 and 5:25, Colossians 3:17, 1st Timothy 2:8-10,

2nd Timothy 3:16, 1st Peter 3:2-5, 1st John 2:15-17, and many more can be found.

My point is this. God ordained and commanded men to work and provide for his family, ever since Adam and Eve, women were created from man, for man to be a helpmate for her husband. To be at home, caring for her husband, his home, his children is an honorable position. Children today return home from school to empty houses. Men return from work to an empty house. Children run out to play, join gangs... or they meet dad while whining, 'we're hungry...where's mom...' Where is mom??? She is outside of God's will and plan, out there in the world, outside of the protection, shelter and authority of her husband.

As a result of this sin, disobedience to God, greed, power, everybody loses, and society suffers. Divorce rates skyrocketed after women left the homes. Drug abuse, alcohol abuse, gangs-a place that children could go to for a sense of belonging, sex-to feel loved, which leads to adolescent pregnancy...abortion, child abuse...

I was reading a book given to me one time just to pass the time, and there was a young lady who gave up herself (selfless sacrifice) to pay for medical bills for her worthless dad and to give her younger sister a better chance at life. She lost herself in being a high-class escort. She was helping everyone except for herself. We must never lose ourselves to this world but to God- doing His will in selfless sacrifice. And while she enjoyed the sex, she found that that isn't where love was to be found, are you hearing this?

You see my dear friends; God's way is the only way if you want true love, peace, joy, tranquility, and success in your life. The husband should be able to return from work to a quiet, happy home, wife, and children. They should welcome him home and celebrate his return, as we shall celebrate our Father's return, and long for that day. Perhaps as he comes through the door, hugs and kisses, the wife may wash his feet as Christ taught, as a show of humility and love, then he may relax in a nice chair, to a nice cup of hot tea, or some cold lemonade. The wife and children may sit beside him and just showing that they are safe and there for him, as he is now back there for them. No television, just nice family time before dinner is served.

Being out there in the world is full of aches and pains, headaches, stresses, turmoil, physically, emotionally, and spiritually. Who wants or needs that? How many men wish that they didn't have to be out there interacting with the world, yet the women are choosing this very thing, to the detriment of their families and society. I am reminded as I write this, of the wise men telling the king to put away Queen Vashti so that the sin wouldn't spread to the other women of the kingdom. The women in the U.S.A. and other countries went astray and today the women in many countries around the world are following them. 2nd Thessalonians 2:4 tells us the effects.

I need also to take you to the Song of Songs 8:6, a very powerful verse. The wife should be a seal to God, those who choose to believe. Jealousy is cruel; therefore, we should not cause or give reasons for our spouses to be jealous, that is why the law was set up to test the wife to see if she was unfaithful or not. We are also tried and tested to see if we are faithful before Christ. If the women are anxiously awaiting their husbands return, then he has no reason to have affairs and be running around committing adultery, think about it. If he knows he's going back to an empty house, the secretary, neighbor, or anyone else that may be willing to give him the attention he isn't getting from his wife. It is not right. But...if the wife was there, these feelings and actions wouldn't be.

I will go on and say that just as we anxiously look for the return of Christ, you should anxiously await thy husband. Thou should prepare for his return, just as we should be prepared for the return of Christ. You should be clean, fresh, happy, have a snack or meal prepared for him, so that when he returns, you have time with him and he with thee. It shouldn't be that he comes home, and you then run to the kitchen and begin cooking. He wants and needs you to be there with him, he has been away and missed you all day. He wants you more than anything else. The house should be clean, and you should be nicely dressed. Open the door for him and welcome him home, make him feel welcome, just as we should with Christ. Examples of greeting the man can also be seen in 1ˢᵗ Samuel 18:6-7, note that they greeted with joy and celebration.

Now, I was compelled by my Lord to write this brief section before we conclude here. The king was admonished by the leaders to put Vashti away, discipline her so that others wouldn't follow her. The other women would see or hear of the discipline, so the consequences and wouldn't follow suit. God tells us to discipline our children as we discussed in the first chapter. God disciplines those whom He loves. Now these disciplines are done with love to get our children, ourselves on or back on the path of God's righteousness, not our own likes and dislikes. They are done with love, not in anger, thus the difference between discipline and abuse. This having been said; in the early years, up until the late 1800's there were strict laws for women...no smoking, adultery... and had very strict penalties. Women were also disciplined by their husbands. The admonishing by the king I believe is still applicable today, but ignored. Just as God disciplines us, His bride, His children, the husbands and dads today, need to return to disciplining their wives in love, when they start to fall from the path of righteousness, God's laws, and refuse to listen or obey you their husband or dads. If men had of continued this practice, children, women, marriages, families, churches, nations wouldn't be in the sorry state that they are in today. We read in Zephaniah 3:1-2 *Woe to her that is filthy and polluted, to the oppressing city! She obeyed not the voice; she received not correction.*

I speak this, my dear sisters, in love, and with a burden for repentance, revival, and restoration of marriage and family as well as our Christian walk. Unfortunately, men have neglected their role and women have taken it over, but this is not God's design. I tried to discipline my daughter once for repeatedly bullying her brother; my wife went crazy. Again, I take you to Esther 1:16-17 and Ezekiel 23:45-48. While much has been removed from society in this regard, I am compelled by the Spirit of the Living God that the husband needs to discipline with love his wife and children as needed. A ruler, God, kings, presidents, and husbands cannot rule unless there are consequences for defiant behavior. I never disciplined my wife, perhaps which is why she left.

People do not naturally submit to authority because of our sinful nature. Resistance appears to be more gratifying than submission, Genesis 3:17-19. The human heart, much like the cursed ground, prefers the weeds and resists nurturing. Women must learn to submit to her dad's authority until married, then she must fully surrender herself and fully submit to that of her husband's authority just as we are to submit to our Father's authority. Many in authority have not earned our respect but that does not in any way negate God's command and example. Having said this, resisting authority is not always bad or wrong, Acts 5:40-42, if the authority is directing you to violate the law of God. Daniel is an excellent example of this.

I steer you now to Hebrews 12:3b-6, 11. Now you wives may be looking at your husbands and thinking or saying Just try it! or over my dead body, but I have spoken with women during counseling who told me that they wish that their husbands would love them enough to discipline them. I am not speaking here of 'fifty Shades of Grey'. Think about it, why are so many women into bondage and discipline? I believe that a woman's (secret) need for discipline has to do with her representing our sinful nature. It has been well documented that many women (around seventy-five percent) dream or fantasize about being disciplined, tied up, or even raped. Why? Because I believe in their subconscious knowledge that they know that they represent the sinners and are in need of discipline (remember that we are all sinners in need of the discipline of our Father, again the symbology). It is interesting that while writing this, I did some research and it seems that an increasing percentage of women are getting involved in bondage and discipline.

I also found that only about eight percent of women like to dominate whereas over seventy-five percent prefer the submissive role. Why? Because this is God's ordained role. While woman's lib is propelling social pressure to be contrary to God's ordained role, most still desire to be submissive. Men, you must be mature enough to be able to demonstrate your ability to be in control in a loving, caring and protective way, you cannot just demand your God ordained life partner to be submissive. Women, be honest with your husband about your willingness to submit unto him and his God given authority. Listen to God and thy husband, not to social pressures, and be honest with each other in all things, including sexual desires, so that you can satisfy one another. Be willing to submit to the discipline from thy husband, just as we must submit to the discipline of God. Remember, like it or not, God created rules for us to live by. Why? In order to protect us from the enemy and bring us closer to Him. Likewise, as man is lord of the home, he must make rules in order to protect his wife and children, and to protect them. If we are disobedient to God's law, there are consequences and suffering, and God disciplines us for our own good. In society there must be rules in order to protect us, and disobedience brings consequences and discipline. Likewise, in the home there must be rules and discipline for disobedience, otherwise how can order be maintained? How can a man protect his family? Discipline is given to us by God, the legal system, and the head of the house because God cares about us, and we should likewise care about our family. Even so within the church, that is why God's word says to cast out for a time people who sin and refuse to repent in order to keep sin out to protect the remainder of the congregation, (Memucan law). Again, we are speaking about discipline, not abuse!

I believe that God's word supports the discipline of a wife and daughter for any ungodly behavior, which would include style of dress, going out of the house without permission, (if there is an emergency, she should contact her husband and get his permission and have an escort go with her for her protection); there should be NO physical contact with anyone of the opposite sex. Remember that the purpose of exercising discipline is not to punish but to restore one back to the path of righteousness.

If you think about it, look at John 5:16-20 with me for a moment. *From now on thou shalt be called my Lord. Thou shalt lead and guide me in my ways. Though painful, thy rod and thy whips shall comfort me by turning me from any wicked ungodly ways. No chastening for the present seemeth* to be joyous, but grievous; nevertheless afterward it yieldeth the fruit of righteousness unto all who are chastened or disciplined with the love of God. This is just as true for wives who represent the sinners, as it is for God chasteneth those He loves (us sinners).

Most women today are as a wild and untamed beast as they have caved in to social pressure and social norms, rather than holding firm to the word of God, and where are the churches? So many young females of today try out so many men and toys, etc. that their anatomy is so used up and stretched out by this adultery that they are resorting more and more to anal. In scripture they speak of the woman being humbled, for example in Deuteronomy 22:24 *Then ye shall bring them both out unto the gate of that city, and ye shall stone them with stones that they die; the damsel, because she cried not, being in the city; and the man, because he hath **humbled** his neighbor's wife: so thou shalt put away evil from among you.* In Ezekiel 22:10-11 *In thee have they discovered their fathers' nakedness: in thee have they **humbled her** that was set apart for pollution. And one hath committed abomination with his neighbor's wife; and another hath lewdly defiled his daughter in law; and another in thee hath **humbled** his sister, his father's daughter.* Now we understand this as representing intercourse, but humbled her. Now you women are perhaps saying whoa! You're going too far and being too hard on the women. But in fact, I'm being hard on the women...as well as the men, for they too are wild and not fulfilling their God appointed role in humbling their wives and daughters (I'm speaking literally here, not sexually). Where are the godly men today who are called to tend to their wives and children? In Matt 7:5 we read *Thou hypocrite, first cast out the beam out of thine own eye; and then shalt thou see clearly to cast out the mote out of thy brother's eye.* We must be able to care for our own families before we can go out and care for the family of God, and bring in His flocks, the lost sheep. The men must humble their wives and teach them the precepts of our Almighty God. After all of their running around and being disobedient to God's word, it is no wonder that so many are wanting discipline today.

Women in general have abandoned their roles as wives and mothers to go to work and exude authority over men, so that when they want a man, they can't find any because a good man needs a submissive woman so that he may fulfill his God-given authority and position in the family.

Wives, you choose-to do your own thing and be like the world, like everyone else and being the property of your husband, just his wife; or to be godly, humble, submissive, trying to please him in all that you say and do, and be the love of his life, just as we are to be before God, our Bridegroom.

Isaiah 5:15 tells us *And the mean man shall be brought down, and the mighty man shall be humbled, and the eyes of the lofty shall be humbled.* But in Jeremiah 44:10 *They are not humbled even unto this day, neither have they feared, nor walked in my law, nor in my statutes, that I set before you and before your fathers.* So, go back now to Jeremiah 13:18 and see his instruction, *Say unto the king and to the queen, humble yourselves, sit down: for your principalities* (angels) *shall come down, even the crown of your glory.* You are the king and queens of your home, and the husband is the crown of the wife. We are just like the Israelites at Mt. Sinai when Moses was communing with God those forty days, then was sent down because the people were gone astray. When Moses went back down what did he find? He found loud music, drunkenness, everyone naked, in a big orgy, wild dancing...God is trying to warn us through the earthquakes, hurricanes, etc.; but mans' hearts are so hardened. He hath sent a few out to try to speak the truth to the world, now, God is speaking through me and once again calling us to repentance that there may be restoration and revival in the family and in Gods family. He needs us to be humbled before this can occur.

2nd Samuel 6:16 Michal, the wife he loved, had no respect for her husband, and therefore God rendered her barren unto the day of her death. He removed her blessing, her ability to give birth to a child. Are you barren? Then evaluate your relationship with your husband. It <u>may</u> be that you are disrespectful or dishonoring to him causing your barrenness. There of course other causes, but you might check this out first.

Sisters, you must remove the pants and follow, submit to your man. My dear brothers and sisters, this must begin from the day that you become betrothed. This is not a democracy with God, 1st Corinthians 11:3. It has nothing to do with equal rights, women's liberation, but it is about what God says.

We have said that wives are to submit to their husband's and that children are to submit to their parents, as well, we are to submit ourselves unto God our father, but what exactly does submit mean? To submit means to place oneself humbly before another person on the basis of **voluntary choice**. One cannot ever be forced to submit. You can force obedience-like teaching a dog, but you cannot force submission, it must be a voluntary choice, just like love. Romans 3:1-2 tells us *Let every soul be subject unto the higher powers. For there is no power but of God: the powers that be are ordained by God. Whosoever therefore resisteth the power, resisteth the ordinance of God: and they that resist shall receive to themselves damnation.*

Men, women are not tea leaves to be used and then thrown away, and women you shouldn't allow yourself to be tea leaves by throwing yourself or flaunting yourselves.

I want you to see than in 1st Peter 3:1, it doesn't start a new thought. It begins with the word likewise, meaning that he is continuing with the thought. So, if you back up to chapter 2 verse 18 on, chapter 3:1 will have even more power, meaning, and understanding.

I found this following message one day, source unknown, but I wish to share it with you in closing out this segment.

A godly woman doesn't just sit there.

She knows that we cannot eat air,

She works hard around the house to keep it clean, safe, and attractive.

A woman is wise

A godly woman dresses modestly,

She does not leave her chest bare,

As she knows that her body is for her husband's eyes only,

She maintains her nails clean,

And her hair neat.

She soaks herself in a hot water bath

Lathered with perfumed soap.

She comes to bed with her husband.

She calls to check on her husband's parents

They laugh on the phone.

She jokes with her in-laws,

And plays with their last-born child,

She advises her brother in laws,

And shops with her sister in laws,

She loves her in laws.

A godly woman cooks delicious meals,

As she knows the way to a man's heart,

She packs some food

And gives to a neighbor,

Or perhaps even to the local police officer or anyone.

She donates some of her belongings to the needy,

She finds favor from those who admire her generous deeds,

And her gracious hospitality,

But most of all from her husband.

We find in 2nd Samuel 6:16 she had no respect for her husband. *And as the ark of the LORD came into the city of David, Michal Saul's daughter looked through a window, and saw king David leaping and dancing before the LORD; and she despised him in her heart.* She remained barren the remainder of her life. There are consequences.

Men, women are not tea leaves to be used and then thrown away, and women you shouldn't allow yourself to be tea leaves by throwing yourself or flaunting yourselves.

Sisters, you must remove the pants and follow, submit to your man. My dear brothers and sisters, this must begin from the day that you become betrothed. This is not a democracy with God, 1st Corinthians 11:3. It has nothing to do with equal rights, women's liberation, but it is about what God says.

Women are to submit to the man-BUT NOT to submit to abuse-physical, emotional, mental, and/or immorality at any time, there a woman must draw the line just as we as believers are to be obedient to the law up to the point where they tell you to do or not do something contrary to God's law. Daniel was an excellent example of this.

There were no female angels in scripture, because God can have no part with sin and the feminine is symbolic of sin. Remember that Satan was an angel, but when he sinned, he was cast out. Only masculine can be justified (declared righteous) so the angels by nature must be masculine- i.e., Michael and Gabriel.

Before closing this segment, I wish to bring you to Romans 13:1-2 which tells us *Let every soul* (hear this my dear brothers and sisters) *every soul be subject unto higher powers. For there is no power but of God: The powers that be are ordained of God. Whosoever therefore resisteth the power, resisteth the ordinance of God: and they that resist shall receive to themselves damnation.*

Going back to early history, in the Garden of Eden, God gave commandments (not recommendations) which included; The second commandment given was 'to leave father and mother (they had none) and become one. Why this command? Because out God already knew that Eve would fall resulting in death and thus mankind would have to reproduce -Genesis 2:24.

The third commandment given by God our Creator was for women to bare children – Genesis 3:16.

The fourth commandment given was That the husband is to rule over his wife, calling the woman into submission, Genesis 3:16

And the fifth commandment is for the MAN to work, if he is able (Genesis 3:17-19, 2nd Thessalonians 3:10)

Moving on, it took around nine months for the ten plagues on Egypt in an effort to develop and grow (Spiritually) the children of Israel, just as it takes around nine months for you to grow and develop that miracle in thy womb, a baby.

MOTHERS

A beautiful passage of scripture is found in the book of Deuteronomy 7:12-15. *...if ye hearken to these judgments* (commandments, God's law), *and keep them and do them...And He will love thee, and bless thee, and multiply thee: He will also bless the fruit of thy womb... Thou shalt be blessed above all people: there shall not be male or female barren among you...*

Let me begin at the beginning here. In Genesis 3:16 we are told that because of Eve's sin that we have previously discussed, there would be consequences. Here we see *In sorrow thou shalt bring forth children, and thy desire shall be to thine husband, and he shall rule over you.* Husbands can only rule over you, his wife, if you submit to the authority that God gave him. This is God's plan and it can work no other way. Now to the point as to why the pain in childbirth, for this is where motherhood begins. The answer lies simply because of the woman's pride and unfaithfulness, Eve's consequences for her actions, which always brings pain and destruction. I can tell you however that I have delivered many babies, and have seen women give birth in the U.S. laying on the gurney with legs up, perhaps the most unnatural position there could be. I have seen women give birth squatting and kneeling, perhaps the best position. I have seen women hanging from tree branches to give birth... and that the quietest and calmest deliveries including my eldest son, and my daughter, were from Christian couples where the woman was comforted by a loving husband by her side that was encouraging and supporting her. What encourages him to be by her side at this time? by the love of God, and by having a loving, supportive wife who always loves and encourages him, and helps him along the way. God stays by our sides, even during times of pain and sorrow, and we make it easier for Him when we are loving and obedient to Him along the way. In Lev 12, we see that if a woman bore a son, she couldn't participate in worship for forty days. If she bore a daughter, no worship for eighty days, no worship for she was unclean, then bring a sin offering and a burnt offering. Although childbirth is a blessed event, it is a reminder to the Christian that sin is transmitted to each of us and thus our need for Jesus Christ in our lives. A woman must nurse her infants, for thus God ordained. Your breasts however big or small they may be, are not there for decoration. God gave them for a purpose, to nurse thy children. They are a practical tool in which to nourish His gift to you, your babies. Your breasts provide the perfect blend of the necessary nutrients, and immune system enhancers, needed by thy child. The formula in thy breasts is such that nothing-cows, goats or man's formula, can duplicate. Your breasts also provide a time and source for emotional bonding and touch, which are necessary for emotional and physical growth. In the developed world, women are so secretive about her breasts, (while men's breasts are freely revealed), in keeping them somewhat covered but yet flaunting them at the same time; whereas in parts of Africa, if an infant's mother is busy, she just passes the infant off to another female to tend to it. This other female may be six or seven on up to very elderly, any of which just open their top to expose their breast and let the infant suck. Mind you a young girl has not even budded yet, but lets the baby to suck as if it is the most natural thing in the world (which it is), and the elderly have no milk left, but allow the infant to suck. Those in the child bearing age group may or may not have milk, but still allow the infant to suck. The child naturally weans himself after two to three years. Look at Lamentations 4:3 *Even the sea monsters draw out the breast, they give suck to their young ones, and the daughter of my people is become cruel.* God nurtures us and expects us to nourish one another, as well as for mothers to nourish their children. Men are to nurture their wives and children with God's word. Also good for emotional support is to allow the infant to sleep in the family bed, sleep with their parents, which again they can be weaned after a couple of years. This also keeps the mother from having to get up all night as well; she can remain in bed and nurse. We are all part of the family of God, and the infant is a part of our family and needs to know this from the start. Nursing your children has also been cited as reducing the incidence of breast, uterine, and cervical cancers, crib death...

We are told in Isaiah 66:9 *Shall I bring to the birth, and not cause to bring forth? saith the Lord: shall I cause to bring forth, and shut the womb? saith thy God.* My point in bringing this verse out is that childbirth is a normal and natural process, event that has occurred since the beginning of time, since Eve, and IS NOT AN ILLNESS, therefore should not be made a medical issue. There is no place on earth with as many bacteria and viruses as a hospital, It is a very dirty place and thus going to doctors and hospitals for maternity care MD's and hospitals also make money by doing more procedures and tests therefore you are placing yourself and your infant at greater risk than staying away from the medical system, and statistics strongly support this fact; some startling statistics are printed in the book Medical Nemesis Making this beautiful and God blessed event into a medical event also considerably increases your emotional stress and removes the spiritual blessings. If I recall correctly, the complication rate is around eighty percent higher in medically assisted deliveries! All of this combined with the fact that nobody but thy husband is to come into the wife or see the partners' body, is clearly violated by the medical system who sees everything and constantly enters into the woman for exams and to assist with the delivery. A dear friend of mine in Africa whose wife became pregnant after several years of a closed womb, who I was admonishing to deliver at home, partially because of this message and partially because of the deplorable conditions in maternity care in the hospitals here, asked me, but what if... God created this child and loaned him to you; if you'll trust Him, He will care for you and this His child. I am not here telling you what to do as I realize that society, government and the medical system has done a great job of brain washing society, but herein are the facts, you decide. There is no greater blessing on earth than the couple being together in the clean loving confines of their home and the husband receiving his child in the loving, peaceful environment which God hath provided.

Please also note in Genesis 18:12 that Sarah considered childbearing a pleasure! Not a curse or burden. Read also Psalm 127:5 to see that children are a blessing, not a curse. They are a gift from our Almighty Father...a blessed gift.

Now you have a baby, you are a mother, congratulations! Now what? Proverbs 22:6 tells us, *train up a child in the way he* (righteousness) *should go.* Proverbs 29:15 tells us, *the rod and reproof bring wisdom, but a child left to himself bringeth his mother shame.* Verse 17 continues *correct thy son and he shall give thee rest. Yea, he shall give delight to thy soul.* Proverbs 13:24 teaches us *He that spareth the rod hateth his son* (righteousness), *but he that loveth him chasteneth him betimes.* Again, in Proverbs 19:18 *Chasten thy son while there is hope.* Proverbs 22:15 *foolishness is bound in the heart of a child, but the rod of correction shall drive it far from him.* You see dear precious children, dear parents, dear children of God, just as God disciplines His children, the truly spiritual, to keep us on the correct path, so must the church discipline those who are wandering off, the husband the wife, the parents to the children. Let this discipline always be done with love of the Almighty God. We are accountable before God for this discipline. Listen to 1ˢᵗ Samuel 3:13. *For I have told him that I will judge his house forever for the iniquity which he knoweth; because his sons made themselves vile, and he restrained them not.* And again, what is the difference between discipline and abuse? Discipline is done with love, abuse done in anger. Discipline is enforcing God's law, not our own, whereas abuse is enforcing our own desires.

My in-laws tried to teach my wife the night before our marriage, that your husband is the head of his home. Whatever he says you do, wherever he goes, you go. Don't step foot on our doorstep without him by thy side, and if he kicks you out, wait on his doorstep until he invites you back in. Now I know by western culture that this sounds terrible in this liberated world of today. But in fact, it is in line with scripture. See how far off track we have become. This kind of love, this sacrifice, this total surrender of self, is exactly what God desires from us sinners. God plans for you women to your husbands are no different. God's word never changes, even if churches, cultures, friends and family change, God's word is firm, and is the foundation that we need to hold onto. I must add in here that the husband should never kick his wife out, just as God will never kick us who truly believe, out. And this brings us to the beautiful book of Ruth, a beautiful love story in its literal, historical sense. Let us now look at chapter 1:16 where she says *intreat me not to leave thee, or to return from following after thee, for whither thou goest, I will go, and where thou lodgest, I will lodge: thy people shall be my people, and thy God, my God. Where thou diest, I will die and there will I be buried. The Lord do so and more also, if ought but death part thee and me.* Do you know that there are cultures today where when the husband dies, the woman must remove her jewelry and walk into the fire of his cremation, because she is to remain by her husband's side? Now, I certainly am not advocating this practice, but definitely **until death do us part.** This passage of Ruth is so powerful, words of complete surrender, complete submission, as we are called to do in marriage and in our relationship with God, so ought women to their husbands. This special passage is read in many marriages, but obviously, it doesn't mean much to most people, or the divorce rates wouldn't be so high. But, as Boaz took the leadership, responsibility, he fulfilled his responsibility, loved and protected her, so must husband's today. We must love our wives and forgive them as Christ loves and forgives us. This is not a license to sin for women, any more than does God's mercy give us license to sin.

After all is said and done, his wife was left with a stroke and brainstem migraines, very severe. One night the Lord touched him, and he awoke, laid hands upon his wife's head and prayed in tongues for her. He said that he didn't know it then, but she was having one of her headaches at the time, God knew. Immediately the headache disappeared and praise God, it never returned. The point is, he could have said to God, "neigh Lord, she deserves this after all that she did, the humiliation, the pain, my poor son" ...but dear friends, God calls us to forgive, to love, as He does us. He had forgiven, and loved her, so he had mercy on her as did God, so he obeyed God; I'm not here to tell you that forgiveness is easy, or that it alleviates all of the pain, but if you make the effort to be Christ-like, He will be with you and help you. She never appreciated what God and her husband did for her, it meant nothing, and many times, I'm afraid, we fail to see the love and mercy of our Lord and Savior. Wives often fail to see the love and mercy of their husbands, this leads to conflict, resentment, and divorce, just as many walk away from God due to a lack of trust and forgiveness when things don't go your way...

And finally, no discussion of wives would be complete without taking a look at Proverbs 31. Look first at the Song of Songs and see how much love Solomon expressed towards his wife. To paraphrase Proverbs 31, a virtuous (behaving in a very good and moral way) woman is worth more than anything else on earth, but very difficult to find. She is a blessing from God. The heart of her husband doth safely trust in her, so if the woman is fulfilling her God given role, her husband can trust her. She will be good for and to him, and he her. She will care for his house and prepares food for the family. His house, because he belongs to God, everything belongs to the husband, even if the law doesn't concur. She is hospitable and helps the poor and needy. She keeps busy caring for her husband, children and home. She isn't out gossiping and wandering around. I like verse 30, *Favor is deceitful and beauty is vain; but a woman that feareth the Lord, she shall be praised.* Just as the sinner that repents and accepts the free gift of salvation. In essence, if the husband and wife fulfill their roles, he is her savior, saving her from this world of troubles.

A woman's role is to be the helpmate for her husband and care for his family. If a man says, my dear, please have dinner ready and some nice clothes prepared for when I get home at 5:00, because I have a meeting at the church tonight at 6:00, remember? Thank you. He goes to work. He returns home at 5:00 as promised, only to find dinner not ready and no clothes prepared. She says, oh, you are home...I'm sorry, I got carried away talking with my friend, then I got carried away with my art work and forgot. He gets dressed the best he can, then he goes to a fast-food restaurant for a bite before the meeting at the church.

Modern society says no big deal, but in reality, it is a big deal. His wife negated her responsibilities and her role caring more about self than her lord, her provider, her savior while he was out there in the world trying to provide for her and his children. She in effect made herself more important than her husband and God. Isn't that a big deal? We as sinners have fallen so far from the path of righteousness, that Christ taught us to walk on, not to turn to the left hand or to the right hand, that we don't even see what is important anymore or why.

Somewhere along the line, we did turn to the left and fell. Nothing in our lives is as important as being obedient and submitting to the authority of God and thy husband. Such should be the heart of women. Should a disobedient, dishonoring wife be disciplined? We did discuss this briefly. God says he who spares the rod spoils his son, hates his son (righteousness). God chastises those whom He loves, then should the husband chastise, nor spare the rod for his wife whom he loves? A rod is used when oxen turn to the left or to the right when plowing. A godly husband who loves his wife certainly should not want his wife turning to the left or to the right and falling off of the path of righteousness any more than God wants us turning and falling. Chastisement is never pleasant for the moment, but the love behind the chastisement is such a blessing, for which we should always be thankful.

There unfortunately are so many women today who are refusing to bear children mostly because of vanity. I wish for you to know that if you are married, that bearing children is a commandment of God (Genesis 1:28), and the same God said that it is a blessing to bear children (Psalm 127:3-5). The second commandment of God is found in Genesis 2:24, that we are to leave father and mother and become one, as He already knew that mankind would sin bringing death unto all, so reproduction was a necessity, thus a commandment was given in Genesis 3:16.

Ruth if you recall her story was childless, but when she was obedient to the Lord, she bore children. Women were cursed for their disobedience by God closing their wombs but were blessed of God for their obedience by opening their wombs and giving them children. Look with me to the Book of 1st Timothy 2:15 *Notwithstanding she shall be saved in childbearing, IF they continue in faith and charity and holiness with sobriety.* A very powerful scripture. Take a moment and reread it and meditate upon it. We see also the examples in the boook of Luke 1:25 that it was considered by mankind as a reproach not to conceive, whereas in 1:30 conception signified honor with God. I must add in here however a verse for you women who are married and have not born children by God's ordination not yours (birth control), from Isaiah 54:1 *Sing, O barren, thou that didst not bear; break forth into singing, and cry aloud, thou that didst not travail with child: for more are the children of the desolate than the children of the married wife, saith the LORD.* Here He is not instructing you not to bear children, nor is He condemning those that do. Leave it to the Lord and praise Him either way as we spoke earlier and will speak more in a subsequent chapter. He is merely saying as did Paul, that without marriage or without children you have more time to serve Him.

If you are in the unfortunate position of being a single mother, are you teaching your daughters to love and submit to the man or to hate them leading them to homosexuality- lesbians; and your sons how to be a man? Are you providing your sons with any role models IE uncles, etc.? Are you teaching or demonstrating that men are bad? Are you making him hate women because of your attitude, behavior, and/or speech, causing him to become gay? The poor parenting of single parents is affecting their future as well as the various social problems resulting, as we are already seeing today.

WOMEN IN THE CHURCH AND COMMUNITY

I'm going to repeat myself here a bit, just to put in context the important point here.

As we just saw, a woman is to be a keeper in the home, not out working and certainly not in positions of authority over a man. Is this because she may not be able? No, some are, but...God said...

In 1st Corinthians 14:34-35, we are told *let your women keep silence in the church, for it is not permitted for them to speak.* Women are commanded by God to be in subjection, not authority *and if they will learn anything, let them ask their husbands at home,* not friends, neighbors, or the world...your husband! *For it is a **shame** for a woman to speak in the church.* Now, if a woman is not to teach or usurp authority over a man, and she is not permitted to speak in the church, how can a woman pastor a Christian Bible believing church? How can a woman be a manager, boss, politician... even more so when she is to be a keeper in the home? The natural progression of this, give them an inch and they'll take a mile, Women weren't permitted by God to speak in the church, but she did, then she sang; now they are taking over the pulpits, such an abomination. I am not saying that women shouldn't sing for God gave them beautiful voices, but...The Israelites were told to destroy all of the Canaanites, but they didn't and look still to this day the consequences. The Canaanites included the Phoenicians, Jebusites, Amorites, and the Hittites, with such well known cities as Gaza,

Megiddo, Jericho, Sodom, Gomorrah, and Jerusalem. Ham, who was cursed for looking upon the nakedness of his father, was the father of these Canaanite tribes.

We must be obedient unto God. Let us go one step further, in looking over in 2ⁿᵈ Chronicles 5:12, those who played the instruments and sang in the temple were men, not women. In 1ˢᵗ Timothy 2:11-12 it goes on to say *let the women learn in silence with all subjection. But I suffer not a woman to neither teach, nor usurp authority over the man but to be in silence.* Quite simply, God ordained, not man, that a woman is to be under submission, obedient to her husband (if single, to her dad), just as we are to be unto God, as sinners. 1ˢᵗ Timothy 2:14 tells us *For Adam was not deceived but the woman being quite deceived was in transgression.* Satan knew that Eve, the woman, was the weaker vessel, so she was who Satan went after, just as he went after Job's wife...He never tried to attack Adam. We already discussed the three-fold transgressions of Eve's sin, but a quick review, first, her disobedience to her husband and to the revealed word of God. Secondly, she believed the lies of the world, of Satan, rather than the truth of God's word. She placed her own will above that of God and of her husband. Third, she took authority from God and her husband, consequently, they were kicked out of the garden, all of mankind, and all of nature was cursed forevermore because of her one decision, her choice. And again, I refer you to Isaiah 3:12 *As for my people, children are their oppressors, and women rule over them. O my people, they which lead thee cause thee to err, and destroy the way of thy paths.* Now, with this in mind, let us jump to the New Testament book of the Revelation to John 2:20, unto the church of Thyatira... *because thou sufferest that a woman Jezebel, which calleth herself a prophetess, to teach and seduce my servants to commit fornication and to eat things sacrificed unto idols.* This will have even more significance after you read chapter six of this message; In other words, false doctrines and practices. Fornication refers here to unbelievers having relationships with other gods, idols. It is not God's will for women to lead, and when the blind lead the blind, they both fall. Are you hearing what the Spirit is saying? If you look over into the book of Acts 6:2-5, you will see that the men were even chosen to serve the tables. There are those churches today, which were founded by women who professed to be prophetesses, but were false and caused thousands to commit suicide, and men today are still following and reading the writings of these women. I read a little, and was appalled at some of the false doctrine contained therein. Oh, the shame.

A man must not submit to the teachings, doctrines, or authority of a woman, anywhere at any time, for that is not God's will or plan. Every matriarchal society has fallen. There is not a single scriptural example that God has revealed unto me, of a female church leader. God is the head. He is the head of the church, He is to be the leader, although most churches today have taken the leadership away and fallen into routines and rituals. God created man to serve Him, and to care for and enjoy God's creation, to tend the flocks. He created woman to help her husband at home, not to lead him. Women are taking the seats in the schools and jobs, away from the men, and society is encouraging this, but it is of the world and opposed to God and His word. You cannot serve two masters my dear sisters, you cannot serve two masters, *but as for me and my house, we shall serve the Lord,* Matthew 6:14 and Joshua 24:15. Men today are under or unemployed because of the sin of women, thus they are unable to care for and provide for their families as God ordained. This leads to depression, alcoholism, drug abuse, crime, and suicide... I challenge you my dear sisters, I challenge the politicians today, to return to Christian values, biblical precepts, and fight the good fight to restore God and His values back into society. Women, I challenge you to quit thy jobs and return to your husband, your home, to your honorable God given roles, and you will be blessed. Men, I challenge you, if you are under the authority of a woman in the workplace, that you discuss your biblical beliefs with your employer, and if no resolution, that you transfer or quit so that you may once again be under God's plan, you will be blessed. And 'ouch', this one will offend many today, if you are in a church under female leadership, female pastor, find a church that seeks to teach and practice the truth of God's word, but be sure to explain to the church why you are leaving, in a loving manner.

In Judges 4:8, we are shown a good example of the way that things shouldn't be. Here we see first the woman as a judge instead of being at home. Secondly, she places herself in authority over the man. Thirdly, the man Barak refuses to take the authority or responsibility and instead he submits to her. Let us look at reality. What would have happened if Sarah, Ruth or Esther had been independent and disobedient unto God (and their husbands)? Sarah and Ruth are in the lineage of Christ! Thus, no Christ to save us! Esther saved the Jews, again Christ, so praise God for the few godly, obedient women, but we need more of these today.

After leading one of the heads of the Apostolic church in one of the countries I was working in, to Christ; while in the Kenyan prison, during the torture and persecution, God sent to me an angel, as He frequently does for me. It was at a point where my airway was so closed down that I could hardly breathe, each breath was a struggle and great effort, and I was too weak to continue. God sent a woman that I didn't know; she identified herself as a Bishop of the apostolic church. I laughed to myself and silently asked God, is this some sort of a joke, I know that you have a sense of humor...but...really! But this woman, who looked fierce on the outward appearance, had a heart of gold, (see why we shouldn't judge!). She prayed for me and that day my airway improved. I praise God for her. I don't agree with, or even consider her as a Pastor or of the apostolic church, but her prayer life is wonderful. Many times, in my ministry, I have called upon women for intercessory prayer (but not in the church services), as they tend to be very strong in this area. In spite of all that I have said about women, I have never said that they are worthless, quite the opposite! They are precious instruments of God, and are here for a purpose just as men are; the purposes are different, but no less important!

I have heard many say that God is a woman, or ask why God couldn't be a woman. If you turn to Genesis, you will clearly see that God made MAN in Their own image, and from man God took a rib and made woman. This is not my doing or my saying, it is God.

Today my dear friends, there are many men in the U.S., numbers are increasing, who are marrying foreign women, have you ever stopped to wonder why? Because many other countries still encourage family values, discourage divorce, and women are still taught to be submissive to their husbands as God hath ordained, and most men still desire this as it is God's plan.

There are those who pray to Mary. Mary was the mother of Jesus, but nothing more than a vessel as we all are, of God, used by God for His divine purpose. Mary was a woman. She died as we all shall. Praying to a woman (sin) much less a dead person is sin and brings about death. In John 14:6 we read *Jesus saith unto him, I am the way, the truth, and the life: no man cometh unto the Father, but by me.* Jesus is the ONLY way to eternal life in heaven, the ONLY way and He is the truth, for He is God.

Another issue I am compelled to address here is menstruation. Many women, and men, feel that this is dirty, ugly, a pain... but, I am here to tell you that a woman's menstrual periods are in fact another wonderful and beautiful creation of God, it is not dirty or ugly, and it certainly is no mistake. In Ireland, I've been told that the women refer to this time as 'our ladies' gift', very positive reference.

Jesus Christ died on the cross and spent three days in the tomb. There was a time of separation between Jesus and God because Jesus took upon Himself our sins. He was 'dirty'. He died. There was a sloughing off of the old covenant through His precious blood and His resurrection, God ushered in the New Covenant. cleansing of sin- Christ bled only after taking on our sins.

I see menstruation as symbolic of the sloughing off of the old (tissue) and building up the new cells and tissues, with the possibility of a new life, just as we have the possibility of a new life IF we accept Jesus into our temples. All of this done so that a new life could be created, through conception, by accepting our Lord and Savior Jesus Christ, our Husband, and His shed blood. Women menstruate (shed blood) as a symbol of the shedding (Hebrews 9:12) of our sins, (women being again symbolic of the sinfulness of mankind) which Christ did for us, Hebrews 9:22. People see menstruation negatively, In Lamentations 1:17 pain and sorrow...pain, the women are filthy and are not allowed into the sanctuary, they cover themselves up- spiritually here to cover their sins.

You see, it is not dirty, it is so beautiful. It is a time of cleansing, purification, and restoration in the temple of God. God didn't have to design women to have menstrual periods, but He did. And God saw that all was good (perfect). There is a purpose, a reason for thy periods, thus should we rejoice and praise God. Hebrews 9:22 tells us, *and almost all things are by the law purged with blood; and without shedding of blood is no remission.* In the Old Testament book of Leviticus, it was considered dirty so that her husband could not enter in. In the New Testament, we are told that now we enter the Holy of holies, the presence of the Lord...by His blood. Romans 14:14 *that there is nothing unclean of itself; but to him that esteemeth anything unclean, to him it is unclean,* but God says all things are now clean. This period, these few days may well be used as a period of sanctification, of fasting (abstaining from intercourse) for a time of prayer. Again, in the Old Testament, after the temple was defiled by the Babylonians, the Spirit of God came not in until it was cleansed once again. The blood itself is not dirty; it represents life, and death, death which is the result of sin that makes us dirty, but life for those who accept the sacrifice of the shed blood and life of Jesus Christ. We see instructions in Leviticus Ch. 15 about that time of month.

Along the same line as we prepare to close this chapter, menopause is a very sensitive issue in a woman's life. You husbands need to show her God's love, mercy, and compassion during these tough times for her. She often will have no interest in sexual intercourse, which is okay as long as you remember the words of 1ˢᵗ Corinthians 7:5 fast and pray for a time but then come back together; for just as a man must meet his wife's intimacy needs (emotional), so must a woman meet a man's (physical). Men, this is a great time to demonstrate the love and patience of God to thy wife. She often feels useless because she believes her fertile period is over, which may or may not be so, my wife had our daughter a few years after menopause, and she isn't alone in this, because of prayer and fasting. Sarah, and others in scripture were late but God has ultimate control of thy womb. But also, extremely important, you aren't put here just to be an incubator, you are here as a helpmate for thy husband, so get back on your feet and serve your husband and God. They shall appreciate you fertile or not, and you shall feel better about yourself when you realize this, feel the appreciation, and reap the blessings of thy presence in the life of your husband and of God. It is ironic but women morn their periods, then when they stop coming, the women morn. Also remember the ark was lost to the Philistines. When returned, they found it missing all but the rod, but...they still rejoiced for the ark was back. So shall thy husband rejoice when you are back. You wish to see just how important women are? Just look into the Books of the Kings and the Chronicles of the kings, where you shall see that when the kings died, their sons took over. The sons were influenced by their mothers, which influenced the entire nations of Israel and Judah!

We are told in 1st Timothy 2:11 that likewise, we as sinners (women) need to be in silence before the Lord, listening to Him and subjecting ourselves in obedience unto Him.

It is important in review of Paul's first letter to Timothy that he mentioned three key areas of discipline for the Christian woman; that they are to be proper, modest, and discreet. Are you living up to these? This reminds me of the movie entitled 'Pretty Woman' where a prostitute was changed into a beautiful and well-mannered woman who became proud of her new self. Today as we discussed, women believe that they are equal with men, but it is important to understand that they are equal with man, but it is important to understand that equality is not synonymous with identical. Jesus shares equality with God but yet still submits unto His authority and was obedient even unto death.

Before closing I need to refer you to 1st Corinthians 12:18-25 and say that women are so important, but must be in the role where God placed them just as men must. Women are to be in the submissive role to assist men.

Titus 2:3-5, an extremely powerful commandment to women. *The aged women likewise, that they be in behaviour as becometh holiness,* **not false accusers,** *not given to much wine, teachers of good things; That they may teach the young women to be sober,* **to love their husbands,** *to love their children,* **To be discreet, chaste, keepers at home, good, obedient to their own husbands,** *that the* **word of God be not blasphemed**. Emphasis I added, please note the seriousness of this passage. If the women would be obedient to God in this way, there would be so few divorces and much happier marriages. Please note however that I am not making this one sided, as men must share in the responsibility for the failed marriages as well, but if the woman would heed God's advice here after all He was the Creator of women and of marriage, marriages would be much better. If my wife had of listened to and obeyed her husband, our son would have been saved as well as our marriage, and then she closed it off by not being discreet and became a false accuser and liar to the government. These same do so many women today. Most men simply desire a woman to come home to, to share with trusting that everything discussed shall stay between them. They desire happy children, and a clean organized home. When women refuse to stay in the home, obey their husbands, refuse to bear children, broadcast things in the home to outsiders, much discouragement and frustration occurs within the husband, then marital strife and contention sets in, all preventable by simple obedience to this one scripture. Again, this is not one sided, but...

I would invite you to read and review the following scriptures: Exodus 15:20, 38:8; Numbers 12:6; Judges 4:4; 1st Samuel 2:22; 2nd Chronicles 34:1-2; Ezra 2:64-65; Esther 1:16, 1:22b Jeremiah 31:22; Mark 16:9-10; Luke 2:38, 8:1-3, 23:55-56, 24:1-7; Acts 9:36, 21:9; 1st Corinthians 11:8-11; Ephesians 4:11; 1st Timothy 2:9-10; 2nd Timothy 1:4-5; Titus 2:3-5.

PERSONAL NOTES

PERSONAL NOTES

Genesis 2:24 *Therefore shall a man leave his father and his mother, and shall cleave unto his wife: and they shall become one flesh*

CHAPTER 4

An Introduction to Betrothal

Dear brothers and sisters, we thus far have introduced you and spoken about men, women, and children in the literal and spiritual aspects. Now it is time to move on. We shall explore when a man meets a woman, again both in the literal as well as in the spiritual aspects. The first three chapters were foundational to assist you in understanding the remaining chapters. We are going to get seriously into the Scriptural aspects of dating, marriage, sexuality, and family matters.

Paul in 1st Corinthians 7:7 says that it is best to remain single, but he says this not to condemn marriage, for marriage is God's plan for some people, to populate the earth, as well as typifying or as a parable of God's family relationships. But you read in verse 32 that when you are a virgin you are free to serve God, when you are married you must fulfill thy responsibilities to thy spouse.

We see in 1st Corinthians 7:36-37 that a father should care for and protect his daughters, but if she feels the need to marry, then the father should arrange for her marriage. It is best if they remain single though and serve the Lord God. Note that the girl wasn't out hunting for her prey, but her dad's choice. We need to erase the social stigma of being single. It is not wrong, it is not sin, it is not bad to be single.

I was talking with a young man years ago who told me that a big advantage of not being married is that on a couple of occasions he had the opportunity to go serve in the mission field and he was able to accept the offers to serve our Lord without hesitation because he had no family to prevent it.

Marriage is not ordained for everyone. Remember Jeremiah was told by the Lord not to marry, Jeremiah 16:1-3. God took Ezekiel's wife from him in Ezekiel 24:15-18. **Our life must never be defined by our marital status**! Do not look for a lifelong partner just because you are lonely, often people end up worse and more this rarely resolves the problem and more often the individual ends up in a worse condition than before. There was a true story in a big city, where a woman had been found dead in her apartment. The sad but amazing part of this story is that she had been dead for ten years! People are so alone that they can die and not be missed for ten years! Find a friend that you can talk with, this doesn't require necessarily require marriage, unless God so ordains.

Naomi took Ruth out of the cursed land (Moab from Lot's incestuous relationship with his daughters), into the land of hope and promise for Ruth-Bethlehem, where she got plenty of food, found a husband, and became the great- grandmother of David and in the genealogical line of our Lord and Savior Jesus Christ.

Note also that neither Ruth or Boaz never said that she was beautiful, he was fair to look upon, comely, etc. as in other areas of Scripture... but instead saw and commended Ruth for her heart in verse 2:11, and they looked at the heart, not the race or age in 3:10.

Men and women, especially my young brothers and sisters, God says that we are to dress modestly, and we discussed this briefly earlier. If you'll look at Genesis 24:65, you'll see that Rebekah covered herself until she came before her lord, and was accepted by him. Then he covered her. We come before our Lord as sinners. We confess (uncover) our sins, He accepts us and covered our sins with His blood. I'll go a step further in saying that Miss America doesn't stay Miss America forever.

She grows up, gets married, has children, grows old...Men and women's appearances change, so cover thyself so as not to reveal your physical self, but reveal thy inner self, who you are for that should never change. In Isaiah 53:2 we see that beauty is more than skin deep. True beauty is found in one's heart, soul and mind, not in one's appearance. Look over at Isaiah 53:2 now, *For he shall grow up before him as a tender plant, and as a root out of a dry ground: he hath no form nor comeliness; and when we shall see him, there is no beauty that we should desire him.* Who is being spoken of here? Our precious Lord and Savior! We see that there is now outward beauty described here, so why should we desire Him? because of the inward beauty. They will know that we are Christians not by our appearance or attire, but by our love!

In Nehemiah 13:26 Satan has a way of using women to bring men down, to cause him to sin, to fall. This is why God placed men in authority over the woman, to protect him and her...as we saw in Gen 3:16, because the woman is the weaker vessel (we are the weaker vessel before God), 1 Peter 3:7 when one is in authority, he must do three things. First, he must love. Second, he must discipline with love in order to protect and save them, and third, he must sacrifice for them. Jesus has done and is doing these three for us, and we should do these for our wives. Just look at John 3:16 and compare with what we are saying here, for God so loves you and I that He sacrificed His only Son, Himself, that whosoever will believe in Him and confess Him before man, he shall be protected, sheltered, and have everlasting life with our Father, (My paraphrase). He will never divorce us dear friends.

When a man's strongest passion is to be satisfied in a beautiful marriage, he becomes unreasonable and desperate, actually making the thing he desires less likely to occur. But when his passion is to the kingdom of God, he becomes more attractive to his woman.

I need to say here before proceeding that if you aren't married but hugging, kissing, touching in any way, living together or engaging sexually, you should stop NOW...this very minute... and await any such activities until after you are formally married. Is this what you culture or friends say? Probably not. Read John 4:18 what Jesus said to the woman *For thou hast had five husbands; and he whom thou now hast is not thy husband: in that saidst thou truly.* Is this what God says about you? Absolutely, and if you are going to call yourself a Christian (being Christ-like) then it is time to be obedient unto Him. Are you an orphan or coming from a broken or dysfunctional home? Sex and marriage are not the way to find love. Only through God and through His ordained life partner for you can you find true love, peace, and happiness in your life. Offering of yourself as a chaste virgin to your marriage partner, after you are married, is the best gift that you can offer to thy partner and God. If you do so, then I believe you spiritually remain a virgin unless you commit adultery, fornication, or divorce. We read in Ruth 3:10-11, *And he said, Blessed be thou of the LORD, my daughter: for thou hast shewed more kindness in the latter end than at the beginning, inasmuch as thou followedst not young men, whether poor or rich. And now, my daughter, fear not; I will do to thee all that thou requirest: for all the city of my people doth know that thou art a virtuous woman.* You see, she was considered virtuous because she didn't chase after men (read the story in Ruth to fully understand this).

It is important also for you, young people anxious to enter into sexual intercourse prematurely, to understand that this may lead to conception EVEN if you use birth control, and that the female pelvis doesn't rotate out and mature until around twenty-five years of age. Giving birth before maturation of the pelvis often leads to a much higher risk of delivery, including the possibility of infant and/or maternal death.

Both Ezra chapter 10, the end, and Nehemiah 13:23-31, both end in warnings for marriage to the Jews, the believers. Be sure to take time now to read these passages of Scripture.

People tell you to choose your friends carefully, wisely; the same is true even more so when choosing your life partner. Friends come and go, but your marriage covenant is until death do you part. Adam had it easy because God designed the perfect woman for him, and gave her to him. Today we have so many to choose from, but the same God that gave Eve unto Adam is the same God that can and will give you the perfect woman, if you will just pray and wait on Him. The women today are not perfect but then, neither was Eve, was she.

There are many who fear not getting married because of social pressures and/or loneliness; whereas there are many today who fear marriage because of fear of failure and getting hurt, or because of history of a dysfunctional marriage/family that they were reared in, broken, single parent upbringing, abuse, etc. To this I am compelled to say that fear is not of God, but of the enemy. We must leave the fears that we carry at the foot of the cross, then we must listen to God-for His direction. If you are obedient unto God married or not, He will never let you down. Again, I must repeat that there is nothing wrong, bad, or sinful about remaining single.

You should always be honest with everyone, but especially if you are going to begin relating with someone of the opposite sex in regards to seeking a life partner, then it is essential that you always be honest with each other from the begining because the truth always comes out. Let each other know the real you, and that way you are better able to make an informed decision. It is better to find out early on rather than after betrothal. Ephesians 4:25 tells us *Wherefore putting away lying, speak every man truth with his neighbor: for we are members one of another.* This is especially so with a life partner.

You don't need any pick-up lines, you need honesty. Speak truth from the very beginning, from the heart.

DATING

In Genesis 2:18 we are told that *The Lord God said, It is not good that the man should be alone; I will make an helpmate for him.* God determined that man should have a companion and a helper, thus He created women special for the man.

I wish to start out this segment by saying Do not look for a lifelong partner just because you are lonely, often people end up worse and more this rarely resolves the problem and more often the individual ends up in a worse condition than before. There was a true story in a big city, where a woman had been found dead in her apartment. The sad but amazing part of this story is that she had been dead for ten years! People are so alone that they can die and not be missed for ten years! Find a friend that you can talk with, this doesn't require necessarily require marriage, unless God so ordains.

I was talking with a young man years ago who told me that a big advantage of not being married is that on a couple of occasions he had the opportunity to go serve in the mission field and he was able to accept the offer s without hesitation because he had no family obligations to stand in the way.

As I said earlier, marriage is not ordained for everyone. Remember Jeremiah was told by the Lord not to marry, Jeremiah 16:1-3. God took Ezekiel's wife from him, Ezekiel 24:15-18. Our life must never be defined by our marital status! I said this before but it bears repeating.

Many women and their families look more at the man's bank account than at the man. My dear friends, Money and material possessions do not create a marriage nor do they hold a marriage together. The rich get divorced perhaps more than the poor. We read in Job 23:12 *I have esteemed the words of his mouth more than my necessary food.* God will provide, just look at His promise in Philippians 4:19. Love comes only from God. If you don't know God you can never truly love. Whenever money enters into the love equation, then it is lust and not love. Love will last and endure all things, but lust will only last until something better comes along. This includes dowry, marrying for money... Love of money is the root of all evil because it is lust not love, and thus is not from God. A person may be quite comfortable, and then get married. When you get married, cut your money by give or take, one third, and then have children, divides that much further; these figures are very rough just to give you an idea, but not to worry because God will provide IF you stay close to Him. While the money decreases, love increases, and grows. People work all of their lives for money and material prosperity which they cannot take with them unto the grave. If only people would work that hard on love- of God, spouse, and family, that which is eternal, and is much more precious than money, and this doth not perish.

Money and material possessions don't strengthen a marriage; create a healthy marriage, or a happy marriage. Actually, in reality, quite the opposite is true. God desires obedience more than sacrifice. One must have a solid foundation, Jesus Christ in your life and in thy personal relationship. A relationship or marriage built upon anything else is sure to collapse one way or another. God however will be there for you even when money, possessions, friends, or family aren't. A house may burn down, your business may collapse, the banks may fail, but God never fails. He will still be there for you if He is your firm foundation, Amen? Hallelujah, Thank you Jesus.

Many put my wife and me down because we were of different races. We were kicked out of an Assembly of God church in the middle of the service, because of this. Others may be put down because of age differences, etc. What I wish for you to realize and see here is that we are not to judge, nor to listen to what people say, see 2nd Chronicles 19:6. What God hath joined together, let **NO** man put asunder. If God brought the two together, why worry about what others think or say? We are all sons and daughters of Noah and of Adam, red, yellow, black or white, all are precious to Him. You may say wrong, Pastor, the Bible says not to be unequally yoked. To this I'll respond that this passage does not even relate to marriage per se if you read it in context. It refers to our day-to-day walk. Applied to life and marriage this passage in context refers to a believer not having fellowship with non-believers, to which I certainly will not dispute. A Christian would not desire to marry an unbeliever. And one must also look at Boaz and Ruth, when people start talking about age differences, In Ruth 3:10, we see that Boaz was around the same age as her dad. Then look over into Genesis 29:12 where we see Rachel who married Jacob who was her father's brother. Rebekah could easily have been her husband's daughter rather than wife, as she was so much younger. Also, in Genesis 11:25-29, we see that Sarai was ten years younger than Abram and Nahor took his brothers daughter to wife. Then look at Exodus 6:20 where we see that Amram married his father's sister, who bore him Moses and Aaron. Age differences are not so important, love and God's plan are what is important.

Naomi took Ruth out of the cursed land (Moab from Lot's incestrial relationship with his daughters), into the land of hope and promise for Ruth-Bethlehem, where she got plenty of food, found a husband, and became the great grandmother of David and in the genealogical line of our Lord and Savior Jesus Christ.

Note also that Ruth and Boaz never said she was beautiful, fair to look upon, comely, etc. as in other areas of Scripture... but instead saw and commended Ruth for her heart in verses 2:11, and they looked at the heart, not the race or age in 3:10.

The races were apparently formed at Babel, though nothing is truly said about this, so the mixed racial marriage takes on an altogether different hue. While in reality there is no black or white, red or yellow people, we are all brown, just with different shades, some lighter and some darker while others are in the middle somewhere. The Jewish race has a very light complexion. All skin color is the product of the curse. Color, languages, and race are the product of a universal sin. It is not the sin of one person. Race distinction reveals the curse which was aggravated by sin. When a black and white unite in marriage it personifies the curse, and that is why so many are opposed, but God is not opposed, we are all His children. This is usually socially embarrassing to those who have melted into the socially acceptable background of the prejudice; some of these people have formed an evil prejudice that is very strong. Although mixed racial unions are perfectly legitimate, they nevertheless will be unions that experience social tension, i.e., the tension of societies own embarrassment which is a reminder of the sin of all men at Babel. The loving couple will not personally know the embarrassment; they will however wrestle with the embarrassment of others. God is not prejudiced; we all came from the same Father and have the same blood.

The question of the mixed marriage, the believer with the unbeliever surfaced in Corinth, just as it seems to surface still today. Paul only instructs the believer not to be unequally yoked together with unbelievers, this in context isn't even related to marriage, but certainly does apply. His primary instruction is that the believer should not put away the unbeliever. It is important here to mention that mixed marriage is not a matter of missed race as many people claim, but rather a mix of a believer with an unbeliever. The **believer** is commanded to stay with the marriage; it is the unbeliever who is not commanded. The unbeliever appears to have the right to control the outcome of the marriage. Paul gives the unbeliever the right of choice. The instruction to the believer in the first place is not to be unequally yoked...with an unbeliever, but... sometimes an unbeliever can pretend, and then, the marriage is up to the unbeliever because **the believers are under the command not to leave**.

We see in Judges 21:20-24 a great example of mixed marriages and women not having a say in the marriage.

From the very beginning of courtship or dating, the man should assume the position of headship of the family so that she can follow him. If he doesn't then she assumes that position and this is outside of God's plan. The man needs to be the head and the woman must follow him. He must be the prayer leader, he must be the worship leader, he must lead daily Bible study; he must be the leader in his family. He must set family time where you all shut off your phones, the TV, the radio, everything and lead worship and then time to talk and plan for their future. He must exude confidence in his role as leader so that the woman and her parents can feel comfortable in following him.

I did a random search across different cultures on an international matchmaking site and listed below the basic characteristics that the women of today are looking for in a man. My dear brothers consider these when you consider a woman and carefully and truthfully challenge yourself, do you meet these standards? The list includes:

Caring
Comfort
Faithful
Family oriented
Honest
Listen to them
Love
Protect
Respect
Responsible
Romantic
Simple
Support
Tenderness
Knows what they want in life

In 2020 I signed into an Asian dating site to see what was going on there. I was amazed! I signed in with just a name and basic info- age, height, weight, hair and eye color, nothing more. There was no photo or profile, no personal info. With a week I had over three thousand letters, from ages eighteen to sixty, many were very rich, but are undervalued so they want to marry foreigners. Many mentioned that they were ready for marriage and would come here to meet me. I never responded to any of the notes. Within one week I received over three thousand hits!!! The girls from eighteen to seventy-two years of age responded and wanted quick marriage, they would love and support their husband. All were dressed, most very nicely dressed. This was the same as I found in the African dating site. Why isn't it the same with American women? I found in there, naked photos in obscene poses, sex talk, no humility at all.

But if the unbelieving depart, let him depart. A brother or a sister is not under bondage in such cases: but God hath called us to peace, 1st Corinthians 7:15. The believer must permit the unbeliever the choice. This coincides with 1st Corinthians 5:12 *For what have I to do to judge them also that are without? do not ye judge them that are within?*

A believer might even argue that the unbeliever does not have the right to depart based on Jesus' command, *Let not man put asunder*, and *They twain shall be one flesh.* Although this is so, it is nevertheless true that God permits man, the unbeliever, the right to choose, even if the choice is sinful or leads to his or her destruction; *For whosoever shall call upon the name of the Lord shall be saved.* This right of choice must be extended to the unbelieving partner regarding their marriage, but **never to the believing partner**. The doctrine of marriage and the doctrine of salvation are one in the same.

The believer is not bound to force the unbeliever to remain, however the believer is bound to permit the unbeliever to leave in peace with the hope of a future restoration; **RESTORATION AND RECONCILIATION, THE MARK OF SALVATION**. The Christian must extend to the unbeliever the invitation to return to the marriage bond and must remain unmarried as taught in verses 10 and11, thus permitting the indissoluble union to physically reunite. To the believer this is the true essence of love. As with the grace of God, he waits for the return of all unbelievers. God keeps the door of His heart ready to open; all we have to do is come and knock. We as pastors must teach our dear people to do the same for the lost husband or wife. The believing partner must keep the door of his or her heart ready to open and must keep the literal door of his or her home ready to open. Hope must not be abandoned, hope that the lost partner will find true repentance and faith upon their return and be saved.

What better words can be said than these found in 1st Corinthians 7:16, *For what knowest thou, O wife, whether thou shalt save thy husband? or how knowest thou, O man, whether thou shalt save thy wife?* The extension of love to the departed is intended to bring the loved one to salvation, *thou shalt save thy husband, or thy wife.* I find this statement very interesting since the salvation of the departed loved one is now the target of the believers' love. He or she must pray for the departed loved ones to be saved and return. The question this verse raises is, when do we stop praying for them to return to the Lord, and to us? This verse indicates that the believer permitted the unbeliever to leave in peace, and with the condition that when they return which implies the hope that they will also accept Christ as their own personal Savior, and thus be saved. You never stop praying for your loved ones until your or their dying day. Therefore, this verse states that unless the unbelieving spouse returns there is to be no remarriage for the believer this-side-of-death. Again, this verse speaks to the permanency of marriage, even if that partner is never heard from again, or even if the believer has no knowledge of whether they are dead or alive. This is the complete translation of Ephesians 5:25, *Husbands, love your wives, even as Christ also loved the church, and gave himself for it.* That verse could just as well read: Wives love your husbands, even as Christ also loved the church, and gave himself for it, but it says husbands to love because again, male represents righteousness.

Paul repeats his appeal for men to be content with their calling when he said in 1st Corinthians 7:20, *Let every man abide in the same calling wherein he was called. Art thou bound unto a wife? seek not to be loosed. Art thou loosed from a wife? seek not a wife.* Paul is using simple language to make a point. To be bound to a wife simply means to be married, and to be loosed from a wife means the person is single or a widow. It means this and nothing more, nothing less. From this chapter we have shown that the unmarried are people who have never been married, or widows(ers).

In each case where a believing married person experienced the departure of a living mate, that believer was commanded to remain unmarried or to be reconciled. And of course, as Paul opened the chapter with his *it is better to marry than to burn* he now continues that theme with *if a virgin marry, she hath not sinned.*

In the beginning of our spiritual journey, we must see God for who and what He is. He must show His true colors, so to speak, that we may have faith and trust in Him. We must be justified before Him. Likewise dating, if you believe in dating, that the man must be himself, honest, not a pretense or showing off, so that the woman may decide if she can love, trust, have faith in him and to be justified so to speak by him.

Likewise, the woman needs to be open and honest about herself as she humbly comes before him, just as we sinners must do before our Lord.

Today, men don't want to lead and women don't want to submit or follow. It has nothing to do with the amount of education that you have, the number or type of degrees that you have, the amount of money you have, or anything else; The Bible says! When looking for a life partner, pray and find someone that you can respect. Men, you can't be a coward, lazy, or anything, God gave you a powerful position-the king, lord, the pastor, the leader of your family, so wear the pants. Sisters, you must remove the pants and follow, submit to your man. My dear brothers and sisters, this must begin from the day that you become betrothed. This is not a democracy with God, 1st Corinthians 11:3. It has nothing to do with equal rights, women's liberation, but it is about what God says.

We must remember that men represent God and righteousness. In Ezekiel 44:22 we see that the priest (the man is the high priest and lLord of his home) *neither shall they* (priests) *take for their wives a widow, nor her that is put away* (divorced)*, but they shall take maidens* (virgins)*, of the seed of the house of Israel* (believers in Christ)*, or the widow that had a priest before.*

Dating is **NOT** a time for hugging, kissing, touching, or revealing any part of thy body, and I'll be explaining why shortly in greater detail. If you find it hard or difficult to keep your clothes on and hands off, then find another friend, for this is lust, not love, and is not of God. Do not yield to the lustful temptations out there.

Dating is a time to truly get to know each other. God and man, man and woman, and begin to build a sincere and true relationship if you feel that this is truly God's choice for you after fasting and prayer. In some cultures, the virgins still go out on dates with a chaperone, a great idea as it protects the both of you. It protects the woman from any pressure or advances, and it protects the man from any allegations or any undue advances or pressure. Young men and women ought to respect one another including their bodies.

I mentioned a bit ago that if you believe in dating. What did I mean? Today more and more people are using dating web sites to meet someone, and there seems to be some degree of success, though it is still too new for any long-term statistics. Be careful however because the person on the other end may or...may not be the person that they present themselves as. They pretend to be something or someone other than themselves, and people lose a lot of precious time and money, only to get hurt badly in the end. Even though it sounds foreign to the American psyche, from early on, in the Old Testament times, and still held in parts of the east today, and is in fact growing stronger in the U.S., especially amongst Christian home-schoolers, is match making. Take a quick look at Genesis 38:6; 24:4, Judges 1:13, Exodus 2:21, 1ˢᵗ Samuel 18:17...look at Genesis 41:45 where the woman was given as a gift, which occurred as well many times throughout scripture, the list goes on of giving the daughter or the man taking a woman to wife. You may say ugh, but...my dear friends, they have a higher degree of success than marriages from dating. There are several reasons for this among which are, dating people often pretend to be someone that they aren't...until it's too late, whereas matchmaking you learn to love the partner for who and what they are. There is also more family and social encouragement to make the marriages work and not divorce in matchmaking societies. Dating societies tend to have advertising for divorce and divorce attorneys everywhere you turn, like hungry wolves. Dating societies tend to marry with the idea that if it doesn't work, there are other fish in the sea, mentality, and the couple has little or no family, church, or social support or encouragement to make the marriage grow or survive. Match-made marriages have a statistically lower divorce rate compared to those from dating.

Take a look with me at Ezra 9:12, again an important reminder not to be bound to unbelievers. In the book of Ruth, Boaz's brother was greedy and selfish, Boaz who was humble and faithful. He covered Ruth with the wrap, and sheltered her under his wings. He provided for and protected her and loved her, as God does for us. In the old times and still in some cultures, women have no choice. We have no choice, we are born into sin, just as women have no choice to be women when born, nor do men. But...we have a choice whether or not to accept the Lord and Savior into our lives; and thus, I believe that a woman should have a say, a choice to enter into a relationship with the man or not. And...looking from the Spiritual perspective, God's view, are we not match made unto Christ? Those who date, trying out different gods, get lost in the weeds, but when we are match made with Christ, we have the firm foundation, and a strong marriage which lasts for an eternity. For match making let us look at Genesis 24:40, 51, where we see Rebekah and Isaac were match made, never knew each other. Rebekah traveled some five hundred miles with a stranger to meet Isaac. She was given away by her family; Isaac took her to wife. You may also wish to take some moments now to look at the following scriptures about this. Judges 14:7-8; Genesis 29:24, 30:4, 9, 41:45; Exodus 2:21; 1st Samuel 25:39. In Isaiah 62:5 we see *for as a young man marrieth a virgin, so shall thy sons marry thee: and as the bridegroom rejoiceth over the bride, so shall thy God rejoice over thee.* A couple of points have I to shed light on. First, you again must notice that the man is to marry a virgin. You see, God only accepts the pure, the clean, undefiled, and the only way for us sinners to qualify is to accept Jesus Christ, and be justified by Him. So, just as God's bride must be pure, clean, undefiled, a virgin, so must men marry virgins. What this must bring to light for you is the importance of boys and girls keeping their clothes on and hands off. At the cross, Jesus carried our sins with Him. God cannot and will not have any fellowship with sin. He will not marry the defiled, the sinner, for He is perfect, without sin. Men, are you hearing this? You are called to be Christ-like, be pure, clean, undefiled, and only date a woman who is likewise. My dear sisters, are you listening?

In the late twentieth century, there was a song if I said you have a beautiful body, would you hold it against me. A proper response my dear sisters and brothers would be to say, I won't allow my body, the temple of the Almighty God, to be held against anybody until marriage, and I don't care how you feel about my body until marriage, I want someone who will love me for who and what I am...and yes, I would hold it against you for you have no business speaking to me this way.

Boys and girls, men and women, my dear brothers and sisters, A common misconception in our societies today is that one way to be or feel 'loved' is to engage in sexual activity, but this is not God's way. That one way of being accepted by the crowd is to engage in sexual activity, or see how many you can get... but this is not God's way. It is not right, and more often than not, you'll walk away feeling worse than before and quite empty, used... God's way is the only way. God loves you, and when the correct person at the correct time comes along, all will be well, but you must walk on God's path, or you will miss His blessings for you, amen. I personally never dated, never looked for a wife, but God brought my wife in my path through matchmaking. I was asked in 2013, do you still believe that it was God's plan for you to come to Africa since you ended up in a Kenyan prison. Do you still believe that your wife was God's chosen after all that she did to you? To both of these questions, my answer is always YES! Oh yes, my friends. I know spiritually what happened and why, I know why I am here, and I know that God knows where I am, for He is here with me, and He has demonstrated this repeatedly, for many to see and witness. He has used me in a mighty way. I could have never of imagined the way that my Lord hath chosen to use me, and I know that He isn't through with me yet or I would have long ago been dead, five MD's have told my escorts and I that it is a miracle that I am still alive. I always tell them, it is my God, and to Him I give the praise and glory. I have no regrets having married my wife, she was God's choice just that later, she made some bad choices, but that isn't God's fault. She failed God and I, but God ordained her for me, I have no doubts, and if she were to return and ask forgiveness, I would accept her, and my children back, with open arms, for God ordained us to be one... until death do us part...God is in control and God is so good... So...are you ready to commit?

We discussed clothing earlier, so allow me to just briefly remind you young people that the type of clothing you wear reveals a lot about you and will attract a certain type of person, so be careful.

Also, I want to say that if you date you are never obligated to go out with a certain individual, and never obligated to go 'further', touching, kissing, hugging...NEVER! And a lunch or dinner does not obligate intercourse!

In the Exodus 3:17, we see that the Canaanites are Ham's descendants, cursed twice over- by Cain, and Ham, so God told Israel to destroy them. He will take His chosen in the end time out of this world, into heaven. This is also why God specifically told them not to do as the Canaanites do because they were evil and why God told them to destroy all of them, so that there could be no contamination amongst the chosen people. This is also why unbelievers are not allowed into the temple (be ye not unequally yoked with unbelievers) this includes marriage (allowing intercourse between a believer and unbeliever).

Having said all of this, I wish to give you two final things to consider before becoming betrothed. Many people get hurt when you divorce but nobody gets hurt by you staying single.

One of the biggest misconceptions of the world is that love makes the world go round. It doesn't, God does that. Love is what makes the ride easier.

I covered all of this to prepare you before making the commitment of

BETROTHAL

Assuming all goes well with dating or match making, you've both prayed this through and feel God's presence, His blessing, then the next step in our Christian journey is betrothal, where we sanctify ourselves unto each other and God sanctifies the couple. If it didn't feel right, one should never be afraid to sit down with the other and in an honest and loving way, explain that they have prayed through this and that it just doesn't feel right. Rather than leading the other along, it is better and far less painful to cut the relationship and remain friends rather than to mislead, or worse enter into betrothal only to end up in trouble down the line. Betrothal...In this context the woman separates herself from any and every other man, for this one man. This one man holds onto her, emotionally but not physically yet. He protects her and encourages her, he loves her as they continue their journey, just as we are to separate ourselves from the world and live for Christ, 1st John 2:15. God then holds onto us, eternal salvation for those who are faithful and true. Now, notice that I have not said man separates himself from other women, why? because like God, he only desires his chosen bride, his woman, he's not out playing around.

Before entering into this sacred event, you must take it step by step-

> Pray and seek guidance from the Holy Spirit- does He wish for you to marry, not your heart, or pressure from family, friends, church, society.

- Do an intensive self-evaluation.

    ○ **Men,** are you a leader,

    ○ are you physically, emotionally, and spiritually mature enough to take on such a responsibility?

    ○ Can you demonstrate to the woman and her family that you are ready and able to care for her and be responsible as required of a husband?

    ○ Are you confident and mature enough that she can feel comfortable in trusting and submitting fully unto you?

    ○ Are you strong enough spiritually so that she cannot bring you down and you can build her up?

    ○ **Women**, are you physically, emotionally, and spiritually mature enough to take on such a responsibility?

○   Can you demonstrate to the man that you are able and ready to take on such responsibilities as required of a wife?

○   Are you confident and mature enough to be willing and able to fully trust and submit thyself unto thy husband?

-     Then carefully and prayerfully evaluate your potential life partner. Men, is she someone that you can trust fully and feel comfortable with? Will she build you up, support and encourage you? Women are you confident and mature enough that he can feel comfortable in trusting and submitting fully unto you? Will he build you up, support and encourage you?

-     The man should never ask a woman to marry him in public, where the woman can feel trapped. They should never be out alone anyway. This special moment should be done in the presence of her parents and/or the pastor, where she can feel comfortable being honest with her response.

-     Try to get to know your in-laws and seek their blessings. This is especially true for the man, as he must be able to convince his in laws and demonstrate to them that he is willing and able to love and care for their daughter, for they are relinquishing any and all responsibility to whomever takes their daughter.

As you are praying through this, be certain to read and understand 1ˢᵗ Corinthians 13:4-7 *Charity* (love) *suffereth long, and is kind; charity envieth not; charity vaunteth not itself, is not puffed up, Doth not behave itself unseemly, seeketh not her own, is not easily provoked, thinketh no evil; Rejoiceth not in iniquity, but rejoiceth in the truth; Beareth all things, believeth all things, hopeth all things, endureth all things. Charity never faileth.* And ask yourself, am I mature enough to be able to love my potential life partner like this? Because love is not something that you fall into nor is it something that you can you fall out of. Love is a choice that you consciously make. You can choose to love someone or you can choose to hate them, there is no in between. Love is not mere words, but rather is an action that cannot stop. We see Solomon talking of his bride in his Song of Songs 2:2 *As the lily among thorns, so is my love among the daughters.* Then in verse 4 we see *He brought me to the banqueting house, and his banner over me was love.* You can see here again that love is the banner, the bond. Love is the central focus, the key theme throughout the Scriptures from the creation in Genesis through the end of time as we know it as recorded in the book of the Revelation. God's love for us was demonstrated time and again, especially through sacrificing His only Son, Jesus Christ, now we must as followers of Christ show His love one to another.

Just as in the case of faith and our Christian walk, I wish to take you to Luke 14:28-30 and say that Jesus is our tower. Do you have the faith and the love to endure the Christian walk as well as a marriage, through the winds of adversity, trials, and temptations, in possible sickness, poverty, worst of times? Do you have the firm foundation upon which to build your eternity and til death do you part upon? Israel kept saying 'I do' then kept falling away, is that you? This is exactly what is happening in our marriages today as well as within our churches. Remember that as soon as you say I do in accepting Christ as your Lord and Savior, as well as saying I do to your life partner, the Lord, His angels and people around you are all witnesses and are all watching, and God said 'I hate liars and hypocrites!'

My wife and I were match-made. I flew several thousand miles to meet her, pray, and ask through an interpreter, her dad to stop arranging proposals for her, that I would like to have her **with** their blessings. This is God's way.

Hosea 2:20 tells us *I will even betroth thee unto me in faithfulness: and thou shalt know the Lord.* Betrothal, the couple, the man and the woman are as good as married in God's eyes. It's just not consummated yet, and shouldn't be until after marriage. Once the man has asked the woman to be his helpmate, his wife, his companion until death, the two commit themselves, they vow unto God, sanctifying themselves unto each other. This my dear friends, is a vow before God, it is legally binding in the heavenly court, so should not be entered into lightly, but prayerfully.

It is still not the time for hugging, kissing, touching, or removal of any of thy clothing, exposing any part of your bodies unto one another.

It is the time for continued growth of the relationship, continuing to get to know each other, and planning.

One is loved because one is loved; no reason is needed for loving, for love is of God. God gives you love, He gives you someone to love, and you should do this and accept this with all of thine heart.

Betrothal is biblically as binding as marriage, so be ever so careful before making that vow, that commitment! Be very prayerful and very careful. It's not just 'give me a kiss and a ring and let's see what happens.' Whoops, no ring, remember what we said about jewelry. This vow is very important to God. We cannot be betrothed to God and just walk away; Very serious consequences, and likewise between a man and a woman. Take a look at Matt 25:1-3, you must be ready before you enter into this vow.

As soon as you become betrothed you must surrender all, become selfless doing all that you can for thy partner, just as our God gave His all when He surrendered Himself to come to earth in the form of Jesus Christ and gave His all to us, wanting the best for each of us. He gave us His best that He had and surrendered even unto death so that we may be saved. Likewise, you must give up self, surrender your all, the best that you can give to God and thy partner. Marriages fail because of selfishness.

We see in Matthew Chapter 1, Mary was betrothed unto Joseph, not Joseph to Mary, though he is, but the wording is very specific, for a reason. You see, the woman has a choice to accept the man's call to her, just as God gives us a choice... a free choice, no pressure. I need to point out a few important points here. God chooses the humble, not proud; the obedient. In Matthew 1:18 it is translated espoused, and in verse 19, her husband. They were not yet married, but by Jewish law, by God's law, betrothal was and is just as binding. Because of the betrothal, Joseph had to take Mary with him to pay the taxes. In Ruth 1:16 *where thou goest, I shall go.* It is important to note also that even though betrothal is as binding as marriage, they weren't married. Mary and Joseph remained virgins! They traveled approximately sixty miles to Bethlehem, so obviously they spent several nights together, but separate! Hello...are you with me on this? There was no place for Joseph and Mary in the inn, more exciting details, and important points on this in my book on Christmas. They stayed in a cave of a rock, where the manger- the feeding trough for animals, was found, my friends, and used to lay our Savior, the Christ Child in. Joseph and Mary stayed in the cave together, alone and isolated, but... they remained virgins! Also, my dear sisters, did Mary ever complain to Joseph, her betrothed, of inferior lodging conditions? Here she was pregnant, about ready to give birth, uncomfortable, and yet, Joseph puts her up in a filthy cave... Then Jesus is born, without a midwife, natural birth my dear sisters, and in the filthy environment. Then Joseph laid the newborn baby, their firstborn child, into the feeding trough. The cave must have smelled from all the animals that used this cave, and was dirty. Mary never said, no way...find me something comfortable or I'm leaving, I'm out of here...and this is my firstborn, I want something special, something better for Him, no, she humbled herself, and she was patient...I feel the need to stress this important point further, but will explain the reason why it is so important in a bit. Turn with me now to the book of Numbers 31:15-18. You shall see that the woman caused Israel to sin, and then all but virgins were to be killed. Virginity is so special to God and to thy betrothed. Only the virgins were spared.

Betrothal among the Jews in biblical times took place nine to twelve months before marriage. The bride being in all respects bound as a wife, she could be freed only by death (God's law) or divorce (Mosaic law), under the same divorce laws as the married woman. During the espousal period of between nine to twelve months before the marriage **proper** took place, the woman who was betrothed or espoused was regarded as the man's wife and he as her husband, even though they had not sexually come together or made their marriage vows. Deuteronomy 22:23 (Sleeping with a betrothed/espoused damsel was regarded as sleeping with another man's wife). Matthew 1:18-21 (Mary was only betrothed/espoused to Joseph when she was found pregnant. They were not properly married and thus, according to Hebrew custom he could put away his espoused wife by giving her a writing of divorcement. Death (not divorce) was the penalty for adultery in Old Testament times. Leviticus 16:15 (A man committing adultery with another man's wife must be put to death). Leviticus 18:20 (Adultery defiles a man and makes him ritually unclean) Deuteronomy 22:22 (A man and a woman committing adultery: both must die).

Men, when you are out looking for a car, you check out more than just the exterior body styling. Are you with me? You check the inner works as well. The engine-the HEART of the vehicle is more important. The exterior is nothing without a good engine, the heart of the vehicle. You need to be as careful when selecting a wife. Don't go out looking for a husband or a wife, let God place that right person in your path at the correct time. People waste so much time and money running around, just pray! Let God place that correct person, His choice, into your life. God never makes mistakes. Theology should be the first thing that you check out, for you don't want to be yoked together with an unbeliever, even if the body style is beautiful! Friends, Miss World doesn't stay Miss World forever, she grows up...and sometimes grows out, but God and God alone is the one who will build and sustain the marriage. In 1st Samuel 16:7 we read *For the Lord seeth not as man seeth; for man looketh on the outward appearance, but the Lord looketh on the heart.* When you are in crisis, it should be your godly spouse who stands by and encourages and helps you through, they pray with and for you. And!!! DO NOT check out the plumbing until after the marriage! I assure you, God of all creation does not make mistakes, and if this is the person that He hath ordained for you, don't worry about the plumbing, leave that to God. AND NEVER trade your partner in for a newer model! No deposit, no return! Again, the reason for this shall be explained in full detail shortly. In retail they say try on the merchandise before buying, but in relationships, you should never try out, take the other for a test drive, you take the person and learn to love them-plain and simple. This brings us to marriage. Leviticus 21:7 tells us *They (priests) shall not take a wife that is a whore, or profane, neither shall they take a woman put away from her husband: for he is holy unto his God.* Verses 13-14 go on to tell us *and he shall take a wife in her virginity. A widow or a divorced woman, or profane, or a harlot, these shall he not take: but he shall take a virgin of his own people* (believers) *to wife.*

In Ireland, I've been told, that there is an expression that 'if a man kisses you, never, on no account, let him put his tongue in your mouth.' Wise advice which can and should be interpreted two ways, which I won't elaborate on here. Men, you should never place a woman in the position of temptation; and my dear sisters, you should never lead on or encourage a man, wait for the wedding night.

The person you love is rarely worthy (except for God) of the magnitude of your love, because no one is worthy of that, and perhaps no one deserves the burden of it either. Women, are you worthy of the love of your husband? Are we worthy of the love of our Husband in heaven? You'll be hurt, disappointed, they may break thy trust. You'll have good days and bad. You win, you lose. The dreams don't last forever, and life is never happily ever after, but if you roll up your sleeves and work hard at it all, you're growing up. I heard this one time and there is a lot of truth to it. I would add however that if you look to God and work daily at your relationship, you'll be blessed, regardless of the outcome, and if you follow God, regardless of the outcome of the marriage, you will be blessed. God allows us free choice in our lives, and sometimes people make the wrong choices and it can ruin a marriage, but as a Christian, keep looking to Him, always pray for your partner, leave the rest to God. Love can hurt, but it can also be rewarding, it is a gift from God. His love cost His Son His life! Praise God daily for the love that He places in your life, your partner. Marriage takes effort, so before entering into betrothal, be prepared for the work, it isn't for the lazy.

Before we move on, I need to bring you to 1st Corinthians 7:38 telling us *So then he that giveth her in marriage doeth well; but he that giveth her not in marriage doeth better.* The issue of marriage or remaining single is one which should be discussed earlier in a young man and ladies' life with her dad (and perhaps her mother present), read this verse in context when you get a chance. Because it is good for them to remain single to serve the Lord, but if they are unable (or unwilling) to do so, then it is her dad that shall decide and give her away, so this is a very serious matter that he must seriously pray through as well. In Luke 1:36 we see that Mary and Elizabeth were cousins, Elizabeth was old, so Mary was also perhaps much older than most people perceive. In 1:38 Mary had many cousins, but after the marriage to Joseph, there was no mention whatsoever of her family as she became one with Joseph her husband. You also didn't hear about his family because they created a new family.

The betrothal should be a time of transition of authority from the woman's dad to her betrothed. Initially, the man should approach her dad, and alone (the woman not present) discuss his intentions, and ask her dad about her if he has any questions, and her dad should answer honestly, and feel free to ask the man any questions that he may have. Then the man should ask for the woman to be brought into the room and propose to the woman in front of her parents, so that her parents may be the witnesses. After the proposal, I believe that the betrothed husband should contact his Pastor as quickly as possible and arrange for a betrothal ceremony which I believe should be initiated into the church.[1] Virginity should be confirmed both by the woman and her parents. At the proposal, the woman should be given a choice without any pressure from her parents or the man. Throughout scripture you see that the woman has no say if her family gives her, or the man takes her to wife. She only has some say in how she treats her husband, though is commanded to love and serve him. We have a say, our Father, Creator, Savior loves us so much and takes us, we do have a choice however whether or not we will accept Him into our lives and how we shall treat Him. It does take so much more energy however to hate and resist, than to surrender and love. Think about it. It doesn't matter how perfect or imperfect a person is, the question is are you the right one for each other, as God ordained you to be together...for better or worse, sickness or health, richer or poorer, no matter what trials come your way, do you have that kind of love, that conviction? Betrothal is a vow before God, and should be a time of celebration, and should be witnessed. From betrothal to marriage should be a special time of getting to know each other better and making plans for the future. He should begin providing for her though she remains at her parents' house. She may begin cooking and cleaning for him, but no touching, kissing; and there should be NO body exposure, and the couple should not be alone together, lest Satan tempt them. Any questions or problems during this time should be discussed amongst themselves, and if necessary, be taken to the Pastor for resolution. This is also the time to be consolidating bank accounts, etc., and women, it is time to quit thy jobs, and adapt to your new career, and new life as a wife. Since you are now one in God's eyes, it is also I believe appropriate that the woman's name should be included on her husband's passport instead of having her own, and to travel by her husband's side. Just as we need to come before the Lord for guidance and direction, as well as for protection, so should a woman before her husband or father. Voting is politics and should be left to the men, however on certain issues; a man may discuss issues and seek the input from his wife and/or daughters. She should surrender her driving license and vehicle as she should be tending to his home, not out running around. She should put in for name change on all of her documents. With all of this, it also men, increases thy responsibility for thy wife! The woman surrendering her driver's license, passport, etc. is a beautiful example of her willingness to surrender all and submit unto His and his authority. Again, an allegory of our relationship with Christ. It is a time of total surrender and sacrifice. As the woman surrenders her driving license, passport, her family name, etc. she transitions into **BECOMING ONE** with her husband. Likewise, the husband must be worthy just as God is worthy.

In one xmas movie, a flight attendant gave up her dream position in Rome to be with a man that she fell in love with. In another xmas movie, a woman was putting a man down for giving up a position in a San Francisco law firm to live on and operate a xmas tree farm, only to find love with him, and she subsequently gave up her job as a top wedding planner to be with him. I don't recall the names of these movies, but they are examples of selflessness and sacrifice for what and who you love. I use xmas here, you can see detailed reason in my book What about xmas.

Love is an action. You choose either to love or to hate another person. One of those you choose to love may very well be God's anointed angel-life partner for you. People move away because someone comes in from a different race in to their area, or even into the church. Do you love me or hate me because of my skin color? Do you love me or hate me because of where I was born? Do you love me or hate me because I come bringing you the truth of God's precious word? Love is an action my dear friends, not an emotion, it is something that you choose to do as none of us is worthy. It is putting the other person above yourself and happy not jealous or envious when they succeed, selfless rather than selfish. Any two people can have sexual intercourse, but is it love or lust? Are you engaging in such activity (inside or God forbid outside of marriage) to make yourself feel good or to make your partner feel good, pleasing self or thy partner? Think about it. The act of sex is not love. If you are making love you are engaging in any act of making your partner more important than yourself. Do you touch, caress... your partner because you want to or because it pleases them, makes them feel better, special, comfortable, safe... Is this hitting home? Is this a convicting message? I pray that this entire message will be convicting and bring each of us back to the path of righteousness, a life changing conviction.

This is a very serious period of time because refusing to surrender all and submit to the authority of thy husband at this stage (not sexually) is dangerous and leads to destruction just as when we refuse to surrender and submit unto our Husband-God! The Christian walk requires total surrender, sacrifice, submission unto our Bridegroom just as does the Christian marriage. But to you men, I say, God has more than proven Himself worthy and so must you prove your worthiness to the woman and her family.

The man must demonstrate that he has a vision for his life-career, family, etc.

Following the betrothal ceremony at church[1], there should be a banquet to celebrate with your church family and friends. This ceremony should be within a week or two of the proposal. Ezekiel 16:8 ...*behold, thy time was the time of love; and I spread my skirt over thee, and covered thy nakedness: yea, I swore unto thee, and entered into a covenant with thee, sayeth the Lord God, and thou becamest mine.*

In Ruth Chapter 3 verse 3 *Wash thyself therefore and anoint thee, and put thy raiment upon thee...* then in verse 9, we see the skirt again. This skirt is used as a pledge to marry, a sign of marriage. Scripture is not referring to an uncovering of herself, nor is she unclothed! Nakedness in Ezekiel 16:8 represents our sins. In Nahum again we see in 2:13 *Behold, I am against thee, saith the Lord of hosts; and I will discover thy skirts upon thy face, and I will shew the nations thy nakedness, and the kingdoms thy shame,* Nahum 3:5. Where this is a literal meaning but also as the skirts are symbolic of marriage, here the removal of the skirt could be symbolic of divorce. The other issue that must be addressed before the betrothal ceremony is setting the date for your marriage, which should be set and announced at the church betrothal ceremony.

Everything that either of you do once betrothed, is a direct reflection on both of you and your family. Be careful, be prayerful.

Now, allow me to go into another area that will raise many eyebrows, while adhering to God's precious word. Since you are betrothed and have been speaking to your Pastor about your betrothal and now marriage, one thing most are going to tell you is...you need to go and get a marriage certificate from the government office. I pose the question to you now, should you do this? You may be asking now, why would a Pastor ask such a question, but I believe that it is important to point out that it is wrong to get one and here I shall attempt to briefly explain a few points to consider on this matter.

First let me share with you the legal definition of License according to Black's Law Dictionary, the permission by competent authority to do an act which without such permission would be illegitimate In my computer dictionary, I found it defined as official permission to do something, either from a government or under a law or regulation. The point here is that why do we need the governments' permission and authority to complete an act ordained and authorized by God our Creator in Genesis 2:18-24? The simple answer is that we don't need the government's approval or license to do what God ordained, nor should we as Christians participate in such activities. Now you may ask what harm is there in doing so. First let me say that you must understand that the authority to license implies the power to prohibit, to prevent a man and a woman to do the very thing that God ordained for us to do. A license by definition confers a right to do something or not. The State cannot grant the right to marry for it is a God-given right, from the beginning of creation, and nothing has changed in God's eyes.

Secondly, with a marriage license, you grant the government complete jurisdiction over your marriage. When you obtain a marriage license, your marriage belongs to the State. Therefore, they have jurisdiction over your marriage including the fruit of your marriage. What is the fruit of your marriage? Your children and every piece of property you own. There is plenty of case law in American law which proves this to be true.

In 1993, parents were upset with one of the States when a test was being administered to their children in the government schools which was very invasive into the privacy of their families. When some of the parents complained, they were shocked by the school leaders who informed them that their children were required to take the test by law and that they would have to take the test because the school had jurisdiction over their children. When these parents asked the leaders just exactly what gave them jurisdiction over their children as well as their privacy, the leaders answered, your marriage license and their birth certificates. There was another situation whereby the school was doing female exams without parental consent for the same reasons. Who knows what else the government is doing without us knowing? This is another great reason for Christians to homeschool their children, and to keep the FREEDOM to educate your own children alive, as the government is trying to remove our rights, and are doing so little by little. Legally, your governmental marriage license has far-reaching implications into your rights and your privacy.

The marriage license removes our God-given, and God-ordained parental authority. In reading God's word, you will see that God intended for parents to train up their children in the ways of the Lord, not for the pagan governments to do so. God also ordained our precious children to have their father's blessings regarding whom they married. We see in Deuteronomy 22:16; Exodus 22:17, as well as in 1st Corinthians 7:38 that daughters were to be given away in marriage by their fathers. We have retained a portion of this instruction in some of our countries today when the bride's father takes his daughter to the front of the altar and the pastor asks, "Who gives this woman to be married to this man?" Now here it is also important to see that it is a requirement for the girl to seek her father's permission to marry, something that has long gone by the wayside and needs to return into the Christian life today. I recall that when I flew to Malaysia, I respectfully asked her dad to allow me to marry his daughter and then sought his blessings, and I truly believe that this is the way that it should be, the way that God ordained.

By purchasing a marriage license, the government is telling you that, you no longer need your parents' permission, you need our permission. If parents are opposed to their child's marrying a certain person and refuse to give their permission, the child can avoid the parents' authority or even their knowledge, by obtaining the governments permission to marry. This is an invasion and removal of God-given parental authority by the government.

When you obtain a marriage license, you are subjecting yourself to an immoral and unbiblical law, of sinful leaders, rather than unto God, our Creator. You become subject to the family court rather than unto the Court of God. Under these immoral laws, you can divorce for any reason or for no reason at all, and who do these civil courts side with? As you will see in my case as well as most, they side with the guilty, the wicked, the ungodly, because they are ungodly! They side with the side that is being rebellious and disobedient to God, and strongly criticizes or rebukes the Christians behavior, see 1st Corinthians 6:7,9. Especially amazing are judges calling themselves Christian and granting divorces!

Actually, when you say your marriage vows you enter into a binding legal contract, to which there are three parties, you, your husband or wife, and the government. This dear friend is not the way that God ordained. Yes, He ordained the binding, legal contract, but it was to be between you, your husband or wife, and Him (trinity)! My dear brothers and sisters, bring Christ, our Living and loving God back into your lives, and that of your marriages and families.

As a Pastor, I have no desire to perform a marriage which would place people under this ungodly body of laws. In doing so I also would have to sign the marriage license, and send it back to the Government, making me an agent for this ungodly issue. Given the governments demand to act as a god and take over the family regarding marriage, and given its unbiblical, immoral laws to govern marriage, (homosexual marriages, birth control in schools, abortion...), It would to seem hypocritical for a Pastor to do so.

With the government legalizing same sex marriages, a Christian must ask, if a woman and a woman marry with a government issued marriage license, and a man and woman marry without a government issued marriage license–who's really married?

So how do you prove that a marriage took place if you have no license? In order to determine whether a marriage existed or not, you need to have at least two witnesses. This is why you have a best man and a maid of honor. They should sign the marriage certificate in your family Bible, and guest book should be kept of your wedding day.

So, this is just one more example of how we have strayed and need to be brought back to repentance and revival. Think about it.

In the book of Numbers, chapter 30, we see the law for vows. Take a look at verses 2, 6-7, and 15. You must note that a man is accountable for his vows (including marriage vows until death!) and that a woman in the presence of her husband (betrothed is husband and wife) is bound in marriage until death! Furthermore, in verse 15, the woman vowed in the presence of her husband to love until death, so if a husband leaves, he has violated the law of God and the results are seen in verse 15. Betrothal and marriage are serious business, a vow to cherish...and uphold...no matter what! So, before making this commitment, pray through it, and be certain that it is God's will for you to marry, and be certain that if so, that this person is the person to which God hath ordained to be your life partner, then: Women- 1st John 2:15 and James 4:4. You must trust God, and you must trust your God ordained partner for you. Whatever he says, you do; wherever he goes, you go without complaint. You must surrender ALL unto him, your lord, this includes your heart, soul, mind, respect, devotion, obedience, your possessions, your money, your all. This is a sacrifice which true believers must make to our Bridegroom and one in which all of you my dear sisters must make to thy husbands. Being a true Christian requires complete and total sacrifice and surrender, just as Christ Himself surrendered His all and sacrificed Himself upon that old rugged cross while we were yet sinners. This takes real faith (Hebrews 11:1) in your Christian walk as well as your earthly walk and your relationship. The Christian walk is very lonely because you are walking on a path not well traveled. And marriage requires often times a change of friends because some of the old friends can be destructive to the marital relationship. You are to try to bear him children (*be ye fruitful and multiply*) just as we are to bear fruits bringing more of God's children unto Him.

And men, this is not one sided!!! 1st John 2:15 and James 4:4 also applies to you. You have been given an awesome responsibility and you'd better be certain that you are up to it before entering into betrothal so that you don't let your wife or God down. You must love thy wife (and children) as Christ loves His church. This too requires sacrifice and surrender. Your life is no longer work, parties, beer with the boys, football games... it is now a total devotion to God and thy family. We are told in 1st Corinthians 13:11 *When I was a child, I spake as a child, I understood as a child, I thought as a child: but when I became a man, I put away childish things.* You are to be the lord and savior of your family, a pillar in the family, church, and the community. You have been given an awesome responsibility, doing whatever is necessary to provide for her needs, protect and defend her, comfort her...Isaiah 53:4a, and just as Christ intercedes for us, so must we as men intercede for our wife and children, just as Job did.

From the very beginning of courtship or dating, the man should assume the office of headship of the family so that she can follow him. If he doesn't then she assumes that position and this is outside of God's plan. The man needs to be the head and the woman must follow him. He must be the prayer leader, he must be the worship leader, he must lead daily Bible study; he must be the leader in his family. He must set family time where you all shut off your phones, the TV, the radio, Everything and lead worship and then time to talk and plan for their future. He must exude confidence in his role as leader so that the woman can feel comfortable in following him.

In Matthew 12:39, we see that the nation was called adulterous by Jesus because they were unfaithful in its vows to the Lord and adulteresses will not be accepted into heaven, 1st Corinthians 6:9.

I believe that the true church must once again take an active role in preparing young people for dating and marriage, and not leave it up to society to prepare them, look at where that has taken us. Ideally the parents should be doing this, but unfortunately, they have their own problems, and neither is home to train up their precious children. The churches need to be preparing Christian young men and women for dating and marriage, in order to keep them from straying from the path of righteousness.

One final and very important note here, Salvation is not for cowards for we need to deny self- selfless, and we must take up the cross and follow Him. Cowards can do neither of these. John 15:20, Revelation 2:10, 21:8. A coward is unable to withstand the trials of marriage or the Christian walk and will eventually walk away. Acts 8:30, and 1st Corinthians 14:20. If you are a coward, be fair to the other and be honest about it before entering into a covenant with God and them, also pray for God to help you to overcome the cowardiceness.

When we commit ourselves to another person, such as in becoming betrothed or bringing forth children, there must be a willing surrender of our freedom because these choices affect our lives and our future, and once the choice is made, it cannot be changed, so careful and prayerful choices, decision must be made before making that choice. Don't just think about today, because these choices are eternal. And remember that you cannot expect the best if you don't give your best.

There is something very special, wonderful and intimate about knowing one another's secrets in marriage and holding those in ABSOLUTE trust and confidence. They say don't kiss and tell, I say don't hear secrets and tell. This takes faith and genuine love.

People tell you to choose your friends carefully, wisely; the same is true even more so when choosing your life partner. Friends come and go, but your marriage covenant is until death do you part. Adam had it easy because God designed the perfect woman for him, and gave her to him. Today we have so many to choose from, but the same God that gave Eve unto Adam is the same God that can and will give you the perfect woman, if you will just pray and wait on Him. The women today are not perfect but then, neither was Eve, was she, and neither are you.

In Genesis 29:17-18 we must note that love is more than skin deep. He loved the beauty which later betrayed him

While I was going through and doing the appendix, the Holy Spirit gave me this thought, so I'm inserting it in here. You know, the woman normally passes a single cell every month, called an ovary. The man passes millions of cells each time that he ejaculates, but only one cell, if God so ordains, will meet the woman's single cell. My dear brothers and sisters, when the female cell and the male cell meet by God's ordaining, the two **BECOME ONE** and cannot be separated, no matter how hard man may try, it is impossible! The same is with marriage. If God so ordains, the male and the female come together and **BECOME ONE**. I also want you to see that the woman's cell is just passing, it is the male cell that must go looking for her. Also, of note, only one male cell is ever allowed into the female cell. These last two points are significant as well in the relationship between a man and a woman.

[1] The betrothal ceremony should be announced as the wedding ceremonies are today. The ceremony should be as the wedding ceremonies today EXCEPT for the you may now kiss the bride!

The wedding ceremony should just be brief at a formal dinner for family, friends and pastor. The pastor should pray for them then You may now kiss your bride The bride should serve her husband, then the husband should feed his bride the first bite in a reverential manner where the dad then completely relinquishes all parental rights of his daughter over to her husband in ceremonial fashion at the dinner. Then the groom should publicly thank her parents for their daughter, and thank all the guests present for celebrating with them. After the dinner, the bride and groom go and consummate the marriage and honeymoon.

PERSONAL NOTES

_____

_____

_____

_____

_____

_____

_____

_____

_____

_____

_____

_____

_____

_____

_____

_____

_____

_____

PERSONAL NOTES

Ephesians 5:23 *For the husband is the head of the wife, even as Christ is head over the church.*

CHAPTER 5

The Sacred Marriage

This message began with a summary of the roles of men, women, and children, along with the spiritual parallel, and then we began putting it all together to see how it all works together in God's plan beginning with the betrothal. Now we shall continue. You are now betrothed, and a marriage date was set and announced. That marriage is a parallel, marriage and family is an allegory of our relationship with God our Father, in the Family of God.

We said that it is okay to remain single and Paul supports this in 1ˢᵗ Corinthians 7:8-9 when he says *I say therefore to the unmarried and widows, it is good for them if they abide even as I. But if they cannot contain, let them marry: for it is better to marry than to burn.* But again, I say, you must choose your friends very carefully. A friend is someone who accepts you as you are and doesn't force you to change. You must choose your spouse even more carefully. Friends come and go, but marriage is until death do you part. Adam was so blessed in that God made the PERFECT woman for him, and he didn't have to choose between different models. The rest of us have a more difficult time because there are so many to choose from, and none is perfect. Perfection here isn't about being without flaw, it is rather about being exactly what the other person wants, needs, and desires, without having to try. Choosing a lifetime partner is the second most important decision in one's life (the first is accepting Jesus Christ into your life), so choose your partner carefully and prayerfully. Ideally if you think that you have found the right one, take her to your pastor and allow him to talk to the two of you and give you guidance, which hopefully will come from the Holy Spirit.

We spoke of dating and betrothal and their spiritual parallels. Now my dear brothers and sisters, it is time to get to the heart of the matter, so that your marriage may be strengthened. Those marriages which are in trouble, that this special message may place your marriage back on the solid foundation and rescue it, that thy marriage may be saved. Those who are separated or divorced, I pray for restoration, for this is God's will. Those who are contemplating marriage or are betrothed already, that you shall enter into a Holy matrimony until death do you part. Amen.

Mal. 2:11-12, *Judah hath dealt treacherously, and an abomination is committed in Israel and in Jerusalem; for Judah hath profaned the holiness of the LORD which he loved, and hath married the daughter of a strange god. The LORD will cut off the man that doeth this, the master and the scholar, out of the tabernacles of Jacob, and him that offereth an offering unto the LORD of hosts.*

Marriage takes effort (work), it is not for lazy people, Hebrews 6:12,15.

There are many opinions as to what is a proper marriage. There are constantly changing legal and cultural definitions that often distort the clear picture which God gave us in the Bible. Since God Himself is the author of marriage, only His opinion matters.

People today say marriage is hopeless. If you go along with the ways of the world, this statement is true. If people will read and understand God's word, God's plan, it is God's will as be written in the Word of God, His purpose and plan for marriage, and depart from the ways of the world, all will be well. If you are separated, divorced, or having troubles in thy marriage, return unto thy marriage partner and to God, for

God's sake as well as for thine own sake. Then and only then can the marriage, family, church, and society all benefit, and flourish, Amen. You see how important you are? Why are there sixty-seven verses on the marriage of Isaac you may ask? It is a valuable lesson on hearing God's word, God's voice, obedience, and God's grace and provision, faith.

Jesus told us in Matthew 5:17 *Think not that I am come to destroy the law, or the prophets: I am not come to destroy, but to fulfill.* Jesus didn't come to abolish the Ten Commandments but knowing that we are sinners, came to teach us and show us the way unto salvation, and to justify the truly spiritual believer. The New Covenant, the interesting thing is that there was absolutely no change in the marriage covenant with the New Covenant, in fact, Jesus Christ confirmed and explained how important the marriage covenant is to Him! The marriage covenant was never changed by God because from the beginning, it was designed by our Creator as a physical representation of our salvation and our position in the family of God.

God made marriage-earthly and heavenly, so beautiful. The image of God in Genesis 1:26-28, is literal, but also shows the relationship as in the three Persons being One in the Trinity. From the very beginning men and women were not created equal; they were created differently, for different purposes. Adam was created from the dust, Eve from Adam, both with different functions and purposes. They had different appearances.

Creation dictates the aggressive nature of the male, the passive yet thoughtful nature of the female. The Shulamite speaks in the Song of Songs 1:2, *Let him kiss me with the kisses of his mouth.* She anxiously awaits her aggressor with a permissive spirit. Jacob approached the well, rolled the stone away, and kissed Rachel. Consent must be won. The man must be gentle, strong, romantic, and practical, but... God aggressively guards' man's right to choose the bride, and the woman's right of consent.

It must be stated here that to leave father and mother, and to obey the command to honor thy father and thy mother, implies that parental blessing will be sought by the pair. Nevertheless, should the pair make a choice/consent, which does not receive parental blessings the union is still defended by the Creator who aggressively protects free choice and consent.

It is so important to maintain virginity until marriage, we'll discuss this in more detail in the next chapter, but important for us to see now, in the context of marriage is found in Deuteronomy Chapter 22 beginning at verse 13, that if a man and a woman marry and he comes into her to find that she is not a virgin, that he could take her before the church and expose this, a shame and humiliation for her and for her family, and he could annul the marriage. Should we return to this practice today? Perhaps; If I were to ask a group today how many are virgins, nobody would raise up their hands, but decades and centuries ago, people would have been proud and honored of being a virgin (if unmarried) as it was the expectation and the norm, just as it SHOULD be today. We need to return to God's value system contained within His precious word to us.

In 1st Corinthians 7:28 *if you marry you shalt have troubles in the flesh: but I spare you.* Why this profound statement? Is God teaching against the same marriage that He created and ordained in Genesis 2:22-24? Certainly not, for He saw that all He created was good!

No, He is allegorically speaking here that when you marry or join into sin, it brings trouble, women represent the sinfulness of mankind; but He spares His children from the troubles, look at Proverbs 1:10-15. This is confirmed in verse 33-35. The first wife is the woman ordained for thee. Subsequent marriages and their offspring don't receive the blessings. Numbers chapter 2, one must look carefully here to understand that when it was time to march, the Levites carried the tabernacle. Levi was the son of Leah, the first wife. Rachel's son was to the west (left) and front of the tabernacle. In other words, Rachel's (second wife) sons were to protect and defend the tabernacle. They in essence served their brother of the first marriage. Who bore Judah, in the lineage of Christ? Leah, the first wife did.

In the prophet Hosea's time, the people were so married to the world, the lusts and entertainment, that they forgot God and were giving God's gifts, the gifts given to them by God, to the idols, false gods. Dear friends, what are you doing with the gifts that God has given unto you, including thy spouse, children, money, possessions...? Are you living for God truly, or the world?

A beautiful show of God's love and protection is shown in Ruth 3:9. The kinsman redeemer spread his skirt over Ruth as a pledge of marriage, just as God in Ezekiel 16:8; *and I spread my skirt over thee, and covered thy nakedness: yea, I swore unto thee, and entered into a covenant with thee, sayeth the Lord God, and thou becamest mine.* This is also reflected in Psalms 36:7, 57:1, 91:4, and 63:7.

Just as God covers us with His love with the blood of Christ, covering our sins in His mercy and grace, so should men cover their wives with their love, mercy, and grace, protection and guidance, as God covers us with.

Here is where we shall start going into more detail, explain, and focus more upon the spiritual aspects, God's views, God's purpose and plan.

Marriage is one of the first gifts from God. It was created for us by our Creator; no parent chooses to have a permanently dependent child, do they? Any good parent teaches their children to walk, talk, feed themselves, clean themselves, to think for themselves... to bring them to a state of independence. You see God creates us perfect, but we are born into sin. The Bible teaches a parent to train up a child in the way he should go... but love and marriage is just the opposite. The man and the woman both have complete freedom, just as sinners in the world have. Yet just as we give up or surrender our sinful natures unto Christ at the foot of the cross, so must the man and the woman give up complete freedom, and surrender all, including that freedom, in order to become one, dependent upon God and each other. We must submit to one another, to sacrifice, the Bible teaches, and this is never easy. You cannot be unified, become one, and be independent! Did you catch this? You cannot be one with God and do your own thing; you cannot marry and do your own thing. We must become one with each other, and forsake the world. When you add zinc into a cup of hydrochloric acid and stir, what happens? In any healthy marriage, the submission must be by choice, voluntary, just as accepting the free gift of salvation through Jesus Christ into thy life is a free choice, never forced.

If we look back to the book of the Song of Songs 8:7, Solomon shows us that true love can never be bought or sold-prostitutes or women, who marry for money, never find love.

Again, we must be careful what we vow, for a vow is binding, it **must** be kept, as God is the witness, and He will **not** forget the vow. Hannah in 1st Samuel 1 made a vow to the Lord. She gave Samuel, her first born son, to the Lord in keeping her vows. How difficult this must have been. Here a barren woman makes a vow, I will if you will. She gets pregnant and delivers a precious, beautiful, perfect firstborn son. Then because of a vow, she must fulfill and give up her son, her only son, unto the Lord. Hannah didn't say 'well, I was just kidding', or 'I didn't really mean it.' She never said 'well, the next one I'll give, this is my firstborn and he is so special'... No, she made a vow and the vow she kept without any hesitation, matter of fact, she nursed the child to strengthen him for the Lord and His service. Hannah's husband supported her in keeping her vow. She loved and cared for and feared her Father God. God loved Hannah and blessed her for honoring her vow. Again, in Judges 11, he made a rash vow and later became frustrated and bitter because of the vow that he made, and thus had to sacrifice his daughter. Note here, the sincere heart, vow-a son, the rash vow-daughter. Marriage is also a vow recorded in heaven, that so many break apart. We shall first discuss marriage, then later divorce, the consequences of breaking this precious vow.

In Luke 1:38, Handmaid or female slave- Mary referred to herself in this way as a show of humility and respect for Joseph, her betrothed. We are bound likewise to Christ and to serve Him, so technically, a woman is bound, or enslaved to her lord, and is never to leave him. If you wish to go so far, just look at the natural position that a person uses to urinate. A man stands upright, yet women squat. I say this so that you may see just how magnificent the Creator is, and the perfection of His creation. God is upright righteous, whereas the sinner needs to be on their knees before Him. Squatting or kneeling is a sign of humility, humbling yourself before the other. So... you can see that God designed EVERYTHING to reflect our relationship with Him and each other.

If we develop a relationship with God apart from our life situation or circumstances, in the good times and the bad, we are better able to hang on when the trials, the disappointments and injustices in our lives strike us and engulf us like a dark cloud. Jesus is the calm in any storm. Jesus is our light in the times of darkness, so hold on to Him, and hold on to one another. We can hang on to and trust God in all things and not walk away. My dear friends, the same is true in marriage, we must hold on to the one we love, regardless of what is going on around you, whatever is happening to you.

So, marriage is the emotional, physical, and spiritual joining of one man and one woman to form a new single unit that is indissoluble and inseparable according to God's law.

Trust is so very important in any relationship, and especially within the marriage. You are to trust God completely (or do you?) regardless of what happens. I was held hostage as a prisoner for Christ in a Kenya prison, but did I lose trust or faith in Him? No, so why can't we believe in our marriage partners that He hath blessed us with? I saw a film where this couple received a photo in the mail of him in bed with another woman. He told his wife I didn't do it. The marriage broke down, violence erupted (by his wife who finally walked out) they say that a picture is worth a thousand words, but I wish to tell you that nine hundred ninety and nine of those words aren't necessarily true! We must trust God though we can't see Him. I'm a pilot and I trust that the air which I can't see is there and will hold me up. If we can trust things that we cannot see, how much more should we be able to trust those things which we can see? We must build trust and faith in God, as well as in our marriage partner. If you don't have faith and trust, then you have nothing, because love is based on these. Sometimes this trust may be a day by day or even during trials and tribulations, minute by minute, but we must endure unto the end!

If you are spending your time looking for troubles or reasons not to trust, you are wasting your (God's) time, anything can look like something which you are seeking to find. I must also say here that nobody can make someone else believe and trust them, trust is something that each must find within themselves.

Living together or common law marriage is not the way that God ordained; He wants the public statement, the sacred vows, and the covenant relationship to be present.

In the Code of Eshunna of 1925 B.C. we see that the woman who cohabits without a formal marriage contract is considered a prostitute, however a formal contract will qualify her to be a housewife. Again, here we see adultery considered as a capital crime, punishable by death.

In John 8:1-11 the scribes and Pharisees claimed that the woman that they had arrested was taken in adultery. If this was true, where was her male counterpart, the adulterer? They failed to meet the criteria of the law, and consequently Jesus threw the case out. First of all, they wanted to stone the woman without a trial. They did not present the two required witnesses. But the real problem with their story was that the adulterer was missing. The case against the woman could not be proven without the male counterpart. Of interest is the fact that in this passage, it was the law that both parties involved in the adultery were to be killed. Only she was there indicating that the folks there may have been hiding the man or perhaps one of them was guilty, or perhaps there was no adultery (false accusations) to test Jesus, but that is one reason that she wasn't stoned. Also, Christ said he who is without sin... He knew that it was a sin to enforce death to only the one party involved. He also would have been breaking the law by accusing her as he was not an eyewitness to the sin.

The elements of adultery or even the suspicion of adultery have the gravest consequences for the man. A woman, however, never has this total fear. She knows the man, or possible men that impregnated her. The mystery of iniquity is that a woman could conceive a child by adultery and her husband probably would never know.

The former vice-president Daniel Quale, stated that a single parent mother, bearing children out of wed-lock, should not receive the honor of a true family, and this is consistent with scripture.

We see in Genesis 38, Tamar played the harlot, deceiving Judah, and was found with his child. In Israel the penalty for Tamar, had she actually played the harlot, would have been to be burned to death. However, since Judah was her father-in-law, and she was only playing the harlot so as to receive justice, Judah was obliged to confess in verse 26, *And Judah acknowledged them, and said, She hath been more righteous than I; because that I gave her not to Shelah my son. And he knew her again no more.* Although it is reported that Judah knew her again no more, it does appear that along with her pardon Tamar was supported by Judah for she was given a place in the genealogy of Jesus, as we see in Matthew 1:3 where she appears as a wife of Judah. She was considered by God to be his wife because he came in to her!

What others are saying is irrelevant, even when the dark cloud is settling down between you, hold on tight and wait for the cloud to pass, just as it did Job in his time of crisis. If my wife had of held on, she and my children would have been blessed, and been a part of a growing ministry, not to mention the blessings from keeping one's vows. They would have seen firsthand God's miracles in our relationship and through the ministry. Talk with each other, always keep the line of communication open, and pray without ceasing. Friends, are you listening, are you hearing what the Holy Spirit is saying here? Open and honest communication, consistent communication is critical in your relationship with God and to each other in marriage.

The question of dowry has come upon me on several occasions, and as always, I prayed for answers. As of this time, He has not seen the necessity of revealing the answers to this question. However, I wish to provide some different angles on this subject briefly. In the U.S.A. this isn't even an issue, but in all other countries I have lived, it is.

If you will look at Exodus 21:7 and 8, you will read *And if a man sell his daughter… If she please not her master, who hath betrothed her to himself…* You see, selling (paying dowry) and betrothed to himself showing ownership just as we belong to God, but God gives us a choice, and the woman should have a choice as well. When you pay for something, it becomes your property. Is a wife or husband property?

Although marriage by purchase is not God's will (Human trafficking), it nevertheless played and plays a part in the customs of marriage from antiquity. Man assumed that a wife was a mere possession, and he had the right to buy as many as he could afford. If he had enough money, he could afford a harem, and since the king was the wealthiest individual in the kingdom it was only fitting that he had the most wives. Harems were the possession of the ancient kings. The Lord God set the rules for Israel's king, *Neither shall he multiply wives to himself that his heart turns not away: neither shall he greatly multiply to himself silver and gold,* Deuteronomy 17:17. Nevertheless we know David had eight wives named, and when he took up residence in Jerusalem, we are told that he took more wives and concubines. Solomon of course had seven hundred wives and three hundred concubines. But God commanded the king not to multiply wives. The concept of ownership spilled over to other members of the family as well, for even in the Mosaic Law we find legislation which regulated the sale of a daughter, Ex. 21:7-11. I can honestly tell you that I have been offered $15m to marry a woman and another $8B, and millions for others as well as millions and billions to impregnate women by their parents. Another offered me $5B if I would get their daughter pregnant! Oh, the shame! Of course, I declined all offers! I could have used the money to further the ministry but right is right and wrong is wrong!

We see that not only did Isaac love the woman of his father's choosing, but he also expected his father to acquire him a wife, and Abraham did just that. The price of Rebecca was paid in jewels of gold, jewels of silver, and garments. What was the meaning of these gifts? On the one hand they could have been a purchase price and on the other hand they could have been compensatory to a family who was losing a daughter. It should be pointed out that oriental women feel sorry for the brides of America and the west because they are given away for nothing. They take pride in their price, believing that the higher the price the greater their self-worth. It was also unlikely that the man who invested good money in his bride would divorce her for nothing. However, some cultures sell the daughter, pay the man a dowry.

In Genesis 31:16 the girls said, *For he hath sold us.* When you pay for a woman or a man, what is it called? Prostitution! And when you pay for a woman or a man to marry, is it really any different? In Asia, the girls' family must pay the man (a dowry) to marry their daughter. Isn't that selling or human trafficking? Because of this fact, and the poverty so abundant there, females are frequently aborted or killed after birth, because they don't have the money to pay dowry to marry her off. The girls are a financial burden on the family, thus infanticide. A precious life lost because of sales. I also lived in a country where baby girls not even walking yet, were sold into prostitution just for money. Babies!!! When I married my wife from Malaysia, an Indian girl, her dad asked how much I wanted, fearing that I was an American so would want a lot more than he could afford. So, what was my response? I told him politely, that all I wanted was...his daughter and...their blessings and that I didn't believe in buying or selling women or people in general. Friends, God doesn't pay us to come unto Him, and we don't pay Him for the relationship. It is a free gift, amen? In Africa, the man pays the girls family the dowry with goats, cows, etc. for the girl. How many goats is a woman worth??? I met several depressed young people who were so much in love and wished to marry, but were prohibited from marrying because the man simply could not afford the goats, cows, chickens, whatever. God tells us in the scriptures that He desires our love and obedience more than sacrifice. Isn't our love and commitment to one another enough? It's enough for God; it should be for us also. Praise God that we don't have to pay a dowry in order to be with Him! And remember, who provides for us? God is our provider. Love is more precious

than riches. Look at Genesis 34:11-12, where a dowry was used
by Satan to buy the believer and in the New Testament Christ
was offered the world...but He refused it. I am reminded of a
great movie (musical) called 'Fiddler on the Roof, if you hav-
en't seen it, it's worth seeing. It is a story of an old traditional
father of a young lady, who believes in following the traditions.
His daughter is in love with a man he doesn't like because he
doesn't have much money, so he tries to match her to an elderly
butcher with money. The story is well done, clean and enter-
taining, and with a good message. I need to bring thy attention to the book of Ruth 4:10 Where Boaz said *moreover Ruth
the Moabitess, the wife of Mahlon, have I purchased to be
my wife...* Here you must note that no money changed hands,
he is merely saying that he acquired her legally in front of the
witnesses. In many countries today who use wedding rings, I
see this as a form of a dowry as well in that a piece of metal
containing a sliver of a rock can impress so many and is used
as a status symbol more than anything else today.

Here we are discussing marriage, but allow me to ask you
two quick questions. First, what is marriage? Sounds simple,
but... Marriage is defined as a 'legal relationship between a
man and a woman,' period, end of story. Not between two men
or two women, not between one man and two or more wives...
We as believers, children but sinners, women, the bride of
Christ- men. This leaves out any possibility for homosexuality
or polygamy, more on these shortly.

The second question is why marriage? Is it for sex? No...!
People frequently have sex without being married, though it
is wrong. Marriage is a parallel of the Christian walk and our
relationship with Jesus Christ and God our Father.

I believe that it is noteworthy that the first wedding was
in the Garden of Eden, the first miracle of Christ was at the
wedding of Cana. Jesus was at both. He united Adam and Eve;
He turned the ninety to around one hundred and twenty-five
gallons of water into the finest wine, and that is a lot of wine!

The joy and celebration of a wedding should remind us of
the rejoicing and celebration in heaven whenever one is saved,
and who will be present at the marriage supper when God will

bring His bride, the truly spiritual believers, to heaven with Him in the final days. Isaiah 62:5 *For as a young man marrieth a virgin, so shall thy sons marry thee and as the bridegroom rejoiceth over the bride so shall thy God rejoice over thee.* I would also invite you to take a quick look at Revelation 19:6-9.

So...You've made all of the preparations during your period of betrothal, and the joyful day arrives.

Men, the Bible teaches that before the high priest came into the temple, he had to sanctify himself, and surrender all. Ezekiel 44:21 says that *neither shall my priest drink wine, when they enter the inner court.* I have heard that there was so much fear at the entering into the holy of holies, that they tied a rope around their ankle so that they could be pulled out by the congregation, should they die in there! Men should have a reverent fear, respect, love, and honor for God and for his wife.

Before a woman comes to a man, she must surrender all like all to Jesus I surrender... She must surrender all to and for her lord, her husband. I need to make one thing perfectly clear. I am in no way putting men on a pedestal, men and women are sinners alike, but God hath designed marriage as an allegory, a parallel as I said earlier. Men represent God and righteousness, which he needs to live up to as much as humanly possible. Women represent all of mankind, the sinners. So, just as we must before coming before God, before He comes into us, we must sanctify ourselves and surrender all, just as women must do for her husband. Deuteronomy 13:4 says, *Ye shall walk after the Lord your God, and fear Him, and keep His commandments, and obey His voice, and ye shall serve Him, and cleave unto Him.* Are you listening?

THE CEREMONY

To begin this section, I must say that the ceremony should not be the big deal that people make of it these days. Most women get married in outrageously expensive white dresses that they will never wear again. They wear white supposedly as a sign of purity, virginity (although that was not its origin), but honestly, how many women get married as virgins (pure) today? Also, the ceremony as discussed earlier should be at the time of the betrothal as that is the time that the lifelong covenant begins. Furthermore, if you look over and over again, there was no wedding ceremonies in scripture, for example just look at Genesis 29:21 and 24:67, where you will see there was just a dinner.

The details of the wedding custom are not significant and it varies from culture to culture. I do wish for you to note that in a wedding ceremony, the woman comes to the man, not the man to the woman, for again the marriage is symbolic of us the sinner, coming unto our Lord our Bridegroom; the historical event is significant, I refer you here to Genesis 2:22. The verbal and written contract is complete in the public testimony-the ceremony.

It is also significant that the bride's dad escorts her down the aisle and there gives her away to the groom (even though he already did that when he accepted the proposal or betrothal). This is to be a finality of his/her ties and responsibilities, and his relinquishing all responsibility over to her husband. Please note that it is always the man (dad) that is to give away his daughter in marriage, not the mother. If she has no dad, then who can give her away properly?

The ceremony is usually short, with the usual formalities... the vows to love, honor, cherish, respect, and in the woman's case-obey, in <u>sickness</u> and in health, for richer or <u>poorer</u>, in good times and <u>bad (for better or worse)</u> ...life has its ups and downs, the down periods are no reason to split apart, in fact, the vows conclude with...until death...until what? ...until death do us part! Until death dear brothers and sisters, until death!!! Nothing but death is to separate you! This is a vow you make or made before the Almighty Witness, our Father God! And further my dearest brothers and sisters, nothing but death is to separate you! Nothing and nobody! What therefore God, who? God hath joined together, let no man (or woman) put asunder (separate). You may ask where is that found in the Bible? The answer is in Matthew 19:6. This of course is beautifully illustrated in Ruth 1:16-17, in which Ruth tells Naomi, *Entreat me not to leave thee, or to return from following after thee: for whither thou goest, I will go, and where thou lodgest, I will lodge, thy people shall be my people and thy God my God. Where thou diest, I will die, and there be buried, the Lord do so to me and more also* (indicating the worst possible death if she violated this vow), *if ought but death part thee and me.* I already discussed briefly the cremation ceremony in Asia where the woman walks into the fire to be by her husband's side when he dies and is cremated, and again I do not advocate this and do not believe that this is God's will in any way! However, the point I wish for you to get here is until death we should honor our vows!

Furthermore, it has been said that the creation of woman removed a physical part of man, the loss of which drives man to be rejoined with his missing being.

The Hindi has seven steps of marriage, a beautiful illustration, and a part of this celebration is beautifully portrayed in the movie 'Gandhi'.

I heard a woman say to her new husband at the marriage banquet, You should never steal, lie, or cheat. But if you must steal, steal away my sorrows. If you must lie, lie with me all the nights of my life. And if you must cheat, then please cheat death and stay with me. At first, I laughed to myself, but as I thought about this statement, I realized how much love and truth is contained therein this plea.

One thing that I do need to point out here though about the ceremony is the fact that the wedding vows which are recited routinely are not even biblical. When a pastor asks a woman 'do you take... to be your lawfully wedded husband in sickness and in health...' is not biblical. Where in Scripture do you see the woman taking the husband, or even having the choice? You don't, so why is she asked this during these ceremonies? Better would be to ask her if she is willing to accept her roles and responsibilities and become one with ... (the husband's name). But in scripture the man chose the woman or his parents (or a servant of the family) sent for a woman for him. The Scriptures say 'and he took her...' and she became his wife. A perfect example of this is the story of Rebekah in Genesis 24. Please don't misunderstand me, the man also has very critical roles and responsibilities to the woman that he is choosing to be his helpmete. Among other things, he is to love her unconditionally just as Christ loves the church. He is to care for her spiritually, physically, and emotionally, and provide for her needs just as God does for us. This must include the intimate time that she needs or desires, which unfortunately a growing number of men, especially those calling themselves pastors are neglecting. A helpmete is a very important position and is to be a permanent position...until death, according to God's perfect design. When a man goes for a job, the owner of the company or his designee makes a careful evaluation and assessment before hiring you, correct? The man therefore should be extremely diligent in evaluating and assessing the woman before becoming betrothed unto her, because once betrothed, this is a binding covenant until death do you part. In fact, one night I was awakened again by my best friend, and He began talking to me some more about marriage issues and I asked Him a question, which I don't even recall now, but He asked me a question throwing me completely off track. The Spirit asked me, my son, where did the marriage ceremony come from? Did I create it? Why is all of this money and time squandered on such frivolities? Well, I went and did some research and found some very interesting and somewhat amusing though sad bits of information, which should make any truly Spiritual person think seriously about this and anything else that we do in our Christian walks. It is so easy just to follow along with the world, the trend, the traditions of our forefathers, but we truly must sit and analyze things sometimes because we need to be followers of Christ rather than man or their vain customs and traditions, especially because so much of what the world does today comes from...Rome...Roman Catholic...Are you protestant? Really??? Then why are you following the teachings of the Roman Catholic Church rather than God and His word? So here please allow me a few moments and I will share with you just a small bit of what I discovered. Let us look at some history of marriage and the ceremony, and even the vows. Here is what I have found.

The period of waiting between the engagement and marriage was started in 1214 by Pope Innocent III, and used the engagement ring as a show of commitment. The diamond was added to it in 1477.

The use of the white dress started in 1840 when Queen Victoria wore a white dress for her wedding. Before that the woman wore red dresses.

In England many years back, often times the bride and groom first met at the altar. Thus, the bride wore a veil to hide her features to keep the groom from backing out of the deal if he didn't like what he saw. Romans also used the veil to **ward off any evil spirits** that may be jealous of her joyous day.

The bouquet originally was a bag of spices and herbs to again **ward off evil spirits.** Also, in days past, the bride and groom threw the bouquet of flowers as a distraction immediately after saying I do, so that they could go quickly and consummate the marriage then he would throw the garter to symbolize that the marriage was...official.

The bridesmaids were to dress similar to the bride and surround to again **ward off or confuse the evil spirits** who may be trying to destroy the brides' joyous event. Originally in Rome, there was no ceremony, the bridesmaids dressed up, lit candles and escorted the bride to the man's house, protecting her along the way from any man who would try to steal her away.

The best man began as an expert swordsman. Weddings used to be a business transaction, and the groom needed a swordsman to protect the groom from an angry family of the bride or prevent the bride from running away. Also, sometimes when the bride's parents didn't agree to the marriage, the bridegroom would be sent to kidnap the woman so that the groom could marry her. The kidnapping of the bride began in ancient Rome. This was abolished in 1753. But the kidnapped bride stood on his left side so that he could fight off any trouble with his right hand.

Wedding cakes originally were simple and made of wheat and symbolized fertility and prosperity. The cake originally was thrown at the bride, or crushed over her head. The guests would gather around the bride to pick up the pieces to eat.

The wedding ring originated in Egypt. The diamond later was added by the Sicilians who believed that this stone was made by the fire of love. It was placed on the 4th finger of the left hand believing that there was a vein from there that ran directly to the heart. Originally, the ring symbolized ownership, and only the woman wore the ring. Apparently, the early Roman rings were made of Iron.

The throwing of the garter came from France and England, other cultures, where guests would tear pieces from the wedding dress for good luck, so her dress was essentially torn to pieces. So, to satisfy the guests, the groom began throwing the garter to protect his wife and her dress.

The dad originally walked his daughter down the aisle to give her away as an exchange of ownership.

Carrying the bride across the threshold originated again to **protect the bride from evil spirits**, believing that her feet were susceptible to evil spirits.

Remember that I mentioned about kidnapping the bride from her family and other men trying to kidnap the bride? Well, it appears that the origin of the honeymoon was to hide the girl away for a month so that nobody would know where to find her.

As for the ceremony itself, it has evolved over time, but apparently was started in Rome (here we see Rome, Catholic, again in the picture creating traditions of man rather than God). In the earliest ceremonies there was a feast where the groom would give the woman the iron ring, followed by the woman being escorted by her maid of honors, to the man's house carrying a candle or torch. He would meet her and carry her over the threshold as we discussed earlier. The couple would hold hands and vow and consent to the union, before his dad. Interestingly, **the wife's family was expected to pay for everything**. Later, at the house, the couple would be led to the bed by the guests and then they would return to the feast, while the couple consummated the marriage. There were gods involved in all of this over the centuries in Rome and Europe, but I'm saving time and space.

So, what about the vows, after all, that is where we left off. To have and to hold, from this day forward, for better, for worse, for richer, for poorer, in sickness and in health, until death do us part. It is interesting that with all of the evolution in the marriages worldwide, they have held onto til death do us part, even though the divorce rate is so high. The first wedding vows again is traced back to none other than the Roman Catholic church, specifically here, Thomas Cranmer, Archbishop of Canterbury, I, ____, take thee, ____ to be my lawfully wedded husband, to have and to hold from this day forward, for better for worse, for richer or poorer, in sickness and in health, to love, cherish, and to obey, till death us do part, according to God's holy ordinance. But did God ordain this? Whose law are you referring to? In truth, God never created or sanctioned the verbal vows, just the commitment, however they are consistent with His teachings. If vows are to be recited, I like best the vows that I found from the Quaker Church (a conservative Christian denomination) "Friends, in the fear of the Lord, and before this assembly, I take my friend ____ to be my wife, promising, through divine assistance, to be unto her a loving and faithful husband, until it shall please the Lord by death to separate us," and likewise the woman would recite also.

Marriage is a vow to one another and to God, binding until death, and our Almighty God is witness to this. There simply are no exceptions! You may say, Whoa Pastor, what about Matthew 5:32, where it says except for fornication? To this point, permit me to say two things. First, Matthew 5:32 known as the exclusionary clause, is the only place in Scripture where this is found, not saying that it is wrong but it is unsupported by any other scripture. Secondly, Fornication relates to sex after betrothal and before marriage is consummated, with someone other than your betrothed. This is why Joseph could have, and did consider, putting Mary away (divorce her). Joseph considered putting Mary away (divorce) due to his belief of her being guilty of fornication, where fornication is practiced by a woman after being betrothed but before the couple had begun living together as husband and wife. But Joseph didn't put her away and so was called a just man in Matthew. 2:19.

Mathew 19 Therefore shall a man leave his father and mother, and shall cleave unto his wife; and they shall be one flesh. Jesus declares that the married can never be two again. He acknowledges God's involvement in marital joining and Man is not to separate the married. Moses suffered from the hardness of the hearts of men, but Jesus reiterated about divorce, From the beginning it was not so. Was Jesus' response to except for fornication, which is prior to marriage.

The context of this chapter shows that the intent is not encouraging divorce, but rather a higher way of looking into our own hearts, resisting the anger, retaliation, pride, lust, and hatred which leads one to forsake their marriage covenant which is a grave sin. One must observe that in Mark and Luke, the exception clause is not even included, and Jesus and God outright condemn divorce.

How did Mary feel when all this happened? The Scripture is silent as to Mary's thoughts or words when the Spirit over-came her and she was with child; however, Joseph is being moved by thoughts and emotions that are devastating. We should note here that Mary was one who pondered the deep things of God in her heart. She waited for God the Holy Spirit to inform Joseph. This faithful pondering woman is a tribute to the life of faith; she certainly was one of the heroes of faith recorded in Scripture and we should be likewise minded.

It is unbelievable that today everyone from the student to well educated in our present intelligent generation refuses to at least admit to the difficulty and contradiction of the modern interpretation that the exception clause permits man to put asunder that which God joined together.

Since the modern interpretation of the exception clause permits divorce for adultery this fact absolutely qualifies the exception clause to be defined as an obscure text: murder is murder, and adultery is adultery. When Jesus describes murder there is no question, no exception to his dialogue; the same is true of adultery, and to forswear. So, the evidence that the exception clause is an obscure text cannot be denied. The context must dictate the meaning of the obscure text; like it or not. Scripture must interpret Scripture. The modern interpretation of the State civil marriage and divorce laws CANNOT dictate the interpretation of the exception clause to the church.

It is of interest that Mark was allowed to write *And he saith unto them, Whosoever shall put away his wife, and marry another, committeth adultery against her. And if a woman shall put away her husband, and be married to another, she committeth adultery,* Mark 10:11, 12 as this is a very obvious comment regarding the woman. The argument states that Mark was writing with the Gentile Christians in mind, since the Gentiles permitted the woman the right to sue for divorce, an act quite foreign to the Jew.

In Rom. 7:1-3 we read *Know ye not, brethren, (for I speak to them that know the law,) how that the law hath dominion over a man as long as he liveth? For the woman which hath an husband is bound by the law to her husband so long as he liveth; but if the husband be dead, she is loosed from the law of her husband. So then if, while her husband liveth, she be married to another man, she shall be called an adulteress: but if her husband be dead, she is free from that law; so that she is no adulteress, though she be married to another man.*

The body is for the Lord, and the Lord for the body. The body will experience redemption and resurrection. A believer's body is a member of Christ's body; it is a temple. By having sexual union with harlots, a believer was taking the members of Christ and uniting them to the harlot. *For two, saith he, shall be one flesh.* We should be one spirit and one flesh with Christ.

Fornication should not be committed in the temple of God, and your body is the temple of God and the Holy Spirit. You no longer own your body; it has been bought or redeemed by Christ, purchased for a price, that of the precious blood of the Lamb of God, our Lord and Savior Jesus Christ, who taketh away the sin of the world. For this we have been admonished and called on to repent; being offered complete Christian restoration: for after he rebuked them, he proclaims that they have been bought with a price, this statement means that we are redeemed.

Marriages at first weren't even religious or legal, the earliest marriages were essentially casual agreements between families or clans, to establish peaceful relationships, trading relationships, and mutual obligations. Even looking back into the Old Testament of our Bible, you see that kings exchanged their daughters for peace, contracts...The girl was just a piece of property to be traded in exchange for political purposes, for example, see Genesis 41:45 and 1st Samuel 18:17.

The New Testament church should have a higher standard for marriage than others. Believers are the priests of the new temple, the body of Christ. And like the Levitical priests we have a higher standard than the world. Leviticus 21:7 tells us that a priest must not marry a harlot, a violated virgin or a divorced woman. Jesus' teaching on divorce in Matthew 19 was directly related to his eschatological view of the new Temple in the kingdom age, and the regulation of the priests of the new Temple: *Neither shall they take for their wives a widow, nor her that is put away: but they shall take maidens of the seed of the house of Israel, or a widow that had a priest before,* Ezekiel 44:22. Although the position of Levitical marriage and new Temple priesthood marriage is a high standard, it does not reach the height of perfection which Jesus reaches for all men: What, therefore, God hath joined together, let not man put asunder. I teach that this rule of Jesus applies to all men of all time just as all of Scripture does.

The Law regulated every aspect of Jewish life, including their time. The Sabbath, the primary holy day, was followed with numerous holy days, holy weeks, and holy years. Their clothing, diet, and sacrifices were regulated; but if you look at each of these, they all relate to the Spiritual walk, and while none of these can impart righteousness, they could impart guilt leading to repentance and revival.

Now, the man is a significant point of the family and receives the inheritance according to Jewish law, whereas the women children are up for grabs, they will get married and leave. But the men also must leave and cleave unto his wife. Jesus left heaven (home) to come to earth and cleave unto His bride, us. Jesus left His family to serve His bride, the church when He was twelve. But in both cases, He still returned home, and the men are responsible in many cultures to care for their elderly parents as needed. You may also look at Romans 8:15-16.

To cleave is as binding together with glue. When two pieces of wood are glued up and allowed to dry, then you try to break it apart, the wood will split rather than the glued-up joint. What God hath joined together let not man put asunder. William J. Hopewell says, in regards to scripture saying that the two shall become one flesh, that one is the smallest indivisible unit there is, so it is impossible to divide the unit of one flesh once it has been glued together. Sacrifice is the glue that bonds marriage and the family; selfishness fractures that bond. When splitting occurs, it is usually the new twigs that have sprouted from our sides that suffer the greatest, those twigs are our children.

In 1ˢᵗ Corinthians 7:3-5 it is important to note *let the husband render unto the wife due benevolence* (debts) *and likewise also the wife unto her husband.* This shows responsibilities to and for one another must be met, selfless rather than selfish, just as God calls us to be for Him. Jesus Christ showed a wonderful example to us in His life. *The wife hath not power over her own body but her husband: and likewise also the husband hath not power over his own body, but the wife*; Again, responsible to and for each other. We give God power and authority over our lives when we listen and obey Him and surrender all unto Him. *Defraud* (refuse)*ye not one another, except it be **with consent for a time**, that ye may give yourself to fasting and prayer* (sanctification) *and **come together again** that Satan temp ye not...* Wives must return to their husbands as we are called to return unto the Lord, see Joel 2:12-13. Remember we are the bride and He is the Groom. See also 2ⁿᵈ Chronicles 24:20 and 14:7.

Genesis 2:24-25 tells us *Therefore shall a man leave his father and mother and shall cleave unto his wife and they shall become one flesh.* Unity! Cleave, I wish to discuss this term with you briefly at this time, as it is one word that has two completely different meanings yet the same. Both are used in scripture. First, split apart. Second, stuck fast, be faithful. The cloven-hoofed animals were considered dirty, and so are we if we split apart from God or our spouse. We are called as believers to cleave unto Him, we are called as husband and wife to cleave to one another, stick together, and be faithful. We see in Deuteronomy 11:22 that we are to obey His laws, love Him, walk with Him, and cleave unto Him. He is our redeemer, so must a wife unto her husband.

One cannot be independent or liberated, and united at the same time for they are opposites! Marriage is unity, where two become one. In Genesis 2:25 we read *And they were both naked, the man and his wife, and were not ashamed.* Within the confines of marriage, God desires to have you enjoy each other in every way, including thy bodies, and there should be no shame.

Women, you may feel picked on today, but the man is also. First my sisters, women are symbolic of both men and women for we are all sinners. But marriage takes two, a man and a woman. It is like a bank account. You must make deposits before you can make any withdrawals-bad moments, stress, trials and tribulations... You can earn interest on your deposits by love and favors, but you must maintain a minimum balance. You can only withdraw so much before your marriage goes bankrupt. Dear brothers and sisters, avoid withdrawing as much as possible, and concentrate as much as possible on making deposits, to build up your marriage. Start today and try to make a deposit at least once every day, and your marriage shall be rich in love and blessings. Some people are never satisfied with the size of the account and always want more. If God brought you two together, rejoice and be glad, be satisfied always! Your job is to help your partner be the best that they can be for the Lord.

Isaiah 54:5 says, *For thy maker is thine Husband, for the Lord of Hosts is His name and thy Redeemer the Holy One of Israel, the God of the whole earth shall He be called.* Our

Creator, the Creator of the whole universe is God, our Father. For the woman, if you are truly submissive, thy husband will make you better than before, as you grow together in love and serve him, you'll be serving God, who is our Redeemer. In Hosea 2:16 He says, *...at that day that thou shalt call me Ishi (meaning my husband); and shalt call me no more Baali (my owner).* Though you belong to your husband as we belong to God, He later adopts us as sons, and calls us friends.

Ephesians 5:33 *Let every one of you in particular so love his wife even as himself, and the wife see that she reveres her husband.*

You know dear friends; today, in so many marriages the couple have separate careers, separate vehicles, separate friends, separate bank accounts, etc. The only thing that they share, the only joint possession is their bed, where they produce unwanted children, then throw them away to baby-sitters, day care, so that they may continue to enjoy their separate lives, or God forbid worse, they abort their poor children. Is this marriage? Unity and independence are opposites, they cannot mix, and you cannot serve two gods.

Husbands and wives are not equal! God never intended for them to be equal, any more than He intended for us to be equal with Him. Romans 12:4 tells us *For as we have many members in one body, Christ, and every one members one of another.* The eyes, ears, feet, heart...they all have different functions, but are all equally important in God's overall plan. God's church has many members with different functions, but all are important. God and Jesus NEVER used a woman to teach a man, preach, lead, and in fact, He taught against such practices. Jesus didn't have any female disciples (equal opportunity quotas), not even women followed the star to see the Infant in Beth-lehem! We read in Luke 1:40 *And entered into the house of Zacharias, and saluted Elisabeth.* We must note the house of Zacharias not Elisabeth, Mary didn't go to Elisabeth's house, no, she went to Zacharias' house and greeted Elisabeth. Why? Because women represent sin and God calls the righteous. There are many good women and many bad men, so let me make this point clear. For the three major events in the life of Christ, His birth, death, and resurrection, unbelievers only witnessed His death, not His birth or resurrection.

Please allow me to place this in context. Today women want to be equal; Equal rights, equal salaries, etc. Listen my dear sisters, women join construction firms but how often do you see them out paving the roads? No, in the developed world, she's there holding the stop sign. We discussed this earlier. Dear friends, we can never be equal with God, and Women are not to be equal with the men, it just isn't God's plan or will. It is time for you my sisters to remove your pants and return them to thy husbands, or fathers if you aren't married. We as sinners cannot bear the shame and humiliation, the pain and the cross that Jesus did. We are called to have faith, trust, and obedience, to submit and surrender all unto Him, just as women are called by God to do unto their husbands or dads. I've had several women tell me, Oh, but Pastor, my husband is so irresponsible, I could never... Listen my dear sisters, what God says, No if's, ands, or buts. You must...maybe thy husband is the way he is because you are the way you are. Perhaps he is this way because of Eve. The women took the pants away from him, he now is naked and walking ashamed and humiliated. Give him back his pants, show him some respect, honor, pray for him... and see the miracles take place in him, in you, in your family! God's covenant with us is I will IF you will. You must take the first step, and then leave the rest to God. See God work in thy husband, yourself, and your family, church, and nation, Amen! Salvation can only come when we surrender all and submit, trust and obey our Lord. So, women, remove thy pants, return them to thy husbands, you are not oppressed, this will free you from oppression, and you shall be blessed. You are saved from the stresses of the world when you are under the shelter of thy husband and in God's will. Look at the awesome responsibility of thy husband. He didn't ask for it any more than you asked to be a woman with your God given roles and responsibilities. Sisters please, heed the instruction of the Lord. Let us turn please to the book of Matthew 18:12. You must leave the world behind and cleave unto thy husband. Husbands, encourage thy wives and daughters to stay home, for when they wander off, there is a mountain (trouble) everywhere, the enemy is out there just waiting to strike, and is waiting for that chance, just like it struck Eve, when she wandered off from her husband. God created the universe perfectly. He didn't make a mistake with women, who He created to help the man at home, not out in the world. In my book '**ONLY BELIEVE**', I go into some depth explaining the mountain and its symbolism in scripture. In Genesis chapter 3 we see that God created woman for the man, not man for the woman. We see that man shall rule over the woman, not woman over the man, because of Eve's sin, but this was already His plan. See Titus 2:5 and 1st Timothy 2:12 also. Pride prevents women from accepting their God given roles, as it also separates us from God. Women need to humble themselves, and men need to humble themselves, and take back the authority in their families, the church, and the nation. Men need to lovingly encourage their wives and daughters to humble themselves and to submit to the authority of their husbands or dads. Looking back to Genesis 16:2 we see *Sarai said unto Abram, behold now, the Lord hath restrained me from bearing: I pray thee, go in unto my maid; it may be that I may obtain children by her. And Abram hearkened to the voice of Sarai.* There are a couple of points here that I am compelled to point out. First, no woman should invite her husband to sin or to take another woman. It is wrong; it is not God's will! The husband belongs to his wife until death. Furthermore, a woman should not tell a man what to do (authority) and here again we see the woman leading the man into evil, into sin, just like Eve did. She lacks the faith and leads him off of the path of righteousness. Think about it my dear brothers and sisters. Secondly, Abram, the men, need to be in authority, look to God in all things, and not yield unto temptation, even if it comes from thy wife. Remember, Satan uses friends and families those closest to us to pull us off the path of righteousness, who better than thy wife?!!

Now concerning the things whereof ye wrote unto me: It is good for a man not to touch a woman, 1st Corinthians 7:1. The word touch in classical Greek literature, and in the Greek

Old Testament, is a figurative expression for sexual intercourse. But God ordained marriage and commanded men to engage in the sexual relationship in order to bring forth children, **WITHIN THE CONFINES** of the monogamous marriage. *What therefore God hath joined together, let not man put asunder.* The other important doctrine here is the doctrine of reconciliation that must remain a permanent option for this New Testament marriage, this reconciliation speaks of salvation by grace alone, not by any works.

This revelation to us must be considered vital to the doctrine of Christ and the subject of marriage. We are clearly told that Joseph was a just man. This of course means that Joseph was slow to anger, and was willing to investigate the matter, and come to a reasonable decision as to his action.

But I want you to see that even here where Mary was pregnant with child before they got married and consummated their marriage, He hadn't been with her or known her, God, who? God said no! Hold on to thy wife. My dear brothers and sisters, are you listening? Hold on!!! Betrothal is so binding that it would call for a certificate of divorce to split apart during or after this time.

Let's return to Isaac and Rebekah in Genesis 27, we see Rebekah changed. She deceived Isaac, lied to him, and involved her children in her schemes. My dear friends, this happens so much today also. Just as Satan used Eve, so parents often use their children against their partners. This ought not to be. This time of marital problems is hard enough on the children, much less, involving them and using them in lies, deceit, and siding one against the other. This is not fair to them, its ungodly behavior to begin with, and is worse before God and thy children when you involve them in the problems.

Okay my dear brothers and sisters, let us return to the celebration now. Vows said, now what happens next in most marriages? The exchanges of rings; where in Scripture my dear friends, do you find this ritual? You can't, because it is not there. God's word teaches against jewelry. The wedding rings stem from none other than the Catholic Church. There is absolutely no Christian basis for doing this, in fact as a protestant;

you shouldn't do it for three reasons. First, it isn't God's plan, or it would have been in His word, where in fact He teaches against any jewelry. Secondly, as a Protestant, we must stop following the Catholic Church and return to Luther's protesting against her, thus protestant. Thirdly, a ring does not keep you together, God does. Rings are a form of idolatry, especially gold, diamonds-wedding. Some cultures use a special necklace...it doesn't matter it is jewelry, and won't keep you together, and is contrary to God's word. The marriage is our accepting Christ as our personal Lord and Savior. We become His bride, the bride of Christ. In some Indian cultures, the woman wears a putuh – a painted dot on her forehead, the color red or black denotes if she is single or married. At the ceremony instead of exchanging rings, it would be great for the man and woman to take her train and wrap it around both of them, demonstrating the union of the couple becoming one.

The ceremony closes with...you may now kiss the bride. This, my dear friends, should be the **very first** kiss. Respect each other enough to wait. You are now legally married and married in God's eyes, and thus the kiss is proper and acceptable. Eve's passiveness in Genesis speaks submission and permission. In the kiss is promise. Each person should promise admiration, trust, faith, and sacrifice in the kiss.

AFTER THE CEREMONY

Typically now the bride goes somewhere and changes out of her wedding dress into something else for the remainder of the day. Now, we talked about dress earlier, but the Spirit led me to add more here. Dresses as I write this, the fashion is short and extremely tight so that every curve right down to the butt crack and the abdominal muscles coming together down between your legs. The top is split down below the breast line so that everything is hanging out for all to see. This is not godly, it is not modest apparel, and it entices lustful thoughts in those around you and can lead to rape. You wish to call yourself a Christian, then be a Christian. Be obedient to God and His word, and separate yourself from the ways of the world, and that must include fashion. It is interesting that as I write this, while here in Africa the trend is short and tight while in China the trend of young ladies is going back to the hanfu, the traditional Chinese attire that is full length, loose, high neck and back, very large hanging sleeves, and even a light robe like covering over that. I have also been told that the kimono is gaining popularity among the Japanese young ladies, these are all modest dress and so beautiful. My wife until the 9/11 incident used to wear sari's a lot, and her sister taught me how to tie them, so I got to dress my wife, and it was such an honor each time that I wrapped her in a sari, and they also are modest and so beautiful. To see an American or African in a nice long loose-fitting dress or a long loose skirt and blouse makes them so much more beautiful, but in tight, short dresses or these pants, especially the stretch pants that must take them an hour to stuff themselves inside of these, or jeans... is anything but attractive. But as beautiful as the former are, the beauty is much more than physical, but seeing the beauty of her self-respect and the godliness, the inner beauty shows forth. I am sure that the same is true when women look at how a man is dressed.

Let us again speak here about dress, for the wedding day has come. Men typically wear a suit, and that is fine. Today the wedding dresses are getting shorter, tighter, lower cut, sleeveless, and without shoulders...The woman is already betrothed so she belongs to her husband, and nobody else needs to or should be seeing any part of her body. The color is unimportant. Many countries still use white which is a sign of purity, but how many women today wear white when they are no longer pure? In Malaysia, the women wear gold and scarlet... God does not care the color, He looks at the heart, but He does care about modesty. 1st Timothy 2:9 teaches ...*that women adorn themselves in <u>modest</u> apparel*... Another issue here is jewelry and makeup for the wedding ceremony. I told my wife no jewelry or makeup because it's not right. She chose again to defy and deceive me and came down the aisle wearing a little makeup and a little gold jewelry, to appease her family, her third act of deception before we were married, in order to appease the world (her family, rather than God and her husband. I was disappointed because of her disobedience and deception, so was God Almighty. The temple was completely covered, as was the Holy of Holies, so should the woman be completely covered. A woman wears a veil for the marriage ceremony and the veil is lifted, but this is only an external show, what really and truly needs to be taking place is an unveiling, circumcision of the heart, that of the man and the woman. Circumcision is just the removing of the veil also, just as Christ was circumcised and He removed the veil at the time of His death removing forever the veil separating us from Him. I draw your attention here to Romans 2:25-29.

Panties, dresses, pants. We discussed clothing-modest apparel but I feel that a bit more needs to be said, not wanting to get too personal, but it is important in caring for God's temple. People, especially women-young teen agers and young adult women especially, like to wear nice cute sexy panties (not that anybody should see it) but these are almost always made of nylon, acrylic, polyester or other plastics. These fabrics are one of the leading causes of urinary tract and vaginal infections in women. This plastic material doesn't breathe so it traps in the natural moisture, which is a great medium for bacterial growth, and then you end up with the infections. You should use cotton panties to enhance your health and prevent such problems. The cute little things may perhaps be used for just a few minutes IF YOU ARE MARRIED, to make things a little more interesting for you and your husband if you so desire.

The wedding is complete, now the feast. In some cultures, then and now, the feast lasts for seven days. In keeping with the context of this message, I believe that the man should bring food to the wife, and then allow her to serve him, as he is to be the provider for his family just as God is our provider, but we the bride are to serve Him. At the feast traditionally there is a cake, which the bride and groom cut together, they get the first cuts and feed each other. This originally was and should still be a sign of humility and of serving one another. I believe that the man should first serve his wife, then she should serve her husband, then she should go and serve her new in-laws then her parents and return to her husbands' side. Unfortunately, this has become a joke, a fun time, shoving as much as possible in the partners' mouth and all over their face, making a mess. Unfortunately, I believe that this joke is an indication of how they view the marriage, as many soon divorce. Dear friends, this ought not to be. This is no laughing matter and should be done with love and humility; it should be revered and respected by the bride and the groom, a humble time of servitude. Let's get back to God and away from the world, the ways of Satan.

THE WEDDING (FIRST) NIGHT

N̲ ow the wedding, the feast, the photos are all completed and the bride and groom go home, to a hotel, or wherever they planned for their first night. Now comes a very special time, spiritually, emotionally, and physically, usually reserved for the bedroom. In Amos 3:3 *Can two walk together except they be agreed?* Ecclesiastes 4:11, *Again, if two lie together they have heat: but how can one be warm alone?*

Now prepare thyself because I am going to go into some detail here for a very good reason, but shall be as discreet as possible to get the message across. I had over twenty years in medicine and studied medicine for over thirty years.

The wedding event is climaxed in the conjugal act of physical consummation, the private physical contract. Thus, the physical consummation is totally an important part of the wedding. In scripture most all of the covenants were sealed by a blood sacrifice; thus, the marriage must also be sealed by the blood sacrifice, i.e., the bleeding from the breaking of the hymen, but this shall be discussed more in the following chapter. We see in Genesis 17:10 thata covenant is ratified by blood including the covenant of marriage, the reason virginity is so important. A woman should ratify the covenant the night of the marriage (consummate) allowing the hymen to be torn (The veil) and shed blood to ratify thy covenant.

If necessary, however consummation can be delayed if both parties previously agreed to its absence. A delay may also be caused by many human activities, for example if one must travel suddenly, menstrual period at the time of marriage, etc. Where fraud or the unknowing inability to offer physical consummation exists, most states permit annulment. The church has no doctrinal position in these matters except til death do us part. Could the law be exercised in such matters? Where fraud is the question, the law should be exercised, unless repentance exists. Impotence on the other hand could be overcome by love, and may be just God's timing. Like Abraham, his first wife, Sarai was eventually blessed with the promised seed, so Jacob's first wife, Leah, gave birth to both Levi and Judah. Leah was the mother of Israel's priests and the mother of the promised seed, for *the scepter shall not depart from Judah, nor a lawgiver from between his feet, until Shiloh come; and unto him shall the gathering of the people be,* In Genesis 49, Shiloh, a reference to Christ. Most civil judges would award an annulment to the victim of a fraudulent marriage, God here blesses the union.

The quality of the Sinai marriage was as magnificent as you could expect from the Creator, the Father of creation and marriage. It was bound permanently; Inseparable. Thou shalt fear the Lord thy God; him shalt thou serve, and to him shalt thou cleave, and swear by his name. *For if ye shall diligently keep all these commandments which I command you, to do them, to love the Lord your God, to walk in all his ways, and to cleave unto him,* Deuteronomy 11:22. Leaving Egypt and cleaving to Jehovah, Israel was married as she confesses that she would keep the commandments. Moses was the pastor who performed the ceremony: *And Moses came and told the people all the words of the Lord, and all the judgments: and all the people answered with one voice, and said, all the words which the Lord hath said will we do;* (I DO), Exodus 24:3. The betrothal led the bride into the tabernacle of her lover where the Glory of God entered and the marriage was consummated. The vehicle of the seed of the woman and the marriage was now in the hands of the children of Abraham, the Jewish nation of Israel.

God created man from the dust of the earth, in Their own image, then breathed into Him the Spirit. He who hath the Spirit hath life, here we see this profound statement in its physical sense, but in its Spiritual sense, only with the Spirit of God can we confess Jesus as Lord, so without the Spirit, there is no life, for without Christ there is only death, the second death. He breathed in the Spirit, the breath of life. We are created from dust, and will return to dust, but in the end, our bones will be restored and we will resurrect again to be with God or face the second death, just as is illustrated in Ezekiel, where the bones in the field were resurrected. God created Adam to serve Him.

God next determined that Adam needed a helpmate. He took a rib from Adam and created Eve, Genesis 2:21-24. It is interesting to note that every creature and the universe were made from...nothing. Man, however was created from dust of the earth, Material that God had already created. Then, God created woman from the man. She is special and truly a part of him, as we are a part of God and His family. The significance here is that they were literally one flesh and blood. Blood cells are created in the marrow of the bones; Bone of his bone, flesh of his flesh. God equates this to marriage, thus cannot be separated from her husband, they are one. In Hebrew, the word for man is ish, similar to the word for dirt- (Adam/adamah), and the word for woman is ishah, see how closely related the husband and wife are, and so should be our relationship with God. In the Bible, God says you shall no longer call me Baali (my owner), but Ishi (my Husband), if we are truly Spiritual. When God created Adam and Eve, the intense closeness, the intimacy was so pronounced. Intimate is defined as a close and private personal relationship, and this is what our Father desires from us, and for us with our spouse. We are His children; we are His bride, and He desires for us to have such a relationship with Him, and in our marriage, with each other.

We are in the bedroom, remember? God is not opposed to romance. In fact, God is a romantic, and He is the Creator of romance. There is no example in scripture of a kiss between a man and a woman before marriage, only after, and then only in the Song of Songs, nowhere else. Also stop for a minute and think. The Bible is a history book. What history book have you ever read that had stories like that of Ruth, Song of Songs, or Esther? Now, the kiss, you already had one at your wedding ceremony, and perhaps (probably) snuck one or two in on the way to where you will be spending your, hopefully first, night together. But one must be ever so careful also, and why should it be saved for marriage? We find in scripture the answer. The scriptures show us the kiss of love, and the kiss of deception, are we together? For the kiss of deception, I refer you to look at Genesis 27:27 and Luke 22:48, Matthew 7:21, and Luke 6:46. For more on the kiss see 2nd Samuel 20:9, and Matt 26:49. The kiss of someone you don't know or don't know well (adultery) can lead to death.

Typically, now comes the time...in the bedroom, the man prepares for bed as his new bride goes into the bathroom and prepares herself for her husband. She then enters the bedroom and presents herself unto her bridegroom. This is highly symbolic of us needing to prepare ourselves-our hearts and minds before presenting ourselves unto our Bridegroom-our Lord God. Then He (he) welcomes her with open arms.

Now that they are undressing, I have this note that needs to be added somewhere so, I snuck it in here, and bear with me for a moment while the couple is undressing. The Spirit told me to say a bit or brief word about weight. In some cultures, the men like big women. The mother begins fattening up the poor child from a young age to make her desirable. In still other cultures that I have been in, if the man is not big, the woman is criticized because she isn't taking care of him. Listen, I am not here to discuss culture or tradition, but the Bible and only the Bible. The Bible is clear that the body is the temple of the Lord, therefore we have an obligation, of good stewardship, to care for our temples as well as that of our marriage partner. Being overweight is not godly. It is extremely hazardous to our health.

Obesity is a leading cause of cancer, heart disease, strokes, diabetes, joint disease, especially knees and hips As Christians, we should want ourselves and our marriage partners to be healthy, therefore we should follow a healthy diet and style of eating, and encourage our marriage partners to do likewise. What is more important, a wife who is the size of Mt. Everest and dies a long slow debilitating death, or a wife who is healthy and happy, and lives a long, full life? Same applies to the husband. This must include adequate exercise for both parties in order to stay healthy. Sitting in front of the TV drinking beer and eating bowls full of popcorn saturated with salt and dripping of butter, is not healthy-mentally, physically, or spiritually. Getting outdoors, taking nice evening walks hand in hand is extremely healthy. Are you unsure if you are overweight or obese? Go to your local doctor or clinic and ask them to check your "BMI". It is just a matter of checking your height, weight, and your blood pressure, then they can calculate it from there. But if you are using X sizes or larger, you already know that there is an issue. Also, your breasts need proper support, proper fitting bras. Breasts that are too large also are unhealthy. There is an increased chance of breast cancer, as well as back problems, etc. Use of high heels is also a major cause of back conditions and other joint conditions. How you dress is a direct reflection of how you think of yourself (self-respect) and affects how others will view you, treat you and respect you. I have done many rape exams and I can honestly tell you that by far, the majority of cases of rape, the female was dressed very provocatively. I am in no way justifying rape, it is a very serious and horrible crime, but if you cannot respect yourself, how can you expect anyone else to respect you? I have rarely seen a nicely dressed young lady coming in with such complaints. I speak this not to say that size matters in the context of love, but as a life partner, one should desire for their partner to be healthy. Okay, moving on now.

Moving along here, still in the bedroom, kisses, hugs, the whispering of sweet words, then...off come the clothes. One must be certain that the woman is not menstruating, Leviticus

20:18. A man shall not lie with a woman menstruating, as we discussed earlier, the two sides of this detail; however, it is not the best time for the first time, as she may be moody, uncomfortable, not enjoy the experience, messy, and will not be able to witness the tearing of the hymen. Acts 15:20, just as we aren't to partake of the blood of animals, we are not to partake of the woman, intercourse during her period, blood is life, but as I said there are two sides to this, and I am still praying through this issue.

Jesus shed His blood that we may partake with Him, that we <u>may</u> <u>have</u> <u>life</u>, a woman sheds blood that life may come forth from her. The blood of Christ cleanses us; the blood of a menstruating woman cleanses her womb. Let us stop here and examine this critical point of time.

First, I need to tell you that nakedness is not sin...Adam and Eve were created naked, without any clothing. Genesis 3:7 Nakedness was not a sin! What lay naked that they were ashamed of was the sin and their sinful nature and that is what they were hiding from. 1:31 *God saw that everything that He had made...was very good.* He didn't create sin or evil, or bad. Nakedness was not sin. Chapter 3 verse 8 continues *they hid themselves from the presence of the Lord God* Why? because God does not and cannot commune with sin. Sin creates a distance, a barrier between God and us, symbolized by the clothing, which God made from animals that were killed, were sacrificed for our sins, because of our sins, and ultimately causing the death of our Lord Jesus Christ- the sacrificial Lamb so that we may be saved.

A sideline here, please note that Adam didn't choose Eve and Eve didn't choose Adam. God chose...God brought them together...God married them... THEN they learned to love one another for who and what they are. Love is a choice; it's not something you fall into or out of!

We read in the Song of Songs 8:6 Set me as a seal upon thine heart; as a seal upon thine arm: for love is strong as death, jealousy is cruel as the grave... Do you have this seal?

They were sinless before the fall, they were completely naked, not ashamed or embarrassed. God created them and He saw that all was good (perfect). It was natural. The body is so beautiful, God created it. You, each of you are created beautiful, special, and unique. Be proud and honored how God created you, your color, sex, shape, hair color, height, eye color...even any human deformities are not deformities in Christ's eyes, for He makes no mistakes. You are fearfully and wonderfully made; God tells us in Psalms 139:14-15. We are created in the image of God, by God. You are special, and God loves you just the way that He created you. It was only after the fall that **God** covered or clothed mankind...Why? Not to cover our bodies, His beautiful creation...then why? My precious and dear friends, God covered our sins and our sinful nature, not His creation! Remember the story of the Prodigal Son? He returned to his father. He repented for his sin. Hello...are you listening? And the father what? His father covered him with the best of robes, Luke 15:22. He wasn't covering his body, but his sins, signifying that his sins had been forgiven, welcome home my son. God our Father clothes us, He covered our sins, justification, and we have been sanctified by the precious blood of Jesus Christ. Our sins have been covered, washed away. Now this has a two-fold meaning here. First, God placed the clothing, the veil, which separates us from the Holy of Holies, God, because He is perfect and can have no part with sin. This is why God desires all of us to receive His Son Jesus Christ, to be washed from our sins, which can only be accomplished through Jesus Christ our Lord and Savior, so that we can be cleansed from our sins and be reunited with Him. Oh, dear friends what love! Hallelujah! If we accept Christ, then He will justify us before God our Father, and declare us clean, that we may have fellowship with our Father. More on Justification and sanctification in my book '**ONLY BELIEVE**'. Jesus can do this because of His great love and that He bore our sins upon the cross of Calvary, buried them with Him in the tomb. Then when Christ was resurrected on the third day, He left our sins in the tomb, Hallelujah. On the cross, Christ cried out to God in Matt 27:46, *Why hast thou forsaken me?* God never forsook Jesus, His Son. He forsook the sins, our sins! God can and will have no part with sin, so while the perfect Christ carried our sins upon the cross, God separated Himself from the sin, until our sins were buried. If we accept Jesus Christ, then our sins are forgiven, we were already judged at the cross of Calvary. We need to bring all of our sins and burdens to the cross, confess our sins before Him, repent of our sins and accept the forgiveness that God offers to each of us. Then we need to leave them behind and walk away in the newness of life.

The husband is also called upon not only to prepare to die for his spouse but to live for her. He is to labor with her to make her beautiful and glorious, without the blemish of any sin. He must be determined to teach her, or assure that she is taught the truth of the scriptures that she may be spiritually clean not having any spot or wrinkle of sin. She can only be glorious if she is steeped in the Word.

In a healthy and happy marriage both partners feel safe and protected, safe and secure. To accomplish this takes an effort on both sides, and keeping God in the center.

Churches should have a early married support group to encourage and support young couples and prevent problems.

When God says that we're forgiven, we need to leave the guilt at the cross and praise Him. When the unbelieving partner returns, the believer and the unbeliever need to leave the guilt behind and start afresh.

My dear brothers and sisters, we are sinful and must be forgiving of one another, confess our sins to one another husband and wife, and to God, then forgive and be forgiven, and carry on, back on the path of righteousness. Pray one for the other. Amen. Husbands and wives, children, forgive and stand by your partner, you parent, your child. Don't ever leave. God never forsook His precious Son, He will never forsake you or I, He forgave us our sin, our sins, if we truly repent, and accept what His Son did for us. He will justify the truly spiritual before our Father God, Hallelujah. The Christian marriages are being tried and tested and many are falling away. The men and women are falling away as well. I praise God that my roots were firmly planted, deeper than I ever realized. I have a very solid foundation in Christ, stronger than ever before, who has never left me or forsaken me. I have withstood all that has been thrown my way and have endured unto the end. I have grown and been strengthened, ye I have received greater blessings because of the trials and tribulations, the persecution that I have undergone. I always recalled 2ⁿᵈ Timothy 3:12 which tell us, *Yea and all that live godly in Christ Jesus shall suffer persecution,* so I tried always to praise God for finding me worthy to suffer so, not an easy task when you are undergoing such torture and persecutions. This message is being delivered to you with love and in hopes of deepening thy roots, and strengthening your foundations, though with fear for I know that many who read these words will reject them and the one who gave me these words. We see in Hebrews 13:17 *Obey them that have the rule over you, and submit yourselves: for they watch for your souls, as they that must give account that they may do it with joy.*

Before we move on, I will say that romantic hugging and kissing should be kept in the house or private places, not out in the open public. Simple greeting hugs or a small kiss is acceptable. However, I have lived in areas where even that was not acceptable, simply a handshake like with anyone else when in public, even in the hospital as a respect for yourselves and for those around you. When you see these young people fondling, kissing...in public, it makes them look so cheap and disrespectful. If you truly love and respect your life partner and those around you as we are called by God to do, then show thy partner respect, they and those around you will respect you much more.

I heard a song that was so beautiful at a wedding, which said 'As long as you love me, we can be starving, homeless, we can be broke; as long as you love me, I'll be your platinum, and I'll be your silver and your gold.' Oh, how precious are these words, if only more would have this kind of love!

Back to the bedroom where we left off, hugging, kissing, and the sweet whispers of love, while completely disrobed. Before we go any further, let us stop here and discuss what **should** happen next, but rarely does.

The first thing that you as a married couple should do is to get down on your knees, together, and worship God! When you get into your home, a new home, a new car, a new job, your **marriage**, you should sanctify thyself and worship God, our provider. Praise Him, thank Him, glorify Him for providing your life partner for you, ask God's blessings upon thy marriage, your home, and your vehicles, that you will always be safe, protected by the grace and mercy of God. Then blessings will come, Genesis 35:7. Put God first!

Before moving on, I would encourage you to read Song of Songs 8:6.

It is that special moment; you both remove thy clothes, the veil. Your clothing created a separation between you, just as it prevented people from entering into the Holy of holies, approaching Mount Sinai-the Holy Mountain, etc. Now the veil is removed and you may now approach each other. You kiss again. After the death of Christ, the veil was torn in two so that we could have an intimate relationship with Him. You kiss again, hug.

The first evening with my wife took me back to the creation of love, where everything I saw was good! The world seemed to stand still and all was good. It was only my wife and I...and God, in the entire world. And then...

PERSONAL NOTES

John 17:11 *That they may be one, as we are.*

CHAPTER 6

Behind the Veil

Virginity is so important as I pray you have already seen, but will see a bit more in this chapter.

Do you realize that in the Old Testament times, only the virgin women were saved from the massacres, see Numbers 31:18?

We see in Leviticus 21:13 that a priest could only marry a virgin. My dear sisters, do you want to marry a priest, a godly man? Then you must keep yourself unstained and pure for him.

Note in Genesis 31:4,9 that Abraham never entered into the handmaidens until they became his wives.

It is also important to note that physiologically, a woman's' pelvis doesn't rotate and mature until she is around twenty-five to thirty years of age and then returns around thirty-five years of age, so these are the safest years to conceive and bear children. When a girl is under aged, the lack of pelvic maturity considerably increases the risk of maternal and/or fetal complications including death.

And again, we return to the book of Hebrews chapter 9 verses 16 and 22 where we read For where a testament is, there must also of necessity be the death of the testator. *And almost all things are by the law purged with blood; and without shedding of blood is no remission.* Here we are discussing two different issues with a common thread, that of losing one's virginity. First of all, we see that there must be the death (shedding of blood). When a man and a woman become betrothed and then marry, they must sacrifice themselves and surrender all unto God and His ordained life partner if the marriage is to be successful. The failure to do so is resulting in the high number of divorces so prevalent today. We see also that the covenants are sealed in blood. The marriage covenant must likewise be sealed by blood, by the shedding of blood, the tearing of the hymen when a woman's virginity is surrendered.

In 2020 I signed into a local dating site solely for purpose of this message, using a fictitious name and made no introduction, submitted no photo, and made no replies to any hits. I did this just to gather some data for this message. In just a couple days I received around seven hundred responses. The respondents ranged in age from eighteen to seventy-three years of age. Of these around eighty percent were exposing their breasts, naked between their legs, or their buttocks, many had toys and vegetables hanging out of their orifices, showing no respect for themselves or others that may be looking for love. They ranged from slender to massively obese. Imagine! I was shocked. I did this as an experiment to see how they women would respond in such a small sparsely populated area. Their careers ranged from sales, housekeepers, waitresses to doctors and attorneys! Most of the females that weren't married were divorced. A couple were widows. I would say that more than fifty percent were married looking for sexual encounters outright!!! Many said that their husbands were not satisfying their sexual needs. Others said that their husbands are never there. A couple said that their husbands were infertile or had low sperm count, and a few said that their husbands were very ill. Many of them spoke of their husbands or boyfriends in a very negative manner, no respect for them. But men and women respect must be present in any relationship. None of those excuses are a reason for violating the sacred covenant! However, men, I want you to see how the women are feeling, but not justifying their behavior. They want and need you around. They want and need your attention-physically, emotionally, and spiritually. Many of these women said that they are lonely (lonelier married than before marriage!), that they need someone to talk to, listen to them. I hope that you are hearing this, men. But women, there is no excuse for divorce, none of these reasons are grounds for divorce or for adultery. A few women said that their husbands are cheating so they want to also as revenge! The shame! I do have to say that the few African or Asian women there were generally nicely dressed (none naked) and most were looking for loving relationships, not sexual encounters! That is how it should be folks. Furthermore, about thirty percent wanted or wanted to try anal intercourse in addition, and at least five percent outright wanted disciplined (spanked, flogged, whipped... and some of these wanted bondage and pain as well, why? Because they know that they are bad, sinful. There were probably thirty percent that just said kinky but left it unspecified. There were many Asian women that just wanted someone to take their virginity! Why?!! That is something to cherish! Many also wanted tied and spanked, as well as anal!

Intercourse... Don't panic! Intercourse was also created by God, and I shall go into some detail here as it is critical to understand in an amazing way, it shall be more special to you, and you shall view your partner in an entirely new way. This shall assist you in understanding more about intercourse, and God's view of major life issues which we shall also discuss in this chapter. This message should also strengthen your Christian walk. Bear with me, follow along and hear what the Spirit of the Living God has to reveal.

What is intercourse? Intercourse is defined as communication between individuals. Intercourse isn't the physical act as you don't truly communicate with your genitals, it is more in the heart and manifested through the eyes, touch, and soft-spoken words. The physical closeness brings you together. It is demonstrating a complete trust in one another. It is a time of so much communication with so few words, and remember that old cliché, actions speak louder than words. If you rape someone or are physically rough with your partner, or playing the karma sutra circus, is there any demonstration of love? absolutely not!

It has been said that the pure sexual act is ninety-nine percent spiritual and one percent physical. This mixture aroused in Adam the aggressiveness to bond to the woman, enthusiastically surrounding her with his masculinity. Her attraction is both spiritual and physical. He senses her promise of companionship as well as being attracted to her physically. Her silence speaks of approval. She was created with the power of speech and could have rejected Adam's advances, but passively and with a sense of delight the woman joins the man and is not ashamed- this is in accordance with God's plan and purpose. She immediately consents to his proposal. The Shulamite speaks, *LET HIM kiss me with the kisses of his mouth.* She ANXIOUSLY AWAITS her aggressor WITH A PERMISSIVE SPIRIT.

Why marriage anyway? Is it for sex? No! The body is made up of some ten trillion sells, perhaps twelve thousand square cm of body surface area, yet people focus so much on a tiny ~ twenty-four square cm area, the one area usually kept covered. The Bible consists of one thousand one hundred and eighty-nine chapters, of which only two are really about creation; there are fifty or so chapters on the holy tabernacle and more on the Temple of God. The temple of God was a permanent structure, but we are tabernacles for the fact that our bodies on earth are temporary, at death we become temples thus we look at the construction of the tabernacle in this chapter. The body, the temple is so important, that tiny area-the holy of holies, the most special and important of the tabernacle that only the one high priest could enter into the veil. Yet there is an entire body area to enjoy, and in fact, isn't the face of thy wife, husband far more beautiful than that tiny area? 1st Corinthians 12:23 tells us *and these members of the body, which we think to be less honorable, upon these we bestow more abundant honor, and our uncomely parts have more abundant comeliness.* Think about it. I mentioned the cells, the largest cell in the human body is the sperm, and second largest is the ovum. In fact, I think (as I believe many others likewise) that a nice backside, or nice legs, not to mention her face, are far more beautiful that a woman's little flower, and I think that certainly there must be parts of a man's body that are far more attractive than his male organs, nevertheless, that little area brings great intrigue and is in fact, a very important part as it allows the high priest to enter into the temple which is to be a very holy and sacred time and event, just as in the Old Testament period.

Is sex necessary? Couldn't God have made man without woman and made him unisexual as some other organisms are, so that he would be able to procreate, reproduce? Sure, God could have...but...He didn't. Remember God created Jesus Christ without man. We see in 1st Samuel 2:20-26 that the Lord visited Hannah so that she conceived; and bore three sons and two daughters. Now, no doubt here, God used her husband, but...it was the LORD! She had been barren for so long, but her submissiveness and obedience to God and her husband brought them blessings. God could have made it so that man could fertilize an egg laid by the woman, but He didn't. You should get the idea here and now that God created anatomy and sexual intercourse the way that He did with purpose, and as a parallel of what Jesus Christ did for us. The way God created humans allows the parable that we shall begin discussing, but also allows pleasure for both the man and the woman, and allows the physical closeness of being one. We are talking about one very small opening, when there are seven openings in the face, but these meet with much less interest, even though the eye is so beautiful.

The head god of the Canaanite religion was El, and his wife was Asherah. He also married his sisters, one of whom was Asterah. Asterah was probably the nickname of Istar (Babylon), Asteroth (Canaan), goddess of fertility. As we study the ancients we are impressed with the omnipresence of this female deity. She appears as Astarte (Phoenicia), Isis (Egypt), Demeter (Greek), Aphrodite (Greek), Ishtar (Assyrian), Venus (Roman), Artemis (Assyrian). Virgo.

The consequence of false worship is wrong conduct; conversely the result of true worship is moral or right conduct.

God gave us marriage for two principal reasons. First, literal as a helpmate for the husband, not a slave, but someone to love, encourage, assist each other along the way, along the pathway of life; Secondly, spiritually, as a parallel, a parable of God's relationship with man and man's relationship with God. Now, don't get me wrong, I loved and cherished and miss those intimate moments with my wife, where the veil was removed and we became united as one flesh physically, emotionally, and spiritually. However, I think about it, and those times are the same moments that I cherish most with my Father God, These intimate times with Him, the quiet, uninterrupted time of fellowship with God; The world behind me, God before me. You see God designed the intimate relationship in marriage to depict what He accomplished through His Son, Jesus Christ for us, showing His magnificent, beautiful love that He has for us and the relationship that He desires from us, that in the end, we have become one and we may each sit at the marriage supper with our Bridegroom, and God did this only for mankind who was created in His image, amen. Every detail of God's creation is so perfectly designed to show us of Himself and His extreme love for us, His bride. fourteen years later, I miss the sexual intercourse of course because it is such a wonderful, intimate moment, but what I miss so much is having her to hold and be held, to talk with and listen to, making one another laugh and bring joy after the long day apart, speaking of her day, our children, her joys and sorrows... An infant must be held and touched-human contact or it will not survive. I believe that we all have this need; it is not limited to infants. After an old person loses their partner, they frequently will die within six months or so. Why? Perhaps it is because they lose that human contact and the listening ear.

These intimate, personal times together, what is intercourse anyway? Oh, get your minds back my friends. Intercourse is defined as a communication or exchange. Intimate is defined as a close, personal relationship. Whew! We got through that hurdle. In 1st Corinthians 7:4, we receive some shocking information. As we are standing there naked, we are still in the bedroom, in front of our spouse, listen closely to this, dear brothers and sisters. *The wife hath not power over her own body, but the husband: and likewise also the husband hath not power over his own body, but the wife.*

It's not so much the physical act of intercourse for he places his organ into her orifice whereby they experience a couple of minutes of pleasure before he climaxes, then it's over and all returns to normal. No, the pleasure of these magic moments, making these moments so special and so wonderful is derived from the emotional, the spiritual unity, and the time whereby we literally are **BECOMING ONE.** Just as the best times in one's life is when we are one in the Spirit with God and we sense His presence inside of us, that He is there right beside us.

Evolutionists say that sex is just a reward mechanism to encourage us to pass on our genetic material, but...that's not what God says. God created man in Their image as I have said earlier, but...He needed a relationship with another to reflect God's relationship with us as well as the relationship between God, Jesus, and the Holy Spirit.

In Genesis 2:20 we see that Adam was naming all of the animals as God brought them to him two by two. He must have felt alone not having a mate like all of the others.

God could have created Eve at the same time as Adam, but He didn't. He made them on the same day but not the same time, Adam had to wait. This waiting (patience) should have encouraged him to appreciate the precious gift from God, are you listening my dear friends? God could have created Eve by speaking her into existence; He could have created her from the dust like He did Adam, but He didn't. He took a rib from Adam, a piece of Adam! I believe that this has multiple meanings to be aware of. God made from Adam, for Adam, indicating unity and oneness. He made Eve from a rib, not a foot bone, head bone, back bone, but a rib. The rib is next to the heart, from which to love her. It was taken from Adam and given to Eve. Man is to give of himself and care for his wife, just as God gives and cares for us. In Genesis 2:22, we see that God brought the woman to Adam, not Adam chasing after or looking for Eve. God's precious gift, when you wait patiently, God will provide. She is to give of herself to her husband only and to submit to his authority since she is in fact a part of him.

In Psalm 23:4 God says *Thy rod and thy staff they comfort me*. This statement has a two-fold meaning. First, is the chastisement, the discipline that keeps us on the right path, protects and guides us. Secondly, He is our rod-the vine, is there ever a time that you women feel as safe, secure, protected and loved as when you are one with thy husband in a loving embrace? I think not, and neither is there a time when we as sinners can feel as loved, safe, and secure as when we fall into God's precious, loving, outstretched arms and become one with Him. He waits for each of us with such love and mercy. We are the branches. We fall away but He in His infinite mercy is always ready to graft us back in. He is our rod, our strength, our protector, our shield, and our guide. But He can only do so much for us unless we...surrender ourselves, our all to Him, submit to His authority. Likewise, my sisters must surrender all to thy husbands. It isn't always easy...but it is absolutely necessary for a successful marriage. Likewise, we must do so for a successful marriage to Christ.

In Genesis 4:1 we see that Adam didn't know his wife (consummate) until after God gave her to him, Genesis 2:22. Adam didn't seek a wife; God gave him the gift of a wife. Are you listening? Again, he didn't go looking, he waited upon God and God created a wife for him, special for him, and gave her to him.

So, where are we? We are still standing naked in the bedroom. Intercourse, the woman **after** marriage, **welcomes her husband** to come into her, just as when we accept Christ, we allow the Holy Spirit to come into us, and we should welcome Him. She is still a virgin, has the hymen intact, you notice as you get to know and explore each other.

I need here to also say that as you touch and explore each other's bodies, that the real art of touch is not so much selfish, enjoying yourself, but selfless, trying to make the other, the one being touched, feel good and loved.

I have written some material on the Song of Songs, Esther, and Ruth, but let us look at the Song of Songs for a minute, 4:12-16, *A garden inclosed is my sister, my spouse; a spring shut up, a fountain sealed. Thy plants* (don't shave my sisters) *are an orchard of pomegranates, with pleasant fruits, camphire, with spikenard and saffron, calamus, and cinnamon, with all trees of frankincense* (purity), *myrrh* (death) *and aloes, with all the chief spices; A fountain of gardens, a well of living waters, and streams from Lebanon. Awake, O north wind, and come, thou south, blow upon my garden that the spices thereof may flow out. Let my beloved come into his garden* (note into his garden, not my garden, because her body is his), *and eat his pleasant fruits.* In Leviticus Chapter 15 her labia are referred to as flowers, though some believe that it refers to menstrual impurity. The original word niddaw translates impurity, filthiness, menstruous, set apart.

At this point I feel compelled to take you back to the Old Testament. We are the temple of God are we not? So, we need to return to the Old Testament and there explore the construction of the tabernacle as God gave the instruction, and look at how this relates. I know that for those of you who read thy Bibles, most skip over this part. There was an outer curtain and an inner curtain. The outer curtain was the access into the tabernacle. The inner curtain was for access into the Holy of Holies, where the Ark of the Covenant, the treasure, was kept. The outer curtain or veil; your clothes, have already been removed by now and now you have gained access into the beautiful temple, the tabernacle of God, and Oh, how beautiful it is. Now, the inner veil or curtain was strong, actually it was reported as being four inches thick, and was so designed to keep out any and everyone except for the High Priest. The inner veil we are talking about here and now is the hymen that now must be entered into in order to consummate the marriage. He came into her and they became one, we see this time and again in scripture, for example in Deuteronomy 21:13. The hymen is a tissue (veil) covering the vaginal entrance, a veil over the holy of holies. The hymen really has no physiological function, only spiritual. Stay with me here, because it is all starting to come together. Again, let us return to the Old Testament. Who was allowed to enter into the inner curtain, into the Holy of Holies? Only the high priest ordained by God! We see in Hebrews 5:1-10 the qualifications for the high priest. First, he had to be a man (righteousness and no homosexuality-gay or lesbian) verse 1. Secondly, he had to be compassionate verse 2. Third, he had to learn through suffering verse 7-8 which leads us to patience.

On the wedding evening, during the act of copulation, and the man found reason to deplore his bride i.e., during his attempt to consummate the marriage the man found a barrier, He sensed that his wife, who obviously claimed to be a virgin, was not or in his mind he believed the woman that he married to be a harlot; Therefore, at that instant, before the conclusion of the wedding day, the marriage was in a serious crisis. Is it possible that the when of Deuteronomy 24:1 is a reference to the marriage night? Could it be that the man saw some bodily flaw, physical disease, or other physical unpleasantness which caused him to loath the woman he married— *she find no favor in his eyes.* I believe that the text in Ephesians 5:25-27 is appropriate here: *Husbands, love your wives, even as Christ also loved the church, and gave himself for it; That he might sanctify and cleanse it with the washing of water by the word, That he might present it to himself a glorious church, not having spot, or wrinkle, or any such thing; but that it should be holy and without blemish.* You are married, you vowed before God for better for worse in sickness and in health!

Sampson, the thirteenth and final judge, violated Israel's special marriage code by choosing a bride over his father's wish, and choosing that woman from the ungodly Philistines. Fortunately, Jehovah oversaw the entire affair and redeemed Sampson by inflicting judgment upon Philistia through Sampson's anger. It would be good if we could end the downfall of Israel as recorded in Judges right here but we can't. Chapter nineteen opens a very ugly bag of worms.

The Levite was returning to his home in Mount Ephraim, with his wayward concubine (concubines were again the invention of man's polygamist nature).

The Book of Samuel opens with another sad story. Here the priest Eli fails as a father, his son's, Hophni and Phinehas, taught and practiced heathen doctrine of the worst type; they offered unacceptable sacrifices to Jehovah. But their most well-known act was their propagation of the doctrine of temple prostitution. Hophni and Phinehas committed sexual acts with the women who assembled at the door of the tabernacle of the congregation.

During this period of gloom another ray of hope shines into this darkness, that of Ruth the Moabitess. This beautiful story is actually made even brighter by the background of all this sin. This love story is a picture of the day that the Son of God would offer his Holy Life as a ransom for His friends- you and me. Boaz in his love spread his skirt over Ruth in claiming his bride. Jehovah in his love affair with Israel did the same: *Now when I passed by thee, and looked upon thee, behold, thy time was the time of love; and I spread my skirt over thee, and covered thy nakedness: yea, I sware unto thee, and entered into a covenant with thee, saith the Lord God, and thou becamest mine,* Ezekiel 16:8. Boaz, after redeeming Ruth, marries her and brings her into the realm of marriage.

Dear brothers and sisters, the husband that God ordained for you sisters, is to be the high priest the lord of your family. Remember in Job 1:5, Job was acting as the high priest of his family when the calamity struck. That is actually why the calamity struck. When we serve God with a pure heart, Satan seeks to destroy you, and your marriage, and God allows you to be tested and tried, but He never leaves you alone, He is there to see you through, it is up to you to hold on, or fall into the fire. He and the angels are watching you, Amen. There was a great fear entering into the Holy of Holies, so after the veil was torn, do you think that they were anxious to enter in? I believe that there remained a great fear and reverence for the Holy of Holies. So, don't be so anxious, but enter with fear and reverence into thy wife, into the holy of holies.

Just as only the High Priest could enter into the Holy of Holies, so likewise, **only** your high priest, the lord of thy family, your husband, may enter into the sacred, sanctified area of thy temple.

Dear brothers and sisters, God designed only one key for each lock, are you listening? God told the Israelites that they could only offer sacrifice in the designated altar, likewise only one man and one woman as clearly ordained by God, the

Creator of all. It isn't a matter of trying different keys to your heart, it's a matter of finding the right heart, and then the correct key will be attached, amen? The woman should not touch another man or the man a woman until married. Look at Deuteronomy 25:11-12 ...*and putteth her hand, and taken him by the secrets: thou shalt cut off her hand...* Now, in context she was trying to help her husband, but...

Before we go any further, I need to take you to Genesis 35:7, where we see that the first thing again was to worship God! When we get a new house, car, job, spouse, child, whatever, the first thing that we should always do is to sanctify ourselves and worship God, our Provider. Then shall the blessings come. Even a husband or wife- how many of you men after getting married and before enjoying her in consummating thy marriage, bothered to sanctify thyself and worship God, thanking Him for this precious gift, and asking God's blessings upon her, and thy marriage. Perhaps if this was done, we'd have fewer divorces amongst Christians. Before we go any further, I need to say that, yes, you both are now naked and anxious, but... Who gave thee thy partner? Who is going to sustain thy relationship and provide for your family? You both at this point need to get down upon thy knees and praise God, thank Him, for this blessing, and ask for Him to bless each other, thy marriage and family, thy possessions...

In the bedroom don't be shy to show thyself to thy God ordained life partner, variety is the spice of life and we are all a little bit different from one another physically. And don't be afraid to allow your life partner to enjoy you and your body. Try something new and different that you both can enjoy. Try different positions within the confines of biblical teaching which includes first and foremost love and respect; vary your routine so that neither of you get bored. If there is something that you desire to try within the confines of biblical teaching, discuss openly with your life partner and see if they are in agreement.

Now, as you prepare to enter into the temple, you should sanctify yourself. You should enter in prayerfully, humbly, and respectfully. The temple of God is not a toy, nor a playtime, but an ordained and sacred temple created just for you. It should be a time of worship- of the Creator, not the creation, a time of praise and thanksgiving. Just as the High Priest entered into the Holy of Holies; you should leave the world behind during this intimate time. This time is holy and sacred.

We are back in the bedroom, still in the bedroom, naked, man and wife. They have explored one another's bodies, their temples. Now the woman welcomes her husband to enter into her, just as a believer welcomes the Holy Spirit to enter into our lives, our temples. It was by the Holy Spirit coming into Mary that she conceived Jesus Christ. Just as we are to submit to the Holy Spirit of God, so must women their husband.

Again, I am not ashamed to repeat myself. This time of entering in should be done with reverence and a totally unselfish manner, doing everything to please and comfort thy partner rather than thyself. It is not a time for a karma sutra circus. If you think about it, in the love stories, they are always in the missionary position, why? Because the woman lies down submitting her all unto her husband, the high priest of the family. They are then in a position whereby they can look into each other's eyes making the act of intercourse (communication) to be more intimate, but looking deep into each other's souls, their innermost being, communicating in the deepest way possible. Missionary position may seem boring in light of all the karma sutra circus stunts that are being so widely spoken about today, but...intercourse is not designed to be an exciting event, but rather an extremely intimate period of time where the husband and wife can be so close physically, emotionally, and spiritually, with skin to skin, heart to heart, and the ability to look deeply into one another's eyes looking deep into their souls and literally **BECOMING ONE**, just as we should have this intimate time with God, being so close and searching His heart, His desire for you. This cannot be accomplished when you are looking at her backside and she is looking at the sheets or whatever.

Inside the clam shell is a treasure, a pearl of great price,

Inside the bird's egg is a great treasure.

Behind the veil of the Temple was a great treasure-the ark and commandments.

Likewise, when one enters a woman (she allows her lord to enter) you will find great treasure if you are her chosen and ordained priest.

This should be an extremely intimate period of **BECOMING ONE** with God and thy partner which He hath ordained for you.

We see in Genesis 38:2-3 *and Judah saw there a daughter of a certain Canaanite, whose name was Sarah; and he took her, and went into her and she conceived.* She became his wife. In Deuteronomy 21:13 ...*thou shalt go in unto her, and be her husband, and she shall be thy wife.* You see this time and again in scripture. He came into her and they became one... married! Remember Adam and Eve were husband and wife, Genesis 2:24-25; 3:17. There was no ceremony, only consummation. So, my brothers and sisters, be careful, be prayerful, and be married before you go entering or allowing entrance into the holy of holies of the temple of God. The sabbath must be honored so no sexual intercourse as it is work by definition and one is considered dirty til the night- see Leviticus 15, thus cannot go to church.

The husband enters into his wife, not into another woman, not into a man or woman into a woman, tearing the hymen and bleeding occurs. This is so important! When Christ died upon the cross, shed His precious blood, the veil was torn in two, because God wanted us to become one with Him, no longer anything between us, to separate us. After the veil was torn, we no longer were two, but the truly spiritual becomes one with Christ, hallelujah! Brothers and sisters, man and wife become one when that veil is torn. We shall discuss this more shortly, but my dear friends, condoms separate us, they create a barrier between us, which is against God's will. Jesus died, tore the veil that we no longer needed a mediator, nothing between God and us. A barrier also wastes seed, which is a sin in itself. He calls us to become one, united, to love one another and trust God. When Christ died upon the cross and His blood was shed for us, the covenant, the testimony, which always had to be sealed by the shedding of blood, so tearing of the woman's hymen and subsequent shedding of her blood seals the marital vows, the Holy covenant, until death do you part. Are you seeing why people should not expose themselves to extramarital situations? One must recall that if there was no bleeding, she was declared not to be virgin, damaged goods so to speak. The man could return her before the church, thus humiliating her and her family, and the marriage could be annulled. Christ shed His precious blood for you and for me. No bleeding indicates adultery or fornication both of which are sin; More on this shortly. The veil is torn; it is a parallel of the removal of sin that separates us from God. Since His death at Calvary, the veil torn means that we no longer need a mediator, we have direct access to God through His Son Jesus Christ. No priest or man need mediate for us any longer. Through His death, shedding of His blood, we can now be one with Him. The woman (sinner) dies (bleeds) to self and the marriage is consummated. Consummation means to make complete or perfect. We die to self and commit, submit, to God and He will consummate our relation, through the justification through His Son Jesus Christ. The marriage is now consummated. And he came into her and the two became one flesh, see also Ephesians 5:31, *And he came into her and took her as his wife.* We see the Holy Spirit came upon Mary and she conceived a child. Elizabeth and Mary are the first recorded in the New Testament to be Spirit filled. The Holy Spirit God, dwells in all who believe, who are truly spiritual. You may look also at Genesis 24:67; Exodus 22:16. Also whereas Christ bled and the veil was torn once and for all, the woman bleeds and veil torn only once.

Is there really any need for breast or especially vaginal exams normally? Or is it simply another form of fornication or adultery. Read also 1st Corinthians 6:16. If you truly believe and are obedient to Christ, He will keep you well, and if by chance you become ill God's word says to go before the elders and be prayed for. Again, I am not telling you what to do, just giving you things to consider in your life and your Christian walk, and please, don't take me wrong, as there is a time and place for doctors.

One becomes guilty of adultery when they are unfaithful in their vows to the Lord. Matthew 12:39, and t is a form of blasphemy against the Holy Spirit when you say it was a mistake (God never makes a mistake!) and break covenant with God in seeking a divorce as blasphemy is attributing the Spirits work to Satan. And permit me to take this one step further to Matthew 12:36-37 where Jesus says *But I say unto you, that every idle (useless) word that man shall speak, they shall give account thereof in the Day of Judgment. For by thy words thou shalt be justified, and by thy words (broken vows to man and God) thou shalt be condemned.* For Jesus says in Matthew 7:21 *not everyone that sayeth unto me Lord, Lord, shall enter into the kingdom of heaven.* In Hebrews 4:1 we are told *Let us therefore fear, lest a promise being left us of entering into His rest, any of us should seem to come short of it,* for only an unbeliever would dare mock the Spirit of God and break covenant and the bond of unity which God hath created-to honor and serve Satan and the world. Divorce is serious my dear brothers and sisters. Paul says in Hebrews 3:19 *So we see that they could not enter in because of unbelief.* In 4:2 **For unto us was the gospel preached, as well as unto them: But the word preached did not profit them, not being mixed with faith in them that heard it.** As if this sin of adultery is not bad enough, I read a poll of pastors... PASTORS! As well as of MD's, the two professions that one should most be able to trust; the number who admitted to having had relations with a woman, man, patient and/or of rape was staggeringly high! People submit themselves unto the authority of these professionals rather than to God and obedience to His word. Part of the reason for this is ignorance...most don't know the word of God because they never or rarely read it, study it, instead they go to church once a week (maybe) and trust whatever they are told. Women especially transfer their husband's authority over her to these other men. Friends, this is such an abomination! We read in the law found in the Book of Leviticus 20:10 *And the man that committeth adultery with another man's wife, even he that commiteth adultery with his neighbor's wife, the adulterer and the adulteress shall surely be put to death* (hell is the second death). This is so serious to God! I want you to understand that in the NT after the church began you don't see any cases of adultery, because it ought not to be found within the church.

Malachi's prophecy declared that John would be sent to prepare the way of the Lord. Then Malachi goes on to say that John would be a swift witness against sinners, and he specifically mentions adulterers in Mal. 3:5. John certainly fulfilled this prophecy as we follow his ministry. As a matter of fact, one could argue that his sermon on adultery and incest was his greatest sermon. Matthew chooses to reveal the fullness of John's sermon in chapter fourteen of his Gospel. The Old Testament closes with this promise found in the book of Mal. 3:1, *Behold, I will send my messenger, and he shall prepare the way before me: and the Lord, whom ye seek, shall suddenly come to his temple, even the messenger of the covenant, whom ye delight in: behold, he shall come, saith the Lord of hosts.*

The striking accusation is that if a man only with his eye looks upon a woman to lust after her, to contemplate even the smallest mental initiative to think of seeing through the clothing, undressing the woman, touching the woman sexually, or of proceeding into sexual contact with the woman—that man is guilty of committing adultery, likewise a woman to a man. He then emphasizes his comment by saying in Matthew 5:29, *If thy eye offends thee, pluck it out, and cast it from thee; for it is profitable for thee that one of thy members should perish, and not that thy whole body should be cast into hell.* Jesus accused every man who has ever looked upon a woman or a woman upon a man, with the sinful pleasure of lust, of committing adultery with that woman or man. That man or woman broke the Seventh Commandment; Thou shalt not commit adultery, nobody is exempt! Jesus intended to convict all; His purpose was to call all men to repentance and He did accomplish that. But the provocative way that women dress is causing men to sin, women again are bringing men down.

The Law of Moses protected the marriage covenant in the case of adultery. The adulterer and adulteress were to put to death. It was that simple. When the death penalty was no longer practiced, the State of Israel lost its authority because of the apostasy; men employed the death penalty in a different way, divorce. To the human mind this was equal to capital punishment. Many believe that life in prison is equal to the death penalty since society has eternally excommunicated the social violator. Some denominations actually teach that in the case of infidelity in the marriage bond, the innocent partner has the right to put to death the offender by executing a divorce, but this is wrong and not scriptural.

The salvation of God is by grace through faith and not of works. Our marriage to Christ is a great mystery as seen in Ephesians chapter 5. This is an analogy of our salvation by grace to God and His Son Jesus Christ. Oh, so great our salvation! The very meaning of the word salvation teaches perfect safety. Should we commit some sin and depart from the Lord and Savior Jesus Christ for a time, we can be assured that He will never leave us or forsake us. He will never divorce you or me, however, so many walk away from Him.

The Apostle Paul counseled the innocent partner to peacefully wait for the return of the sinning partner as we see in 1st Corinthians 7:16 *For what knowest thou, O wife, whether thou shalt save thy husband? or how knowest thou, O man, whether thou shalt save thy wife?* If any God ordained marriage can be put asunder then the salvation of God; Christ's marriage to the believer *(For we are members of his body, of his flesh, and of his bones)* can be put asunder. That divorce doctrine equates that the salvation of God can be lost because of sinful works and if that is the case you are confessing to a doctrine that you obviously gained your salvation, your marriage to Christ, by good works. If one believes they can lose their salvation by evil works, then you believe that you can gain salvation by good works. You cannot have it both ways: *What therefore God hath joined together, let not man put asunder.* Only legalism teaches divorce. The foundation of divorce is the law of man. The foundation of *the* God ordained marriage is grace; it completely contradicts the law.

We see in Luke 1:5 that Zacharias was the father of John the Baptist. Herod and his family played a significant role in the lives of Jesus and John the Baptist. The Herod mentioned here in Luke chapter 1 is Herod the Great; Herod I. Herod the Great had ten wives and many sons. His wife Malthake, a Samaritan, was the mother of Herod Archelaus, and Herod Antipas. Another wife, Cleopatra of Jerusalem, bore Herod Philip. Antipas ordered the bloody decapitation of John the Baptist.

Repent for the Kingdom of Heaven is at hand. To John repentance was the first step in making the way of the Lord straight. To Jesus repentance was the first step in dealing with any and all the sins of the people. All the marriage sins of his day were relegated to that first step, repentance. My dear brothers and sisters, are you listening to this?

John's last and greatest sermon was aimed at the marriage sin of the political ruler of his time, Herod Antipas. His last sermon cut to the heart of Herod Antipas and Herodias. Antipas' half-brother by his father, Herod Philip was previously married to Herodias. She became embittered with Philip because he was disinherited by his father Herod the Great.

This Philip was disinherited through the treachery of his mother and lived privately in Rome with Herodias and their daughter Salome. Herod Antipas was a son of Herod the Great and the Samaritan Malthake and thus a half-uncle of Herodias, and was married to the daughter of Aretas, King of Arabia Petrea. While he was on a visit to Rome, Antipas and Herodias eloped, and the wife of Antipas, not waiting to be divorced, returned to her father, and a war followed between Aretas and Herod Antipas.

It was not Philip the tetrarch, but this Herod-Philip, whose wife Herod, Antipas the tetrarch had married, and in that her first husband's lifetime, and when her first husband has issue by her; for which adulterous and incestuous marriage John the Baptist justly reproved Herod, Antipas the tetrarch; and for which reproof Salome, the daughter of Herodias by her first husband Herod-Philip, who was still alive, occasioned him to be unjustly beheaded. So now we have Matthew describing another case of special fornication regarding marriage, which is incest. This is remarkable to say the least. Matthew reports two cases of each (fornication) in marriage and both cases required divorce to conclude them.

In Mathew 5:32; 15:19; 19:19 and others, the actual translation Is fornication instead of marital unfaithfulness as is written in many of the modern translations.

Matt 5:5,7,9, 24, 33, 38, 40, 44-45, 48 The higher way, as described here could not allow for divorce for marital unfaithfulness or fornication.

She remembered it all only too well— her stormy, reckless past. The daughter of Aristobulus, the ill-fated Asmonaean princess Mariamme (I), she had been married to her half-uncle, Herod Philip, the son of Herod the Great and of Mariamme (II), the daughter of the High-Priest (Boethos). At one time it seemed as if Herod Philip would have been sole heir of his dad's territories. But the old tyrant had changed his will, and Philip was left with great wealth, but as a private person living in Jerusalem. This didn't set well with this woman's goals. It was when his half-brother, Herod Antipas, came to visit him at Jerusalem that an intrigue began between the Tetrarch and his brother's wife. It was agreed that, after the return of Antipas from his impending journey to Rome, he would reject his wife, the daughter of Aretas, king of Arabia, and marry Herodias. But Aretas' daughter heard of the plot, and having obtained her husband's consent to go to Machaerus, she fled then to her father. This, of course, led to enmity between Antipas and Aretas. Nevertheless, the adulterous marriage with Herodias followed. To be brief, the story may be completed. The woman proved the curse and ruin of Antipas. First came the murder of John the Baptist, which sent a shock of horror through the people, and to which all the later misfortunes of Herod were attributed. Then followed a war with Aretas, in which the Tetrarch was ousted. And, last of all, his wife's ambition led him to Rome to solicit the kingship, which had recently been given to Agrippa, the brother of Herodias. Antipas not only failed, but was deprived of his territories, and banished to Lyons in Gaul. The pride of the woman in refusing favors from the emperor, and her faithfulness to her husband in his fallen fortunes, are the only positive points in her history. As for Salome, who was first married to her uncle, Philip the Tetrarch, Legend has it, that her death was retributive, being the consequence of a fall on the ice.

Jesus' departure into Galilee was not for fear of Herod Antipas, but rather Jesus retired to Galilee, correctly noting that Galilee was also the territory of Anitpas. Jesus was going to take over where His witness left off. He would now begin His preaching. Again, His first sermon was one of repentance; for His first words, like John the Baptist, was Repent! *Repent for the kingdom of heaven is at hand.*

Now while John was in prison for accusing Herod Antipas and Herodias of being unlawfully married, Jesus was preaching His first sermon, *Repent for the kingdom of heaven is at hand.*

I feel compelled to add here, that when the Holy Spirit came into the temple, the Holy Mountain, none dare draw near, showing God's protection over us, as our bodies are also holy, the temples of God. My dear sisters, once your lord, your husband, Sarah called Abraham lord, comes in, you should never show or allow another man or woman to see or approach thy temple. It is sacred, and your relationship must be revered. Your temple is holy and must not be entered or seen except by your high priest, and him alone, no other gods, are you with me? When Israel was getting bit by the serpents (snakes), God told Moses to make a golden serpent and place it around the stick. They did and if they were bit and looked at this then they were healed. Later this same became an idol that people worshipped and God said to destroy it. They did, but unfortunately it was later resurrected and is the symbol of the medical system, which people again tend to worship. In the medical system, there is a syndrome we eloquently call the god complex. Doctors have this complex and people worship them instead of going before the Master Physician our Creator, to heal us and care for our temples. This is an entire subject also covered in my book **'ONLY BELIEVE'**. We are to surrender ourselves fully, submit to only the One True and Living God, and He alone should be allowed entrance into our temple. Each of us is sanctified to and for one God. Each of us are sanctified to only one spouse, ordained by the Living God from the time of betrothal until death do you part.

So, why should you keep your panties up (I say this not to be rude, but a woman can pull up her dress or skirt, but nothing can happen as long as her panties are up), your veil, your clothes on before marriage? In Judges 21:11 we see God orders that *ye shall utterly destroy every male, and every woman that hath lain by man.* It is a sin, an abomination to lay with a man other than thy husband, to serve other gods, or to defile thy holy temple of God Almighty. Deuteronomy 22:14-21. Men if righteous will also keep their clothes on and not yield unto the temptation of falling into the deep pit that leads to eternal death. Even many bathing suites cover less area than one's underwear! We as true Christians need to return to a modest mindset and cover ourselves, out of respect for God, our marriage partner, our families, and ourselves.

As with all gifts, sexuality comes with a set of rules; an instruction manual so to speak, found within the Bible, the Creator created the gift and the instructions for its use! Now, I need to remind you my dear friends that as I said earlier, women represent all of us sinners in the scriptures, so men and women need to honor and care for their temples, God's temples. Furthermore, in a practical sense, if a woman keeps her clothes on before marriage, and during marriage other than with her husband, men couldn't defile or desecrate thy temples and vice versa. My brothers, you represent God and righteousness. God won't ask any of us to sin, or serve other gods, or to defile His temple, His creation, so neither should we. Are you getting this message? Only one husband, one wife, there is no other way.

God, with outstretched arms, calls us and says '*Come unto me and I will give thee rest,* I will give thee peace, I will protect and guide you,' I will, being a covenant promise. I will provide all of thy needs in sickness and in health, in good times and bad, for richer or poorer. There is no death for the believer, so He does not include this portion. Death is reserved for those who choose not to believe, who shall part and be cast into hell. As true believers, the truly spiritual, there is no death, but merely a waiting room for the marriage supper, with everlasting life, joy, peace, no more pain, no more tears, Hallelujah! My dear brothers, you must do your part for your wife as God does His part for us. I am not suggesting in any way that men are God! Never, we are but allegories and we are in fact to be Christ-like. He gives us the most precious earthly gift, that of a wife, and we must cherish and care for this gift. She is so special. She was made by God just for you! Nothing is more precious on this earth, nothing so special. Aside from the precious blood of Jesus Christ, we can receive no greater gift. Take your God given responsibility seriously, because of God's love, let it so shine through you; and my sisters, you must remember the covenant promise with God.

Now, the husband is in the temple and climaxes, they both climax, defined as the most intense point of an experience. Then the seed is planted and the garden watered.

God breathed into us the breath of life, men, you are giving the seed of life unto thy wife, a miracle of miracles, just as God gives us the seed of life through His Son Jesus Christ. God plants the seed in us through the Holy Spirit, for eternal life, should we accept it by faith, just as the husband plants the seed for life and future generations of believers, children, grandchildren... should God so choose, and He opens the womb of the wife, God's choice, not ours.

Sexual intercourse is a reminder of God as Creator, and we see in Romans 1:25 *that man changed the truth of God into a lie and worshipped the creation more than the Creator.* This, my dear friends is simply idolatry. It is important that we don't lust after sex or women, men, but worship God and God alone. Proverbs 6:24-32 evil always looks pretty. Evil seeks after the righteous. You mess with sin and evil, be sure that there are consequences. Exodus 20:17 tells us that thou shalt not covet thy neighbor's wife, thy neighbor's property. You chase after sin or lust after it; you shall be guilty before the great Judge. Back to Proverbs 6:25, lust not after her beauty...verse 26... the adulteress will lust for the precious life (the righteous). In verse 29 we see *So he that goeth into his neighbor's wife,* (and who is our neighbor? Everyone...) *whosoever touched* her **shall not be innocent.** Continuing in verse 32 *but who-soever committeth adultery with a woman lacketh under-standing: he that doeth it destroyeth his own soul.* Jeremiah 5:7-9 *How shall I pardon thee for this? Thy children have forsaken me, and sworn by them that are no gods: they then committed adultery and assembled themselves by troops in the harlots' houses. They are as fed horses in the morning every one neighing after his neighbors' wife. Shall I not visit for these things? Saith the Lord: and shall not my soul be avenged on such a nation as this?* Now turn with me over to Proverbs 11:16 which tells us *A gracious woman retaineth honor: and strong men retain riches.* These riches are your family and your relationship with God and His kingdom, and gifts of the Holy Spirit.

There is a big difference between love and lust, love and sex. Don't confuse these terms. One lusts after that which one doesn't see, you don't see the Ferrari in your yard, so you lust after it. People lust after the parts of the body always covered. Naturists don't because everything is exposed, and they honor and respect the sexual relationship within the marriage. The eyes are so beautiful and marvelous, yet you see them all the time, so don't think about them. Lust only cares for the act, not the person, whereas with love you care about the person more than the act. Look at what happened in 2nd Samuel, chapter 13. You can read that now for yourself. We are called to be Christ-like. He set the example for us to follow, of selfless love, not selfish, not self-gratification, anger, and dominance. God with such love gave up His Son to die for us-selfless love. Christ suffered and died for us- sacrifice with selfless love, this is the way marriage should be. In lust, you only crave sex. In love, you willingly await the person that God ordained for you, and thus should we do in marriage, with no sneak previews. It is like xmas, which is another message altogether and in my book **WHAT ABOUT THE BIBLICAL PERSPECTIVE OF CHRISTMAS?** As every child knows (and adults), waiting for xmas dinner, hovering around the table, smelling the numerous and wondrous aromas emanating from the stove and oven, and working up an appetite is immensely better than the actual consumption of the meal. Love and sexual inter-course are the same, waiting for the correct person and after marriage vows are exchanged, makes the experience that much better. It's like opening gifts the night before; those who open the gifts before xmas have no surprise, and actually a letdown come xmas day. Same way with sex, you can't wait to see and try out the new model (lust), then come the wedding day? If there is a wedding, there will be no surprises, just another night of sex. If you wait, that first night will be so wonderful, so special... Dear brothers and sisters, who are single, please listen to this. If you can't keep your clothes on and your hands off, find someone else who you can truly love, for this is just lust. God will reward you.

Many ask if it is appropriate for a woman to ask her husband for intercourse. Absolutely! Just as we come and invite the Holy Spirit to come into us, it is totally proper for a woman to invite in her husband.

Now, we have discussed a lot of very important material and I pray that it hath strengthened you. But there are some serious issues that I feel compelled by the Spirit of God to discuss here and now, to help you understand the right and wrongs of some issues regarding sexuality and why, from a biblical perspective. If you are struggling with any of these, I pray that this will assist you and set you free and on the straight and narrow path. This knowledge may help some of you to assist friends or family members who are struggling with some of these issues. Before we move any further however, I wish to share another passage with you, please turn with me to Song of Songs 4:8. *Come with me from Lebanon, my spouse: look from the top of Amana, from the top of Shenir and Hermon, from the lion's dens, from the mountain of leopards.* One must see that he has called her unto himself, and taken her from her old life and her family in Lebanon, to begin a new (and better) life with him, just as God does for us. He calls her to look back one last time at the life and the hardships, to gather herself, leave her hurts, fears, and frustrations behind, and give herself entirely unto him. We are called by our Savior to leave our past behind, our old life, leave the worldly ways and walk anew with Him.

Okay, moving along here, 2ⁿᵈ Corinthians 11:2 tells us *I am jealous over you with godly jealousy: for I have espoused you to **one** husband that I may present you as a chaste virgin to Christ.* Dear friends, God ordained only one person for you.

By the shedding of the blood- Ezekiel 16:38 *and I will judge thee as women that break wedlock and shed blood are judged...* Could this shed blood be also the tearing of the veil before marriage? Think about this. Shedding of the blood and tearing of the veil before or outside of marriage is fornication or adultery, the allowing of other gods, idols, men, women, objects, other than thy spouse, it is a sin against God and against His temple, the temple you are desecrating, as well as thyself. You make thy temple and your partner's temples desecrated, dirty, and sinful. Now my dear brothers and sisters, let us read Deuteronomy 22:22-25, *if a man be found lying with a woman married to a husband, then they shall both of them die, both the man that lay with the woman, and the woman: so shalt thou put away evil from Israel. If a damsel that is a **virgin** be **betrothed** to an **husband,** and a man find her in the **city,** and lie with her,* (mind you, the woman should be at home taking care of the home, then she wouldn't be susceptible in the city);*then ye shall stone them with stones that they die; being in the city* (her place is in the home not the city); *and the man, because he hath humbled his neighbors wife...But if a man find a betrothed damsel in the field* (not in the city but at home), *and the man force her, and lie with her, then the man only that lay with her shall die.* Verse 28-29, *if a man find a damsel that is a virgin, who is not betrothed, and lay hold on her, and lie with her, and they be found: then the man that lay with her shall give unto the damsels father fifty sheckles of silver, and she shall be his wife; because he humbled her. He may not put her away* (divorce) *all his days.* We see in 2ⁿᵈ Samuel 13:15 where Amnon raped his sister Tamar. After the rape *Amnon hated her exceedingly* (it was lust not love): *so that he hated wherewith he hated her was greater than the love wherewith he had loved her. And Amnon said unto her,* *arise, be gone. And she said unto him, there is no cause: this evil in sending me away is greater than the other that thou didst unto me.* He was to marry her, so by sending her away was worse than the rape to her.

In Numbers 18:7 *therefore thou and thy sons with thee shall keep your priests office for everything of the altar, and within the veil; and ye shall serve* (man protect and serve thy wife): *I have given your priests office unto you as a service of gift* (being a husband is a gift from God, your wife is a gift from God) *and the stranger that cometh nigh shall be put to death!* Dear friends are you hearing what the Holy Spirit of God is saying, how sacred our temples and marriage is to God?

We see in Genesis 38:14, where Tamar set herself up to have relations with her father-in-law, a double sin, relations outside marriage, and with a family member. In Genesis 38:18 tells us that your sin shall find you out. God sees what we are doing, and He cares!

Women, when you start removing the veil, and allowing men and women, other than your husband into your holy of holies, the temple of God, the living God, becomes desecrated, and defiled. This adultery, mentioned eighteen times in Proverbs alone, even Doctors and nurses, especially if in disobedience to thy husband. This adultery is nothing other than spiritual idolatry. Your husband is thy lord, high priest, and anyone other than the high priest who entered into the Holy of Holies was to die. The king burned incense one time and was a leper unto his death! When people worship other gods, where does the Almighty go? You cannot serve two masters, Luke 16:13. God loves you, but He won't stay where He isn't wanted, it is your choice, because He loves and wants you so much and desires to be a part of your life. There is no place in your temple for God and Satan, only one or the other. 'Those who are not with me are against me.'

You have and will hear me refer to adultery and fornication. What is the difference? The prophets and Jesus spoke mostly of adultery because as believers, we are to be betrothed unto Christ. Adultery is intercourse with a married person. Fornication is sex with an unmarried person. Heathen are unmarried (to Christ), whereas believers are married to Christ. In Ezekiel 16:29, we see fornication with Canaan, the Canaanites didn't know God, were not married unto Him. In Proverbs as I began to say, adultery is mentioned some eighteen times in one quarter of the chapters! Why so much emphasis on adultery in a history book? Dear brothers and sisters, the truly spiritual believers are the bride of Christ. If we, being His bride, serve other gods (adultery) or divorce Him to worship and serve other gods, leaving the church and God, is clearly a sin, hurting God so very much. God sacrificed His only Son for us, whom He created with such love, and Jesus suffered tremendously for us and sacrificed His life all out of love for you and for me. This adultery and divorce have a huge price to pay-pain and suffering emotionally and physically in this life, then for eternity pain and suffering in hell. Psalm 119:133 tells us *order my steps in thy word, and let not iniquity have dominion over me.* In Matthew 12:39 we see that the nation when called adulterous by Jesus because they were unfaithful in its vows unto the Lord!

It takes great strength to resist a woman who wants you to come into her. The woman again in sin seeks to bring the man (Joseph in the case of Genesis 39) down. In 1st Samuel 19:1 we see again where a woman is used to snare a man and take him away from the path of righteousness. Again, please note that in Joshua 2:13 that it was first a woman again to entice the men to sin against God and Israel is paying the price still to this day. And Genesis 3:16 because she listened to and obeyed Satan rather than to God and her husband, she was made subject unto man, her dad then husband.

In 1st Kings 1:2-4, I wish for you to note here two important points. First, where was his wife? She should have been there by his side to keep him warm and meet his needs, but, where was she? She was nowhere to be found just as when he was returning the ark to its rightful place. She was quick to put him down but not to honor or assist him. Secondly, though they found David a virgin maiden, she served him and cared for him, kept him warm, but...he knew her not...he had no sexual relations with this virgin!

In 2nd Timothy 3:6 we see that women and men are easily lured into the bed of adultery and fornication by various lusts and enticements of this world, and the powers of darkness.

A woman takes hours to prepare herself-why? To turn heads. Proverbs 7 says she is not in her house (verse 10), her attire (verse 9), her eyelids (6:25), her speech (7:21). She makes herself up to be someone other than who God designed. She does up her hair; she does all of this to attract a man or men, or to get attention. But a man, a husband should look at the heart, not outward appearances, nor should she be out trying to attract others. She should spend more time in building her heart and mind, instead of outward appearances. We need to build up our hearts and minds on God, for God, through His precious word. God gives you, each of us, a choice who we shall serve, it's your choice. Seek and ye shall find, knock and it shall be opened unto you, but you must seek Him with a sincere heart and mind. You must repent of thy sins and sinful nature, your adultery and idolatry.

Adultery, read the book of Proverbs, in it you will find Solomon speaks about adultery eighteen times, as well as lust, and of course he is speaking literally, as well as spiritually! When you read through the thirty-one short chapters in one sitting keeping in mind this fact, it will have a whole new meaning for you.

We are talking here of adultery, so allow me to share a couple more verses for you to ponder. In Ezekiel 16:25 God tells the people *thou hast built thy high place at every head of the way, and hast made thy beauty to be abhorred, and hast opened thy feet to everyone that passed by, and multiplied thy whoredoms.* Turn back with me to Jeremiah 3:1-2 where He tells us *They say, if a man put away his wife, and she go from him, and become another mans, shall she return unto her again? Shall not that land be greatly polluted?* (Think about this my dear friends.) *But thou hast played the harlot with many lovers; yet return unto me, saith the Lord. Lift up thine eyes unto the high places, and see where thou hast not been lien with. In the ways thou hast sat for them...and thou hast polluted the land with thy whoredoms and with thy wickedness.* Oh, what a powerful statement! Let us now turn to Proverbs 6:29 where we are again told not to go into thy neighbor's wife, literally, but we are also not to join in with the sins (wife, woman, sinner) of others, look at Proverbs 1:10 and again 1st John 2:15.

Proverbs 6:32 tells us that if you fall into sin, you lack understanding of God's word. Proverbs 6:24 tells us to avoid the lusts and enticements of the world, of Satan, but rather to keep focused upon God. Back to Proverbs chapter 7, sin is lurking everywhere, but if you keep focused on God, you can resist her. The world seeks to candy coat sin, but sin is sin. Also, in Proverbs, time and again, we are told to resist the adulteress, this must include porn. One must remember, adultery is a relationship with a married person, and that as believers we are already betrothed unto God, not to sin, Proverbs 6:26. Finally in this regard, let us look at Proverbs 23:27 where God reminds us that *For a whore is a deep ditch; and a strange woman is a narrow pit.* The whore (sin) is a deep ditch, hard to get out from it without the help of God. A strange woman, a non-believer, sinner, not your own, is a narrow pit, easy to fall into, but again needs God's help to get out of and back on thy feet.

Turn with me now to Hosea 1:2. If you find your wife in bed with another man, how would you feel? Then imagine how God feels when He sees you engaging in spiritual adultery, when He sees you entering into other gods- tobacco, alcohol, drugs, sex, money, false religions, fashion, career, fancy cars and houses, greed, power... When He allowed His only Son to be hung on the cross for us!

But like Peter, we have a hard time staying awake and keeping on guard against the evils and focused on God. But just as God is so loving, merciful, and forgiving, so should we be. He never divorced His bride, as hurt as He was and is today, He still loves His bride; all those who love Him, should repent and return unto Him. We need to love our spouse with this agape love and forgiveness, because God's wife, the truly spiritual, is no different than Gomer.

Furthermore, an unfaithful wife was to be stoned, killed. Imagine in this type of a culture taking back, lovingly, your unfaithful wife, along with thy illegitimate children that she may have had through other men, gods; imagine how your family, society would respond or react to you, to both of you. I think about this, as we are illegitimate children, the unfaithful wife of our Lord. We are deserving of death, but... He bought her back for a price, what love!!! Just as...God bought us back with such a great price-the death of His precious Son upon that cross! By the shedding of His precious blood, sacrificing Himself for you and for me, oh what great love He has for us!

This woman spoken of earlier became disobedient to her Lord, and to God. She paid others to commit whoredoms. The idolatry brought curses upon her and the death and disability of a son, whom God created to be perfect. It also led to the destruction of her marriage, which God hath ordained until death. Choosing continued idolatry and friendship with the world of darkness, of sin, over God and her vows, and walk away from all that was sacred, all for the world. Just as God is faithful to forgive us, so must we forgive our spouse. I did forgive my wife before and after she walked away into outer darkness. If she should decide to return, turn from her wicked ways, and seek me as well as God once again, I would be there with outstretched arms, just as our Father does for us. Friends, it must be this way. In 2021 while I was on the site mentioned elsewhere, an add popped up for Asian friends, so out of curiosity, as I was working on marriage issues. What I found was shocking. While these women aged eighteen to sixty-one were dressed, some were selling themselves, offering one, five, ten million and five to ten billion dollars! One dad was offering one million dollars to impregnate his daughter! One asked is five million dollars enough to marry me and she was physically attractive, but! A few were orphaned or had been sold to other families because they weren't boys. Many just wanted sex. I looked at several to see what they were looking for in a man (husband) for the purposes of this message. Few mentioned love faithfulness... rather they wanted romantic, passionate, good in bed... Few of these ladies claimed virginity. Several wanted a man for her and her friend, or sister, and the abomination of wanting a man for her and her mother! And many of these wanted a man for her along with a friend, sister or mother or daughter, offering threesomes! Oh, the abomination! Again, on a Russian site the girls were more subtle but were still offering themselves up for sex. What is this world coming to? One local woman on a site for local friends, said that she was 43 and still a virgin and wanted someone to take her virginity! Rather than being honored and proud of her virginity, she wanted to freely surrender it to anyone! I must say that now days, a young man who finds a pure young lady has found a rare gem and he should respect and cherish her!

God is so good and so faithful, and that is how we must be to and for Him. We must love, respect, honor, and cherish our temples of God, as well as our precious gift from God-our husband or wife, children-your parents. Just stop for a minute to ponder this. Realize that God cleanses us from all unrighteousness, so once thou art cleansed, honor and care for thy temple as well as for the temple of thy spouse; defileth it not. Remember that when the temple was defiled by the Babylonians, it had to be cleansed and sanctified once again before worship of God could resume and before God would enter in.

This having been said, from the toddler stage of development on, people love to put things into holes. We love to make holes, and we love to fill them. We see a hole; we look for something to place in that hole. God's temple unfortunately is no exception. The holy of holies is ordained and sanctified for the high priest only! God created this inner sanctum even with a protective covering, the veil. But there is an entrance. It is for nothing and nobody but the high priest and him alone, are you with me? Other men, other hands, toys, dildos, vibrators, douches, fruits and vegetables, cans and bottles, tampons, birth control, IUD's... these are all off limits, they have absolutely no place in God's temple or in the Christian walk. Some birth control can cause permanent infertility. IUD's can cause massive infection, destruction of thy uterus and death! Also, IVF-in-vitro fertilization and fertility drugs should not be included in the life of a true believer, Prayer should be and let God's will be done. Just as we need to clean our lives and our marriages, the church also must be cleansed. We must teach

God's word and not permit the weeds to grow and choke out the blossoms. Please read at this time, 2nd Corinthians 6:14, Matthew 18:15-17, and 2nd John verse 10. We must cleanse the church of sin so that others are not enticed to follow along with it. God won't allow sin into heaven. God could have no fellowship with sin, the reason for the separation when Jesus was on the cross, therefore neither should we allow sin in the church and fellowship with it. We need to remove adultery and idolatry from the churches, and from the pulpits and the teachings thereof. Don't allow a sinful pastor in thy pulpits. Don't idolize thy pastors, God and God alone should be honored. We turn now to Psalms 81:11-12 where we read *But my people would not hearken to my voice; and Israel would none of me. So, I gave them up unto their own hearts lust: and they walked in their own counsels.* If you want to continue to see the pain in His heart, continue into verse 13. James 4:8 *Draw neigh to God, and He will draw neigh unto you. Cleanse your hands, ye sinners, and purify your hearts...*

I, as was the man earlier was working on my Doctoral dissertation and my wife destroyed it, but what Satan seeks to destroy, God will protect, and I stand here today with my Doctorate, Praise God! The title means nothing to me, what matters is that I didn't allow, nor did my Lord, to allow Satan to prevail. He got my wife, who I pray for daily, but he didn't get me. Dear friends, choose thy friends wisely and carefully. They may claim Christianity but actions speak much louder than words. Friends, I will tell you as I told my wife many times, a true friend is someone who loves, cares, and respects you for who and what you are, and doesn't try to change you. True friends pull you to Christ and not away from Him and His word.

How God has blessed me and how I was tried and tested, persecuted is beyond my imagination, beyond anything I ever dreamed possible, and is included in part in my book **'ONLY BELIEVE**

Now my dear brothers and sisters, having said all of this so far, some of you may be saying, 'this is all well and good, but I'm single', and may be feeling like you are missing out on something so special and beautiful, the intimacy, the intercourse. Do not fear, where did God concentrate when He entered the temple? Where was His treasure? Paul states that it is best to remain single, that you may sanctify thyself unto the things of God, God's service. If you are pure, a virgin, and single, then praise God! For this is a precious gift, that of serving God Almighty is the greatest gift. Isaiah 54:1 *Sing, O barren, thou that didst not bear, break forth into singing, and cry aloud, thou that didst not travail with child; for more are the children of the desolate than the children of the married wife saith the Lord.* The single man and woman can bring forth more fruit (children) unto the Lord than the married who are concerned with taking care of each other.

If you are married, praise God, for all of this. Whether single or married praise God, sanctify thyself to God and for God. Amen.

If you are single (or married), man or woman, and masturbating, or inserting objects into thy temple not ordained to be there, these are idols, false gods, desecrating His holy temple. It is a sin. Men, are you wasting seed? We see in scripture that this leads to death. In Genesis 38:9-10 *Oman knew that the seed should not be his; and it came to pass, when he went into his brother's wife, that he spilled it on the ground, lest that he should give seed to his brother. And the thing displeased the Lord; wherefore He slew him also.* It is no light matter. Dear friends, this is nothing to play around with, thy temple is sacred before our Lord God Almighty! This type of activity is not good and there are consequences. In Kenya, there are many that still take their brother's wives whether or not they had children!

While in Kenya I had the opportunity to counsel several people, one of which a young lady a couple of times. We spoke. She had trouble holding a job. We discussed this. She also had a young daughter that she was trying to support. I asked her about her husband, but she said that she was never married. I wish to point out here...friends...that this is a woman who professes Christianity and attends a local Pentecostal church. She was prostituting herself! If this isn't bad enough, and I am not judging her, but her actions and beliefs, and her pastor encouraged her in this path, A Pentecostal pastor! After we got through the why and wrongs of this, I had to ask her (my point of consequences), aren't you afraid of contracting AIDS or other sexually transmitted diseases? I was absolutely amazed at her response, and I later found out that this also was reinforced by her pastor, was Oh no Pastor! I'm a Christian and God would not allow that to happen to me. I then asked her if she knew her HIV status. No, because God will protect me. My dear brothers and sisters, you cannot walk in sin, bow to Satan, profess Christ, and think that there shall be no consequences. You cannot serve two masters, Luke 16:13. There are consequences for sin, and if truly you are a Christian, you will not continue on in sin. I also need to remind you that time and again God's word teaches *and went into his mother's tent and took her (his woman) as his wife,* Deuteronomy 21:13. ... *thou shalt go into her, and be her husband, and she shall be thy wife.* 1ˢᵗ Corinthians 6:16-17 *What? Know ye not that he which is joined to a harlot is one body? Sayeth he, shall be one flesh. But he that is joined unto the Lord is one spirit.* Again, I refer you back to Deuteronomy 22:28-29, which in summary says intercourse outside of marriage is adultery; idolatry, it is a sin. A woman who can't keep her clothes on and her legs closed, apart from her husband, and allow in anyone else is the sinner that brings down the righteous into sin and the pits of hell. Remember Aaron's sons in Leviticus Chapter 10, and the king Uzziah who went into the temple. They died, and the king became a leper until his death, Genesis 20:3. Now we move along, I pray that you are beginning to see the relevance, the spiritual side of sexuality, or you may be asking why we are even discussing this. It is meant to enhance your spiritual walk as well as your marriage, as well as to better understand these issues so as to better understand the remainder of this chapter, and be better able to help others.

The Greek word for sexual immorality is pornea, which covers everything from pornography to any sexual activity outside of marriage of one husband and one wife. Jesus' use of the exception clause indicates that there is a difference in circumstances involving pornea, or fornication than those that do not.

The Greek root word pornea is different here than adultery, which is always translated from the Greek root word moiceia. In this passage, and the one to follow, Jesus was referring to the Jewish betrothal process. He was speaking to Jewish lawmakers on legal matters. A translation of this verse could be written as But I tell you, anyone who puts away his wife, except for fornication (pornea), causes her to become an adulteress (moiceia), and anyone who then marries the woman put away in such a way, commits adultery (moiceia). We further read in the book of the Proverbs 30:20 *Such is the way of an adulterous woman; she eateth, and wipeth her mouth, and saith, I have done no wickedness,* but it is my prayer that today you shall see and be convicted of just what a sin this is.

Matthew 19:9 *And I say unto you, Whosoever shall put away his wife, except it be for fornication 'pornea', and shall marry another, committeth adultery (moiceia): and whoso marrieth her which is put away doth commit adultery (moiceia).* John 8:41 *Ye do the deeds of your father. Then said they to him, We be not born of fornication* 'pornea'; *we have one Father, even God.* Acts 15:20 *But that we write unto them, that they abstain from pollutions of idols, and from fornication* 'pornea', *and from things strangled, and from blood* 'pornea'. You may do the same substitute in Acts 21:25, 1st Corinthians 5:1, 6:13 and 18, 2nd Corinthians 12:21, Galatians 5:19, Ephesians 5:3 and 5, and others.

We see in Leviticus 18:6-20; 20:10-14, 17; and Genesis 14:31-32, I'm not going to print these, you may read these in your Bible now. Please read them. You must not have intercourse with any of thy relatives or with thy spouses' relatives, for this is a sin.

Marriage with one's daughter was and is not allowed. This is probably because it was already accepted that such a union was illicit, Genesis 19:30 Lot and his daughters. In other words, these regulations extend the prohibition on incest already accepted in other parts of the ancient Near East.

In Egypt, the land of artifacts, it is surprising that no ancient code of laws has been uncovered, nevertheless we have evidence that reveals the nature of its supreme court; since

Pharaoh believed he was the supreme court who protected the rights of his people. The rights of the people are their customs. Therefore, knowledge of their customs will reveal their laws, or the rights of the people, and book of Leviticus indirectly reveals the accepted customs of Egypt. The following is a list of sixteen certain customs that were practiced in the land of Egypt and the pharaohs: They uncovered the nakedness of their fathers. They uncovered the nakedness of their mothers. They uncovered the nakedness of their step-mothers. They uncovered the nakedness of their sisters. They uncovered the nakedness of their step-sisters. They uncovered the nakedness of their grand-children. They uncovered the nakedness of their daughters-in-law. They uncovered the nakedness of their aunts. They uncovered the nakedness of their sisters-in-law. They uncovered the nakedness of their step-children. They uncovered the nakedness of their step-grandchild. They approached a woman during her uncleanness. They lay carnally with their neighbor's wives. They burned their children to death in sacrificial worship. Their men would sexually lay with other men. They sexually lay with animals–Leviticus 18. No wonder God told Israel, His bride, not to follow the ways of the land from which you came (Egypt)! When I was gathering info from an Asian site, I was amazed that several of the young ladies and their mothers and sisters play with each other, and want a man to take both them and their mother or sister! Times haven't changed! Such abominations must not be seen in the Christian walk!

Even in Eden there was a condition placed on marriage; that it must be sought outside the parental relationship; incest was forbidden. This was not the case of the fornicator of Corinth, who had taken his father's wife. The condition was clearly commanded, that the pair would have to leave father and mother. The Mosaic Law would clearly define the forbidden degrees of marriage within the limits of family.

Polygamy is a sin. Yes, dear friends, there were polygamous marriages in scripture, most notably David and Solomon, but look at what happened because of the polygamy, sin. The men fell because of their wives, and suffered the consequences. A few patriarchs married sisters-Jacob with Leah and Rachel...

a sin, how did they get away with this abomination? How did these Patriarchs get away with polygamy when we see Do not marry a woman as well as her sister to distress her by having intercourse with her while she is alive, Leviticus 18:6-18, people ask me? Well, it was during this period in Sinai, where the law was first given. When I was hosted on National TV in one nation, discussing marriage and family, the host took me right to divorce. But one of the questions that he asked was, is God a polygamist if we are all His bride. The answer is quite simply No! God is not a polygamist. The handful of true believers comprise the true church and the true church is His bride.

The king was not to multiply horses in an attempt to return to Egypt. Neither could he multiple to himself gold or *wives*, for the multiplication of wives would cause the king's heart to turn away from his God.

Abraham may have justified acquiring an heir through the provisions of the ancient codes and customs, but his failure to trust the Lord God for a son from the bowels of his marriage to Sarah should be marked as one of the greatest sins of mankind. The son of custom, Ishmael, became the alleged father of Islam. Later giving rise to the likes of Mohammed, Kohmeni, Kadaffy, Hussein, and Arafat. What would the world have been like without Ishmael, and Islam—One of the most profound verses in the Bible for the twenty-first century must be the prophesy regarding Ishmael: *And he will be a wild man; his hand will be against every man, and every man's hand against him; and he shall dwell in the presence of all his brethren.* Genesis 16:12. God had promised Abraham greatness if he would walk by faith.

Solomon later even said it is all vanity. Genesis 4:19 introduces us to the first recorded polygamist-Lamech. In 1st Samuel Chapter 1, we see another man, Elkanah, who had two wives, Hannah who was barren, and Pennuah. The Jewish law allowed Elkanah to have a second wife because his first wife, Hannah was barren, but still not allowed in God's plan, His will, and Samuel carried on the Levitical line, the Son of the **first** wife, not the second. If you look at the definition of marriage, it is a legal relationship between **a** man and **a** woman, note please a man, not men, a woman, not women. This clearly leaves out polygamy and homosexuality-gay or lesbian relationships! I refer you here to Proverbs chapter 7. In Genesis 24:67; 29:21; 30:9 the concubine was given to wife, but only in man's eyes, not God's, and only the offspring of the first wife was generally blessed. Harem is a Hebrew word and means...utterly destroyed, and is used in the sense of belonging to a god. Listen friends, even animals know to have sex with the opposite sex!!! Have you ever seen any animal having sex with its own sex?

Sodom's horrible sins and other homosexual acts may have been out done by the Americans. Reports have surfaced of acts of homosexual abominations, which are not fitting to even reiterate in this message. Billy Graham is not far from the truth when he exclaimed that God will have to apologize to Sodom, if he further delays the judgment of America. Just take a minute to read Leviticus 18:24-27!

Today, this destructive ideology is being imposed on the world by the United States and the European Union (the reigning political and social powers) with the support of almost uninterrupted media propaganda and the coerced sex education, by new age immoral groups with the support of the governments, of school children. It is really a modern case of mental tyranny or brainwashing. The public must believe that the homosexual orientation is as normal and healthy as heterosexuality and that a homosexual relationship is equivalent to the authentic marriage between a man and a woman, or they are considered abnormal. So, we have a case of where normal and correct is socially considered abnormal and where the abnormal and unhealthy is considered socially normal. Oh, how far man has passed from the path of righteousness!

The garment of the sin of mankind is polygamy. Rather than commit adultery, a man divorced his wife, and married his lover. Rather than raping the beautiful young maid, man invented polygamy; he just married her. Now, women are having multiple husbands, so it applies to both. God allowed man to invent divorce and polygamy. He permitted them to exist, as he permitted sinful man to exist. These feeble coverings for sin are actually the sinful acts and inventions of man.

God did not invent divorce or polygamy. Remember that the first recorded sin was the eating of the forbidden fruit, the second was the murder of Abel, and the third was the polygamy of Lamech.

Polygamy is nothing more than the extension of the sin of bigamy. Realizing that more than one wife gave man the ability to have many sons, he must have imagined that he had discovered the doctrine of marriage that would make him the savior of the world- polygamy, a Satanic deception. Lamech reminds one, of the antichrist of the last day, 2ⁿᵈ Thessalonians 2:4 tells us *Who opposeth and exalteth himself above all that is called God, or that is worshipped; so that he as God sitteth in the temple of God, shewing himself that he is God.* In the midst of the Garden, the Lord God planted the tree of knowledge of good, *tohu,* and evil. When the Sethites who were godly priestly men called the sensual women, *tohu,* they were confusing good and evil.

Homosexuality-gay and lesbian relationships are an abomination unto the Lord. I can't say homosexual marriages, because a marriage is defined as one man and one woman, but countries are beginning to allow homosexual marriages, remember what I was saying about marriage licenses! We see in 1ˢᵗ Corinthians 6:9 *Know ye not that the unrighteous shall not inherit the kingdom of God? Be not deceived; neither fornicators, nor idolaters, nor adulterers, nor effeminate, nor abusers of themselves with mankind* (gay/lesbian) ... In Leviticus 20:13 He tells us that they (homosexuals) shall be put to death. The second death is eternal damnation in hell. In the book of Jude, we are told in verses 7 and 8, *Even as Sodom and Gomorrah, and the cities about them in like manner, giving themselves over to fornication, and going after strange flesh, are set forth for **an example**, suffering the vengeance of eternal fire. Likewise, also these filthy dreamers defile the flesh, despise dominion, and dignitaries.* This is referring to homosexuality, and the dignitaries are a reference to the angels. Further references for homosexuality include Genesis 19:5; Leviticus 18:22, 29; 20:13; Romans 1:26; 1ˢᵗ Timothy 1:10. Take the time now to read Genesis chapter 19. Romans 6:12-13 tells us *Let not sin therefore reign in your mortal body, that ye should obey it in the lusts thereof. Neither yield ye your members as instruments of unrighteousness unto sin: but yield yourselves unto God.* The homosexual is like a wild unbroken mare that refuseth to be humbled. The custom of Sodom had become a terrible weapon; a Satanic attack upon the Seed of the woman. The success of the Sodomites would have resulted in the destruction of man's power to propagate, preventing the birth of the Savior, and causing the death of mankind. Homosexuality is atheism and death. The United States of America is failing to control the sin of homosexuality because the government is protecting this evil custom by creating laws in its defense. In 2014, The then President of the U.S.-Obama, was traveling to Africa and telling the African Nations to accept and embrace homosexuality! Some embraced it but when one of the presidents stood up and said NO! and outlawed homosexuality in his country, Obama cut off funding and support to them according to their media! Had the U.S. Congress been the government of Sodom they could have issued in the possible extinction of the human race. God interceded to govern Sodom; he destroyed the city and its inhabitants. Today He needs to step in once again, but is allowing the bad seed a chance to repent and seek his face, if not to face future judgment! The Sodomite generation melted in the fire of sulfur; will this American generation melt? The fiery annihilation of Sodom is God's opinion and view of homosexuality. God does not make mistakes! Our God is a consuming fire. Perhaps however the independent woman, the black widow murders, and the marriage for profit has discouraged marriage and encouraged homosexuality, but this doesn't make it right in God's eyes...it is wrong!

Homosexuality has become, not the 'love' which dares not to speak its name, but rather the 'love,' that never shuts up, for the word and activity has permeated our society. It along with some other words that one used to just see occasionally painted in a hidden wall someplace, are commonplace now in word and print, for example, fuck and screw. These words are so cold, without any feeling, and yet they are nowadays freely spoken by most males AND females. I hate to be so crass, but...would you rather fuck (or be fucked), or make passionate love with someone you love? We as Christians MUST be more conscious of what we say and how we say it. We furthermore should avoid reading or watching any material that is not so selective of their terminology and values.

God did not ordain man to enter the woman from behind like animals, nor the woman on top where she is in control, and in authority. In 2nd Corinthians 4:3-4 *But if our gospel be hid, it is hid to them that are lost: lo when the god of this world* (Satan) *hath blinded the minds of them which behave not, lest the Light of the glorious gospel of Christ, who is the image of God, should shine unto them.* Read please also, Leviticus 18:22; Romans 1:26; 1st Timothy 1:10. Men, don't have sex with thy wife from behind like animals, but face to face so that you can see and appreciate her and this intimate time with her, as you both become one, love and celebrate together, not a Karma Sutra circus. This special time, ordained by God, is beautiful, precious, one to be revered, and should be a humbling experience. I now take you to Genesis 39:12 *and she* (Pharaoh's wife) *caught him* (Joseph) *by his garment, saying, lie with me: and he left his garment in her hand and fled, and got him out.* This is a perfect picture of 2nd Timothy 2:22 where we are taught to *Flee youthful lusts*, instead of accepting the invitation and falling into the pit of lust, Satan's detour. While in third world countries, I had plenty of invitations, but as quickly as I told them that I was a pastor, they walked away. Hold on to God and righteousness. Joseph held onto God and righteousness. We men and women need to take lessons from Joseph, both of them.

Homosexuality-gay/lesbian. God never makes a mistake and the worst thing one can do is blame God for their own wrong and evil choices, you are what God wants you to be, accept it and move on. I honestly believe that many homosexuals are victims of single or broken family units.

I am compelled also to ask why would a man desire to be a woman, or a woman desire to be a man. It is a sin. It is telling

God that He didn't know what He was doing when He created you, making God imperfect. The entire universe works perfectly, should one person be an exception? I believe that God is in fact perfect and made all perfect, the way that He wants you and me, He made us. You further are telling God that you refuse to be the person that He created you to be, and if you refuse His will, His purpose and plan, the deity of Christ; then there is only one judgment and it is condemnation.

Prostitution...God says, *know ye not that your body is the temple of God*? I briefly spoke on this earlier, with the young lady from Kenya. Have you or are you prostituting yourself? If you think about it, even bees go around collecting pollen (nutrition), but they always return to the same spot to deposit to make honey! Men and women can get their nutrition in various places, but the seed deposit should be in only one place! Like false gods, idols, like a trash can- drop the money, the can opens up, then dump the trash (which in this case is the precious, sacred seed of life) into the holy of holies, then the lid closes and off you go. Dear brothers and sisters, don't prostitute thyself to the world, marry Christ and remain a chaste virgin before Him and Him alone. There is power in the blood of Christ. The world offers nothing but death. Are you dear brothers and sisters getting the picture?

We read in 1st Corinthians 6:16 *What? Know ye not that he which is joined to an harlot is one body? For two, saith he, shall be one flesh*. Are you hearing this? Let me go to 1st Corinthians 3:17 *If any man defile the temple of God, him shall God destroy; for the temple of God is holy, which temple ye are*. This applies to men and women, but I pray you can see just how serious all this frivolous play is. It may seem harmless, enticing, everyone else does it...but God!!! God says NO!!!

My dear friends, the very first commandment is that ye shall have no other God's before me. You cannot serve two masters! This includes adultery, affairs, polygamy, fornication, prostitution, masturbating, homosexuality, etc.; all of which are forms of idolatry and adultery; this is for your good, for your sake, and takes us over to Romans 1:25 *Who changed* the truth of God into a lie, and worshipped the creation more than the Creator... Dear friends, why look at or chase after my spouse when you have your own? God hath blessed you but what do you do with your blessing? ... If you want her in heels, put her in heels. If you want her to be a size twelve instead of sixteen, take her out walking, but always remember that beauty is what's inside not outside, but sometimes for health reasons, some changes may be in order, and you should appreciate one another for who they are not how they look. God hath given you a blessing, a garden to tend, a spouse. The first thing that God told Adam was to tend the garden, be fruitful. We must tend to (care for) our spouse. Work is not a curse but a blessing that God hath given to us and we must work to be fruitful and productive; then the money will come. Don't work for the money, work for God. Don't worry about failing because failure is not a curse either, just God's way of saying that there is a better way, amen.

In Nahum 3:13-18 we read a very powerful passage. *Behold, thy people in the midst of thee are women: the gates of thy land shall be set wide open unto thine enemies: the fire shall devour thy bars. Draw thee waters for the siege, fortify thy strong holds: go into clay, and tread the mortar, make strong the brick kiln. There shall the fire devour thee; the sword shall cut thee off, it shall eat thee up like the cankerworm: make thyself many as the cankerworm, make thyself many as the locusts. Thou hast multiplied thy merchants above the stars of heaven: the cankerworm spoileth, and fleeth away. Thy crowned are as the locusts, and thy captains as the great grasshoppers, which camp in the hedges in the cold day, but when the sun ariseth they flee away, and their place is not known where they are. Thy shepherds slumber, O king of Assyria: thy nobles shall dwell in the dust: thy people is scattered upon the mountains, and no man gathereth them.* What are we shown here? There are several points here to see and understand. The gates set wide open, the women are opening or giving themselves to anybody, and everybody. The virgins even became the temple prostitutes. The fire shall devour, fire is destruction and purging, there is a penalty for these sins.

Multiplied thy merchants, they were having many partners, not monogamy as God ordained. As grasshoppers; hopping from one woman to another. When the sun ariseth they flee away, the darkness/night are symbolic of evil, because the Light shines upon all of thy sins. Thy shepherds' slumber, where are the pastors today? They are asleep, ignoring God's word and have been washed away by the ways and sins of the world. Because of the multitude of grievous sins, the believers have scattered away from the modern church, and no pastors are out there gathering up the flocks and leading them back to the paths of righteousness. We could go into more detail here but I believe that you must be getting the main points here. I have written messages about a few of the seven churches in Revelation and how they relate to us today.

I personally know of many cases of adultery, all with their own stories, but allow me to summarize briefly to again demonstrate the consequences of the sin of adultery. First, a married man had a onetime sexual encounter with a married woman. He ended up in jail and the woman was murdered by her husband when she tried to divorce him, so her husband ended up in prison. Another case, a married man had a one-time encounter with an engaged woman, his secretary. The man's wife divorced him, the woman's husband called off the marriage, and she had a baby from the encounter, lost her job, and then committed suicide. You see my dear friends; there are consequences, physical, emotional, spiritual; Keep thyself pure-physically, emotionally, and spiritually pure. 2nd Chronicles 21:11 refers to spiritual impurity, fornication. A friend told me about a similar situation that happened to a friend of his.

Are you men...and women into pornography? Are you watching God's precious creation- men and women, having sex, or reading romance novels (women's form of pornography).... rather than watching and waiting, sinning, find God, trust God? Seek God and allow Him to come into thy life, into thy temple. I know of a man who as a child, his dad had some Porn magazines, and he looked through them out of childhood curiosity. Later, as a scout, he did paper drives, where he collected newspapers and magazines for people and recycled them. One day on a drive, he picked up a stack of porn magazines and they were quickly set aside, and again out of curiosity, he glanced at them. Dear friends, the Bible says that if your eye causes you to sin, pluck it out... but I want you to know that it is best never to see in the first place, as once you see it, even if you pluck out thy eyes, the images are permanently ingrained into your mind. It cannot be erased. Pornography has destroyed many a marriage, family, and many lives. It is not harmless in any way and it hurts many, both those who pose, as well as those who view it. One must never look at pornographic materials as it is the equivalent of looking at other gods, and brings your mind into adultery. And be certain that at some point thy innocent children shall find it and this will be embedded in their minds the rest of their lives.

Abstain from all such activities and if you are currently involved in pornography, repent and leave it behind you. Fathers, don't get involved in this and expose thy children and women, don't pose or watch! When I was held hostage, one day, the Embassy with good intentions brought me a magazine, not one I was really interested in, but for something to do, I glanced through it. One of the ads was for I think it was a purse, but the ad showed a very famous singer, in extremely tight stretch pants in a sitting position that revealed **all** of her genitalia to be viewed. I doubt seriously like myself, that most people will even see the purse...I burned the magazine so that nobody else had to be exposed to this material. We read in Leviticus 20:10 *the adulterer and the adulteress shall surely be put to death.* This is no joke. The woman is not to tempt or tease the men of God!

There is only one entrance ordained by God, to penetrate, to enter into, only one, the others are ordained by God for discharge of waste material from the body. Are you with me?

In the Song of Songs 4:16 *Awake O north wind: and come thou south: blow upon my garden that the spices thereof may flow out. Let my beloved come into his garden* (remember the husband has power over his wife's body and she hath power over his) *and eat his pleasant fruits.* In verse 5:5 we read *I rose up to open to my beloved; and my hands dropped with myrrh, and my fingers with sweet smelling myrrh, upon the handles of the lock.* We need to keep pure until death, frankincense in scripture is symbolic of purity, Myrrh is symbolic of death, pure until death in marriage as well as in our Christian walk; the purity and death to self, and a total surrender unto our Lord.

Let us look a bit more at what God thinks of adultery. In Hebrews 13:4 we read *Marriage is honorable in all, and the bed undefiled: but whoremongers and adulterers God will judge.* Turn with me now to the book of Jeremiah 3:8-9 in which we see *and I saw, for all the causes whereby back-sliding Israel* (true believers) *committed adultery. I had put her away, and given her a bill of divorce, yet her treacherous sister Judah feared not, but went and played the harlot also.* Please listen my dear friends, *And it came to pass through the lightness of her whoredoms, that she defiled the land.* You see, God figuratively divorced her because she left Him for other gods, and God hates divorce! We'll see this in a later chapter. The land was defiled, consequences for our actions, our free choices. You are not the only one hurt. Turn now to Ezekiel 16:32-34, 36, 38. *But as a wife that committeth adultery, which taketh strangers* (other gods, unbelievers) *instead of her husband!* Don't allow in the stranger or the defiled lest it corrupt others. A little leaven leaveneth the whole lump. Have not fellowship with unbelievers. When Judah learned that his daughter-in-law was pregnant by harlotry, he unleashes the ultimate condemnation on the girl, bring her forth, and let her be burned. The ancient's penalty for harlotry was a bitter form of capital punishment.

Let's stop for a minute and digest this because there are many who will ask, 'what's the big deal?' We are the wife remember? We are the sinners, and when we chase after other gods, strangers, the unbelievers, the lusts of the flesh, like our wives chasing after other men; it is a direct disobedience to God, our Husband. Are you with me? We read on now, *They give gifts to all whores: but thou givest thy gifts to all thy lovers, and hirest them, that they may come unto thee on every side for thy whoredom.* Women do this today, but spiritually let us see God's perspective here. When we give tithes, offerings, or gifts to evil churches, religious organizations, worldly people to feed their lusts, rather than to God and His service; or we serve the world rather than serve God, we are doing the same thing. God seeks those who give one hundred percent of themselves and their God given resources, all that you possess, think and do, surrender all unto and for Him. Like the woman found in Mark 12:42-44 who gave little, but she gave all that she had. In 1st Samuel 8:8 he gave all that he had. Remember also the rich man in Matthew 19:21 who asked Jesus *What must I do to be saved*? Jesus said obey my commandments. The man then replied 'I have.' Jesus responded, then sell all that you have, give to the poor and follow me. The man walked away. No matter how much or little that our worth, our talents...God doesn't look at the amount that you have, He looks at the heart, the attitude, remember that God loves a cheerful giver. One may only be a cheerful giver if he is giving from the heart. Do you think that God should or would reward a selfish heart? Was God selfish when He sacrificed His Son? We are told in Ezekiel 16:36, *Thus sayeth the Lord God, because thy filthiness was poured out, and thy nakedness discovered through thy whoredoms with thy lovers, and with all the idols of thy abominations, and by the blood of thy children* (abortions), *which thou didst give unto them...and I will judge thee*, did you hear that! Back in the Old Testament times, they burned their sons and daughters to their gods. Today they just abort them though some still burn them in fire, I have met a few who have done just that! I will judge thee, as women that break wedlock and **shed blood**. A woman who leaves the marriage, breaks her vows to her Lord and her lord, a woman who murders, an adulteress, idolater, are all equal in God's eyes! And I will give thee blood in fury and jealousy. Oh, my dearest brothers and sisters, please hear what the Spirit of God is saying, for He hath sent me with this message to warn you, to bring you to repentance and revival. Revival of your marriage and/or bring it to a higher level, as well as by reviving thy walk with Christ down the straight and narrow path of righteousness. Too many have turned to the left or to the right and have fallen off, gotten lost. God loves you and He is striving to get you back on the right path. Do you truly wish to stand before God, before the wrath of an angry, furious God??? I tremble at the thought and take the Christian walk very seriously, thus I have been blessed. In Romans 1:26-27, God is so tired of the sinfulness; you can just hear it here, *For this cause God gave them up.* You hear that? He gave them up to their vile affections *for even their women did change the natural use into that which is against nature* (lesbian), *and likewise also the men, leaving the natural use of the woman, burned in their lust one toward another, men working with men that which is unseemly.* Listen friends, *and receiving in themselves that recompense of their error which is meet.* You see just how odious homosexuality is to God? Oh, my dear brothers and sisters please listen and hear what the Spirit is saying today!

I also must speak briefly about birth control. Just as God gives a woman to her husband so that she may bear children, so God takes us so we can bear fruit for Him. There is an organization that is a demon possessed organization, and is prevalent worldwide (it's precepts), pushing for legalized abortion (murder of unborn children, our blessings from God) and promoting abortion and population control. God, my dear friends, is in full control. He does not need man to control wildlife populations or the population of man. When a woman is with child, it is no accident, God is in full control, and that child was designed by God for a purpose, a part of His plan. There is a place that you are to fill and no one else can fill, something you are to do which no one else can do. The place God calls you is where your innermost and deepest joy and peace, meets the world's deepest hunger and needs. I want you to please Note in Ruth 4:13 the Lord, who? The Lord gave her conception! Not Boaz, but God gave her conception.

God desires for us to be fruitful in our physical and Spiritual lives. Again, being fruitful in our physical lives is analogous to our being fruitful in our Spiritual lives.

Blasphemy can denote a claim of equality with God (see John 10:33 and Matthew 26:63-65) so the action of usurping His authority is a form of blasphemy, see Mark 2:7, and trying to take control of your fertility or trying to prevent conception is usurping His authority-blasphemy.

Look at 1st Samuel 15:33, ...*as thy sword* (scalpel, suction, etc.) *hath made women childless (abortion, hysterectomy or needless C-Sections, so shall thy mother be childless among women. And Samuel hewed Agag in pieces before the Lord in Gilgal.* Now while this doesn't refer actually to abortion, hysterectomy, or needless C-Sections, it certainly could be as it indirectly is the same. This same organization is pushing their agenda worldwide to all nations, especially the third world nations, to use birth control to control the populations (mind you that many can't afford sanitary pads, yet are expected to pay for birth control?). Now there is an organization that wishes to control populations, insinuating that the population is out of control, thus that God is out of control. My dear friends; my God is not out of control, the Creator of the universe, the Creator of each and every life- man, plant, animal, is in full control! Amen! You will see in scripture, so many women wanted children; there were no men or women, who didn't want children! Look at Genesis 29:32-30:24. Barrenness was believed to be a sign of God's disfavor.

This brings us to Ruth 4:13, where we shall explore two facts that I want you to understand from this passage. First of all, the fact that as is shown elsewhere in scripture, He came into her and she became his wife, intercourse consummates marriage, the unity, they became one! Secondly is that we are talking here of a barren woman who God chose to open her womb as soon as she married Boaz, a man older than her, the age of her dad. She never conceived when married to Mahlon. This verse also reinforces that children are indeed a precious gift from God, a blessing.

Furthermore, the same Lord who sent His Son to cover our sins with His blood is the same God who commanded man to populate the world. He never called us to limit or to destroy life, just the opposite, so who are we going to listen to, the world and the above-mentioned organization and Satan, or God? I had a couple of religious leaders tell me that I shouldn't teach against birth control because 1) it is not politically correct and 2) because it is better to have one or two children and provide a good education than to have several. Where is the faith and trust in God? We are called to be Spiritually correct above all else and God promised to supply all of your needs, where is the faith and trust in God and His faithful promises?

Abortion is another slap in God's face, throwing away, murdering God's precious gift to you that He chose to bless you of all people with. Do you realize that abortion is the leading cause of death in North America? He chooses to bless you with a precious gift and you go and destroy it and throw it away? What a display of hatred towards the Almighty, the giver of good gifts. This also violates the sixth commandment that thou shalt not kill. The heart starts pumping between three and eight weeks depending on the literature that you read, you are murdering a precious life which God hath chosen to bless you with and to fulfill His purpose and plan. Remember that each of us was created by God not the parents, for a specific role in His purpose and plan, Jeremiah 29:11. This does include the IUD (intrauterine device) and the morning after pill which goes by different names in different countries. Cells are reproducing-this is life. Dead cells can't and don't reproduce. Each of us was created by God, not by our parents! Each of us was created by God for a specific purpose in His overall plan. When you kill the masterpiece of God, you destroy His creation and a part of His divine plan, like a missing piece to a ten-thousand-piece jigsaw puzzle. You may conceive a child, whether you wanted to or not, but...God wanted that child at that particular place and time. God chose the particular husband and wife to incubate and nurse; rear this particular child, to prepare him or her for the service of God as did Hannah, the mother of Samuel, as did the mother of Moses. Man says 'you can't afford so many children', my God is not limited and is faithful, He is the Creator all and will supply all of thy needs and more if you if you'll only trust and obey, amen! And man says 'there isn't enough food supply for so many', again my God is the Creator of all, all was perfect, my God has supplied all of my needs and more, as well as those of my friends, and He will provide for thee **IF** you will only trust and obey. As I said at the beginning, my friend with so many wonderful blessings, didn't take a second job, he cut his hours in half.

Remember that Jesus Christ our Savior was an unplanned pregnancy! Imagine where we would be today if Mary had of aborted our dear Savior! The child you carry is NEVER unplanned by God, He creates each and EVERY child with a purpose!!!

I saw a report indicating that a fertility rate of two point one per family is necessary to maintain a constant population. The prime factor contributing to the present low fertility rate is individualism, which plain and simply is selfishness and an unwillingness to be obedient unto our Father God. How can we maintain that two point one if we continue to have such a high divorce rate coupled with the high murder/divorce rates and birth control? And I propose to you the question, is it our right as the created beings to attempt to control what the Creator is in control of already and has instructed us to leave it to Him? Think about it.

Marriage and family place heavy demands on individuals, and tends to limit the freedom of both partners. For a couple, having children further limits opportunities and activities, in addition to the direct costs. At the same time, children's utility has declined. They are no longer either expected or legally required to support their parents in old age or help with family finances in most cultures today. But we forget the blessings of children, and again this is selfishness and disobedience unto God.

The words mother and papa remind us of what a family ought to be and that without one we are incomplete. The world is one of unbridled selfishness. Sacrifice is the glue that bonds marriage and the family; selfishness fractures that bond. When that splitting occurs: it is usually the new fruits which have sprouted from our sides that suffer the greatest; those fruits of course are our children.

I was reading God's word and a few passages came my way, and I prayed unto my Lord for understanding. In the middle of the night, I was awakened with answers, and I once again thanked and praised Him for enlightening me. He often speaks to me in the quiet of the night, as He is the Light that shines in darkness.

Adultery, if you have ever noticed, is the first of many sins listed in Galatians 5:19 and Romans 1:29; 13:9, as well as the third in 1st Corinthians 6:9 following fornication and idolatry. As well as literal interpretation of adultery, He is referring as well to spiritual adultery, and is very serious, so much so that it is number one on the lists of sins. Allow me to explain. Turn with me to 2nd Peter 2:14. It tells us *having eyes full of adultery, and that cannot cease from sin; beguiling unstable souls: a heart they have exercised with covetous practices; cursed children.* You see, in God's eyes this adultery is very serious. Now let us return to the book of Romans 7:2, where you will see that *the woman* (we as sinners) *which hath a husband* (we have God) *is bound by the law to her husband as long as he liveth.* What law my friends? God's law, your husband shall die, but our marriage to God brings eternal life with Him, Hallelujah. Then we continue in verse 3, *So then if, while the husband liveth she* (us), *be married to another man* (God) *she shall be called an adulteress.* Now let us return to the book of 1st Corinthians 6:18-20 *flee fornication. Every sin that a man doeth is without the body; but he* (righteous) *that committeth fornication sinneth against his own body;* and now this includes you my sisters, if you are righteous, you are he, also if you don't go along, a man can't commit fornication or adultery and vice versa. Look my dear friends, if you kill, rob, lie, whatever, it's against something or someone else, but sexual immorality including adultery and fornication is a denial of our Lord-the God of thy holy temple, and going after other gods, such an abomination! Then He continues in verses 19-30, *what? Know ye not that your body is the temple of the Holy Ghost which is in you, which ye have of God, and ye are not your own? for ye are bought with a price. Therefore glorify God in your body and in your spirit which are God's.* Amen.

245

The biochemistry and psychological components of intercourse cause it to be very addicting, and if you are addicted to your spouse, I guess that is okay as God is the Creator and ordained intercourse, but if the addiction pulls you into any relationship outside your marriage, then you are in sin and need the help of the Lord. In Hebrews 13:4 *Marriage is honorable in all, and the bed undefiled: but whoremongers and adulterers God will judge.*

In parts of Asia, they still put people guilty of adultery to death, the classic story of the Scarlet Letter (the original), but... is it okay in other countries because there is no law against it? NO! There is still a law against it, the supreme law of God!

My dear brothers and sisters, know thou that we, through our sins, nailed Jesus Christ to that cross. He accepted this death with such great love for us and still forgave all the sins of those who choose to believe in Him. When you commit adultery, you create such a huge wound through God's heart as well as thy partner's heart. IF they choose to accept you back, know for certain what great love they have for you, appreciate and respect that great love of Christ and of thy partner, repent of thy sin and never return unto it. Just as God erases the sins from His book when we accept Him and His Son Jesus Christ so that those sins are never again brought to the light, so must we forgive. We can never as humans forget, but when we forgive our partner, we should never again bring up the past sins, it must be deleted.

Prostitution is just another form of adultery and fornication.

Now rape...is a horrendous crime, because it is a merciless defilement against the temple of another child of God. Whereas God is a God of love and mercy, and men are to be types of Christ so likewise should we show love, mercy, and respect to our brothers and especially our dear sisters. There is no love or mercy in a rape. We see in Romans 13:10 that when you rape someone, you are raping more than just a child of God; you are raping the temple of the living God, and desecrating it. This is a very serious crime! Take a look at 1st Corinthians 3:17. This passage reminds us that if any man defiles the temple, he shall God destroy: for the temple of God is holy, which temple you are. This admonition must also apply to the women who are raping men. I need to say that MANY rapes are preventable, by 1) wearing proper, not provocative clothing and behavior, 2) being at home under the protection of the father or husband, and 3) having a chaperone when she goes out. This is not absolute, but gives you a safer chance and should not be seen by women as demeaning, but rather a deep respect and honor for her as God hath so designed. Also look at Exodus 22:16!

Also, rape, when you uncover another god (goddess), be it sex, money, false religions, fashion, fancy cars, whatever; and go into her (ways) then you are guilty of rape.

Now, in recent years, there has been talk about marital rape, and much debate about the issue. I wish to say that marriage should constitute 'implied consent'. However, when two become one, the two should ALWAYS seek to please and serve the other. Therefore, the one should never force themselves on the other, nor should the one ever deny the other, it is that clear.

In Kenya, they were boasting in the paper that Generation gerrit where virginity is no longer considered cool, where lesbianism and multiple partner sex orgies is the in thing. Oh, dear friends, the atrocity of all this. Imagine how God, our Master Designer feels as He looks at us today! We need to turn from our wicked ways today and be on our knees in repentance!

The Bible teaches that even lusting after another is a sin. Matt 5:28 tells us that *whosoever looketh on a woman to lust after her hath committed adultery with her already in his heart.* Look at 1st Corinthians 10:6 which tells us that we should *not lust after evil things...neither be idolaters...neither let us commit fornication.* Why? Because lusting after someone or something of the world is the same as lusting after sin. Romans 13:14 tells us to *put on the Lord Jesus Christ and make not provision for the flesh, to fulfill the lusts thereof.* Men, you shouldn't look, but women, you should dress modestly so that there is nothing for them to be looking at.

I must return you to 2nd Corinthians 11:2 which tells us *For I am jealous over you with godly jealousy: for I have espoused you to one husband* (God), *that I may present you as a chaste virgin to Christ.* This reflects His love for us and our relationship with Him.

Oh, my dear friends, as I write these words here, I am in tears. These precious words from the Holy Spirit of the Living and Almighty God, bring the harsh reality of the condition spiritually of the world today...and in His church. I am praying that you are listening and hearing the Spirit of God today, and that it is piercing your heart, soul, and mind, that your life will never be the same again, that you are getting on or back on the straight and narrow path that leads to the promised land of heaven for all eternity. 1ˢᵗ Corinthians 5:1 *It is reported commonly, that there is fornication among you, and such fornication as is not so much as named among the gentiles* (unbelievers)...*and ye are puffed up* (proud) *and have not rather mourned, that he that hath done this deed might be taken away from among you.* Then we see in Revelation 2:20, 22 *because thou sufferest that woman Jezebel, which calleth herself a prophetess, to teach and seduce my servants to commit fornication, and to eat things sacrificed unto idols...behold, I will cast her into a bed, and them that commit adultery with her into great tribulation, except they repent of their deeds.*

My dear brothers and sisters, I sit here thinking about the condition of the world today. Men AND women having sex with dogs, horses, chickens, and anything else, sex with children. This is so sinful. Didn't we just read about this in Leviticus, they shall be put to death...hell! One man was beaten and killed by a group of prostitutes because he was found having sex with a chicken or dog, I don't recall. They were irate yelling if you have to have sex, we are available, why go after animals! They showed this on the news! Women were raping dogs... Oh the shame of how low we have fallen, and yet people want to condemn Sodom and Gomorrah! Yet God says that adultery and divorce is worse than what they were doing there in Sodom and Gomorrah! And look at the amount of adultery and divorce we have today, not to mention the atrocities of homosexuality, polygamy, sodomy, pedophilia...Oh my dear brothers and sisters, we must get to our knees and repent!

The epidemic proportion of adultery. Friends, the command to love thy neighbor **DOES NOT** include lust and coveting after thy neighbor's husband or wife! Domestic violence, in which just as many women are guilty as men, as they are killing for money, property, etc. Married women are out prostituting themselves on the streets while their husbands are at work. Women not at home for whatever reason when their husbands arrive home from work, so he goes and finds someone else who will keep him company. Oh, the apostasies, the shame, just like the Israelites at Mount Sinai and Sodom and Gomorrah. We must stop this and return to the good old family values and Christian precepts!

For all of you, who are married, God says, commands you to procreate. Look at Jeremiah 29:6, where God says *Take ye wives, and beget sons and daughters, and **take** wives for your sons, and **give** your daughters to husbands, that they may bear sons and daughters; that ye may be increased there and not diminished.* God needs more servants. Do you know, I was told that one reason that the Islamic religion calls for polygamy is to have more children for their armies! Dear friends, don't listen to the world, but to God and let us build up the army of God, Amen! In Exodus 12:17 *I have brought your armies out of the land of Egypt...* Here we see that He delivers us from evil also. In Philemon 2, goes on to say *And to our beloved Apphia and Archippus our fellow soldier...* God **never** anywhere in scripture, tells any man or woman, 'if you like children then...' no, He never said 'limit yourself to one or two children', no dear friends, my God is in full control! And God said bear children, populate the earth! My friends who had ten or more children were blessed, as they, we allowed God to be in control instead of trying to take control ourselves. I was blessed with four, God's choice, and what is impossible with man or man's understanding, is still possible with God. Look at Sarah, ninety years old and conceived. Rebekeh and Abraham were married twenty years before her womb was opened by God and she conceived Jacob and Esau. The barren woman is symbolic of the unfruitful person. Look at Judges 13:2 Manoah and his wife were barren, but God opened her womb to bring Samson into the world. Jump over to 2nd Samuel 6:23, because of Michal's behavior to her husband David, God never opened her womb and she was barren unto her death. Look also at Ruth 4:13. You must note that Ruth was barren in her marriage, when her husband died and she remarried, she conceived. God is in control, not man. My wife was two and a half years into menopause, when God heard my prayers and reopened her womb to give me a daughter. God is in control and He can open or close thy womb at any time. It is by His power only that brings the flower to fruit. God doesn't need the man to fertilize the ovum. Behold a virgin shall conceive. He can open, He can close a womb. In Psalm 113:9 we read, *He maketh the barren woman to keep house,* **and** *to be a **joyful** mother of children.* In Genesis 38:9-10 we see Oman didn't want children with his deceased brothers' wife, so he spilled his seed on the ground, and...the thing displeased the Lord. Wherefore He slew him also, withdrawal method my dear friends, is a sinful act.

Menstrual periods are a beautiful process, created by God. It is not necessary for the pad companies to advertise this personal issue and I would recommend avoiding use from the companies that do. All men and women know that the pads are needed and which are available, it doesn't need to be advertised, and not advertising would cut the cost of these products as well, but I want you to know that if you use any form of birth control, every period then becomes a missed blessing from God, a potential blessing flushed down the toilet or tossed in the trash. Do you honestly believe that this could in any way be pleasing unto our Creator? in addition to being disobedient to His commands.

In Kenya there was a frequent television advertisement that said love without regrets; it was an advertisement for condoms. My dear brothers and sisters, condoms are for sex which is a sin, not for love. The act of intercourse, loving one another-husband and wife, must have no barrier, just as there is no barrier between God and us. God loves us so much that He removed the barrier once and for all, the curtain and priests, so that we could have direct contact and be one with Him, if husbands and wives truly love one another, then there should be no barrier between them, and in love there are no regrets, children are a blessing, not a regret. Children IF God opens thy womb, are a blessing, not a regret. Children are a gift from Almighty God, have you ever received a gift from anyone that you regretted? Another advertisement in Kenya was for a manufacturer also of contraceptives-barriers and injections. As I heard the name, what immediately came to my mind was Female's plan is not God's plan. I call you to recall that the feminine is symbolic of sin. Also, any barrier contraceptive is actually a veil that separates you from the love of thy spouse. Children don't have to be a burden; they can and should be an integral part of a happy and healthy family. Plan thy family wisely, by leaving it all in God's able hands, be His instruments. One must remember that sexual intercourse is not about having children, but about a time of intense personal communication exchange between a man and his wife, whatever else happens is in God's hands. If He chooses to bless you, receive His blessing with praise and thanksgiving, if not; still praise Him for your blessings.

There is all the talk today of Safe sex...do you use a mask when kissing your mate...to be safe? Of course not, so why wear one down lower? What are you protecting yourself from in safe sex? From the possibility of disease? The organisms that one is trying to protect themselves are smaller than the pores of latex, so not much protection. Furthermore, if you are uniting yourselves only within the confines of marriage, you needn't worry about such diseases. So, what are you protecting yourself from? From the possible precious gift from God? Mind you that up until this present age, children were considered the blessing that they are. Infertility or barrenness was considered with so much pain and disgrace. Today, people are paying men to play god, to sterilize themselves as children are now considered as an inconvenience, Oh what a tragedy-the reversal of the minds of mankind-the evil, completely opposite of God's precious intentions.

Speaking of birth control, no form of birth control is one hundred percent effective in preventing pregnancy except by the removing of sacred parts of the temple of God called a total hysterectomy, and no form of birth control can prevent HIV/ AIDS, or other sexually transmitted diseases! We must surrender all, and allow God to be in control of our lives! Birth control is wrong because in addition to being disobedient to God and wasting financial resources that He hath given unto you, and wasting precious seed, it is man's **attempt** to take control away from God, even though God is still in control. You can use a condom, foam, and withdrawal all together and still conceive, still become pregnant-I have seen a case, in a friend of mine. I also know of a couple of young people that exposed themselves to one another outside of marriage, they were only fourteen and fifteen years of age. She wouldn't let him in at the last minute, and told him that if he needed to release, he could outside of her. He did ejaculate on her pelvic area while she watched. Remember, she is still technically a virgin, but...she conceived! The seed seeped into her and ... You can have intercourse one time and get pregnant, or you can have intercourse as often as you wish and not get pregnant, it all is in God's control. The womb open or closed is in God's control. Look at Genesis 29:31, earthly reason, but God was going to fulfill His promise to Abraham, and it needed to be the son of his first wife! God assured this here by closing the womb of Rachel and opening the womb of Leah, who also bore Levi (priesthood), and Judah (lineage of Christ). Look over in the New Testament book of John 1:18, God is in control, not the parents' choice. We saw that Michal's womb was closed because of ungodly behavior, she was disgraced by childlessness, whereas look at 1st Samuel 2:21-22 where God visited the godly Hannah, and opened up her womb. Hannah was humble, obedient, and full of worship and devotion to God and to her husband. I knew a young lady, who got married, had twins. She was considering a hysterectomy, which again, is a destruction of God's Temple and a removal of sacred parts. I tried to discourage her, and to pray. As she was praying about it, she conceived again, and had twins again. Instead of being blessed, they saw God's blessings as a curse, and were pulling for the surgery again, but before she could have the surgery against my advice, she conceived again and had triplets. Was this a curse? Absolutely not! God

knew what He was doing. He always does. Then without surgery, God closed up her womb. Blessed is the man whose quiver
is full. Look again at Genesis 19:31-36. What are the odds of a
man who is so intoxicated that he didn't know his own daughters, or that he was even having sex, could ever become erect
or ejaculate and impregnate two daughters in two days, who
would have both been fertile at the same time?... Father God
is in control of thy womb!

Abortion is simply not birth control; it is murder of a precious gift from God, a life God blessed you with. The intrauterine device (IUD) does the same thing in destroying the
developing fetus, baby. The tortuous murder is clearly shown
in the movie "The Silent Scream" which is a movie showing an
ultrasound of the fetus, the baby, being murdered, torn apart,
and extricated from the womb. Several million precious gifts
are murdered by abortion every year; this is a bigger atrocity
than the holocaust! Indeed, this is a holocaust of its own rank
and magnitude. This is a violation of the commandment thou
shalt not kill. From the moment of conceptions cells are repro-
ducing, breathing, and within days there is a heart and brain!
Thus, the fact that this is life can further be confirmed by the
fact that these are the same criteria that Doctor's use to pro-
nounce death in an individual. **There is no justification for
this murder**, this violates the sixth commandment, never is
murder acceptable to God, of a helpless, innocent gift from
our Father. It wasn't man that planted that life in her womb,
it was GOD! I had a young lady one time that came to see me.
She explained in great detail how she was raped, and now was
two months pregnant, wanting to abort. This was a difficult
case for me. I prayed and prayed as she continued to speak. I
was finally convicted to tell her to keep this precious life that
God gave her, that this precious gift isn't from the rapist, but
from God, as He could have closed her womb. I proceeded to
explain that this was a gift from God, and not the child's fault
to justify the murder. That God chose her to carry this child,
nobody else, to be blessed with this precious life from God,
this gift from God to her, this gift from God! In spite of the bad
situation, she listened to me, and became a wonderful loving,

caring mother of twins- a son and a daughter. She thanked me every time that she saw me after that for encouraging her in God's way, not mans.

In Leviticus 18:3-4 we read *After the doing of the land of Egypt* (the sinful world) *wherein ye dwelt* (We live in a sinful world but are called by God to separate ourselves from it in 1st John 2:15), *shall ye not do: and after the doings of the land of Canaan, whither I bring you, shall ye not do: neither shall ye walk in their ordinances. Ye shall do **My** judgments, and keep **mine** ordinances, to walk therein.*

I am the vine; ye are the branches God tells us in John 15:5. Any branch that yields not fruit shall be pruned away and cast into the fire. Marriage is selfless, not selfish, just as our spiritual life can only blossom and bear fruit if we are self-less, humble, to God AND to each other, then produce the fruit that God intends for you as you continue to look to Him and serve Him.

PREGNANCY

Let us look briefly at pregnancy. In Exodus 40:17 the tabernacle was erected in nine months, a human pregnancy takes nine months-coincidence? I think not. The tabernacle was constructed nine months after their arrival at Sinai, no coincidence since the body is in fact the temple. They got to right to work; they didn't waste time or procrastinate. They didn't wait for the 'right time' because God's time is always right.

There are millions of men in the world, but only one (if God wills) woman is ordained for you, and vice-versa. Likewise, there are millions of sperms in each ejaculate, but only one (if God wills) is ordained to enter into the ovum. Sperm cells are the largest cell in the human body; the ovum is the second largest.

Menstruation if no fertilization has taken place is a sloughing off of the old, just as our sins are sloughed off-our old self, by the cleansing blood of Jesus Christ. Our old self is washed away and a new, pure, clean self is created.

Only when the Holy Spirit comes into you can there be a new life, just as only when the husband comes into his wife, can new life be created. When you refuse your husband and/or don't invite him into you, is the likeness of refusing Jesus Christ, the Holy Spirit, into your life. Without Him is death. Likewise, any birth control or abortion is a sin, in that it violates God's law, as well as the command to be fruitful and multiply. Remember, God judge's men by the fruits of his labor; this is one of his fruits! A woman's labor is in serving her husband, offering of herself willingly, as well as the labor of bringing forth children for God.

So...Why does a woman menstruate and not a man, since Jesus Christ shed His precious blood? The woman again represents the sinner. Eve gave birth to sin for all of mankind. She changed the world, vegetation, weather, wildlife, thus she represents the sinner. Man cannot represent sin for he was made in the image of God, in His image (Christ-like). The sinner needs the shed blood of Jesus Christ to cover our sin, to wash, to cleanse us white as snow. Menstruation is a symbolic reminder of the sinners' need of repentance, humility, and complete surrender, for restoration and that of God's love for us. The blood of Jesus was shed only after He took on our sin. The woman menstruates because it was the woman that brought sin into the world, the shed blood serves as a reminder of our need for repentance and of what Jesus did for us on the cross. God's saving grace and mercy, as He washed away our sins by the blood of His Son Jesus Christ. This is my body broken for you...this is my blood, shed for you. Menstruation should serve as a monthly reminder for husbands and wives, that Christ shed His blood for the sinners and this should bring us to our knees in repentance.

The Holy Spirit knocks at our door and wants to be invited in, to bring us, the sinners, to new life in Him. The husband needs to be welcomed in, invited in by his wife for new life to be created if it is God's will.

Jesus died, shed His precious blood for our sin, that those who accept Him into their temples shall be cleansed from the inside out, and create in us a new life. While there are many today who are quick to tear the precious veil- no big deal, I'm hoping and praying today that you are seeing just what a big deal this desecration of thy temple really is, by allowing many gods in, serving them rather than the Almighty God and thy husband. Many say Lord, Lord, but I know them not Matthew 7:22-23, many are called but few are chosen. Who will be chosen? Those who accept Him and forsake the world; those who will cleave unto God and God alone are those who shalt be the chosen. So, what if everybody else does it? So, what if you are the only virgin in the class, in the church, only virgin in the world! Rejoice for God will be happy and honor you, what better reward could you seek, a moment of pleasure or an eternity with Christ? In 1st Corinthians 7:23, *Ye are bought with a price; be not ye the servants of man,* for we are to serve Christ.

Erectile dysfunction and premature ejaculation are growing problems in men today and can be caused by diet, medication, drugs, alcohol, stress and spiritual condition. It is harder to have sex with someone who is not ordained for you.

In some countries, female genital mutilation (FGM) is still practiced. This is simply cutting off the clitoris so that the woman feels no stimulation from intercourse, so has no desire, thus, doesn't go running around... but women need to feel the warmth and satisfaction, the love and closeness of her Lord, just as we need this from our Lord God, we need Him to come into us.

A growing problem in women today is vaginismus. They have found the Lord, but are afraid to accept Him, they are unable to fully surrender unto Him and allow Him into their hearts, their lives, and their temples. I can call this spiritual vaginismus, but the physical vaginismus is also a growing problem. She will not surrender fully to her husband and allow him to enter in or to give him **complete** control of her life.

We now are going to go into even more historical background and deeper into the scriptures to understand about sexual practices and divorce.

We see in Romans 1:28-32, *And even as they did not like to retain God in their knowledge, God gave them over to a reprobate mind, to do those things which are not convenient; Being filled with all* **unrighteousness, fornication, wickedness, covetousness,** *maliciousness,* **full of envy, murder(abortion),** *debate, deceit, malignity, whisperers, backbiters, proud, boasters,* **inventors of evil things, disobedient to parents, without understanding, covenant breakers, without natural affection,** *implacable, unmerciful: Who knowing the judgment of God, that they which commit such things are worthy of death, not only do the same, but have pleasure in them that do them.* In 1st Corinthians 7:2 we read *Nevertheless, to avoid fornication, let every man have his own wife, and let every woman have her own husband* I wish for you to note here that man, woman, husband, wife, are all singular, not pleural!

Egypt grew wicked in domestic violence and became notorious for its practice of incest. The moral decay of the Roman Empire is marked in history as one of the underlying causes of its fall, and Greece can boast of its invention of the word lesbian, not to mention its contribution to male homosexuality.

Uncovering the nakedness is a Hebrew term for sexual intercourse; thus, the customs of Egypt included incest of every kind, homosexuality, and bestiality. The Lord God introduced this section of Leviticus with these words: *And the Lord spoke unto Moses, saying, Speak unto the children of Israel, and say unto them, I am the Lord your God. After the customs of Egypt, wherein ye dwelt, shall ye not do; and after the doings of the land of Canaan, to which I bring you, shall ye not do; neither shall ye walk in their ordinances,* Leviticus 18:1-3.

From the language of Leviticus, it appears that incest and wife swapping was ordained as a right of an Egyptian. When Deuteronomy 24 was written, the Jewish people had followed the terrible sin of the Egyptians in wife-swapping. *After the doings of the land of Egypt, wherein ye dwelt, shall ye not do*, the doings of the land were their customs, and as we said, it appears that the listed items may have been the legal rights of the citizens of Egypt. This is not surprising since America

257

protects the rights of the homosexual, the adulterer, and the abortionist and former President Obama had gone on a campaign trying to force feed this immorality on to other nations. When in February of 2014, I applauded one President who rebelled and signed laws against homosexuality the US cut off this country, and many others were appalled. Unfortunately, months later he backed down and allowed it into his country because needed funds were cut off by Obama. We need men who will stand up for the truth, what is correct by God's standards! I have heard it said that morality cannot be legislated, but as a Christian, you must know that this simply is not the case, because God, our Creator, wrote the greatest laws of all time, which clearly legislated morality! We as Christians need likewise dare to take the stand for God's word and morality, and not allow non-Christian leaders in or to continue to destroy our nations because the more we allow them to whittle away our country's Christian morals, values and ethics, the less we have, and we can never get it back.

There is said to be evidence that Ramses II married two of his own daughters and that Psammetik I married his daughter. Artaxerxes married two of his daughters. The Ptolemies adopted this practice. The family married in and in for generations, especially brothers and sisters, although sometimes of the half-blood. Indicating the Ptolemies by numbers according to the order of their succession, the II married his niece and afterwards his sister; IV his sister; VI and VII were brothers and they consecutively married the same sister; VIII married two of his own sisters consecutively; XII and XIII were brothers and consecutively married their sister, the famous Cleopatra. Under the Emperor Commodus two-thirds of all the citizens of Arsi had married within the family. Marriage with a sister shocks our moral sense, but seemed most natural to the Egyptians, just as in modern Egypt marriage with a cousin is considered to be most sensible and right.

(AP) Moscow news release read, Soviet paper blames incest for infant deaths in village. In order to prevent paying dowries, the people of the Central Asian Republic of Turkmenia resort to incest, another case against dowries. The Russian medics attribute the high mortality rate here on intermarriage within the bonds of consanguinity. We are powerless in the case of the death of a child of related parent. Among the Akamba in East Africa (Kenya), a law of avoidance is in force, which one would have expected to encounter more frequently. A girl must carefully avoid her own father between the time of her puberty and her marriage. She hides herself if she meets him on the street and never attempts to sit down next to him, behaving in this way right up to her engagement. But after her marriage, no further obstacle is put in the way of her social intercourse with her father.

In the end, one must consider the cause of the fall of the Egyptian Empire. A civilization which introduced the world to medical procedures, the chemistry of dyes, cosmetics, and embalming, they excelled in letters (hieroglyphics and demotic (unofficial informal language)) as well as inventing the paper to write on, constructed the pyramids and sphinx, raised up the Pharaoh's, King Tut, and Cleopatra, and left behind that mathematical solution $\prod$ (in Egypt 3.16), (today, after some four thousand years: 3.14159265). It is difficult to identify exactly what condition caused Egypt to fall from its brilliance, but we cannot eliminate the corruption from incest. Just how powerful can one wicked, evil woman who is not God fearing, be? Just look at my book on Daniel, chapter 11 and read about a woman by the name of Cleopatra.

If brethren dwell together, and one of them die, and have no child, the wife of the dead shall not marry without unto a stranger: her husband's brother shall go in unto her, and take her to him to wife, and perform the duty of an husband's brother unto her. And it shall be that the firstborn which she beareth shall succeed in the name of his brother which is dead, that his name be not put out of Israel, Deuteronomy 25:5 and 6. There are still some tribes that practice this today! Most commentators agree that the levirate custom or law did not interfere with the living brother's existent marriage. In other words, within these limits the brother-in-law's marriage might co-exist with the prohibition of marriage with a brother's wife.

259

Women, my dear sisters, I'm going to be very blatant here for just a minute, but please listen. If you are menstruating and are leading a truly spiritual life with God and thy husband (if married), or a virgin, saving thyself, then menstruation is a beautiful time, a reminder of what God hath done for us. But!!! If you are menstruating and out playing around with different gods (men), and/or use birth control, then you are playing with fire. Each period then becomes a judgment representing the death of a life that God may have given thee, a gift from God that thou hast refused and thrown away.

Pregnancy It is interesting to note that while Caucasian ladies refuse to have children and do everything including murder to avoid them, Asian and African women deeply desire to have children. We see in 1st Samuel how she craved a child!

Pregnancy is a beautiful time of life, but requires prayer and tender, loving care (TLC) from her husband throughout. God didn't create then abandon us. He remains with us to care for, to nourish, and to help us grow in strength and wisdom. Fathers, you need to do likewise. From the time of conception, love and care for thy wife and unborn gift from God, never leave or forsake them. Husbands, each time thy wife conceives, you men should lay thine hands upon the head of thy wife and pray for her, and ask blessings upon her, sanctify her, praise God for her, and pray for her safety, God's protection over her throughout the pregnancy. Then youshould lay thine hands upon her womb and pray for this thy child, this precious gift, and reward from God. Bless this thy child, sanctify this child, praise God for this precious gift, and pray for God's protection and blessings upon the life of this child that they may be servants of Almighty God. He must intercede for his family and for the protection of both mother and child throughout the pregnancy. He should also praise his wife for carrying this his child.

We see in Isaiah 26:17-18 *like as a woman with child that draweth near the time of her delivery, is in pain and crieth out in her pangs, so have we been in thy sight, O God. We have been with child; we have been in pain...*

My dear friends' childbirth is a nine-month experience. We have already spoken about the lord entering into the holy of holies. Then there is the nine-month waiting, patience, a period of growth and development. This is time where two cells become ~ten trillion all working together in unity, in perfect harmony. If growth and development are halted or interfered with in any way (bad food, worldly teaching rather than God's...) then there is a major risk of problems and/or death. Likewise, we are in this nine-month period-the exile, where we should be growing and developing in Christ, but unfortunately, like the Israelites, we have had the growth and development interfered with by the world, false teachers in the churches... We are in need of emergency treatment to get back on the correct pathway, before death and eternity in hell occurs. We all look forward to a beautiful, healthy, and perfect little child, don't we? My dear friends, so does God so desire. The time of delivery is at hand. In this and my other books, I am striving to call all of us to repentance, to restoration onto the path of righteousness. I want each of us to be on the correct path in our marriages as God hath ordained as well, so that our marriages may return to perfection, that beautiful, healthy child in God's eyes, Amen.

Some of the penalties seem exceptionally harsh to our age partly because discipline has virtually disappeared in many parts of the modern church, but the Bible, God's word never changes even if culture does. Each of us must decide who we will follow-the customs and traditions of man, or God our Father and Creator, you cannot serve both, two masters. We are clearly shown in Matthew 18:15-18; 2nd Corinthians 2:5-11 and 2nd Thessalonians 3:14 that excommunication however, was a regular feature of the New Testament church for various sins including sexual offences, 1st Corinthians 5:1-13. We do not know how long such a sentence would have lasted, though presumably it could not have been revoked until the offender showed signs of repentance, 2nd Corinthians7:7-13 and 2nd Timothy 2:24-26. In Malaysia certain tribes have a custom and tradition the night before a young ladies wedding where a group of women get together and have a ceremony. A part of that ceremony includes her being undressed and bathed by these women. I said no because it's not right. My wife went for the ceremony anyway, what happened, I know not for she never would tell. Her second act (first that I knew of at the time) of defiance-before we were married. I need to say that cultures worldwide have their own unique customs and traditions and there is nothing wrong with complying with these AS LONG AS it does not conflict with what God teaches us in His precious Word.

Jesus was conceived in Mary by the Holy Spirit rather than by man so that He may be perfect, without sin. This is not to say that the man imparts sin into the woman, but that only by being born of God, through faith and trust in Him, can we be justified. God is our Father, when we accept Him and His free gift of salvation, of adoption and marriage into His heavenly family. The seed is coming from the man and is planted into his wife. His wife incubates the seed and gives it back to him in nine months. What I am trying to show here is that men must be careful what seed you plant, be careful about what you give and how you treat thy wife because all that you say and do will be incubated and returned back to you. God planted in each of us the seed of faith and love. We too need to incubate these seeds so that they may grow to maturity and that the fruits of these may be returned unto Him, in the souls saved and the lives touched by our faith and love in its maturity.

Please turn now to Exodus 1:16 and read it based on what you have learned so far in this message. Can you see the message? Yes, it was a literal command, but it is also spiritual, saying to destroy the righteous, just as we see clearly in Matthew 27:20.

The act of sexual intercourse requires a woman to totally surrender herself and submit to her lord, to invite him in and welcome him into her inner sanctum, just as we as sinners must totally surrender ourselves completely and submit to the Holy Spirit of the living God. We must invite Him in and welcome Him into the inner sanctum of our hearts and our total being, allow Him to create for us a new life in Him. Perhaps because of this analogy, more women accept Christ than do men. God has given to us such a beautiful picture, a reminder of His supreme sacrifice for us in giving to us a life partner, and sexuality, if viewed and kept in the clean, pure, manner in which it was designed. A lot to think about here, May God bless you.

It is a sad commentary of today's society that everyone from little children on up, know what is on the other side of the veil (the anatomy) long before they ever get married. My dear Christian friends, this needs to be halted. Our precious children need to be protected from this, and let the anatomy and the act of intercourse be a pleasant surprise and experience on the night of their wedding day.

We have spoken about intercourse but...remember that Intercourse is defined as a communication or exchange. For women the most intimate moments are when you give her undivided attention and allow her to talk, talk about anything, and to cry, for she was created different from man, remember? Women were created emotional beings and men must realize and remember this. She is delicate and fragile and should be treated with love and tender care, and a truly godly woman will sincerely desire to be treated in such manner and will be ever so thankful and grateful to be treated in this manner! Men are physical beings and so for men, intercourse is their intimate moments. To be successful you must balance the two, mix the two. For most women, they just lay there and allow the man to do their thing, but men, you must satisfy your wife by listening to her, talking with her, care about her feelings. Talk before the physical act, and talk afterward, don't just roll over and go to sleep! Christian men, know how to treat thy wives; Christian women, know how to honor love, and appreciate thy husband. Men desire the physical, but more and more women have become as men in their physical desire. My dear brothers, you need to have self-restraint against such women and temptations. My sisters, you need to return to humility and shyness when it comes to men. Yea, ye should not be dressing provocatively in tight, transparent, low cut clothing or skimpy bathing suits (they used to be loose fitting with a small skirt attached and we should return to this); ye should not be chasing after, flaunting, teasing, enticing, etc. a man as Eve did in that garden, but to act, talk, behave in a humble and respectful heart, mind, and manner as is becoming a Christian, respect yourself and the men, don't try to bring him down in fornication or adultery. Don't make yourself to be the cause of his or your fall. In Leviticus 26:12-16 we read *And |I will walk among you and will be your God, and ye shall be my people. I am the LORD your God, which brought you out of the land of Egypt, that ye should not be their bondmen; and I have broken the bands of your yoke, and made you to go upright. But if ye will not hearken unto me, and will not do all these commandments; and if ye shall despise my statutes, or if your soul abhor my judgments, so that ye will not do all of my commandments, but that ye break my covenant* (Marriage is a covenant) *I also will do this unto you; I will even appoint over you terror, consumption, and the burning ague, that shall consume the eyes, and shall cause sorrow of heart: and ye shall sow your seed in vain, for your enemies shall eat it.* We have discussed much in this chapter, both the ordained and the abhorrent. But there are blessings...or curses, depending upon which path you CHOOSE to walk.

In August 2019 I was awakened with another Revelation from the Holy Spirit, taking me back to the building of the tabernacle. Right after the people said 'all that He said we will do' Exodus 24:3 God gave the commandments to them and what did they do? They immediately started following after other gods, the golden calf. Then they built the tabernacle, why? Did the Israelites need a place to come to worship God? No, they were worshipping Him all along, weren't they? Everything in scripture is symbolic. Everything that God does has a purpose. The tabernacle was a temporary structure and portable, just as is our body-temporary and portable. There was the outer covering Exodus 28:33, which was made modestly to assure privacy of the worshippers, just as our clothes are to keep our tabernacles private, not revealing anything. The priests had to be consecrated (set apart) from family and any others and dedicated to the tabernacle, his wife. Then there was the altar of incense in Exodus chapter 30 to sanctify themselves before the Lord just as we are to come before the altar to sanctify our marriage. And then we are told that before the High Priest could enter into the Holy of Holies, he must be sanctified, meaning that he must wash and be clean, he must put on clean garments. Here we see that the husband before he may enter in, must be clean-spiritually, physically, and be pure (virgin). He must put on clean garments. This shows a respect for thy wife and yourself as well as before God. It also is symbolic of changing thy old ways and being afresh with thy wife. Then I want you my brothers and sisters to realize that the Levites, the priestly responsibility was for the tabernacle. He was to care for and carry the tabernacle which he was responsible for, men, i.e., your wife (Numbers 30:3-15); and my sisters, he can only carry you, care for you IF you will humble yourself and submit fully unto his authority. Please note that over and over again God told the Israelites, (men to your wives) I will...IF...you will... Then in Deuteronomy, you see IF you will listen and obey, then I will bless you, but if not, then I shall bring curses upon you. Men, humble yourselves also. I have been given great Revelations from the Holy Spirit. I have been given prophecy. I have been used to heal (for real, not pretend). I have been used to cast out legions of demons from people, even a couple of witchdoctors, and bring all of these folks unto our Lord Jesus Christ. I say this to show you that I could (as many do) become very proud. But instead, God hath given me a humble heart, as this responsibility that He hath entrusted unto me comes with a tremendous amount of responsibility and accountability, as you represent the Lord in all that you do. Being the lord of your home is no different. You must humble thyself, and be responsible for thy wife and children.

The priests had to be sanctified. Do you understand the word sanctify? It means that he was set apart from the rest, to minister. The husband has been set aside by God and should be also by his wife, in order to minister unto her and her needs. Now again, remember that God is faithful to provide for our needs-food, clothing, etc., not necessarily our desires. I hope that you are getting this powerful message, this revelation from the Spirit of the Living God.

The people said 'all that He said we will do' Exodus 24:3 God gave the commandments to them and they immediately started following after other gods, the golden calf. My dear friends, this is (spiritual) adultery. Your marriage is between husband, wife, and God, nobody else. Your body, the tabernacle is for your husband or wife, and God, nobody else. Anybody else comes into the picture; it is adultery, plain and simple. In Leviticus chapter 4 we see the results of adultery and abuse of the temple- abuse of your marriage partner or child, in the story of Nadab and Abihu who misused the tabernacle and were destroyed by God. This includes any form of abuse or misuse of the body, yours or that of your marriage partner, thus no karma sutra circuses in the bed. God destroyed the Idolaters after the commandments were given and they committed the idolatry (golden calf) God says I hate idolatry, I hate adultery, I hate divorce, I hate hypocrites and liars. How can you call yourself sanctified and holy (set apart) and go chasing after other gods (other men and women)? Again, please note that there was even special clothing to be worn for the service of the Lord. Are we not all called to be servants? So, ought our bodies to be clothed modestly and respectfully for God, for our marriage partner, as well as self-respect.

I also was shown in this revelation that with the temple there were all of the frills-the altars, the Laver, the pillars, the golden lamp stands...BUT!!! Then there was the inner veil which covered the Holy of Holies. This was sacred and NOBODY entered into this inner sanctum, the Holy of Holies other than the High Priest, and then with great fear and reverence. I hope that you are getting me without me having to get more graphic, just how important this point is in our marriage lives.

I wish for you to see that in the tabernacle, anybody could have entered into the Holy of Holies behind the veil-curtain, but nobody did because it was sacred-only one man was to enter behind the veil into the Holy of holies, that was to be the high Priest chosen by God. This area was so sacred that they (even the High Priest) feared to enter therein. This same heart and mind should still be with the temple of God- our bodies. Rape or any sexual anomaly should never cross one's mind. It is estimated that thirty five percent of women worldwide are raped or sexually assaulted, and men of late have also become widespread victims of rape by women. That area behind the veil is to be held sacred to all, not to be entered into by anyone but the high priest chosen by God for you. Likewise, we must hold this area and our bodies in general as sacred, to be covered modestly and discretely and not to give our bodies away freely (or for profit), hold your body as sacred especially that area behind the veil. As of 2012, there were an estimated forty-two million prostitutes in the world. Is sex work or use of these people respecting God's temple? Is it holding this area behind the veil sacred? I think not! Now there are so many single parents in the world. It used to be unintentional-caused by the death of a parent, but today it is rampant and the major causes are divorce, accidental pregnancies and single parenting by choice! Today seventeen percent of children aged one to fourteen live in single parent homes in the world. Each year there are approximately eighteen and a half million girls aged fifteen to nineteen worldwide-developed and underdeveloped countries giving birth and two and a quarter million girls under sixteen years of age giving birth! And the mean age of first marriage is around twenty-five, which means that well over twenty-one million females are engaging in sexual activity outside of marriage. Where is the sanctity of God's temple, the sanctity of the holy of holies? And choosing single parenting, and so many births outside of marriage, where is the sanctity of thy temple or of Holy Matrimony? Please note here, if you were the victim of rape, I am not including you in this criticism, you were a victim, not a willing party.

Today, people need to focus less on sex and more on love!!! If we would, the sexual intercourse would be much better for both parties, and there would be far less sexual crimes, adultery and divorce. We are shown in the Song of Songs the mutual love and respect for one another in marriage Come with me to chapter 4:8 *Come with me from Lebanon, my spouse, with me from Lebanon: look from the top of Amana, from the top of Shenir and Hermon, from the lions' dens, from the mountains of the leopards.* You must notice that it was an invitation, not an order of Solomon. Then her response in 4:16 *Awake, O north wind; and come, thou south; blow upon my garden, that the spices thereof may flow out. Let my beloved come into his garden, and eat his pleasant fruits.* Where she invites him in *Let my beloved come into HIS garden.* She is allowing, and claiming that she has given him ownership thus authority over her and her body, 1st Corinthians 7:4. There was no force, demanding, just a mutual love and respect.

When the scriptures are talking about knowing her, it wasn't just saying the physical union of **BECOMING ONE** but a joining of the two hearts and minds as well.

It is good to note that she was a virgin as he discovered and confirmed in the Song of Solomon verse 4:12 *A garden enclosed is my sister, my spouse; a spring shut up, a fountain sealed. You see a garden inclosed, and a fountain sealed...*

In a true union, intercourse becomes another language between the two of you. A type of a song without words, a coming together, **BECOMING ONE**, and needing no explanation or consideration.

Solomon had seven hundred wives, three hundred concubines. Imagine one thousand women...His...This is sin...even he said later, vanity of vanities. Also imagine with one thousand women, the number of children, but never spoke about birth control or abortion. God provides, and Solomon's wealth was beyond measure!

The rose pedals and the branch (female and male genitalia) are nothing compared to the beauty of one's face and hair so why so much emphasis on that tiny part of the body? Simply it amounts to the ability to conquer and humble another, and this ought not to be-except in marriage. Let's get right down to it. What is attractive about the man's penis or the woman's labia? There is nothing attractive, but their face and hair is beautiful. The only beautiful thing about those unseemly parts of one's body is the coming together and **BECOMING ONE** with thy God given life partner.

A woman's face and hair can be enticing, a woman shaved for example doesn't attract much attention, and this is part of why the Bible teaches a woman to cover her hair.

I saw a couple of films where the women were saying that 'sex complicates things', young people I hope that you are hearing this. You create heat during sex (work by the scientific definition). This heat bonds the two souls together like two cubes of butter whose edges are melted together or two wires soldered together. The world can pull the wrapper or sheathing, your bodies away but the bond is still welded together by the Spirit of our Living God. When tremendous tension is pulling the two apart, that weld is actually the strongest point. The butter, wire, or your life can snap anywhere else but that bond cannot break. The same is true in our marriages and in our spiritual lives. The world can pull us, try us, but once you truly have been saved, nothing can separate us from the love of God, no trials, tribulations, persecution, words of adversity... you become one with Him, you become one with your God ordained life partner.

In 1st Corinthians 10:31 we are instructed *Whither therefore ye eat, or drink, or **whatever you do**, do all to the glory of God.* Amen!

PERSONAL NOTES

_____

_____

_____

_____

_____

_____

_____

_____

_____

_____

_____

_____

_____

_____

_____

_____

PERSONAL NOTES

Ephesians 3:15 *Of whom the whole family in heaven and earth is named*

CHAPTER 7

Marriage and Family

$\mathfrak{I}$ said earlier that I would be discussing marriage and family more as it fits in with scriptural teachings, as well as answer those questions that I asked you to ponder at the beginning. You perhaps can say that you have already received the answers, or you still may be uncertain. We have discussed the practical roles of men, women, and children, as well as betrothal and marriage. We have just discussed sexuality. We have seen the literal as well as the spiritual aspects for us today.

We discussed earlier selfless not selfish attitudes as this is the way that any true Christian must walk, including within our marriage, Philippians 2:3-4. We discussed the significance of him and her in scripture. If you look over at Revelation 17:3-7, the woman is not necessarily a female, but representative of sin and evil, most probably represents Rome and/or the Pope. I need to add something here, and that is mother and father. Please turn with me to Proverbs 1:8 Father in the scriptures represents instruction, whereas mother represents the law. This is important when reading and trying to interpret God's word. In Daniel 11:6 the end time prophecy, the daughter is the unbeliever, the sinner (feminine) whereas in verse 10 the sons (the righteous, masculine), shall be stirred up...verse 17 the daughter of women was given to corrupt! Then we see in

Joel 3:3 where was given a boy for a harlot-given up righteousness for sin. You see why this symbolism is so important? It helps one to understand God's word. Jesus spoke in parables; God's word is a parable that the blind not see. I am here today to remove thy blindness and bring some light to thy life. He who hath eyes let him see. I believe that the literal as well as the spiritual aspects are critical in the life of the true believer, the truly spiritual person; and these precepts are what we need to strengthen, save, and restore our marriages as well as our Christian walk. Satan is working hard to destroy the Christ-centered families, so don't let your guard down. If you don't continually fight the enemy, you will lose...your family, and your life.

Man was created a single pair, apparently in contrast to the animals. Genesis 1:20, *And God said, Let the waters bring forth **abundantly** the moving creature that hath life, and fowl that may fly above the earth in the open firmament of heaven.* The animals were created, not only in a rich variety of genera and species, but in large numbers, which is in remarkable contrast to man, the Single Pair.

Marriage made God's creation *very good.* Man was created married. Man was created in love and instructed to love. It is no wonder that since the garden love scene, all creation has been filled with reports of love. *Let him kiss me with the kisses of his mouth: for thy love is better than wine,* Song of Songs 1:2.

Why is it so important to God and why is it discussed so much in God's word? Simply my dear friends, it exemplifies our relationship with God, which is everything to Him. In Matthew 12:50 we are shown that obedience to God takes precedence over responsibility to family, not to neglect the family, but God comes first. The Bible tells of family to show us our position in the family of God.

The primary building block of society is the biblical based male–female family unit. It is what separates us from a complete social and spiritual breakdown. Without it we are threatened with an unrestricted immoral free for all of hate, lust and selfishness not unlike that of Sodom and Gomorrah. Satan hates marriage and loves divorce, anything and everything that is opposed to God. It allows him to curse the minds and hearts of all involved, turning what once was love and peace into hatred, bitterness and deceit.

In the beginning God created man and woman. He created man in their own image, in the image of God created He them. This image is physical, but equally so, in character, in our relationship with Him as well as in the relationship between man and woman. We should make every effort to be Christ-like, not to be Christ or God, for this we can never be.

Proverbs 30:11 tells us *There is a generation that curseth their father* (God)*, and doeth not bless their mother* (law)*. There is a generation that is pure in their own eyes, and yet is not washed from their filthiness.* Sound familiar? This is the condition of today.

These relationships between God and us, as well as our relationships between man and wife, children and parents, require humility, they require responsibility and accountability in addition to a real and genuine love. Just as a child yearns to please and be like his parents, so should our behavior be as true spiritual believers, to be Christ-like in our relationships with Him, our spouse, our children, our parents, as well as our relationships with one another in general...as brothers and sisters in Christ.

Marriage is sacred. It is ordained by God, just as remaining single is for others, both can be and are used by and for God. All true believers are married to God. We who are truly saved are the children of God, adopted as sons (righteous) into His precious family, Romans 8:15-17, as well as being the bride of Christ, Ephesians 5:22-23; Jeremiah 3:14.

I believe that the true churches should have an early married support group to encourage and support young couples and prevent problems, assisting them in building strong foundations and problem solving.

We are to be Christ-like, therefore we must be examples of Christ in all that we do and all that we say, in the home as well as in the community. Any inappropriate touching, speech, etc. is not being a good example of Christ. Holding hands when walking together is a wonderful example if married, but is rarely seen anymore. A friendly hug can also be appropriate. Jesus when He walked, He touched, He laid hands upon...but all was done in an appropriate manner, and brought honor unto God! We as the children of God, need the guidance and direction that can only come from above, we need the discipline that only our Father can provide.

In 2nd Corinthians 11:2 we are told that we are virgins espoused to **one** husband, God, and He says let not the marriage bed be defiled. We serve a very jealous God my dear friends, and with very good reason. He loves us so much that He sacrificed His only Son Jesus Christ, that we may have everlasting life, John 3:16. We, who are saved, are married to Christ, those of us who are truly spiritual. He is very jealous and wants nobody and nothing to come between us. He comes into us through His Spirit, and we become one with Him, united unto Him as one flesh. We are the temple of the Almighty God, Creator of the universe. When we go out into the world, we commit adultery, or spiritual idolatry. Again, and again, God tells us in Luke 16:13, that you cannot serve two masters as you will hate the one and love the other, strong reason against polygamy. God and God alone my dear friends, amen! We must hold on tight, cleave unto Him, become one with Him and to our spouse as well, and not permit Satan, friends, money, family, anyone or anything to separate us from the love of God or each other as husband and wife. This is a type of the Trinity, God-husband-wife; we are to be one, though separate. Oh, the mysteries of God! Just as God told me, He gave my wife a choice. He gives each of us a choice, the freedom to choose...the world...or His precious word and promises, His love and grace. Those of who are divorced and not remarried still have a choice.

As we shall see later, there is absolutely NO provision for divorce in scripture, but because of the hardness of heart, like the Pharaoh's, mankind created divorce, not God. Divorce was and is never a part of His plan or of His will, but of Satan's. God in fact hates divorce and there are consequences whenever you turn to the left or to the right from God's will, God's law.

Divorce is not a part of God's plan and He will never divorce you. Salvation is a free gift, and He will not take it back. Secondly, Divorce is an allegory of turning away from Christ. He says clearly that a woman (sinner) is not to leave her husband (righteous God). Remember, the truly spiritual is the bride; He does not want us to divorce Him, just look at the parable of the lost sheep. The husband is not to put away his wife, because God will never put us away. This is a promise of God; you made or perhaps will make the same vow. The same promise before God when you got or get married to your God ordained partner, or will when you receive salvation. God is witness, as are the angels, of the promises made between a husband and a wife, to love honor, and cherish (no matter what) until death do us part. This is the same as when you accept Jesus Christ as your precious Lord and Savior. It is a vow to cherish and protect at any and all cost, as long as you both shall live, and friends, eternity is a very long time, for the true believer and God never die! When two people divorce one another, it is another slap in the face, and Jesus Christ my dear friends, has already received too many slaps already before being crucified for you and for me. You are bound to God for eternity, Romans chapter 7, and if you have married God and marry another god, you are an adulterer, and there is no inheritance in the kingdom of God for them, Galatians 5:16-21. When we make a choice for the world over God; riches, other gods, other men or women, advice from friends, etc. over our Lord's word, there are consequences leading to destruction! The Egyptians were destroyed; the Israelites were destroyed, all but whom? Joshua and Caleb both were saved; both of whom had faith; the others suffering and death. For those who choose to be adulterers by choosing the world-friends, riches, greed, pride, etc. then there is suffering and death, for you cannot serve two masters. God desires with all of His heart to adopt each of us, to marry us and takes us home with Him, Hallelujah. But many are called, few chosen. Why? It is because most choose to marry and love the world rather than God. He doesn't want you to suffer now...or forever more. We are told in Proverbs 10:12 that *Hatred stirreth up strife: but love covereth all sins.* IF we choose to remain faithful to our Husband, God, He promises to take us home, the Promised Land, heaven, a home prepared for us. It is a home where there is no pain, sorrow, no suffering or death, just ask anyone who has suffered a divorce. I had a heart attack, and such sorrow. I know my wife and children are suffering out there in the world of darkness, all because of her choice. Look at Ezekiel 16:39, my wife's lovers broke down her eminent place in marriage. They stripped her and after destroying her and our son, left her wounds wide open and her naked. They brought up the team to destroy her and tore her apart with scalpels (the swords). Then...look at verse 44-45, my poor daughter! People, including some pastor friends of ours asked me if I would accept her back after all of her adultery, idolatry, lies, theft, and broken vows...my answer has always been an emphatic yes. I love my God, I cherish my vows, and will accept her until or unless she remarries and I will not go looking for another. I love my wife and children. We are all sinners; we all make mistakes. If she repents, seeks forgiveness, she is still my wife in God's eyes and mine. It is also a testimony for others to restore a broken marriage, but God's will be done. Do I wish and pray for their return? Absolutely! Just as God desires for His lost sheep to return unto Him. If God restores my wife and children unto me, Praise be to God. If He chooses for me to remain as I am, I will not cease from praising Him. Also, of note, I never signed the divorce papers. Why? Because it is wrong. You as a Christian must never leave your marriage partner as Scripture clearly dictates, however, if your partner leaves, you should never sign the divorce papers because this is completely contrary to God's teaching, and you should never agree with something so contrary to God's Word and teachings. It is a sin against the living and Almighty God, and they mean nothing for with or without these papers, she is still my wife in God's eyes, and He is who I honor, not the world. Regardless of what He does-restoring my family as He did Job, remaining as I am, or whatever, one thing is sure, the remainder of my life shall be spent in full time service unto Him. My experiences with my wife, and held hostage, etc., have only strengthened my resolve to serve Him, and the tremendous burden that He hath placed in my heart is unchangeable.

My dearest brothers and sisters, are you single? Seek not a partner, wait upon the Lord.

Are you a single sister and not willing to be humbled? Do not worry. Are you a single brother and unwilling to take full responsibility and accountability? Don't get married, God may have other plans for you. Praise God and keep your hands off anyone else. Are you married? Rejoice and praise God. Don't allow anything or anyone to come between you. I know that I am repeating some but this is so important! But never choose single parenting or this absurdity they are calling friendship with benefits. Listen, parenting is an awesome responsibility. It takes a father and a mother to properly rear a child, (you raise plants, and you rear children). Children learn certain things from the dad and certain things from the mother. To be reared well, they need both parents. If one is missing, the child is unbalanced. They need to see the love between the man and the woman. They need to see the leadership of the papa, and the submission of the mother, to be well grounded for their earthly lives as well as their spiritual and eternal lives. I discussed single parenting briefly in the previous chapter. Why is this such a bad choice? First of all, it is ungodly, fornication or adultery is an abomination before God. It also has catastrophic consequences on the children. I have already mentioned the increased incidence of homosexuality in these children. Parents tend to balance each other. Children depend on their papa for support-physical, emotional, and spiritual; as well as affection, guidance, and as a role model. The men need to set priorities and God must come first, family second and work last. Having had said this role of the papa, one of the most important things that a papa can do for his children is to love their mother unconditionally. Alongside of that is leading the children to God. This is accomplished both by teaching as well as by example.

We see in Isaiah 62:4, *Thou* (Israel) *shalt no more be termed Forsaken, neither shall thy land anymore be termed*

Desolate: but thou shalt be called Haphzi-bah (My delight is in her), and thy land Beulah (married)...

When the woman disrespects, dishonors and is disobedient to her husband; it is the likeness of when we as sinners do so unto God our Father, our Bridegroom. Now there are those who teach that man has no authority or rule over his home or family, but to say this is to say that God has no authority or rule over His home or family, as God hath created and ordained the marriage to be a likeness of His marriage and family.

Sometimes one partner isolates or tries to isolate their partner due to insecurity, fear of losing them. But instead of isolating them, do all you can to please your partner so that they will desire to stay with you and not look elsewhere.

Having said this, if your daughter or wife are just allowed to cook, clean, and be a sex slave, it is abuse, but if she is given some latitude within boundaries (as God does us), she should be grateful for it is not abuse, though most women today want the latitude without boundaries and this cannot work, that is why women and families are running into so many problems today. This is called independence, and as I stated earlier, marriage is both man and woman giving up their independence to become one- unity. We as true believers, truly spiritual, as the bride of Christ, have latitude within boundaries to keep us from the sinfulness, evils of this world for our own good and for our protection. Many professing Christians today reject His boundaries and want to be independent, and it cannot work! We step out of the boundaries then we are in Satan's domain and out from under the shelter of His wings and His protection. When we step outside, He disciplines us or allows us to be destroyed by the evils of this world.

In 1st Samuel 1:23 we see an example of the husband supporting his wife with her vows. In verse 28 he could easily have said 'no way are you giving up my son, my first born son'! but He supported his wife who was worshipping the Lord. In 2:1 she rejoiced, not sorrowed. Imagine, she yearned for this child, she prayed for this child, then she rejoiced in giving back to our Lord. She gave willingly unto God with a joyful heart. This was a child, the first born of a barren woman, and she rejoiced giving unto God!!! How many people do you see rejoicing when they give unto the Lord today?!! Then He will bless you, 1st Samuel 2:21.

Are you truly married to the Bridegroom? Seek not a divorce; commit not adultery with the world. God does not force His bride to let Him come in, He knocks and asks, pleads with you, with such love, to allow Him into your heart and life. In Deuteronomy 6:4 and Genesis 2:24, the same word in Hebrew for one is used in both of the verses. Echad, for oneness, is a complete unity of distinct parts, inseparable. God, husband, and wife are to be one just as God, Jesus, and the Holy Spirit are one, in the Trinity.

I am reminded here, of 2nd Chronicles 7:14 which I shall talk more about later, but I need to say here that God tells us to seek His face, turn from thy wicked ways... and when you women get married, a woman needs to seek her husband in all things and nobody else (no other gods), turn from your selfish ways and become selfless to serve thy Lord and thy husband, and you must invite him in and allow thyself to be humbled.

Dear brothers and sisters, don't separate thyself from the love of God, or of your spouse, but rather *be ye separate from the world and the things of it* 1st John 2:15, for you cannot serve two masters. James 4:4 tells us that *Friendship with the world is enmity with Christ*. There is no gray area or best of both worlds; your choice one or the other but not both. You separate from thy spouse, you separate from God and commit adultery, idolatry, and there will be consequences, pain and suffering guaranteed. It may not be immediate, during the period of numbness there may be fun and games, but the numbness will settle and the pain shall come. Sooner or later, pregnancy, spouse finds out, divorce, AIDS, STD's, emotional pain...and most importantly, God knows, as you cannot hide from God, just ask Jonah or David. If pregnancy from adultery, then compound that with the guilt, pain and suffering from a... God forbid...abortion. Like David, Adultery then murder! All of this as a reminder of adultery, or rearing of an unwanted child, as if it is his fault that you played with fire and got burned... Both of you suffer, all because of YOUR sin. There are always consequences-in this life and/or in the life to come. Whether or not you planned or wanted your first-born son, he is a blessing and is to be given unto the Lord. Encourage and support him. He is God's precious gift to you. Receive him with praise and thanksgiving. You should receive all your children with joy and thanksgiving, praising God for these precious gifts, but especially your first-born son.

Please note that of Israel's twelve sons, that both Levi (the priesthood) and Judah (lineage of Christ the High Priest) came from Leah, Israel's first wife (through man's deception but God's providence), not from Rachael whom he loved most but who proved to be evil time and time again.

When in hell, the people will be crying out, why? I'm a Christian... Remember Lazarus and the rich man? Why didn't I listen to my husband and obey him, my God, my Savior, and my Creator, why didn't I listen? Friends, be at peace with God, be at peace with one another, in marriage, love one another, for love is of God. If single, love and respect thy parents and others. Most of all, be at peace, love and respect, obey our Bridegroom, our Lord and our God. He never promised us an easy walk, a rose garden; in fact, He promises trials and tribulations, persecutions in order to be blessed. Remember that even the roses have thorns! He tells us to ever be on guard against the enemy. He promises never to leave or forsake us, He promises to provide for our needs in Philippians 4:19. He promises never to give us more than we can handle, but my dearest friends, I pondered and pondered this passage in some of my darkest moments, during trials, tribulations and persecution. One night the Spirit of God spoke to me and said, my dear son, often the simplest of things are the most difficult for people to understand. You shall never have more than you can handle, because you have Me, and with Me, nothing is impossible, nothing is too difficult for Me. Amen!!! As we go through the valley or wilderness experiences in life, we seldom understand why, why me Lord? But when the dust settles and we look back, we can see God's hand. I think of the beautiful poem 'Footprints in the Sand,' which I have included a copy in appendix D. When we lost Joshua eight- and one-half months into the pregnancy, totally healthy! Why God!??? God promises never to give us more than we can handle, but my friends, there have been many times in my life when I've felt that I was at the edge of a ten-thousand-foot cliff leaning over and looking down defying the laws of gravity! But when I look up again, like Abraham when he was to sacrifice Isaac, I look up to Him; there is restoration and revival in my life. He allowed me to lose Joshua, knowing that I could handle it, having Him and His peace in my life, and then...He placed other couples in similar situations in my path. I had been through it so that I could relate better with them and help them through their crisis. He allowed our loss. He allowed me to lose my precious God given family, so that I could be a missionary deep into the villages of Africa. Our sorrows, God can turn into joy and blessings. One must recall that the flood because of sin, brought destruction, but from the one righteous man and his family, there was restoration, just as in the case of Job.

Eve's passiveness speaks submission and permission. The male announces his intentions with forwardness; the lady submits and signals permission to her lover. Kiss is plural; it requires two players. One alone cannot kiss. The act can only be accomplished with two sets of lips Each person's lips must desire the others. Kiss is irresistible. Each person is drawn by an energy of love which each cannot resist. Kiss is promise. Each person promises admiration, trust, faith, and sacrifice in the kiss.

In 1st Timothy 2:15 we see *Notwithstanding she shall be saved in childbirth if they continue in faith and charity and holiness with sobriety.*

My dearest brothers and sisters, just as we as Christians, the truly spiritual, true believes are to be examples of Christ unto the world, through our submissiveness, being subject to, and obedient to our heavenly Father, so is a woman to a man. Just as God loves, forgives, and cares for us, so must the husband/father be to their wife or daughter.

In discussing marriage and family, I need to remind you that Job in chapter 1 served as Lord of his family and they respected his authority. I bring you now to Genesis 35:2-3 we see *Then Jacob said unto his household, and to all that were with him, Put away the strange gods that are among you, and be clean, and change your garments: And let us arise, and go up to Bethel; and I will make there an altar unto God, who answered me in the day of my distress, and was with me in the way which I went.* Here we see a man named Jacob, a man called by God to return to bethel and build an altar. Before he went or did anything at all, he first called his family to revival. The man must care for and be lord of his family, and his family-wife and children must be subject unto him as we are to be subject to our Lord and Father.

As a further security of the bond of Holy Matrimony, I believe that there is strong reason for the husband and wife to drop their family names and only use their first names (or nicknames). I liked the system in Malaysia, where both drop their family names, for we are to leave our family and cleave to our new partner, and the family name becomes the husband's first name, so we became Enchik dan Puan John (Mr. and Mrs. John). I believe that the Hispanic tradition of holding onto and adding more and more family names defeats the whole meaning of marriage as we are to let go, not hold onto our families; We are now a new family that God has created, and we need to honor Him through praise and obedience. Family names serve no purpose other than to identify nationality and tribe, as well as for genealogical purposes which the Bible tells us not to participate in 1st Timothy 1:4 *Neither give heed to fables and endless genealogies, which minister questions, rather than godly edifying which is in faith:* so do Fatima Rajaratnam, Vicky Chan, Rose Babirye, Evan Nymwaro... without the family name, we are just a person...the way that it should be! That way there is no prejudice or discrimination, no tribalism. We are children of God, pilgrims upon this earth.

In-laws are not and should never be or consider to be out-laws. They are a part of the family, and without them you wouldn't have your partner. While it is important for the extended family, it is equally important that the in-laws give space to the couple. They may make suggestions, but are never to be the decision makers for your new family. In-laws also should close the door when you are married, meaning that once married, you stay in your new home with your partner. You should never feel that it is a place to return to if...nor should in-laws ever encourage their child to return to their home, but rather if problems crop up, and what marriage never has a problem once in a while? Then they should encourage the couple to sit down and discuss and resolve the issue(s). If they are unable, then you or preferably a pastor or Christian marriage counselor may be of assistance. The problem with parents stepping in, they always (naturally) will tend to take sides and that can be very dangerous.

Inviting each other for a Sabbath dinner, a picnic once in a while, and things is very healthy for all parties, and you are all family so if someone needs some assistance, some encouragement, etc. help one another.

If the in-laws begin to be controlling or manipulative, then it is important to sit them down and explain your feelings and concerns and attempt to resolve them. If it doesn't work, then you must pray and distance yourself from them before they become an obstacle between husband and wife.

Just as in war, as in marriage, there must be rules of engagement, A few of these must be:

- Joined in **Holy** union (matrimony)

- There must be mutual respect

- There must be mutual trust

- There must be no barrier between you emotionally or physically including birth control.

In Genesis, God created Eve from Adam's rib- that she was literally a part of him, they actually were originally one flesh, and was to be his help-meet. In Genesis 3:4-6, She was created perfect as was Adam, but then she allowed herself to be deceived by the devil. Eve brought Adam down with her. In verse 13, Eve confessed her sin, so that they could move on.

Then sentence was pronounced in verse 16- your desire shall be for your husband, and he shall rule over you. Thou shalt fear the Lord thy God; him shalt thou serve, and to him shalt thou cleave Deuteronomy 10:20. Turn, O backsliding children, saith the Lord: for I am married unto you Jeremiah 3:14, Thou shalt make no covenant with them, or with their gods Ex. 23:32.

This is depicted in the story of Ruth and her mother-in-law, Naomi. It cannot go unnoticed that Ruth clave unto Naomi, not merely remaining her companion but remaining a companion till death do us part.

I have spoken about marriage, but little about family, which began at the end of the last chapter. Allow me to enlighten you on a few points in this regard. Family is very important to God, and is one of the first gifts that He gave to man at the beginning of creation. This is why He desires to be a part of your family, just as He desires you to be a part of His family, the family of God, with Jesus Christ and the angels as our relatives. He went to prepare a place for you and for me, all who truly believe, and all who are truly spiritual. In 1st Timothy 5:9-10 note brought up children. It is biblically incorrect not to want children if you are married, selfish rather than selfless and trusting God. Blessings are given because of and through children, Psalms 127:3.

God disciplines us His children to keep us on the correct path of righteousness and to keep us from falling into the hands of the enemy. This discipline is a blessing and is done with love. In Deuteronomy 7:14 you shall see that **IF** you are humble, submissive, and obedient unto God, that there shall be none barren among you, why? because children are a blessing from the Lord, Psalms 127:3 and 5.

It likewise is good for us to discipline our children as God hath commanded us to do, if we truly love and care for our children, not to spare the rod. This is to protect our children, God's children, and to keep them on the path of righteousness, and should always be done with love.

Likewise, also, wives should be disciplined as needed in order to protect them and to keep them on the path of righteousness, to keep them from falling into the hands of the enemy and from falling from the path of righteousness-gossip, adultery, rape, etc. and this too should be done only in love.

In Kenya a father beat his daughter to death and got twenty-four hours in prison, whereas an elderly man stole two chickens to feed his starving family was sentenced to five years in prison.

No discipline at any time should be done in anger, or from self-will, discipline is for the righteousness of God, not for our own likes and dislikes. Regarding discipline, I want to bring you to Jeremiah 10:24 which tells us *O LORD, correct me, but with judgment; not in thine anger, lest thou bring me to nothing.*

I used to live beside a group of eucalyptus trees, which housed turkey vultures and hawks. I loved to watch the turkey vultures teach their young to fly, one parent on the one side and the other on the other side, to keep the young one from falling, as they learn. Both parents work together with so much love and support, encourage, train, and assist their young. But in our families, where are the parents today, both parents? The child is left all alone in this vast lonely and scary desert laden with sin and temptations. Children today are lost, wandering aimlessly. Parents, it's time for the women to return to their nests, their homes, to care for their children and their husbands, for the family, and men, you are to assist them. Remember men that your wives are given unto you as helpmates, not slaves to do all of the work for you. A helpmate, a helper is there to assist not do your job for you. Let us relearn from the vultures.

Not all of us come from such wonderful families. I didn't and neither did some or may I say most of you. But I wish to point out that after very careful and thorough study, neither did...Joseph, Japhthah (book of Judges), or...Jesus Christ. Our dear Savior was from a poor family as evidenced in Luke 2:21-28, Mark 6:2-4, and Leviticus 12:8, He was from poor and 'normal' people. As you read Luke 2:23, I would encourage you to read along with it, Exodus 13:2, 22:29, and Numbers 3:13.

Listen my dear friends, Jesus was born the Son of Mary, and was the half-brother of James, Joseph, and Simon. He also had sisters, whose names are not recorded, see Mark 6:3. His family was less than perfect. Does this sound sacrilegious to say this? Well just listen to His story, because most people think or assume that since Jesus was born of a virgin and that He was perfect, that He had a perfect life, He was perfect and all was perfect. Well listen and follow with me in this and we shall see the other side, the real life of Christ. Did you have a problem of family not understanding or appreciating you? Take heart my friends; neither did Jesus' family understand or appreciate Him, even after the virgin birth and God speaking to them. Does this sound astonishing? Let us look at what Jesus said in Mark 6:4. *A prophet is not without honor, but in His own country, and among his own kin* (family and friends), *and in his own house.* Look at David and Joseph, neither were they understood or appreciated. Very little is said about the next several years of His life, but then Jesus grew...twelve years old, and we pick up again in the accounts of our dear Saviors life. We pick up His life again with Him remaining behind in the synagogue. When His parents returned looking for Him, He was found, was found teaching in the Synagogue. Imagine for a moment, twelve years old and teaching the elders and the priests! But everyone was so happy and perhaps proud of Him, after all, here is one of our own people preaching, teaching the elders and priests...until...Jesus referred to Himself as the anticipated Messiah, the fulfillment of prophecy. Wow, everything changed from that moment on. Everything changed; His life as well as the attitudes of those around Him. The truth hurts. The people questioned, 'is this not the carpenter, the son of Mary? Mark 6:3. How can He be the Messiah, He is just...well...He's just like us. The Jewish priests and even His brothers were jealous. Imagine how hard it must be to be perfect, and how people would react to you.

The people forced Jesus out of the Synagogue, and completely out of their town, and they took Him to the edge of the hill upon which the town was built. How did Jesus react? Let us look to the book of Luke 4:29-30 *And rose up, and thrust Him*

*out of the city, and led Him unto the brow of the hill whereon
their city was built, that they might cast Him down headlong.
But He passing through the midst of them went His way.* He
went His way...alone. My dear friends, the friends and family
of our dear Savior desired to kill Him! But...Take a look around,
where was His family? Where was His mother, where was His
step father? Where were His brothers and sisters? Here we see
Jesus was in trouble for nothing, and His family and friends
were nowhere to be found. They weren't there for their first
born, miracle (virgin birth) son.

We turn back now to Mark 3:21, where we see that His
family were talking unto Him, and in fact were seen with Him
in public, but let us listen in to the conversation and hear what
is going on. There was sorrow, shame and humiliation, rather
than pride and joy. His family went to get Him because they
believed Him to be beside himself, mentally unfit, lost His
mind. There was no pride or joy; they were embarrassed and
ashamed of our Savior! Jesus' brothers tried to get Him to
leave town. Jesus never tried to control, manipulate or change
His family, nor did He ignore them. He also never allowed
them to control Him for He answered to His Father in Heaven.
He was God. Jesus didn't complain, or withdraw when they
cast all of the insults at Him or when they put Him down and
criticized Him, in fact even on the cross He never complained,
just uttered those precious words, *Father...forgive them for
they know not what they do,* Luke 23:34. His (God's) mission
was not to please His family, but to serve God, to accomplish
God's purpose and plan, just as should be our mission while
upon this earth. His and our parents are nothing more than
instruments of God to bring God's children into this temporary
life on earth for His purpose and plan. Jesus never disobeyed
or disrespected them either. The same people who worshipped
Him in Matthew 2:11, those in Luke 2:17, as well as the priests
and elders of Luke 2:47 are the same who denied and offered
up Jesus to be crucified.

He was sold to His enemy by one of His own disciples,
Jesus was falsely accused, despised and rejected, but...Jesus
forgave His enemies, all who rejected Him and joined together

in nailing Him to the cross. All of the evil actions against Him were tolerated and accepted out of His great love for you and for me. He sacrificed and surrendered all unto His Father, and to us, if we choose to believe and accept all that He accomplished for us. Doesn't this sound like the life of Joseph in the Old Testament? Doesn't this voluntary sacrifice and surrender sound like Isaac in the Old Testament?

When both husband and wife are working, they tend to fall into a rut of meeting their own needs rather than those of our families, I know that it happened even to me. We must put God and our family first.

Not all families can be like 'Little House on the Prairie', or 'the Walton's. Jesus told us in Mark 3:35 *For whosoever shall do the will of God, the same is my brother, and my sister, and mother.* God also works all things for good for those who choose to believe. Even look at Pharez in Genesis 46:22 who was the son of Tamar. After playing the harlot with <u>Judah</u> her father-in-law of all people, is still in the lineage of Christ.

Jesus fully realized that His spiritual family could and in fact would provide for what His earthly family didn't and couldn't, including that of eternal life. Friends, we have no control over how people treat us, even how our family treats us, but we can control how we listen to and obey our Father, God. Mary was seen at the cross, the tomb, and in the upper room at Pentecost in the book of the Acts of the Apostles. But...where was she all of Jesus' life, when He needed her, and...where was Joseph? Joseph was there to betroth Mary, pay his taxes and deliver Jesus Christ, and then...Where is he? We know that he brought forth a couple of sons and daughters but... where was Joseph through Christ's' life?

What was important in Joseph was the importance in God's eyes of betrothal-a binding vow, and against divorce.

In Genesis 44:9 we see that we must be careful what we vow before God, because a vow can and usually will be tested, including marriage! And your faith!

What did Joseph think about the ministry of Christ? We are never told, but in Matthew 3:17 we know that God had confirmed the ministry of His Son, saying *This is My Beloved Son in whom I am well pleased.* Your family may or may not give you their blessings, but if you listen to and obey our Father in heaven, you'll receive His blessings, and those are the most important of all. He will bless you for His ministry, including the ministry of marriage. It is one thing to accept God as Lord; it is an entirely different thing to accept Jesus as your Savior. It is an entirely other issue to accept Him as thy Father. Lord recognizes Him as the Supreme Being over everything and everybody. Father accepts Him as our Guide and protector, one to look up to and His promises made to us, it is a personal and close relationship. Savior accepts His free gift of salvation that He offers unto all who choose to believe.

God has proven Himself time and again as Lord and Savior, as Friend and our precious Father. He is just and faithful who always keeps His promises. He will always stay by our side and never leave or forsake us. The question is...are you ready and willing to accept His free offer, accept all that He hath done for us, are you willing to trust and obey Him? Are you ready and willing to be faithful to Him? Do you listen to our Father? Are you listening to Him now? Do you ever take the time to talk to Him as your Father and best friend? In Galatians 4:7 take a look at it quickly. Likewise, ye wives are you ready and willing to be obedient unto God, and honor thy vows made to thy husband? Are you willing to trust and obey, submit and surrender all unto thy husband...until death? It sounds scary to completely surrender and submit unto another person, or to God, but this humility is what will bring the greatest blessings, including that of salvation and a happy marriage until death do you part. All of us walking in here, into this message, carrying the past and the past will haunt you. God and Jesus told people don't look back. In Luke 9:62 we are told, *No man having put his hand to the plow, and looking back is fit for the kingdom of God.* The people of Israel died looking back, Lot's wife also died looking back...Please my dear friends, leave your past, all the hurt, pain, sorrows, wrongs done you...leave it all at the feet of Jesus, **this very minute** leave it all behind, then carry on down the path of righteousness. Praise God for sending us His Son to take our pasts, our pains and sorrows, our hurts and our wrongs done us, our burdens, He took them all, leave them behind and don't look back, just Praise God and thank Him for all that He has done. Pray that thy life may be revived, restored, our marriages, our Christian walk, and let's walk hand in hand with Christ, with our God ordained partner, or if single with thy parents, now back to the life of Jesus.

Jesus never allowed His friends or family to interfere with His ministry, from obedience unto God, and neither should we. I am speaking here from personal experience!

Let us now jump over to the book of Acts 1:12, 14. What a change! Now Jesus' mother, Mary, and His brother worship and pray for Him. If Jesus had of disowned His family, ran them off, disrespected them or tried to force them to change earlier on, then...who would have been there for Him? But, because of how He accepted them for who they were and I'm certain that He prayed for them, God changed their hearts. Are you seeing how you may apply this into your life, your relationship with thy parents, with thy spouse...? Then we look awhile later and see that one of His brothers became an Apostle (Galatians 1:19), others became missionaries (1st Corinthians 15:7). This reminds us again in the Old Testament story of Joseph, with his parents and brothers, and should as well be applied in our lives and our relationships. After many years and shortly before my being taken hostage in Kenya, my parents responded to an e-mail that I sent them, and said that they were proud of me and happy the way that I was serving the Lord, and though they said they didn't have much, they wanted to help the ministry financially. I was so happy, more for their change of heart than for the offering itself, though that would have been a blessing also. A local church also approached me saying that they would like to know if I would accept some monthly support from them also. Then after a couple of years as a hostage, the Embassy related to me that they had been in contact with my parents and that they said that they loved me and knew that I was guilty of no crime. I told them to let my parents know that I always loved them and that truly I was not guilty of anything save that of serving the Almighty God. Then after four years, I get a message that they didn't know if

I was dead or alive, in the hospital or what/where. I prayed for them for that must be a tremendous amount of unnecessary stress for my elderly folks, Oh the shame on Kenya and the American Embassy.

I did a message on marriage and family awhile back, and afterwards I invited couples to come and recommit their marriages and families, as well as their lives to Christ and to each other. I was surprised with tears of joy as I watched an elderly couple come forward. They were supporting one another as both were very weak and unstable, they both had difficulty walking. I stopped everything, gave them both a big hug, and asked them a few questions quickly. They were married. He replied, I knew her from the day that she was born, as we were neighbors. We then grew up together. We got married and have been married for over seventy years! I asked him if he would mind sharing a word of wisdom and encouragement for the others, of their success. He responded, "you covered it in your message, we love God and I love her". Then with tears in her eyes, still holding onto her husband, she looked up at him and said, "I love him, I trust him, and I obey him." Oh, dear friends, you heard their response, so simple, and that is what God wants, and that is the secret for a successful marriage on earth and in our marriage to Christ. This is how it should be for us to each other and to God. It isn't complicated, very simple-love...trust...and obey, Selfless not selfish. Strive to be your best as a child of God, strive to be your best for your spouse, and strive to be your best for thy parents if single.

Months after I was married, a pastor friend asked me how I could marry someone that I didn't know. I looked at him and replied simply, that I didn't need to know her yet, because I knew God, I trust God, and that is more than enough for me. He asked me, but what about your wife? I told him, The God that I serve doesn't make mistakes. I know my God and trust Him; I now have the gift that He loaned to me and I trusted her through Him. After she left twenty years later, I've been asked several times if I still believe these words; my response? Absolutely, my God doesn't make mistakes. Did my precious wife make a bad choice? Absolutely, but not God. We are all sinners and we all make mistakes, we all fall short of the glory of God, but as long as God wills, I'll be there to take her back, just as God does for us. It isn't that hard. I'm nobody special, just one who loves and trusts God enough, and appreciate all that he hath done for me, that I want to be Christ-like and be forgiving and welcoming as well. My dear wife made mistakes. I made mistakes. Instead of condemning her as well as the many other women who do the same thing without realizing just what they are doing; I ask that you, like I do, pray for her to return to God and her marriage. We are all sinners, hmmm. No matter how perfect we'd like to be, sometimes mistakes are difficult to own up to, accept responsibility for, and we desire to appear perfect (pride), but...overall, she made one big mistake as do so many. She walked out on God and her husband for the world, just like Eve, and it caused so many other problems. Aside from that, she was a wonderful young lady, who had so many beautiful and wonderful qualities. I was always honored to have her by my side, and to walk hand in hand with her. I rarely read any secular books, but was recently impressed when reading a book that was lent to me, where a successful man in the world had been a leader of a troop in a war many years prior in the army during an atrocity that killed around a hundred civilians including women, babies, nuns, and babies, from various countries. Then all these years later, a member of his troop wrote a book about the atrocity and exposed him. His wife told him to flee to another country and that she would join him. He said fight or flight. She told him that if he stayed to fight, that she wouldn't wait around while he was in prison. Awhile later, he was inducted back into the army to stand court marshal and was confined to base. Shortly thereafter, his wife showed up on his doorstep to move in with him, saying 'I was reminded by several women, that a woman's place is by her husband's side, and I love you and I respect you for standing up for what you believe. This reminds me of the passage in Matthew 21:28-31, and this is the way that it should be. After he was convicted but while being held in jail before sentencing, his wife sent him a note through his attorney stating that she loved him. She had previously stated that she wouldn't wait, but here she is and is still reminding him that she is with him and loves him.

We shall return now to the book of Matthew 18:4-6, because there are a couple more revelations to be seen here. We need to humble ourselves in our marriages, drop the pride (and laziness), and accept the roles that God hath ordained for us, and be the people that God created us to be, not pretenders. Men, humbly assume thy roles, and women, humble thyself, submit unto the God given authority of thy husband. Remember that you never asked to be a woman and neither did thy husband ask to be a man. Remove thy pants and return them unto thy husband and you husbands, rejoice, gladly accept the pants and put them back on. Be the responsible husbands that God ordained you to be, your wife is counting on you. This alone could eliminate many divorces.

Verse 5 is so important as shown here, how important, what a blessing these precious children are. Don't neglect or reject God's precious gifts, God's blessings for you. People today are too selfish to have children anymore. We send out the elderly to nursing homes, so that in the end...people are all alone.

Don't even think for a moment of birth control or abortion, rejoice and accept thy lord into thy temple and if God so desires, rejoice and receive God's precious gift, the little child that He has entrusted unto **YOU** in His name, amen! If you respect and cherish God's gift, then there shall be showers of blessings, but if you reject God's gift, then there shall be judgment because you dared to defy His purpose and plan for thy life, and chose to reject His love and gifts.

One or two children tend to be spoiled, self-centered, materialistic, and greedy; whereas children of larger families learn to get along and share, care for one another, and appreciate what they have. They help one another and love each other so much.

Children continues from chapter 1, but... while rearing thy children, God's blessings to you, you parents must never forget that your first blessing is your partner; That relationship must never be forgotten due to the children. Your marriage must be continually nourished-otherwise when thy children are gone, you experience the emptiness of the empty nest syndrome. This can and should be avoided by nourishing your relationship with one another throughout your family life. Include your children but don't base your life on your children for they go away but thy partner is forever. Never lose sight of thy first blessing-thy husband or wife. Just as we as Christians must never lose sight of our primary blessing-Jesus Christ by getting lost in all of the earthly blessings, otherwise we may lose sight and fall away from the path of righteousness.

Mark 7:10 parents, are you being honorable by lying and teaching your children and keeping pagan festivals?

To a large extent, the unity and harmony within the church is dependent upon the unity and harmony within the individual homes. The apostle Paul emphasized a lot on the unity and harmony, the love and respect that must exist between husband and wife, and this should serve as a clear illustration of the love of Christ, the self-sacrificing, selfless love that Christ has for His church. This Christ like love within the home as well as within the church is essential for husbands and wives as well as the church members. This same selfless love must as well be seen between parents and children, and employers and their employees. This type of love, harmony, unity, and peace should spread through our homes and church life. Thus, as I said at the beginning, marriage and family exemplifies our Christian walk and our relationship within the family of God, and consequently is why God created marriage, and why marriage is so very important to God.

Society and our church are only as good as the family. Society and the church are the way they are because of the family. Perhaps you cannot change the world, but you can be a lighthouse to those around you through your marriage and family values which must be Biblically based.

My dear brothers, before you were conceived, God knew if you were to be married or not, and to whom. Women likewise, God also knew just how many boys and girls **He** wanted you to bring into this world for Him in order to fulfill His purpose and plan. Don't deny God for thy own plans and pleasures, He knows best as He is the Master Designer, and with submitting to Him in total faith and surrender, there shall be joy and blessings...curses if you deny Him. And you know what? God loves children...so should we.

I know that this is contrary to modern cultural teaching and thought. I know about X and Y chromosomes and the science, the chemistry of reproduction...But we are not talking science here. Who created science, and who is in control of the universe? God knows better than scientists, for God created science! He created the universe, and He who created the universe is in full control of the universe and all that it contains, He isn't out of control and He doesn't need any help.

Dear brothers and sisters, I know that this sounds strange, and perhaps difficult, but God, the Almighty God is simple, **ONLY BELIEVE**, have faith, trust and obey, and remain under the shadow of His wings. Oh, glory my dear friends, what did we ever do to deserve such love? We didn't, we sinned against Him, we nailed Him to the tree, but He still loves and forgives the righteous. This needs to be carried into our marriages. It's hard in our human nature but with God, it becomes much easier. If you only knew what I've been through...but part of that story is in my book **ONLY BELIEVE**, but the trials and tribulations, the persecutions I've been through, I feel like Job, Daniel, Paul, Joseph all rolled into one, but...I and my faith are stronger now, just as we see in these stories of the Bible. No, it's not easy, but I can tell you that God is there each step of the way. If there are one thousand steps between God and you, He will take the nine hundred and ninety-nine, but He will wait for you to take that first step. Once you take that step, there are no regrets and your faith, as well as your marriage; your life shall never be the same. God pushes us to be all that we can be, He pushes us to the impossible to show us that with Him, nothing is impossible, think about this, apply it to your life today, to your Christian walk, your marriage, and see what God can do, then sit back and count your many blessings. That first step is a most difficult step, it usually defies all human logic or understanding, but once you take it, you'll never regret it. When you jump from an aircraft, you trust that the chute will open. God is always there for us if we look to Him.

What are the indications of Spiritual indicators of the need for family reformation?

Lost fear of God- In Proverbs 1:7 *The fear of the Lord is the beginning of knowledge: but fools despise wisdom and instruction.*

Abandoned absolute truth- John 8:31-32

Accept divorce- Malachi 2:16- I hate divorce. Old Chinese proverb, in the broken nest there are no whole eggs. Divorce is destroying children, families, churches and cultures.

Lost clear distinction between male and female roles- everything has become unisex causing social confusion, and is in direct opposition to what the Bible teaches.

Abandoned our children- In Psalms 127:3, it says, *Lo, children are an heritage of the Lord: and the fruit of the womb is his reward.* They are a gift from the Lord.

Feel powerless to effect change. We need to break from pride to humility. Change must begin in the individual, then the church, and then the community; and one must ask, Lord, what needs to change in my life, for a family reformation to occur in my home? As He has to work in us before He can work through us.

We are in severe need for family reformation, which involves knowing God's truth, applying God's truth in your life, experiencing, embracing, and proclaiming God's truth of marriage and family to others. God's Plan for reformation includes personal repentance and purity, Psalms 139:23. Repentance is a climbing into the fiery furnace to burn away pride, selfishness, greed, immorality, fear, and apathy Psalms 51:10-13.

Honor the Sacred covenant of marriage

Sanctity of God ordained roles within the marriage Psalms 127:3

In order to bring reformation and revival you need to pray with your spouse, read scriptures daily to your family, living a life separate from the ways of the world. You must forget the ways of your parents and look to the ways of thy Father in heaven, you can't be middle of the road; be marriage and family mentors for newlyweds, and remember the godly patri-archy, godly husband and father.

I have outlined part of the answer for the family but where does the church come in to reclaiming the sanctity of marriage within the churches and bring revival? Don't get married unless you plan to keep your vows, as vows are very sacred before God. Don't advocate divorce under any circumstance. Divorce needs to become shameful again. Churches should refuse to marry people who refuse to go through biblical marriage training, and sign a document that they will never divorce or even men-tion divorce. They should refuse to remarry anyone who has become divorced and/or refusing to try reconciliation. Fulfill your vows by staying married. Divorce is NEVER the solution. Fulfill your vows by praying faithfully with your spouse. Fulfill your vows by caring faithfully for your spouse, meet each oth-er's needs for affection, emotional, and sexual needs, fulfill your vows by maintaining emotional and moral fidelity, main-tain a healthy sexual relationship with your spouse, guard your heart in relation to the opposite sex, and fulfill your vows by finishing strong.

Be Courageous— Don't Compromise

Men, do you regularly pray with and for your wife? Do you read the Bible together and lead her spiritually in the truth? Are you passionately loving God's most holy human gift to you, your wife? Are you spiritually leading, loving and protecting your children? Do you model a humble and teach-able heart for God by asking for forgiveness when you have wronged a family member?

And churches, In the book of Joel we see all of the inhab-itants of the land to gather into the house of God, fast, and cry out to the Lord annually, to rid the Christian families of divorce, immorality, violence, abuse, perversion, murder, drugs, alcohol, materialism plaguing the homes like swarms of locusts, are you doing this?

Are you honoring the sacred vows of marriage and providing church or Christian based mentors for families beginning before marriage and lasting at least through the first few years, and thereafter as needed?

In the Songs of Solomon 5:3-8, I wish for you to note that her husband was out working. He returned home and his wife refused to open the door for him. This may be translated actual or sexual, but then after he was gone, we see in verse 13, she repented and searched for him just as women today should be doing for their first husband if they are separated or divorced, and brought about restoration which is God's desire. So often we close the door on Christ, but we need to seek Him with a whole heart and mind and restore our relationship with Him.

The family is only to be severed by the departure of the child in marriage; thus, permitting its members to join in a new family unit; or death. One is the smallest indivisible unit that there is, so it is impossible to divide the unit of one flesh once it has been glued together. Man and woman are two entities before marriage, but following marriage they become an indivisible unit of one in marital status, one entity, thus they cannot be divided. Again, Jesus said, they shall be two in one flesh.... not three or four. But if they marry a second time, or more, then their oneness no longer exists; there will not be two in one flesh, on the contrary, many in one, thus polygamy, and adultery.

Just like everything else in our lives, God allows our marriages to be tried and tested, because He allows our faith and trust to be tested. Either we grow in faith and trust, and our strength in Him; or we fall away. This applies also to our marriages. We must be strong in the Lord and in each other. Any weakness when tried and tested, and one falls into the fire, then the marriage dissolves.

As Christians, we need to be careful and guard ourselves from the outside, from the world and unbelievers; from the enemy. We need to build the great wall of defense, and we do this only by staying in His word and in prayer. We need to be alert and on guard twenty-four hours per day, seven days a week, and men, we must be on guard for our families. But families, the men can only guard you IF you are willing to submit to and obey his authority.

Man and woman are an allegory, an illustration of God's promise and plan. Every detail has a purpose in God's creation. We are all sinners, deserving of death, but God in His infinite love, mercy and grace, still cares for us and desires to use us for His glory. The question is, do you trust and love God enough to leave the world behind and cleave unto Him forever, to allow yourself to surrender all unto Him and be His helpmate? Not to live by thy will any longer, but His? Are you willing to trust God enough to carry this into thy marriage and family? My dear sisters, are you able and willing to demonstrate this by doing this for your husband? My brothers, are you willing to demonstrate to the world God's love by demonstrating this to thy wife? Allow me to illustrate briefly. A husband gets called by God to go out into the remote parts of Guinea. He tells his wife. What is her response? 'No way, I like my life now, our home, car, and...go out there in the village with...nothing...and the cannibals...' or like Ruth who responded in 1:16, *Whither thou goest I will go, where thou lodgest, I will lodge, Thy God my God,* I love our God and I love you, my lord. And my brothers, will you listen to thy wife like Adam did and disobeyed God, or listen to God as Job did and follow Him rather than his wife who told him to curse God and die...

A message on marriage and family wouldn't be complete without some further discussion on Proverbs 31:10-31.

Verse 10, *Who can find a virtuous woman?* Virtuous refers to ability, efficiency and strength. *For her price is far above rubies.* This is the way a wife should be to her husband and how that we should be for our Lord.

Verse 11 continues *The heart of her husband doth safely trust in her, so that he shall have no need of spoil.* Are you women such that your husband can trust you? Are either of you keeping secrets from the other, secrets always surface sooner or later and cause major problems. Honesty is the best way to prevent future troubles. We cannot hide from God or from each other if we truly love and trust one another. Likewise, God calls us to confess our sins, and so should husbands and wives to one another, then the love and mercy for one another. Pray for one another, encourage one another down the right path. Can God entrust you with His word and service?

Verse 12 *She will do him good and not evil all the days of her life* (till death do us part). My dear sisters? We see Israel in the wilderness; they kept wandering further and further from God, and did evil...and died without ever entering into the rest, into the Promised Land. They repented on occasion but not with a clean or pure heart, just lip service in order to avoid the consequences, but the truth shall always find you out. I asked a church one day, 'how many of you are truly saved Christians?' One hundred percent raised their hands, yet... this was asked inside of a prison where many were known to be doing illegal business, stealing, homosexuality, liars... Then I asked them, how many of you faithfully read thy Bibles on a regular basis, and they looked around and only a couple raised their hands. Is this truly a saved Christian? My God be the judge. Dear friends are you hearing what the Spirit is saying? Will you apply this to your life and your marriage today?

Verse 15 *She riseth while it is still night, and giveth meat to her household and to her maidens.* She rises early to prepare the day and breakfast for her family, and is hospitable to anyone in need. I wish to note here also that night represents darkness and evil, so she the wife and believer must arise from the darkness of sin and stand firm upon His word and promises, then avoid falling back into the darkness. This strength can only come from God and is a part of the virtuous wife, as well as ourselves before God.

Verse 20, I'm skipping some, as I'm just highlighting some points here. *She stretcheth out her hand to the poor: yea, she reacheth forth her hands to the needy.* Our wives must be good stewards of family resources, while not neglecting the care of others in need. We as truly spiritual, must be good stewards of God's resources, and always be willing to open our hearts and our hands to reach out to the poor and needy, the sick and the prisoners, the down and the lonely-physically, emotionally, and spiritually...

Then in Verse 23 *Her husband is known in the gates, where he sitteth among the elders of the land.* She brings honor and respect to her husband, who serves God in society. We must bring respect and honor to our Father and make Him known wherever we go, unto the ends of the world, as He will sit as judge at the gate in the end times. I want you to see the other side of this and read it as God is our husband and He is known... what are you doing women, to make your husband known and respected in the church and community? Men and women, as the bride, what are you doing to make God our Father known to those around us and around the world? I personally have been in villages who have never heard of Jesus Christ! Now they know Him and many accepted Him into their lives and the villages will never be the same, Praise God!

Verse 26 goes on to say *She openeth her mouth with wisdom, and in her tongue is the law of kindness.* She isn't a gossip, slanderer, full of hatred; but rather full of wisdom and kindness, knowing what to say, when to say it, as well as when to keep silent, so should a wife be, so should we as God's children, as the bride of Christ. When we speak, we are God's spokesmen, so we should speak with love and honor at all times.

Verse 27 *She looketh well to the ways of her household and eateth not the bread of idleness.* As the wife stays busy caring for her household and not out running around gossiping, and away from the shelter and protection of her husband, so should we be as God's children and bride.

Verse 28 goes on to say *The children rise up, and call her blessed: her husband also, and he praiseth her.* Do you wish to be blessed and praised by our Father? Also rise up, this is two-fold. Rise up in the morning, as well as rise up in wisdom and knowledge and social status, all from the stay-at-home wife, who loves, teaches, and cares for his children.

Verse 29 *Many daughters have done virtuously, but thou excellest them all.* Many do the works of the law, but God desires those who do it from a pure heart, and who stand strong, stand out of the crowd, and be a lighthouse, to lead others unto Him, to serve as a living example by being a living sacrifice. Do you my dear brothers and sisters stand out of the crowd or are you just blending in with everyone else? Can you my brothers honestly praise thy wives? Do you my brothers love thy families; love thy wives as Christ loves the church? All of us need to ask ourselves if our Husband-the living and Almighty God, can say *Thou excellest them all* about you…about me? *Many will say to me in that day, Lord, Lord, have we not prophesied in thy name? and in thy name have cast out devils? And in thy name done many wonderful works? And then will I profess unto them, I never knew you, depart from me, ye that work iniquity.* Matthew 7:22-23, Divorce in the end times.

Finally, in verse 30, *Favour is deceitful and beauty is vain, but a woman that feareth the Lord, she shall be praised.* A sinner that repents, fears God, shall be praised in the end times, the man beside Christ on the cross. My dear sisters, you need to love, fear thy Lord, whom God ordained for thee, with a pure and clean heart. Likewise, we must fear God so that He can praise and bless us. Remember, spiritually we are all women and we all must fear God our Father. The beauty of a wife, the beauty of a believer is in the heart, not the outward appearance.

Let us go further and look at the Titus 2 woman; (some of this was from a note that an office handed me one day, source unknown, but I felt it such a wonderful outline.)

REVERENT BEHAVIOR

Ecclesiastes 12:13; Hebrews 12:1-2; Rom. 12:1; Psalms 90:12; Gal 2:20; Colossians 3:2; Rom 12:2

Are you committed to God and your family?

Are you devoting yourself to spiritual maturity?

If I were to ask those who know you intimately (who know the real you), would they say you are undoubtedly a spiritually minded person?

If God was looking for a living illustration of a spiritually mature reverent woman, would He select you?

Do you regularly read, study, and apply God's Word in your life?

How is your prayer life? Is it powerless because of some besetting sin? Is it hindered by haste, irregularity, unbelief, etc.?

Have you set aside all sin in your life as well as any hindrances?

Are you conformed to the world in your dress, speech, actions or goals, etc.?

Do you have a reputation of humility?

CONTROLS HER TONGUE

Not false accusers, slanderer

A person who reveals personal facts. Sharing private information about others with those who are not part of the problem or part of the solution. See also

1st Timothy 3:11; James 1:26; Ephesians 4:29-32; Proverbs 26:20-23

She must ask herself; Is this appropriate to say right now? To this audience?

Have I personally verified all of the facts? Or is this something I overheard, been told, or assumed from what you thought was obvious evidence?

What is my purpose in repeating this information? Am I trying to make someone else look bad? Am I trying to make myself look good? Am I thinking the best of others? Am I trying to build others up?

Does the hearer really need to know this information?

Do I enjoy sharing negative or bad information about others?

If this incident I am relating were about me, would I want it repeated to others?

Can the person I am telling really do anything to help or to correct the situation?

Matthew 5:7,7:1-5, 18:15-17; 12:34-37; Proverbs 6:16-19, 20:19,26:17,11:11-13,13:3, 29:20, 18:13, 10:17-19, 17:28; 1ˢᵗ Peter 2:1, 3:10; Rom. 3:23, 13:10; 1ˢᵗ John 1:8-10; 1ˢᵗ Corinthians 13:5; James 5:9-10; Galatians 5:14-16; Ephesians 3:10, Ezekiel 13:10.

Do you talk too much?

Have you learned to overlook the transgressions of others?

When it is not possible to overlook a transgression, do you faithfully practice the principals found in Mat. 18:15-17?

Do you assume the best about others?

> Do you take up offenses for others?
> Do you avoid negative talk about others?

Rom. 6:18; Galatians 5:22-23

In Titus Chapter 2, it teaches that a woman is to love her husband. Paul is speaking here of a friendly love in which godly wives choose to have for their husbands. This is not based upon a husband's worthiness, but on God's command. God says that young women are to be taught to love their husbands. There are no conditions or exceptions to this command. If a wife does not love her husband, she must in obedience to God train herself to love him. Loving a husband involves being a friend and companion to him, even when a wife does not feel like it. Even ungrateful, unkind, husbands are to be loved. It involves putting his interests and welfare above her own. Are you hearing this my sisters? And men, you must try to be worthy of such love, surrender and sacrifice.

Respect found in Ephesians 5:33, is defined as a reverential obedience.

1st Cor 7:1-6; Ephesians 4:31-32; Hebrews 12:14-15; Jeremiah31:34; Psalms 37:7; Proverbs 31

In 1st Corinthians 7:34 the definition of please is to accommodate one's self to the opinion's desires and interests of another.

Look for ways to please him

Ask his advice and preferences rather than asking your family or friends

Study your husband to discover what he likes and dislikes, and then adjust your housekeeping, cooking, etc. to fit his tastes and preferences

When he asks you to do something, do it well, just as his boss expects him to do at his job.

Be mindful to obey his smallest wishes, to submit to his desires, and seek to please him in all things.

Ask him what he thinks your responsibilities as his wife are and then seek to fulfill them, just as we should seek to fulfill God's (our Bridegroom's) desires.

1st Peter 3:1-4; 1st Corinthians 14:35; 1st Corinthians 7:2-6

Do not resist your husband's physical affection. Avoid allowing exhaustion, bitterness, fear, etc. to mold your receptivity to your husband. Do not withhold yourself from your husband in order to get back at him or punish him. Freely give your love and affection to your husband. Joyfully receive his love and affection in return.

Hebrews 13:5-6; 1st Timothy 6:6-11; Proverbs 14:29, 15:1, 10:19, 27:15-16, 21:19,28:13, James 5:16; Colossians 3:13; 1st Peter 4:8; Luke 17:3; 1st Peter 3:1-21; 1st Thessalonians 5:11; Ephesians 4:29; 1st Corinthians 15:33

I want you to see something very special and beautiful in God's word. Women, you are special and are loved! In John 3:16, we are told *For God so loved the world that he gave his only begotten Son, that whosoever believeth in him should not perish, but have everlasting life.* God (righteousness), so loves you and me, the sinners, the women or the bride, though we are but sinners. He loves us so very much. Now look at 1st John 3:16, *Happily perceive we the love of God, because he laid down his life for us, and we ought to lay down our life for the brethren.* This includes our wives, men. God (righteousness) laid down His life for us sinners (women) so ought we for our wives. Now, look over at Genesis 3:16 which tells us *Unto the woman he* (God) *said, I will greatly multiply thy sorrow and thy conception; in sorrow thou shalt bring forth children;* penalty for our sin men and women, *and thy desire shall be to thy husband,* my sisters did you hear this? *And he shall rule over thee.* Who is our husband my dear brothers and sisters? God is our Husband, our Bridegroom and we need to respect, honor, and obey Him, just as the women should respect, honor, and obey thy husband, submit unto him and allow him to be the lord over thy home and thyself as God hath ordained. We see in Judges 15:6 that the woman was married to Samson and knew better than to go with another man and so was punished by God. The woman after marriage is to remain faithful to her husband, as her father gives up all rights, just as we after we accept Christ, and marry Him, must remain faithful unto Him and Him alone.

Women need to tell and remind constantly in word and deed that she and God are one with their husbands, and that they love them. Men are not verbal beings like women are; they are not able to communicate their inner feelings, fears, and troubles like a woman can.

You know, when Jesus was twelve years of age, His mother went and pulled Him out of the temple, away from His ministry. Instead of being proud and honored, she pulled Him away. Years later when He was around thirty, Mary and His brothers came and again tried to interrupt His ministry and He cast them away, *'who is my mother and brethren'*...? Are there people in your life trying to pull you away from the Lord and His ministry, His purpose and plan for your life? Satan uses family, friends, church members, and others...but you must cast them away if they are pulling you away. And wives, are you hindering your lord from fulfilling the ministry that God ordained for him or are you encouraging him?

Jesus twice went into the temple and cleansed it out because of all the uncleanness, the evil. Is there uncleanness in your life, your home, in your heart? Is there uncleanness in your family or your church? Is the Lord convicting you, is He angry trying to cleanse your temple but you are refusing to allow Him access?

Once a year the Israelites entered the temple to cleanse it from top to bottom...entirely. Perhaps today is the day... to cleanse your heart, your family, your home, your church... Don't fight or resist Him, He wants the best for you, allow the cleansing. Make right your hurting or broken relationships (separation or divorce) as we are told in 1st Corinthians 11:27 *Wherefore whosoever shall eat this bread, and drink this cup of the Lord, unworthily, shall be guilty of the body and cup of the Lord.* Holy communion, I hope that you are hearing this, read also Exodus 12:48.

Come now, let us reason together. Parents need to return to teaching the precepts of the Bible. We need to practice and teach our children to abstain from worldly entertainment-Movies, television, radio, books, magazines, etc. which is both sexual and violent, and in direct violation of God's word. How can we call ourselves Christian and partake of the lusts of the world? Rather, we should be and must return to teaching our young boys and girls instead of sexual education which should NOT be taught to our young children, they will learn when the time is right (after marriage), But boys to respect girls, and girls need to be taught to respect and submit unto the boys (but not sexually until after marriage). Teach the precepts of God as we see in 2nd Timothy 2:22 Flee also youthful lusts: but follow righteousness, faith, charity, peace, with them that call on the Lord out of a pure heart, Titus 2:12 *Teaching us that, denying ungodliness and worldly lusts, we should live soberly, righteously, and godly, in this present world;* 1st Peter 4:2 *That he no longer should live the rest of his time in the flesh to the lusts of men, but to the will of God,* and 2:11 *Dearly beloved, I beseech you as strangers and pilgrims, abstain from fleshly lusts, which war against the soul.* We need to think on these things-Philippians 4:8 *Finally, brethren, whatsoever things are true, whatsoever things are honest, whatsoever things are just, whatsoever things are pure, whatsoever things are lovely, whatsoever things are of good report; if there be any virtue, and if there be any praise, think on these things.* Let us stop all these epidemics of rape, incest, adultery and fornication, birth control, abortion, violence; and do as David did in Psalms 96:1-6 *O sing unto the Lord a new song: sing unto the Lord, all the earth. Sing unto the Lord, bless his name; shew forth his salvation from day to day. Declare his glory among the heathen, his wonders among all people. For the Lord is great, and greatly to be praised: he is to be feared above all gods. For all the gods of the nations are IDOLS: but the Lord made the heavens. Honor and majesty are before him.* In the Indian culture and traditions, women have been highly respected in many ways, but rape should not be tolerated in any culture. It is totally disrespectful and there is no love in the act. But the Indian and Asian women today are losing respect because they are fighting to leave the home and marriages to be a man in society and usurp his authority and positions, just as has happened in the U.S.A. They are deciding not to marry, and not to have children when they are married, and this should be God's choice not the man or woman's choice.

Parents, Isaiah tells us in 23:4 *Be thou ashamed, O Zidon: for the sea hath spoken, even the strength of the sea, saying, I travail not, nor bring forth children, neither do I nourish up young men, nor bring up virgins.* Parents should be ashamed because they have neglected God's gifts to them, their children and have gone their separate ways, do their own thing, and who is rearing thy blessing-thy children? Where are the young godly virgin men today? Where are the virgin young ladies today? Most children have become sexually active from the age of around ten to twelve years of age! Oh, the apostasy, where are you oh Christian parents, where are your churches and church leaders?

In Genesis 6:12 *And God looked upon the earth, and, behold, it was corrupt; for all flesh had corrupted His way upon the earth.* Imagine what He would say today. Then look at Genesis 19:13 *For we will destroy this place* (Sodom); *because the cry of them is waxen great before the face of the Lord; and the Lord hath sent us to destroy it.* Dear friends if God doesn't judge and destroy the U.S., He needs to go and apologize to the people of Sodom and Gomorrah! Then in Genesis 6:8 out of all the people on earth, Noah found grace in the sight of God, many are called but few are chosen. Will you be the one man today? But I want you to see also in verse 18 that the righteousness of the father saved his family! Men, are you listening? The righteousness of Christ can save us. Did the animals sin? No, but God is in control, and everything pays the price for our sins.

In the book of Esther 5:14 Here as in Eve and Delilah, as well as Job's wife and others, women are used by Satan to destroy their husbands. This ought not to be and women you need to guard yourselves against this ploy of Satan's. Always strive for peace and love, encourage and support the ministry of thy husband, for if you are married, this is thy ministry. Don't be fooled by Satan and the world! One must always be careful not to take their life partner for granted, after the marriage has endured for a while. It is a natural tendency, so you must watch and be careful. Every once in a while, do something just to rekindle the fires, don't ever let the fire burn out. The fire can be rekindled, but it is much easier to keep the fires burning.

Men, you have an awesome responsibility to demonstrate to the world God's love, mercy, grace, and forgiveness to us sinners by how you treat thy wife. And my sisters, you have an awesome responsibility to demonstrate how we as sinners are to love, respect, submit and obey our dear Heavenly Father by using these attributes towards thy husband. Understanding this will bring you to a much closer relationship with God and thy marriage partner. It will create much more balanced children. We don't always understand God's ways, but we trust Him and surrender ourselves to His authority, while He loves us while we were yet sinners, He forgives us seventy times seven and provides for our needs.

Our children now do not have the living example of enduring, committed and selfless love. Sex is everywhere and parents are engaging in adulterous affairs, the children see this, they see it on TV, books, magazines, movies. They hear their friends and everyone talking about it, so they go and engage in it themselves, not fully comprehending the consequences-spiritually, emotionally, and physically, and it has become a vicious cycle. Hardheartedness is a transgression against God and the social order of His creation. This vicious cycle can be broken! It had degraded to the point that one young lady told me love doesn't matter anymore, but sex you can't live without. How sad!!!

We, who are saved, truly spiritual, have been welcomed, adopted into the family God, with the angels as our brothers (righteous). This in spiritual terms is what we call justification (discussed in more detail in my book **ONLY BELIEVE**) When Jesus declares us righteous before God and welcomes us into His family, to the marriage feast. We should not be selfish as our Father desires a large family; He desires all to be at the marriage feast in the last days. We need to share the true word of God to the world, by word and deed, to our neighbor, share the precious love of God with all, so that they may also be a part of God's and our family. We also should not fight amongst ourselves and cause divisions, i.e. Denominations, divorce... amongst ourselves, as our precious Father desires for us to be one, unity, love one another, and to live in peace and harmony. Likewise, ought we to do in our earthly families. Debbie Boone's song 'You Light Up My Life', just as applicable to marriage as to God, you light up my life, you give me hope to carry on...it can't be wrong when it feels so right... and Endless Love, where two hearts joined as one...you are my endless love.

The Canadian Government reported that forty percent of the murders in their country are related to violence in marriage. Violence is such a grievous sin, but within marriage I believe is even a much greater abomination, and as Christians, we need to reverse this devastating abomination.

We see in Genesis 13:10 that Lot's greed took him to the sin-filled land of Sodom, and the loss of most of his family. Lot chose the land that appeared the best, for himself (selfishness), but it turned out to be such a sinful and unclean land. We need to look at the inside not just the outside!

In the early church, families

- Opened their homes for Bible study

- Prayed and even ate together

- Shared money and possessions

- Cared for one another

- They witnessed to one another and to unbelievers with boldness, even at the risk of their lives

What, are you afraid of what others may see physically and/or spiritually in your home? If that is the case then clean up your home. When someone comes, do they feel hospitality, love, kindness, generosity? Opening the doors of our homes is a form of ministry. It is a means of others seeing what a Christian marriage and family should be like so that they can learn and grow.

What happened? Where are these Christian families today? If one looks back, they can easily see that Viet Nam was the turning point. Before the 1960's there was strong family, strong church and strong social life. I can remember back to the days of Leave it to Beaver, Andy Griffith, and Little House on the Prairie. I remember back when around July 4th, grandparents and the entire family would gather with many other families at a big park and have picnics, swimming, a game of horseshoes... But during the Viet Nam crisis, many people were opposed to what was going on, and the American intervention, etc. and rebellion set in rapidly. Communes started. Make love not war, all we are asking is give peace a chance... We had the flower children, the peace flowers on all the Volkswagen beetles, popular at that time. People wanted peace, but rebellion set in and what happened? The women went to work sewing uniforms for the military, etc. Nobody at home so the children began going out. The young people staged huge demonstrations in Berkeley and San Francisco, not long after it sprang up at Kent State, then throughout the country. Free sex, drugs, alcohol, and suicide! Military men began coming home. The women refused to return to the homes so there weren't enough jobs for these men who were able to work, so they began drinking. Many of the men returned physically and/or mentally damaged and were unable to work. The family unit was gone. The church just as quickly decayed, following the family decay, and following that was the social decay. It became a me culture, and as always, the entire world follows the United States for good or bad. So, the world decayed, all because of American intervention in Viet Nam. I say that we must once again get back to the word of God and away from all of this frivolous teaching and worldly entertainment and return to being Christian marriages and families and boldly embracing the word of God at any cost. I have, and I have suffered the trials and tribulations, the persecution that Christ promised those who believe, but I have endured. I have kept the faith; in fact, my faith and boldness are stronger than ever before because of this. Will you repent, turn from the wicked ways of this world, and join with God, join me and the ministry that God hath entrusted me with? Believe me, it is truly worth it all, as I have seen Jesus, face to face and He hath transfigured me to a garden in heaven where we talked a lot on a few occasions and look forward to be with Him in heaven for eternity. The restoration of the family is the ONLY chance of reviving the church, community, and the world. It only takes a spark to get a fire going. Will you be that spark? The Lord through this powerful message is giving us the solution, the rest is up to us. Will we humble ourselves and seek once again the true and Living God and forsake the ways of this world at any cost, to save or restore our marriage, our church, our community? We read in 2ⁿᵈ Chronicles 7:14 that If my people will humble themselves and pray, seek my face, and turn from their wicked ways, THEN...THEN...THEN!!! Will I hear their prayer, forgive their sins, and heal their land...their marriages and families. You have heard, now are you willing to humble yourself and pray to the true and Living Almighty God and turn from all of your wicked ways-these demonic entertainment centers in the name of church (see the message that the Holy Spirit inspired me to write called The Pentecostal Movement), your sexual perversions, your pride and disobedience...Men, will you take back your leadership and authority given you by God in your home, your church, and your community? Women, will you return to your husband's home, tend to it, bear children to your husband and tend to his home and children, remove the pants and submit unto his authority as God hath so ordained for you?

I also wish to briefly take you to a critical verse in scripture which is the source of another message, but easily fits into this topic as well. I have preached on this many a time. Turn with me please to 2nd Chronicles 7:14. *IF my people* the truly spiritual, *which are called by my name,* shall what?

shall
1. *Humble themselves and pray-* humility is the FIRST step!
2. *Seek my face*
3. *Turn from their wicked ways*

...THEN...THEN...THEN Will I

1. *Hear their prayers*
2. *Forgive their sin*
3. *Heal their land,* their marriages, and their families...

We read God's promise in Revelation 21:9-10 *And there came unto me one of the seven angels which had the seven vials full of the seven last plagues, and talked with me, saying, Come hither, I will shew thee the bride, the Lamb's wife. And he carried me away in the spirit to a great and high mountain, and shewed me that great city, the holy Jerusalem, descending out of heaven from God.* Listen my dear friends, If God can give us, His bride, His children, such a great promise, such a great gift of everlasting life in such beauty, shouldn't we also love our life partner and our children likewise? God's promise to us His bride is everlasting, shouldn't our promise, our vow to cherish be likewise to our God ordained life partner?

My dear brothers and sisters, if you desire God's blessings in your life, in your marriage, your land, have God hear thy prayers and forgive you, and then you must humble thyself, drop the pride of the world, which comes from Satan. Humble thyself, turn back to God, and return to thy husband, He will help you. Turn from any and all of thy wicked ways, the ways of the world, and back to God. Then do not look back. Once thou confesseth thy sins, leave then at the feet of Jesus. Don't be like the people of Israel who, like Lot's wife, kept looking back...and were destroyed. Rather, look forward to the finish line, walking hand in hand as husband and wife, and with God. In Deuteronomy 30:19-20 God tells us *I call heaven and earth to record this day against you, that I have set before you life and death, blessing and cursing: therefore choose life, that both thou and thy seed shall live: that thou mayest love the Lord thy God, and that thou mayest obey His voice, and that thou mayest cleave unto Him: for He is thy life, and the length of thy days: that thou mayest dwell in the land which the Lord sware unto thy fathers...to give them.* My dearest brothers and sisters, this message is for each of us, all of us, but it also applies to wives with their husbands in marriage. Reread Proverbs 31:10-31, and replace wife with who God or your husband is talking to. This is a very powerful message.

I wish to close this section with a scripture from Exodus 19:5 and 6 which tells us *Now therefore, if ye will obey my voice indeed, and keep my covenant, then ye shall be a peculiar treasure unto me above all people: for all the earth is mine: And ye shall be unto me a kingdom of priests and an holy nation. These are the words which thou shalt speak unto the children of Israel.* Amen?

Our earthly existence is but a blink of an eye but eternity is eternal. The Christian walk is a full-time position. Being a husband or wife, dad or mom is likewise and it is time for those calling themselves Christians to wake up and take their positions in life seriously, for time is running out.

To a large extent, the unity and harmony within the church is dependent upon the unity and harmony within the individual homes. The apostle Paul emphasized so much on the unity and harmony, the love and respect that must exist between husband and wife, and this should serve as a clear illustration of the love of Christ, the self-sacrificing, selfless love that Christ has for His church. The Christ like love within the home as well as within the church is essential for husbands and wives as well as the church members. The same selfless love must as well be seen between parents and children, and employers and their employees. This type of love, harmony, unity, and peace is not a weakness but rather a strength and should spread through our homes and church life, then it will be clearly reflected throughout the condition of our communities. Thus, as I said at the beginning, marriage and family exemplifies our Christian walk and our relationship within the family of God, and consequently is why God created marriage, and why marriage is so very important to God. If we cannot get along here on earth which is a preparation for eternal life, how can one expect things to be better in our eternal lives?

I heard "Perfection in a relationship is not about being without flaw. It is about being exactly what the other person wants, needs, and desires without having to try." I am not sure that this is exactly correct but it certainly should be a goal. We all have flaws and we must be able to overlook and compensate for each other's flaws and weaknesses.

Please take a few moments also to read Judges 21:23 and Psalms 90:12

Let us live happily ever after (eternity) starting from today, as a member of the family of God. Marriage is a precious gift from God, and it is sacred. We are human though and make mistakes so...

PERSONAL NOTES

Deuteronomy 18:21 *Lord, how oft shall my brother sin against me, and I forgive him?*

CHAPTER **8**

Forgiveness is a Form of Love

We covered very briefly forgiveness in the previous chapters, but I felt compelled to add in this brief but critical chapter. As humans we all sin, we all fall short of the glory of God, and from our loved one, our mate. Forgiveness is critical in our walk with God (repentance), and in our human relationships, especially so in marriage. Sin carves out the Grand Canyon and forgiveness can build a bridge over it.

Forgiveness is a subject for a book by itself and many have been written, but as I said, I felt compelled to share a few words here, a few thoughts that the Spirit of God laid upon my heart, before proceeding to the next chapter. This may be the shortest chapter in this message, but perhaps the most important.

We are all human. We all make mistakes-men, women, husbands, wives, parents and children, pastors and congregations, bosses and workers. Many of these mistakes hurt others, even those that we care most about. We also hurt ourselves. Because of this, we need to be able to forgive, and we need to be able to ask for forgiveness. God in His mercy forgives us, so ought we to forgive others as well as ourselves.

In Matthew 18:22 we are told to forgive how often? Seventy, times seven. God has such love for us that He sacrificed His only Son, who from the cross cried out *Father...forgive them for they know not what they do.* He died as a substitute for our sins, yours and mine. Matthew 18:32-35 says, *O thou wicked servant, I forgave thee all that debt, because thou desiredst me: Shouldest not thou not also have had compassion on thy fellow servant, even as I had pity on thee? And his Lord was wroth and delivered him to the tormentors till he should pay all that was due unto him. So likewise shall my heavenly Father do also unto you, if ye from your hearts forgive not everyone his brother their trespasses.* The king is God, the servant is us, the fellow servant is our spouse, our neighbor. Nehemiah 9:28, speaks of Israel, the believers, God's chosen, that they did evil yet *when they returned and cried unto thee, thou heardest them...and many times didst thou according to thy mercies.* If God can forgive such sins, why can't we as well?

If one or both of you make a mistake, you may ask your partner why if you wish, in a loving, non-accusatory manner, in case it is something that you can change to prevent reoccurrence, but then move on and forgive, don't look back but rather always keep focused on the finish line. You must have faith which comes from love, love from one another as well as the love from God our Creator, the author and finisher of our faith.

We all must make choices in our lives and we must live with the consequences of those choices. However, often times there are bad choices that we later regret. Sometimes the consequences are disastrous and can lead to destruction...of our marriages. It is essential to understand that there can be forgiveness, restoration, and healing for these, by turning back to our Lord and Savior.

It is important to understand that forgiveness is not designed to numb or in any way excuse the sin or the pain from the sin. Sin is sin, from ourselves, others, or just the pain of life in general. We need to allow ourselves to go on living as God ordained, in peace and love. This is impossible without forgiveness, and forgiveness would be difficult without the love of God.

If we hold on to the pain, it causes a cancer figuratively and literally as well, that spreads into bitterness and despair, hatred and disease, cancer...none of which is God's desire for our lives.

I was friends with one family before they moved away. A couple of years later I received a phone call asking me to come. I went to visit them. He was in tears. His wife was dying of cancer and was a different person, and asked me to see her and pray for her, for them. I went and saw her, and the sweet, kind, and loving woman I remembered was gone. She and I talked for a while and I found out by her own admission, some things happened in the marriage and she couldn't forgive, and now was angry and very bitter, with her husband, herself, and with God. I told her that the only way to fight this cancer and bitterness, and to live, is to forgive all who hurt her, and to forgive God. She said John, I can't...I just can't. She died two days later, a very angry, bitter woman Emotions are very powerful forces that can sustain or kill a person. This is why Jesus taught so much on love and forgiveness, that we *may have life and have it more abundantly.*

In Matthew 5:39 Jesus says to turn the other cheek. Why? Because it diffuses a situation and shows others how God treats us. This is different from the Old Testament teaching of 'an eye for an eye', but listen my dear friends, an eye for an eye leaves everyone blind. Think about it. If you seek revenge, remember... you in your sinful nature, deserve death and hell, but Jesus died, He sacrificed Himself, so that we, the sinner may live, Acts 5:31. Also remember that God says vengeance is mine! So, we don't need to seek vengeance because as always God has everything under control. Also seeking revenge necessitates the digging of many graves because it always destroys the person, yourself, as well as those around each of you... including your mate and children. Romans 12:19-20 *Avenge not yourselves, but rather give place unto wrath: I will repay, sayeth the Lord. Therefore if thine enemy hunger, feed him; if he thirst, give him drink...*

This cancer of unforgiveness requires emergency treatment or it becomes terminal and kills, as it is better to humble thyself and seek forgiveness in order to keep peace within the family, even if you don't feel that you are the guilty one.

So, what is the treatment? Simply to look to your Creator, the love and forgiveness that He has offered unto you and me, as well as the gift of the person in your life to love, cherish, and to share thy life with, Oh what a precious and wonderful gift from God. My wife was so precious to me, as were my children. They still are and not a day or night passes that I don't think about them and pray for each of them; for friends, true love can't quit, you cannot fall out of true love! No man, no court, nobody, and nothing can separate me from my God; this has been proven in my life through many trials and tribulations as well as the persecutions. They are still in God's eyes and mine, my wife and children.

I was counseling a couple in their late thirties. I was talking about the gift. They both laughed and she responded that he wasn't a blessing but a curse. They were long separated. The next session, I had a friend, a female, wrap the woman with ribbons and a big bow, while in another room, and I placed a bow on him. I then brought the two together in the office for the session. When they saw each other, the both laughed so much, followed by some very sad and hurtful, hateful words. The gift wrapping however, broke the ice and communication began for the first time in months. After several tough sessions, they got back together, praise be unto God!

Anger, bitterness, and hatred destroy one physically, mentally, socially, and spiritually. In Matthew 6:12 and 15 we must remember that Jesus Christ taught us to love as He loves, and to forgive as He forgives, as we are to be Christ-like.

Do you know why forgiveness is so difficult? The love truly never left. The problem is...pride. You cannot forgive until you can humble thyself. But this same humility is required for redemption, which is what salvation is all about, saved from our sin, but...what is sin? Sin is the disobedience to the ways of God. What keeps us from obedience? Pride! What are the ways of God? They are love, forgiveness, mercy, sacrifice, total surrender. One must humble oneself; only then can you forgive and carry on. We as true Christians, truly spiritual, must believe in the miracles of God, and that God gives us the strength and courage we need to do all things, and be able to overcome all things, through Christ. ..Including being able to love and forgive, Philippians 4:13. As I said before, if we wish to be forgiven by God and others, we must be able to first forgive, and be able to receive forgiveness. In scripture there is only one unpardonable sin in marriage before God (Blasphemy against His Spirit!!! And there can be no unpardonable sin in marriage on earth!!!

I counseled a young woman who came from an unhappy, divorced family background, who then tested her boyfriend too much, because she wanted so much to have the perfect husband that he left. I spoke with both of them and it was quite obvious that there was a lot of love there, but also fear on her part. Most of the time people see what they want to see rather than what is really there-both good and bad. You keep testing and comparing, looking for the perfect relationship, not seeing that you may already have that. In marriage and our relationship with God, we must trust each other, not always test them. Those who look for trouble, usually find it. If something happens, you blame your partner (we fail God), you must remember that we all make mistakes, we are all sinners saved by grace and mercy. Love can cover the hurt that we cause in others as well as the hurt that they may accidently cause us. If you truly love your partner, be with that person and trust, don't test them. It isn't a matter of deserving another chance, for who says that we are deserving of one another's love, but without forgiveness, your love, your relationship doesn't stand a chance. Love is not about pass or fail, it's about honesty, trust, and total sacrifice, surrender and commitment. Think about this. This couple did get back together and later married, having learned important lessons for their relationship.

Jesus was tortured and persecuted for our sins, yet remember those powerful and tear-jerking words *How often did I want to gather you and you would not,* this also is reflected in Psalms 91. In Isaiah 53:3-5 and 7 we see *He is despised and rejected of men; a man of sorrows, and acquainted with grief: and **we** hid as it were **our** faces from Him; He was despised and we esteemed Him not. Surely He hath borne our sorrows: yet we did esteem Him stricken, smitten of God, and afflicted,* *but He was wounded for* **our** *transgressions, He was bruised for* **our** *iniquities...He was oppressed, and He was afflicted, yet He opened not His mouth,* Such humility and such love. This same Jesus took and carried our sins, our burdens, to the cross, from which He cried out with such love found in Luke 23:34, *Father, forgive them* (forgive John, (just insert thy name here)) ... Bless those who persecute you. Bless your husband, bless thy wife, bless thy children, and bless thy parents. Men as lord of your house have you tried to gather your blessed wife and children together, to share, to care, to love and protect, but they wouldn't come, they wouldn't listen to your calling? Imagine then how God must feel. He is calling and so few are listening, so few hear His sweet voice, and fewer still are obedient to come unto Him. So, few are separating themselves from the world and cleaving unto Him, surrendering all unto Him. But He is merciful and forgiving **IF** you will humble yourself, repent, seek Him, turn from thy wicked ways. These ways may not seem wicked because the world clouds them over, everybody else does it...but they are wicked if it is not the way of God even IF everybody else does it. My dear sisters, is your lord calling you? Are you listening to him and being obedient? Children are you listening to thy father? Think about this-all ye who are the children of God.

If you want peace in your life, your marriage, your family, your church, and your community, then there must be forgiveness, for all have sinned and fall short of the glory of God, Romans 3:23. And to have forgiveness, there must be love.

Jesus teaches us to love, forgive, bless. To repeat this I have no regrets, for Jesus taught this and the life of Christ, as well as the entire word of God focuses on love and forgiveness. God teaches us not to permit the sun to go down on our anger, Eph 4:26, so we need to forgive now, don't wait. The problem is unfortunately, we tend to return hate for hate, just to multiply the hatred, making it fester up and become an infectious wound, but two wrongs don't make a right. The best way to get rid of an enemy is to love them. They will either become the best of friends, or they will leave, their choice, but...your spouse, your children, your parents, **should never** be your enemy. In Philemon 18 *if he hath wronged thee, or oweth thee ought, put that on my account;* This is forgiveness and love my dear friends. This is what God calls us to do.

Martin Luther King once said We shall overcome. Friends, you can only overcome through love and forgiveness. In the 1960's the hippies frequently chanted 'All we are saying is give peace a chance.' Peace can only come from love and forgiveness. Husbands and wives, parents and children, men and women; are you listening? Those of you who are separated or divorced, are you listening?

I am talking about forgiveness. Forgiveness is much more than mere words; it must be sought and given from the heart. I must also tell you that forgiveness does not ignore the problem or the wrongs done, but it does two things. First, it clears the way to resolve and restore a relationship, and secondly, it clears any obstacles so that you can carry on and continue living.

A good recipe for a healthy marriage is to daily forgive one another, always love one another. Don't allow the sun to go down on your anger. In the 1960's again, there was a popular saying 'make love, not war'. I believe that this fits in well into the context of marriage, even if that wasn't the context in which it was originally intended. Bitterness, frustration, doubts, and anger settle in like the dust and piles up in mountains of hatred and even cancers, heart disease, strokes and other diseases, unless you keep dusting. Likewise, these feelings fester up if they are not dealt with in a positive manner. Good, open, honest communication is where it all begins. Communication requires listening and speaking. Always remember during the communication however, that God gave us two ears and one mouth, that we may listen twice as much as we speak! When we speak, it should always be done with love and respect, in a positive and restorative manner. When you point a finger at the other person, there are always at least three pointing back to yourself! You as a couple, as a husband and father, should always pray together as a couple, as a family, and always be praying with and for thy family. Keep God in the center of your conversations and you can't go wrong. A few don'ts in communication includes but are not limited to;

Don't look for faults, rather look at and find strengths and blessings

Don't blame each other

Don't demand your rights

Don't judge each other, but remove the speck from your own eye before trying to pull the log out of your partners' eye. Remember the old adage, 'an ounce of prevention is worth a pound of cure', is certainly true in our marriages today.

Do listen more than you speak to thy partner

Do put thy partner above yourself. Do all you can to please them and keep them safe and happy.

Do share quality uninterrupted time daily with thy partner, doing whatever they desire-talk, take a walk, whatever.

Read God's Word daily with thy partner, and pray together.

Many couples share nothing more than a bed, and frequently this is because there was never love in the first place, just lust, and/or a lack of forgiveness.

Forgiveness must be accompanied by a change of heart. Words without action are worthless.

Children were or are your parents less than perfect? Forgive them so that you can remove the burdens of your past and carry on with your life, and remember that nobody that you will ever meet upon this earth will be perfect.

Finally, if someone just refuses to accept thy forgiveness, that's their problem, not yours, just as those who reject God's forgiveness. You can still forgive them from thy heart and leave the rest to God. Jesus died on the cross for all even though most reject Him, but God will separate those who have been redeemed, who have repented and sanctified themselves from those who haven't. So, my friends, forgive thy mate, Children, forgive thy parents. Forgive thy neighbor, and leave the rest to God. Colossians 3:12-15 tells us *Put on therefore, as the* elect of God, holy and beloved, bowels of mercies, kindness, humbleness of mind, meekness, longsuffering, forbearing one another, and forgiving one another, if any man have a quarrel against any: even as Christ forgave you, so also do ye. And above all these things, put on charity (love), which is the bond of perfectness.* Remember that the greatest command- ment Jesus said is to love. *And let the peace of God rule in your hearts, to the which also ye are called in one body; and be ye thankful.* Colossians 3:16-17, *Let the word of Christ dwell in you richly in all wisdom; teaching and admonishing one another in Psalms and hymns and spiritual songs, singing with grace in your hearts to the Lord, and whatsoever ye do in word or deed, do all in the name of the Lord Jesus, giving thanks to God and the Father by Him.*

In Ephesians 4:31-32 we are told *Let all bitterness, and wrath, and anger and clamor, and evil speaking, be put away from you, with all malice* (separation and divorce), *And be ye kind one to another, tender hearted, forgiving one another, even as God for Christ's' sake hath forgiven you.* Psalms 133:1 tells us *Behold, how good and how pleasant it is for brethren to dwell together in unity!* Amen. In Titus 3:3 *For we our- selves also were sometimes foolish, disobedient, deceived, serving divers lusts and pleasures, living in malice and envy, hateful, and hating one another.* Titus 2:12 *Teaching us that denying ungodliness and worldly lusts, we should live soberly, righteously, and godly, in this present world.*

When you have been hurt, it is important to sit down, dis- cuss it openly, and honestly, Lay all the cards out on the table. This way they know what is going on and can explain and/or apologize to you. Then the rest is up to you. If you truly love the person (as God calls us to do), then you will trust and find forgiveness and peace in your heart. Jesus taught to forgive seventy times seven, which means to infinity, God doesn't keep a count our sins, and neither should we forgive those of others.

When you have been hurt, it's so easy to hold on to it, but when you look to Christ, His wisdom and His strength, then it is much easier to let it go. Remember Philippians 4:13 which tells us that *I can do **all** things through Christ who strengtheneth* *me.* And in John 14:27, my peace give I unto you, it's a peace that the world cannot understand. Just as God forgives all of our sins, shouldn't we likewise forgive one another rather than fight, divide ourselves and/or divorce? Look at Matthew 18:21-35. In John 8:11 we see that after the men brought the adulteress before our Lord for judgment, Jesus said unto her after her accusers left, *Neither do I condemn you but go, and sin no more.* You see here that first, Jesus and God forgive us, and secondly, that after being forgiven in the spiritual as well as the earthly sense, we should not continue in the sin. Forgiveness is not a license to continue in our sins.

In Ephesians 4:1-3 we are told, *I therefore, the prisoner of the Lord, beseech you, that ye walk worthy of the vocation in wherewith ye are called, with all* **lowliness** *and* **meekness,** *with* **forbearing** *one another in love.* (humility, forgiveness and love) *endeavoring to keep the* **unity** *of the spirit in the bond of* **love.** Then Paul tells the people of Philippi and us in 3:13 *forgetting those things which are behind, and reaching forth unto those things that are before, I press toward the mark for the prize of the high calling of God in Christ Jesus. Let us therefore, as many as be perfect be thus minded.*

There are so many scripture verses about love and forgiveness but allow me quickly give you just a few for you to consider. Romans 13:10 tells us *Love worketh no ill to his neighbor: therefore love is the fulfilling of the law.* Is not thy partner thy neighbor? Turn now to Leviticus 18:26 *Ye shall therefore keep my statutes and my judgments, and shall not commit any of these abominations; neither any of your own nation, nor any stranger that sojourneth among you,* now God called abortion, sexual immorality, adultery, divorce...abominations, didn't He? Deuteronomy 18:9 and 20:18 *When thou art come into the land which the Lord thy God giveth thee, thou shalt not learn to do after the abominations of those nations, That they teach you not to do after all their abominations, which they have done unto their gods; so should ye sin against the Lord your God.* In Isaiah we are told in 66:3, *he that sacrificeth a lamb, as if he cut off a dog's neck; he that offereth an oblation, as if he offered swine's blood; he that burneth* incense, *as if he blessed an idol. Yea, they have chosen their own ways, and their soul delighteth in their abominations.* Look also at Ezekiel 8:17, 14:6, and 18:13 *Then he said unto me, Hast thou seen this, O son of man? Is it a light thing to the house of Judah that they commit the abominations, which they commit here? For they have filled the land with violence, and have returned to provoke me to anger: and, lo, they put the branch to their nose. Therefore, say unto the house of Israel, Thus saith the Lord God; Repent, and turn yourselves from your idols; and turn away your faces from all your abominations. Hath oppressed the poor and needy, hath spoiled by* **violence**, *hath not restored the pledge, and hath lifted up his eyes to the idols, hath committed abomination, Hath given forth upon usury, and hath taken increase: shall he then live? he shall not live: he hath done all these abominations; he shall surely die; his blood shall be upon him.* Now, I'd like for you to turn and look at Jeremiah 4:1, *If thou wilt return, O Israel, saith the Lord, return unto me: and if thou wilt put away thine abominations out of my sight, then shalt thou not remove.* I direct you as well to see the following verses on forgiveness; Matthew 6:12, 14 and 15; 18:35, 2nd Corinthians 2:7, Ephesians 4:32, Luke 6:37, 7:47; and you will find many others throughout God's word. Is it easy? No, but if God can forgive our many and horrendous sins, why shouldn't we try to forgive those relatively small sins of our partners, our children, and our parents, compared to those we commit against our dear Lord?

Jesus said that if we do not forgive others that have hurt and damaged us, we will not be forgiven by God. Unforgiveness, resentment and using the sins committed against us as a justification of our own sinful reactions is not an option if you know Christ. We are to let God's love shine through us. When you forgive someone, you don't ever hold it above their head; you have to let it go for both of you.

Sometimes you can be so blinded by all the raging anger, that you can't see the truth and go crazy, doing stupid and sometimes very dangerous things, which may cost lives, and/ or landing in prison.

For those trying to help troubled marriages, right is right and wrong is wrong. We must not take sides but always speak the truth of God's word.

A quote from an anonymous individual, You can't make someone love you; All you can do is be someone who can be loved. The rest is up to the person to realize your worth.

Take a look around you-touching, hugging, kissing...but... true love is hard to find and is something to hold onto at any and all cost, both your partner and to God.

I heard a woman who was asked why she stayed with her husband after he had an affair, I chose to stay with him for all the things that he did right, not for the one thing that he did wrong, Wise words.

Whenever an injury is done to us, we will never recover until we forgive. Forgiveness is the door to peace and happiness, and cannot be opened without love and humility.

Forgiveness is not a matter of right and wrong, fairness or excusing, but rather the seeing beyond the situation and carrying on with life.

What is done cannot be undone, but when you can see through to the other side through love and forgiveness, then you can begin once again moving on with your life.

Without forgiveness there is a drive for revenge, and revenge necessitates that you dig at least two graves-one for the person, one for yourself, and perhaps for others as you affect many around you.

Without forgiveness, bitterness, anger, frustration, etc.; build up inside of you and eat away like a cancer. They cause cancer and other physically destructive conditions. They are destructive both to self as well as all those around you.

Take a look at the 'Lord's Prayer'. We must recognize our need for forgiveness before we can forgive, for we are all sinners and evil, wicked in nature. Despite our guilt, we are all still fellow human beings. There is no us and them, for we are all neighbors, there is only us. We are in need of the Lord's forgiveness and He says that if we want to be forgiven, that we must forgive-forgive others as well as forgiving ourselves.

Jesus said that we must forgive but then He went further to say in Matthew, to bless those who persecute you. He told us that we must love our neighbor, our enemy, as ourselves. Returning hate for hate, a wrong doing for a wrong doing, only serves to multiply the problem, look at the world today! It is time that we become Christ-like and stop this cancer which is eating away at our culture and our very existence worldwide. Love is an extremely powerful force. It has the power to transform. It can turn an enemy into a friend; it can...save a marriage. Hate destroys whereas love builds.

Martin Luther King Jr. said that we shall overcome, but he knew that he could only overcome by love and forgiveness.

Upon the cross at Calvary, our precious Lord and Savior, Jesus Christ, after being mocked, beaten, spit upon, bleeding and wounded, and hung upon that cross, never said curse them, kill them, or anything negative or wished anything bad upon them or us. No, He simply and humbly said *Father forgive them*. My dearest brothers and sisters, if this innocent man could endure all of that and still ask God to forgive them/us, why cannot we forgive one another for these little infractions in our marriages and families, and carry on...endure unto the end, for whosoever shall endure shall receive the crown of glory...and salvation.

In Mark 11:25-26 we are told *And when ye stand praying, forgive, if ye have ought against any: that your Father also which is in heaven may forgive you your trespasses. But if ye do not forgive, neither will your Father which is in heaven forgive your trespasses.* We are further told by our dear Lord, Lean not on your own understanding. Forgiveness is critical in any relationship for we are all sinners and fall short of the glory of God. So, as He is faithful to extend His grace and mercy to forgive us, so must we forgive one another. This is especially true within the marriage and family setting.

We all must make choices in our lives and we must live with the consequences of those choices. However, often times there are bad choices that we later regret. Sometimes the consequences are disastrous and can lead to destruction...of our marriages. It is essential to understand that there can be forgiveness, restoration, healing for these, by turning back to our Lord and Savior.

I invite you now to look at Matthew 25:37. Now read John 15:12. Now, please carefully consider the difference between these two important scriptures about love. What (if any is the difference)? Simply the answer in the former, we are told to love as man loves, and many don't love themselves so how can they love another (marriage); whereas the latter is to love as God loves, regardless of how you feel about yourself.

It is better to humble thyself and seek forgiveness in order to keep peace within the family, even if you don't feel that you are the guilty one.

And in closing of this critical chapter, I wish to bring you to Paul's letter to the people of Colosse chapter 3 and verse 13, *Forbearing one another, and forgiving one another, if any man have a quarrel against any: even as Christ forgave you, so also do ye.*

We as Christians must also remember that we are all sinners in need of forgiveness and that God loves us in spite of our sinful nature. He loves us, not the sin! We need to have this heart toward one another, in that we should never hate our partner or our neighbor, even though we have every right to hate the sins. We must always separate the sin from the person. I will even add to this in saying that the refusal to forgive the person (not the sin) is a selfish act, and we are called to be selfless. I should also remind you that in the end, we shall not be judged for what others did unto us-good or bad, but rather for what we did unto them. Did we love; did we forgive our partner, our neighbor? Or did we walk away?

<u>The moments that turn your life upside down are the very moments which define who you are.</u> God gives us the choice on how to respond-in a godly way, or the way of the world.

Remember the words of the Psalmist in 103:10-13 *He hath not dealt with us after our sins; nor rewarded us according to our iniquities. For as the heaven is high above the earth, so great is his mercy toward them that fear him. As far as the east is from the west, so far hath he removed our transgressions from us. Like as a father pitieth his children, so the Lord pitieth them that fear him.*

Zech. 3:4 tells us *And he answered and spake unto those that stood before him, saying, Take away the filthy garments from him. And unto him he said, Behold, I have caused thine iniquity to pass from thee, and I will clothe thee with change of raiment.* This change of garment represents forgiveness and putting away (hiding) the sin(s), putting them out of mind. In our marriage and families, we need to do this just as God does for us.

I must remind you of David and Peter among others, who messed up badly, but yet look at the mercy and grace God gave unto them. We who are truly spiritual must be Christ like and extend the same, especially to our marriage partners and our families.

As I sat hostage in those prisons, there was not a day that went by that I didn't pray for my wife and children, that they will come to know the Lord and Savior Jesus Christ; that He will reach out and touch their hearts and that was released, somehow God will rejoin us as He did Job; while at the same time praising Him for saving them from this trial of me being held hostage and made to be deathly ill.

True love withstands the test of time and the wiles of the devil, through the trials and tribulations through the fires of life, and will remain faithful (*Many are called but few are chosen*). If there ever was love then your wife, my wife will return home and rekindle the marriage set by God; just as some of us have had our faith tried and tested by fire through trials and tribulations and choose to hold on to our faith, our Bridegroom in heaven, holding firm. The true test of love- time and persistence through the fire, knowing that the cloud will soon pass on.

Salvation is by grace alone, not by good works, and this belief must be carried into the marriage as well, for we are all sinners and by grace are we saved, and only by grace can a marriage survive and/or be saved.

A man by the name of Will Durant wrote in 1941, Year by year marriage comes later, separation earlier; soon no man will go down the hill of life with a woman who has climbed it with him, and a divorceless marriage will be as rare as a maiden bride.

Luke 17:4 *And if he trespass against thee seven times in a day, and seven times in a day turn again to thee, saying, I repent; thou shalt forgive him.*

Luke 23:34 *'Then said Jesus, Father, forgive them; for they know not what they do. And they parted his raiment, and cast lots.*

David was a great example of not an eye for an eye but to turn the other cheek. He loved as we are to love, even those out to kill him, but killed them not, in fact he protected them-Saul, Abner...See 2nd Samuel chapters 2 and 3. Also note the love between Jonathan and David in 2nd Samuel 1:26.

Only the life of Christ can tell us to true cost of love

Lean not on your own understanding. Forgiveness is critical in any relationship for we are all sinners and fall short of the glory of God. So, as He is faithful to extend His grace and mercy to forgive us, so must we forgive one another. This is especially true within the marriage and family setting.

As we near the closing of this critical chapter, I wish to bring you a few additional words from God's precious word here. We shall begin with Matthew 6:12 which tells us *And forgive us our debts, as we forgive our debtors.* And verse 15 continues with *But if ye forgive not men their trespasses, neither will your Father forgive your trespasses.* Luke tells us in 17:3-4 that *If thy brother trespass against thee, rebuke him; and if he repent, forgive him. And if he trespass against thee seven times in a day, and seven times in a day turn again to the, saying, I repent; thou shalt forgive him.* Jesus said in Luke 23:34 *Father, forgive them; for they know not what they do.* Mind you that He was hanging from that old rugged cross, hands and feet pierced with those spikes, dying for you and for me while we were yet sinners! In 2nd Corinthians 2:7-11 we read *So that contrariwise ye ought rather to forgive him, and comfort him, lest perhaps such a one should be swallowed up with overmuch sorrow. Wherefore I beseech you that ye would confirm your love toward him. For to this end also did I write, that I might know the proof of you, whether ye be obedient in all things. To whom ye forgive any* thing, *I forgive also: for if I forgave any thing, to whom I for-gave it, for your sakes forgave I it in the person of Christ; Lest Satan should get an advantage of us: for we are not ignorant of his devices.* Then we turn further to Ephesians 4:32 and read *And be ye kind one to another, tenderhearted, forgiving one another, even as God did for Christ's sake hath forgiven you.* And lastly in 1ˢᵗ John 1:9 we see *If we confess our sins, he is faithful and just to forgive us our sins, and to cleanse us from all unrighteousness.*

In Acts 1:8 Note that Jesus made it a point for His disciples to go to Jerusalem and all the world (gentiles) but made a special point of mentioning Samaria. Love your enemies, do good to those who hate you. Samaritans were enemies of the Jews. He didn't hold any grudges; He had no hatred for anyone and neither should we.

We read in Deuteronomy 8:2 *And thou shalt remember all the way which the Lord thy God led thee these forty years in the wilderness, to humble thee, and to prove thee, to know what was in thine heart, whether thou wouldest keep his command-ments, or no.* and further in 10:12-13 which should be one verse and not separated, *And now, Israel, what doth the LORD thy God require of thee, but to fear the Lord thy God, to walk in all his ways, and to love him, and to serve the Lord thy God with all thy heart and with all thy soul, To keep the commandments of the Lord, and his statutes, which I command thee this day for thy good?* And of course, we must recall the words of Jesus found in John 13:35 *By this shall all men know that you are my disciples, if ye have love one to another.* And finally, in closing, allow me to leave you with a verse from Ephesians 4:32 which tells us *And be ye kind one to another, tenderhearted, forgiving one another, even as God for Christ's sake hath forgiven you.* Amen! And this was demonstrated in Matthew 18:21-35 the king is God, the servant is us, the fellow servant is our spouse, our neighbor.

When you get a wound as all marriages do, you cannot just slap a band-aid on it or it may fester up, get infected and may cost you your life or limb (your marriage). You must first render first-aid. You must first elevate the situation, the wound. Control the bleeding. Clean it up, wash it clean. Then perhaps apply some antibiotic ointment or stitch it up, then dress it and nurse it back to health. The same is true within our marriages. You must sit down together, evaluate in a loving, non-judgmental manner, not saying who is the problem, but rather what is the problem and why. Don't just address the problem but get to the root of the problem so that it can be resolved and hopefully not be repeated. You then must figure out a plan together on the best course of treatment, what can be done to heal the wound. Then render the first-aid.

We read in Numbers 30:2 *If a man vow a vow unto the Lord, or swear an oath to bind his soul with a bond; he shall not break his word, he shall do according to all that proceedeth out of his mouth.* If or when God blesses you with the precious gift of a life partner, you should praise God for that gift, then appreciate it, respect it, love it, care for it, and protect it. Are you hearing this?!

We read in Philippians 3:13-14 *Brethren, I count not myself to have apprehended: but this one thing I do, forgetting those things which are behind, and reaching forth unto those things which are before, I press toward the mark for the prize of the high calling of God in Christ Jesus.*

Marriage is all about humility. The women are to serve and care for the men, to be his helper, whereas men as leaders are to serve and care for one another and the women, John 13:1-15.

I would ask that you read these additional verses before moving on, Nahum 3:18-19, Ephesians 4:1-2, 31-32; Matthew 6:12; Luke 17:3; 23:34, Colossians 3:8, 12-15.

If you can keep the original spark/fire alive, always love... regardless, as Christ loves you and I, who are far from perfect, so should we be able to love and forgive one another, and keep that precious fire burning, that as Christ taught us to do, and demonstrated this love to and for us, as well as the act of forgiveness, on the cross of Calvary, then...we would have no need for the next chapter, but...sadly...mankind is sinful, with hardened hearts full of pride, so...

337

PERSONAL NOTES

PERSONAL NOTES

This chapter on divorce is a must read whether you are unmarried or happily married or anywhere in between and/ or separated or divorced. This chapter is for everyone! It is dedicated to the children of broken families and especially to Obadiah, Caleb and Naomi, who by God's love and righteousness deserve and have the absolute right to have it so be with their parents. And to all the creation-marriage husbands and wives who have been betrayed by the unfaithful spouse as I have, some who have been divorced by the unfaithful spouse, and are being faithful to our Lord and Savior Jesus Christ by remaining alone praying and waiting with great long-suffering for the full repentance and return of their departed beloved spouse.

Ruth 1:17 *The Lord do so to me, and more also if ought but death part thee and me.*

CHAPTER 9

Divorce

irst of all, when the Spirit of the living God began talking of divorce, I put down the paper and pen and asked, Why God? After all, a Christian should not divorce. He replied 'hear what I have to say.' I listened, so we shall now take some time to speak of divorce, because it is such an accepted social practice, abomination today. It is so prevalent and accepted even by many churches today, but such a grave sin and slap in the face of our Lord and Savior Jesus Christ.

In Deuteronomy 24:4-5, We know that it included every kind of indecency, such as going about with loose hair, turning in the streets, intimately talking with men, ill-treating her husband's parents in his presence, brawling, that is, 'speaking to her husband so loudly that the neighbors could hear her in the adjoining house', a general bad reputation, or the discovery of fraud before marriage. Other improprieties include: poor cooking, no sons, or anything else that displeased her husband. They divorced them for the most frivolous reasons: if she burnt his biscuits, or didn't season his food right, or if he did not like her manners, or if she was a poor housekeeper, even if he finds a woman more beautiful than she, violation of the Law of Moses, or of Jewish customs, such as the woman causing her husband to eat food on which a tithe had not been paid; not setting apart the first dough; appearing in public with disheveled hair; exposing her arms in public; speaking disrespectfully of her husband's parents in his presence; in general, according to Moses, not God, they could divorce for any reason! How many girls could live today like that!!!

In Mark 14:72 we see the finale of a story that most of us are familiar with, Peter's denial of Christ and the cock crowed. What most people fail to recognize in this story is what led up to his denial. I want to share with you a few things that I have found in my studies. First, he was Overconfident, verses 29 and 31, wasn't praying verses 37, 40-41, not listening to Jesus in verse 47 and Luke 22:49-51, and associating with the wrong people verse 54, returned to old habits verse 71, then in verse 71, outright denial. You may be asking why I am mentioning this scripture here and now. If you look closer at these scriptures, they are the same that led my wife to leave and so many millions of others to leave breaking their covenant vows, promises before God and their God-ordained partner. Essentially, breaking covenant vows are a denial of Christ as He taught everything contrary to this.

I looked up the statistics a few years ago on divorce, and what amazed me was that for the past several years, divorce rates among Christians were greater than for non-Christians. The low moral and ethical standards of the Church are appalling. The divorce rate exceeds that of much of the unbelieving pagan world.

The figures claim that sixty percent of modern American marriages are destined to end up in the divorce court. The world always follows America good or bad. Those suing for divorce customarily charge their spouse with irreconcilable differences, or cruel and abusive treatment among other things. The difficulty here is to define abusive treatment (anything that doesn't suit their desires) and irreconcilable (was any effort ever made?) But going back further, God says that there are **NO** excuses for divorces, **NONE,** what part of none are people not understanding today, in today's church! Again, this is not giving license to illegal or immoral behavior, or any disobedience to God's law (incest, adultery, homosexuality, polygamy, etc.) but this also doesn't give license to break covenant promise with God and His law to commit the horrible crime of divorce! This is a capital crime against God and it is one that has so many victims! We see in Romans 1:28-32 *And even as they did not like to retain God in their knowledge, God gave them over to a reprobate mind, to do those things which are not convenient; Being filled with all unrighteousness, fornication, wickedness, covetousness, maliciousness; full of envy, murder, debate, deceit, malignity; whisperers, Backbiters, haters of God, despiteful, proud, boasters, inventors of evil things, disobedient to parents, Without understanding,* **covenantbreakers**, *without natural affection, implacable, unmerciful: Who knowing the judgment of God, that they which commit such things are worthy of death, not only do the same, but have pleasure in them that do them.*

Take a look at Deuteronomy 28:56 where we see *The tender and delicate woman among you, which would not adventure to set the sole of her foot upon the ground for delicateness and tenderness, her eye shall be evil toward the husband of her bosom, and toward her son, and toward her daughter.* He continues in 31:20 *For when I shall have brought them into the land which I sware unto their fathers, that floweth with milk and honey; and they shall have eaten and filled themselves, and waxen fat; then will they turn unto other gods, and serve them, and provoke me, and break my covenant.*

We see the condition of the world and read the divorce statistics of every country and then we must ask ourselves, 'what is going on?' Well, this question takes us to Isaiah 24:5-6 *The earth also is defiled under the inhabitants thereof; because they have transgressed the laws, changed the ordinance, broken the everlasting covenant. Therefore hath the curse devoured the earth, and they that dwell therein are desolate: therefore the inhabitants of the earth are burned, and few men are left.* You see here that the breaking of the everlasting covenant (til death do us part), transgressing the laws (committing adultery, divorce, polygamy, homosexuality, pedophilia, beastiality, etc....) See Exodus 22:19 and now we are reaping the consequences, the whole earth has become defiled and we need to return to our first love (God and our life partner). Ezekiel goes on in chapter 16, take a few moments and read this chapter, then return to verse 59 and see that he is also in agreement with what Isaiah was just saying, why? Because they were both prophets of the Most- High God and God doesn't change. We see in Leviticus 20 that there are consequences for such abhorrent behavior and that is death-hell. I will refer you to 2nd Thessalonians 1:9 we should still love our enemy and pity them, hurt for them, but your partner can never be your enemy. Can we be an enemy of God or God be our enemy? God forbid!

There is a significantly higher divorce rate amongst those identifying themselves as born again Christians, than the rest of society as a whole, more than even amongst those claiming to be atheists and agnostics. Bible professing Churches, proud of their Bible Believing theology most often take the lead in the divorce rates. According to the statistics, in the Bible belt of America, where the greatest concentration of evangelical Christians practice their faith, the divorce rate is fifty percent higher than the nation as a whole. In addition, a recent study determined that ordained ministers themselves now have the second highest divorce rate of all the recognized professions in North America. Where are the truly spiritual, true believers today?

In a recent survey according to statistical data published by Christianity Today magazine of Pastors and evangelical Church leaders, only four percent believed that remarriage is a sin that the Church should refuse to either participate in, or to recognize. A full ninety six percent believed that remarriage while a spouse lives could be acceptable under at least certain conditions. Essentially the Church and the world are now becoming yoked together in common beliefs and practices, instead of being obedient to God's word found in 1 John 2:15 and James 4:4, and over fifty other verses that the Holy Spirit revealed to me saying the same thing; if you can't beat them join them mentality, especially nowadays where most of the leaders now are just after money (see my message Called **The Pentecostal Movement**, another revelation from God to me to be shared with all who are serious minded). Subsequently, evil is rampant and escalating both inside and outside the Church. In the next decade or so, if the present rate of moral decay continues, little if any of the basic precepts of God's law will be known, let alone adhered to in society. This was prophecy from God given unto me back in 2012 and now in 2019 it has already come to pass! I praise God for entrusting me with prophecy as well as revelations. Anyway...When the blind lead the blind, they both fall into the pit. Faced with the same type of apostasy Jeremiah wrote in 6:13-14, *For from the least of them even unto the greatest of them every one is given to covetousness; and from the prophet even unto the priest every one dealeth falsely. They have healed also the hurt of the daughter of my people slightly, saying, Peace, peace; when there is no peace.*

Jeremiah 17:9 tells us that *The heart is deceitful above all things, and desperately wicked: who can know it?* Isaiah 64:6 tells us further *But we are all as an unclean thing, and all our righteousnesses are as filthy rags; and we all do fade as a leaf, and our iniquities, like the wind, have taken us away.* Divorce was not an invention of heaven, it was one of the manufactured garments of sin; it is of the earth, nothing more than an attempt at covering the sins of man.

God didn't cause but allowed Israel to leave Him. He tried hard to keep her, to hold on to her and protect her, save her, but He allowed her (the unbeliever, the one who separates themselves from the sacred covenant of marriage) to leave and told her (them) go...and see if your gods will save you. They couldn't, only God Almighty can and will IF we obey Him and stay within the boundaries, He hath set for us.

We are told in Micah 7:6, *For the son dishonoureth the father, the daughter riseth up against her mother, the daughter in law against her mother-in-law;* ***a man's enemies are the men of his own house***. Friends, this ought not to be!

There is so much of uninformed opinion as to what God teaches us in regards to marriage and divorce. The Bible clearly spells out exactly what our Lord expects us to do, and gives us complete direction on how to do it. I believe that we must obey God's Word in discovering and defining what His will is concerning marriage, divorce and remarriage. We must go to the Bible, the Word of God, and search prayerfully for the truth. We read in Malachi 2:13-17 *And this have ye done again, covering the altar of the Lord with tears, with weeping, and with crying out, insomuch that he regardeth not the offering any more, or receiveth it with good will at your hand. Yet ye say, wherefore? Because the Lord hath been witness between thee and the wife of thy youth, against whom thou hast dealt treacherously: yet is she thy companion, and the wife of thy covenant. And did not he make one? Yet had he the residue of the spirit. And wherefore one? That he might seek a godly seed. Therefore take heed to your spirit, and let none deal treacherously against the wife of his youth. For the Lord, the God of Israel saith that he hateth putting away: for one covereth violence with his garment, saith the Lord of hosts: therefore take heed to your spirit that ye deal not treacherously. Ye have wearied the Lord with your words. Yet ye say, wherein have we wearied him? When ye say, every one that doeth evil is good in the sight of the Lord, and he delighteth in them; or, where is the God of judgment?* Then we read in the book of Hebrews 8:9b *because they continued not in my covenant, and **I regarded them not, saith the LORD.*** Are you hearing this my dear brothers and sisters?

The breaking of the covenant by a wayward spouse results in a severing of their relationship with God as He refuses to hear or pay attention to offerings or prayers, no matter how sincere. Obviously, repentance must be sincere and restorative as a vow. God was party to the marriage covenant as a witness and an active participant by making the man and woman His own personal possession, and uniting them as one. Faithfulness to the marriage covenant is absolutely necessary to produce godly offspring. Without it the future of God's people is threatened. Even though one of the parties may be unfaithful, as described here, to the original covenant, it remains in force for God says that the betrayed one remains the partner. This dispels the notion entirely that adultery dissolves the marriage covenant. In fact, we see in 1st Corinthians 5-6, an example of the marriage covenant being upheld in the event of marital unfaithfulness. In 1st Cor 6:15-16, we see the instruction. I was introduced to a website for friends in the local area. It turned out that it was nothing but ladies from 18-72, most naked in different positions that wanted nothing but sex, and most were married!!! I was deeply saddened by this and immediately closed out of the site.

David was no Job: *I made a covenant with mine eyes; why then should I think upon a maid?* Job 31:1,7,9,11. That look formed into lust then conceived the sin of adultery, and deception, which brought forth death. The deception, a failed attempt to create a lie which would have had Uriah raise a son which was not his own, one of the greatest fears of all men, gave David one final evil choice, to murder Uriah. It almost appears that Uriah knew that Bathsheba was with child of the king, the reason for his refusal to return to his bed although the king made every arrangement to persuade him. Whatever the reason, we know that God had intervened in the heart of Uriah to prevent David from orchestrating his lie. Even if Uriah knew the truth, he wouldn't be able to win a case in convicting King David of committing a capital crime; a crime which was punishable by death.

Regardless, God left David the choice to repent. David chose to murder. And when the wife of Uriah heard that Uriah, her husband, was dead, she mourned for her husband. Was she a part in this plan? The Bible doesn't indicate. And when the mourning was past, David sent and fetched her to his house, and she became his wife, and bore him a son. But the thing that David had done displeased the Lord. 2nd Samuel 11 the marriage of Bathsheba to David is in stinging contrast to the penalty of the law, which required the death of both individuals. How could this be reconciled with the law? That is a good question. Did David conjecture that since polygamy was allowed to exist, and since Bathsheba was now a widow that he had the right to marry her?

He would go on to reveal his confession in Psalms 32, and 51 Is it here that David was truly born-again; I believe this is exactly what occurred; David got saved; he was born-again.

There is, however, no record of Bathsheba's repentance, nevertheless later we do see her in need of comfort. Their son of adultery ended up dying the death of the law for each of them; not atoning for their souls, but for their lives. The final element, which weighed in David's forgiveness and maintenance, must be seen in the covenant of 2nd Samuel 7:12-16. David was a chosen vessel. He was promised, unconditionally, a son upon whom God would establish His kingdom forever. Although David has other sons, he did not have any sons of promise. With the death of his son by adultery, and with the pure confession of David, it appears that God chose to expose his doctrine of grace on this repentant sinner. The spirit of grace is to show that where sin abounds grace will much more abound. So, in other words, God was forgiving and restoring David on the basis of his un-merited favor, God's grace. He was forgiving David because David truly repented. On that basis God wanted to forgive David; and that He did, just as He is faithful to forgive those who shall truly repent of their sins today.

God wanted to forgive David because David believed in the Lord Jesus Christ the only begotten Son of God. This is the total idea of grace; and Satan is Satan because he is ignorant of the matchless grace of God. David knew the Son of God: And David comforted Bathsheba, his wife, went in unto her; and she bore a son, and he called his name Solomon; the Lord loved Solomon. And he sent word by the hand of Nathan, the prophet; and he called his name Jedidiah, beloved of the Lord, because of the Lord, 2nd Samuel 12:24, 25. Several interesting comments can be received from this text; Whereas Bathsheba was distressed by the death of the son of adultery; was she distressed by her sin? God blessed the widow/marriage with the birth of a son, Solomon, (peaceful), Jehovah has a special love for the child and gives him a personal nickname, Jedidiah, beloved of the Lord. The Lord is telling us that the entire David and Bathsheba restoration was a matter of God doing something for His Beloved Son. He was freely exercising his grace because of the loving sacrifice of His only begotten Son, our Lord and Savior Jesus Christ. With this said, let us not lose sight of the total corruption and death which the world's most published sin of adultery produced. The Scripture cannot be broken, *Then when lust hath conceived, it bringeth forth sin: and sin, when it is finished, bringeth forth death,* James 1:15. David committed adultery and murder and was forgiven; God did not require the death penalty for the king because of his repentant heart.

But his murder and lust conceived more than his own sin; it also produced sin in his family. Amnon, the elder son of David, saw a chance to explore his lust and follow in his father's footsteps, children always learn the lessons our own acts teach them. Tamar, Amnon's step-sister, was an especially beautiful virgin, and Amnon had an unnatural lust for her. He was literally sick with lust over his sister. With some help from a cousin, Amnon, manages to lure Tamar to his bed, where he viciously rapes the innocent and lovely virgin, Tamar. Shortly thereafter Absalom avenges his sister, by killing Amnon. Absalom continues his rebellion against his father, even threatening the throne. Forming a faction against his father, the king. He enters Jerusalem, and defiles the king's concubines. Setting up a tent on the top of the king's palace, he enters the tent of his father's concubines in the sight of all Israel. In the sad end of Absalom, we find him caught by the hair hanging in an oak, and struggling to get free when he is found. Joab, the captain of David's army, manages to reach the site in time to thrust three staves through the heart of Absalom. One act of adultery and now David is faced with three murders, one rape, and the death of a child. Yes, David was forgiven, but when lust is conceived, it bringeth forth death. This is the law of sin.

Now just how should we interpret David's adultery and murder? Consider the following facts, David was a sovereign king, David fully repented, i.e., he confessed his sin and discontinued his sin; and he was fully forgiven of his sin. He lived during a period that permitted polygamy, as explained before. Bathsheba was now a widow and free to take another husband; Therefore, David's marriage to Bathsheba was legitimate under those conditions. This means that David's future intercourse with Bathsheba was not a continuous act of adultery; under the permission of polygamy, Bathsheba did not have another living husband. Think this through. These elements are not found in the act of remarriage today. In most cases of divorce and remarriage that I have counseled both partners are alive and therefore any remarriage for them is an act of continuous adultery, the act of having sexual relations with another during the lifetime of a previously married partner is adultery and polygamy. No one is inculpable of the law. Modern adultery is no less subject to this law: *Be not deceived; God is not mocked: for whatsoever a man soweth, that shall he also reap,* Galatians 6:7. This is in no way suggesting or encouraging murder in order to gain a new spouse, as this too is an abominable violation of God's commandment, thou shalt not murder, as well as thou shalt not covet thy neighbor's wife (husband) or property. Also, though David repented, he continued in his sin by remaining with Bath-Sheba. You simply cannot continue in your sins and justify it by repenting.

Every time that I hear someone say I do at a wedding, I cry inside knowing that there is only approximately a thirty percent chance that they are being honest with God and their partner, yet they profess Christianity. Over sixty eight percent of Christian marriages end in divorce! Then I got to thinking and praying about this. This coincides with the changes in the church, and the liberation movement, the Pentecostal Movement, again I have written a message from A Revelation from God on this topic. Also, the fact that Satan doesn't need to attack unbelievers, so he spends his time attacking the believers, and seeks to destroy them and their marriages, for each time that he destroys a Christian marriage, others see this and it weakens their faith as well. These are two very good reasons for us to be always on our guard to protect our marriages and our walk. We cannot allow the enemy to get any foothold. The statistics are a sad commentary that Christians are not on guard, and...where is the church??? God teaches love...love... love...LOVE!!! So, my dear friends, where does divorce fit into this picture??? Where does divorce fit in to the spiritual picture?

One landmark commitment you make in life is to your spouse when you marry him or her. Many lose the character of cherishing their spouse after marrying, and others spit upon the vow they made by divorcing their partner, and divorcing God. My wife removed her head covering one day, threw it on the floor and spit on it. My dear friends, you will never know the pain that I felt, I still remember that moment until I die.

David tells us in Proverbs 10:12 that *hatred stirreth up strife; but love covereth all sins* Very wise words. Divorces are rampant today; jails and prisons are full today because of pride and jealousy, domestic violence.

In Exodus 21:4-6, we are told that if God gives you a wife and children and you say I love God, my wife, and my children, that He hath blessed me with, I will serve Him forever, and accept that I am sealed by His blood, and that this seal cannot be broken and **NO** attempts should ever be considered or attempted. Remember Ruth who said *entreat me never to leave thee...* Ruth 1:16; *I will never leave thee nor forsake thee,* the precious promise of God. A true believer plain and simply will never leave or walk away from a marriage, because they vowed before God and the angels of heaven as witnesses, also before men as witnesses, to be bound, to be one until death do us part. So if anyone leaves a marriage, their Christianity must be called into question as the pastors had reminded me, and God will sit to judge the people who break wedlock, who break their vows to God and to their husband or wife, and when you stand trembling before the awesome throne of judgment, what are you going to say my dear friends? for there simply is **NO** excuse, **NO** justification for divorce, of breaking thy covenant promise to God, anywhere in God's word or plan. Look again at Luke 1:56, Mary conceived by the Holy Spirit, then she left for Elizabeth's place where Luke 1:56 tells us *And Mary abode with her about three months, and returned to her own house,* that is before returning back to Joseph. By this time, she was around four months pregnant. Having never been with Joseph, her betrothed, don't you think that Joseph may have had reason to question and/or doubt Mary? If there ever was a cause for a divorce, this certainly could be it, but...Joseph loved

Mary, and the Holy Spirit told him not to put her away, God hates divorce! And there was and is no cause for divorce. In Matthew 19:6 *What therefore God hath joined together, let no man put asunder.* Man represents righteousness, the believer, and includes not only other people but the husband and wife as well. She leaves him for four months and returns pregnant, but Joseph loved and trusted Mary...He loved and trusted God... therefore, he accepted Mary. Now, the Spirit spoke to him, but don't you think that the remaining ~ five months as well as during the delivery and thereafter, that Joseph wondered about this whole event? A very strong statement is found in the Song of Songs 8:6 *For love is strong as death; jealousy is cruel as the grave.* True love is so very strong and one must fight for it and hold on to it, not allow anything...including jealousy, friends or family...to get in the way, or to come in between the two of you, for you are now one! Don't give reason for jealousy, and be ye not jealous. If you will turn to the book of Luke 18:53, you will find all sorts of relatives against relatives, BUT!!! Nowhere will you find husband against wife or wife against husband, why? Because the husband represents God, the wife represents us the sinners, and **NOTHING** can separate us from the love of God, Hallelujah! And nothing should be allowed to separate us from the love of one another.

Ashtaroth's worshipers praised her as The Virgin, The Virgin Mother, and the Holy Virgin. This merely meant that her lovers were free from all obligation of wedlock. In Babylon, she was the goddess of war as well as love, of prostitutes as well as mothers. Aren't these the identical names, which the Roman Catholic Church gives to Mary, the mother of Jesus? The true virgin, however, would be a humble Jewess. A young virgin who would forever ponder, in her heart, the miracle of being overshadowed by the Holy Ghost, and then the joy of delivering the world it's Savior.

If one or both of the partners in the marriage bond are guilty of adultery, this **does not** give the innocent or guilty parties Scriptural grounds for divorce. Marriage is to be regarded as a binding life-long **covenant**, which can only be terminated by the death of one of the partners. They both need to repent and seek forgiveness from one another and from God. Turn from their wicked ways and have restoration and revival in their marriage. Contrary to popular opinion, none of the following are biblical grounds for divorce: Adultery, Homosexuality, Fornication, Abuse, Unfaithfulness, Alcoholism, Desertion, Prostitution, Cruelty, Insanity, Sodomy, etc.... This fact does NOT make these sins okay, but the marriage vows made to each other before many witnesses, the minister and God, are binding and hold each other accountable **for better FOR WORSE, till death do us part.** Love the sinner, not the sin. Each partner in this marriage bond is to realize that, as opposed to being a contract**, which** has escape clauses and penalty clauses; marriage is a sacred covenant, which binds the couple together with an unbreakable vow made to God.

God's word teaches us in 1ˢᵗ Corinthians 7:10-11 that a woman is not to leave her husband, so women, don't leave your husband and let not a husband put away his wife-verse 15. *But if the **unbelieving** depart, let him depart. A brother or a sister* (the believer) *is **not** under bondage in such cases: but God hath called us to peace.* is not under bondage to what? Under bondage to the vow. The unbeliever may leave, they can run but they can never hide from God and His judgment, just ask Jonah in the first chapter of his book or David. There are NO exceptions! There are no ifs, ands, or buts...Dear friends; there are **NO** biblical grounds or basis for separation or divorce! None! In fact, God says that He hates divorce, Malachi 2:16. If we look at Romans 7:2, we see that she is bound to her husband by law. Whose law?... God's law binds her to her husband until death. When you made or make your vow in marriage, it isn't just before man, but before God and His angels. Until death, and I am not advocating murder, for that violates another of God's commandments as well! Look over at Jeremiah 3:20. *Surely, as a wife treacherously departeth from her husband, so have ye dealt treacherously with me.* You see how serious this is. I must comment here also, that you must notice that the instructions are to the wife and not to the husband here, why? Because God will never divorce us sinners, He is our Husband.

Though we are but sinners, a man represents God, thus should never put his wife away.

In 1ˢᵗ Cor 7:10-16, it talks about if an unbeliever departs or separates from the marriage. Any person that violates the oath, the sacred covenant of marriage is an unbeliever, having not the faith that God will fulfill His promise in your relationship. The believer is not to grant servitude to the unbeliever; coercing their marital involvement. He is not to try to cleave to the departing mate. The peace from God does not come until the believer submits to the reality of their partners of them and of God and His law. For as Paul said, *For how knoweth thou, O man, whether thou shall save thy wife?* This faithful action of the believer may at some point cause the unbeliever to be saved.

God expects the unbeliever who departs from the marriage to repent for violating our vows to Him and to seek Him for the grace to fulfill those vows.

Malachi 2:10-3:5 states clearly that God calls marriage a covenant and is witness unto it. And Malachi speaks of the Lord coming near to you in judgment; and I will be a swift witness against those who fear not me, saith the Lord of Hosts. And remember that the penalty for breaking covenant was death, eternal damnation, separation from God.

If one or both of the marriage partners are guilty of adultery, fornication, unfaithfulness, desertion, cruelty, sodomy, homosexuality, abuse, alcoholism, drugs, prostitution, insanity, etc., this does not give any innocent or guilty parties Scriptural grounds for divorce. Marriage is to be regarded as a binding lifelong covenant, which can only be terminated by the death of one of the partners. The guilty parties should repent and seek forgiveness, then forgiveness should be extended, and every endeavor should be made to re-build the marriage relationship.

If you are separated or divorced from your marriage partner, God has provided you with a command, a purpose and a mission that only you can carry out. The future of you and your family is at stake, but you need to repent of your sins and seek God's help.

A bad wife or husband cannot destroy us, discourage us yes. The International Bible Encyclopedia states that, though the Hebrew wife and mother were treated with more consideration than her sister on other lands, even in other Semitic countries, her position nevertheless was one of inferiority and subjection. The marriage relation from the standpoint of Hebrew legislation was looked upon very largely as a business affair, a mere question of property. A wife nevertheless, was, indeed, in most homes in Israel, the husband's 'most valued possession.' Frequently we find this belief regarding the From Whence Cometh basis for Israelite and Semitic marriage. **MARRIAGE WAS THE COVENANT NATURE OF THEIR RELATIONSHIP WITH JEHOVAH, and it still is.** The covenant was obviously a powerful force with the sons of Noah, as a marriage contract was required.

The one who marries a divorced spouse sins not only by committing adultery with another's spouse but also sins against God by acting as a barrier to reconciliation and revival of the original marriage. They are as well guilty of polygamy, for now they have two wives or husbands.

We look now at yet another book, Malachi 2:13-16, and let us examine a few points here. He says, *And this have ye done AGAIN, covering the altar of the Lord with tears, with weeping, and with crying out, insomuch that he regardeth not the offering anymore, or receiveth it with good will at your hand.* Why? As we shall see in a minute, God hates divorce! When you marry, you vow to Almighty God and your life partner until death do us part. When you walk away from God's precious gift, you break thy vow-thy promise to God that you will NEVER leave. You then became a liar, as you lied to God, your partner, and the witnesses in heaven and on earth. You lied to God and there are always consequences for our choices. *Yet ye say wherefore? Because the Lord hath been witness between thee and the wife of thy youth, against whom thou hast dealt treacherously, yet is she thy companion, and the wife of thy covenant* (promise...vow). *And did He not make one? Yet had he the residue of the Spirit; and wherefore one? That he might seek a godly seed,* as we discussed earlier. *Therefore take heed to your spirit and let none deal treacherously against the wife of thy youth,* Malachi 2:14-15. Deal treacherously here means to put away, to divorce. *For the Lord, the God of Israel sayeth that He hateth putting away.* Divorce...He hateth divorce.

In Numbers 13:6,8 we note Caleb who first gave good report with faith after spying out the promised land in verse 30, was from the tribe of Judah, the lineage of Christ, from Jacob's FIRST wife, whereas Joshua came from Rachel, the second wife whom he loved. Leah, the first wife was given to Jacob by deception, he didn't choose or want her, but... note that he never put her away either.

In Matthew 5:31-32 we are shown *It hath been said, whosoever put away his wife, let him give her a writing of divorcement.* Now note, he put away his wife, because it hath been said that a woman is not to leave her husband. But we are also told that from the beginning divorce was not God's plan or will, only mans because of the hardened hearts. Does a truly spiritual man or woman have a hard heart? In reality, God desires all of us, but if we choose to leave Him or go a whoring after other gods, then...Note in 1ˢᵗ Corinthians 7:15 *But if the* **unbelieving** *depart* (why not the believer? Because a truly spiritual person will not leave or break their vows before God), *let him* (or her) *depart. A brother or sister* (the believer) *is not under bondage in such cases: but God hath called us to peace;* Under bondage to what? Bondage to the vow, for the believer didn't break the vow, the covenant, the unbeliever did. I could say that men should call the police, have their wandering wives (divorce and separation) and have them captured and returned to their rightful husbands, like they used to do for runaway children, but...this isn't right either, for God gives us free choice- to sin and serve, follow the enemy, or to love, serve and follow our God.

Soon no man or woman will finish the path of life, the mountain, with the woman who had climbed it with him, and a marriage not ending in divorce will be as rare as a virgin bride.

Friends, there is no more severe form of domestic violence than that of divorce, murdering your marriage and breaking covenant with God our Father! If you truly love someone, even God, you simply don't do this to thy partner. You stick with it and make it work. The true believer will not bow down to the ways of the world or seek/listen to the advice of ungodly friends, and the unbeliever will not look to the precepts of our Father, Creator, and our Bridegroom. We read in Habakkuk 2:10 *Thou hast consulted shame to thy house by cutting off many people, and hast sinned against thy soul.* Think about this seriously.

We read in Zechariah 8:17 *And let none of you imagine evil in your hearts against his neighbor; and love no false oath: for all these are things that I hate, saith the LORD*

And then we cannot forget to mention Paul's words found in his letter to the Romans 8:38-39 *Foe I am persuaded, neither death, nor life, nor angels, nor principalities, nor powers, nor things to come, nor height, nor depth, nor any other creature, shall be able to separate us from the love of God, which is in Christ Jesus our Lord.* Paul goes on to say in chapter 16:1-18 *Now I beseech you, brethren, mark them which cause divisions and offenses contrary to the doctrine which ye have learned; and avoid them. For they that are such serve not our lord Jesus Christ, but their own belly; and by good words and fair speeches deceive the hearts of the simple.* Don't you believe that the same precious words must also apply to our marriages and those who try to separate marriages?

DIVORCE AND THE CHURCH

One problem in the church today is conformity with the world. If you can't beat them, join them, or stoop to their level, rather than holding on to God's precious word and standing firm as a sheep among the wolves, again I refer you to 1st John 2:15 and James 4:4. The Bible is so clear, that a woman is not to leave her husband and that a husband is not to put his wife away...no exceptions. My dear brothers; God tells us to love our wives as Christ loves the church, as a weaker vessel. He didn't leave us even though we are sinners. God in fact says *I will **NEVER** leave you nor forsake you,* brothers, are you listening? This doesn't give license for the woman to do whatever she pleases, just as we are not free to sin, if we love Him, we will serve Him and do whatever we can to please Him, obey Him. My dear sisters, are you listening? All have sinned and fall short of the glory of God, but He still loves us. He does not love the sin, but He loves us. We are all sinners and will fall short sometimes of each other's expectations, but we must forgive and still love one another, not walk away. He is faithful to forgive us if we repent of the sin and turn from our wicked ways; this is how husbands need to treat their wives as well. Your partner will never be perfect, but still love them and hold on to them, neither shall you be perfect. Remember men and women, husbands and wives, forgiveness seventy times seven-infinity!

The understanding of our Christian forefathers is substantially different from that of the present generation of Church leadership, especially in matters concerning the necessity of Christians to maintain strict separation from worldly corruption.

It is a wrong understanding to believe that it is simply one's right to divorce a spouse. Even though human law may permit such a thing, God strictly forbids it. Anyone who follows human customs and laws regarding marriage, divorce and remarriage, instead of Divine laws should stand in fearful awe of God. All lawmakers, in and out of the Church are warned, to hear and obey the Word of the Lord. Jesus' command is reaffirmed: What God has joined together, let no man put asunder, and that my dear friends must include yourself and your partner!

Quickly let us turn to 1st Samuel 25:3 in which we see Abigail, the wife of Nabal, (Nabal means fool), and a fool he was, a worthless man, but...After his wicked behavior, you see that she remained loyal in love, and cared for him to save her family. She never thought about the wrong choice of packing her bags and leaving him, for in reality, that would have made her just as worthless, if not more so, for Nabal sinned against man, breaking vows is a sin against God and man.

I mentioned a couple of cases on a previous page, I also know of a case where when the couple was young, he had an affair with a co-worker. His wife considered divorce, but in her heart and mind knew that he was the father of their children, and that divorce was wrong. They stayed together and now many years later, they are still together, stand by your man. This woman earlier played the harlot, she sinned as do we all, but remember, when the men brought the woman caught in adultery before Him, He said in John 8:7, 11, *He that is without sin among you, let him first cast a stone at her.* and they all left. Jesus said, *Neither do I condemn thee: go, and sin no more.* If Jesus can forgive us sinners, ought we not to forgive one another, especially our spouses who are gifts from Jehovah Jireh? Forgiveness is not a license to continue in your sins! I met a young man who got married to a beautiful young lady. Four months later, He went and was drinking, got mad at a drunken man who was acting stupid, actually they were fighting over a girl. They got into a fight, the man took off in his car to clear himself of the situation, and this young man shot him. The man was killed and this man ended up in prison, condemned to death. Four years later, still in prison, His wife is still standing by him, still holding on to the vow that she made, for better or for worse, until death do us part. Oh, dear friends, if only more men and women could be like this precious woman. As I said from the introduction, I am not casting stones or condemning my precious wife, but using her as an example for most women fall into the 'socially acceptable' behavior, but this is NOT biblically acceptable, and that is exactly why this message is so important for all of us to read and understand, as well as to apply God's word and law unto our lives and leave the world behind!

There is no salvation in the act of adultery. Permit me to explain. By permitting remarriage after divorce, the church is condoning the continual act of adultery, to permit willful sin. There is no forgiveness for willful sin but a certain fearful judgment as we see in Hebrews 10:26, 27. To teach that adultery on the part of the married is a license for divorce and remarriage is to teach that the first marriage is dissolved by adultery and we know that in Christ, there is no divorce.

Under the doctrine of Grace, the innocent partner must extend to the guilty partner the offer of grace, that is to offer the opportunity of repentance and restoration of the marriage till death do they part just as Jesus does for each of us.

Woman's place is in the home and I believe that as Christians, we need to go to male checkers, tellers, etc., do business with men, not women as she is to serve her own husband (or papa), and nobody else. We now look to Hosea 3:3 and see, *And I said unto her, thou shalt abide for me many days, thou shalt not play the harlot, and thou shalt not be for another man, so will I also be for thee.* Period; should be the end of the story. But God hateth divorce! *But I say to you, that whosoever shall put away his wife, saving for the cause of fornication...* Whoops, so there is a ground?!! Let's stop here and look closely at this verse. This verse in Matt 5:32 often referred to as the exclusionary clause, but my dear friends, if you read this carefully, it is not giving permission to divorce. In reading from various bibles, we have the following words being used for the Greek word **pornea**; Fornication, sexual immorality, adultery, illicit sex, marital unfaithfulness, unchastity. However, which best fits the context and situation, as pornea is both used in a narrow sense and a broad sense throughout scripture. I am convinced that fornication is the best when using the example of Joseph and Mary. Fornication is after betrothal and before the marriage is consummated. And even so, let us look at Matthew 1:19. Here we see that Mary was betrothed to Joseph. **Then** she is pregnant and Joseph hadn't consummated this marriage yet. That certainly is incriminating evidence. Joseph could, by the Jewish law, not God's law, have put her away. Then we look in verse 20, where we see the angel of the Lord appeared unto him and said *fear not to take thee Mary, thy wife...* We turn to the Old Testament again and see that there was a very strong and affectionate bond between Abraham and Sarah. Abraham never abandoned Sarah during the many years (twenty) of barrenness, but instead, he prayed for her. In fact, it was only by Sarah's insistence that Abraham took Hagar as his surrogate wife or concubine. In Genesis 24, a long chapter, records Abraham's servants' journey to find Isaac a wife. When he returned with Rebekah the account begins another beautiful love story.

Don't prostitute thyself to the world, marry Christ, for there is power in the blood...There is no biblical prerogative for divorce after marriage, not even before marriage. I hate divorce. Not convinced yet? Let us jump to Matthew 19:3-10. The Pharisees asked Jesus about divorce. Jesus answered *Wherefore, they* (men and women) *are no more twain, but one flesh.* In this unity is reflected the Trinity. You have God the Father, the husband, and the wife, all in one spiritual union, one spiritual body. *What therefore God...who?...* **God** *hath* **joined** *together, let not man put asunder.* In Romans 8:35-39 *who shall separate us from the love of Christ? Shall tribulation, or distress, or persecution, or famine, or nakedness, or peril, or sword? Nay, in all these things we are more than conquerors through Him that loved us. For I am persuaded, that neither death, nor life, nor angels, nor principalities, nor powers, nor things present, nor things to come, nor height, not depth, nor any other creature shall be able to separate us from the love of God which is in Christ Jesus our Lord.* My precious and dear friends, this equally should apply to thy marriage. Moses gave permission to divorce because of their hardness of heart, but again this was of man's doing, not Gods. **From the beginning,** it was not so, not God's will or plan. Let us now look at Romans 7:2, *For the woman which hath a husband is bound by law,* God's law, *to her husband so long as he liveth, but if the husband is dead, she is loosed from the law of her husband.* Now as I write this, God hath revealed to me another parallel. She is loosed from the bonds if her husband is dead (or vice versa), but remember we said earlier that the believing spouse is free from the vow, no longer bound, if the unbelieving spouse leaves, which is to say that the unbeliever is dead in their sins. I pray that you are seeing just how important marriage and NO divorce are to God and to each of us. Because of this freedom after the death of a spouse, Ruth was able to marry Boaz. I am not advocating, nor is God advocating murder to be free of the vow! That violates several of God's laws-thou shalt love not hate, thou shalt not kill, thou shalt not leave the marriage... We see in Hosea 3:1 He is asked to take his wife back whom he had divorced and to love her in spite of the fact that she had committed adultery: we read *Then said the Lord unto me, Go yet, love a woman beloved of her friend, yet an adulteress, according to the love of the Lord toward the children of Israel, who look to other gods, and love flagons of wine.*

There is no question of what the Law taught regarding adultery. It was not a matter of divorce. It was a capital crime requiring the death penalty. *If a man be found lying with a woman married to an husband, then they shall both of them die, both the man that lay with the woman, and the woman: so shalt thou put away evil from Israel.* Deuteronomy 22:22. *And the man that committeth adultery with another man's wife, even he that committeth adultery with his neighbor's wife, the adulterer and the adulteress shall surely be put to death,* Leviticus 20:10. In Deuteronomy 22:13 the woman was put to death if she was found not to be a virgin on her wedding night; the indecency, èrwat dabar, translated: a matter of shame, or literally nakedness.

This expression is usually interpreted to mean something shameful or repulsive, without going into any detail as to what it is that arouses the husband's loathing for his wife. The expression occurs in another passage in the Old Testament; in Deuteronomy 23.14. Verse 12 of chap. 23 mentions that there is to be a place outside the camp at which all of the fecal material from the camp is to be buried. This is to be done lest Yahweh, when he walks through the camp, should find something exposed. It is clear that here dabar stands for human excrement. It is accordingly a euphemism. Yahweh must not see excrement lying about exposed. The expression is similarly used as an euphemism in Deuteronomy 24:1 but here it does not stand for human excrement but for the female pudendum **somebody's external genitals:** the human external genital organs) with reference to the mention of the female token in

Deuteronomy22 here means a cloth or garment of some kind, as a covering for the female pudendum, which the husband gave his wife at their marriage as a sign that she was his for example see Ezekiel 16:8: *Now when I passed by thee, and looked upon thee, behold, thy time was the time of love; and I spread my skirt over thee, and covered thy nakedness: yea, I sware unto thee, and entered into a covenant with thee, saith the Lord God, and thou becamest mine.* While Leviticus speaks of uncovering the nakedness of a father in Leviticus 18:7 and 20:11, Deuteronomy speaks of uncovering the skirt of a father 23:1 and 27:20. Thus here also Deuteronomy avoids directly mentioning the pudendum. In Deuteronomy 24.1 it cannot be a matter of some other man having lifted the covering and exposing the wife's pudendum. This would have been tantamount to adultery and in that case, there could be no question of a new marriage for the wife, since both parties would be stoned to death. Probably it is a question here of the wife having exposed herself voluntarily or involuntarily. **All other exposure of his wife's pudendum than that which the husband himself is responsible for** arouses his loathing. That the husband's improper exposure of himself in the presence of any other person of the opposite sex than the woman he was married to aroused the wife's contempt is clear from the story of how Michal despised David when in his dance before the ark of the Lord, he exposed himself (not apparently his genitalia) to the crowd in 2nd Samuel 6:12-20. Michal interpreted David's exposure of himself as a deliberate exposure to the servant maids. But it is only licentious people for see example 2nd Samuel 6:20 who expose themselves in this way. No modest Israelite woman (believer) will dress in an immodest manner or expose herself to ANY OTHER Person than her own husband. The wife will no longer find grace in her husband's eyes when he discovers her exposing her nakedness, unless he is willing to be Christ-like and forgive her IF and when she truly repents. This is also clear from Ezekiel 23:18, in which it is said that *So she discovered her whoredoms, and discovered her nakedness: then my mind was alienated from her, like as my mind was alienated from her sister.* We see here that the man's soul turns away from the wife who exposes her naked-ness. The term èrwat dabar can be used to mean as we stated earlier, human excrement, or it can be used to mean nakedness.

Therefore the two remaining uses belong to Deuteronomy 24 and here: *Thou shalt have a place also without the camp, whither thou shalt go forth abroad: And thou shalt have a paddle upon thy weapon; and it shall be, when thou wilt ease thyself abroad, thou shalt dig therewith, and shalt turn back and cover that which cometh from thee: For the Lord thy God walketh in the midst of thy camp, to deliver thee, and to give up thine enemies before thee; therefore shall thy camp be holy: that he see no unclean thing in thee, and turn away from thee,* Deuteronomy 23:12-14. This we should note is the same reason that a woman is to keep her head covered. We must note here also that back in the garden when the Lord saw the sinfulness of man after Eve sinned, the first thing that He did was to cover her (them). The camp was to be kept holy, because the Lord walked in the midst of it, in order that he might not see the nakedness of a thing, i.e., anything to be ashamed of in the people, *and turn away from thee.* There was nothing shameful in the excrement itself; but want of rev-erence, which the people would display through not removing it, would offend the Lord and drive him out of the camp of Israel. Exposed excrement, the èrwat dabar within the camp of Israel, would have been the act, which would have caused the Lord to be offended, thus driving him out of the camp. Likewise, in Deuteronomy 24:1 the èrwat dabar, unclean thing, would have caused the wife to find no favor in the eyes of her husband. Today just like these days of old that we are showing here men, that divorce has become so common and accepted that men and women need have no excuse to divorce, they blanket it under the excuse of irreconcilable differences. What God hath joined together there are NO irreconcilable differ-ences, anything in God can be worked out and solved, as God ALWAYS has a solution! The fact that men and women, Judges and attorneys, especially those calling themselves Christian, today so freely accept the culture and laws of man rather than the precepts of God goes to show just how ignorant and far off the path that mankind has become! Even the leaders of the Seventh Day Adventist church promised to publish this message, and then read it, and told me that this is not of the SDA doctrine, so refused to publish reneging on their promise. A Catholic priest printed copies for me without me even asking and said that they were great, but that he couldn't justify publishing them because they weren't with the Catholic doctrine. I praise God that it isn't! My friends, this is non-denominational-this message is from the Spirit of God and His precious word, and that is what we are to follow and the only way unto salvation! Denominational doctrine, laws of your land or culture and traditions will never lead you to the gates of heaven!

The marriage was forever put asunder: kerithuth, karath, to cut off; hew down; is used for hewing down timber in 1st Kings 5:18 and amputation in Leviticus 22:24; as well as decapitation in 1st Samuel 17:51. It indicates severing of what was once a living union.

Thus, the law of man not God, permitted polygamy and divorce because the heart of man was so totally evil that man could not conceive of a marriage that was permanent.

God was married to Israel. The Law was a marriage contract with His beloved lady. He loved her. In His Song of Songs, He composes her song of songs, and pledges His love, *Set me as a seal upon thine heart, as a seal upon thine arm: for love is strong as death; jealousy is cruel as the grave: the coals thereof are coals of fire, which hath a most vehement flame*, Song of Songs 8:6. His love was everlasting. We will see throughout this message that as Israel deserted Him, He pleaded for her to return, always keeping the door of reconciliation open. His perfect love required Him to discipline her, but He never forsook her. We shall see that although Israel was the blessed and chosen nation, and the wife of Jehovah God, she nevertheless was given to marital apostasy, just as Eve, Jezebel, David's wife, etc.

When we return to Christ, we return with a repentant heart, we return with a clean slate, and that is exactly how it must be when the unbeliever returns to the marriage. This is forgiveness and true love, being Christ-like. We read in Hosea 2:7 *And she shall follow after her lovers, but she shall not overtake them; and she shall seek them, but shall not find them: then shall she say, I will go and return to my first husband, for then was it better with me than now.*

We see in Exodus 34:14-16 *For thou shalt worship no other god: for the Lord, whose name is Jealous, is a jealous God: Lest thou make a covenant with the inhabitants of the land, and they go a whoring after their gods, and do sacrifice unto their gods, and one call thee, and thou eat of his sacrifice; And thou take of their daughters unto thy sons, and their daughters go a whoring after their gods, and make thy sons go a whoring after their gods.* With this idea as a concept of deception Balaam convinced Balak to arrange for the daughters of Moab to play the harlot with the children of Israel on its Plains of Moab. These women were experts in the sin of licentiousness, and the prostitution of idolatry. *And Israel abode in Shittim, and the people began to commit whoredom with the daughters of Moab. And they called the people unto the sacrifices of their gods: and the people did eat, and bowed down to their gods. And Israel joined himself unto Baalpeor: and the anger of the Lord was kindled against Israel. And the Lord said unto Moses, Take all the heads of the people, and hang them up before the Lord against the sun, that the fierce anger of the Lord may be turned away from Israel,* Numbers 25:1-4. We see this same behavior in the plains of Sinai while Moses was atop Mt. Sinai communing with God.

The worship of Baal Peor was known to be attended by women and virgins who prostituted themselves to this practice of the Moabites, for the god of fertility. Archaeological discoveries have revealed that the devotees of Baal practiced prostitution as a regular part of their worship. This sordid practice was adopted by the Israelites. We see in the Book of Revelation 2:14 and 15 it is revealed that this fornication was associated with the doctrine of the Nicolaitans. Although some see Nicolaitanism as clerical hierarchy, others see it as a licentious sect advocating complete and free love. So, the daughters of Moab prepared their licentious worship which required the participation of the standing men of Israel. The

Moabite harlot decked her bed with tapestry and covered it with aloe to perfume it. She whispered her offer of lust/love to the interested Jewish males who hovered around on the desert lands. The army of Israel soon fell into the idolatry of sexual and spiritual fornication. This was the plan of Balaam to curse Israel. Revelation states that it is Balaam who cast this stumbling block before the children of Israel. But to the surprise of Balaam, the children of Israel were not consumed. God's anger was kindled and He began cursing the people with a plague, and ordering Moses to hang up the heads of those guilty of fornication. This hanging consisted of a form of crucifixion, which was practiced by the ancient people.

A spark of hope springs out of Jericho. Here in this heathen stronghold abides the harlot of the city, Rahab. The miracle of Jericho was more than the fall of its walls. It was the conversion of its harlot—the LXX translates the Hebrew word, harlot, as porne. The fear of God and his servant, Joshua, drove the harlot, Rahab, to her knees in repentance for her sinful life. She thrust her life into the hands of this heroic soldier-savior and finds atonement for her soul. She is born-again, converted from harlotry to become the great grand-mother of the promised seed-king David. What a miracle. The power of God's men is always salvation, and when that salvation is the salvation of his enemies, oh, so great is the salvation! So, with the opening of the Book of Joshua, Rahab's conversion and marriage appeared healthy and promising, unfortunately this was for a moment. By the time we reach the end of the Book of Judges we will find Israel at the lowest moral state in their recorded history. Shortly after the death of Joshua we read in Judges 3:3-7 *Namely, five Lords of the Philistines, and all the Canaanites, and the Sidonians, and the Hivites that dwelt in Mount Lebanon, from mount Baal hermon unto the entering in of Hamath. And they were to prove Israel by them, to know whether they would hearken unto the commandments of the Lord, which he commanded their fathers by the hand of Moses. And the children of Israel dwelt among the Canaanites, Hittites, and Amorites, and Perizzites, and Hivites, and Jebusites: And the children of Israel dwelt among the Canaanites, Hittites, and Amorites, and Perizzites, and Hivites, and Jebusites: And the children of Israel did evil in the sight of the Lord, and forgat the Lord their God, and served Baalim and the groves.*

As God and Moses were planning the future of Israel and their salvation and worship in the heights of Sinai, Satan and Israel were committing fornication with a golden calf at its base; dancing naked and sensually, the nation worshiped in the customs of Egyptian idolatry. The fertility cult represented idolatry throughout their desert journey, and every time the nation strayed into idolatry, she experienced fornication, that is physical AND spiritual fornication and adultery.

There is another factor here, which most people fail to recognize from God's word. Look over at 1st Corinthians 6:1-2. When you divorce you go to court don't you? Here He tells us *Dare any of you* (truly spiritual), *having a matter against another, go to law before the unjust, and not before the saints? Do you not know that the saints shall judge the world? And if the world be judged by you, are ye unworthy to judge the smallest matters?* Verse 6 continues, *But brother goeth to law with brother and that before the unbeliever. Now therefore there is utterly a fault among you, because ye go to law one with another before unbelievers for judgment.* Think about it my dear brothers and sisters. He refers to brothers because He is talking about the righteous people, not the unbelievers. If we were quicker taking our problems to God than to court, how much better off we would be, and how much less sin and pain. All divorce breaks the sacred covenant promise made at the time of marriage. Also, how can any judge break the vow of God, much less a Christian judge?

I have a small idea of how God feels. I gave twenty years of my life to my dear wife, along with a lot of work and sacrifice, as well as monetary resources and made her dreams come to pass. Then she just up and walked away into outer darkness, taking my precious children, all because of the lusts and enticements of the world. All that I did meant nothing to her; all that we went through together with many good times and the few hard times meant nothing to her. When you love someone so much you always desire them to be by your side, and then they walk away, that is analogous to God loving us with such great love and then we choose to walk away from Him. The world pulls many of God's brides, His children away from Him after all that He has done for us. Furthermore, she hid, I found out later, to me throughout our marriage, just as many people claim to love God, but serve themselves and the world instead. Things got worse before she broke covenant and left; lies grew-to the U.S. Government, to the court, to many people, just as many make false promises to God, but all just lies to accomplish self-seeking goals. A vow is something sacred, something to be cherished. A vow to God and a vow to thy husband or wife, until death do us part, not allowing the world to tear you apart or put asunder (separate parts or pieces). The world and the lusts thereof, the enticements are strong, but my God is stronger and so can we be victorious in our marriages and our Christian walk. But this strength comes from Christ and only if we cherish our vows to God and to each other, and hold on tight.

Communication is so important, open, honest communication with each other, and in our prayers unto God. What is said or confessed, as well as any problems should NEVER go out to friends or family, all communication should be kept in the house between the two of you ONLY. How can you open up and trust or confide in a partner who spreads everything everywhere?

Unfortunately, marriage today is like a menstrual rag. Apply it...use it...then throw it away, but this is not marriage and certainly not the way that God ordained it to be. Dear brothers and sisters, we need to return to the path of righteousness. Marriage is to be unity not independence. Many ladies today are advertising themselves as independent while seeking a marriage partner. The two don't mix! Marriage is until death, no in-between. God is not a male chauvinist, He is the potter, and we are the clay. If we are obedient and take our role seriously, in accordance to His will, all will be well, but if we refuse God...just look at the world today, look at the church today.

Another aspect to this, men don't ever leave your families as God doesn't leave us. We see in Zech. 9:6 *And a bastard shall dwell...* A bastard is a child without a father. A child needs a father very much, just as we need our heavenly Father. Without him, children are lost. Children also learn how to relate to God by learning how to relate with their dads. The dad is the lord of the family, and is such an important part of that family. See how important you men are? So, don't ever leave thy wife, and my dear sisters, don't ever leave thy husband or chase him away, for God's sake as well as the sakes of your children and thyself.

Divorce judges should never give children to the parent seeking the divorce. If it is a joint application for divorce, then the children should go to the dad, just as we belong to our Father until or if the enemy, the evil one takes us away. Children out of wedlock should likewise be reared by their dad.

I was told a story a few years ago that on the computer, there was a nest of birds-Bald Eagles. After raising several eaglets before, this time after laying eggs, a young female came and started playing with the male. The female who had laid the eggs left and the eggs eventually died. As viewers around the world I guess, watched, many wanted the female to return. Men and women, are you listening? God is watching us and He takes the unity of the family very seriously. He is heartbroken each time a partner leaves a marriage and breaks covenant, and the children dear friends suffer, but the parents are usually so focused on their own problems that they are unable to care about their children. The children then become lost and sometimes die folks, all because someone fell off of the path of righteousness. Things will never be perfect, but...God calls us to love and forgive!!! Studies have shown that children of divorce have very high rates of alcohol and drug abuse, suicide, violent crime, domestic violence, etc.... Who is caring for them, the poor, precious gifts, the children entrusted unto us by God our Father, which He hath blessed us with, when an unbelieving partner tells lies and destroys God's union? I also feel compelled to say that while what my wife did was wrong that began the problems, she and many other women, compile the problem by denying or trying to justify it, and then worsened it by turning their children against their papa, just as Satan uses the unbelievers to turn away the believers from our Heavenly Father. My dear friends, you see how devastating this is?

I had been called to do a crusade in one area, and on my way, I felt led to speak on marriage and family of God, along with repentance. Later, I received a call from a pastor who said that there was a woman who really desired for me to meet with her daughter. I went out there days later and found that the nineteen-year-old daughter was having trouble accepting the love that a young man was trying to offer. He wanted to marry her, but she was afraid of marriage. In talking with her, I found it stemmed from her parents, so I asked her to bring her parents so we could all talk. She returned with her mother, and we talked. Then the girl looked at her mother and asked her, was dad the right man for you and if so, why did you divorce? Her mother cried, and said, my dear daughter, yes...your dad was the perfect man for me, ordained by God. I made a huge mistake and listened to a man who desired to...use and hurt me. Your dad tried so hard to warn me and told me not to go, but I was stubborn and didn't listen. I got hurt badly, and afterward, your dad reminded me that he tried to protect me. I couldn't accept this, so I made the huge mistake of leaving him and taking you, his daughter from him. After hearing this dear brother preach on marriage and the family of God, I realized just how wrong I was and I immediately went to apologize and ask your dad to accept us back, but when I found him, he had passed away. I so regret all I have done and pray that you will learn from my mistake, accept Joseph as your husband and **ALWAYS** listen to him, not the world.

We continued talking, but I had a waterfall of tears inside hearing this confession and repentant heart, while thinking about and praying for my dear wife and precious children with such great love for them, and wondering if one day that is what my dear wife will be telling my children. I have heard similar stories time and again, and my dearest brothers and sisters, this ought not to be so, because God ordained man to care for, protect, and be in authority over the woman, that is why the girls' dad GIVES, not sells, her to her husband at the marriage ceremony. Does divorce affect children? You bet!!!

There is so much emphasis on career today, but I challenge you today to remember, the jobs will never love you the way your family will. The jobs don't love you back and you are expendable!!! We see this all the time, men put everything into a job or career, only to be let go... But God ordained a partner for you, who will love you and will leave a big hole when you depart, nobody is expendable in a marriage, you are irreplaceable! There isn't a sea full of fish for you, only the **ONE** that God ordained for you and nobody can fill your shoes or those of your partner. Nobody can fill your place in your family! So where should you focus your time and energy? With the family, that God ordained for you, and He will provide for your needs. My precious wife of twenty years left a hole in my heart, physically and emotionally.

I counseled a couple one time, two professionals. She wanted a divorce. We spoke at length and as always, I was praying as we spoke, to seek God's guidance. Then finally, I asked 'are you now ready for God's solution?' They both replied yes. I began...To him I said, you must love this woman, this wife of thy youth with all of thine heart. You must forgive her faults and pray for and with her. You must leave thy work at work, and when you are not at work, your time belongs to her and her alone. His wife began laughing in agreement with all of this. I then looked at her and continued, and you...You must quit your job today (she made in excess of one hundred thousand dollars per year). You must stay at home and care for thy husband and his home. You must have meals prepared for him before work, and on the table when he arrives home. You must submit fully to his God given authority in full surrender and obedience. She, needless to say was no longer laughing... in fact they were both speechless for a few moments. Dead silence in the room as I allowed them time to absorb this information. They could hardly manage to get their jaws back up off the floor, before they both finally said that they couldn't afford for her to quit work as they couldn't live on the one salary alone (He also made in excess of one hundred thousand dollars per year). I said, then downsize your lifestyle, sell your wife's vehicle. Since she is to stay at home, she doesn't need her own vehicle. Sell the house and purchase a smaller home, but upsize thy marriage, God will provide. She replied, But I already filed for the divorce anyway. I told her gently, then cancel it for the love of God and your husband. Strike the original match, find that spark that you once had, and rekindle the fire. You know that if you don't feed a fire that it goes out. Then I asked her what the grounds for the divorce were and she replied, Irreconcilable differences. I told her that there are no irreconcilable differences when the husband and wife will sit down, talk out the problem(s) and LISTEN to one another.

About five months later, I received a phone call from this young lady, please Pastor, I have to talk to you, please! I told her that she could come by, as I pondered and worried about the urgent request. I was so surprised however when she arrived with her husband hand in hand. They were both smiling joyfully and appeared ten years younger. They told me that they had done all I had suggested, and that they have never been happier. I praise God for this. He also opened her womb and she was expecting! Praise God again! Another marriage saved, simply by applying God's precepts to the marriage, and bringing these two young people back onto the path of righteousness, His perfect plan, Amen!

So...what happened to my wife you may be asking? I don't honestly know exactly, because she had the court order a no communication order, but! I serve a mighty God! Also, I'm being held hostage in Kenya without being allowed any communication with the outside world, not even my parents or ministry. I have in over eight years, since I was taken hostage, not been allowed any communication with family or ministry. A group of American attorneys came and asked to speak with me, I was not allowed. There is a group of Voluntary Christian Attorneys but they have had no interest in assisting an innocent pastor being held hostage! Satan seeks to destroy but God turns it all around. He allowed both of us and our marriage to be tested. We read in the book of Deuteronomy 11:22-23, For if ye shall diligently keep all these commandments which I command you, to do them, to love the Lord your God, to walk in all his ways, and to cleave unto him; Then will the Lord drive out all these nations from before you, and ye shall possess greater nations and mightier than yourselves. I passed and was taken to a new and greater level of ministry, far exceeding anything I ever dreamed of, and into the mission field in Africa, a stronger faith, and a stronger servant of God. While Satan is holding me in prison because he knows what I was doing and will continue to do, meanwhile, the Lord is using this time to strengthen me and enlarging the ministry He has plans for me to continue, as well as using the time to allow me to write these messages for the world to read and reach perhaps more people than I ever could in person. He hath showed me time and again His mighty and awesome power, and His great love, and hath used me in such a mighty way; I can never thank Him enough for all that He has done for and through me. I never dreamed of the life that He hath bestowed upon me. Even now in my suffering, God has **NEVER** left me and I know that my Redeemer lives and hath great and mighty plans for me, whether or not my wife will rejoin me, that is between her and my God.

My wife had a sister whose husband cheated on her, and another sister who was abused by her husband, but neither divorced, what was the difference? What was the difference between her and her sisters? The answer is simple. Her sisters remained in a culture that encourages marriage and rejects divorce, whereas my wife came to a country that unfortunately encourages divorces for any or no reason. Again, I must refer you back to 1st John 2:15 which tells us to hate the world and the things of it. God tells us in His word to forsake the ways of your forefathers and the ways of the world, and this absolutely must include divorce. Then in Luke 16:15 we read that whatever is highly esteemed by man is an abomination to God. *And he said unto them* (Jesus said) *Ye are they which justify yourselves before men; but God knoweth your hearts: for that which is highly esteemed among men is abomination in the sight of God.* My wife cheated on me, but the biggest cheat and deception was in her leaving the marriage after twenty years. She lied to everyone including our children, God and I.

Divorce is so serious, and it hurts so many people; the God ordained partner that was left behind, stranded, the children suffer, and you will suffer in the end because God will judge the covenant breakers, those who lied to God when they vowed to remain one until death do us part...so help me God... God allows free choice but...there are consequences! It may seem good at the moment, but in the end, you will have to answer to the final Judge and He is the One who you lied to and broke covenant with!

My wife cheated on me, but the biggest cheat and deception was in her leaving the marriage after twenty years. All too often, though the person be forgiven by their partner, they cannot forgive themselves, so they run. The problem is that they are running from themselves and from God, and you can't hide from either. They must forgive themselves, repent, restore, then can they find forgiveness from God and live in peace.

My wife was taken to America where everyone professing Christianity are so numbed by divorce and social standards (which are at an all-time low) that they no longer discourage it, rather in violation of the very Gospel that they claim to believe, they go against and conform to the world and encourage divorce, as well as homosexuality, homosexual 'marriage', and other grave sins, hypocrisy plain and simple. What are we told in Deuteronomy 18:9? *When thou art come into the land which the Lord thy God giveth thee, thou shalt not learn to do after the abominations of those nations.* She was in America and listened to drunks, adulterers and porn addicts-the world, rather than to the Gospel, pastor friends, or her husband. We then turn over to the book of Ezekiel 8:17 where we read *Then he said unto me, Hast thou seen this, O son of man? Is it a light thing to the house of Judah that they commit the abominations which they commit here? for they have filled the land with violence, and have returned to provoke me to anger: and, lo, they put the branch to their nose.* Then we jump to 14:6 *Therefore say unto the house of Israel, Thus saith the Lord God; Repent, and turn yourselves from your idols; and turn away your faces from all your abominations.* Then a little further, we read in 18:13 *Hath given forth upon usury, and hath taken increase: shall he then live? he shall not live: he hath done all these abominations; he shall surely die; his blood shall be upon him.* Per her Christian friend's advice, she lied to the U.S. government, police, state, and court as well as to my children. If you are going to claim Christianity you must live it otherwise you are nothing more than a hypocrite-which God hates! You choose God or the world, but you cannot serve both. I chose God while my dear wife chose the world, while claiming Christianity. Where my dear friends, in scripture, does God tell us to listen to the world, lie to the government and your family, to divorce your God anointed partner and break your vows unto God? All who are considering, seeking, or already divorced, please consider God's words today. Please reconsider this because friendship with the world and the things of it are enmity with God, and thousands around the world have or are doing this very thing-divorcing, violating the very Scripture that they profess to believe in, all for the sake of the world. This simply is hypocritical and breaking covenant-divorcing from God Almighty, as well as breaking covenant with thy partner and God's commandments. Again, I can't stress 1st John 2:15 and James 4:4 enough! Take a quick look at Proverbs (book of wisdom) 4:14 and 15, where we are told *Enter not into the path of the wicked, and go not in the way of evil men. Avoid it, pass not by it, turn from it, and pass away.* Later in Proverbs, 6:26 we read *For by means of a whorish woman a man is brought to a piece of bread: and the adultress will hunt for the precious life.* My dear friends, the world seeks to destroy the righteous, but regardless of what the world tells you, you CANNOT enter into the sins of others, of the world and not get burned both now and at judgment day; you CANNOT enter into the sins of others, of the world and be declared righteous. You want to be declared righteous, then if separated or divorced, women return unto thy husbands today and be reconciled unto him, you cannot serve two masters! My wife along with thousands of other wives failed the test, broke covenant and allowed friendship with the world to destroy a twenty-year marriage. She returned to the wilderness, the world of darkness. Our Pastor friends all argued that she was never truly a Christian, just a pretender, because a true believer would not have forsaken God or her husband. God gives us all choices, but there are always consequences. I pray daily for my family and I pray also that God would somehow reach her and bring her back into (into) fellowship with God and I. My dear friends, as a believer you will be tried and tested, persecuted, Matthew 5:10-12, John 15:20. If you aren't, you aren't on the path of righteousness. Whenever there is a period of crisis, the Lord puts us through suffering and distress so that we may call out to Him and get to a higher position with Him, or...we will not get through, but fall away. If we pass, and are strengthened and we will not be so easily snared the next time.

In addition to my wife's sin of divorce, her leaving was a premeditated departure, filled with lies and deceit, and included my innocent children in her scheme. Toward the end of our marriage, even my children were caught lying. Please read Ezekiel 16:44. She ended with the kiss of deception just as Judas did. Her lies 'I love you', kisses, sex, etc., all while her heart was far away in sin. Including my children in her scheme made it all the worse, as children of God; we are never to leave our Father for any reason, much less to serve the world, and false gods.

My dearest sisters, if you ever contemplate a deception such as so many women today do and as my wife did, think again and pray, because God will judge as you compile the sin day by day, for the Bible, God's word, tells us in 1st Corinthians 7:5 *Defraud not one another except it be* (first)***with consent***(second)***for a time*** *that ye may give yourselves to fasting and prayer* (sanctification is three days), *and* (third**) come together again**, *that Satan tempt you not.* I also need to take you back to the Old Testament in the wilderness of Sinai where the first laws were given to us by God. We see in Exodus 23:1-2 *not to raise a false report...Thou shalt not follow a multitude to do evil.* Yet so many people fabricate events or exaggerate them in order to accomplish their evil mission, and many follow the multitude to sin, to do evil... 'everybody else does it so why can't I?' 'My friend...my mother...my...told me to...' If these people told you to jump off the Golden Gate Bridge, would you do it? If these people told you to cook a nice dinner and bake a nice cake for your marriage partner to celebrate the good times (instead of leaving because of a situation), would you do it? So, what makes lying to your marriage partner, the police, the courts...and most of all to God, correct and following the multitude in doing evil? *Come now, let us reason together*, God's precious word tells us. Repent and return to God and His word, His law, and return to your life marriage partner if you are separated or divorced, or if not then renew your relationship with your marriage partner, bring it to a stronger level today.

In Proverbs 27:6 *The kisses of the enemy are deceitful.* Remember that Judas betrayed Jesus with a kiss, and my wife betrayed me with the kiss of deception. In Romans 6:12-13 we read *Let not sin therefore reign in your mortal body, that ye should obey it in the lusts thereof. Neither yield ye your members as instruments of unrighteousness unto sin: but yield yourselves unto God.*

When children are pulled away from their dads, like a believer being pulled away from God, there is a high rate of violent crime, troubled marriages, divorce, alcoholism, drug and tobacco abuse, depression and suicide in our youths. Why? It is because they have literally been pulled away from the lord of the home, whom God gave the authority over these precious gifts. They have literally been pulled away from God and God's plan; their foundations have been shaken and destroyed by the unbelieving spouse. Why does God teach for a woman not to leave her husband, but not for a husband not to leave his wife? Because we as sinners are not to leave God our Father for any reason, much less to serve the world or other gods, but God will never leave us or forsake us, His children, His bride. My dear friends, it is that simple. Even Michal in 2nd Samuel 6:16, David's wife, should have been by David's side, but she wasn't; then when she saw him worshipping God, she despised him, but!!! She didn't leave or divorce him. If you find and truly love your partner, and God, that love that is genuine will never die, it is an endless love, you just need to love, forgive, and hold on, stand by your man or woman. Hold on to thy marriage and to God and get the fires burning once again. Remember gold when mined is worth little, but when it is tried by fire, it becomes beautiful and worth much. Don't allow the trials and tribulations in your lives to destroy you, be what God wants you to be. Look to Him and allow the trials to strengthen you. Don't be as the world wants you to be, but what and who God created and wants you to be.

Furthermore, there are no irreconcilable differences in God's kingdom. If you and your partner can't work out an issue, pray about it and for each other. You both should be praying daily for your marriage and partner anyway! Study God's word together and see what God says about your problem(s), that's why this book in part, to bring God's word to you to build, rebuild, strengthen your marriages and your Christian walk, back to God's word and the path of righteousness; Still no resolution or agreement on an issue? Seek godly counsel; Your Pastor or I, but you must make certain that it is a person of God, and not worldly wisdom givers. Confirm that the counsel is in accordance with God's word and not mans. Then you must humble thyself and accept if you are wrong and seek forgiveness from God and thy partner as well as from yourself. Quite often both partners have created the problem. Both of you must be willing to forgive and be forgiven, just as God forgives us so must we forgive one another. This isn't Pastor John's way; this is God's way! I can tell you that separation and divorce is not God's plan. You wish to be right with God? Then you must be right with the partner that God ordained for you.

1st Peter 5:5-7 tells us that *God resisteth the proud, and giveth grace to the humble. Humble yourselves therefore under the mighty hand of God, that He may exalt you in due time: Casting all your care upon Him; for He careth for you.*

In Ruth 1:17, we see that when you are divorced, and you die and get buried somewhere, thus placing the curse upon thyself for this sin. *Do so to me and more also,* invokes divine punishment with the worst possible consequences if the vow is broken, until death do us part. Then jump back to Ruth 1:14, 15, where we see that divorce takes all your blessings away. A house destroyed by a hurricane must be rebuilt from the foundation up. Sometimes marriage likewise, but...the foundation, if properly laid initially, in Jesus Christ, will still be there. The rebuilding begins with humility, love and forgiveness.

My dear sisters, just as we are to be on our knees before God, our Bridegroom, get on your knees before thy husband, honor him and love him with all your heart. My dear brothers, be worthy of this love and honor, just as God is worthy. Again, though I reiterate, that man is not God, but is a type, a symbol, an example of God.

A song by Rick Wren called 'When Love is Hard, says when love is tried as loved one's change, hold still to hope, though all seems strange, till sane returns and love grows through listening ears and opened eyes. My dear friends remember all of the good things and forget the bad. This sounds impossible, but nothing is impossible with God, only then can you carry on.

Look over into the book of Hosea, a very powerful book, 4:1-2, 6. ...*there is no truth, nor mercy, nor knowledge of God in the land. By swearing and lying, and killing and stealing, and committing adultery, they break out, and blood toucheth blood. My people are destroyed for lack of knowledge: because thou hast rejected knowledge, I will also reject thee... seeing thou hast forgotten the law of thy God, I will also forget thy children.* Oh, my dear friends, you have been given knowledge today, are you listening to what the Spirit is saying? In sickness and in health, in good times and bad, for richer and for poorer, until death do us part; In God there is no death, only everlasting life, joy and peace. Those who choose to be disobedient to Him, divorce Him, shall stand before that great white throne of judgment and be cast into hell, for there is no explanation for disobedience to Him or His law. Men you must do your part as God does His, and women you must do yours. Divorce, see also Leviticus 26:15-31. Your body is the sanctuary. You need to confess and return unto the Lord and to thy husbands.

A beautiful song and biographical movie are Stand by Your Man by Tammy Wynette, which says it all. Sometimes it's hard to be a woman (being a sinner makes our life difficult-men and women), but stand by your man (God and your husband). Her husband became an alcoholic and if I recall correctly, a drug addict, still a singer. He was a wife abuser, but through it all, she kept her faith and stood by him. I'm not saying that marriage is easy, and I am not justifying domestic violence, but neither is the Christian walk easy, however, we must stand by our God. If we can hold on during the trials and tribulations as Tammy did, as Jesus did, why are so many Christians walking away? Marriage and our Christian walk take constant prayer, faith, trust, obedience, submission, surrender, and sacrifice. The rest, leave to God.

God sometimes brings us down to a state of nothing, He drains us, He makes us ever more conscious of our weaknesses and our dependence upon Him. He empties us of self... **self**-importance, **self**-sufficiency, **self**-conscious, self-awareness, self...so that we may be fit for God's calling. We see in Micah 2:9 the world teaches that there are other fish in the sea, but there is nobody that can replace the one that God ordained or anointed for you. God says, *Live joyfully with the wife of thy youth.*

The Bible, God's word says that the fools, lazy, and the cowards will not see heaven. In the book of Proverbs alone the writer speaks of the fool some ninety-eight times. That is how significant this is. Revelation 21:8 *But the fearful, and unbelieving, and the abominable, and murderers, and whoremongers, and sorcerers, and idolaters, and all liars, shall have their part in the lake which burneth with fire and brimstone: which is the second death.* In 1st Corinthians 14:20 we are told *Brethren, be not children in understanding: howbeit in malice be ye children, but in understanding be men.* And in the book of John 15:22 we read *If I had not come and spoken unto them, they had not had sin: but now they have no cloak for their sin.* We must be strong in the strength of the Lord for Revelation 2:10 tells us *Fear none of those things which thou shalt suffer: behold, the devil shall cast some of you into prison, that ye may be tried; and ye shall have tribulation ten days: be thou faithful unto death, and I will give thee a crown of life.* 1st Tim 4:13 *Till I come, give attendance to reading, to exhortation, to doctrine.* Does this sound like it is written to a lazy person? We must not only read but understand and be obedient unto His word, remember the words of Acts 8:30 *And Philip ran thither to him, and heard him read the prophet Esaias, and said,* **Understandest thou what thou readest?** The **coward,** she will not withstand the trials of marriage and will leave. Proverbs 18:2 *A fool hath no delight in understanding, but that his heart may discover itself.* And 19:3 *The foolishness of man perverteth his way: and his heart fretteth against the Lord.* We must leave our foolish ways and return unto the Lord our God. The liars...divorcing thy partner makes you a liar to God, thy partner, and all of the witnesses. If you don't want an eternity in hell separated from our Almighty God, then you need to repent and restore thy marriage.

Every purpose of the Law is destined to prove to man that he is guilty of sin...capital sin. This fact must be kept in mind when we approach any element in the study of the Law; polygamy and divorce are elements of the law. *For whosoever shall keep the whole law, and yet offend in one point, he is guilty of all.* James 2:10 *For as many as are of the works of the law are under the curse; for it is written, cursed is everyone that continueth not in all things which are written in the book of the law, to do them.* Galatians 3:10

To the non-Jew (the unbeliever) the Decalogue is the Law (the Ten Commandments), but to the Jew (the believer) the entire revelation of God is the Law. The problem is compounded because the church as a whole regarding marriage has embraced the Gentile governments dictates of marriage-law. The state propagates laws regulating marriage, and the church foolishly over-embraces those laws. This creates a problem. The problem is that the church because of their belief in and embracement of governmental marriage laws is failing to regulate marriage according to the dictates of the God of all creation. Regarding marriage, believers often see the state and the church as the same law-giver.

Look at Judas, one of the twelve closest to Christ, who Christ served, taught, washed his feet, and provided for, those three years; But in the end and with a kiss, led Christ to His killers. I provided and loved, cared so much for my family. This man I spoke of earlier and myself helped save the life of our wives and sons, we taught our wives scripture, the law and love of the Lord, but...in the end and with the kiss of deception, they hardened her heart, refused to listen to God, her parents or I; she betrayed with the kiss and left. She never even allowed me to say goodbye or kiss my children goodbye as we also see in Genesis 31:28. It is painful to write this chapter because of what she did, and too many others are doing today. Divorce shouldn't even be in the vocabulary of the true believer. When my wife left, she took little, not even my children's eyeglasses, but she took my Bible, given unto me by my grandparents the day that I was baptized! This was not the work of my wife but the work of Satan for why would an unbeliever need the Bible? Satan took my Bible, he took my family, but I the next day went and purchased another, for nothing can keep me from God and His word. She took my Bible. Dear friends, there is a big difference between knowing about God (by reading the Bible), and knowing God, bringing the true and living God to life in your life, and begin living for Him. Let Him, not the people of this world, be your guide. It is my prayer that after reading and hearing this message that you will never be the same again. That this message, so powerful from the Holy Spirit, will bring you to repentance and revival in your personal life, your marriage/family, and in your Christian walk, that Jesus Christ will be brought to life and that you will surrender **ALL** unto Him, and allow Him to be the Lord of your life; for only then will you truly begin to live and experience the joy that He desires for you. When you live for Him, it's a wonderful life, but never easy. Too many people wander throughout their lives, but never begin to live, so sad. At the end my wife destroyed my doctoral dissertation that I had been working on, but again, Satan seeks to destroy, but God makes a way for His plan to be accomplished, especially for those who choose to love and follow Him, and surrender all. He took me a different road after the dissertation was destroyed, and here I stand today with my Doctorate, and was taken abroad and used in such a mighty way for Him, in ways far beyond my imagination before my wife left, but that is another story, partially covered in my book '**ONLY BELIEVE**', Again even though she was and is in sin leaving me, she made her choice, but God didn't leave me while she left, He remained faithful and by my side, Hallelujah. I always wished that they were by my side also, to encourage and assist me, as well as to see God at work, but... God gave her the choice. Look at Genesis 50:20 *Ye thought evil against me; but God meant it unto good.* I lost ALL of my property valued at over one million dollars and possessions, some of which are irreplaceable, the point being that the past is gone, look forward and see what God will do. I pray for them daily, but I also praise God that I had the strength (through Him) to hold on to Him and not make the bad choices like she did. I survived the heart attack, my heart actually stopped and I had to be resuscitated, while my wife apparently told my children that it was a suicide attempt, but God allowed me to live and used me in such a special way and though I hurt from her decision, I rejoice that I am God's child and He is such a wonderful Father to me. I pray my wife and children will contact me, and /or return for their leaving never stopped my love for them. God gives us choices- she chose the world. I am lonely and miss having her by my side to talk to, share with. I have had other offers and have simply told them that I am married. The love is not gone but her choice to love the world is stronger than her love for God and her husband. God used this to free me for His service but the demons of the evils of the world, the sins of lies, betrayal, broken vows, deception, were introduced into her through her friends. Looking back, I could see the ugliness of sin, but love is blind. Look at Judges 16:15-17 *And she said unto him, How canst thou say, I love thee, when thine heart is not with me? Thou hast mocked me these three times, and hast not told me wherein thy great strength lieth. And it came to pass, when she pressed him daily with her words, and urged him, so that his soul was vexed unto death; that he told her all of his heart...* Then you know the rest or can read on in this chapter of Judges. When you love someone, you tend to see the good and don't look at the bad; only in the absence of love does the ugliness show its colors. God causes all things to work together for good to those who love Him Romans

8:28, Romans 13:10, 1ˢᵗ John 4:7. And while you forgive and anger dissolves before the sun sets, the pain is long lasting and your forgiveness does not absolve that person of their sin. The daily breaking of that vow before God, until they return to their ordained partner, they remain in sin. I have been asked by many, how can you honestly forgive such behavior? The answer my dear friends, is simple. First, we must never forget what sinners we all are, what we did to Jesus Christ, yet He still loves and forgives us. Even while suffering on that cross, Jesus cried out to our Father, God, *Father forgive them, for they know not what they do,* Luke 23:34. We must likewise forgive if we truly desire to be Christ-like. Secondly, this wasn't my wife's doing, but Satan. The choice of my wife was of Satan over God, just as Eve did, but Eve stayed with Adam! My wife did what her 'friends' told her to do, she didn't know to do all that she did; it was Satan through her 'friends'. My wife is still my wife, just as yours is. I've likewise been asked if I would take her back, and again the answer is simple. If she repented, humbled herself and returned to me, I would welcome her back with open arms and celebration, just as God welcomes us back though we are sinners. Look at Matthew 6:12, and just because she left, my love for her didn't. Women need to humble themselves, repent, and return, restore the marriage, but men, just as God receives us, His bride back if we repent turn from our wicked ways and return receives us back into His family, so must we humble ourselves and receive our wives back if they repent, turn from their wicked ways and return. No matter how much she has hurt you and/or you have hurt her, she has humbled herself and returned to thy marriage and we, my brothers need to find the grace and mercy of our Lord, just as He does for us, and welcome her back into the family. This is a humbling thought isn't it my dear brothers?

She listened to her friends, but after they destroyed, where are they? We see in the book of Lamentations 1:2 *She weepeth sore in the night, and has tears on her cheeks; among all her lovers she hath none to comfort her: all her friends have dealt treacherously with her, they are become her enemies.* We are told in Isaiah 47:10-13 *For thou hast trusted in thy wickedness: thou hast said, None seeth me. Thy wisdom and thy knowledge, it hath perverted thee; and thou hast said in thine heart, I am, and none else beside me. Therefore shall evil come upon thee; thou shalt not know from whence it riseth: and mischief shall fall upon thee; thou shalt not be able to put it off: and desolation shall come upon thee suddenly, which thou shalt not know. Stand now with thine enchantments, and with the multitude of thy sorceries, wherein thou hast laboured from thy youth; if so be thou shalt be able to profit, if so be thou mayest prevail. Thou art wearied in the multitude of thy counsels. Let now the astrologers, the stargazers, the monthly prognosticators, stand up, and save thee from these things that shall come upon thee.*

Anger, is it a sin? Don't allow the sun to set on your anger. Ephesians 5:26 tells us, *Be angry, and sin not: let not the sun go down upon your wrath.* When you awaken in the morning, praise God together! Yesterday is gone, leave it behind. Today is a new day with fresh blessings, all of which are lost if you awaken with thy anger and resentments. In other words, forgive. Did God get angry? Yes! And He destroyed all living things except an ark full of animals and a few people who God found to be righteous.

Did Jesus get angry? Yes! and twice He overturned the moneychanger's tables and chased them out of the temple. Did God or Jesus sin? No, never my dear friends, did Jesus ever sin. Anger is not a sin but a natural reaction to hurt. What you do with that anger is what may become sin.

As we already briefly discussed the devastating effects, consequences of divorce on children. I have held on to my vows, as I consider marriage sacred. The time that we were together was very special, we had many good times. Before she left, she used me through deception and lies, to obtain her U.S. citizenship by fraud and deception. She used me to get her dentures, dental and eye care at my expense under false pretense, in preparation for her premeditated sin. Oh, dear friends, how crafty and evil the enemy is. We cannot rest; we must always be on our guard every minute of every day, and fight the enemy with the power of God. We who truly believe are never alone, God along with His legions of angels are with us, Hallelujah.

Turn with me quickly to Isaiah 2:12. *For the day of the Lord* (the time of God's judgment) *of hosts shall be upon every one that is proud and lofty, and upon every one that is lifted up; and he shall be brought low.* My dear friends, it all begins with humbling ourselves, go back and review 2nd Chronicles 7:14, it all begins with humility.

How does God feel? This message is from Him. Look at Isaiah 1:2-6. *Hear, O heavens, and give ear, o earth: for the Lord hath spoken, I have nourished and brought up children, and they have rebelled against me. The ox knoweth his owner and the ass his master's crib: but Israel* (the believers) *doeth not know, my people doth not consider. Ah sinful nation, a people laden with iniquity, a seed of evildoers, children that are corrupters: they are gone away backward. Why should ye be stricken anymore? Ye will revolt more and more: the whole head is sick, and the whole heart faint. For the sole of the foot even unto the head there is no soundness in it; but wounds, and bruises, and putrefying sores: they have not been closed, neither bound up...* Oh dear brothers and sisters, can't you just hear the pain in His voice as He cries out these heartfelt words, to the people today, for the condition has not changed. Hearts are still hardened; people have fallen way down off of the path of righteousness. I feel His pain as I write these words, for it happened in my family, just as it is in God's family, but you can make a change, a difference, and I will tell you how shortly, but for now, I will say repentance and restoration, only then can there be a revival in our lives, our marriages, our churches and our communities.

The cause of marital discord and divorce is simply a separation, from (divorcing) Christ. If both partners will hold on to Christ, all will be well, and nothing can separate you. If you return unto thy partner, then Christ will accept you back, hear your prayers and forgive your sin, but if you choose not to return unto thy partner, then there is likewise eternal separation from God!

What should be the role of the church? The church has some very crucial roles to play here.

- First is preparation for dating for young people.

- Secondly, good Bible based premarital counseling.

- Third, Good Bible based marriage classes and support groups for the married couples,

- Fourth is programs for support of broken families and <u>victims</u> of divorce, NOT for the ones who effect the divorce as they are in violation of God's plan and have broken their vows to their partner AND to God. The church should do everything possible to restore the marriage, rekindle the fire to prevent divorce. These programs MUST be led by a Christian who is fully knowledgeable about the biblical precepts of marriage as is outlined in this critical message **BECOMING ONE.**

  - playing an active role Sin teaching God's love, mercy, grace and forgiveness,

  - What marriage is really all about, which is why this message.

  - The church should NEVER be found encouraging or aiding in any way, a married person who has left their God ordained partner and broken her (unbeliever) vows. They should be admonished in the Lord to return to their partner and honor their sacred vows, and to love, honor, and cherish their God ordained partner.

  - The church may and should offer any assistance to the victim be it man or woman, as necessary when their partner walks out.

  - Godly counseling, encouragement, and any physical assistance as is needed.

○ The exception is in the case of abuse, then both need extensive biblical counseling to resolve the issue, then they should restore their marriage and come together again.

The church today needs to:

- The deacons/elders of the church should approach any divorced or separated male pastor who has been the instigator of the separation and advise him of these precepts and to return unto his wife. If he refuses, the congregation should be advised and they all should find another church, If he returns to his wife, then the congregation should forgive him, this is the biblical way.

- If there is a female leader, then again, she should be addressed by the deacon's/elders about the biblical precepts of women's role in the church and community, and if she steps down, forgive her, if not, again the Deacons/Elders should address the congregation and they should find another church. This is what the Bible teaches very clearly.

- Return to the precepts of God and His word, and teach them.

- NEVER suggest, encourage, advocate, support, or assist in any divorce or separation of a married couple except- Encourage and promote the divorce from any 2nd or subsequent marriages so that they may return to their first love.

- Disfellowship any woman who is divorced or separated refusing to return to her first husband; and any man who refuses to accept her back with the love of God.

- Not perform remarriages to divorced individuals, either or both having been previously divorced should not be remarried.

- Not accept into the fellowship, and disfellowship any existing single mothers or dads, who effected the separation or divorce, thus discouraging unmarried people from engaging in sexual affairs, guilty of adultery or fornication, bringing those guilty unto repentance.

- Participate in better and Bible based, Christ centered premarital counseling,

- Be available twenty-four hours a day, seven days a week.to mentor, assist, encourage, and counsel young married couples. Christianity and the true Pastoral calling, is not a nine to five job, but an always available for the Lord job! Being a true Pastor is not meant to be easy work.

Women, if you want to do what's right in God's eyes, what's best for your children and yourself, don't ever leave thy husband, but stand by your man! Demonstrate to thy children God's love, mercy and grace by how they see you treat thy husband. Pray for him, but leaving him is sin. It violates all of God's precepts and all of His teaching by word and by His example of love, and...He hates divorce! Men, demonstrate to thy children God's love, mercy and grace. Everyone gets hurt because it is of Satan who seeks only to destroy. God's plan is till death do us part. Allow me to tell you something else. You went to court and received a divorce certificate? So what? It means absolutely nothing to God. Once the vow has been made, even before the marriage has been consummated, it is until death do us part, no exceptions, no man can separate, so if you are holding such a certificate, be ashamed, be convicted, return to your love, your God ordained life partner, and fulfill thy vows until death do us part. I must also say that the believer should never sign the certificate. It is one thing to let the unbeliever depart, but quite another to agree with it (by signing the certificate) Rejoice and be glad. If you read in Isaiah 1:27-31, God promises redemption for those who return and repent. Zion, His bride, but destruction for them that stay away! The world takes divorce so lightly, but God is dead serious about it, and so should we be if we are to be called Christians, Christ-like. Shame and curses upon divorce attorneys and judges who separate husband and wives in violation of God's law, especially those calling themselves Christian!

I must include the children in the marriage and divorce picture. What is the bottom line of the divorce controversy? Is it not the children; the orphans of divorced-broken families. Don't these orphans have any rights? Well, Jesus said that they sure do have rights. Suffer little children, and forbid them not, to come unto me: for of such is the kingdom of heaven. And he laid his hands on them, and departed thence. Yes, He laid his hand on them. He touched them. Marriages are to be built on Christ. What God hath joined together. The most powerful evangelistic tool in the hand of God is a truly saved mama and papa. The heart of a true believing parent prays fervently for their child; presenting the Gospel with great care so as to ensure that their child truly gets every opportunity to get saved; to have his or her own experience of repentance and faith in the Lord Jesus Christ. This is difficult to provide to the child of a broken family. In the dedication of this book, you will read that I have honored the faithful spouse who is awaiting the return of a departed sinful spouse; in all actuality dying for the beloved departed one. I believe that is what it means to give your life for your wife, to wear yourself out till death, if necessary, for your departed spouse. These faithful men and women are offering the grace of God to their unfaithful and abusive mates to the Glory of God, waiting lovingly for their reconciliation in this lifetime if possible. The second person I honored are the children of divorce. especially that little daughter, or son who wish they could live with their biological father and mother and have all their love, not be limited to only one parent or; not being required to share it with alien children or an alien parent. These children should also have rights.

You can be assured dear believer, as God said in Malachi 2:16 that, *I hate putting away* be assured that Christ will never divorce me, and he will never divorce you. Jesus just does not teach divorce nor does He believe in divorce; to Him it is a mere imagination, and the invention of the prince of darkness, the devil. But Christ is the Prince of Light and He has faithfully promised each believer an eternal union with God the Father through Him and this union is indissoluble and eternally permanent. If we are to be Christ-like, Christians, we cannot put away what God hath ordained for us, and united us as one with.

Consider the possibility of the judgment of western civilization, likened to the judgment of the flood and Sodom; and the violence of measure today would be man's violent treatment of God's ordained command regarding marriage as He created it, then as we look about our once 'Christian America', especially the 'Bible believing church', as well as the other Christian countries of the West, the state of the marriage is quickly collapsing, thus we can say the next day of judgment draweth nigh. Yes, as mentioned in the Introduction of this book, the fate of marriage and perhaps the fate of mankind may depend on your interpretation of those five words: *except it be for fornication.*

The consequences of rampant divorce and remarriage are not only dissolution and destruction of the family, which are especially harmful to the children, but this has also opened the door to denial of scripture in other important areas.

Malachi 2:11 *Judah hath dealt treacherously, and an abomination is committed in Israel and in Jerusalem; for Judah hath profaned the holiness of the Lord which he loved, and hath married the daughter of a strange god.* It is important to realize that holy means to be sanctified or set apart, and as believers, we are to be set apart (sanctified) and are instructed to act accordingly. In Malachi 2:13 we again see *And this have ye done again, covering the altar of the Lord with tears, with weeping, and with crying out, insomuch that he regardeth not the offering any more, or receiveth it with good will at your hand.*

We have eternal life, eternal security, in Christ IF we truly accept Him and will forsake the ways and things of the world, pick up the cross and follow Him, *For God so loved the world that he gave his only begotten son, that whosoever believeth in him should not perish but have everlasting life; For he that believeth on the Son hath everlasting life; He that hath the Son hath life. My sheep hear my voice, and I know them, and they follow me: And I give unto them eternal life; and they shall never perish, neither shall any man pluck them out of my hand. My Father, which gave them me, is greater than all; and no man is able to pluck them out of my Father's hand. I and my Father are one.* The great mystery of being one with Christ is salvation. Oh, how great our salvation! Our heavenly marriage to Christ is everlasting. And dear born-again reader, if you in some way believe that you have departed from Christ and his doctrine, be assured that if you repent and return to Him, He will receive you with open arms for Jesus said, come unto me, all ye that labor and are heavy laden, and I will give you rest. He is a faithful husband that is still waiting by homes door since the day you left him. He is ready to receive you back into his arms. And my dear friends if you have never found repentance and faith unto eternal life, I invite you today to turn from sin to God and come unto Jesus the only true God and Savior and believe in Him for your salvation which he purchased with His own precious blood on the old rugged cross. *I Jesus have sent mine angel to testify unto you these things in the churches. I am the root and the offspring of David, and the bright and morning star. And the Spirit and the bride say, Come. And let him that heareth say, Come. And let him that is athirst come. And whosoever will, let him take the water of life freely,* Revelation 22:16-17. Jesus promises you eternal life, that is absolute everlasting life, and Jesus is not a liar, His word is sure and everlasting; heaven and earth shall pass away but His word endureth forever, and so will you if you trust in Him. He will never divorce you, for that, I am sure.

The sinning partner must be offered salvation; the fornicator of 1st Corinthians Chapter 5 eventually repented and was received back into the church of Corinth we see in 2nd Corinthians chapter 2. Marriage is an illustration of our salvation. Salvation is permanent, and for that reason marriage is permanent. One cannot divorce Christ; so, divorce does not fit into the Christian married person's life. Furthermore, the concept of the abomination has been overruled to the permanent believer since Jehovah God himself told His sinning wife Israel to return to Him, Jeremiah3:1. The reason God could justly take Israel back as His wife in purity was only because God never endorsed, and never will endorse divorce. The divorce that Israel experienced was only an illustration. God hateth putting away, He hateth divorce. God is a God of love. Marriage as God created it is a type or illustration of Salvation, it speaks of eternal life with eternal security; *For by grace are ye saved through faith; and that not of yourselves: it is the gift of God,* Ephesians 2:8.

Paul gives the approval of remarriage after the death of a partner. Here he appropriately chooses the death of the husband. It seems that antiquity even declares that women outlived the men. Consequently, the church as a social unit had to manage widows, to which the New Testament confirms.

Another principal teaching in the marriage doctrine of the church is that marriage like other partnerships is to be between two believers. A partnership between a believer and an unbeliever is *unequal*. We are so instructed in 2nd Corinthians 6:14 *Be ye not unequally yoked together with unbelievers: for what fellowship hath righteousness with unrighteousness? and what communion hath light with darkness?*

In the first few chapters of Ephesians Paul strives to explain the position of the believer specifically using the terms *in* Christ. Paul adamantly states that the believer is in the box of marriage forever, literally in heavenly places in Christ. Permanently. This is an extremely important theological truth. This is the doctrine of grace. To be one with Christ is to be in the box. Ephesians 1:22, 23 *And hath put all things under his feet, and gave him to be the head over all things to the church, Which is his body, the fullness of him that filleth all in all.* The believer joined in one (married) to Christ is the Church, His body.

So, **the solution to any marital problem can only be solved with true repentance, forgiveness, and reconciliation**. *But if the unbelieving departs, let him depart. A brother or a sister is not under bondage in such cases: but God hath called us to peace. For what knowest thou, O wife, whether thou shalt save thy husband? or how knowest thou, O man, whether thou shalt save thy wife?* If an innocent spouse denies their partner the opportunity of repentance with full marital reconciliation, then the analogy of the church and marriage has failed. The greatest sin in the discussion of marriage is actually caused by the false teachers, pastors, who are leading millions into darkness and the apostasy. Allow me to explain. When a pastor counsels a person away from the permanency of marriage and teaches that their marriage can be put asunder, for what he decides is a legitimate reason, and approves remarriage he is leading that person into apostasy. Any act of sexual intercourse for a married person with someone other than their living spouse is adultery. Divorce in other words for a married couple is impossible. By advising toward divorce with remarriage the false teacher is leading his listeners into apostasy, the falling away from the truth. The Scriptures clearly declare that the latter-day apostasy will be marked by people who divorce -covenant breakers, trucebreakers, *Without natural affection, trucebreakers, false accusers, incontinent, fierce, despisers of those that are good, given to marital divorce,* 2nd Timothy 3:3. So, these false teachers enter the world of apostates themselves. I constantly pray for my wife to receive the salvation that only Christ can offer and for restoration of our marriage, but I leave it to my Almighty God. Worse yet is when they divorce and remarry themselves setting an example for others to follow... down the path leading to destruction!

They take a clean holy vessel, a spouse who never committed physical adultery, and have led that spouse directly into an adulterous situation and have accomplished even a greater feat in that they have called the unholy act of adultery, holy matrimony.

The word for divorcement is apostation. The writing of divorcement can thus be referred to as a writing of apostasy or renunciation of faith: the abandonment or rejection, denial of a religious or political belief or allegiance, and what is renunciation but the denial or rejection, a denial or rejection of something or somebody, usually for moral or religious reasons.

We bring you now to 1st Peter 2:18-25, which again may be applied to the relationship of a husband and wife, showing the submissiveness required by the wife (us sinners) towards her (our) husband. In verse 25 we see once again the call to return and restore.

Salvation assures sinners that by repentance and faith they are saved; Ephesians 2:8-9 tells us *For by grace are ye saved through faith; and that not of yourselves: it is the gift of God: Not of works, lest any man should boast.* The false teacher's doctrine slaps 'by grace' in the face. By teaching holy adultery, they have created an act whereby the sinner is at liberty to willfully sin and live comfortably, especially in the church, with a mind whereby they believe that they are righteous. This is a grave insult to the Gospel of Jesus Christ by excluding the sin of adulterous remarriage from the act of repentance. Now the sinner cannot be forgiven because they do not know they are living in sin. And if the innocent remarries, he closes the door for the sinner to repent and restoration of the marriage, which God ordained. It is the same as teaching a homosexual that he or she has been born as such. This is an abomination and apostasy for certain. *Woe unto them that call evil good, and good evil; that put darkness for light, and light for darkness; that put bitter for sweet, and sweet for bitter!* Isaiah 5:20. Ephesians 5:26,27 continues *That he might sanctify and cleanse it with the washing of water by the word, That he might present it to himself a glorious church, not having spot, or wrinkle, or any such thing; but that it should be holy and without blemish.*

My dear friends, the Bible is not just a history book, it is just as practical for us today as it was for those people to whom it was first written, and will be until the end of time. Times change, but people don't, and neither does God's word!

REMARRIAGE AFTER DIVORCE

So what about remarriage? Many people have asked me, and I asked my Lord this question as the one verse that stood out in my mind was 1ˢᵗ Corinthians 7:15 *But if the unbelieving depart, let him depart. A brother or a sister is not under bondage in such cases: but God hath called us to peace.* He answered me and now I see that the Bible is clear that the unbeliever, the one who leaves a marriage (the unbeliever), is not to remarry. In Mark 10:11 we are told, If you put away a spouse and marry another, you commit adultery and polygamy. If your partner dies, not because you killed them, then you may remarry a believer. But... what about the believer who is left after a divorce? God in reality doesn't recognize a divorce so remarriage would constitute polygamy under normal circumstances.

Often Christians will endeavor to vigorously defend their marital position by justifying their remarrying whilst their previous partner is still alive. To do this they will use Scriptural references that often center on God's mercy and forgiveness. They will say something like When I confessed my sin, God's mercy was extended to me and it is forgiven and I am covered under the Blood. I am now a new creature in Christ Jesus. To this we would add: If we want to stay under the grace of God and thereby enjoy the mercy of God, we need to be balancing mercy with truth, like two oars of a boat. Proverbs 3:3 says *Let not mercy and truth forsake thee: bind them about thy neck; write them upon the table of thine heart.* Using God's mercy to cover our willful disobedience to God's word is only presuming upon the Grace of God. Paul challenges the Christians at Rome with this thought-provoking question: *What shall we say then? Shall we continue in sin, that grace may abound? God forbid. How shall we, that are dead to sin, live any longer therein?* Romans 6:1, 2. We must never substitute a prayer of justification for an act of obedience. As people say today, two wrongs don't make a right. Always make your commitment because it is right, not because it is easy! Deuteronomy 23:21-23 God views all vows (including our marriage vows) in a very serious light. They must be kept at all times. Numbers 30:2-4, Ecclesiastes 5:1-6, Romans 7: 1-4 a husband and wife are bound by a covenant commitment to marriage. Deuteronomy 23:21-23 God views all vows including our marriage vows very seriously.

Initially, I saw no clear-cut answers to the issue of remarriage for the believer, so I prayed and searched His word for the answer. Then once again God poured His heart out to me. In fact, even in the case of 1st Corinthians 7:15, the later Catholics interpreted to permit a believer deserted by an unbeliever to remarry, but Jesus and the early church fathers said that the deserted Christian had no right to remarry.

In Deuteronomy 24:4 the man could not marry a former divorced wife who had been another man's after he put her away. *Her former husband, which sent her away, may not take her again to be his wife, after that she is defiled; for that is abomination before the Lord: and thou shalt not cause the land to sin, which the Lord thy God giveth thee for an inheritance.* However, she was permitted to marry another by Mosaic Law but not by God's law.

You see blessings from the offspring of Leah (Caleb), because she was the first wife...He who leaves his wife (or vice versa), and marries another commits adultery; supportive of once saved, always saved, once married, always married. Your vows are more than just for good times, for wealth and health. No, but rather in sickness and in health, for richer or poorer, in good times and the bad...until death do us part. True love, God's love can take you through the toughest of times.

Sin separates us from God, sin separates husbands and wives, sin separates children from parents. God however is willing to forgive and welcome us, His bride back, **IF** we will humble ourselves and pray, repent and seek His face, and turn from our wicked ways, the evil and sinful ways of the world. Separate yourself from the world, not from God's gift to you, your ordained and anointed partner. Then we must look at Deuteronomy 24:1-2 here which tells us, *When a man hath taken a wife, and married her, and it come to pass that she find no favor in his eyes, because he hath found some unclean-ness in her: then let him write her a bill of divorcement, and give it in her hand, and send her out of his house. And when she is departed out of his house, she may go and be another man's wife.* This is not God but man authorizing divorce for God hates and does not recognize divorce in any way or at any time. God will never leave or forsake you, so, the next time that you ask 'where are you God?' ask yourself 'where am I, why aren't I by His side?'

For the Law (of divorce) was given by Moses, but grace and truth (the permanency of marriage) came by Jesus Christ, John.1:17. The day of grace and the truth would be radically different from the age of law. It has a superior Priest, and a superior doctrine.

The wives are to keep submitting themselves to their own husbands in the Lord. Genesis 3:16, *Unto the woman he said, I will greatly multiply thy sorrow and thy conception; in sorrow thou shalt bring forth children; and thy desire shall be to thy husband, and he shall rule over thee.* Stating that Paul is only applying the doctrine of the marriage of Genesis to having the husband rule and administer the home but God has a purpose for the man and the woman and this is God's will for the wife. In a godly manner, the wife is to submit to the husband as she submits to the Lord. This must be a voluntary submission in that as the Lord loves her and she submits to His care for her, the wife is commanded to submit to her husband who cares for her. Paul then goes on to say in Ephesians 5:23, 24 *For the husband is the head of the wife, even as Christ is the head of the church: and he is the savior of the body. Therefore, as the church is subject unto Christ, so let the wives be to their own husbands in everything.* That the husband is the Head of the wife, even as Christ is the head of the church. In Ephesians 5:22-23, There is no latitude granted to either mate to view themselves as separated or divorced because that is hating rather than nourishing and cherishing one's own flesh. Divorce must be considered unthinkable behavior within the body of Christ.

This can be supported by 1st Corinthians 11:3, *But I would have you know, that the head of every man is Christ; and the head of the woman is the man; and the head of Christ is God.* Christ to the church is Savior. The church submits to her Savior, because a woman's husband is to be her savior-type here on the earth, she must need to submit unto him.

As Christ hung on a bloody cross and died, dying for his beloved wife, the church, every husband is commanded to submit to God and to love his wife as Christ loved the church and if need be, be ready to give himself in death for her. This is the matchless definition of love. Now dear reader it also means that the forsaken believing spouse must wear themselves out till death, if necessary, waiting for their departed loved one to return. This is biting the real bullet of death for your beloved spouse. Oh, so great love as He loved us; this is the actual matchless grace of God. What a wonderful testimony of a believing spouse and what a sacrifice!

The analogy that God makes between marriage and the church dictates that, as salvation is permanent and sure, so marriage is to be permanent and sure. Therefore, the preacher who promotes the doctrine of divorce is at the very same time teaching that a believer can lose his salvation; thus, teaching that Christ will divorce the believer if He so wishes. That is a false doctrine. The primary problem with the one who teaches that salvation can be lost is that at the same time he is confessing to the doctrine that a man can gain or work for his salvation. By teaching that salvation is gained by man and his works, that same one must teach that it can be lost by man as well. This is the false doctrine of works.

Therefore, marriage is binding even in the event of adultery. Remember that Jesus took on the church while we were yet sinners, and reconciled us while we were enemies. **Love is at heart of the matter.** One does not fall into or out of Love, for love is a choice. Remember Christ called us to love our neighbor and who is our neighbor, but everyone, even our enemies! Therefore, you should always choose to love the partner which God hath ordained for you in the union of marriage the innocent partner must provide the way for the adulterer, or any other marriage breaking sin of the partner, and permit the door of repentance to remain open as the way for the departed unbelieving spouse to return to full marital union. Thus, marriage is as I have been saying, a picture of salvation.

The only time that God's offer of salvation is removed from the spouse, *for God so loved the world that He gave His only begotten Son that whosoever believeth in Him should not perish but have everlasting life,* John 3:16; is when the spouse is dead. Jesus by equating His marriage with His church to human marriage declares that marriage on the earth is eternal, eternal as a measure of the time one lives on the earth. And that since a man establishes his salvation by faith, without the deeds of the flesh, and then the door and way of faith in the marriage of earthly married couples must be kept open for their guilty partner during their lifetime. To believe in divorce is to believe in works to acquire salvation. By divorcing a spouse, you are saying that the failed spouse lost the salvation of the marriage, and is to be accursed. This concept terribly fails to meet the analogy of marriage that God teaches us in Ephesians 5.

On the other side of the coin here is that if the innocent (believer) spouse sues for divorce, they deny the partner the promise of full marital reconciliation upon repentance. It's as if that person is denying salvation to the guilty unbelieving partner, since marriage is a picture of salvation. The most degrading event occurs when the partner sues by the false doctrine of divorce and then the partner remarries under the law of man.

RETURNING TO THE PATH OF RIGHTEOUSNESS

Many, perhaps most people later regret choices that they have made. Many live with the shipwrecked lives from wrong choices that they have made long ago. Praise God that there is forgiveness. There can be redemption, revival, and healing, even for the worst of decisions, including in marriages.

1st John 2:15 Friendship with the world brings divisions in the churches as well as divisions within marriage. One must be wholly committed unto God and thy partner.

Remember that God says in His word, Matthew 10:22 *he who endureth unto the end shall be saved.* Do you wish to be saved? Do you wish your marriage to be saved? Then in James 1:12 *Blessed is the man who endureth temptation.* Don't allow Satan in to tempt you. Marriage is a vow, a covenant promise to thy partner and to God. Don't ever allow thyself to be tempted and don't allow anyone around you to tempt you to leave thy life partner. Satan seeks to destroy, but God gives you free choice, obedience to Him or to the enemy, the great deceiver; you cannot serve two masters.

The Love of God is best expressed in forgiveness of others. Scripture repeatedly states that God considers the absence of forgiveness on our part an unforgivable sin. Jesus said in Matt 6:14-15, *FOR IF YE FORGIVE MEN THEIR TRESPASSES, YOUR HEAVENLY FATHER WILL ALSO FORGIVE YOU: BUT IF YE FORGIVE NOT MEN THEIR TRESPASSES, NEITHER WILL YOUR FATHER FORGIVE YOUR TRESPASSES.* Jesus gave many examples of forgiveness of thy enemies. In fact, there is no better example of this than when Jesus included all possible enemies and acquaintances, as illustrated by His forgiveness on the cross for all of mankind. About what kinds of hateful actions that should be forgiven, He specified everything from stealing, beating, lying, adultery, murder, and everything in between.

In regards to the number of times one must forgive others, he indicated that the obligation to unconditionally forgive has no end, seventy times seven equals infinity in the scriptures. Does Jesus count our sins and when you reached the limit, say no more? Absolutely not, He said seventy times seven! Jesus placed no criteria required to enable forgiveness, He gave none, except the one single condition, that there be an offence, whether repented of or not. So as Christians we are required by God to go forth and to set a standard of forgiveness for the betrayal by a husband or wife. When we truly forgive, we let the power of the Holy Spirit flow through us to the ones who need it the most, the fallen. What's the alternative? hardhearted wickedness and entering eternity unforgiven, just as we have been unforgiven. In John 8:7, Jesus told the men who wanted to stone the adulterous woman He that is without sin among you, let him first cast a stone at her. And again, Jesus said in Luke 6:41-42, *And why beholdest thou the mote that is in thy brother's eye, but perceivest not the beam that is in thine own eye? Either how canst thou say to thy brother,*

Brother, let me pull out the mote that is in thine eye, when thou thyself beholdest not the beam that is in thine own eye? Thou hypocrite, cast out first the beam out of thine own eye, and then shalt thou see clearly to pull out the mote that is in thy brother's eye.

We all have heard the stories of dogs going great distances to find their masters. When a dog is left behind, his natural instinct is to seek her master no matter how long or difficult the road for they know not the distance. No matter how rough or rocky, rain or sunshine, they will keep on going. There would be no giving up until death, no matter how tired or weary, hungry or thirsty they become. They would get water from a puddle or fresh mountain stream. They would take whatever scraps of food that they could find to keep going. No matter how hot or cold, with the help of God, they will return to the master. Marriage and separation (divorce) should be the same way. God brought the two of you together, take whatever scraps you can get and appreciate them, and feed the fire. Remember that if a fire is not fed it burns out, but if you feed it, the fires grows and you can sit back and enjoy its glow and heat as long as you keep feeding it. The dog will one day be welcomed home and rest by their master's side and all will be forgiven and life goes on. The fire will burn once again.

Go back in time to the believer who is left after a divorce. Take a look at Nehemiah 9:28; which tells us that a woman is not to return to her husband if they have separated and she has had another man, but...God in His infinite mercy, accepts us back even though we commit spiritual adultery. One must not take this as a license to sin however, for we know not the day nor the hour in which we shall be taken from this life, and we must always be ready, lest the Day of Judgment catch us unaware or unprepared.

If you look at Ezra 10:2-3 we see *And Shechaniah the son of Jehiel, one of the sons of Elam, answered and said unto Ezra, We have trespassed against our God, and have taken strange wives of the people of the land: yet now there is hope in Israel concerning this thing. Now therefore let us make a covenant with our God to put away all the wives, and such as*

*are born of them, according to the counsel of my Lord, and of
those that tremble at the commandment of our God; and let
it be done according to the law.*

God gave man a helpmate just as we are to be His helpmates. When a wife leaves, oh the pain!!! So, I can feel a little
of the pain of God when any of parts of His bride leave Him
for the world. I know the agony of how God's heart must be
shredded in agony seeing His bride, His children leaving for
and wandering aimlessly in the world.

When the Jews left God, He took in the gentiles, in essence,
He allowed those who rejected, turned away from Him, to go,
and He betrothed those who would accept Him. This message
is reinforced in the Parable of Jesus Christ in the marriage
supper found in Matthew 22:1-14. See also Isaiah 50:1 and
Deuteronomy 24:4. Mind you that at this time the church (His
bride) is composed of the truly spiritual believers. Christ is
betrothed to His bride (the true church), the wedding will take
place at the wedding supper in the end of time as we know it.

My dear brothers and sisters, I have cheated death more
than ten times in my life, pronounced dead for several hours on
three occasions, and have been told that I should be dead now,
but God has plans for my life, He isn't finished with me yet, for
me to serve Him and get the powerful message of repentance
and revival out to the world.

I told my wife how wrong her actions were, but forgave
her, and then God gave me this message reinforcing it. God
allowed her to make her choice; the problem was that her faith
and trust in my Almighty God wasn't strong enough to stand
up to the weeds, the tares of this world. It is my prayer that
she will find a copy of this message for I know not where she
(they) is, and that she will read it and be convicted, humble
herself, repent, and seek my face that we may be restored, and
that you also may repent and restore your relationships or that
your marriages will be strengthened through this message. It
is my prayer to see marriages restored and that my wife also
shall humble herself and return because I love her, because of
her vow for her sake spiritually, and because of what a testimony for God this would be. She kept asking me Why do you

have to be so different? Why can't you be like everyone else? I praise the Living God that I didn't curse God and die; I'm still alive by God's providence, still praising and serving Him, my Almighty God!

Quite simply, allow me to say that you cannot serve two masters- choose who ye shall serve. If there was love, joy, happiness in your marriage, they were blessings from God. When you threw all of that away because of the evil one, you broke covenant, your vow unto Almighty God, and lost blessings from above, and God continues to say choose who ye shall serve- God or the enemy- but blessings can only come from God, so drop the pride, admit your error, fight the good fight and fight against the enemy, return unto thy husbands. Honor and cherish them and thy vows, receive once again the blessings that can only come from doing so. They only come when you are in fellowship with Him and His chosen one for you, your mate. Remember the good times which came from God through thy mate, forget the bad that came from the enemy. Return unto God and thy husband today, return unto thy first love. God says over and over again, I will... IF you will and in Judges 11:14 *Go and cry unto the gods which you have chosen: Let them deliver you in the time of your tribulation.* God hath given unto you a most precious and special gift, chosen just for you with His love, your mate who He ordained for you since before you were born! Don't throw away His blessings for the evil one, return unto God, return unto thy husband, receive God's blessings and fight the enemy. Actually, if you are obedient unto God and resist the enemy-the devil, God will do the fighting for you. Isaiah said in 1:3 *The ox knows his owner and the ass his master's crib: but Israel doth not know, my people doth not consider. Ah sinful nation, a people laden with iniquity, a seed of children's children that are corrupters: they have forsaken the Lord, they have provoked the Holy One of Israel with anger, they are gone away backward,* then go on and read verse 10-16 and 19-21. In Micah 6:8 *He hath shewed thee oh man what is good, and what doth the Lord require of thee, but to do JUSTLY, and to love MERCY, and to walk HUMBLY with thy God?*

Dear Brothers and Sisters in Christ, we did not intend to fall into Satan's trap. We stepped off the narrow path into a deep ditch once we tried to be all things to all people. We believed that we could mix God's solutions with the worlds. We were wrong. The church was led away and enticed by the evil of unconfessed sin and the lure of adultery of the world. By neglecting the teaching and instruction of our Lord and His Apostles thereby producing bad fruit, the modern church has done great evil in the eyes of the Lord. We have led many astray, we have scattered the flock. We are now faced with the terrible consequences of our sin.

All sin is eradicated and atoned for by the Blood of Jesus Christ by sincere and genuine confession and repentance. As the church and we as individuals have sinned publicly then so must the confession be equally public. Confession means that the truth of God's instructions must be proclaimed as well as our own disobedience to them. As we know that 1ˢᵗ John 1:9 reminds us that *If we confess our sins, he is faithful and just to forgive us our sins, and to cleanse us from all unrighteousness.*

Repentance means that we must turn away from sin and follow God's plan from that point on. This means that the church as well as we as individuals must refuse to recognize and facilitate any further divorce and remarriage.

In the end we all shall sleep and await judgment. Those who have truly accepted and served God have already been judged and justified by Jesus Christ upon the cross of Calvary, and shall spend eternity with our precious Father in heaven hallelujah! Those who don't shall stand before that great white throne of judgment and shall be cast into eternal fire and brimstone, which we call the second death, however it isn't truly a death, just a separation from Christ and God. *Many are called but few are chosen.* Few shall pass on the straight and narrow gate that enters into the kingdom, and I pray that you shall be one of them, but it is your choice! Those who are cast into the lake of fire and brimstone shall spend eternity cursing the deceiver, whereas those in heaven shall spend eternity praising and celebrating joyfully our Creator, your choice. Those who are divorced are the same. I've spoken with so many women who were deceived and left (or the husband shamefully sent them away) from their husbands and always regretted it and cursed their deceiver(s). Then they were afraid, ashamed, embarrassed, or too proud to return unto their first love, their husband. But we must repent and return to our First Love, our God Almighty, and thy husband or you shall forever regret and live in hell, in the hands of the deceiver. Your first love is waiting for your return with His arms outstretched. Men, are you listening? Women, are you hearing this? Men and women, are you hearing and listening to this critical message? So, humble thyself and repent today, this very moment and bring revival into thy life. Return to thy First Love, thy Bridegroom. Love one another, women don't ever leave thy husband, and if you have, return today unto him and seek his forgiveness. If you have walked away from our heavenly Father, return unto Him and seek His forgiveness. 1ˢᵗ Peter 3:9 *Not rending evil for evil...* If one sins and you divorce, this evil of divorce is returning evil for evil and much more than that, in that you are also adding to it the evils of breaking covenant with God! He continues in vs. 11-12 *Let him seek peace and ensue it. For the eyes of the Lord are over the righteous, and His ears are open unto their prayers: but the face of the Lord is against them that do evil.* Romans 5:10 goes on to say *For if when we were enemies, we were reconciled to God by the death of His Son, much more, being reconciled, we shall be saved by His life.* We as believers need to repent and be reconciled unto God, as well as with one another, especially in marriage where we have vowed unto God...until death do us part! Walking away doesn't solve anything and in fact severely hinders your relationship with God our Father and Bridegroom.

If your husband kicks you out, wait on his doorstep, pray for him and for your marriage, sacrifice and surrender your all, your will unto him until he invites you back in. Men, this is serious. You must love as Christ loves the church, unconditional love of the sinner, which we all are. If you are without sin, cast the first stone. If you are not without sin, then remove the beam from your own eye so that you may more clearly see the mote, the speck in your...partner's eye. It is no surprise that this story from John 7:53-8:11 is excluded from many modern translations.

There is no greater sin in marriage than divorce. Divorce shows a complete lack of hope, faith, love, trust, respect...for God, for thy partner, and for thyself. No matter what happens in a marriage it can be repaired, forgiven, as nothing is too difficult or impossible for God! But divorce is an act of hatred and lies unto God and thy partner. If you divorce your spouse, you are an unbeliever for you have not only divorced thy God given mate, but God Himself. You MUST repent, humble thyself, seek His (his) face, and turn from your wicked ways, the ways of the world, and return to thy mate and to God. God is what binds a marriage together, and the absence of God in the heart of the unbeliever is what destroys a marriage, for God is love...Satan is hate. You cannot serve two masters.

Just as in marriage and divorce many shall come- many are called, but many fall away, and few are chosen. But how much better is it for the one who holds on to marriage and to Christ in the good times and the bad, he that endureth unto the end shall be saved!

If you have read or heard this message and understood even a little of it and of God's word, you will easily see why there are no biblical grounds for divorce. Matthew 19:8, Because of the hardness of man's heart... Are you having troubles in your marriage or family relationship? *Let him deny himself* (righteous) *and take up thy cross and follow Me*, Jesus said in Luke 9:23. Pray and be Christ-like...love...forgive...sacrifice...surrender...
AMEN.

In Matthew 5:44, Jesus said *Love your enemies, bless those that curse you, do good to them that hate you, and pray for them which despitefully use you, and persecute you*; And in Luke 6:31 we are told, *And as ye would that men should do to you do ye also to them likewise.*

The basic plan and purpose, the basic premise throughout scripture from Genesis through Revelation, is Love...love... love! Love thy neighbor as thyself...love your enemy...bless those who persecute you...from the cross, Christ cried out Father forgive them (us), why? Because He loves us so much that He forgave us. If Christ and God can love and forgive us sinners so very much, and this is the basis of all scripture (John 3:16), cannot we also love and forgive? And if we can't love and forgive the most precious and wonderful earthly gift from God our Father, our partner, how on earth or in heaven, can we love anyone or anything else? Think about it. And if we can't forgive and love the precious gift from our Father, how can we love the precious giver of that gift?

The Bible through and through teaches us to love...as God loves...and to be in unity, not to be divided, 1st Corinthians 1:10...Psalms 133:1 tells us *How good and how pleasant it is for brethren to dwell together in unity.*

God forgives us the sinner after we have gone astray, and accepts us back into His loving arms just as in the parable of the Prodigal Son. If God and parents can forgive and accept back the repentant sinner, can't the husband and wife do likewise? This is not giving license to go out and sin, but license to be accepted back for God and man, for all who have divorced are walking in sin day by day and are outside of God's will. Will God forgive? Yes, but only if you repent and forsake thy wicked ways and seek His face, therefore as long as you stay away from your first marriage partner, you continue in sin, for you are also away from God. You lied to God promising, vowing until death do you part, you would remain with the person that He ordained for you and made one, God cannot and will not forgive those who remain in sin; *For the law was given by Moses, but grace and truth came by Jesus Christ,* John 1:17. *And the Lord spake unto Moses, saying, Speak unto the children of Israel, and say unto them, I am the Lord your God. After the doings of the land of Egypt, wherein ye dwelt, shall ye not do: and after the doings of the land of Canaan, whither I bring you, shall ye not do: neither shall ye walk in their ordinances. Ye shall do my judgments, and keep mine ordinances, to walk therein: I am the Lord your God. Ye shall therefore keep my statutes, and my judgments: which if a man do, he shall live in them: I am the Lord,* Leviticus18:1-5. In Leviticus 11:44 we continue reading *For I am the Lord your God: ye shall therefore sanctify yourselves, and ye shall be holy; for I am holy:*

neither shall ye defile yourselves with any manner of creeping thing that creepeth upon the earth.

The truth is, according to Malachi 3:13 – 16, God says he won't accept their offerings anymore. Why? -Because they have dealt treacherous with the wife (or husband) of their youth who remains the wife of their covenant.–I plead with Pastors to count the costs. Not only do they put themselves *in* danger of missing Heaven (no adulterer will enter Heaven), but they endanger all who follow their teachings–And as a Pastor you WILL be held responsible as well.

Actually, please back up with me to verse 5, where we read *And I will come near to you to judgment; and I will be a swift witness against the sorcerers, and against the adulterers, and against **false swearers**, and against those that oppress the hireling in his wages, the widow, and the fatherless, and that turn aside the stranger from his right, and fear not me, saith the LORD of hosts.* Do you hear this?

Please allow me to summarize using scripture on the abomination of divorce, the issue of remarriage, and the Christian walk.

But King Solomon loved many foreign women; in addition to the daughters of Pharaoh, women of the Moabites, Ammonites, Edomites, Sidonians, and Hittites, of the nations concerning which the Lord said unto the children of Israel, Ye shall not go in to them, neither shall they come in unto you; for surely they will turn away your heart after their gods. Solomon clave unto these in love. *And he had seven hundred wives, princesses, and three hundred concubines; and his wives turned away his hear,* 1ˢᵗ Kings 11:1-3 Like father, like son. David's life of polygamy and adultery would bear fruit in the beloved son, Solomon. Although these wives and concubines were the common gifts and peace offerings of foreign kings, nevertheless many of them were wedded by Solomon. We are clearly told that Solomon sinned: Did not Solomon, king of Israel, sin by these things? Yet among many nations was there not a king like him, who was beloved of his God, and God made him king over all Israel; nevertheless, even him did foreign women cause to sin. Nehemiah 13:26.

Jehovah God was married to Israel, His beloved. We are clearly told that He was her husband: In Isaiah 54:5-7 we see that *For thy Maker is thine husband; the Lord of hosts is his name; and thy Redeemer the Holy One of Israel; The God of the whole earth shall he be called. For the Lord hath called thee as a woman forsaken and grieved in spirit, and a wife of youth, when thou wast refused, saith thy God. For a small moment have I forsaken thee; but with great mercies will I gather thee.* Mal. 2:14 *Yet ye say, Wherefore? Because the Lord hath been witness between thee and the wife of thy youth, against whom thou hast dealt treacherously: yet is she thy companion, and the wife of thy covenant. Saith thy God, for a small moment have I forsaken thee, but with great mercies will I gather thee.* God betrothed Israel on the foothills of Mount Sinai.

In her youth she was a slave of the kingdom of the Pharaoh, where her infant sons were persecuted. One of those infants, Moses, led the children of Israel to the altar where she betrothed Almighty God; she became one with Him, an allegory of marriage. Later Israel's conduct as a wife became disgraceful, and illegal. The law set certain conditions on the marriage relationship; Adultery was a capital crime; certain acts could result in divorce with a prohibition to any future reconciliation of the original marriage. Israel committed adultery and those acts; yet, God never put her asunder. His perfect love required Him to chasten her, but he never put her asunder. He created the institution of marriage and He was bound to her forever, by choice. Let us follow this marriage.

The Lord God was betrothed to the twelve tribes of Israel: In Jeremiah 3:14 we read *Turn, O backsliding children, saith the Lord; for I am married unto you: and I will take you one of a city, and two of a family, and I will bring you to Zion.* We must remember that although Israel and Judah committed many crimes against their marriage with God, He nevertheless was faithful to them. Malachi speaks firmly regarding Jehovah God's commitment to the nation as their Husband: *For I am the Lord, I change not; therefore ye sons of Jacob are not consumed,* Mal. 3:6. Both Israel and Judah had committed the capital crime of adultery. Both kingdoms could have been destroyed from the earth for their sin, but God makes no mention of their utter destruction. He does however describe His anger.

The illustration here is that Israel was put away (divorced) by her captivity, figuratively given a bill of divorce. She had committed adultery with foreign gods, and God put her away. She then went and became the wife of another god, another man. Then in reference to Deuteronomy 24:1-4, God annuls the abomination and pleads for the return of His harlot wife. We see here strong evidence that the thought of the divorce and remarriage of Deuteronomy 24:1-4 was not God's will. God says, they say, indicating that He did not say it. But the primary concern of the verse in Jeremiah is the fact that God accused the nation of committing adultery, this was certainly not the same uncleanness, or same indecency of Deuteronomy 24:1. Adultery was a capital crime; in Jeremiah 3:1 God goes on to say, even though you have been defiled by another during our separation, return to me. In Jeremiah 3:1 the abomination is annulled. Their reunion was holiness. Why? In spite of Israel's adultery and harlotry, and in spite of her symbolic divorce, she was married to Jehovah!

The long arm of the law, the sword of the law is absent from this scripture. The adulterer and adulteress were not executed, but were graciously offered a pardon. The text is bursting with mercy, and reason: Jehovah argues that He is married to Israel. He is the faithful Husband. Jeremiah labors to portray the first love of Israel, her apostasy, her metaphorical divorce, and her offer of reconciliation: Go and cry in the hearing of Jerusalem, saying, *Thus saith the Lord, I remember thee, the kindness of thy youth, the love of thine espousals, when thou wentest after me in the wilderness, in a land that was not sown. Israel was holiness unto the Lord, and the first fruits of his increase; all that devour him shall offend; evil shall come upon them, saith the Lord. Hear ye the word of the Lord, O house of Jacob, and all the families of the house of Israel.* In Jeremiah 2:2-4, the illustration here is the betrothal period when Israel was rescued from the armies of Pharaoh and was romanced by Jehovah God in the wilderness. She then became His wife.

Thus saith the Lord, What iniquity have your fathers found in me, that they are gone far from me, and have walked after vanity, and are become vain? Neither said they, Where is the Lord who brought us up out of the land of Egypt, who led us through the wilderness, through a land of deserts and of pits, through a land of drought, and of the shadow of death, through a land that no man passed through, and where no man dwelt? And I brought you into a plentiful country, to eat its fruit and its goodness, but when ye entered, ye defiled my land, and made mine heritage an abomination. The priests said not, where is the Lord? And they that handle the law knew me not. The rulers also transgressed against me, and the prophets prophesied by Baal, and walked after things that do not profit, Jeremiah 2:5-8. Here the Northern Kingdom is indicted for adultery, i.e., their apostasy into the idolatry of Baalism. The prophesying by Baal was the same as being married to another.

The forsaking of God by Israel, the fountain of living waters, and her adultery were acts of marital violence, but her marrying Baal, the hewed out man-made cistern, was a second and more violent evil. This act under the law would have prohibited any further reconciliation. She became the wife of another after a divorce from her first husband. Thus, according to the law, she was now defiled to her original Husband, Jehovah God: *Is Israel a servant? is he a homeborn slave? why is he spoiled? The young lions roared upon him, and yelled, and they made his land waste: his cities are burned without inhabitant. Also the children of Noph and Tahapanes have broken the crown of thy head. Hast thou not procured this unto thyself, in that thou hast forsaken the Lord thy God, when he led thee by the way? And now what hast thou to do in the way of Egypt, to drink the waters of Sihor? or what hast thou to do in the way of Assyria, to drink the waters of the river? Thine own wickedness shall correct thee, and thy backslidings shall reprove thee: know therefore and see that it is an evil thing and bitter, that thou hast forsaken the Lord thy God, and that my fear is not in thee, saith the Lord God of hosts,* Jeremiah 2:14-19. The desolation of Israel is a direct reference to a type of divorce. It was a divorce, which was self-inflicted. God permitted her to exercise her free evil will. He permitted the divorce for which she sued. He gave her the *bill of divorce,* she requested. **In this sense, God never divorced her.** He continues *For of old I have broken thy yoke, and burst thy bands; and thou saidst, I will not transgress, when upon every high hill and under every green tree thou wanderest, playing the harlot. Yet I had planted thee a noble vine, wholly a right seed. How, then art thou turned into the degenerate plant of a strange vine unto me, saith the Lord God. How canst thou say, I am not polluted, I have not gone after Baalim? See thy way in the valley, know what thou hast done; thou art a swift dromedary traversing her ways, a wild ass used to the wilderness that snuffeth up the wind at her pleasure; in her occasion who can turn her away? All they that seek her will not weary themselves; in her month they shall find her. Withhold thy foot from being unshod and thy throat from thirst; but thou saidst, there is no hope. No; for I have loved strangers, and after them will I go. As the thief is ashamed when he is found, so is the house of Israel ashamed; they, their kings, their princes, and their priests, and their prophets, Saying to a tree, Thou art my father; and to a stone, Thou hast brought me forth; for they have turned their back unto me, and not their face, but in the time of their trouble they will say, Arise, and save us. But where are thy gods that thou hast made? Let them arise, if they trouble; for according to the number of thy cities are thy gods, O Judah. Why will ye plead with me? Ye all have transgressed against me, saith the Lord. In vain have I smitten your children; they received no correction. Your own sword hath devoured your prophets, like a destroying lion,* Jeremiah 2:20-30. The nation has been plainly caught in the bed of adultery, and that with her lover, Baalim. Furthermore, she claims that her adulterous marriage is not polluted. In her imagination her adultery was a holy religious experience. But God tells her, *For though thou wash thee with lye, and take thee much soap, yet thine iniquity is marked before me, saith* *the Lord God. O generation, see the word of the Lord. Have I been a wilderness unto Israel? A land of darkness? Why do my people say, 'We are Lords'; we will come no more unto thee? Can a maid forget her ornaments or a bride her attire? Yet my people have forgotten me days without number. Why trimmest thou thy way to seek love? therefore hast thou also taught the wicked ones thy ways. Also in thy skirts is found the blood of the souls of the poor innocents; I have not found it by secret search, but upon all these. Yet thou sayest, because I am innocent, surely his anger shall turn from me. Behold, I will plead with thee, because thou sayest, I have not sinned. Why gaddest thou about so much to change thy way? Thou also wast ashamed of Assyria. Yea, thou shalt go forth from him, and thine hands upon thine head; for the Lord hath rejected thy confidences, and thou shalt not prosper in them,* Jeremiah 2:31-37. Her apostasy was preceded by fornication; she changed her ways to seek love. She left her wedding gown behind. *They say, If a man put away his wife, and she go from him, and become another man's, shall he return unto her again? shall not that land be greatly polluted? but thou hast played the harlot with many lovers; yet return again to me, saith the Lord. Lift up thine eyes unto the high places, and see where thou hast not been lien with. In the ways hast thou sat for them, as the Arabian in the wilderness; and thou hast polluted the land with thy whoredoms and with thy wickedness. Therefore the showers have been withholden, and there hath been no latter rain; and thou hadst a whore's forehead, thou refusedst to be ashamed. Wilt thou not from this time cry unto me, My father, thou art the guide of my youth? Will he reserve his anger forever? Will he keep it to the end? Behold, thou hast spoken and done evil things as thou couldest. The Lord said also unto me in the days of Josiah the king, Hast thou seen that which backsliding Israel hath done? she is gone up upon every high mountain and under every green tree, and there hath played the harlot.* Jeremiah 3:1-6.

In the book of Acts 15:19 and 20 we are told *Wherefore my sentence is, that we trouble not them, which from among the Gentiles are turned to God: But that we write unto them,*

*that they abstain from pollutions of idols, and from **fornication**, and from things strangled, and from blood.* And he
continues in 15:29 *That ye abstain from meats offered to idols,
and from blood, and from things strangled, and from **fornication**: from which if ye keep yourselves, ye shall do well.
Fare ye well.* Then in 21:25 he concludes saying *As touching
the Gentiles which believe, we have written and concluded
that they observe no such thing, save only that they keep
themselves from things offered to idols, and from blood, and
from strangled, and from **fornication**.* Remember that fornication is the word pornea as we discussed earlier.

Israel had been divorced and remarried. Now God says,
They say, regarding the abomination of Deuteronomy 24:1-4.
It was not his will. The They of the verse refers to Moses as
the author of the permissive section of the law. For Israel in
her marriage to Jehovah, the abomination did not exist. It did
not exist because her marriage was eternal; it was permanent
marriage. He was the Guide of her youth; in her youth she was
his bride. *The Lord said also unto me in the days of Josiah
the king, Hast thou seen that which backsliding Israel hath
done? she is gone up upon every high mountain and under
every green tree, and there hath played the harlot. And I said
after she had done all these things, Turn thou unto me. But
she returned not. And her treacherous sister Judah saw it.
And I saw, when for all the causes whereby backsliding Israel
committed adultery I had put her away, and given her a bill
of divorce; yet her treacherous sister Judah feared not, but
went and played the harlot also. And it came to pass through
the lightness of her whoredom, that she defiled the land, and
committed adultery with stones and with stocks. And yet for
all this her treacherous sister Judah hath not turned unto me
with her whole heart, but feignedly, saith the Lord. And the
Lord said unto me, the backsliding Israel hath justified herself more than treacherous Judah.* Jeremiah 3: 6-11!!!! It is
no wonder that the princes in the book of Esther advised the
king to put away Vashti so that she couldn't infect the others.
Judah, the southern kingdom, is charged with adultery. The
entire nation is equally guilty of capital crimes and of those

certain acts which caused her to be metaphorically divorced, entering into further relationships that prohibited her return to her husband, God. It is said here that God, had put her away, and given her a bill of divorce. Her putting away and bill of divorce was her captivity and destruction by Assyria. These were temporary for shaming them, not permanent judgments as the law permitted under divorce. Had God actually wrote a bill of divorcement He would have had no further authority over His wife. She would have been permitted to be wife of another. But she was never so permitted. This is further evidence that God never endorsed as a legal divorce procedure. *Go and proclaim these words toward the north, and say, Return, thou backsliding Israel, saith the Lord; and I will not cause mine anger to fall upon you: for I am merciful, saith the Lord, and I will not keep anger forever. Only acknowledge thine iniquity, that thou hast transgressed against the Lord thy God, and hast scattered thy ways to the strangers under every green tree, and ye have not obeyed my voice, saith the Lord. Turn, O backsliding children, saith the Lord; for I am married unto you: and I will take you one of a city, and two of a family, and I will bring you to Zion,* Jeremiah 3:12-14. Her acts of adultery and uncleanness reaped neither divorce, execution, nor the abomination of Deuteronomy 24:1-4. Jehovah God, her Husband, pleaded for her return. After her adultery, and uncleanness, God says, I am married unto you. The illusion of divorce is only a gentle rebuke to the temporary captivity with which He chastised His beloved wife, Israel. God did not practice divorce at all. God was not a divorce´. He was forever married to Israel. Divorce was the practice of men; men with hard sinful hearts, not ordained by God. As we said, Israel had committed spiritual adultery. The metaphor of adultery would be complete only with the death of Israel. God did not subject Israel to the law, and stone them to death. Neither did he literally divorce his beloved wife, His companion. *Turn, O backsliding children, saith the Lord; for I am married unto you* Jeremiah3:14. Rather than hate her husband she now used a new weapon: separation and divorce. But these are not an invention of heaven, but rather one of the manufactured garments of sin, just as Adam and Eve clothed themselves after the fall.

A careful study will reveal that God is not divorced. And that is important. There are no grounds for divorce, which is the foundation of the covenant marriage of God with Israel.

No, this does not affirm that God was no longer the Husband of Israel. The metaphor does not literally mean that the event really occurred. God told us that my covenant, they broke, although I was a husband unto them, saith the Lord. His use of divorce, putting away, and the bill of divorce were illustrations intended to chasten Israel to re-think their rebelliousness. The idea that God divorced and remarried Israel after she was the wife of another is to accuse God of committing the sin of abomination. The idea that God divorced Israel and remarried her is totally against any sound doctrine.

The powerful force of a prophet who literally lives with a wife of harlotry serves as the perfect picture of Israel, the harlot wife of God. This is an overwhelming picture of the truth of God's unthinkable marriage to Israel, as was Hosea's marriage to Gomer.

The wording of the text supports the actual consummation view which seems a fitting message from God to his sinful wife. Further the children of that marriage certainly appear to be literally born, and are given names which suggest judgment for the purpose of conveying God's message: Jezreel, meaning scattered, the judgment of the northern kingdom; Lo-ruhamah, meaning unpitied, no mercy to the northern kingdom; Lo-ammi, meaning not my people, you are not my people, and I will not be your God. The one definite theme throughout the book of Hosea is that this adulterous wife in not judged; divorced or put to death. She is not totally destroyed. She is not stoned to death. But she is pleaded with to return.

I must point out that although the judgment of Israel would be severe, as noted in the meaning of the names of Hosea's children, there is also an unconditional promise of complete and full restoration for both the northern kingdom, Israel, and the southern kingdom of Judah. The putting away in the divorce metaphor was figurative for a temporary chastising of Ephraim, the northern kingdom, and her adulterous sister Judah. It certainly was not the irrevocability of legal marital divorce as practiced by the previous generations, the west, and the church today. It is not what it is often taken to be, a threatening of God's abandoning of the idolatrous nation ... the very fact Hosea was prophesying to call Ephraim from his sin showed that God had not let Ephraim alone, but was persuading him through His prophet, and seeking to win him back by the words of his mouth. God was doing all that He could do, rising early and sending His messenger and calling to Ephraim: 'Turn ye! Turn ye! Why will ye die?' For Hosea, in the very act of pleading with Israel on God's behalf, to have declared that God had abandoned it, and ceased to plead, would have been a complete absurdity and contradiction. This is why we see in the New Testament as well in Matthew 18:14-17 that *Even so it is not the will of your Father which is in heaven, that one of these little ones should perish. Moreover if thy brother shall trespass against thee, go and tell him his fault between thee and him alone: if he shall hear thee, thou hast gained thy brother. But if he will not hear thee, then take with thee one or two more, that in the mouth of two or three witnesses every word may be established. And if he shall neglect to hear them, tell it unto the church: but if he neglect to hear the church, let him be unto thee as an heathen man and a publican.* (disfellowship for a time until he repents and turns from his wicked way).

Chapter two begins with Hosea speaking to Gomer of divorce and chastisement. As we shall see this was only a metaphoric divorce, a temporary punishment. *Plead with your mother, plead: for she is not my wife, neither am I her husband: let her therefore put away her whoredoms out of her sight, and her adulteries from between her breasts,* Hosea 2:2 In a spirit of jealousy God, declaring that although the nation had apostatized to the point of calling God, Baali, they would be restored and call him Ishi, *my husband.* And then he drifts into a beautiful song which God sings to His lady, speaking to her with the language of love.

In chapter three Hosea is asked to take the wife back whom he had divorced and to love her in spite of the fact that she had committed adultery: *Then said the Lord unto me, Go yet, love a woman beloved of her friend, yet an adulteress, according to the love of the Lord toward the children of Israel, who look to other gods, and love flagons of wine.* Hosea 3:1.

Initially Hosea supplies Gomer will all her needs. She unsuspectingly believes she is being sponsored by her lovers. Then Hosea removes his support, leaving her to be caught in a society without any wealth but the flesh of her life. She is reduced to a slave and is auctioned for a price. As God remained the husband of Israel even though she committed adultery, so Hosea purchases her from the auction block and restores Gomer to the full status of a beloved wife: *So I bought* (God's redemption for us) *her to me for fifteen pieces of silver, and for an homer of barley, and an half homer of barley: And I said unto her, Thou shalt abide for me many days; thou shalt not play the harlot, and thou shalt not be for another man: so will I also be for thee,* Hosea 3:2-3. Hosea did not practice divorce. God did not practice divorce. In chapter three however he immediately takes her back on the command of God. Are you getting this? He took her back in spite of the sins that she committed, the doctrine of mercy and grace.

Our Lord, the God of Israel, saith that he hateth putting away (divorce) Mal. 2:16. Metaphors are figures of speech, and are used to permit the speaker the liberty to drive home his thought by creating a picture of the idea.

Ezra, the scribe, Nehemiah, the governor, and Malachi, the prophet, were three prophets all concerned with how the Jewish remnant were conducting themselves while returning to Jerusalem. While in Babylon the children of Israel learned the customs of the unbelievers, divorce with remarriage, and marriage with the heathen, and other atrocities. When these prophets found divorce, remarriage, and heathen remarriage in the ranks of Israel, they began rebuking them. Ezra pulled his hair out, Nehemiah pulled out the hair of the guilty, and

Malachi warned the perpetrators that God will cut off those who divorced their Jewish wives and married the daughters of the heathen. The solution included the putting away of both the strange women and their children. As Ezra saw it, this was not a question of breaking up legitimate marriages but of invalidating those which were contrary to the law of Deuteronomy 7:1-11. Although the separation of the wives with children is especially difficult, it nevertheless was the fruit of true repentance, and perhaps we need to follow suit today.

I was in one country where I was invited to speak on national television about divorce and remarriage. This was during a time when an extremely wealthy and prominent religious leader there was tired of his wife so he was divorcing her to marry his secretary! People are watching...people are following. We as religious leaders must set a biblical example to the world, selfless, and must remember that God is watching and will hold us doubly accountable.

The concept of illegitimate marriages is simple. A marriage within the forbidden degrees would be illegitimate, or a matter of incestuous or consanguineous marriage. A marriage to a previously divorced wife, who had another husband during the interim was illegitimate and an abomination. Therefore, a marriage to a person who was to be annulled would have been an illegitimate marriage, and an abomination. Marriages built on adultery may be classified as illegitimate or adulterous marriages. In each case, the shame of sin belongs to him who unites such marriages not to him who puts them asunder. These illegitimate marriages simply are not joined together by God, and they should be put away. Since these illegitimate marriages were never marriages their disunion cannot legally meet the definition of divorce; however, the term divorce would be appropriate in the common meaning of the act. But to justify the act of divorce on the basis of the text in Ezra is wrong. Technically, there was no divorce in Ezra; it was legal annulment or legal separation.

This traitorous act of no longer cleaving to their wives was being committed by many Israelites; priests included, and are fiercely attacked by Malachi. He explains the reason for his anger. God had chosen the nation to be a holy nation; a nation, set apart which would be a blessing to all other peoples; a nation that married Jehovah God in holy covenant. The chosen covenant nation, which would be the progenitors of the Holy seed, the Infant Son of Bethlehem. By departing from the wives of their youth and marrying foreign women the nation was breaking their covenant marriage with God, falling into idolatry, and corrupting the Jewish marriage, the ultimate hope of mankind; that would bring forth the victorious seed of the woman of Genesis 3:15, the Messiah the Savior of mankind.

Yet she was thy companion, who shared thy joy and sorrow, and the wife of thy covenant, with whom thou didst make a covenant for life. The amazing thing about these blessed marriages was that the Jewish men mentioned had dealt treacherously with their wives, divorcing them. The pleasing thing about these divorced wives was the fact that God saw the divorcees as still married, *yet is she thy companion, and the wife of thy covenant.* The divorce was not recognized by the Lord God. *For the Lord, the God of Israel, saith he hateth putting away,* Malachi 2:16. The God of Israel hates divorce!

God cries out, 'I love marriage just the way that I created it, and I hate divorce.' As a mother bear closing in to revenge someone or something disturbing her cubs, the God of these Israelite divorced women was raging with fury to re-establish justice. The treacherous act of divorcing these women caused the altar of Israel to catch the tears and the voices of these weeping women. Their cries caused God to condemn their Jewish husbands in Malachi 2:12, *The Lord will cut off* (kill or to destroy) *the man that doeth this, the master and the scholar,* God continues His indictment, *He accuses these men of wearing blood-stained garments, for one covereth violence with his garment.* His cries will not stop until He intercedes and puts an end to it all.

John the Baptist was sent to make the way of marriage straight. His sermon was a call to *Repent for the kingdom of heaven is at hand.* Here Malachi cries against adultery. His cries were provoked by those who dealt treacherously by divorcing their wives (husband's). Malachi calls on his hearers to repent, to return to the ordinance of the Lord, the Christ centered marriage saying *Even from the days of your fathers ye are gone away from mine ordinances, and have not kept them. Return unto me,* (Repentance and restoration) *and I will return unto you, saith the Lord of hosts,* Mal. 3:7.

The marriage covenant is a natural symbol of God's covenants, especially His covenant with the nation He married, Israel (the believers). For a man to break his marriage covenant is diametrically opposed to the entire nature of God.

Our salvation is by grace through faith, not of works, lest any man should boast; it is permanent, inseparable, and indissoluble; just as God created marriage to be. Divorce is non-existent and incomprehensible to God's created marriage.

Allow me to add here that **even if you divorce and remain single**, that each and every day you are walking in sin, because you don't return to your God ordained partner. Even if you repent for the sin of divorce, you are still deliberately living in disobedience to God's word and breaking covenant with Him and His chosen partner for you, thus it is not true repentance and not accepted by our God. Until you return and honor thy vows and responsibilities, God will not hear thy prayers 2ⁿᵈ Chronicles 7:14 tells us that we must **HUMBLE** ourselves and **pray**, **seek His face**, and **TURN FROM OUR WICKED WAYS** (not their wicked ways, but allow God to work on your partner) **THEN...THEN...THEN...** will He hear your prayers, forgive your sins, and heal your land (life, and your marriage), are you hearing this my dear brothers and sisters? There can be no salvation for the divorced, because a true believer will do everything possible to please God and fulfill His law-which is summed up as loving and forgiving, being honest to God and your partner. You may be living single, but you are still married!

Divorce is such an accepted and encouraged part of modern culture worldwide, destroying more people than the covid, but it is such an abomination to God and should never even be considered in the life of a true believer in Jesus Christ for it is diametrically opposed to everything that He taught from the beginning to the end. God outright said I hate putting away.

The answer or solution lies within this message which takes you back to His word and His instruction and purpose. You must be prayerful and return to the precepts of God's precious word, leaving the world behind. You cannot serve God and man, you must choose, but only the path of righteousness will bring favor with God.

Christians must stop making excuses for and trying to find justification for divorce and more so for remarriage. None of it stands before God, and must not be considered at all when applying the Word of God in the Church or to our individual lives. A marriage is for life, and no matter what a spouse turns out to be or how they may act or the sins they commit, the covenant, remains fully in effect. God does not divide the one flesh relationship. A spouse that is separated or divorced for any reason, no matter how provoked or how circumstances came to be as they are, is still bound to the marriage covenant.

The Gospel being taught today in many Bible believing Churches, insofar as the moral standards required by Christianity are concerned, is diametrically opposed to that taught by Jesus Christ and His early church. I believe that the modern church is presenting a different, powerless version of a Christianity that denies the essential Truth of God, which does not recognize the complete transforming power of the Holy Spirit to regenerate degenerate man.

As I mentioned at the start of this chapter, I resisted writing this chapter because divorce is such an evil abomination of the world, but God led me to write, and it since has become the lengthiest chapter, as the material is in fact so important for the world to hear today. I sincerely desire the salvation of marriages and the salvation of all the unbelievers. Marriage in a way separates the believers from the unbelievers, as the believers honor God and their vows, whereas the unbelievers pack their bags when the going gets tough and walk away.

There are so many men and women who are saying 'I'm tired of this model, it's time for a new one'. Brethren, this works for cars, but not for LIFE partners. God says no way!

We read in Num. 14:43 *"For the Amalekites and the Canaanites are there before you, and ye shall fall by the* sword: because ye are turned away from the LORD, there-fore the LORD will not be with you." You simply cannot dis-regard God and His law and expect Him to be there for you. This includes those who break the marriage covenant (divorce). The world will tell you that it is okay, but you must choose who you will serve, God or the enemy. In the Songs of Solomon 6:13 note that the women, her friends, are trying to pull her away from her beloved just as they do today. Also, as the world (again women representing sin) try to pull the follower of Christ away from Him, our Beloved, and away from the path of righteousness.

God says over and over again I will...IF you will. And in Judges 10:14 we read *Go and cry unto the gods which ye have chosen; let them deliver you in the time of your tribu-lation.* God hath given you a special gift-your partner whom He ordained for you, don't throw away His blessings for the evil one, return unto God, return to your husband if you are divorced or separated receive God's blessings and together fight the enemy. Isaiah said in 1:3 *The ox knoweth his owner and the ass his master's crib: but Israel doth not know, my people doth not consider.* Are you listening to God's call for repentance and revival here, in your marriage as well as in your Christian walk? You know, most marriages that end in divorce are not bankrupt or even close to it, people are lazy and just don't want to work at it...there are other fish in the sea... perhaps it's time for a newer model... but! The next marriage won't be any different if you are unwilling to work at it, as well as being in violation of God's law! I was reading in a book on China that the divorce rates are less than two percent because if one applies for divorce, then they along with family, friends, coworkers, neighbors, etc., sit down at a table and talk, and... usually work things out by mutual agreement! If that works in China, it can and will work anywhere, especially if God remains the third string in the cord binding the two of you together!

They say unto him, why did Moses then command to give a writing of divorcement, and to put her away? He saith unto them, Moses because of the hardness of your hearts suffered you to put away your wives: but from the beginning it was not so, Matthew 19:7, 8; this text has been discussed at length in earlier chapters of this message. Jesus explains that *the* writing of a divorce was not an ordinance of His law but rather it was a Mosaic concession to the horrible hardness of man's heart. Jesus strongly and clearly throws their ideas out of His court forever.

My dear friends, marriage is so important to our Master Designer and Creator, our Almighty Living God, and divorce such an abomination that a law was passed that the woman had to wait for three menstrual periods (three months) in order to finalize a divorce, in order to give a cool down period and allow time for forgiveness, restoration and reconciliation, revival of the marriage! Even the three-month plan isn't God's plan.

The emotional mine field of divorce from my opinion, appears more wretched and life-altering than coping with a mate's physical death. In death, God takes, whereas in divorce Satan takes. It has become unthinkable to me that God would sanction such tearing apart of the human heart.

I had met personally Jim Jones as I had a few friends that attended his church. After speaking briefly with him, I spoke with my friends and pleaded for them to come out of her. A couple of them did, but there was one lady, who I actually had personal as well as spiritual interest in, who refused to listen and heed my warnings. She went to Guyana with him and his group, obviously drank the poison punch and is now dead.

I am reminded here also, of a horrible incident analogous to what I am saying here. There was an evening when I had res-cued an eight-year-old girl and her six-year-old brother, their parents had just been executed and they were to be killed as well by enemy hands. I ran and stood between the bullet and them. The enemy waited, then gave up and retreated when after a while some of the friendly local men came with their weapons to rescue me. I went to them and instructed this girl (Esther) to grab her brother (Christopher) because they were quite a distance from me; I still remember their names to this day, and come to me. She stood for a minute then grabbed her brother as I continued to call her to come. She ran the other way and before I could catch them, she landed upon a land mine and all that was left was a couple small pieces of skeleton. I cried and wonder to this day, why...why do women have to be so disobedient to those who care most for them? This Sharon, Esther, my wife...each of you can relate your own personal experience here, but you must realize that while the women need to fight this urge to be independent and do your own thing, as Eve did from the very beginning, we are all sinners and do the same to our God who loves us so much; we must all fight this urge to be disobedient to Him, and surrender our independence and become dependent on Him. In China, many young ladies single, divorced, widowed are looking for husbands. Many are very wealthy, but most are saying that they are independent. Independence and unity are opposites! It cannot work both ways! Sharon, Esther, my dear wife and millions of others have made a bad choice and the dead cannot change their minds now but the living can- my dear wife and so many others. I laid in bed and mourned Sharon for days as I'm certain did the angels and God Himself. I sat in the mine field for hours holding a piece of Esther's jaw bone just crying as I'm certain did the angels and God Himself. After my wife left, I sat there in the empty house and mourned for days until I landed in the hospital with the heart attack. I mourned the loss as I am certain did the angels and God Himself. I believe that each and every time that we make a bad decision (one against God), the angels in heaven and God Himself mourn. The millions of you who have chosen to separate or divorce, it's not too late to turn from your wicked ways and return to your husband, husbands accept back thy wife, and thy vows unto God. Each day that passes when you are in violation of God's law, and broken vows unto Him, is another day in sin and wickedness, separating you from God. You must seek His face, turn from thy wicked ways, repent and be restored...this includes most assuredly your marriages. Wives return to thy husbands, husbands welcome them back with total forgiveness and tender love, just as Christ will do for you once thy marriage is restored. You cannot pray for forgiveness and continue to walk in sin! You cannot say that you are godly and continue to walk in hatred and disobedience unto thy husband and God. It just cannot work that way. Hot or cold, there is no in-between. If you are still married but just passing the days, rekindle that original flame forgive, restore and revive thy marriage...for God's sake and yours! Judgment day WILL come and the ability to repent and be restored is too late- and this decision is eternal. Marriage is symbolic of our relationship with our Father in heaven. If you reject thy husband (husbands reject thy wife), you are in fact rejecting the giver of that most precious gift, and if you reject Him and His gift, then He will reject you. My dear brothers and sisters, your marriage is a life and death matter for eternity, you must care for it, and cherish it...until death do you part! Your eternal life depends upon it. Neither of you will ever be perfect, so forgive and move on, start afresh...TODAY! We are all sinners, saved only by grace. For Esther, there was no second chance, you have this minute for a second chance, the next step that you take could be your last as well, make it a positive...and godly step of turning from thy wicked ways, return to God and thy husband, husband's welcome thy wife back, repent, restore, revive and get all excited go tell everyone that Jesus Christ is Lord and is indeed thy Savior...For He saved thy marriage and thy eternal life. And let go of the past-don't look back, for that is when all turns to ash, remember Lot's wife and the Exodus!

Divorce is one of the greatest if not the greatest problem in the world today. We have divorced one another in the guise of independence when Jesus taught us to love our neighbor, and unity. Many have divorced their God anointed marriage partners, and most people, countries, and churches have divorced... God, and are in such need of humbling ourselves and pray, repent and turn from this wickedness and return to God, our marriage partners, and our neighbors...the path of righteousness and forget all this selfishness.

I was asking God while in the minefield as well as in my empty house, Why God, why do women have to be so stubborn, so obstinate, but then the Lord reminded that females are symbolic of our sinful nature, our stubbornness and unwillingness to listen to and obey our Bridegroom, our Father.

We all have heard women foolishly claim that 'anything a man can do; a woman can do better'. This is pride and an absolute lie of Satan! It is in direct opposition to God's plan and teaching. Then men saying 'women, you can't live with them, and you can't live without them'. Why is this? Because Men are symbolic again of the righteousness of God and women are symbolic of the sinful nature of the devil, and the two are diametrically opposed. However, God ordained for some men and women to be together in marriage, and the couple can only accomplish this peacefully if and when both parties learn and understand this and their God ordained roles. Then and only then can peace be found within the home, church, and community.

If we say that God allows divorce for believers who experience their mate's adultery, we are saying essentially that adultery is greater than the effect of the blood sacrifices of Christ. That adultery is a sin that is great enough to break covenant. It is not the higher way of redemptive thinking reflecting Christ's power to bring about healing and change the injured and the injurer for the sake of the godly seed and a witness around the earth.

What is so heartbreaking about the popular interpretation of Mathew's exemption clause is that it evidences the faithlessness of all who believe and follow it. Instead of reaping righteousness in the face of sin, we are sowing and reaping sin upon sin and we are reaping the harvest of confusion. Those who leave the covenant are no different than the world they are choosing to serve, since they are no longer salt and light but rather covenant breakers through and through. Sadly, people will pray for parking places, weather, finances, etc., but fail to even consider the power of Christ to turn the tide against adultery.

God says that He hates divorce. (Malachi 2:16). God does not set Israel aside but gave them time for the repentance and salvation of Israel, His people. He continues to stand patiently at the line of reconciliation for Israel, as He has promised, so He has promised us for our marriage. He waits until the last breath of sinners to repent and to turn to Him-till death do us part. Also, in John 13:35 Jesus tells us straight, *By this all men shall know that ye are my disciples, if ye have love one to another.*

I don't believe that He could have made it any plainer or simpler. When you call yourself a Christian, can you divorce? Can you choose to stop loving your God anointed partner? God and His Son Jesus Christ are so very clear on this. ABSOLUTELY NO with no exceptions!!!

In the story of the prodigal son, the father waited expectantly for the recovery of his son. So, God waits for us. This is the kind of love spoken about in wedding ceremonies. God's love as should ours be, *is long-suffering, not willing that any should perish but that all should come to repentance,* 2nd Peter 3:9.

Since marriage reflects the image of God, through Christ and the church, Satan is determined to destroy that image of enduring, committed, selfless love.

The number of divorces is a direct reflection of the spiritual condition today, the churches lack of response is a direct reflection of the spiritual condition of the church today. Let us return to our first love, our Lord and Savior Jesus Christ, and stop the divorces, and return to our first love, whom God ordained for us, your marriage partner...until death do you part.

I call your attention to Zech. 7:10-13 which tells *us And oppress not the widow, nor the fatherless, the stranger, nor the poor; and let none of you imagine evil against his brother in your heart. But they refused to hearken, and pulled away the shoulder, and stopped their ears, that they should not hear. Yea, they made their hearts as an adamant stone, lest they should hear the law, and the words which the Lord of hosts hath sent in his spirit by the former prophets: therefore came a great wrath from the Lord of hosts. Therefore it is come to pass, that as he cried, and they would not hear; so they cried, and I would not hear, saith the Lord of hosts.* Don't allow this to happen to you. If it has, then now is the time for repentance, revival and restoration of your marriage...your covenant promises.

If you wish to honestly call yourself a Christian, you must never think or consider divorce. If you are separated or divorced, you MUST repent, restore, return to your marriage partner and revive that which you vowed unto God to do until death. This is God's plan and will. If you consider yourself a Christian, a follower of Christ, then you MUST follow Him and His will for your life; as well as to keep thy covenant vows made unto Him and thy marriage partner. Trust and obey God.

The basic premise throughout Scripture is LOVE and is focused to restoration and revival following our humbling and repentant heart, ever since the fall of mankind in the Garden of Eden. Therefore, taking the easy way out and walking away from thy God ordained partner, from your covenant promise and vows to God and thy husband is not the way. There can be no repentance with your restoration in your walk with Christ and upholding your vows, your covenant promise. Taking Holy Communion without a repentant and forgiving heart and mind, and restoration brings sickness and death-earthly and second death. Again in 1st Corinthians 11:27-29 *Wherefore whosoever shall eat this bread, and drink this cup of the Lord, unworthily, shall be guilty of the body and blood of the Lord. But let a man examine himself, and so let him eat of that bread, and drink of that cup. For he that eateth and drinketh unworthily, eateth and drinketh damnation to himself, not discerning the Lord's body.* It is interesting that the church leaders today choose willfully to leave out this important verse during communion services. Do you honestly expect that God does or should welcome home those who willfully break covenant promises and who refuse to truly repent and restore their walk?

There can be no salvation without true repentance and restoration in your walk.

One last thought here. You may say that after all I've told of what my wife did, and what a wonderful woman she was before her friends destroyed her, and perhaps all you have done...why should you return or how could you return to thy partner after leaving them. We should ask the same question of why Christ should accept us back after we have left Him. He welcomes us back as should your husband, and believe me, the strength of

returning, repentance, restoration, revival over-powers anything that happened in the past. Dearest friends, please hear
what the Holy Spirit is saying today. Some say that love is blind.
If that were true, we wouldn't see the faults in each other. But
the God who brought you together is not blind. Think about it.

Furthermore, while it takes great love, forgiveness, courage
and strength for God and husbands to accept the sinner or
wife back; it takes great strength in humility and surrender
for us sinners and wives to return unto God or their husbands.
It takes great strength and courage on both sides; this is not
a one-sided thing, and in a marriage situation, almost always
both sides have forgiving to do.

Rom. 8:39 isn't that what you are told when you marry, let
no many put asunder?)

The church has a few roles to play here. First is preparation
for dating for young people. Secondly, good Bible based premarital counseling. Third, Good Bible based marriage classes
and support groups for the married couples, and fourth is programs for support of broken families and victims of divorce,
NOT for the ones who effect the divorce as they are in violation
of God's plan and have broken their vows to their partner AND
to God, and the perpetrator of such covenant breaking should
be removed from the church fellowship until or if they repent
and restore their vows to God and their life partner. The church
should do everything possible to restore the marriage, rekindle
the fire to prevent divorce. Church leaders must set a biblical
example to the flock in their own lives and families.

I would also steer you to read 1st Corinthians 6:7.

As I was retyping 1st Corinthians 13:4-7 for the chapter
on betrothal, I was struck once again about the strength and
encouragement that these verses have if one would only take
the time to read and truly grasp these concepts before betrothal,
after betrothal and the remainder of their lives together. All
betrothed and married couples need truly to sit down in a quiet
setting and review together these powerful verses. If they or
you would, there wouldn't be the marriages and divorces that
we see today. Look my dear brothers and sisters, Love is willing

to suffer (as Christ did). Love is kind, not envious or proud, is not inappropriate or rude, selfish, it isn't easily provoked and is without any evil thoughts. Love doesn't rejoice in evil but does rejoice in the truth. Love enables you to bear and endure whatever comes along, and it never fails. Here we are discussing the issue of divorce so I wish to especially repeat that latter part as I paraphrased the verses for you, LOVE is not inappropriate or rude, selfish, it isn't easily provoked and is without any evil thoughts. Love doesn't rejoice in evil but does rejoice in the truth. Love enables you to bear and endure whatever comes along, and it never fails. If this is true and you truly love someone, why cannot you bear the situation, endure unto the end? Divorce is a selfish and destructive act and it is not love and bears serious consequences both now and eternally. Love bears all things and endures unto the end.

Again, in reviewing the various dating sites from various areas of the world, I found that women today are very sexual-physical needs, and that many married women feel bored or their husbands have lost interest. I see that many feel that they don't get as much attention as they wish, yet they claim to be independent. I find that passion and romance are foremost on most agendas and few mentioned that they are looking for a loving partner for marriage. Yes, they want loyalty and honesty. A few actually said that they had given up on finding love, just wanted sex. What a sad commentary for today's society. I wish that I could access the opposite side to see what men are saying. But I pray that you men are hearing what the women are saying here and that both sides are hearing what this entire message is saying, and the bottom line is love first. With love there must be forgiveness because we are all sinners, repentance, compassion, and restoration in our marriages and in our Christian walk with Christ.

There are no New Testament examples of an offended mate being allowed to divorce in the case of marital unfaithfulness or any other cause. The Bible says to love your enemy, bless those who persecute you, don't you think that applies to your God ordained partner? Remember that Jesus, our teacher by word and example used Samaritans in His parables, He healed Samaritans, He chose one to be His disciple (Simon called Peter) who turned out to be one of the most spoken about disciples.

The two shall become one. One cannot be divided except into fractions. Any other number can be divided, but one cannot be divided!

A cord is weak but when three cords (God, husband, and wife) are braided together, interwoven, then there is such tremendous strength. When one decides to separate (and that one will never be God), or divorce from the other two, she is weak and can easily be torn apart, because you are now outside of God's will and plan for you.

And I shall conclude this chapter with a few verses from the book of Hebrews Chapter 10 verses 21-27 where we read *And having an high priest over the house of God; Let us draw near with a true heart in full assurance of faith, having our hearts sprinkled from an evil conscience, and our bodies washed with pure water.* **Let us hold fast the profession of our faith** *without wavering; And let* **us consider one another** *to* **provoke unto love** *and to good works: Not forsaking the assembling of ourselves together, as the manner of some is; but exhorting one another: and so much the more, as ye see the day approaching.* **For if we sin willfully after that we have received the knowledge of the truth, there remaineth no more sacrifice for sins, but a certain fearful looking for of judgment and fiery indignation,** *which shall devour the adversaries,* Let us continue in verses 29-32, *Of how much sorer punishment, suppose ye, shall he be though worthy, who hath trodden under foot the Son of God, and hath counted the blood of the covenant, wherewith he was sanctified, an unholy thing, and hath done despite unto the Spirit of grace? For we know him that hath said, Vengeance belongeth unto me, I will recompense, saith the LORD. And again, the LORD shall judge his people. It is a fearful thing to fall into the hands of the living God. But call to remembrance the former days, in which, ye were illuminated, ye endured a great fight of afflictions.* And then verse 38 *Now the just shall live by faith: but if any man draw back, my soul shall have* *no pleasure in him.* Men, you are to be the high priest of your Christian home. Hold on to your faith in God and teach thy family to do likewise and run the race enduring unto the end, til death do us part, don't go the way of the world. Just because everyone else does it, doesn't make it right, only by following God, being Christ-like, can you receive the prize at the end, of eternal life with Christ. If you truly believe and have the true righteous faith, can you receive the strength from Him.

Many, perhaps most people later regret choices that they have made. Many live with the shipwrecked lives from wrong choices that they have made long ago. Praise God that there is forgiveness. There can be redemption, revival, and healing, even for the worst of decisions, including within marriages. I want to take you to Isaiah 54:8 and 10 which tells us *In a little wrath I hid my face from thee for a moment; but with everlasting kindness will I have mercy on thee, saith the LORD thy redeemer. For the mountains shall depart, and the hills be removed; but my kindness shall not depart from them neither shall the covenant of my peace be removed, saith the LORD that hath mercy on thee.* Now my dearest brothers and sisters if God has such love, mercy, and forgiveness for us sinners, shouldn't we likewise be Christ-like and be able to love, show mercy, and forgive our God anointed life marriage partner?

Malachi 2:13-15, shows us that all divorce breaks the sacred covenant promise made at the time of marriage, and remarriage violates God's plan which He established at creation when He made only one wife for Adam, thus no polygamy either.

Bloom where you are planted, in marriage no going outside of marriage and never breaking the sacred covenant Ezekiel 18:38-48

I would also encourage to read Ezekiel 18:23-24, 27-28, 30.

*** Please note that the few cases that I counseled and included herein, are very delicate situations which confirm what God teaches, but each and every situation is different and **must** be handled by prayer. ***

PERSONAL NOTES

Proverbs 3:7 *be not wise in thine own eyes: fear the Lord, and depart from evil.*

CHAPTER 10

Building Blocks For Building Bridges

Dear Friend, if you do not know Jesus Christ as the Savior of your life, you need to settle some urgent matters with Him. Before we go any farther, and continue this message, let's go to God together and do business. God Himself promised us in His Holy Word, the Bible, that when we sincerely come to Him with a broken heart, He will hear and answer our prayers. The first thing to do is for you to make peace with Him by having all your sins forgiven. That way, the barrier between you and God is torn down so that the two of you can get to know each other. This will be a very brief chapter as most everything was already covered, but I was asked to include this section just to put it all together and help people to begin the process of building bridges, but there are a few new important points that I included here so please don't skip over this chapter.

Just take a few minutes and pray, after which I will give you a few minutes for your own private prayer.

Dear Father God,

Please give me faith as I pray this. We are in so much trouble, and I need your help. Please forgive me of my many sins. I am sorry that I have lived mostly for myself up until now. I confess that I have wasted so much of the life that you gave me by making such a mess of it.

I have read Thy words today and have been convicted. I repent of my sins and I want to make a fresh start from this minute on. With your help, I will live for you from now on. Please come into my life in a real and powerful way. I surrender all of me, everything that I am to you. I wish to hold nothing back. Please take control of my heart and come and live in me.

Father God, search my heart today and forgive me of all my sins and help me to forgive others who have hurt me, my family, parents, spouse, children, as well as any others. Give me the strength and courage to do what is right by you. Cleanse me and restore me unto the path of righteousness. As I recommit my life unto You and unto my family once again, I ask you to give me the courage and strength to do what I need to do to restore and revive my walk with you, my family, and my marriage.

I lift my family before you at this time as well, that I may be an example for them and that they also may be convicted and change their lives, surrendering their all unto you.

Cleanse us, strengthen us, encourage us, and guide us to the path of righteousness and help us to stay thereon.

Please be my God, my Husband, and help me to be your child, your wife. I place my life completely in your hands forever. I ask these things in the name of your Son, Jesus Christ, who died for me, whom you raised back to life, so that I too can live forever more in your family. I accept your Holy Spirit into my heart and will celebrate this, my new birth. Thank you for accepting me back.Amen

Are you hurting following abusive or divorced parents? It is time to kneel before the cross of Christ and leave your past before Him. Leave your burdens with Him and walk away anew and move on in your life, looking towards the finish line rather than the past, which only is an instrument of Satan to destroy.

If you are divorced or separated, I would admonish the women to return unto their husbands and pray them the same, and for the husbands to welcome them back and accept/forgive them just as God is faithful to do for us. Even if you are still together in marriage, praying this can restore and revive, strengthen thy marriage, for we all sin and fall short. None of us are perfect, but the ONE who brought us together as husband and wife is perfect and can revive and strengthen, restore our marriages.

I was finished with what the Lord had given me to write, then one man read this message and asked me, 'you told us where we should be and where we are, but how do we get back to where we should be? He advised me that I should write a sequel to this message to cover this important point, and if the Lord so inspires me, I shall, but I prayed and felt convicted to include in this brief chapter.

It is true that man somehow, somewhere fell along the time line, slipped onto an iceberg and drifted away from land, oceans apart. Now we see that there is a problem, we lost sight of where God desires us to be, so now the question remains, what is the solution?

Quite simply, we need to build a bridge, block by block, to return to the land of promise from whence we began, and the path of righteousness.

There is a saying Change doesn't happen overnight, and Rome wasn't built in a day, change takes time. But is this really true? I think that it needn't be. With sincere prayer, love, faith, trust, surrender, and repentance, God is able to change lives... your life in a single heartbeat! In this brief chapter it is my desire to assist you in understanding the basic building blocks with which you may begin to bridge that gap. This is only a beginning, but with these, the precepts contained throughout this message, and God, you will be amazed at what can happen in your life...and it will affect your life for all eternity! God desires and I desire to assist you with building blocks to assist you in getting back over that vast ocean and back to the path of righteousness and the promised land of God. This is of course completely contrary to the social norm liberated mindset of today, but is on track with what God teaches us in His word and plan. I am not here to tickle your ears, but to bring God's word and plan unto you, to pierce you and bring thee unto repentance and bring revival into thy life.

Before we proceed in this chapter, I wish to say that the best things that a couple can do is to;

- pray and hold fast to God

- make sure with Scripture that you are being obedient according to your gender

- Communicate!!!!!!! This last point I will discuss further in this section.

First of all, **children**, obey, honor, and respect thy parents in the Lord. This includes all of us as we are all children of God. In other words, if you want true revival, joy and peace in your life, and want to live long (eternity), then you must love, obey, honor, and respect the Lord our God, our Father, our Savior. This is the first step that must be taken, and it must be taken with a clean, pure, and sincere heart, not just words.

Children need to be taught God's word, His precepts. It is the most important thing that one can do to, with, and for their children. In order for us to be able to do this, we must study God's word, listen to and speak with our Father in heaven, so that we may gain this understanding. Teaching God's word is more important than anything else, as everything else that is important may be learned through life experience.

Men, you must love thy wife as Christ loves the church. Your wife needs to hear and see that you love her, that you are proud of her, that you respect her. You need to set the godly, Christ-like example for her, and take the authority of her and thy household responsibly and respectfully. You need to bless thy wife and household just as Job did, routinely. Tell your wife with sincerity and love just how beautiful and how wonderful she truly is, for she is God's gift to you, you need to praise God for her and let her always know just how much you appreciate this most precious gift. Did she make you pancakes that looked more like waffles, a cake that dropped, the steak not done just right...is the garbage not taken out because she was trying to have the children ready for you when you walked through the door? Forgive her and praise her for what she has done.

You must NEVER compare her with other women, for she alone is God's chosen gift for you and you alone.

Become selfless rather than selfish. If you aren't sure, just ask your wife for her opinion, what can I do to be more selfless and less selfish?

Read God's word faithfully on a daily basis and meditate after reading- what is God saying here, and what is He trying to say to me? How may I apply this in my life? Then apply it!!!

Love thy wife and children as God loves the church.

Teach thy children God's word, read it and teach it, and live it!

Women, your husband needs to hear and see that you love him, that you are proud of him, that you respect him. Even if he makes mistakes, look for the good, and praise him. He may not have gotten the promotion, the new job, the raise, he may not have fixed the broken pipe, but he tried, praise him!

Wives submit unto thy husband, surrender your all unto him including the authority.

Be a living example unto thy children in all things. Always speak highly and praise their father always so that they learn to respect and praise him and our heavenly Father as well. How you treat your husband should be a direct reflection unto your children and all the people around you wherever you go, of how we are to treat God.

One of the biggest problems that we have in our marriages and in our Christian walk is that we always want to be independent and in control. We cannot be married to God and be independent, any more than we can be married and be independent. We are not in control of God, nor can we be; and a wife is not to be in control of her husband, nor can she be IF she is going to be a Christian, a godly wife!

Feminism is devouring families, imperiling children, blurred the lines between male and female which is clearly a violation of Scriptures, and seducing the churches. It must be denounced- feminism is a genderless society. It existed in at too many cultures, none of which survived more than a few years. It is a threat because it devalues marriage and child rearing. Women who choose to be a wife and mother as God ordained them to be, should not be devalued, but praised. Feminism is demeaning man's uniqueness and importance, and it is denying woman's invaluable and incomparable role as a nurturing mother and helpful wife.

In the Scripture there are six very specific words- *Male and female He created them*, they are two distinct sexes. They were created differently, appeared differently, and were for different functions!

If you are **single**, wait upon the Lord, live for Him, praise Him, and accept joyfully His plan for thy life.

Marriage is a serious covenant, which affects many lives, including your own. Don't get betrothed (engaged) until you are certain that you are ready for marriage until death, with this particular partner. Don't jump into it, but pray about it. It is far more than just a piece of paper. Marriage is a sacred vow and bond between God, your partner, and thyself. It is a very serious matter and must be handled carefully and prayerfully!

There can be NO prenuptial agreements. You must trust God and trust thy partner. A prenuptial agreement demonstrates a lack of faith and trust in both God and thy partner, as well as in thyself. It sets you up for failure in your marriage and thy life.

Don't ever compare thy partner, marriage, or thyself with any other- be what God wants you to be and be satisfied with His precious gift to you.

Instead of allowing disagreements to fester into cancerous wounds which will destroy your marriage or family, just forgive and move on. Always honor and cherish thy wedding vows even if times get rough, God is still there with you and your family. Everybody makes mistakes, forgive your partner, forgive yourself, and move on.

Sex is not a game, nor a time for sexual gymnastics. Sex is not a toy. Intercourse is the most intimate moments of time you may ever have in this earthly life. It is to be a precious time of exchange of an intensely deep form of love and a complete giving of yourself to thy partner. It must be completely selfless, wholly respectful of thy partner. If done properly with a godly heart and mind, can be the most intensely beautiful and precious moments in earthly life for both the man and the woman. If not done properly, it can be the most painful and deadly experience in your life.

You should not participate in any form of sexual activity except with thy husband or wife.

You should never use or even consider using any form of birth control or abortion, but rather give God complete control over thy life. Trust God and trust thy partner.

Parents, teach thy children God's word by word and by example in your lifestyle and habits.

If your children are married, don't interfere in their marriage, it is their marriage not yours. Don't ever take sides, seek God if you are asked for assistance from another couple. Pray daily for them, encourage them continually in good times and bad. If patient, the sun will shine once again.

Divorce...Don't ever even consider divorce or even separation! If the thought even crosses thy mind, kneel down at once and pray to bind these evil spirits that seek to destroy you and thy marriage, and then confess to thy partner, and seek forgiveness. What God hath joined together let no man, nothing and nobody tear apart. Do whatever it takes...sacrifice, surrender, love unconditionally, and forgive one another's faults, for we all have faults, and focus upon the good in thy partner., and most of all, trust God! Forgive seventy times seven just as God forgives you!

If you are divorced, return unto thy partner and live happily ever after.

Churches get involved in change. Use this message and encourage, help people to change back to God's way in their Christian walk as well as in their marriages and family relationships Jesus wants us to take life seriously. He wanted love, no playing around, in order to overcome the enemy and be godly. Jesus taught us to do likewise. How do we do this? We can do this by looking to God, His Father and ours, praying, talking with our Father, and living a life that is pleasing unto

Him, a life of love, forgiveness, mercy and grace, sacrifice, and surrender.

These are just a few brief areas to start with but if you will start with these basic blocks, and then expand upon these with other blocks that are found throughout this message and God's word. Soon you shall have a bridge linking God, your family, and yourself back together as God so earnestly desires.

Proverbs 17:14 says it well, when a pipe begins to leak, repair it before it blows. The same is true in our marriages. When there is an issue, no matter how big or small, sit down together and resolve the issue before it blows into disaster.

When you are in the wrong, immediately admit your fault and repent and correct the problem. Confession with repentance softens even the hardest of hearts.

Nagging and quarreling are telltale signs of suppressed anger or frustration. Rather than avoiding the situation or allowing this to separate you, continue to build your spiritual relationship with God and each other. Sit down and calmly and quietly express your feelings, frustrations, your needs, getting right to the root of the situation then the couple should work out a viable solution to resolve these feelings or needs. Don't accuse or be hostile about it, resolve it with love and compassion. Marriage in fact brings special challenges, but remember that conversely, it also brings special blessings, so look to the blessings and cross the bridge rising above any problems or challenges that arise, moving onward and leaving them behind. I am not saying to dismiss or ignore the problem, rather I am saying to resolve them and then move on. Paul had some great advice when he addressed the people of Ephesus 4:26-27 Be ye angry, and sin not: let not the sun go down upon your wrath: Neither give place to the devil.

Before you speak, remember and ask yourself this acronym (T.H.I.N.K.), is it:

- **T**rue
- **H**elpful

- **I**nspiring

- **N**ecessary

- **K**ind

Please take a moment to look at Paul's letter to the people in Ephesus, chapter 6:12-17 and note that these are not only critical for the Christian walk but also for your marriage and family as well.

Allow me to get to the bottom line here friends. Men, although you represent a type of our God, our heavenly Father, and Bridegroom, you are not perfect. You must make every effort to be Christ-like and accept that thy wife will not be perfect either and you must love and forgive her just as Christ does for us. Work on your weaknesses and put God first in thy life, family second, and work and all other earthly pleasures last. Once again become the lord of your family like Job was. Sacrifice and surrender all for your God given family just as He gave His all-His life, for us. You need to lead, guide, and protect thy wife and family, lovingly.

Now, with that said, women, realize that you are not perfect and neither will thy husband be. He is to be the lord of your home, by God's design and choosing for you, allow him to be; love and encourage him in his walk. Be loving and caring, serve him with all humility and submit unto his authority just as we are to do unto our Bridegroom, our heavenly Father, Almighty God. Obey and honor him as thy lord. You are to follow the leading of thy lord and allow thyself to be sheltered under his wings lovingly and learn from thy husband.

I realize that this sounds so foreign and absurd by today's standards, for it's not the way of the world, but it is God's way! And this is the key to a happy and healthy marriage...unto Him and to thy spouse.

I dare say that if people would become less selfish and more selfless, there would be far fewer problems in our marriages, our churches, and in our societies. We became selfish through the sin of Adam and Eve, and it has just festered up into what we have today-me...me...me... But society can't function or survive with that mentality...neither can marriages, so when we act or speak to our God ordained **LIFE** partner, we must consider a selfless mentality and concentrate on not being selfish. Men, yes you are the head of the family, you are in authority, but...this should humble you, not fill you with pride. You must consider the feelings of your wife and children when making decisions. Remember that God even gave you authority over your wife's vows, etc. but you are accountable before God, so be concerned about them and their feelings and what is best for them and the family, rather than on what you want, selfless rather than selfish. Women likewise. You want to go out to work, to... but God hath given you the responsibility of tending to thy husband's home, of bearing him children and tending to them, your responsibility to God and thy husband is to love, respect, obey God and thy husband and keep them happy, selfless, not selfish, no longer independent. When you become betrothed it is no longer I, but we, because you are now one body, even though not yet consummated, and I can and should never again be considered, because essentially, I no longer exists. Think about it. So, if I doesn't exist, then I am no longer of any significance, I am no longer important, because I no longer exist, it is now and forever more, we. Think about this, meditate upon it, repent and change your way of thinking based upon this profound thought that was just given me by the Spirit of the living God. In 1st Corinthians chapter 13, the infamous love chapter, we are told that love is kind and patient, it does not envy, it's not proud. It is **not self-seeking**, is **not easily angered, does not keep record of wrong-doings...** I must add here that while chapter 13 details how we as true Christians are to love; it does not mention the consequences one may face by loving in such a manner. Love can cause a lot of hurt and grief just as it did Christ Himself, but it is the way in which we must live IF we desire to call ourselves Christians. And during these tough times remember 1st Timothy 4:8 *I can do all things through Christ which strengtheneth me.* This includes enduring unto the end as God ordained regardless of the circumstances.

As your bridge continues to grow, keep praying; seek prayer from your church family, godly friends, and if married, from thy spouse. Then read, reread and apply this message and God's word daily and apply it to thy life, and begin living the life of a true Christian, and experience the joys that can be found only by living a godly life. And as Paul teaches in Romans 12:2, *And be not conformed to the world: but be ye transformed by the renewing of your mind, that ye may prove what is that good, and acceptable, and perfect will of God.*

Building... or rebuilding trust doesn't occur overnight or at the snap of a finger. It must be taken one step at a time. It is a period of time that you must be extremely cautious as figuratively, you are walking on eggshells. One little mistake can set you back into oblivion. But when one is trying to build or rebuild trust and confidence, as long as there is an effort, both parties must be patient and understanding of each other's feelings during this trying time. This rebuilding of trust after it has been broken MUST begin with confession and sincere repentance.

Throughout scripture, we are admonished to love one another, bare one another's burdens, live in peace and harmony, to be patient, kind to each other, and of course as sinners this can be hard to do, but with God all things are possible. It is God who gives us the courage and strength to carry on and get across the bridge over troubled waters, and the ability to get to the other side. When in prison, on death's doorstep, there were many times on those gloomy cloud filled days, literally and figuratively, that I would strive to find that one albeit tiny hole through the clouds and see the blue on the other side. This gave me hope. I held onto God, I held onto hope, and God's promise. He never failed me and praise the living God, I made it to the other side.

It is my daily prayer that God will restore my wonderful wife whom God blessed me with as He did Job's family, but... God allows free choice; to abide by His law or to sin and follow the deceiver. Only an unbeliever will leave a marriage partner and break covenant vows with God. God's word teaches *But if*

449

the unbelieving depart, let him depart. A brother or a sister is not under bondage in such cases: but God hath called us to peace, 1st Corinthians 7:15.

If you are divorced, separated, or even thinking about or considering separation or divorce, think again! Consider what you are doing spiritually; think about all who shall suffer because of your sinful act. Sit down and prayerfully recall the first date, the original sparks, your marriage ceremony as you looked into your partners eyes and said I do before God and man; recall your honeymoon...Let us forgive one another and rekindle the original flame, forgive and love as Christ calls us to do. Wives, if you are separated or divorced for a day or twenty years, humble thyself and return to thy first husband, in full repentance, and men receive them back in full forgiveness and love as Christ does for us.

It is easy to find fault, but not so easy to find forgiveness because of our pride, but God can easily find fault in us as well. What God teaches throughout His precious word is LOVE and FORGIVENESS. He is faithful to forgive us, and expects us to forgive one another, not looking for the faults, but for the strengths. My wife wrote that she loved me then left. This is completely contradictory, for love is a bond, and a bond does not and cannot allow any separation. Love is unity, one...just as we are one with God if we truly believe. I believe that my wife loved me and still does, but was confused by the world as so many are, and instead of clinging to God who I taught her about, she became one with the world and Satan, but it isn't too late for her to return or any other of the millions of women who are separated or divorced from their husbands. Forsake the world (James 4:4 and 1 John 2:15) and return to God and your husbands, for God's sake as well as your own.

I have said repeatedly but please allow me to recapitulate this one point so very important for you, for God, and for the world; you don't or didn't fall in love, nor can you ever fall out of love. I still love my wife and children with all my heart. Love is an action not just word, it is an action of choice, that is why God can tell us to love our enemy, and how He can still love us sinners. True love must be voluntary and from the heart, never forced or demanded, it must be an individual choice, a free choice just as God gives unto us. When you say 'I love you to your marriage partner, family member, or anyone, you are in essence saying 'I respect you, I honor and care about you, I will protect you at ANY cost, and will do anything I can for you, putting them before yourself...It is an action and a vow to cherish and uphold and should never be taken advantage of. In the vows that you take to become one, the first thing is do you promise, will you vow before God and man to love...will you choose to love him/her...until death! Separation, divorce, or even staying together in hatred is a choice you make-a choice to hate. You can choose to hate the mistakes that you and your partner made, but you should never hate thy God appointed partner, as God hates our sin but He still loves us. When you choose to hate, separate or divorce, you violate God's command to love; you break your vows to God and man. You chose and vowed to love, and it is time for all to choose to return to thy God chosen partner and choose to love them...no matter what.

There should be laws once again against adultery and fornication (there still are such laws in parts of Asia), but the truly spiritual, must remember that regardless of mans' law, God's law is supreme and is the one that ultimate judgment shall rest upon.

God did not want my wife or any of the thousands of other wives to leave their husbands, but God allows us free choice... who shall you serve, God or man? In my case, God didn't take my family from me so that He could take me out into the remote parts of the world for missions; No, He took me into the mission field because of my wife's sinful decision. He raised me to greater levels. Just as our faith is tried and tested, so are our marriages. Through these times, we make choices. The believer will hold on tight whereas the unbeliever often walks away. This is true in the Christian walk as well as in our marriages. The believer is raised to a greater level of faith, whereas the unbelievers walk away. We see this beautifully illustrated in His parable of the sower in Matthew 13:3-8.

Now I wish to share something else that the Spirit shared with me. Everything was created by God and everything belongs to God, and likewise all property, possessions, including a man's wife and children become his, the minute that the woman's dad gives her over to the man. IF she chooses to abandon God and her husband, she has no rightful entitlement to anything but the clothes on her back, just as IF we choose to leave, walk away from God our Bridegroom, we have no rightful entitlement to anything from Him. Salvation comes from holding on, those who endure unto the end shall receive the crown, see James 1:12 and the Revelation to John 2:10. Man was created by God the Father, not by God the mother, and we are HIS children. In marriage, the wife, the children, and all of the property belongs to the man. The Bible tells us that the world and all it contains belongs unto the Lord. If a woman leaves her man for ANY reason, she should go out empty handed because she is not to leave her husband and the fact that she, his children and all of the property belongs unto him. She walking out on him signifies that she wants nothing to do with him, wanting to be independent of him completely and assuming full responsibility for herself and any children that she steals away from their father, therefore the man should not be required to provide any longer this stray woman any support. And furthermore, she should be thrown in prison for breaking covenant and especially if she steals his children. However, she will be judged in the final judgment!

The Bible is so clear on this important point. If people (and divorce judges) would realize this and enforce biblical teachings, there would be so much fewer divorces in the world today.

It is of utmost importance that one understands that Erasmus was a man who rejected sound doctrine in spite of the serious warnings of the Apostle found in 2nd Timothy 4:3, 4 *For the time will come when they will not endure sound doctrine; but after their own lusts shall they heap to themselves teachers, having itching ears; And they shall turn away their ears from the truth, and shall be turned unto fables.* Don't be an Erasmus, but return please, unto God and the path of righteousness.

One last comment that I feel led to interject here is that sur-render is the simple but profound wisdom of yielding to rather than resisting or opposing the flow of life. Resignation is not surrender-as you may still take action to change the situation, but how you respond-positive or negatively. Non surrender hardens one's heart and separates you from other people and the world. Nonresistance does not mean doing nothing but any response is non-reactive (not retaliatory) but an honest loving and realistic response. We must surrender ourselves to God and to our family, to our marriage partners.

As I mentioned earlier, Christian marriages result in divorce more than secular, meaning that there is something very wrong. What is wrong is the spiritual life of the individ-uals. If the two (you are not to be unequally yoked with unbe-lievers) have strong relationship with God, then they will have a strong marital relationship. But if one or both of the part-ners relationship is weak or non-existent, then the marriage bonds shall also become weak, fragile, and eventually prob-ably will be broken, so the solution is building a good strong relationship with God, preferably building this relationship together, and your marriage will be strengthened as well. God is calling us to come near to Him, 1st Kings 18:30, Matthew 11:28. Behold the day draweth nigh, come, you can't continue to walk in the darkness, lest ye fall. In 1st Kings Chapter 18, the false prophets didn't respond to the call and they were all exe-cuted, eternity in hell.

If you are separated or divorced, take a nice big slice of that humble pie and eat it...return unto thy first love. Turn from thy wicked ways, repent; leave your past, your baggage behind at the foot of the cross and walk on with the hope and faith and the love in your heart that can only come from thy bridegroom and thy Bridegroom. I sadly laugh as I write this thing back to Ezra 10:11, imagining the masses today sepa-rating from their adulterous (2nd or subsequent) marriages and returning to their original anointed partners, what chaos that would be, but what a tremendous blessing!

One big thing about forgiveness is that God calls us to forgive even if the other party doesn't deserve it. God forgave us while we were yet sinners, do we deserve His forgiveness?

People have two choices in marriage, life, and their Christian walk. You can choose to build bridges or to burn them, it is a free choice, but one that varies consequences. Think about it.

You may have good reason to be angry, but don't use that as an excuse to stay that way, Ephesians 4:26 tells us not to let the sun go down on our wrath.

In Hebrews 12:1-2 we are told some excellent words, *Wherefore seeing we also are compassed about with so great a cloud of witnesses, let us lay aside every weight, and the sin which doth so easily beset us, and let us run with patience the race that is set before us, looking unto Jesus the author and finisher of our faith; who for the joy that was set before him endured the cross, despising the shame, and is set down at the right hand of the throne of God*

When I was held hostage in Kenya, it seemed that whenever there was light at the end of the tunnel, it was always an oncoming train, I had to remind myself and now you, that when trials come in your path in your marriage and or life, remember that the bridge may seem long and unending, but there is beauty on the other side.

And finally, I wish to remind you that In Numbers 11:5 the people remembered the good and not the bad back in Egypt. This is how we need to be in our marriages, and in in Revelation 12:11 note that they overcame by the blood of Jesus Christ, by the Testimony of His word, and by being selfless, and so can you by these same three things.

I would encourage you to also read James 3:5,6,8.

...Marriage is sacred, handle with prayer...

In Proverbs 1:2-4 we read, *To know wisdom and instruction: to perceive the words of understanding: to receive the instruction of wisdom, justice, and judgment, and equity; to give subtly to the simple, to the young man knowledge and discretion.* AMEN!

PERSONAL NOTES

_____

_____

_____

_____

_____

_____

_____

_____

_____

_____

_____

_____

_____

_____

_____

_____

Matthew 3:3 *Prepare ye the way of the Lord, Make His paths straight*

CHAPTER 11

The Final Chapter

Shades of sunset, darken as we get older. I was thinking that this message was complete when the Holy Spirit came and told me, not yet my son. Marriage is until death do us part, so we need to address that final chapter in our lives. We both need to be prepared for this eventuality as well as be prepared for the loss of our loved ones. Neither is easy, so it is something that we wish to think about, much less prepare for, but it is important for you and your loved ones.

In Ecclesiastes 3:1-8 we read *To every thing there is a season, and a time to every purpose under the heaven:* **A time to be born, and a time to die;** *a time to plant, and a time to pluck up that which is planted;* **A time to weep, and a time to laugh; a time to mourn,** *and a time to dance; A time to cast away stones, and a time to gather stones together; a time to embrace, and a time to refrain from embracing;* **A time to get, and a time to lose; a time to keep, and a time to cast away;** *A time to rend, and a time to sew; a time to keep silence, and a time to speak; A time to love, and a time to hate; a time of war, and a time of peace.* Death is just a change of residence moving us from earth to heaven or hell.

Seasons come and go. Rhythms are all around us and even inside of us. Some are good and some bad, but to some degree we have control over many, by proper nutrition and lifestyle, healthy relationships, etc. If we treat others well, then it has a positive effect both on you as well as the other people, and can actually prolong your lifespan.

There are seasons in all of our lives, the rhythms of life; they are an integral part of our existence. Our lives go through stages from the time we are conceived until the moment we die. Some we have control over and others we don't. Some are good some are not good. These seasons come and go generally in an orderly fashion. They exist in and all around us. Our interactions with others around us have an impact on these cycles, either positive or negative.

But whether we like it or not, death is in evitable. You have no control over it, it comes when the Lord pleases, and often without notice, so it is best to be prepared. We begin to die from the time that we are born and take our first breath. Some sadly, never even get the privilege of taking their first breath. It is something that none of us can escape or fully comprehend. Though we cling to our lives and take them for granted, most never truly comprehend or understand. Most don't even think about it until something happens to you or someone else around you. While many ponder 'why am I here' the clock keeps on ticking. A few ponder their death- will it be quick or a long slow, painful or not. How soon will it occur, will I be young or old...? While others seemingly never consider or are afraid to consider death and to prepare for it. Even most who do ponder never begin to prepare for it, perhaps because death then becomes more of a reality. According to a world population clock, there are 4 births and 2 deaths in the world/second, 278 births and 110 deaths/ minute, 16,720 births and 6,611 deaths/hour and 401,300 births and 158,686 deaths/day. You may not make it through to the end of this book, you may end up in a fatal automobile accident, an aircraft may drop through your roof, may God forbid any of these things, but my point here is we never know. Nearly ten years ago I was invited to Kenya to be introduced into some villages, but when I arrived, in a split second my world was turned upside down when I was told by CID that we don't need or want white man's God in this country, give me twenty thousand U.S. dollars or else! I ended up in prison for nearly ten years During those years, I fell deathly ill and was in a coma over twenty times, and unconscious more times than I can count. But during that period, I was actually pronounced dead on three occasions. When I left Uganda for Kenya I felt and most people guessed me at thirty years of age, I was healthy, active, always took great care of myself, but...My point is, you just never know. Even when you are terminally ill, you never know. I am terminally ill as I write this with a few terminal conditions and several life-threatening conditions that can't currently be treated. I should have been dead long ago, and everyone thought that I would be the next to go both in the prison and in the hospitals, but guess what. Many died around me totally unexpected, but I by the grace of the Almighty God, am still around, traveling between villages caring for people and sharing the Good News of Jesus Christ. You just never know, so it is best for you and your loved ones to be prepared.

Everybody will die, but you choose how you will live. Yesterday is history, tomorrow is the future, we must live today. We can change yesterday tomorrow is not yet, so all we can change is how we live now.

Many people ask because they are unsure of where we go when we die. In death there are four areas according to Scripture. There is Heaven, Paradise, hades, and hell. I believe that after death our bodies go into the ground and decays-ashes to ashes, dust to dust. Our souls however await the two resurrections. While awaiting the resurrections, the truly spiritual soul goes to paradise (remember that Jesus told the man on the cross today thou shalt be with me in paradise), and those who are not truly spiritual and have denied Christ in their lives shall go to hades (See the story of Lazarus and the rich man). Then after the resurrections the truly saved shall spend eternity in heaven, whereas the others shall spend eternity in hell. Life is eternal. See Luke 16.

Since we never know, it is prudent to make out a will. A will is simply a legal document stating what you wish done with your property, possessions, money, pets, everything in preparation for your departure from this earth. You needn't worry, if anything changes, you can always amend this will. A will is even more imperative if you get married and more so when you begin having children, especially you men, because this protects your family and your assets. If you pass on without a will, most everything if not all will be taken by the government, if you have a wife (husband) you don't wish that to happen, so be prepared, it is just a quick simple trip to the local attorney.

When making out a will, don't forget your best friend, Jesus Christ. He didn't withhold His life from us. He deserves a whole heart even as we pass from this earthly life. Remember all that we have is lent to us from Him, so it is good to give back to Him.

Before going to the attorney, it is good to sit down and list ALL of your assets on a piece of paper and what you wish done with them. Doing so will save time at the attorney's office (time is money), and it may serve as an eye opener to you as well. Take that paper with you to the attorney. You may wish to discuss this with your God ordained life partner (husband or wife) if you so choose. It is good for both to make out their wills at the same time, as it saves you time and trips to the attorneys' office, kill two birds with one stone, forgive the pun.

If either of you in a marriage have secret assets, bank accounts, safe deposit boxes, etc., it truly is better for the other to know so that EVERYTHING can be recovered in the event of... Otherwise it may just sit there for all eternity. Set up your will all of your assets, what do you want done with each, how much to your spouse, and to each child? How much to Jesus Christ-the ministry(s) of your choice, lay it all out, as I said it can always be amended should anything change. Your partner passes on, you are left, but in your will, things were going to be left to them, now go to your attorney and amend your will. You have another child, go and amend your will, no problem, but it is a major problem if you leave this earth and have not left a will.

There is another type of a will that is also good to complete if you are sick or terminally ill, major heart or lung problems, renal failure, etc. This is called a living will. The living will is a legal document telling Doctors what you want to be done in the even that your heart stops and/or you stop breathing. Do you want to be resuscitated? Do you wish life support? Do you just want to be left alone and let you go? That is the purpose of this document, and it is kept as a part of your medical record, you may even wear a medical alert armband stating that you have a living will. This is important, but unfortunately, push comes to shove, when you are unable to make a decision to your care and treatment, that is when this living will comes in to play, but your family unfortunately can overrule this legal document. And since the living relatives are alive, they can sue, so the Doctors generally will comply with the wishes of the family. God be willing, your family will consent to your wishes, but this doesn't always happen, then you are stuck in the middle and you are in no condition to say yea or no.

Some people wish to donate certain organs, their bodies... whatever, for transplants, university studies, etc., and this is done through the Department of Motor Vehicles, and a notation is affixed to your driver's license, but it is good for your doctor to be aware also.

These three documents (especially the last two) are personal choices. It is up to you whether you want resuscitated or not and to what level. I had several different Doctors discuss with me what I wanted and to what level and I explained to them and why. It isn't a big deal, it is good to be ahead of the game so to speak, and ...well I am still here. I made my choice. You need to make yours for the sake of your family. It is stressful enough going through all the hoops when someone passes on, planning the funeral and burying, all the notifications, couple with the sudden loneliness realizing that your partner is no longer around. Now they have to deal with all of this? Leaving a will makes their life so much easier and less stressful. Love your family enough to take the few minutes and sit down, as I said earlier, make a simple list of ALL of your assets and what you wish done with each, and take them down to your attorney, done...you can all rest in peace knowing that all is finished. If or when that day comes, then your family will be so grateful for your love and kindness for having done this.

It is good especially if you are elderly or ill, to let your partner or nearest living relative know anything special that you would like or not like done at your funeral; or do you even want a funeral or just a memorial service? Any special music... Now is your opportunity to speak up, be prepared.

I must be honest with you. I lost my wife and children back in 2007, so I have nobody. I have no will. I felt young and energetic... BUT!!! After I awoke after being pronounced dead the first time...and the second...and even more so after the third time, I laid there thinking... What if... I have no will. What if... I am thousands of miles from my birth country. What if... When I got back to Uganda and told my good friend, my landlord everything, he gave me a place to stay, he told me a few months later that he didn't expect me to survive for even a month, but that he feared and still does, what if...and I realized once again how selfish it is not to have a will, and the stress that it causes others around you. So... I prayed, I sat down at my little laptop where I am writing this from. I opened a new page and I began to type. I said what I wished done with my body. I stated my wishes to not have a funeral service, just a simple memorial service if they so desired and just play a few of my favorite songs that are on my laptop, that because of my condition I do not wish life support. I have very little property right now, so I typed what was to be done with what little I had, where different things were to go, my landlord, my ministry... all laid out nice and neat on one page. Then I sat my landlord down and explained to him that as he knew I cannot fly because of my condition so returning to the states is an impossibility, so I appreciate all that he has and is doing, but that I didn't wish to stress him any longer (we are age mates) I laid out my wishes should anything happen. And I told him it is all in my laptop, and briefly explained about no resuscitation and briefly what he needed to know, the rest he would find here in my laptop, so now he can rest in peace. Well not exactly, he heard me gasping for breath the other night and came banging on my window at 1:30 a.m. bless his heart. But God is so good and I am still here. My point is my dear brothers and sisters, it doesn't matter how young or old you may be. It doesn't matter how healthy or unhealthy you may be. What matters most is to be ready so that your loved ones, those that care most about you don't need the added stress. Accidents happen, schoolyard shootings happen, planes crash, ships sink, heart attacks may strike, lightning strikes, we never know. Where I am mosquitoes kill millions of people, a simple little mosquito! So just love those around you enough to spend these few moments and be prepared.

The period of time after losing a loved one either through death or a divorce is very difficult. You are used to the comfort from your partner, the support, encouragement, the listening post, the warmth, the sharing, etc. But now they are gone. You sit alone on the sofa...where is my partner? He/she is gone... you go to bed, it is cold and lonely, where is my partner? Oh yes, he/she is gone...Yes, you still have the Lord who will never leave you alone, but as human beings, we need company. We read in Isaiah 51:12 *I, even I, m he that comforteth you: who art thou, that thou shouldst be afraid of a man that shall die, and of the son of man which shall be made as grass.* None of us are independent. So, the church should be a good place to turn to, to assist you with your needs. But the church should also be aware of these needs and reach out to such individuals without having to be asked. Also, if anyone sees a person in church looking alone or lonely, someone should approach them lovingly and initiate a casual conversation and feel them out for any needs and then offer assistance, perhaps even invite them to your place to share a meal and conversation. Just ask what would Jesus do? You may not know this person, but if they look alone or stressed, or whatever, just extend a kind loving hand of fellowship and invite them for lunch or dinner. It needn't be fancy, they may not be coming for physical food but for spiritual, or just a friend to talk to. Who knows you may just make a new friend? What did Mordecai tell Esther in chapter 4 and verse 14, *who knoweth whether thou art come to the kingdom for such a time as this?* Perhaps this person hasn't been to a church in years, but they just lost their partner and need, crave the fellowship, need that one person to lend an ear, a right hand of fellowship, so the church and each of its members must be keen on this. I am reminded here, of the passage found in Hebrews 3:2 in which Paul tells us *Be not forgetful to entertain strangers: for thereby some have entertained angels,* remember when the three angels appeared before Abraham on their way to Sodom and Gomorrah?

If you know that someone has lost a loved one, don't be shy or cold. Cook a bit of food and take it to them so that they can get through the grieving process without having to cook this meal. If they have children offer to take them for a couple hours so that they can have time to themselves. You see the lawn needs mowed or a gate coming down, the dog is getting hungry (probably the last thing on their mind), go tend to it. You don't even have to knock or announce what you are doing, just do it. Bring a screwdriver, a lawnmower, or a can of dog food, whatever. What would Jesus do? What would you wish people would do for you under these circumstances? If you haven't endured it, it is hard to say, but I am painting the reality for you because I have been on that end as well, and people tend to just shut you off and that hurts even more.

If you have a loved one who is very ill, it is okay to ask them their wishes, what should I do with... Put your mind at ease and they should be comforted that they are still able to help you and put your mind to rest. I can tell you quite honestly that the hospital I spent most of my time in (I was in four hospitals) was a very cold-hearted facility. Nobody cared and patients were dying by the dozens, literally. They would stack all of the bodies down at the end of the hall where they kept me, my room was usually right next to the bodies in the hall, and every hour or two they would come with a small pickup truck and collect all of the bodies, throw them in the back of this uncovered truck and drive down the little lane to their three-story morgue which looks like a converted motel, and the overflow, they throw in this same pickup and drive them down the road to the city morgue, I am not joking. Anyway, in spite of the coldness of the staff, it actually was comforting when the doctors came and were discussing death and dying and asking me what or how much I wanted done considering my grave condition. I was not at all offended, I was comforted that they cared enough to ask. (In reality I don't think that they would do anything anyway, but still), only one elderly nurse came and did CPR Cardiopulmonary resuscitation) on me one time, right after that she retired.

If you have children, and your life partner is critically ill, ask someone you trust-a friend, a relative, someone in the church to watch the children while you get everything pro-cessed and go through the grieving process. You need the time and many children are not mature enough to fully comprehend all that is going on, and you need a period for yourself. There are stages that most people go through in the grieving process, and it can take days to years, so allow yourself the time that you need. Once you get yourself together, then it is time to sit down on the sofa with your children, hug them hold them tight and gently explain to them what has happened.

If you have been married for many years, I was for twenty years, there is a high incidence of death for the surviving partner within six months of the departure of their loved one. I ended up with a heart attack but I survived. The key to sur-vival after the loss of a loved one after many years of marriage is to pick up and carry on. God took me back into the mission field spreading the Good News and caring for the orphans, the sick... and I have endured. Yes, I miss her. Yes, I wish she was still by my side, but...I have survived this loss. I write this chapter from the leading of the Holy Spirit, but I have been on both ends of this spectrum-the survivor and the dying, so I am speaking from personal experience.

Death is a fact of life that you cannot escape, birth and death. So, you need to find a way to accept this fact and learn how to deal with it. I have lost relatives. I have lost a son eight-and one-half months into the pregnancy; two adopted daughters orphans of war, and a fiancé were murdered; I lost a wonderful wife and three dear children., so I know from expe-rience about death, not to mention being in medicine for over twenty years and dealt with death a lot as I worked in special-ties where there was so much death.

One thing that I have learned through experience is to be so very careful what you say to the survivors as words can hurt so badly. For example, after we lost our son eight- and one-half months into the pregnancy, people were coming and saying things like Oh he was not good so God is cleaning up the mess (Joshua was perfect, it was a problem with the placenta), Don't worry you can have another ...When you aren't sure what to say, say nothing at all, just be there for the person. Look at Job, for what, seven days his friends just sat with him, and it was comforting to him, but then they started opening their mouths and, oh the pain! When I deal with survivors in the hospital/villages I am careful with my words, and sometimes I say nothing. Even orphaned children, I say little to, I pick them up and hold them on my lap just hugging them. If they choose to talk or ask a question, no problem, but generally I say very little and am so careful with my words because the words of others still haunt me, more than the deaths sometimes. I know it wasn't intentional but...be careful what you say or just say nothing at all, just be there. Do you need to be asked to cook a bite to eat? Do you need to be asked for a cup of chai? No, just take care of them with the love of the Lord.

Once dead, they are dead, though I have called two people back to life after being dead for a few days, and I have been dead for several hours three times, but for all intents and purposes, once dead, you are dead. You had your time to make choices, now your time is up. Praying for the dead serves absolutely no purpose. Being baptized for the dead likewise serves absolutely no purpose.

When children below the age of accountability, I believe the Bible, God's Word testifies to this fact, that if they are taken at an early age that they will be taken to heaven (Paradise). They are too young to make the decision for themselves, and Jesus loves the children.

There are seasons in all of our lives, the rhythms of life; they are an integral part of our existence. Our lives go through stages from the time we are conceived until the moment we die. Some we have control over and others we don't. Some are good some are not good. These seasons come and go generally in

an orderly fashion. They exist in and all around us. Our interactions with others around us have an impact on these cycles,
either positive or negative.

Having said all of this I need to add a note that may seem
cold, but it truly isn't and it is scriptural. Grieving should only
be for the lost, the unsaved souls that pass from this earth. If
you are certain that the individual is saved, then it should be
a time of rejoicing, because they are out of the trials, tribulations of this life and are awaiting the resurrection-that my
dear friends is a call for celebration. Yes, sure we shall miss
them, but remember, God calls us to be selfless not selfish.
Remember they are at rest now-no more suffering, no more
tears, no more sorrow... rejoice for them.

PERSONAL NOTES

_____

_____

_____

_____

_____

_____

_____

_____

_____

_____

_____

_____

_____

_____

_____

_____

EPILOGUE

Most of the world seeks to follow the U.S.A. but there is an old cliché 'if I jump off of the bridge are you going to follow? My dear friends, God's word speaks of the U.S. in the book of Daniel. She is a very evil nation that seeks to destroy all others, but who will ultimately be destroyed. The women's equality issue has caused a breakdown of the marriage and family and social values. Countries around the world are following the U.S.A. They are going to face the same problems, because it is not God's plan; and it leads to an increase in divorce, family values, and decreased social values. I am here today to call ALL people, all families, all churches, and all nations to repentance, to open your eyes and see the truth of God's precious word and the revealed truths contained in this message, so that there may be revival and restoration. We shall return to marriage shortly, but allow me first to share a few scriptures to encourage you to a closer spiritual walk.

Malachi 2:11 *Judah hath dealt treacherously, and an abomination is committed in Israel and in Jerusalem; for Judah hath profaned the holiness of the Lord which he loved, and hath married the daughter of a strange god.*

In Malachi 2:7-8 we are further told *For the priest's lips should keep knowledge, and they should seek the law at his mouth: for he is the messenger of the Lord of hosts. But ye are departed out of the way; ye have caused many to stumble at the law; ye have corrupted the covenant of Levi, saith the Lord of hosts.*

I am committed to standing up for my Lord, and to be used by and for Him; please heed these words, and I pray that

I can find a few like-minded pastors and/or individuals who will dare to spread this important message and stand firm on the word of God and not remain in the ways of this world.

Oh, my dear brothers and sisters, I do praise God for His wonderful and powerful message. We have covered so much material in so little time. It is my sincere prayer that this special message from the Holy Spirit of the Almighty God has in one way or another, reached into your hearts, minds, and souls. God hath spoken. He has used around three thousand verses from ALL sixty-six books of the Bible, to encourage and introduce you to each book, and I find it no surprise that the most come from the book of Genesis, the book of beginnings of everything, including marriage and family. It is further my prayer that each of you feel convicted in one way or another, and that your spiritual walk as well as thy personal life, and if married, your marriage will be enhanced through God's blessings. This powerful message has been a very sharp sword, but I wish to end it with **HOPE**. In the book of Malachi, we are shown people going through the motions of worship and the rituals, but without any real heartfelt conviction, much like people in the churches do today. In Ezra 9:11-12 we are told ... *The land...is an unclean land with the filthiness of the people of the lands; with their abominations...Now therefore give not your daughters unto their sons, neither take their daughters unto your sons.* You see again here that we are to separate ourselves from the world, and from the fellowship of those in the world, and commit ourselves once again fully unto God with a clean and pure heart, mind, and soul. In Isaiah 59:7-9 *Their feet run to evil, and they make haste to shed innocent blood: their thoughts are thoughts of iniquity, wasting and destruction are in their paths. The way of peace they know not...We wait for light, but behold obscurity; for brightness, but walk in darkness.* Isaiah 65:12 tells us *Therefore will I number you to the sword, and ye shall bow down, to the slaughter: because when I called, ye did not answer. When I spoke, ye did not hear; but did evil before mine eyes, and did choose that wherein I delighted not.* Then in Ezra 9:1 the believers *have not separated themselves from the people* (non-believers) *of the lands, doing according to their abom-inations.* Then in Ezekiel 33:11 He goes on to say, *I have no pleasure in the death of the wicked; but that the wicked trans-form his way and live.* Hear the love here? Ezekiel 43:9 tells us, *Now let them put away their whoredom...far from me, and I will dwell in the midst of them forever.* Ezekiel 18:30-31 He says, *Repent, and turn yourselves from all your trans-gressions: so iniquity shall not be your ruin. Cast away from you all your transgressions, whereby ye have transgressed; and make you a new Spirit and a new heart.* Now, in Daniel 12:10 we are told that *many shall be purified, and made white, and tried: but the wicked shall do wickedly: and none of the wicked shall understand; but the wise shall understand.* Turn now to the book of Psalms 118:19 and see *Open to me the gates of righteousness: I will go into them and I will praise the Lord.* In Isaiah 55:7 *Let the wicked forsake his way, and the unrigh-teous man his thoughts: and let him return unto the Lord, and He will have mercy upon him; and to our God, for He will abundantly pardon.* And Isaiah 59:2 *But your iniquities have separated between you and your God, and your sins have hid His face from you, that He will not hear.* Psalm 90:12 *So teach us to number our days that we may be apply our hearts unto wisdom.* These few verses say a mouthful, but are so important in our Spiritual walk as well as in our personal lives and mar-riages. If you are saved, does your life reflect it? Have you been pulled out of Egypt (sinful life) unto the land of promise (heaven)? If you are not saved, do you wish to join the Israelites in leaving Egypt (sinful life), and go to the Promised Land of heaven? In Ezekiel 3:19 *Yet if thou warn the wicked and she return not from her wicked way, he shall die in his iniquity: but thou hast delivered thy soul. Nevertheless if thou warn the righteous man, that the righteous sin not, and he doth not sin, he shall surely live, because he is warned, also thou hast delivered thy soul.* Isaiah 58:1 tells us *Cry aloud, spare not, lift up thy voice like a trumpet, and shew my people their trans-gression, and the house of Jacob their sins.* The Lord through His infinite grace and mercy hath spoken through me this mes-sage for all to hear. The next step is up to you. I have issued the warning, I have blown the trumpet, the question now is will you listen, and will you repent and turn from thy wicked ways, and seek His face, and submit, surrender all unto Him and forsake the world? They have rejected me, but more so they have rejected God. I blew the trumpet, I gave the warning, but their hearts are hardened. Is thy heart hardened? In 3rd John 11 *Beloved, follow not that which is evil, but that which is good. He that doeth good is of God: but he that doeth evil hath not seen God.* Then in Obadiah, we see the prophecy of the doom of Eden. Who was Eden? Eden (Esau) was the twin brother of Jacob. The story of good and evil, constantly striving with Israel, they rejected Moses, and King Saul. They fought against David, and oppressed Solomon. Herod, who killed the children in Bethlehem, in the attempt to kill Christ...marriage today and bringing down the believers, In Haggai 2:4 *Yet now be strong O Zerubbabel, sayeth the Lord; and be strong...and be strong all ye people of the land, sayeth the Lord, and work: for I am with you saith the Lord of Hosts.* We are not alone, God is with us, and He is calling us to repentance so that there may be a revival in our Spiritual walk, and in our marriages and families. In the book of Judges 6:13, Gideon cried out to God *and Gideon said unto Him, Oh my Lord, if the Lord be with us, why then is all this befallen us? And where be all His miracles which our fathers told us of...* Dear friends, there are wars and rumors of war, famine, earthquakes, tornadoes and hurricanes... more than ever before, why people ask? God is calling people unto Himself, He is telling us to wake up and smell the roses, see the signs of the times, to repent and return unto Him. **IF** we repent with a clean and pure humble heart, then He will be with us and will revive us to a life better than you have ever seen, then and only then will you truly begin to live, but you must take that first step. I refer you at this time to also read Nahum Chapter 1:2-3 and 6-8; Zephaniah 1:9 and 2:2-3. We see in 2nd John verse 9, *Whosoever transgresseth, and abideth not in the doctrine of Christ, hath not God. He that abideth in the doctrine of Christ, he hath both the Father and the Son.* This message is the doctrine of Christ, based upon the greatest commandment – to love the Lord thy God with all of thy heart, soul, and mind, and your neighbor including your life partner, and if you violate the precepts of this message, thou hast not known or seen God.

The Sermon on the Mount in Matt 5:3-4 preaches the Gospel with simplicity and power. Every word is intended to evangelize the heart of man. Man is given one narrow gate in which to pass, Repent! Repent! Repent! The Kingdom of Heaven is at hand. The first words of the sermon honor this idea, *Blessed are the poor in spirit, (those who repent), for theirs is the kingdom of heaven.* The second words of the sermon are the same, *Blessed are they that mourn,* (those who will repent*); for they shall be comforted.* The third words again repeat the call for repentance in Matthew 5:5, *Blessed are the meek, those who will repent; for they shall inherit the earth.* The subsequent words are the same in 5:6, *Blessed are they who hunger and thirst after righteousness, those who will repent; for they shall be filled.* Jesus drove this hope to those who will repent as the introduction to His sermon because He was about to draw his sword and pierce the heart of every man who ever took a breath. Jesus taught men to repent. The need for repentance teaches the doctrine of total depravity: *As it is written, there is none righteous, no, not one: There is none that understandeth, there is none that seeketh after God. They are all gone out of the way, they are together become unprofitable; there is none that doeth good, no, not one,* Romans 3:10-12. *He who is without sin cast the first stone.*

The Sermon on the Mount teaches man his depravity by the complete explanation of the Law, His Law and the sermon preaches the Gospel to all men. His disciples were in great need of understanding the Gospel. The multitudes had the same need. We have the same need today. Jesus preached the Gospel to the poor. All are poor. Without apology, the Preacher warns His audience (us) that He would use every *jot and tittle* of the law to convict them of sin, and to pierce their hearts asunder. He would drive the spike of the law into the deepest inner secret of man. Jesus was a preacher who was not willing that any should perish, but that all should come to repentance.

Today, men assume the same idea, that men are not sinners unless they have killed someone or break the civil laws. This seems to be their only criteria for qualifying as a sinner. Well, if that is the case, Jesus was to prove that all men are murderers. The Sixth Commandment now takes on an entirely new meaning. If a man is angry with his brother, and curses his brother, Jesus convicts the man of murder. He teaches that any form of anger, Raca to fool is murder. The bottom line of His thinking was to deprive anyone of his listeners, disciple or stranger, Jew or gentile, to escape the accusation and guilt of murder. All men were murderers; there is none righteous no not one. The cry of Jesus grew louder and louder: ***Repent for the kingdom of heaven is at hand.***

Jesus was not willing that any should perish, but that **ALL** should come unto repentance; therefore, he drove men to repentance, as a shepherd drives his sheep from danger.

Genesis 3:1-13 after the fall they were so full of shame, guilt and fear that they ran and hid from God our Creator, but you cannot hide from God! God found them and called out to Adam. Note that they ran and hid, they never went to seek Him or His forgiveness. What a powerful image of what sin does in our lives. We try to run and hide, which only serves to further separate us from the love of God, but He still loves us and is with us. Oh, what love! Then life began anew. We need to meditate upon these words for our marriages.

The Church has lost the respect of the society it has been sent and instructed to transform, and it has completely left its First Love, in order to conform to society for the sake of greed, power, and prosperity which has become now its basic doctrine rather than the precious and life-saving word of God. It has walked away from the power and authority of the Living God needed to accomplish such a task. The failure is not found in the Gospel of Christ, but in the church's refusal to live according to the Divine message it was given to set the example for and teach. It failed to keep out the stranger who entered and took over the church, taking it away from God and His message.

Don't allow in the stranger or the defiled lest it corrupt others. A little leaven leaveneth the whole lump. Have not fellowship with unbelievers are all commandments from God, but because of man's disobedience, the church has been destroyed. As always, God hath saved a small remnant, of which I praise God to be included in, and it is my plea that you *come out of her, my people, that ye be not partakers of her sins, and that ye receive not of her plagues,* Revelation 18:4. Who am I to make this claim? I spoke briefly about this in another of my books, but I have cheated death so many times, and have been pronounced dead a few times now. Each time was for several hours, and during that time, Jesus took me by the hand and transfigured me to a garden in heaven. I will not give details here because of space and time, but we talked and talked. I did more listening than talking. One of the things that He told me as I pleaded at the end of each of our talks, to be allowed to stay, He told me not yet my son, not yet, for I have so much for you to do down there, for behold, I am coming much sooner than anyone, especially those calling themselves by my name, who I know not, are going to be caught unaware. The end is near, that is another revelation that the Lord hath given unto me and told to write it, some revelations/prophecies He has told me to write, and others He has told me just to hold onto.

This message was very difficult for me to write for four reasons. First, I'm not a writer, but God said write, so I wrote. My teachers always told me that one could write a book from just one of my sentences. Secondly, I was attacked continually while putting these messages together. I had guards scramble the hundreds of notes that I had been given by the Spirit, all over the floor of my cell three times, 1 bag of notes was intentionally burned by guards, then the computer was sabotaged and the books couldn't open, so I had to start over, with no notes as all my notes were thrown away as I put them together in the computer, then the computer crashed. Thirdly, the great pain that I was in as well as the weakness, due to my poor health, but praise God, He sustained me throughout. Some of my notes were stolen. I was plagued with evil and wicked thoughts and dreams throughout this writing, Satan again tried to stop the ministry of God through me, but God is more powerful, there were several attempts on my life, and two different times total strangers came to the hospital where I was on oxygen, in critical condition, and told me the same identical message, Satan is very angry with your ministry and has sent his angels to harass you, tear you down, and to destroy you and your ministry. One attorney, not mine, I wasn't allowed one, and a total stranger and a Muslim, in court told me, be extremely careful because these people want you dead so bad that they can taste your blood. They are already dividing up your property knowing that you will not make it out alive and in fact they were taking all my property, men calling themselves Christians, mostly Seventh Day Adventists. But my God is all powerful, and Satan is a liar, a deceiver, and a loser, so now through God's grace and mercy, you are able to read this message. Fourth, Kenya prison 'officials,' most specifically Mrs. Pauline Wanja; Mr. Yuma (who maliciously and in violation of international human rights and Kenyan law, caused me the loss of over One million US dollars of property and personal possessions including medical equipment and supplies for my work in the villages); Omwenga tried on numerous occasions to kill me. Okamba, and chaplain Mr. Kitenge, among others; fought the writing of this message so that I had to resort to other methods of getting this message out; Colossians 3:12-17. The entire manuscript for this book was deleted from the computer; and the flash disc upon which I had backed up all of the information, was so badly infected by viruses from the school's computers, that I was unable to pull up any of the information, and then it was taken by the OIC who had known that I had it, and then the DVD that it was backed up on was stolen by the officer in charge of the school, Mr. Wanjala. So, this book is lacking some of the material contained on that disk, stolen notes, etc. But God has given me I am certain, the material that He wishes you to have at this time. Kenya needs much prayer, people please remember this nation in such grave sin.

I mention this to show you that Satan did not and does not want this message to be seen, heard, or read! That means that this message is exactly what God wants you to hear! It is interesting to note however that a dear friend who encouraged me for a while before he was transferred, copied three of my messages including this one when they were only one quarter complete and printed them for me, but said that he couldn't publish them because they are not according to the Catholic doctrine, God bless him, so many people were able to read them, and some as many as seven and eight times and wanted them again, it saved lives, literally saved the life of a young lady; and everyone that read them said that it changed their life and they will never be the same, and later I spoke briefly with him and was very surprised to hear that he (the priest) had kept these messages and told me that he refers back to them, praise God! And that was when they were far from complete! God is so good.

Romans 1:31-32 *who knowing the judgment of God, that they which commit such things are worthy of death, not only do the same, but have pleasure in them that do them.* but just as Hitler tried to halt the Jews and was unsuccessful, so will be Kenya. I had already made contingency plans to get this message out in the event that I passed on. I fully understand when Paul wrote in Romans 11:3 *Lord, they have killed thy prophets and digged down Thy altars; and I am left alone, and they seek my life.* God's word cannot be halted or stopped, never has been and never will be. Kenya is in a state of anarchy, where everyone does what is right in their own eyes without any regard for justice or their neighbor. It is void of any morals, values, ethics, or dignity. There are no real leaders. It is a nation who asks God's blessings every time they talk, but the only blessings that they receive are the curses from turning their backs on God while hypocritically claiming to be a Christian nation. Their leader is quickly leading his country to a civil war. But I ask you today, how many people today claim Christianity, yet are living only for the world and have no regard for our only Savior? This message is on marriage and family, yet is concurrently a call to repentance and revival. God frequently took me back to the verse 1st Chronicles 28:20 *Be strong and of good courage, and do it; fear not, nor be dismayed: for the Lord God, even my God, will be with thee; He will not fail thee, nor forsake thee, until thou hast finished all the work for the service of the house of the Lord.* I praise God continually, and thank Him for finding me worthy to be used by Him. The more Satan attacks me, even with depression, the more I was compelled to get this and other messages out to the world, to you; for if it was important enough for Satan to try so hard to stop me, I believe that it is important enough to overcome the enemy and get these messages out to you, for the Glory of God, Hallelujah! A good book causes one to think about the issues addressed, as well as to stimulate discussion, and it is my prayer that this message will do both in your life.

I have never been told by anyone that they enjoyed the Spirits messages that I have preached, and I praise God for this in that I am here to speak His word, His message, which is sharper than a two-edged sword and is designed to pierce through, that we may be brought to our knees in repentance, become strengthened, be edified; I'm not sent to areas around the world to tickle people's ears, or to make people feel good about themselves, to entertain the world. There are enough wolves in sheep's clothing doing this already, and why so many people are so far off the path of righteousness. I have been sent to gather the sheep back onto the path of righteousness, and this time He chose to bring me to East/Central Africa. I have always been told that my preaching is such, "we've never heard like that before and it's what we **need** to hear." But this is only because each message that I share is from God not my doing, and never canned. God inspires the message, tells me where to deliver that message and I go.

In Romans 10:12, we see that in the resurrection, there shall be no difference between a man and a woman. All shall rise up for judgment; the righteous shall be saved, while the nonbeliever, the sinner shall be condemned. It is my humble prayer that each of you who hear or read this powerful message, hath been convicted, will humble thyself and seek a closer walk with God, as well as in your marriage and family, that you will get on or return to the straight and narrow path of righteousness, bowing down to His authority, His love, mercy, and grace. Then you too can become LIGHTHOUSE OF BLESSED HOPE.

If you will, we shall see revival in our lives, in our marriages, in our churches, and in our communities; but it all begins inside your heart and mine.

In 2ⁿᵈ Chronicles 29:16 we are told that after Hezekiah was convicted, he spoke to the priests, *And the priests went into the **inner** part of the house of the Lord, to cleanse it, and brought out all the uncleanness that they found in the temple of the Lord...* Malachi 3:14 and 4:3, we see that the people were complaining because there was no difference between the good and the evil, the just and the unjust, just as we see in the world today, but God promised us that the evil, the unjust shall be judged and that the faithful shalt be rewarded as we see in chapter 4 of the book of Malachi.

In Isaiah 24:5 *The earth is defiled; because they have transgressed the law, changed the ordinance, broken the everlasting covenant. Therefore hath the curse devoured the earth, and they that dwell therein are desolate.* Verse 8 *the noise of them that rejoice endeth...* we must get back on the path of righteousness so that we also may rejoice. In the Old Testament times, if we look at the big picture, we see that Israel went in cycles. There was sin and idolatry, followed by enslavement by neighbors, and then they cry out to God. God heard their cries and sent them a king or a prophet, and Israel was restored. Today we are in the sin and idolatry phase, and we need to cry out to our Almighty God in repentance, so that there may be revival and restoration once again. Amen?

Psalms 12:1-2, 4 tells us *Help, Lord, for the godly man ceaseth; for the fruitful fail from among the children of men. They speak vanity everyone with her neighbor: with flattering lips and with a double heart do they speak...who have said, with our tongue will we prevail; our lips are our own: who is Lord over us?* This is the condition of the world today, selfish instead of looking to God, and the conditions of the marriages, for the women are no longer respecting, honoring, or submitting unto the Lord of their homes and marriages. People are proud and look to themselves rather than God, and this is the basis for some of the Eastern religions, where 'I am god.' Oh, such an abomination my friends, we must look to God and God alone.

My dear brothers and sisters, after hearing this message, I pray that you will enter into the inner part of your temple, your heart, mind, and soul, and cleanse it, remove all of the uncleanness that you find, and then sanctify thyself unto God our Father, Husband, Father Almighty, Amen.

Our bodies are comprised of some ten trillion cells and trillions of good bacteria, each with a specific and special purpose. Each must do its part while working together with the others in perfect harmony, or else you get our dis-ease. Likewise, in marriage and family, men, women, and children, all have specific and individual roles to play which are ordained by God, not man, and must work together in unity and perfect harmony. We are all, each of us, a single cell in the body and family of God. We each have a specific purpose that He created us for in this universe. The dis-ease in the world today, in the family, and in the church, is because there are too many cells not functioning properly, all wanting to do their own thing, or trying to be like the other cells, and this has caused a widespread cancer that is continuing to grow and destroy lives. Let us today, be the cell that God ordained us to be and let God bring restoration and revival into our lives and into our marriages and families.

I invite you now to read Isaiah 1:19-20. My dear friends, In Jeremiah 29:11, God says that He has a future and a plan for us, a hope. Each of us was created for a God given purpose, you are no accident! An old slogan said 'everything's better with Blue Bonnet on it, but I say to you today that everything, marriage included, is better with Jesus in it. Are you separated or divorced? Unless remarried (I told you that this message would have a very special ending-read on), be ye reconciled to thy partner whom God hath ordained for you, and with whom you vowed before God to love and to cherish...until death do you part. Please...do it today, don't remain in the sin, don't delay another day! Seek counseling, if necessary, from a godly person, your pastor perhaps, me, or any truly spiritual person. If their advice and counsel coincide with scripture, praise God and heed the advice; if not, find someone else. Note that I said coincides with scripture, not necessarily coinciding with your wishes or desires.

As I stated from the beginning, I didn't write this message. I've never heard or read anything like this before. This message is completely inspired by the Spirit of the Living God, and is consistent with His messages through me on repentance and revival.

You have heard, and I pray, listened to what the Spirit of God hath said; now it is your turn to respond. If there were one thousand steps between God and you, He would take the nine hundred and ninety-nine, but...He'll leave that first step to you. Now, in 1ˢᵗ Corinthians 11:27-30 I want to share with you something very pointed, sharp, and hard to swallow, but... we are told, *Wherefore whosoever eat this bread, and drink this cup of the Lord unworthily, shall be guilty of the body and blood of the Lord: But let a man examine himself, and so let him eat of that bread, and drink of that cup;* **For he that eateth and drinketh unworthily, eateth and drinketh damnation to himself, not discerning the Lord's body.** This portion is never quoted during communion services, I wonder why? And also, in Matthew 5:23-24 we see *Therefore if thou bring thy gift to the altar, and there rememberest that thy brother hath ought against thee; Leave thy gift before the altar, and go thy way;* **first be reconciled** *to thy brother, and then come and offer thy gift.* Then in Deuteronomy 12:26, 28 *Only thy holy things which thou hast, and thy vows, thou shalt take, and go unto the place which the Lord shalt choose... Observe and hear all these words which I command thee, that it may go well with thee, and with thy children after thee forever, when thou doest that which is good and right in the sight of the Lord thy God;* Forgiveness my dear friends. My dear brothers and sisters, are you prostituting thyself physically, emotionally, or spiritually? Now is the time to repent, turn from thy wicked ways, turn back to God Almighty, and seek forgiveness. Leave thy sins and sinful nature at the altar, at the feet of Jesus, walk away from them and never look back, rather look forward to the finish line.

You know two of the biggest problems causing divorce today are first, misunderstanding, which won't happen if you will only talk and listen to one another, rather than to friends or family. Secondly, pride...unwillingness to humble oneself and say I'm sorry. Praying for forgiveness and accepting forgiveness, forgiving one another for any and everything just as our Lord does for us. Humble yourself and accept 'I am wrong, I made a mistake,' whatever, then rejoice together as the spark is rekindled and you carry on in unity, as one.

The enemy is furious today because this message has gone out, it has been delivered. The enemy is seething today because thou hast receiveth it. Let us now reason together, stand firm upon the word of God, repent and restore our Christian walk, our personal lives, and our marriage and families, let us have a revival like never before, for while Satan is seething in anger, the angels in heaven are rejoicing!

Children instead of learning and growing from their fathers' knowledge and wisdom are repeating the same mistakes and making worse mistakes so consequently each successive generation is degenerating, just as in the days of the Exodus and early days in the Promised Land. We haven't learned from the mistakes or the sins of the past, those of our ancestors. It is time my dearest brothers and sisters, to wake up! We need to return unto our Almighty God, our Lord and Savior, and His precepts, again I take you to John 14:27, *Peace I leave with you, my peace I give unto you: not as the world gives, give I unto you. Let not your heart be troubled, neither let it be afraid,* and James 4:4 *Ye adulterers and adulteresses, know ye not that the friendship of the world is enmity with God? whosoever therefore will be a friend of the world is the enemy of God.* What did Elihu tell Job in 36:9-12? *Then he sheweth them their work, and their transgressions that they have exceeded; He openeth also their ear to discipline, and commandeth that they return from their iniquity.* **IF** *they obey and serve Him, they shall spend their days in prosperity, and their years in pleasures* (not necessarily in this life but lay up for yourself treasures in heaven-eternity). *But if they obey not, they shall perish by the sword of* God's word, *and they* *shall die* (second death-hell) *without knowledge.* If you look over into the book of Numbers 14:33, you will see *And your children shall wander in the wilderness for forty years and bear your whoredom, until your carcasses be wasted in the wilderness.* Children pay the price for their parent's sins in that they tend to repeat rather than to learn from them. This is so serious to God, our Creator, and the Master Designer. If you are transgressing in thy marriage by not living up to the roles as outlined in chapters 1-3 of this message, you are transgressing against God and it is a grave sin. If you are separated and/or divorced, or defiling the temple of God you are in grave sin and transgressing against God, as well as thy spouse and/or thyself. This very minute you need to feel the sword piercing thy heart and soul, repent, turn from thy wicked ways. Let us go even further and look at 1ˢᵗ Corinthians 11:28-30, *But let a man (righteous) examine himself, and so let him eat of the bread and drink of that cup, for he that eateth and drinketh unworthily* (with unconfessed sin and unforgiveness) *eateth and drinketh damnation to himself, not discerning the Lord's body. For this cause many are weak and sickly among you, and many sleep* (die). Now, you have heard this message and may still be asking, 'what is the way back? What do I do next? Allow me to briefly outline the way forward for you, and to do this, I take you back to 2ⁿᵈ Chronicles 7:14.

Humble yourself and pray. Have you gotten lost along the way, just wandering without direction in your spiritual walk and/or thy marriage and family? Have you sinned? Then repent, seek forgiveness from God as well as any whom thou hast sinned against or hurt. And forgive thyself! This is something very difficult and most people forget.

Seek my face. Return unto God, read His precious word and apply it into thy life. Pray without ceasing. If you are in a troubled marriage, separated or divorced, women return unto thy husband with a repentant, pure, clean, and sincere heart. Are you troubled in your relationship with Christ? Likewise, return unto Him with a repentant, pure, clean, sincere heart. *Knock and it shall be opened, seek and ye shall find.* Husbands receive thy wives with open loving arms and never let her go again, love her as Christ loves the church (us). I am not saying to hold her hostage but rather give her reason to stay and don't give her reason to leave.

Turn from your wicked ways. If you truly repent, then you will hate the sin and never desire to repeat or return to it. That doesn't mean that you won't slip once in a while, but it will cause you extreme anguish. Love and work for God, looking forward to the finish line of eternal life with our Father in Heaven, through the salvation that He alone offers us. Then He will hear thy prayer, forgive thy sins, and heal you, your marriage/family relationship, as well as your relationship with Him Amen.

If you are having problems in your marriage, if you are separated or divorced and not remarried, I implore thee to reconcile thy marriage; this is God's plan, His plea. My dear sisters, whether or not you or he remarried, return to thy husband just as the story of the Prodigal son who left, but who returned, sought forgiveness, humbling himself (righteousness), and then was welcomed back by the father. It doesn't matter if you left, or he kicked you out, you need to return unto him, just as when we stray from God as sinners, we need to return to Him. Have you strayed from thy marriage? Return unto thy husband and to God. *Be ye not separated except with consent, and for a time of fasting and prayer. Don't allow the sun to set on your anger* but forgive.

If you are still in a marriage, strengthen it, rekindle the original match. Love and honor one another as never before, and don't ever give Satan a foothold to enter in.

My dearest brothers and sisters who are not married, Pray. Seek not a life partner, but seek God. If it is His will for you to marry, He will give you the right person at the right time. But hold fast to the precepts herein, and stay on the right path. No touching, kissing... wear modest attire... Remember I said earlier, that this book saved the life of a chaplains' daughter who was getting ready to get sexually involved with a boyfriend that her dad didn't even know that she had. After reading this, she cut the relationship with the young man, never went through with the sexual relations, he went to her best friend who died a few months later from AID's. If you will adhere to these biblical precepts, young or old, single, betrothed, married, separated, divorced, male, female...the precepts from God's Word are all here for you, the choice now is whether you will choose to follow them or...

Have you strayed from God? Return unto Him. Husbands also, seek forgiveness, and receive thy wife just as the father did the prodigal son, and as God accepts us and forgives us. Please! In the name of our Lord and Savior Jesus Christ receive this message and act today! This calls for both husband and wife to take a big bite of humble pie. In Jeremiah 4:4, 14 we read *Circumcise yourselves to the Lord, and take away the foreskins of your heart, ye men of Judah and inhabitants of Jerusalem: lest my fury come forth like fire, and burn that none can quench it, because of the evil of your doings. O Jerusalem, wash thine heart from wickedness, that thou mayest be saved. How long shall thy vain thoughts lodge within thee?*

Men, I have (God has) repeatedly admonished thy wives to return to you IF separated or divorced. When she returns and repents, you must accept her back with open arms, love her and EXPECT no explanations...the past is gone, the past must be forgiven...then proceed TOGETHER on to the finish line, AMEN!

Are you separated or divorced? Find thy partner in any way possible and humble thyself, seek forgiveness, repent, and pray for restoration and revival in thy marriage. Make the first move; don't put it off any longer. You have heard today what God is saying, and how important marriage and family is to our Lord and Savior. Forget the bad of the past, but remember the good, remember what God used to bring the two of you together. Divorce is man's law, not God's, in God's eyes you are still married even if you are holding the certificate of divorce, you are still one, and always will be, until death. My dear sisters, humble thyself, as hard as it may seem, thou must seek thy husband just as we are to seek God, with a whole heart, mind, and soul. Repent, seek his forgiveness, fall at his feet and plead for forgiveness, then rise up a new and regenerated partner for thy spouse, then stand by your man. My dear brothers, forget the past, humble thyself and welcome back your wife with arms outstretched. It doesn't matter who divorced who. Have you left God and committed adultery with other gods-wealth, sex, greed, power, prosperity, fancy houses, cars, fashion...turn back to God, repent and be restored unto Him?

My dear brothers, if your wife divorced you, pray for her, for her safety, for her to return unto you. She is out there in the wilderness in Satan's domain. If you left your wife, seek forgiveness from God and her, humble thyself.

Likewise, my sisters, if thy husband left you, shame on him, if he kicked you out, put you away, divorced you, shame on him, but...pray for him to accept you back, for he is outside of God's law and so in Satan's domain. Humble thyself and return unto him, seek his forgiveness, forgive him, pray for him.

If joint divorce, pray for each other, you are both in sin. You must in any of the above cases, pray and forgive, and accept each other back. You must forgive, for what does God teach? *Seventy times seven*, my dear friends...*as I have forgiven you.* In Matthew 6:12 Jesus teaches the people to pray saying, *forgive us our debts as we forgive our debtors.* The debts are our sins of omission and those of commission, intentional and unintentional sins. We are to forgive if we desire to be forgiven by God, and without His forgiveness, there can be no salvation, just as without forgiveness in our marriages, there is no marriage.

After seeking forgiveness and forgiving (it is a two-way street), you must be reunited again. Be reunited; rekindle that original spark that brought you both together in the first place. Then forgive, don't look back, but forward together by God's grace and mercy, to God's blessings. God's law, your promise to Him until death do ye part.

I look around and see people and watch them. Most are wandering through life with no joy, no hope, no peace, just day to day drudgery, and existence. Today I've got to go to work. Friday's payday, I need to pay some bills; xmas is coming (see my book on xmas), got to go shopping...Others are walking with pride in their step and faces; Pride, striving for success in career for power, greed, but still no joy or peace. People have become enslaved to existence and never begin to really live. They have become robots on autopilot, controlled by the world, without joy or any hope, but...they don't seek death because they fear death-why? They don't know. Others don't care about the outcome- 'the unknown' and opt to take their own lives just to get away from 'life', because they never began to live. They never began to understand why they were here in the first place; they never opened the door of their heart for God to enter their lives.

My dear brothers and sisters, I'm calling you today, the Lord Almighty is waiting with open arms outstretched, calling out for you to heed this powerful message that you have just heard or read. Humble thyself, seek Him, and turn from your wicked, evil and sinful ways. God wants to set you free from the bondage of sin and the world so that you can begin to live. Habakkuk 2:4 tells us that *the just* (justified, righteous) *shall LIVE by His* (righteousness) *faith*. Then repent and dare to take that first step into the sea (Moses) of faith, stand before the King (Moses and Esther), step into the wilderness (Abraham and Moses), climb the highest mountain (Moses), step away from the world and the things of it (Jesus was offered the world), save yourself and save your marriage. Take that first step today. Sexual immorality, adultery, divorce, selfishness, greed, whatever the sin; repent, turn around and don't look back, but look forward to the heavenly reward. Restore God's gift of marriage, and begin a true, joyful life filled with the hope, promise and blessings that can only be found in Him. Humble thyself, submit to and obey His law, submit and sur-render unto His will, then and only then can you receive life more abundantly, and really begin to live. Turn back to God, Jesus Christ, return unto thy Bridegroom, and thy husband for restoration and revival. **If you are happily married,** do all that you can to maintain it, for this message shows the conse-quences of giving a foothold to Satan. This message shows you how important it is to keep the fires burning. Then dare to be a lighthouse unto others to lead them to a life of joy, peace and happiness through our precious Lord and Savior Jesus Christ. But...you must take that first step the leap of faith. As I said earlier, I have taken leaps of faith a few times over, and it defies all logic or common sense, but...On the other side are such blessings, and a deeper and stronger faith. Humble thyself, seek and submit fully unto thy husband, turn from thy sinful ways and let's see revival in our marriages, churches, and in our communities. Let's begin once again to be Christians, and Christ-like, and truly experience life, real life with the love, joy and peace that only comes through our Lord and Savior Jesus Christ, In John 14:27 Jesus tells us *Peace I leave with you, my peace I give unto you: not as the world gives, give I unto you. Let not your heart be troubled, neither let it be afraid.* Colossians 3:2 *Set your affection on things above, not on things on the earth.* but you must take that first step. Return to thy husband, restore and/or strengthen your marriage if you are still married, and praise God.

If you are with boy or girl friend, engaged (betrothed), please allow this precious message to be a part of your foundation for a healthy, and happy marriage and life.

I desire to see God's love in His children once again...I desire to see real Christians who reflect the love of God, His mercy, and grace reflected through us as, strengthening our marriages or restoring and reviving broken marriages amen! Then the church of God will be rekindled, restored, oh how wonderful that will be! You see my dear friends, people of the world are watching, and when you claim to be a Christian Satan works overtime to destroy you and your marriage, why? Because the world is watching, and when they see Christians falling, many rejoice and laugh, because then you are no different from anybody else...the world. But when you stand strong despite the adversity, holding on to God, and waiting for the sun to shine again, the world watches in amazement, and can see your God! The world and Satan don't watch or care about the unbeliever, for he has already won them. The world is watching you to see if they can see God in you, in your marriage, in your work... When you fail to hold on to Him, love, and forgive, show His love mercy, and grace; the world sees God in the same light. Remember Moses in the Exodus, kept pleading with God; don't destroy thy people, for the world is watching and what will they think? Deuteronomy 9:28 tells us...Lest the land whence thou broughtest us out say, *Because the Lord was not able to bring them into the land which He promised them, and because He hated them, He hath brought them out to slay them in the wilderness.* Then in Joshua, we see the Canaanites feared Israel, because they saw the power of God working through and for them. Are you hearing what the Holy Spirit is saying?

What God is asking you to do today...this very day, not tomorrow, next week, month or year, but this very day, is to humble thyself, repent, and revive.

Again prostitutes, adulterers, homosexuals, bisexuals ... turn from thy wicked ways now, this very minute, repent. Have you had abortions or contemplating an abortion? Please, repent this very minute of this sin.

Are you separated, divorced, or contemplating such sins? Dear sisters, humble thyself, seek thy husband, and men you must welcome thy wife back. God says seek My face, do that also, return unto thy husband, fall at his feet literally, repent, seek his forgiveness and forgive him. Strike up the original match, that spark that burst into flaming love and brought the two of you together. My dear brothers, humble thyself also, forgive thy wife and seek her forgiveness as well, then welcome her back with outstretched arms, take her back as thy wife, fully restored to her rightful place.

Make God the center of thy life as well as the center of thy marriage and family. Forgive each other as God forgives us, seventy times seven, and build up your marriage bank account. If God can and He does, resurrect us into a new life from being dead in sin; is it too much for Him to resurrect thy marriage to life, to new life?

If you are happily married praise God! But He can raise thy marriage to even greater heights, Amen!

My dear friends don't listen to the world, friends or family; but listen to God and each other (if married). Remember, the world tortured and crucified our Savior, and they will try to do so to us as well when we surrender all unto Him, and to each other in marriage. They had long waited for His arrival, and then they rejected and destroyed Him all because of the world and ignorance. The world is blind and ignorant regarding marriage as well. Listen to God! The world will tell you that your partner isn't good enough or isn't right for you, you deserve better, there's other fish in the sea, one is good, two is better, there's good money there, and God won't let you get hurt, he did this, she did that, nothing wrong with divorce, homosexuality, adultery, abortion...everyone else does it, God will understand... What God understands is that you vowed to Him and one another...until death do us part.

I counseled a woman after a message on marriage. She felt convicted and confused. In obtaining her history, she had been badly abused by a man physically, emotionally, and sexually. He became that way only after disillusionment with the church! He subsequently became an alcoholic, smoker, and wife abuser. Friends and family talked her into leaving him, which she did. Now after hearing the message of God through me, she felt convicted and confused. I prayed with her, 'Father you gave me this message to share, this young lady has suffered so'... How do you respond to this type of a situation? Almost immediately, as I looked up, I saw a new person. When we began praying, she was in tears, now she was all smiles. I asked her why. She responded, "Your prayer, and your advice gave me a peace that I haven't had in a long time and I know that God will give me an answer to your prayer." I have spoken to so many people, including family, friends, co-workers, and to pastors, they all say the same thing, leave him and find someone else. I smiled at her, held her hand and said, I can see that He already gave you the correct answer. I don't know your husband, but God says that His word is true, and we must be for Him or against Him, hot or cold, but that He wants us hot for Him, have faith in Him and trust Him. God's word says for a woman never to leave her husband and that God hates divorce. I'm not saying that your husband is correct in what he did, but I must advise you to humble thyself, seek your husband's face, his forgiveness for leaving him, and become his wife once again, and if he is willing, he can come and talk with me as well. We talked for a while, and she agreed to return to her husband after thinking about it, and after she asked me several questions. I continued to pray for her daily, for her, for her safety, for her husband and for the marriage. Almost two weeks later she came to see me, with her husband at her side, hand in hand. "Thank you, pastor, we are so happy. We have talked and talked, and I told him of your message, your prayer. Now my husband wanted to meet you and we would like to attend wherever you preach." Praise the Lord! Her witness in returning to her abusive husband was so powerful, that he returned to church and to God and to his wife and became a changed man. He left the alcohol, tobacco, and the abuse behind and looked forward. My friends this miracle can only happen with faith, trust, and obedience to God, not the world, but the power of God, not that of ourselves, and just imagine the impact on their family and friends!

My dear brothers and sisters, my burden is heavy because as you are seeing, mankind has fallen so far from the path, we see the effects in our marriages and families, in the churches, and in our world today. We need repentance and true revival more than ever before, and to separate from the world, but it's so hard and lonely, as is even more pronounced here in prison. My dear brother in Christ, Paul, wrote most of his letters while in prison for Christ. I sit here and have written these messages unto you within these prison walls awaiting death. While I lay here in Kamiti Maximum security prison in Kenya, terminally ill and with a few life threatening conditions, and over <u>eighty</u> diagnoses inclusive of every system in my body and refused any communication with my family or ministry these nine years, my God is with me and sustained me, Psalms chapters 6 and 7, 17 and 35. I fear not death for I know that I will be with my Father in glory, but I still hope that He will restore me that I may continue to glorify His name and testify of my Father to the world. My heart goes out to all those who are physically imprisoned by incarceration, handicaps, or disease; as well as spiritually, emotionally, and sexually, in bondage, in prison, but God can take care of you if only you will repent, forgive, restore, and be revived; Amen. There is a great war going on between the heavenly angels and the demons. As believers, we know the final outcome; we've seen this from Genesis, Job, and Revelation. My dear friends, it is going on today. We don't understand when we are in the midst of the battle like Job, but be sure that God is the winner and so are we when and if we hold on to Him. Our marriages are testimonies to this and also of the raging battle. Are you in a strong marriage? Hold on ever so tight for a bumpy road ahead in your marriage, as it will be tried and tested as will your faith. Look to God and hold on. Never walk away from God or thy marriage, and in the end with God, you shall prevail. Walking away is spiritual adultery and is a grave sin. When you divorce, you divorce God and His special gift, as well as His blessings inclusive of eternal life, for you vowed unto Him until death. You cannot walk away from God, and if you did, why would He want to take you home to Him? Think about this, and take a minute to read Daniel 10:13 and Revelation 12:11. God says I hate liars, I hate hypocrites, I hate adulterers, I hate divorce...

My dear brothers, shape up in Christ and be Christ-like. When Jacob fled from his home, he did so, weighed down with guilt. He was lonely and separated from those important to him. He wandered aimlessly, outside of the veil and plan of God, even though God can still turn these situations around. Even as Adam when he hid from God, Jonah ran from God, same with many people today, until we receive salvation by faith. Their sin and ours separates us from God, from His will, and His plan. But as with the prodigal son, if we repent and return, accept the free gift of salvation He has for us, then He receives us back with open arms. What is being said here is this, love your God given partner with all your heart, soul, mind, and strength. If you are separated or divorced, my dear sisters, return to thy husband, repent, seek forgiveness. This sounds strange by today's standards, but GOD can and will mend thy relationship if you will only follow His commandments and ordinances, return to your partner, return to God. My dear brothers, forgive thy wife, welcome her with open arms, and then cover the sin of thy separation with the garments, the best robe, of grace for her. God not only forgives us, He heals us. Whatever romantic mistakes you have made, you can still seek his and His face, as well as his and His forgiveness and healing that only comes from the cross of Jesus Christ, Hallelujah. My dear brothers, receive thy wives back, if she doesn't come, you seek her; you contact her and invite her to return. *Behold I stand at the door and knock.* When she returns or you find her, forgive one another, forget the past mistakes, welcome her with open arms, cover her sins with the best robe (forgiveness), then...both of you need to get down upon your knees before the altar, the cross of Jesus Christ, seek His forgiveness, seek His strength, wisdom, and guidance, then give Him all the praise and glory.

In Revelation 19:7-9 we read, *Let us be glad and rejoice and give honor to Him, for the marriage of the Lamb is come, and the wife hath made herself ready. And to her was granted that she should be arrayed in fine linen, clean and white* (purity): *for the fine linen is the righteousness of the saints. And He sayeth unto me, write: Blessed are they which are called unto the marriage supper of the Lamb. And He sayeth unto me, these are the true sayings of God.* Now, obviously this is pertaining to the final days, but is easily applied to us today in our marriages.

So...let us as Christians be true Christians...living examples- Christ-like and put away all the prostitution, adultery of all kinds; Separated or divorced women will please and prayerfully return unto thy husbands today. The existing marriages are being strengthened, and...Satan is going to be so angry... Praise God!!! Satan is going to fight us...so be on your guard, be in prayer, hold on to God and listen not unto the world. Resist the enemy. Oh, my dear friends, what a lighthouse ye shall be if you heed these words. This won't be easy, but with God and His strength, *I can do all things through Christ which strengtheneth us*, Philippians 4:13.

Couples, are you pregnant with child? I ask this very day that you both kneel down together before Christ, and ask God's blessings upon your marriage, each other, and this child, this precious gift from God.

Are you married? I pray ye now, this very day, ye my dear brothers that thou takest or bringest thy wife to the altar, the cross of Christ, on your knees, and pray for her, and for your marriage. Do you have children? Have them join you and pray God's blessings for each of them as well. Ask God to forgive each of your family members including yourself, for any wrong-doing, as well as for His strength, courage, and wisdom to get back on the right path, bringing your marriage and family to new heights. Is your marriage being battered by the enemy? Today, pray for forgiveness, repent, pray for restoration and revival in your marriage and thy family.

Are you involved in pornography, romance novels, adultery, prostitution, masturbation, homosexuality, polygamy, and any other sexual sins? Are you abusing thy spouse or thy child in any way? Pray for forgiveness, turn from thy wicked ways, leave them before the altar-the cross, and never look back. Have you aborted a gift from God? Repent upon your knees today. Are you on any form of birth control? Repent on your knees and turn from thy wicked ways, trust God for He knows what is best for you, He knows His plans for you. Just trust and obey Him! See how much nicer that intimate time is when you trust God, and don't have to worry about anything anymore. There are no what if's... your experience shall also feel much better physically, mentally, and spiritually when there are no barriers or chemicals between the two of you. Do you have multiple wives; you must release all but your **FIRST** wife. If you have concubines or mistresses, release them today, repent and never return unto them.

There is forgiveness from all of the sexual and marital sins that we have discussed except for one, IF you repent with your whole heart and turn from thy wicked ways. There is however, no forgiveness for divorce, for this is a result of lying to God, and the breaking of vows made unto Him, as well as disobedience to God and His laws, for we are to leave only for a brief time for fasting and prayer, with consent, and then we are to return. Only when you repent, return and restore thy marriage then and only then can you find forgiveness from Jehovah and peace in your life.

My dear brothers and sisters, make a ceremony when you first arrive home tonight. Remove all jewelry, makeup, and then proceed with the following.

My dear brothers, who are married, take thy wife today, pray with and for her. From this day on, I pray thee to be the lord, the high priest of your home. Dedicate today thy marriage, your wife, your children, your house and your possessions unto the Lord. Then I pray thee, that ye wash thy wife's feet. I'm serious, become the humble servant, the lord of thy home. Take the responsibility that God hath ordained for you.

My dear sisters, I pray on behalf of my Father in heaven that today, after thy feet are washed, that ye remove thy pants literally (unless you are already not wearing pants) then bow down upon thy knees before thy husband and call him lord, just as Sarah called Abraham, lord. Then put on a nice long, loose fitting dress or skirt, with a vow never again to wear a pair of pants. Quit thy jobs and return unto thy house where God hath ordained thee to be, and serve thy husband (or parents if single). I refer you to Ruth 2:10. When bowing, washing feet...it must be done with a pure and sincere heart and mind otherwise it is not worth doing.

From this day forward, I pray ye my brothers to be worthy of the respect from thy wife. I pray ye my dear sisters not to return to pants, burn them, and allow thy husband literally and spiritually to wear them once again for thy family. My sisters, wear no more makeup, nail polish, jewelry; cut not any of thy hair, and begin to cover thy hair with a hat, bonnet, or scarf... my dear brothers, get rid of any and all of your hats and cover not thy heads.

Sin brought disharmony into the relationship of Adam and Eve, later between their children, just as sin today leads to the destruction of marriages and children. Don't allow Satan any foothold; don't allow him to interfere in your family. Look at Matthew 13:19-23. And how do we do this? Remember always to love and to forgive.

In Zech. 3:3-4 *Now Joshua was clothed with filthy garments and stood before the angel, and he answered and spoke unto those that stood before him, saying, take away the filthy garments from him. And unto him he said, behold, I have caused thine iniquity to pass from thee, and I will clothe thee with change of raiment.* The filthy garments symbolize the people's sins which were removed. He is cleansed and forgiven, and replaced with clean garments that are symbolic of righteousness, the process of justification and sanctification. Notice that the dirty was not removed and replaced with the clean until after he in humility, confessed and repented of their sins. John 15:22 *But now they have no cloke for their sin* No covering, as the covering only comes after humbling and repentant confession of the sins.

If thou shalt make a vow today before God and thy partner, and heed these words today and everyday hereafter, but start today, I believe honestly that thou shalt be amazed at what God will do for you personally, in your marriage and family, your church, and your community. You know that it only takes a spark to get a fire going. Be that spark today. Take a few minutes to read Psalm 95 and 2nd Chronicles 30:9-12 now. In Revelation 21:7-8, *He that overcometh shall inherit all things; and I will be his God, and he shall be my son. But the unfaithful, and unbelieving, the abominable, and murders, and whoremongers and sorcerers and idolaters, and all liars, shall have their part in the lake which burneth with fire and brimstone: which is the second death.* 1st Peter 4:2 reminds us *that he no longer should live the rest of his time in the lusts of men, but to the will of God.* We look at Hosea 4:6 *My people are destroyed for lack of knowledge: because thou hast rejected knowledge, I will also reject thee...* but 1st Peter 2:1-2, *Wherefore laying aside all malice, and all guile, and hypocrisies, and envies, and all evil speakings, As newborn babes, desire the sincere milk of the word, that ye may grow thereby.* You are getting fed this milk today that ye may grow strong in the Lord. He goes on in verses 17-18 *Honour all men. Love the brotherhood. Fear God. Honour the king. Servants, be subject to your masters with all fear; not only*

to the good and gentle, but also to the froward. Then in 2ⁿᵈ
Peter 3:17 and 18 he tells us *For it is better, if the will of God
be so, that ye suffer for well doing, than for evil doing. For
Christ also hath once suffered for sins, the just for the unjust,
that he might bring us to God, being put to death in the flesh,
but quickened by the Spirit.*

In Isaiah 16:8 we are told that *Thou* (Israel) *shalt no
more be termed Forsaken, neither shall thy land anymore
be termed Desolate: but thou shalt be called Haphzi-bah (My
delight is in her), and thy land Beulah (married), for the Lord
delighteth in thee...*

Solomon reminds us in Ecclesiastes Chapter 2 that God has
given to us a life to enjoy; it is His gift to us. This joy can be
realized only when we live in obedience to Him. We will never
understand life's problems, so just leave them to God. This
message was not intended to be exhaustive but as an introduction to marriage and family, as well as our Christian walk.
God's word is precious and speaks for itself if one will only read
it and listen to His word and Spirit who shall guide you. It contains so much more about marriage, and I can't encourage you
enough to start a habit of daily Bible reading and explore it for
yourself. Read it to your family, read it in the morning with thy
wife before you rise up. We have covered all of the books in the
Bible to introduce you to each of them here.

God's word is the key that can unlock the door and open
your life, and your marriage to a new world of the joy and peace
that God desires for each of His children, the love in God and
one another.

In Philippians 4:8-9 we are encouraged to stand firm in our
faith. Pray for all of the martyrs in prisons around the world
including me as I sit here hostage for the cause of Jesus Christ,
that I may continually speak boldly the truth of our Lord and
Savior Jesus Christ, and that if it is His will, that the gates shall
swing wide open for me to leave here and return to the mission field. Paul wrote most of the letters contained in the New
Testament. Most of his letters were written from within prison
walls. I like Paul and so many others am being held hostage for
serving Christ, for which I carry no regrets, and have written

these six letters to the world from within these cold and lonely prison walls. It is my prayer to get out of here alive that I may continue to teach and testify of the Wonderful Savior Jesus Christ, but also have no regrets of dying as I know where I am going and being with my Lord and Savior will be far more wonderful; but whether I survive this ordeal or not, these letters that were inspired by the Holy Spirit of the True and Living God, will live on as did Paul's, and if even one person is saved, one marriage rescued, it will be worth it all, but I know that through the Spirit, these messages shall touch many lives and marriages and for this I give praise unto my God, and being a martyr is worth it all. Jesus taught in Matthew that the true believer, the truly spiritual, shall endure fiery trials and tribulations and shall suffer persecution, so I praise God that I was found worthy to suffer such and now can await my crown of glory and hear those precious words-well done thou good and faithful servant. But to Kenya (as well as China, USA, etc.) I refer to Matthew 26:24 which says *The Son of man goeth as it is written of him: but woe unto that man by whom the Son of man is betrayed! It had been good for that man if he had not been born,* as I believe that this is just as pertinent to the Martyr today, the few servants of Almighty God, as it was for Christ Himself. Kenya, China, USA, and others who are trying to halt the work of the Lord and His servants, woe unto you.

I have been taken hostage, beaten, poisoned, inflicted with life threatening and terminal conditions, starved, refused nutrition and medical care even though ordered by several MD's and the high court of Kenya; been drowned, strangled, habitually abused, harassed, humiliated, tortured by the Kenya authorities because of my serving God...We don't need or want white man's' God in this country, and then they wander why countries are pulling people out, and why the daily violence, killing, bombings, etc. in their land! Christians, be warned against Kenya! But whether I make it out of here alive or not, my God is in control. I know where I am going, and as I said earlier, am anxious to be with Him in the end. God knows my innocence and He is faithful and shall judge the wicked-woe unto you Kenya! Woe unto you American embassies in Dominican Republic, Kenya, and Uganda! John 15:19-21, 16:2-3.

Pray for one another for this is the greatest thing that we may do for one another. Pray as husband and wife, parent and children, pray for thy boss, and thy neighbor. The best thing that we may do one for another, the best gift that we may give, is to love and pray for one another. Love ye one another for love is of God. Love ye one another as Christ so loves us. Pray for troubled marriages. Pray for the good marriages. I am praying for each of you who read this message. I pray that His word today has been an encouragement to you, that you are already growing, that it hath pierced your heart, soul and mind and is bringing you unto repentance and sanctification, resulting in a spark, a revival in thy life, that it will be contagious and that others will see the change in you and follow after you. I pray for revival in your life, your marriage, and your church. I pray that a spark hath been set in your life and will start a forest fire of revival around the world, that we shall all walk straight the narrow path and not fall, and that we may all praise and truly worship God our Father, our Bridegroom.

I fully realize that much of this is totally contrary to today's teachings and values, but this is God's word and it never changes. He created us, He gave us an instruction manual in which to live by, but...many are trying to live without reading or following His instruction manual, the Bible, His precious word to and for us. It is too much to digest in one reading, so it is my prayer that you will read and reread, and reread many more times over, as I believe that like the first person that read this message who read this six times and is still asking for it again, I've read it many times over and each time I am strengthened, encouraged, and brought to tears as my burden is so great for the marriages and the spiritual condition today. I believe that the Lord shall also speak to you and strengthen and encourage you as well if you will read with an open heart and mind, listening to the Lord as He speaks to you. He cares about you and your marriage, He desires a close personal relationship with you, and His relationship is so wonderful. Grow and become a lighthouse, let His light shine bright through thy life. Begin a daily reading of God's precious word keeping in mind what He hath shown you in this message, and you shall see the Bible in a new light, the Light of God's Spirit and shalt gain a new and deeper understanding.

Also, share this book with others or encourage them to pick up a copy so that you can keep reading and so can they. As you read this message, always pray for God to reveal His truths for your life, and pray for the marriages today-restoration and strengthening. Go back and review and apply the notes that you wrote on the PERSONAL NOTE pages.

Read Proverbs 31:10-31, remembering that the woman is symbolic of all of us sinners, and our Husband is symbolic of God. Read it carefully, read it prayerfully and see the profound message for us contained therein.

I praise the living God for revealing to me this precious wisdom and for the ability to write it, so that I could share His message with you. I thank you for taking the time to pick up this message and reading it. I believe that it was no accident that you chose this particular message out of all the books on marriage and family available today. God is speaking to you this message; you just need to open your heart, listen to Him, and submit unto Him. Love Him with all thy heart, soul, and mind, amen.

Thomas was anxious to see the holes in the hands and feet of Jesus, as well as the hole in His side. While I am anxious to see Jesus again, those holes in His outstretched hands cause me extreme shame and humiliation, for it was for MY sins that He bears those holes, that He suffered so and died for ME. It is for Kenya's sins that I and many others are suffering, but Kenya will be judged. The point here is that women should never leave their husbands, and if her husband kicks her out for whatever reason, she should wait upon his doorstep until he invites you back into his life. Never leave thy husband but always stand by your man. Never leave thy lord, for when you do so the scars are there for all the world to see your shame, and for God to see also.

In Mark 4:19-20 we read, *And the cares of this world, and the deceitfulness of riches, and the lusts of other things entering in, choke the word, and it becometh unfruitful. And these are they which are sown on good ground, such as hear the word, and receive it, and bring forth fruit...*

I could go on and on, but I shall close here with a couple last verses, then allow you to read and study God's precious word for yourself. First let us look at Galatians 1:9. ...*if any man preach any other Gospel unto you than that ye have received, let him be accursed,* For there is only one God, our Father, and He hath given unto us only one word, His word, contained in the Holy Bible. Then let us turn to the book of Joshua 22:5 which tells us *Take diligent heed to do the commandment and the law, which Moses the servant of the Lord charged you, to love the Lord your God, and walk in all His ways, and keep His commandments, and to cleave unto Him, and serve Him with all your heart, and all your soul.* In Joshua 24:14-15 ... *put away the gods which your fathers served...and serve ye the Lord...Choose ye this day which ye will serve...but as for me and my house, we will serve the Lord.* These verses pertain to our marriage on earth as well as our walk with...our marriage to God.

In the Psalms 1:1-2 we read, *Blessed is the man* (righteous) *that walketh not in the counsel of the ungodly, nor standeth in the way of sinners, nor sitteth in the seat of the scornful. But his delight is in the law of the Lord.*

Rejoice always...pray without ceasing...prove all things and hold fast to that which is good in the Lord. Abstain from all appearance of evil...

All single or married individuals need to come before the altar (cross) of the Lord, upon thy knees, in repentance with a pure and sincere heart and mind for all of thy sins; confessing them with a pure and sincere heart and mind, then accept His forgiveness, leave thy sins at the cross and proceed down the path of righteousness in faith, trust, and obedience to our Heavenly Father, our Bridegroom. Then allow the revival in thy life to be a reminder and encouragement to remain on the path of righteousness and serve the Lord by serving and loving one another.

And now my dearest brothers and sisters, all the congregation, all who read this message and heed His word, may worship the Lord God our Father, we may sing and praise, and glorify our Father for His love, mercy, and grace for us, and may His love abound in thy life, thy marriage, thy family. And now, if married, go and humble thyself before thy partner and heed the instructions that you have just heard. May the love and peace of God our Father, His Son Jesus Christ, and the Holy Spirit be with you always. God bless you richly, may God bless your marriage and your family forevermore, amen and amen!

One must be careful to avoid legalism, but this message is not legalistic, but rather the word and the commandment of God, our Lord, Savior, and Judge. The Author and Creator of all life, and His word never changes, it is for yesterday, today, and forevermore, Amen.

At the end of my marriage crusades, I invite all involved, to bring all of their idols and sinful materials including but not limited to birth control, tampons, sexual toys such as vibrators, dildos, ben wa balls, fruits and vegetables, etc., woman's pants, all nylon, acrylic, polyester panties-men and women, togos, thongs, G-strings-both panties and bathing suits; men's hats, pornography, romance novels, etc., and then we have a big burning ceremony. If God or I came to your house today and looked around, is there **ANYTHING** that you wouldn't want us to find? Then bring it to the fire and rid thyself of the evils and idols from thy life. You who are reading this message I encourage you to do the same or even get your local church(es) to do the same. We read in 2nd Chronicles 29:5 *And said unto them, Hear me, ye Levites, sanctify now yourselves, and sanctify the house of the LORD God of your fathers, and carry forth the filthiness out of the holy place.* And in 31:1 *Now when all this was finished, all Israel that were present went out to the cities of Judah, and brake the images in pieces, and cut down the groves, and threw down the high places and the altars out of all Judah and Benjamin, in Ephraim also and Manasseh, until they had utterly destroyed them all. Then all the children of Israel returned, every man to his possession, into their own cities.*

All who read this message, single or married, betrothed or widowed should come before the altar (cross) of our Lord upon thy knees in repentance for each and every sin that you have committed either by commission or omission knowingly or unknowingly, confessing them with a pure and sincere heart and mind; accepting His forgiveness, then leave them at the cross and walk away from them down the path of righteousness in complete trust, faith, and obedience to our Father in newness of life.

Just as marriage is a new life, so is marriage unto our Heavenly Father, our Bridegroom. Then let the revival in thy life be a reminder and encouragement to remain on the path of righteousness and serve our Lord by serving others, and being a lighthouse unto the world.

Just as we are to be examples for our children, Christ came and set the example for us. The example that He set for us is the same example that we are to set for our children and to all those around us. We are also called to go unto the ends of the world and teach this example of Jesus Christ, in word and deed to all people, leading them unto salvation. We do this by our words and deeds, as well as the way that we dress, behave, the music that we listen to as well as the type movies/TV programs that we watch, and the people that we fellowship with. Everything that we say and do affect those around us as well, impacts how they see us and Jesus through us.

This book certainly is not all inclusive, in fact this is just the beginning, but it is intended introduce you to what God says about some of the major issues plaguing the family today, and to show you just how important thy vows of marriage and marriage are, our position within the family of God, as well as to introduce you to God's word and encourage each of you to begin reading it for thyself, and with a greater understanding. As a Pastor, I have and will, Lord willing, continue to expound upon each of these chapters in various messages that I preach. This message is not intended to have all of the answers to life's problems, but to guide you to the One who does have all of the answers, the Creator of the universe and all that it contains.

It is my prayer that this message has helped you in your spiritual life, your Christian walk, and in your personal life, and that of your family and marriage as well. If it has, I would love to hear from you. Also, if you have any questions or comments about God's word and/or marriage and this message, I would welcome these as well. My contacts are listed in appendix D in the back of this message, and though difficult right now, I will attempt to answer you back as quickly as possible. Remember that God sends us angels to help in times of need and He certainly has for me while here in this prison. Again, I pray that you have been blessed through this His message, and will continue to bless you as you strive to walk down the straight and narrow path, and be a lighthouse for God. I cannot write or read this message without tears, so now through tears of joy and sorrow, for I know a few shall listen and act upon this message, and many will reject it. I will close by sending you, my love. This isn't the end of this message, but the beginning of new life for all who will accept Jesus into or back into your life, as well as your spouse if you are separated or divorced.

My Personal Note to You

We have gone through many important issues in this message, and it is my earnest prayer that it has invoked a life change for you, both in your family as well as in your Christian walk, your relationship with our Father God, our Bridegroom, and that your life will never be the same again. I pray that marriages may be restored and that troubled marriages shall be restored and strengthened to new levels.

I need to bring you back to the book of John 3:17-21. Here we are told that *For God sent not his Son into the world to condemn the world; but that the world through him might be saved. He that believeth on him is not condemned: but he that believeth not is condemned already, because he hath not believed in the name of the only begotten Son of God. And this is the condemnation, that light is come into the world, and men loved darkness rather than light, because their deeds were evil. For every one that doeth evil hateth the light, neither cometh to the light, lest his deeds should be reproved. But he that doeth truth cometh to the light, that his deeds may be made manifest, that they are wrought in God.*

I wish you to realize and remember that it takes three... three to make a marriage work, or one to break a marriage apart, it's your choice. Everything that you do as ONE, affects each other as well as others around you. When you get married, there is a three stranded cord wrapped around the two of you (a type of the Trinity). One represents the husband, the next represents the wife, and the third represents God. Three stranded cord is not easily broken. Life is going to throw you around and try to knock you out, and it can be hard to keep the marriage together when this happens, but you must hold on to your partner and to God. As long as you hold on to thy partner and God, there is such power, but the minute one gets snagged by the devil, the cord will snap, there will be a collapse. Repentance repairs the cord however and brings restoration, hallelujah! Remember, during life's toughest times, many people fall away from God, but that is when we need to hold on the tightest. The same thing is true in a marriage. In your marriage as long as you stay close to Him, your marriage will remain a three stranded cord that the world cannot easily tear apart or break. I must add here that the cord will remain around the two of you unless one of you decides to remove it. Without that cord, you'll usually find yourself sitting alone. Never listen to friends and family, ALWAYS turn to God, not the world.

If you are in a marriage, it is my heartfelt plea that you both fall on your knees and repent for all wrong done to each other and brighten the fire burning between you, bring new and wonderful life back into your marriage. If you are thinking of or are separated or divorced, that you women will return to thy husband, that both of you will fall upon your knees in repentance and restore, revive thy marriage. For all who hear or read this message to fall upon your knees in repentance before God and rekindle, revive your relationship with our heavenly Father, our Bridegroom that we may all be partakers with Him at the marriage supper in that glorious day. Take time also to praise God for this precious gift of thy life partner and any fruits that He hath chosen to give you. I have repeated this many times but it is so very important for the message God hath given unto me is that of repentance and revival, strengthening the Christian Walk which is the theme of my book **ONLY BELIEVE**, and is the theme herein as well as it relates to the family/His family. It is once again time for us to take both our earthly family and heavenly family seriously. My dear sisters, you may think that you have it good being apart from thy husband, but God does not see it that way as I pray this message has reinforced unto you. There is no better place to be than in the center of His will, and that place is with your family-be it your parents, or if you are or were married, with thy husband! And men, I cannot say it strongly enough, love thy wife as God loves you. If you are separated or divorced, welcome thy wife back. Both should forget the past and look forward to the heavenly rewards. The past is past, but how and what you do today will affect the future and eternity.

We live one heartbeat at a time, and when death comes to any one of us, it comes to us all. Divorce as I said earlier, is a form of death and it affects many when you commit this abomination, not just you. The problem is that in this day, there is such a strong push by the world to be strong and independent, that the world leaves out the most important ingredient- that of love. We as people, we as Christians must return to the love and forget the strong and independent factors, for love will lead to much more success and strength. I hope and pray that all who hear and/or read this message will hear these, my words. Don't allow a single heartbeat pass without being together with God and the life that He has chosen for you.

As for my personal experience, it has been painful, but as I sit here in my prison cell and reflect, God hath shown me so much, both speaking to me personally and through this message He has given me to share with the world-**BECOMING ONE.** We had such a beautiful marriage and family, and to this day, I praise God for them and pray for each of them. As the Holy Spirit has given me these words and I have written, read and reread so many times, I too have been convicted and have seen my weaknesses, areas that I failed or was weak in, and need improvement. I can tell you that after hearing the Spirit utter these precious words, and had me write them, I will never be the same, and it is my sincere prayer that having read this message, you too will never be the same. In a relationship there is never a right or wrong person, we are all sinners, we all make mistakes, so if this message appears to point the finger at my wife as being the bad person, forgive me please, for we both made mistakes as we all do. The points that I brought out are simply points that affect so many people today and I was led to share them to try to help you avoid these same problems or find forgiveness if they have already hit your marriage.

What went wrong and why am I including this note here? My dearest brothers and sisters, we are all human, created by the Almighty God. We thanks to Eve, all make mistakes. I am reminded of the old cliché To err is human, to forgive is divine I was working as I said earlier on a Doctoral Dissertation on a very hot and difficult subject. Doing my research and for the Dissertation, there were some photos to support facts. My wife saw them and was upset. I never hid the photos from her, what I was trying to do was complete the dissertation and get my Doctorate as a surprise for her. Rather than talking and praying, she jumped to wrong conclusions, aided by her unbelieving friends. God gives us all choices. My choice of trying to surprise my wife may not have been the best in hindsight, but it was with good intentions. My dear wife of twenty years, made the choice to listen to the world, rather than to God and her ordained husband. She made the choice to lie to the courts and others to accomplish what her friends desired for her, rather than turning to God. She is not alone, many men and women do this today, but there is only one correct pathway, and that is forsaking the world 1ˢᵗ John 2:15 and James 4:4, and look to God and God alone.

When she went to court, she, a foreign woman, was provided legal counsel and all the social service help she desired (all of the world) free, I, a white male was given nothing. In court the judge didn't even listen to me, only her, no justice. I was talking with a family Christian friend during all this, and she said, God told me that you have done no wrong, that everything that _____(my wife) was doing was wrong, it is not of God, but she has been influenced by the world. Not that I have not sinned, for we all have sinned and fall short, but He forgives us and so need we to forgive one another, and she simple was encouraged by her friends not to forgive, but to leave, but in her brief note asked me to forgive her.

I was told by a friend of ours that my dear wife and I had always had a beautiful relationship that everyone looked up to, and the enemy is fighting. You both were given choices you made yours, and she made hers. She is in the world of darkness that you pulled her out from; you...God has something special for you IF you will continue to look to Him.

A while later, I was in fact taken to the remote villages of East/Central Africa to spread His word and His love to these wonderful people. I have been so blessed having been taken by the Lord into villages that have NEVER seen a white man, into villages that have never heard of Jesus Christ! Dear brothers and sisters, so blessed, but the blessing would have been far greater if my family was by my side. I was tried and tested time and again, but God was with me each step of the way. God provided all that I needed. Daily as I was out preaching, teaching children and adults, caring for medical needs, caring for thousands of beautiful orphans, I always had in my mind the thought If only my wife and children were by my side. Then prior to my third journey into Kenya, three people including two local pastors told me Don't go...please. Then finally one said If you go, please, don't ever forget us here.

I went anyway to Kenya. Perhaps I should have heeded the warnings; I don't know the answer to that yet. But I went. As soon as I arrived in Kenya, I was taken hostage by the CID at Jomo Kenyatta National Airport, where many foreigners are arrested because of the corruption in that country. I was told We don't need or want white man's God in this country. They demanded that I give them twenty thousand dollars and leave the country or I was going to prison! I didn't have the money, so... They brought in a portfolio and said that there was heroin in there and that it was mine. I told them that I have never owned a portfolio, please fingerprint it. They said, we don't need fingerprints to get a conviction. The court that they arraigned me in was NOT the court that airport arrests are taken to. They took me to Kibira, whereas the court that airport arrests go to is Makaderos! Then I was transported to prison while awaiting trial. I thought no problem, when the judge hears my case, I'll be free. While waiting, I found out that there are people there who have been waiting ten years for their cases to go to court. My heart sank, but I kept in prayer. I got sick with an intestinal infection from some bad food. They refused treatment and it spread to pneumonia, still refused treatment. Then immune system being exhausted, I contracted TB! I became very sick and wasted away from two hundred and fifty pounds of solid muscle (five percent body fat!) to forty-eight pounds. I couldn't stand or walk, for over two months my entire right lung was completely collapsed, I couldn't breathe, and it got to the point that I had to force a whisper. The Officer in Charge-Pauline Wanja called me to her office; I was carried as I was everywhere because I couldn't stand and kept passing out as well. I got there and was standing for a minute feeling so weak and dizzy. I asked her what she needed. She just sat there looking at me. I asked if I may sit as I was weak and dizzy. She responded These chairs are for people not for prisoners. I passed out and when I awoke, she was still in her chair, and laughing, I asked her, what is it that you need, please? She still laughing said that was all I wanted, take him back. I was beaten on five occasions by guards with rods as well as kicked hard with their boots, and punched, because I didn't speak their language and because I couldn't stand or talk. I had arranged for an attorney Orenge, He was given one thousand two hundred dollars and I thought all was well, except my health. He never once came to see me and never showed up in court. Another attorney Omollo was also paid by a local church but never did anything. While so ill, I was taken to court, drug in and held up by the guards because I was unable to stand or walk, kept passing out and was barely able to breathe. No attorney- he never did show up! The magistrate Kidula didn't care about how ill I was, or that my attorney didn't show up at any hearing, she ignored my request for a translator as she had a hard time understanding me and I couldn't understand or hear her. She at the beginning said, I need to make an example of you. She resigned before she could be vetted out as the magistrates went through a vetting process in 2014. In the middle of the hearings where she only listened to the prosecutor and not to me, one morning a 3 stone came into my room and... well I awoke in the Kenyatta hospital, I found out later, the three stone told me that I didn't see you reading your Bible so I knew that you must be dying. The doctor told me it is a miracle you are alive, that when you presented, you were in shock, your entire body had shut down and you were taking your final breaths, we didn't think you would make it. I asked what my blood pressure was (the medical in me) he told me 34/0! I was in there five weeks with difficulty breathing, the x-ray on admission had revealed the collapsed lung, but still it took four weeks before they put in a chest tube to open my lung back up!

The story just gets worse, but I was convicted of trafficking eight months later-with no evidence, in fact, they by their own admissions contradicted their own story and essentially admitted that I was not guilty, but I was convicted and transferred to maximum security prison, sentenced to another thirteen years with no credit for the time already served! Oh, how I cried out to God. Since then, I have undergone constant harassment, humiliation, hatred and prejudice, sexually assaulted by two guards, treated worse than they treat their livestock, starved, poisoned, strangled, drowned... They have refused to abide by MD or high court orders, or their own constitutional law, and just laugh as they continue their criminal activities-smuggling, extortion, bribes, theft, etc. while guarding an innocent man of God, as well as probably some other innocent people. I have suffered many human rights violations, and nobody cares, not even the US Embassy, but they were quick to help a few young **ladies** who were snagged by the corruption in Kenya! The prison has even refused to allow me my parents contacts, copy of my judgments or court proceedings (Kenyans all have them); and they are refusing to allow me to take my case back to court for a review. The story gets worse but we are talking marriage and family, so... I tell you this to show that the Christian walk isn't easy but God never promised a rose garden, He promised that picking up the cross and following Him (a requirement for a true Christian) brings trials and tribulation, persecution just as it did Christ, but He never leaves us and continues to provide for our needs.

Dear friends, we don't know why things happen until the dark clouds pass over and the sun rises again. In the worldly sense, I know what my wife did, But God showed me that He allows (doesn't cause) the decision people make, but there is accountability, and unlike magistrate Kidula, My God is a just Judge. God tested our marriage. My wife and millions of others, made a very bad choice and failed God's test. I struggled and held on to Him and He took me to new heights, beyond my comprehension, and our relationship has grown so much stronger. The experiences, good and bad, the mighty doors that He opened for me in the ministry, were so wonderful, and I praise Him daily. No matter how bad things get, there is always reason to praise Him.

John the Baptist was sacrificed on the altar of incest and adultery. John's cries were bold against the king of the land. His call was that of repentance: Herod you are corrupting marriage and I am going to make an example of you. He was willing to do whatever was necessary to make his message known to all mankind. I am likewise sacrificed upon the altar of corrupted marriage and I cry against the political as well as the religious leaders.

As I write this from prison, I hate this place, I am hurt and frustrated with the people and the country, the most corrupt in the world and getting worse by the day, but we won't get into that here. I would STRONGLY encourage EVERYONE to avoid going to or even transiting through this land who has forsaken and turned their backs on God, for your own safety, don't listen to the tourist boards, listen to someone who has experienced this forsaken land firsthand, and spoken with many other victims from various countries. I plead to my God to get me out of this hell and place me on the highest mountain so that I may shout praise and glorify His name throughout the world. But...In here, He has given me these messages to write, several books and messages, lots of time in His word. Over nine years here now, and I'm still crying out to Him, but I know that He hears my prayers and He does send angels to me to remind me that He is here with me and hasn't forgotten me. Though Kenya Prisons have denied me all human rights, no communication with my family or anyone else and have caused me immense suffering physically and emotionally, and the American embassy had no interest, I'm starving (Clinically severe malnourished) because the little food that they provide in buckets and eat from an aluminum can like feeding animals, I can't eat the food that they bring because of the health problems that they have caused me, so one of my many diagnoses is gross malnutrition and starvation. Over nine years in this hell, my health has declined, I have been refused healthcare. The Kenyans get some healthcare, they can have food from home, but I'm not allowed to have the embassy bring any food. The Kenyans have phones, internet, visits, I'm not permitted. Oh yes, the embassy, where are they? One said "We are not here to help, only to see the outcome." But when three girls came and were stopped by Kenyan corruption, the embassy was all over it and got them out! Then Another felt that Kenyans could do no wrong and Americans can do no right, and aided Kenyatta hospital in causing my stroke. Then they sent a woman, a Kenyan with no American interest except her passport and money. Yet another came once and took interest, was transferred to the Ukraine two weeks later, He told a woman, his replacement to come every three months...to this day I have not seen her, she sends another peon who has absolutely no interest in helping, so... It is only God and I, but my God is sufficient, and I am still alive by His grace. While the Kenyans have refused to let an innocent man go free and tell the world of their corruption, and have done all they could to kill me, I'm still here. A few guards call me indestructible. It is my God, who is Mightier than this enemy of His and mine-Kenya. I was told by several MD's that I could not survive the flight to the states but the embassy didn't care, but my God cared for me.

I have consistently requested to speak with the U.S. Ambassador but, have not been allowed. I have tried for months to get my case back into the court and the prison refused to allow me to do so.

I encourage everyone to avoid Kenya and Nigeria as well as Kenya airlines as you will pass through Kenya and CID can and oftentimes does pick you up if you are a foreigner (unless you are in a group but even then, you are at risk) so that all may see the horrendous corruption in Kenya and again I encourage a complete boycott and DO NOT travel to this land-or you do so at your own risk, and don't expect help from the US Embassy. Don't even fly on Kenya Air because you will end up in Kenya.

I am nobody special but I hold on to my God who is!

I'm writing this because I feel it is important, and in case anything happens to me, that the world will know that Kenya destroyed an innocent man, but more importantly, that the world will see the message that we all have storms, but we have to endure them and come out victorious, not run from them and face the second death and fierce wrath of the Almighty God! He gives each of us choices. *Many are called but few are chosen.* Those that will be accepted are those who endure the storm and hold on to their God ordained partner and to God, and never let go. What is your choice today? Do you have troubles in your marriage? Sit down and talk it through using the biblical guidelines outlined from Scripture in this message. Divorced? Return to thy first love. Everybody, go home to thy family and kneel down together before the Lord and pray for thy marriage, family, thy partner; then arise anew, regenerated, strengthened in the Lord who created you and ordained your partner, family, parents...for you. Are you single? Then pray with and for your parents and siblings. And remember no matter who you are, you are important or God wouldn't have created you. He has a purpose and a plan for each of us. Pray for one another and pray that God reveal to you His plan (not your plan) for your life, then listen to Him and obey His sweet voice. And as you are praying, pray for the lost, lonely, hurting, and for the victims of the broken marriages. What I have seen in the remotest parts of this planet, just tears my heart. I cry so often thinking of what I have seen, and the suffering beyond human comprehension. God entrusted me with this heart and this mission, and I praise Him. It is through His strength alone that I endured the immense suffering that I have seen, and did what little I could for these wonderful people, as well as the strength to survive hell-Kenya.

We read in Mark 6:4 *But Jesus, said unto them, a prophet is not without honor, but in his own country, and **among his own kin, and in his own house***. Satan seeks to destroy, as a true believer you must hold on to God and fight off the enemy, and the best way is to forsake the world and the things of it, and remain in constant prayer and in His precious word daily, and remember that He chose His children with great love. The stronger your faith, the more Satan fights, in your Christian walk as well as in your marriage, don't listen to these leaders that say, if you have God, Satan can do nothing. God in His word and His apostles and servants, including myself will all testify that God's word is true. You WILL suffer trials, tribulation, and persecution. Jesus said they hated me they will hate you also, they persecuted me and so shall they persecute you. But in Matthew 5:10-12, He says blessed are you when they persecute, and promises a reward of eternal life for those who shall endure unto the end. My dear friends, this includes within your marriage and family! He chose your partner with great love, Hold on dear friends. The road is not easy, the path lonely because it is not much traveled...but on the path of righteousness is where you will always find God and His people, who will be best able to encourage and strengthen you along the way. If you are going the way everyone else goes, you are on the wrong path that leads to eternal destruction. If you hold on to God in your marriage, you can be a lighthouse for others. What a blessing!

Dear friends, pray for me. Don't listen to the world, but look ALWAYS unto God. Hold on tight because the enemy, the world, your friends and sometimes even family seek to destroy your relationship with God as well as your marriage. Hold on to one another with a death grip and never let go! When the storms of life pass over, hold on to God, hold on to your God given partner, and remember that the cloud will pass over and then the sun will shine again! If you walk away during the storm, everything shall be gone when the sun tries to rise again. I am in the pits of hell, but I trust God to raise me to new heights soon, please pray for me as well, as I pray for each person who reads these several books and messages that God hast caused me to write, as well as for all marriages. God bless you all.

John 10:27-30 tells us *My sheep hear my voice, and I know them, and they follow me: And I give unto them eternal life; and they shall never perish, neither shall any man pluck them out of my hand. My Father, which gave them me, is greater than all; and no man is able to pluck them out of my Father's hand. I and my Father are one.*

God has given unto me a great burden for repentance and revival in the world, and for the marriages today. I pray daily for the marriages and for those who have broken covenant and walked away. I pray for your repentance and restoration, for the salvation of your marriage as well as for your marriage to Christ. I daily pray that my wife will repent and return unto my God and our marriage for the sake of the marriage but more importantly for her salvation, and to leave the life of sin... because I love her. God loves us. All men who are divorced should be praying for their wives and children and maintain a heart willing to accept her back with love and forgiveness as God has done for each of us. I pray that each one hearing this message will repent and return to our first love, Jesus Christ our Bridegroom.

My dear brothers and sisters, whatever happened to the era of Leave It to Beaver, Andy Griffith, Walton's or Little House on the Prairie, etc.? Have we really changed that much in such a short period? Look at the way that people speak, dress, love and care for one another, etc. Look at the church today. We have abandoned all Christian morals, values, and ethics and accepted everything contrary to Scripture-polygamy, adultery, immodest dress, abortion, abuse, divorce, entertainment...Birth control because of selfishness and/or don't trust God to be in control, and want to take control of things, independence...from the Almighty God, remember what happened to Jonah when he tried that? People have thrown away their Bibles. The jaws of hell will also engulf you if you don't humble yourself, seek God, repent, and turn from your wicked ways-conform to the ways of God rather than the precepts of man. Regardless of how much you wish to be in control (like Jonah),

God is and always will be in control! And all who sin against Him shall be judged! Rather than listening to government supported pro-abortion, birth control, population organization, homosexuality, etc. that has permeated the world, return to God and His precepts, repent and surrender your all unto Him. Give Him full control of your life, your marriage and family, church and your country. Surrender ALL unto Him. As that song goes, God said it, I believe it, and that's good enough for me. God has never let me down, and He won't let you down either, He loves us too much.

Kenya has laid down the firewood, they have poured the fuel. Sparks from Satan are flying everywhere and it could blow at any time, all the while they are saying that the problem is all external and refusing to realize the fact that ninety nine percent of their trouble is internal, while they keep blaming everyone else. The same is true in human kind. It is so easy to point the finger and say it is your fault and walk away, rather than looking inside oneself and asking what did and can I do to change the situation. It is easier to walk away from God and from your marriage that to pull the log from your own eye and remain with or return to thy marriage partner and thy Christian walk. Their president is telling the world and his own people that Kenya is safe, but as we see in 1st Thessalonians 5:3 *For when they shall say, Peace and safety; then sudden destruction cometh upon them, as travail upon a woman with child; and they shall not escape.* The world is pretending that all is well, but the signs of the end times are upon us, let the reader beware. Don't be fooled by the Kenyan president; don't be fooled by the enemy. I, like John and Jesus, am here today calling each of us to humble ourselves, pray, repent, restore, revive our Christian walk and our marriages. Are you with Christ and me or are you against us? Today it is your decision to make.

The United States had the first non-Christian (professing) president in U.S. history, and his lack of any morals, values, or ethics clearly reveals this-but not the morals, values, ethics of the majority of Americans, but where do they stand? Where do the majority of Chinese stand...or Africans, or...where do you stand? It is time to stand up once again for Jesus. Where DO you stand, with Jesus or with the world? There is no middle ground, no grey area with God; you are either for or against Him.

People watch too much TV which is one of the governments' ways of 'modifying' culture, through their lack of control in some areas and too much control in others. There is far too much TV and far too little family time. TV is so full of stress (action packed), violence, swearing and vulgar dialogue, sex and immodest dress and/or nudity-who needs this, we need to return to the family and traditional family, and godly morals, values, and ethics. Friendship with the world leads to destruction emotionally, physically, and most importantly, spiritually.

I have written much of this with great joy at having been used as a messenger and being entrusted with such wisdom; as well as with great tears of sorrow, and pray daily for the salvation of my dear wife and the millions of others out there in this world of darkness, who have not separated from the evil ways of this world, but to continue to walk ignorantly in this darkness of sin. I pray for the restoration and revival of our marriage and those of millions of others around the world.

Finally, in Colossians 3:12 *we read Put on therefore, as the elect of God, holy and beloved, bowels of mercies, kindness, humbleness of mind, meekness, longsuffering; Forbearing one another, and forgiving one another, if any man has a quarrel against any: even as Christ forgave you, so also do ye. And above all these things put on charity, which is the bond of perfectness. And let the peace of God rule in your hearts, to the which also ye are called in one body; and be ye thankful. Let the word of Christ dwell in you richly in all wisdom; teaching and admonishing one another in psalms and hymns and spiritual songs, singing with grace in your hearts to the Lord. And whatsoever ye do in word or deed, do all in the name of the Lord Jesus, giving thanks to God and the Father by him. Wives, submit yourselves unto your own husbands, as it is fit in the Lord. Husbands, love your wives, and be not bitter against them. Children, obey your parents in all things: for this is well pleasing unto the Lord.*

2nd Chronicles 30:6-9 tells us, *So the posts went with the letters from the king and his princes throughout all Israel and Judah, and according to the commandment of the king, saying, Ye children of Israel, turn again unto the Lord God of Abraham, Isaac, and Israel, and he will return to the remnant of you, that are escaped out of the hand of the kings of Assyria. And be not ye like your fathers, and like your brethren, which trespassed against the Lord God of their fathers, who therefore gave them up to desolation, as ye see. Now be ye not stiff-necked, as your fathers were, but yield yourselves unto the Lord, and enter into his sanctuary, which he hath sanctified forever: and serve the Lord your God, which the fierceness of his wrath may turn away from you. For if ye turn again unto the Lord, your brethren and your children shall find compassion before them that lead them captive, so that they shall come again into this land: for the Lord your God is gracious and merciful, and will not turn away his face from you, if ye return unto him.*

To a large extent, the unity and harmony within the church is dependent upon the unity and harmony within the individual homes. The apostle Paul emphasized a lot on the unity and harmony, the love and respect that must exist between husband and wife, and this should serve as a clear illustration of the love of Christ, the self-sacrificing, selfless love that Christ has for His church. This Christ like love within the home as well as within the church is essential for husbands and wives as well as the church members. This same selfless love must as well be seen between parents and their children, and employers and employees. This type of love, harmony, unity and peace should spread throughout our homes and church life. This, as I said at the beginning, marriage and family exemplifies our Christian walk and our relationship within the family of God, and consequently is why God created marriage in the first place, and why marriage is so very important to God. We see the families have been destroyed as well as the church. They go hand in hand.

God's precious word does in fact explain history from the beginning of time, and prepares us for the future-the end of time on this earth, but most importantly, it is a guidebook, and instruction manual for life...your life and mine. People over the ages have put it aside thinking that they don't need it and have filed it under the history book section. My dear brothers and sisters in Christ, let us retrieve this guidebook and allow it, allow its Author, our Creator, to revive, restore, and begin a new work in our lives, our families, our churches and our nations. He says in Psalms 119:103-106 *How sweet are thy words unto my taste! yea, sweeter than honey to my mouth! Through thy precepts I get understanding: therefore I hate every false way. Thy word is a lamp unto my feet, and a light unto my path. I have sworn, and I will perform it, that I will keep thy righteous judgments.* Just take the time right now to read this entire Psalm, it is so beautiful. Will you vow unto our God, El Shaddai (Almighty God), today these words? Will you return to thy husband, or remain with thy husband and uphold thy solemn vow-until death do you part? Will you vow unto Jehovah Jireh (the Lord provides) to return unto Him and walk in the newness of life, to surrender all unto Him and begin a new life in Him, and in thy marriage? Will you commit to rereading this message and take it step by step in applying it unto thy life and that of your family? God is knocking, He wants to transform thy life and that of thy family, church and community, but you must take that first step. Matthew 7:5 tells us *Thou hypocrite, first cast out the beam out of thine own eye; and then shalt thou see clearly to cast out the mote out of thy brother's eye.* Once we take that first step of repentance and clean up our life, then we may begin to be lighthouses for the Lord God Almighty. Yahweh Shalom (the God of peace) wants to bless you today. Let us humble ourselves and repent of our sins as well as those of our fathers of old, our families, our churches, and our nations. Let us put God first again in our lives, honor Him, His word, His gift of the Sabbath-let us once again make it truly holy, let us become holy-sanctified once again for Him. I believe that this message can be the beginning of a revival in this world of darkness. Yes, as I said at the beginning, there are many who shall read this message and probably never complete it because of the convictions, which it shall bring upon them. But there are those of you that shall endure unto the end, who, if you shall heed these words, shall find God working in your life and in your marriages in ways that you never dreamed possible, AMEN, and AMEN.

I ask you, who are we and who shall we listen to? Society tells us to marry, have children, have a happy family, become wealthy and live happily ever after. But I ask you how many happy families are there in the world today? How many have divorced one or more times? Why? Because this is of Satan, not God. God clearly states that He created each and every one of us with a purpose and a plan for our lives- His purpose and plan, not the world's. His plan for each of us is different, but His purpose is the same for all, to fulfill the Great Commission and to LOVE one another. How many people have fallen short and have lost blessings and perhaps true salvation here on earth as well as for eternity because they listened to the world rather than to God? Matthew 6:33 tells us but seek ye first the kingdom of God, and his righteousness; and all these things shall be added unto you.

There are seasons in all of our lives, the rhythms of life; they are an integral part of our existence. Our lives go through stages from the time we are conceived until the moment we die. Some we have control over and others we don't. Some are good some are not good. These seasons come and go some in an orderly fashion, others random. They exist in and all around us. Our interactions with others around us have an impact on these cycles, either positive or negative.

In Ecclesiastes 3:1-8 we read To everything there is a season, and a time to every purpose under the heaven: **A time to be born, and a time to die;** a time to plant, and a time to pluck up that which is planted; **A time to weep, and a time to laugh; a time to mourn,** and a time to dance; A time to cast away stones, and a time to gather stones together; a time to embrace, and a time to refrain from embracing; **A time to get, and a time to lose; a time to keep, and a time to cast away;** A time to rend, and a time to sew; a time to keep silence, and a time to speak; A time to love, and a time to hate; a time of war, and a time of peace.

Again, I wish to say that my wife is a wonderful woman, beautiful inside and out and I love her so very much. She shouldn't be offended by what I have said herein as what she did is no different from millions of others. She made one big mistake that so many people make and that is listening to the world. One should listen to your spouse and God. Men will never be good enough for their wives and vice versa. She may have meant evil but God turned it too good for His glory in my life as in the case of Joseph and his brothers. But the good news is that the Joseph family was restored and God was blessed. My daily prayer is that my wife will return unto me and that millions of you women will return to your first love. As you can see, there are no blessings only curses for those who choose to break covenant with God and their LIFE partner, and God says that He hates hypocrites and liars! Women repent and return to thy husbands and husbands receive back thy precious wives as God receives us back with loving arms outstretched. If you don't, you will stand before the Great White throne rather than the throne of mercy, and rather than seeing His mercy, you will experience the wrath of God and eternal judgment. When you return and rekindle your marriage, the host of heaven will be singing with joy and celebrating, but also here on earth, you will be such a testimony to those around you, of the love and mercy of God.

Death is just a change of residence moving from earth to heaven or hell.

Before we conclude this message, I would encourage to read Deut. 4:29-31, chapter 30; Joshua 1:6-9 and 24:14; John 13:34-35, Romans 2:13, 13:10, 12 and 14:19.

I asked you at the beginning two specific questions, what is the condition of your marriage and do you desire more? I also asked what is the condition of your spiritual life? It is my sincere prayer that this message has served to enhance both your Christian life as well as your family life.

I'm not interested in the world as it is, I am interested in the way the world should be and so should anyone who calls themselves a Christian.

I must also challenge you who want a deeper and richer life in Christ to read also **ONLY BELIEVE** and **What About the Biblical Perspective of Christmas?** As well as the Revelations given unto me on the Pentecostal Movement, The End Times, etc.

I believe that you have been blessed and will be more so if you will read these special messages to further enrich your understanding of God, His precious word, and thy life.

We read in Exodus 18:20 *And thou shalt teach them ordinances and laws, and shalt shew them the way wherein they must walk, and the work that they must do.* And this I have attempted to do.

God demands righteousness from those who claim a relationship with Him, and the standard of righteousness is the law of God.

A few last thoughts here in closing, the marriage is a very holy covenant, not to be played with. The condition of the marriage and the church are synonymous as the handful of true believers make up the true church body of Christ, which is the bride of Christ.

Galatians 1:8 tells us and I concur that *but though we, or an angel from heaven, preach any other gospel unto you than that which we have preached unto you, let him be accursed, anathema.*

This entire message can be summed up in a single verse found in John 13:35 which tells us *By this shall all men know that ye are my disciples, if ye have love one to another.*

We are told in Hebrews 2:1-3 *Therefore we ought to give the more earnest heed to the things which we have heard, lest at any time we should let them slip. For if the word spoken by angels was stedfast, and every transgression and disobedience received a just recompence of reward; How shall we escape, if we neglect so great salvation; which at the first began to be spoken by the Lord, and was confirmed unto us by them that heard him.* Please take a few minutes to read Luke 10:30-57, so do thou likewise. Love thy neighbor, do good even to those that hate you...

Hebrews 3:7-4:2 tells us *Wherefore as the Holy Ghost saith, To day if ye will hear his voice, Harden not your hearts, as in the provocation, in the day of temptation in the wilderness: When your fathers tempted me, proved me, and saw my works forty years. Wherefore I was grieved with that generation, and said, They do alway err in their heart; and they have not known my ways. So I sware in my wrath, They shall not enter into my rest.) Take heed, brethren, lest there be in any of you an evil heart of unbelief, in departing from the living God. But exhort one another daily, while it is called To day; lest any of you be hardened through the deceitfulness of sin. For we are made partakers of Christ, if we hold the beginning of our confidence stedfast unto the end; While it is said, To day if ye will hear his voice, harden not your hearts, as in the provocation. For some, when they had heard, did provoke: howbeit not all that came out of Egypt by Moses. But with whom was he grieved forty years? was it not with them that had sinned, whose carcases fell in the wilderness? And to whom sware he that they should not enter into his rest, but to them that believed not? So we see that they could not enter in because of unbelief. Let us therefore fear, lest, a promise being left us of entering into his rest, any of you should seem to come short of it. For unto us was the gospel preached, as well as unto them: but the word preached did not profit them, not being mixed with faith in them that heard it.*

Colossians 2:8 tells us also Beware lest any man spoil you through philosophy and vain deceit, after the tradition of men, after the rudiments of the world, and not after Christ.

One last thought. Look over at Matthew 7:24-27 *Therefore whosoever heareth these sayings of mine, and doeth them, I will liken him unto a wise man, which built his house upon a rock: And the rain descended, and the floods came, and the winds blew, and beat upon that house; and it fell not: for it was founded upon a rock. And every one that heareth these sayings of mine, and doeth them not, shall be likened unto a foolish man, which built his house upon the sand: And the rain descended, and the floods came, and the winds blew, and beat upon that house; and it fell: and great was the fall of it.*

You have heard this message and the word of God, over three thousand verses, now the choice is yours. Do you wish to obey God's voice and have a strong foundation upon which to build your Christian walk and your marriage and family, or do you wish to ignore it and await the winds and storms to destroy you and your marriage? Remember that in these verses just read, the WISE man built his house upon the foundation of God.

With that said, I will conclude this dissertation by permitting Scripture to interpret Scripture. I have blown the trumpet and sounded the warning. Remember that those who chose not to hear or obey His message were destroyed for example Genesis 19:14 and even in Noah's time of the flood. I will now allow you time to pray and meditate upon these words. Confess thy sins before our Living God, Father, Bridegroom, repent, then listen for His voice and direction. I sincerely cannot believe that anyone in this world can walk away from this most powerful message without any conviction!

Jesus tells us in the Gospel of John 14:27, *Peace I leave with you, my peace I give unto you: not as the world giveth, give I unto you. Let not your heart be troubled, neither let it be afraid.*

My love be with each of you in Christ Jesus. Amen and amen.

Ephesians 5:32 says, *This is a great mystery: but I speak concerning Christ and the church*

Deuteronomy 32:28-29 *For they are a nation void of counsel, neither is there any understanding in them. O that they were wise, that they understood this, that they would consider their latter end!*

1st John 3:3 *That which we have seen and heard declare we unto you, that ye also may have fellowship with us: and truly our fellowship is with the Father, and with his Son Jesus Christ.*

REPENT FOR THE KINGDOM OF HEAVEN IS AT HAND!

My dearest brothers and sisters, this is not my message as I stated from the start, but an inspired message from the Holy spirit of the Living and almighty God. His message has impacted my life, hit me hard, and revealed some of the weaknesses in my life and given me tremendous insight in which to be able to assist others. I pray that His message has impacted your life as well. May God bless you as you continue to meditate upon these precious words.

I would love to hear from you, letting me know how this message has affected thy life and family-physically, emotionally, and most important spiritually. Also, with any questions you may have regarding this powerful message- God bless you as you allow God and this message to transform and revive your life, AMEN!

May God bless you as you meditate and reread this message and apply it to thy marriage and/or family.

PERSONAL NOTES

APPENDIX A

Index to Scriptural References

GENESIS

1:1	1
1:20	274
1:26-28	1,82, 100,152
1:31	0, 186
Chapter 2-3	1, 50, 176
2:18-24	1, 60, 76,116, 140,153, 163,183, 199,200
2:24-25	31, 93, 100,111, 172,173, 206,281
3:1-13	29,64, 77,80, 186,285, 474
3:15	423

GENESIS Cont.

3:16	31,32, 77, 93, 100, 146,114, 220,286, 307, 400
3:17-19	12, 36, 86,93, 206
3:21	82
4:1	200
4:19	230
6:8,18	311,378
6:12	311
9:21-25	28
11:25-29	118
13:10	313
14:31-32	228
16:2	12,176
16:12	230
17:10	181
18:12	76, 96

GENESIS Cont.

18:19	15,39, 41,42,43
Chapter 19	232
19:5	232
19:13	311
19:14	71,525
19:30	228
19:31-36	28,253
20:3	227
Chap.24	165, 362
24:4	125
24:26	39
24:40,	51 126
24:65	113
24:67	163, 207, 231
25:21	35
25:28	15
Chapter 27	177
27:27	184
29:12	118
29:17-18	146
29:21	163,231
29:24	126
29:31	252
29:32-30:24	242
30:4,9	126,231
31:1-3	59
31:4,9	193
31:16	160
31:28	384
31:35	2, 8
34:1-3	62,63
34:11-12	161
35:2-3	283
35:4	66
35:7	190,204

GENESIS Cont.

37:3	15,52
Chapter 38	158
38:2-3	206
38:6	25
38:9-10	226,250
38:14, 18	219
38:15	68
38:26	158
Chapter 39	220
39:12	234
41:45	125,126,171
44:9	290
46:22	290
Chapter 49	182
50:20	385

EXODUS

General	48
1:16	262
2:21	125,126
3:17	128
6:20	119
12:17	249
12:48	309
13:2	287
15:20	108
16:16	34, 37
18:20	523
19:5-6	316
20:3	77
20:12	3
20:17	215
21:4-6	344,352
21:7-11	159
22:16	207,247
22:17	141
22:19	344

EXODUS Cont.

22:29	287
23:1-2	378
23:32	286
24:3	182,264, 265
28:33	264
28:40-42	82
Chapter 30	264
32:1-2	66
33:5-6	48
34:14-16	367
38:8	108
40:17	254

LEVITICUS

Chapter 4	266
6:10	82
Chapter 10	227
10:9	27
11:44	410
Chapter 12	61,94
12:8	287
Chap. 15	106, 206
16:4	82
16:15	134
Chapter 18	229
18:1-5	257,410
18:3-4	254
18:6-20	134,228, 230, 364
18:22,29	232,234
18:24-27	231,329
19:28	47
Chapter 20	345
20:7,10-14, 17	208,228, 232, 238, 363

LEVITICUS Cont.

20:18	186
21:4-5	46
21:7-14	135,171, 193
22:24	366
24: 16	51
26:12-16	264
26:15-31	381

NUMBERS

Chapter 2	153
3:13	287
11:5	454
12:6	108
13:6,8,30	357
14:33	483
14:43	425
18:1	52
18:7	219
25:1-4	367
30:2-4	337, 398
30:2-15	33-34, 143, 265
31:15-18	133, 193

DEUTERONOMY

4:9	9
6:4	281
6:5	79, 80
6:6-7	9, 13, 14, 21
7:1-11	422
7:12-15	93,286
8:2	336
9:28	489
10:12-13	336
10:20	286

DEUTERONOMY Cont.

11:19	3, 42
11:22-23	173,182, 374
12:26-28	481
13:4	162
17:17	159
18:9	329,376
18:21	319
20:18	329
21:13	201,206, 227
21:18, 21	20
Chapter 22	364
22:1-30	49,52, 82
22:13-21	141,153, 214, 363
22:22-25	134, 218, 363
22:24	88
22:28-29	218,227
23:1-3	364
23:12- 14	363,365
23:21-23	398
Chap. 24	257,365
24:1-4	202, 363, 364,365, 413, 417, 418
24:4-5	342,399, 405
25:5-6	259
25:11-12	204
27:20	364
28:56	71, 72, 344
30:19-20	316
31:20	344

DEUTERONOMY Cont.

32:28-29	526

JOSHUA

2:13	220
22:5	501
24:14-15	39,50, 103,501

JUDGES

1:13	125
3:3-7	368
4:4	44, 108
4:8	103
6:13	472
10:14	426
Chapter 11	155
11:14	406
13:2	249
14:7-8	126
15:6	308
16:15-17	385
Chapter 19	202
19:27	76
21:11	214
21:20-24	120,317

RUTH

General	xx, 59, 97,100, 103, 113, 115,119, 126, 184, 201, 203,286, 363
1:14-15	380
1:16-17	97, 133, 164, 301, 341, 380

RUTH Cont.

2:10	495
2:11	113,119
3:3, 9	139,154
3:10-11	113, 115, 118,119
4:10	161
4:13	241,242, 250

1 SAMUEL

Chapter 1 71,	
	155,202, 230, 260
1:23, 28	280
2:1	280
2:20-26	108,197, 252,281
3:10-14	9,15, 97
8:1-8, 20	9,15, 240
15:23	21
15:33	242
16:7	134
17:51	366
18:6-7	85
18:17,21	125, 171
19:1	220
25:3	359
25:39	126
28:7	63

2 SAMUEL

1:26	335
Chapter 2,	3 335
6:12-21	49, 89,92, 364, 379

2 SAMUEL Cont.

6:20-21	49
6:23	249
7:12-16	10, 349
10:4-5	47
Chapter 11	348
12:24-25	349
Chapter 13	216
13:15-16	218
13:18	52
20:9	184

1 KINGS

General	107
1:2-4	220
1:31	82
2:3	3
2:19	2
5:18	366
11:1-3	411
Chapter 18	453
18:30	453

2 KINGS

General	107
9:30	48, 82
21:1-9	15

1 CHRONICLES

General	107
15:29	80
19:4	47
28:20	477

2 CHRONICLES

General	107
5:12	102
7:14	281,286, 314,315,

2 CHRONICLES Cont.

	388,424, 483
8:11	58
14:7	172
19:6	118
21:11	237
24:20	172
29:5	502
29:16	479
30:6-9	519
30:9-12	496
31:1	502
34:1-2	108

EZRA

General	422
2:64-65	108
9:1	470
9:11-12	125, 470
Chapter 10	115
10:2-3	404
10:11	453

NEHEMIAH

General	40
9:28	321,404
13:23-31	114, 115, 411

ESTHER

General	51,66, 103,184, 417,487
1:12, 16-18	79,80, 85,108
1:22	37, 108
2:7	16
2:12,15,17	48

ESTHER Cont.

4:8,12,16	78-79
4:14	463
5:14	311

JOB

General	xxvi
Chapter 1	283
1:1	26
1:4-5	16,42,203
23:12	117
31:1,7	348
31:9,11	348
33:15-16	xxx
36:9-12	482
41:22	vii

PSALMS

1:1-2	501
Chap. 6,7	491
12:1-2, 4	479
16:7	xxx
Chapter 17	491
23:4	10, 200
Chapter 32	348
Chapter 35	491
36:7	154
37:7	307
37:23	40
37:31	39
Chapter 51	348
51:10-13	298
57:1	154
63:7	154
77:2	39
78:5	15
81:11-13	225
90:12	304,317,

PSALMS Cont.

	471
Chap. 91	324
91:4	154
Chapter 95	496
96:1-6	310
103:10-13	333
113:9	250
118:17	vii
118:19	471
119:103-106	520
119:133	220
119:165	39
127:3- 5	xxxvi,2, 96, 100, 286,298
127:13	20
Chap 128	54
128:3	2
133:1	328,410
139:13-15	2,5, 187
139:23	298
148:12	72

PROVERBS

General	219,221
1:2-15	8,11,31, 71, 153, 222,273, 298, 454
3:3	398
3:7	438
4:14-15	377
5:15-20	38
6:16-19	306
6:24-32	215,216, 221,222, 377

PROVERBS Cont.

Chapter 7	222,231
7:9,10,21	82, 221
7:11	59
8:4	71
10:12	277, 352
10:17-19	306,307
11:4	31
11:11-13	306
11:16	216
13:3	306
13:18	13
13:24	3, 96
14:1	76
14:12	82
14:29	307
15:1	307
17:6	43
17:14	446
17:25	21
17:28	306
18:2	383
18:13	306
18:22	34
19:3	383
19:18	10, 96
19:26-27	21
20:29	51
21:19	306,307
22:6	3,8,15, 96
22:15	10, 96
22:20-21	xviii
23:4	34,36
23:13-14	10
23:27	222
26:17	306
26:20-23	305
27:6	379

PROVERBS Cont.

27:15-16	307
27:23	46
28:13	307
29:15-17	10, 15, 96
29:20	306
30:11	275
30:20	228
Chapter 31	59, 98,307
31:10-31	56, 72, 99,301-304, 316,500
31:25	82

ECCLIASTES

Chapter 2	497
3:1-8	457,521
4:11	181
5:1-6	398
7:25	40
7:28	27, 64
9:9	38
12:13	304

SONG OF SONGS

General	xx
1:2	152,274
2:2,4	131
4:8	217,267, 268
4:12-16	200,238
5:3-8	300
5:5	238
5:13	300
6:13	426
8:6	84,186,

SONG OF SONGS Cont.

	190,353, 366
8:7	155
8:9	64

ISAIAH

1:2-6, 10	20, 388, 406, 426
1:10-16	406
1:19-20	406,480
1:27-31	391
2:12	388
3:12	60,81, 102
5:15	89
5:20	397
16:8	497
23:4	310
24:5-6,8	344,479
26:17-18	260
29:13	xxvi
30:1-9	xxvi, 19
35:2-4	49
47:10-13	386
49:5	5
50:1	405
51:12	463
53:2	30, 114
53:3-5,7	18,144, 324
54:1	100,226
54:5-7	173,412
54:8,10	436
55:7	471
58:1	471
58:6-8	53
59:2	471

ISAIAH Cont.

59:7-9	470
61:1-2	53
62:4	279
62:5	126,162
64:6	346
65:12	470
66:3	329
66:9	95

JEREMIAH

1:5	2, 5
2:2-8	413
2:14-37	415,416
3:1-6	221,394, 413,416
3:6-11	239,417
3:12-14	275,286, 412, 418
3:20	78, 354
4:1	330
4:4, 14	485
4:30	51
5:7-9	216
6:13-14	346
7:29	49
9:20	57
10:24	287
13:18	89
16:1-3	113, 117
17:9	346
29:6	249
29:11	5,243 480
31:9,18,19	13-14
31:22	108
31:34	307
44:10	89

JEREMIAH Cont.

44:15	35

LAMENTATION

1:2	386
1:17	106
4:3	95

EZEKIEL

3:19	471
8:10	61
8:17	330,376
13:10	306
14:6	330,376
16:8	139, 154, 203,364
16:25	221
16:29	220
16:32-34,36,38	75,78, 218,239, 240
16:39	278
16:44-45	278,378
16:59	345
18:13	330,377
18:23-24	436
18:27,28	436
18:30-31	436,471
18:38-48	436
22:10-11	88
22:30	54
Chapter 23	46
23:18	364
23:38-40	48, 66
23:45-48	85
24:15-18	113,117
33:11	471
43:9	471

EZEKIEL Cont.

44:20	47, 49
44:21	162
44:22	124, 171

DANIEL

10:13	492
11:6,10,17	273
12:3	39
12:10	471

HOSEA

General	153,419
1:2	222
Chapter 2	420
2: 2	420
2:7	366
2:16	174
2:20	131
Chapter 3	421
3:1	363,421
3:2-3	81, 361, 421
4:1-2, 6	xviii, 381, 496

JOEL

General	299
2:12-13	172
3:3	274

AMOS

3:2	10
3:3	181
7:7-8	xxix

OBADIAH

General	472

JONAH

Chapter 1	354

MICAH

2:9	382
6:8	406
7:6	346

NAHUM

1:2-3, 6-8	472
2:13-14	139
3:5	82, 139
3:13-19	236,337

HABAKKUK

2:4	487
2:10	358

ZEPHANIAH

1:8	53
1:9	472
2:2-3	472
3:1-2	85

HAGGAI

2:4	472

ZECHARIAH

3:3-4	334,496
5:7-11	63
7:10-13	431
8:17	358
9:6	371

MALACHI

General	470
1:6	43
2:7-8	469
2:10-3:5	355
2:11-12	151,

MALACHI Cont.

	393, 423
	469
2:13-17	298,347,
	356,357,
	392, 393,
	412, 421,
	423,430,
436	
3:1	209
3:5	209
3:6	412
3:7	424
3:13-16	411,479
Chapter 4	479
4:3	479

MATTHEW

Chapter 1	132
1:3	158
1:18-21	41, 133,
	134, 361
2:11	289
2:19	169
3:3	456
3:17	290
4:1-12	vii, 28
5:3-4	473
5:5-6	xxxii,212,
	473
5:7	212,306
5:9	212
5:10-12	378,515
5:17	152
5:23-24	212,481
5:28	247
5:29	209
5:31-32	168,212,

MATTHEW Cont.

	357,361
5:33,38	212
5:39	322
5:40	212
5:44-45	212,409
5:48	212
6:12	323,330,
	335,337,
	386, 486
6:14-15	103,323,
	330,335,
	403
7:1-5	88,306,
	520
7:21	184,208
7:22-23	256,304
7:24-27	524
10:6-16	53
10:22	402
10:27	xxx
11:28	453
12:34-37	208,306
12:39	144,207,
	220
12:48	19
12:50	274
13:3-8	451
13:19-23	495
Chapter 14	209
15:19	212
18:1-6	12, 20,
	295
18:12	175
18:14-18	225,261,
	306,306,
	420
18:21-35	320,329,

MATTHEW Cont.

	330,336
Chap. 19	69, 171
19:3-10	163,228, 321,353, 362,409, 427
19:14	19,20,21
19:19	212
19:21	240
21:28-31	294
22:1-14	65, 405
22:37	xx
23:9	11
25:1-13	48,132
25:37	333
26:24	xxvii,498
26:49	184
26:63-65	241
27:20	262
27:32	45
27:46	187
28:19-20	53

MARK

2:7	241
3:21	289
3:35	290
4:19-20	500
6:2-4	287,288, 515
6:24	69
6:26	38
7:10	296
10:11-12	170,398
11:25-26	332
12:42-44	240
14:29,31,37	343

MARK Cont.

14:40-41,47	343
14:72	343
15:40-41	58
16:9-10	108

LUKE

Chapter 1	211
1:5	210
1:25	100
1:30	100
1:36,38	136,155
1:40	174
1:56	352
2:17	289
2:21-28	287
2:38	108
2:47	289
4:29-30	288
6:31	409
6:37	330
6:41-42	403
6:46	184
7:47	330
8:1-3	108
9:23	409
9:62	291
10:2	45
10:30-57	523
12:15-21	36
14:28-30	131
15:22	187
Chapter 16	459
16:13	37,50, 219,227, 276
16:15	375
17:3	307,335,

LUKE Cont.

	337
17:4	335, 335
18:53	353
22:48	184
22:49-51	343
22:54,71	343
23:34	289,325,
	335,335,
	337, 386
23:55-56	108
24:1-7	108

JOHN

1:17	400,410
1:18	252
3:16	114,276,
	307,401,
	410
3:17-21	505
3:30	40
4:18	115
5:16-20	87
7:53-8:11	409
8:1-11	157,
	329,60,403
8:31-32	298
8:41	228
10:27-30	516
10:33	241
13:1-15	337
13:34-35	336,431,
	523, 612
14:6	105
14:27	329, 482,
	488,526
15:5	254
15:12	333

JOHN Cont.

15:13	xxvii
15:19-21	145,378,
	499
15:22	382, 496
16:2-3	499
16:20	vii
17:11	192

ACTS

General	30
1:8	336
1:12, 14	292
5:31	322
5:40-42	86
6:2-5	103
8:30	145,383
9:36	108
10:1-2	39
10:34	82
13:50	64, 68
15:19-20	186,228,
	416
15:29	417
19:27,35,37	61
21:9	108
21:25	228,417

ROMANS

1:25	215,236
1:26-27	232,234,
	241
1:28-32	245, 257,
	344,477
2:25-29	180
3:1-2	90
3:10-12	473
3:23	306,325

ROMANS Cont.

5:10	408
6:1-2	398
6:12-13	232,379
6:18	306
Chapter 7	277
7:1-4	170,245, 354,362, 398
8:15-17	172,275
8:28	385
8:35-39	358,362, 433
10:12	478
11:3	477
12:1	304
12:2	xviii,304, 449
12:4	174
12:19-20	322
13:1-2	92
13:9	245
13:10	246, 306, 329,386, 522
13:14	247
14:2-3	82
14:14	106
14:19	522
16:1-18	358

1 CORINTHIANS

1:10	410
3:16-17	68, 235, 246
Chap. 5	347, 394
5:1-13	228, 248, 261

1 CORINTHIANS Cont.

5:10-12	121
Chapter 6	347
6:1-2	369
6:6	xxvi, 369
6:7-9	142,145, 232,245, 433
6:13, 18	228
6:15-17	207, 227, 235, 348
6:18-30	245
7:1-6	58,176, 257,307, 307
7:3-5	37,41, 107,172, 199,268, 378
7:7, 32	112
7:8-9	150
7:10-11	78, 354
7:10-16	355
7:15-16	xxvi,121, 122, 210, 354,357, 397, 399, 449
7:20	123
7:23	256
7:28	74, 153
7:34	307
7:36-37	112
7:38	136,141
10:6	247
10:31	269
11:1-34	67,82, 89, 92,

1 CORINTHIANS Cont.

	108,124, 400
11:7	11
11:27-30	309,432, 481,483
12:18-25	75, 107 196
Chapter 13	448
13:4-7	130,306, 433
13:11	31, 144
14:20	145,382
14:34-35	65, 71, 101, 307
15:7	292
15:33	18,307

2 CORINTHIANS

Chapter 2	394
2:5-11	261,330, 335
4:3-4	234
6:14	225, 395
7:7-13	261
11:2	64,218, 247,276
12:14	15
12:21	228
13:5	xxviii

GALATIANS

1:2	viii
1:8	523
1:9	501
1:19	292
2:20	304
3:10	383

GALATIANS Cont.

3:28	82
4:5	22
4:7	69, 291
5:14-16	306
5:16-21	228,245, 277

GALATIANS

5:22-23	306
5:25	82
6:7	351

EPHESIANS

General	395
1:22-23	395
2:8-9	38,595, 396
3:10	307
3:15	272
4:1-3	329,337
4:11	108
4:25	116
4:26-27	325,446, 454
4:29-32	305,306, 307,307, 328,330, 336, 336 337 210, 402
Chapter 5	
5:3, 5	228
5:21-33	77
5:22-24	76, 77, 275, 400
5:23-25	33,34, 36,123, 149
5:25-27	69,202,

EPHESIANS Cont.

	387,397
5:31	207
5:32	526
5:33	174,306
6:1-3	3
6:4	15
6:12-17	447

PHILIPPIANS

2:3-4	273
2:27	vii
3:13-14	329,337
4:8-9	310,497
4:13	324,328,
	493
4:19	117,282

COLOSSIANS

2:8	524
3:2	304,488
3:8	337
3:12-20	3, 34, 47,
	49, 60
	82, 307,
	327, 328,
	333, 337,
	476, 518
3:21	15

COLOSSIANS Cont.

3:22-24	47

1 THESSALONIANS

4:3-5	28
5:3	517
5:11	307
5:21	40

2 THESSALONIANS

1:9	345
2:4	84, 232
3:10	32, 35,
	39, 93
3:14	261

1 TIMOTHY

General	107
1:4	284
1:10	232,234
2:8-10	48,66,
	82,108,
179	
2:11-12	60,65,
	102,107,
	176
2:14	81, 102
2:15	100,283
Chap. 3	4
3:11	305
4:8	53, 448
4:13	382
5:1-2	23
5:9-10	286
5:13	62
5:14	63
6:6-11	307

2 TIMOTHY

1:4-5	108
2:15	39
2:22	234,309
2:24-26	261
3:3	396
3:6	77, 221
3:12	189
3:16	83

2 TIMOTHY Cont.

4:3	452

TITUS

Chapter 2	304-307
2:2	15
2:3-5	61,76, 108, 108, 176
2:6-8	27
2:12 309,328	
3:3	328
3:4	58

PHILEMON

Verse 2	249
Verse 18	325

HEBREWS

2:1-3	523
3:2	464
3:7-4:2	524
3:19	208
4:1-2	208
5:1-10	33,201-202
6:12,15	151
8:9b	347
9:12	105
9:16	193
9:22	106, 193
10:21-27	360,435
10:29-32	435
10:38	435
11:1	143
12:1-2	304,454
12:3-11	14, 86
12:14-15	307
13:4	239,246

HEBREWS Cont.

13:5-6	307
13:17	189

JAMES

1:12	402,452
1:15	350
1:26	305
2:10	383
3:5,6,8	454
4:4	xxix, 9,13, 34,76, 80, 143, 144, 281, 345, 358,377, 450, 482, 508
4:8	225
5:9-10	306
5:16	307

1 PETER

2:1	306,496
2:2	496
2:11	309
2:17-25	90,396, 397,496
3:1-21	78,307
3:1-5	48, 66, 71, 83, 89,307
3:6	76
3:7	36,37,114
3:9,11-12	408
3:10	306
4:2	309,496
4:8	307
4:12-14	vii

1 PETER Cont.

5:5-7 — 380

2 PETER

2:14 — 245
3:9 — 431
3:17-18 — 497

1 JOHN

1:8-10 — 306,336, 407
2:12-14 — 58
2:15 — 80, 82,129, 143, 144, 222, 254, 281, 345, 358, 375, 377,402, 450,508
2:16 — 81, 83
2:17 — 83
3:1 — 58
3:3 — 526
3:16 — 308
4:7 — 386

2 JOHN

Verse 9 — 472
Verse 10 — 225

3 JOHN

Verse 11 — 472

JUDE

Verse 7-8 — 232

REVELATION

2:10 — 145,382, 452

REVELATION Cont.

2:14,15 — 367
2:20-22 — 102, 248
3:20 — xxxii,78
12:4 — 76
12:11 — 454,492
14:4 — 64
17:1 — 63
17:3-7 — 66, 273
18:4 — 475
19:2 — 63
19:6-9 — 162,493
21:7-8 — 78, 145, 382,496
21:9-10 — 315
22:16-17 — 394

APPENDIX B

Topical Index

Abortion

5, 19, 83, 142, 240, 241, 242, 243, 244, 253, 255, 257, 258, 268, 281, 295, 310, 329, 445, 489, 490, 494, 516, 517

Abuse of child or spouse/ Domestic violence

13, 21, 39, 73, 83, 85, 87, 97, 116, 249, 257, 266, 280, 299, 352, 354, 355, 358, 371, 382, 389, 490, 491, 498, 516

Adoption

4, 5, 6, 16, 18, 19, 22, 80, 174, 262, 275, 277, 312, 367, 465

Adultery

xxxi, 15, 37, 38, 43, 45, 60, 64, 74, 75, 76, 84, 85, 88, 115, 134, 144, 157, 169, 170, 184, 194, 207, 208, 209, 211, 212, 215, 216, 218, 219, 220, 221, 222, 225, 227, 228, 231, 232, 236, 237, 238, 240, 245, 246, 247, 248, 249, 258, 264, 266, 267, 276, 277, 278, 279, 281, 287, 300, 310, 312, 329, 343, 344, 347, 348, 349, 350, 351, 353, 354, 355, 356, 360, 361, 363,

364, 369, 376, 377, 381, 391, 396, 397, 398, 399, 401, 403, 404, 407, 411, 412, 413, 414, 415, 417, 418, 419, 420, 421, 422, 423, 430, 451, 453, 482, 486, 487, 489, 490, 492, 493, 494, 512, 516,

Birth Control

2, 12, 19, 100, 115, 142, 225, 241, 242, 243, 244, 250, 251, 252, 253, 255, 260, 268, 285, 295, 310, 445, 494, 502, 516, 517,

Breasts/ feeding

16, 38, 69, 94-95, 155, 178, 185, 194, 207, 243, 420,

Bride/Bridegroom

xxv, xxxi, 23, 29, 32, 34, 37, 48, 58, 60, 79, 85, 89, 126, 128, 131, 134, 139, 141, 143, 146, 152, 160, 161, 162, 163, 166, 167, 172, 174, 177, 178, 181, 182, 183, 184, 198, 202, 220, 222, 229, 230, 275, 277, 280, 281, 282, 303, 307, 308, 315, 316, 334, 335, 357, 358, 370, 379, 381, 386, 391, 394, 399, 405, 408, 416, 417, 429, 447, 452, 453, 487, 499, 501, 503, 505, 506, 516, 523, 525

Clothing

6, 7, 35, 37, 43, 49, 51, 52, 53, 66, 72, 82, 84, 87, 90, 99, 113, 121, 124, 126, 127, 132, 139, 163, 166, 171, 178, 179, 180, 185, 186, 187, 190, 201, 209, 214, 217, 227, 238, 246, 247, 263, 264, 265, 266, 305, 334, 364, 419, 452, 478, 495, 496, 502, 503, 516, 518,

Hair/head cover

47, 48, 49, 51, 59, 66, 67, 68, 73, 91, 121, 187, 221, 268, 342, 343, 352, 365, 495,

Homosexuality

xxxi, 100, 142, 161, 201, 231, 232, 233, 234, 236, 241, 249, 257, 258, 279, 302, 344, 354, 355, 376, 397, 489, 490, 494, 517,

Jewelry

31, 47, 48, 50, 66, 97, 132, 177, 178, 179, 180, 495,

Justification

12, 23, 27, 30, 34, 58, 64, 68, 69, 92, 123, 126, 152, 187, 188, 207, 208, 262, 312, 375, 407, 487, 496

Kiss

83, 114, 124, 128, 132, 134, 137, 145, 146, 152, 178, 184, 185, 189, 190, 196, 251, 274, 283, 331, 378, 379, 383, 384, 484

Makeup

47, 49, 50, 51, 64, 66, 179, 495,

Masturbation

226, 236, 494

Menopause

xxiii, xxiv, 106, 107, 250

Menstruation

105, 106, 182, 185, 186, 201, 250, 254, 255, 260, 370, 427

Polygamy

161, 202, 229, 230, 231, 232, 235, 249, 276, 300, 344, 348, 350, 351, 356, 366, 383, 398, 411, 436, 494, 516,

Pornography

52, 222, 227, 228, 237, 238, 361, 376, 494, 502

Pregnancy

2, 4, 12, 17, 43, 83, 96, 133, 134, 155, 159, 177, 239, 244, 251, 252, 253, 254, 260, 267, 281, 352, 353, 361, 465, 493

Prostitution

17, 20, 38, 45, 48, 49, 63, 65, 75, 81, 107, 134, 155, 157, 160, 203, 222, 223, 227, 235, 236, 237, 239, 240, 246, 249, 264, 267, 353, 354, 355, 362, 367, 382, 416, 417, 420, 471, 481, 483, 489, 493, 494, 496,

Rape

63, 86, 178, 185, 195, 208, 218, 246, 247, 253, 266, 267, 287, 310, 350

Repentance

xvii, xx, xxi, xxvii, xxviii, xxxii, 11, 14, 19, 21, 30, 50, 57, 59, 63, 79, 85, 86, 89, 98, 122, 143, 170, 171, 182, 187, 188, 209, 211, 213, 221, 222, 233, 238, 240, 246, 247, 248, 249, 255, 261, 278, 298, 300, 302, 304, 314, 320, 325, 327, 330, 335, 343, 347, 348, 349, 350, 351, 354, 355, 356, 359, 361, 364, 366, 368, 372, 376, 379, 383, 384, 386, 388, 391, 392, 394, 395, 396, 397, 399, 401, 402, 403, 405, 407, 408, 409, 410, 420, 422, 423, 424, 426, 428, 429, 430, 431, 432, 433, 434, 440, 441, 442, 448, 449, 450, 453, 469, 471, 472, 473, 474, 477, 478, 479, 481, 482, 483, 484, 485, 486, 487, 489, 491, 492, 494, 496, 499, 501, 503, 506, 512, 516, 517, 520, 522, 525, 527

Sacrifice

6, 15, 30, 33, 45, 53, 59, 68, 69, 71, 83, 97, 102, 106, 114, 118, 131, 138, 139, 143, 144, 154, 155, 160, 171, 172, 178, 181, 186, 193, 202, 204, 216, 220, 222, 229, 240, 244, 248, 262, 276, 283, 290, 296, 304, 306, 317, 320, 322, 323, 324, 329, 349, 367, 369, 382, 401, 408, 409, 430, 435, 445, 446, 447, 512, 519,

Single/unmarried

xix, 47, 59, 71, 100, 102, 112, 116, 123, 128, 136, 146, 150, 156, 158, 177, 216, 225, 226, 234, 267, 274, 275, 279, 282, 292, 293, 391, 424, 428, 444, 485, 495, 501, 503, 514

Surrender

2, 28, 60, 65, 71, 76, 77, 78, 80, 82, 86, 97, 132, 136, 137, 139, 143, 144, 145, 154, 162, 172, 175, 193 , 200, 213, 224, 239, 240, 252, 255, 256, 262, 290, 291, 297, 301, 306, 311, 323, 324, 373, 382, 384, 408, 409, 428, 433, 440, 441, 443, 445, 446, 447, 453, 472, 487, 490, 517, 520, 535, 536, 556, 573, 575, 604, 605, 608

Temple

7, 28, 37, 46, 47, 49, 51, 52, 53, 67, 68, 102, 105, 106, 126, 128, 162, 170, 171, 179, 180, 184, 196, 201, 202, 203, 204, 205, 206, 209, 213, 214, 215, 218, 219, 224, 226, 227, 232, 235, 237, 238, 245, 246, 251, 252, 254, 256, 266, 267, 276, 295, 308, 309, 387, 479, 480, 483

Touch

94, 114, 124, 128, 132, 136, 138, 176, 195, 198, 200, 204, 209, 215, 262, 275, 276, 331, 392, 484

Veil

67, 68, 166, 179, 181, 187, 190, 196, 198, 201, 203, 205, 206, 207, 214, 218, 219, 225, 251, 256, 263, 266, 267, 365, 492

Virgin

12, 52, 64, 74, 78, 112, 115, 123, 124, 126, 133, 134, 136, 153, 162, 163, 171, 181, 193, 194, 200, 202, 206, 218, 220, 223, 226, 235, 237, 247, 250, 252, 256, 260, 265, 268, 276, 288, 289, 310, 350, 353, 357, 363, 367

Vows

xxv, xxvi, 33, 34, 47, 68, 131, 132, 134, 136, 142, 143, 144, 155, 157, 158, 163, 164, 165, 167, 168, 177, 202, 206, 207, 208, 216, 220, 223, 240, 277, 278, 280, 290, 291, 299, 300, 316, 337, 343, 347, 352, 354, 355, 356, 357, 360, 362, 363, 369, 370, 376, 377, 380, 385, 386, 387, 389, 391, 398, 399, 402, 405, 406, 408, 410, 424, 425, 428, 432, 433, 444, 448, 449, 451, 480, 481, 490, 492, 494, 495, 496, 503, 520

APPENDIX C

Footprints In The Sand

One night I dreamed I was walking along the beach with the Lord. Many scenes from my life flashed across the sky. In each scene I noticed footprints in the sand. Sometimes there were two sets of footprints, often times there was only one set of footprints.

This bothered me because I noticed that during the low periods of my life, when I was suffering from anguish, sorrow or defeat, I could only see one set of footprints.

So, I said to the Lord, you promised me Lord, that if I followed you, you would walk with me always. But I have noticed that during the most trying periods of my life, there have only been one set of footprints in the sand. Why, when I needed you most you have not been there for me?

The Lord replied. **The times when you have seen only one set of footprints my child, is when I carried you.**

~ Mary Stevenson

Appendix E

**Lighthouse of Blessed Hope Ministry
Pastor and Evangelist Dr. John Bishop D.D.**

We Welcome you to **FOLLOW US** and support the work that our precious Lord and Savior is doing through us,

We invite you to **HEAR** other messages,

We also invite you to **PURCHASE** additional copies of this message or others as they become available

On our website:
Lighthouseofblessedhope.org

PLEASE, if you have questions, comments, if you have accepted Jesus Christ as your personal Lord and Savior and/or if this message has enhanced or saved your marriage, or if you would like this ministry to come to your village or church, **we would love to hear from you at:**

Lighthouseofblessedhopeministry@yahoo.com
Thank you and may God bless you always.

Pastor and Evangelist
Dr. Yokana Mukisa D.D.

Lightning Source UK Ltd.
Milton Keynes UK
UKHW021536061021
391760UK00011B/603